IDENTIFYING A FREE SOCIETY

Studies in Critical Social Sciences Book Series

Haymarket Books is proud to be working with Brill Academic Publishers (www.brill.nl) to republish the *Studies in Critical Social Sciences* book series in paperback editions. This peer-reviewed book series offers insights into our current reality by exploring the content and consequences of power relationships under capitalism, and by considering the spaces of opposition and resistance to these changes that have been defining our new age. Our full catalog of *SCSS* volumes can be viewed at https://www.haymarketbooks.org/series_collections/4-studies-in-critical-social-sciences.

IDENTIFYING A FREE SOCIETY

Conditions and Indicators

MILAN ZAFIROVSKI

Haymarket Books
Chicago, IL

First published in 2017 by Brill Academic Publishers, The Netherlands.
© 2017 Koninklijke Brill NV, Leiden, The Netherlands

Published in paperback in 2018 by
Haymarket Books
P.O. Box 180165
Chicago, IL 60618
773-583-7884
www.haymarketbooks.org

ISBN: 978-1-60846-932-1

Trade distribution:
In the U.S. through Consortium Book Sales, www.cbsd.com
In the UK, Turnaround Publisher Services, www.turnaround-uk.com
In Canada, Publishers Group Canada, www.pgcbooks.ca
All other countries, Ingram Publisher Services International, ips_intlsales@ingramcontent.com

Cover design by Jamie Kerry and Ragina Johnson.

This book was published with the generous support of Lannan Foundation and the Wallace Action Fund.

Printed in United States.

10 9 8 7 6 5 4 3 2 1

Library of Congress Cataloging-in-Publication Data is available.

By most Millian criteria (of liberty), (economically) regimented Scandinavia was freer than my America. For years libertarians have been challenged to explain what appears to most observers to be the greater political freedoms and tolerances that prevail in Scandinavia than in America. I was told that none of this would last, active government economic policy had to result in loss of civil liberties and personal freedoms. One still waits.

SAMUELSON 1964, pp. 226–27

•••

Apply the moral yardstick of certain fundamental human rights to all forms of power and government, to Hitler, Stalin, Amin and Pinochet as to the governments which are responsible for Northern Ireland, the Southern United States and German 'guest workers' [so as not] to call any government legitimate which violates these rights.

DAHRENDORF 1979, p. 110

••
•

Contents

Acknowledgement

I thank Dr. David Fasenfest, Editor of Studies in Critical Social Sciences, for editing and reformatting and therefore helping improve the manuscript.

List of Illustrations

Tables

CHAPTER 1

Introduction: Modern Free Society

The Free, Freer, Freest Modern Society and Societies

What is/are the freest and the least free modern society/societies? This is a question that often arises and is attempted to answer in various ways and on certain bases in the sociology, economics, political-science, and other scientific literatures. It is also posed and answered in contemporary societies themselves, virtually each narcissistically or ethnocentrically claiming to be the freer, freest, and only free, and all others unfree. This is epitomized by such narcissistic or ethnocentric claims in the US expressing supposedly superior 'American exceptionalism' in freedom and their variants in the UK, as well as France, Germany, and most other Western countries and beyond (China, Iran, Russia, etc.). On this account, the above question represents both a sociological and generally social-science problematic or topic and a societal issue or dilemma, with sociologists and other scientific analysts and various non-scientists, including ordinary people and their leaders, alike posing it and attempting to answer it.

The present book addresses this question by providing novel, synthetic theoretical insights into and new multiple empirical grounds to contribute to answer it, while taking account of previous relevant works in the above literatures. It assesses both the prior answers to this question in the social scientific literature and almost every contemporary society's narcissistic claims to the freer, freest and only free one, and all others the polar opposite, particularly their most manifest and salient variant of American freedom 'exceptionalism' as well as its analogs in the UK, France, Germany, and other Western countries and elsewhere. Specifically, it posits and estimates which is or are the freest and the least free modern society or societies combining theoretical considerations and expectations with empirical sources and grounds such as comparative data and rankings of countries on various dimensions of societal freedom and its equivalents and complements.

What is a free and an unfree modern society more generally?—as is even more frequently asked and tried to answer both in the scientific literature and contemporary societies. This seems a perennial or recurrent and even fateful Shakespearean-like question—'to be or not to be a free society' and therefore to exist or not as an individual or group in freedom in his sense and that of Descartes. It forms an equivalent of the Shakespearean existential question so long as individuals or groups can exist in freedom and perhaps wellbeing and happiness—with rare exceptions—only within a free society, and conversely, there is no such thing as a truly free individual or group in an unfree society. In other words, this holds insofar as societal liberty is the prime (though perhaps not only) condition of an individual's or group's existence in the sense of the valuation, dignity, wellbeing, equality, justice, happiness, progress, and full, decent life of humans. Simply, to be in a free society is to exist and persist as a human being, as Shakespeare and Descartes perhaps intimate, and the noted almost universal narcissistic societal claims to the 'freest' societies confirm.

Conversely, societal illiberty prevents, destroys or perverts individual and group existence or life in this sense, instead resulting in the devaluation, indignity, suffering, inequality, injustice, unhappiness, regression, and violent or premature death of humans. Analogously, to be in an unfree society is to not exist and persist in Shakespeare's and Descartes' sense as a human being, as the also virtual absence of societal claims to the most or simply unfree societies confirms. This indicates that the question of a free versus unfree modern society is a crucial sociological and thus legitimate scientific problematic by virtue of being the prime mover and prerequisite of virtually all individual and collective attributes, processes, and outcomes in societies, from equality and justice, wellbeing and happiness to life and death.

And the question as 'what is/are the freest and the least free modern society/societies' is a special comparative and momentous, topical facet of this general and apparently perennial problematic, at least in the context of liberal modernity since the 18th century trilogy of modern revolutions[1] and changes, the rationalistic Enlightenment, the capitalist Industrial Revolution, and the democratic American and French Revolutions. Hence, proposing and estimating 'what is/are the freest and the least free modern society/societies' presupposes redefining and reconsidering the concept of free society itself, in particular its relation to political democracy and capitalism assumed to be a free polity and economy, respectively in view of the frequent conflations between the first and these latter.

Democracy, Capitalism, and Modern Free Society

In this connection, a theoretical and practical problem often arises as to whether political democracy or capitalism thus understood is equivalent to or sufficient for modern free society as a whole. Simply, is a democratic polity

---

1 Frank Knight (1967, p. 789) observes that the 'Liberal Revolution (established) free society, that is, democracy in the broad meaning, especially a political order minimizing compulsory law as well as exercise of arbitrary power, and restricting the latter to acts by lawful agents of the society, approved or accepted by public opinion.'

or capitalism in itself necessarily or enough for modern free society? In particular, the question opens if a formal-procedural democracy as a formally and procedurally free polity is also a free society substantively and effectively in general, with the first typified by a legal code, including a constitution, nominal freedoms and rights for political subjects like the freedom and right to vote and to seek and hold power, and democratic procedures and outcomes such as elections and elected representatives. The same question is posed for capitalism in the sense of a formally free economic system characterized with legal freedoms and rights for the factors of production like capital and labor—unlike official slavery or serfdom denying such freedom to the latter—as well as other non-capitalists and consumers, in relation to modern free society.

Thus, one can ask if the following mostly formal-procedural democracies in terms of nominal democratic rights, rules, procedures, and outcomes and largely capitalist economies in respect of legal economic freedoms constitute substantively or wholly free societies. For example, these[2] are Great Britain during the 19th century, Germany in the 1930s, Mexico until recently, Iran

---

2 The seemingly dubious inclusion of 19th-century Great Britain is justified by that politically it represented an 'exclusionary' and thus spurious democracy, as described by Centeno (1994), and economically a master-servant proto-feudal and so unfree capitalist economy, as Naidu and Yuchtman (2013) show, during most of this period. Centeno (1994, p. 135) observes that an undemocratic 'state had only to consider the wishes of 8% of the population, as was the case in Britain in 1867,' and Lizzeri and Persico (2004, p. 707) that 'in England, where parliament was an influential institution, suffrage was mostly the privilege of the wealthy, and some members of parliament were elected in boroughs with as few as 100 voters, while cities such as Manchester did not have any representative.' In addition, Naidu and Yuchtman (2013, p. 107) make the following observation: 'Indeed, one sees shades of coercion in the world's first industrial economy, in nineteenth century Britain. Until 1875, when it was repealed, Master and Servant law gave employers the ability to criminally (as opposed to civilly) prosecute and severely punish a majority of employees across industries for breach of contract in Great Britain.' Prima facie, the first is a far cry and large deviation from a genuine by definition inclusionary, egalitarian democracy, and the second from a truly free capitalist, market economy. The economic and political argument for including the US South and similar regions in America during postbellum and recent times is probably even stronger and enduring, as Acemoglu and Robinson (2006, 2008) and Amenta, Bonastia, and Caren (2001) and Dahrendorf (1979) suggest, respectively. In particular, Trebbi, Aghion, and Alesina (2008, p. 325) observe that the 'Voting Rights Act (VRA) of 1965 was meant to protect the right to vote for racial minorities, especially in the South. In fact, in a reasonably short time, it resulted in a massive reinfranchisement of black voters through an unprecedented effort of voter registration. White majorities in cities of the South reacted strategically to this federal legislation by changing the electoral rules of their cities in order to minimize minority representation. They only partially succeeded. Had they not been kept in check by judicial intervention, they would have engaged in even more openly strategic manipulation of rules.'

following the Islamic Revolution, Turkey under Islamic governance, South Korea and Taiwan for long and Singapore still, post-communist Poland and Russia, contemporary China, most of South America in the past and present, what Dahrendorf[3] connotes the post-bellum 'Southern United States,' and so on. The probably negative or inconclusive answer concerning these and other similar instances implies that the relationship of democracy in its formal-procedural form or republic and capitalism as a formally free economy to modern free society may be problematic rather than axiomatic, often involving a disjuncture or discrepancy rather than an equivalence or association.

One wonders how to resolve or understand this problem and paradox of a formal-procedural, nominal democracy or constitutional republic and formally free capitalism often not constituting and sufficing for an actually or entirely free society. In order to resolve it, the relationship between democracy or capitalism and modern free society is to be conceptualized and considered as one between a part and a whole according to a holistic, structural sociological approach, including modified social systems theory, treating society in general as a totality of elements considered its social structures or subsystems. Specifically, democracy and capitalism, respectively, constitute a partial political and economic system that is an integral element or subsystem of a free society as a total social system also incorporating an equivalently free culture and civil society as its other elements or subsystems. Formal as well as substantive political and economic freedoms defining and constitutive of democracy and capitalism represent special cases of the composite of societal liberties that also incorporates their cultural and individual forms that define a free culture and civil society, respectively. In this sense, modern free society constitutes the complex of holistic, integral societal liberty in all of its domains,

---

3 Dahrendorf (1979, p. 110) cites the 'Southern United States' for denying and violating 'certain fundamental human rights' in the list of their major deniers and violators, together with the governments of 'Hitler, Stalin, Amin and Pinochet,' etc., and thus totalitarian states. In fact, he implies that there are no fundamental human rights that the 'Southern United States' do not violate, including those of minority groups, the right to vote and seek/hold public office, the right of labor collective bargaining and unionization, freedom from coercive religion, scientific and education freedom, personal choice and privacy, and so on, just as the above governments. The reverse implication is that no 'fundamental human rights' as established by international conventions and institutions (e.g., within the UN) are protected in this American region, just as in these totalitarian states. Therefore, Dahrendorf's citation strongly supports including the 'Southern United States' among those societies listed in the main text, as well as the notion of the 'two Americas' by apparently differentiating these from the other US states in political and ideological, just as historical and geographical, terms.

i.e., of multiple intertwined political, economic, cultural, and individual liberties, typically conjoined and complemented with equality, justice, and related values regarded as complements rather than substitutes, as elaborated below.

Consequently, formal-procedural democracy or formally free capitalism does not necessarily represent and suffice for such a social system of freedom. This is exemplified by the above historical and present examples of formally democratic or republican and capitalist, and yet substantively non- or pseudo-free societies. Alternatively, modern free society constitutes or incorporates not only formal and especially substantive democracy and capitalism as a formally and effectively free economy, but also a free culture and civil society, which are all interrelated in accordance with sociological holism positing interconnections of between the various parts of society seen as a whole. In terms of structuralism or systems theory, modern free society is so defined by being a macroscopic social structure or total societal system incorporating all these elements as substructures or subsystems, thus the configuration of integral liberty encompassing all particular liberties, as precisely epitomized by contemporary free societies.

The holistic sociological approach hence helps address and perhaps resolve the paradox of (formal) democracy as a political regime and (formally free) capitalism as an economic system not being invariably equivalent to or sufficient for modern free society. The paradox persists in the political-science and economics literature insofar as it lacks or downplays societal holism or structuralism that treats a democratic polity and capitalism and economy overall as subsystems or sub-structures of the total social system or macroscopic structure, and political and economic freedoms as particular forms of integral societal liberty. To that extent, the paradox becomes an analog of the 'fallacy of misplaced concreteness' by misplacing the concrete political regime of formal democracy and the particular economic system of formally free capitalism, as done by orthodox or modern 'libertarian' economics, for a free society as a whole. Such a conflation is remedied by realizing that the latter is a total social system incorporating all of its subsystems, and not exhausted by and reduced to any one of them, be it democracy or capitalism/economy, just as a free society's integral liberty incorporates various particular liberties and is not reducible to a single one of these, including political or economic freedom, however important either might be. This realization forms a crucial insight and contribution of societal holism or structuralism to analyzing the relationship and notably resolving the paradox of a disjunction in various societies and historical periods between democracy and capitalism and modern free society, thus preventing the political and economistic 'fallacy of misplaced concreteness' committing reductionism.

In turn, without such an holistic structural-systemic sociological approach, it may be impossible or difficult to understand and explain how, why, where and when many nominal democracies—plus legal republics and constitutional monarchies—and capitalist economies are not considered or experienced as really free societies. Instead, they are deemed or experienced as the latter's opposites or perversions, including aristocracies, theocracies, oligarchies, totalitarian or authoritarian regimes, plutocracies, kleptocracies, master-servant and slave-like economies, capitalist dictatorships, authoritarian, anarchic and mafia capitalisms, and the like. As noted, these societies span from 19th-century Great Britain through Germany in the 1930s to Islamic Republic of Iran, post-communist Poland and Russia, Turkey under Islamic government, contemporary China, South Korea, Taiwan and Singapore, South America, Mexico, the Southern and related states of America, etc. This holistic approach best explains and predicts why they, while being mostly formal democracies or republics and largely capitalist economies (except for, in part, Islamic ruled Iran) were, are and probably will not be substantively free societies.

Hence, in addressing the relationships between democracy or capitalism and modern free society, especially resolving the problem of non-equivalence between the two in many societies and times, the comparative advantages of an holistic sociological theory and approach are salient in relation to political science and economics typically (but not invariably) treating polity and economy as self-contained isolated systems rather than subsystems of the total societal system. As indicated, its related comparative advantage consists in that it analyzes a free society in terms of interrelations between all of its parts—rather than only or primarily as political democracy or capitalism—consistent with the classic sociological principle of interconnections and interactions of social systems within society as the total societal system.[4] If, as Pareto[5] states, sociologists suggest, and sociologically minded economists agree, the 'sociological system' is larger and 'more complicated' than political and economic

---

4   The observed disjuncture between formal-procedural democracy, as well as capitalism, and a free society indicates that the interrelations between its parts, specifically of the first or second with a free culture and civil society, are not invariably positive or always mutually reinforcing, just as the classic sociological principle does not assume that the interactions of social phenomena are necessarily of this nature.

5   Pareto (1935, p. 1442) states the 'sociological system is much more complicated' than the economic system because the first is 'made up of certain molecules harboring residues (sentiments), derivations, interests, and proclivities, and which perform, subject to numerous ties, logical and non-logical actions.' Hence, he suggests that the equilibrium 'states of the economic system may be regarded as particular cases of the general states of the sociological system' (Pareto 1935, p. 1440).

systems as its particular elements interrelated with the others within it as a totality, modern free society is an exemplary variant of the latter and thus more complex than democracy or economy, and integral societal liberty more so than political or economic liberties. In general, democracy or capitalism each relates to modern free society as does a structural component to a structure that is a complex of such components, specifically a political or economic sub-system relating to a societal system as a totality of these and other interrelated and interacting subsystems, including culture and civil society.

The preceding suggests that democracy or capitalism each constitutes the necessary, but not sufficient, respective political and economic condition, element or indicator of modern free society.[6] Each is necessary because democracy or capitalism—if assumed to be a formally or substantively free economy—is necessarily the integral element of modern free society as the total social system, and political or economic freedoms, choices, and rights are an indispensable component of holistic societal liberty, choice and right. Each is not sufficient in itself, however, because democracy or capitalism represents one of the plurality of elements of modern free society, with political or economic freedoms being a particular component among the multiple components of societal liberty. To avoid conflating democracy or capitalism with modern free society, its elements are specified to also include a free culture and civil society, and thus the components of societal liberty to involve cultural and individual liberties as well, along with a democratic polity and a free capitalist or other economy, i.e., political and economic freedoms.

Therefore, democracy or capitalism, political or economic freedom, attains or approaches its full value only when integrated with a free culture and civil society, cultural and individual liberties, as their complementary elements in the whole of modern free society and its holistic liberty. And holistic liberty realizes or approximates its complete 'worth' solely when conjoined and complemented with equality and justice, as Smith with his 'liberal plan of liberty, equality and justice,' and Jefferson[7] with his principles of 'liberty and justice

---

6 Mueller (2009, p. ix) implies this by cautioning that democracy represents 'no guarantee of liberalism' as the foremost principle of liberty and so a free society, citing such examples as India and Turkey and by implication, due to the 'growing importance of religious extremism,' 'conservative America,' first of all, the evangelical South.

7 Even the putatively 'libertarian' but comparatively moderate—compared to Mises, Hayek, and Friedman et al.—economist Knight (1967, p. 783) admits this in depicting America as 'a society claiming to be conceived in liberty (but also) dedicated to equality, according to Jefferson and Lincoln.' Also, he states contra Hayek that 'freedom, correctly conceived, implies opportunity, unobstructed (equal) opportunity, to use power, which must be possessed, to give content to freedom, or make it effective' (Knight 1967, p. 790). Knight adds (1967, p. 794)

for all' and 'all men are created equal' suggest. Conversely, democracy or capitalism fails to realize its societal value if not combined with a free culture and civil society, thus political or economic freedom failing in this respect without cultural and individual liberties, just as does liberty overall in the absence of equality and justice, as well as reason, rationalism and progress. Moreover, especially formal democracy or formally free capitalism can often become virtually valueless from the stance of modern free society and its holistic liberty to the point of not being worth the constitutional and other paper on which their nominal political and economic freedoms are written (or unwritten) if a free culture and civil society, thus cultural and individual liberties, are negated or suppressed. This is precisely exemplified by the societies mentioned previously, from 19th-century Great Britain through Nazi Germany to post-communist Poland and Russia, China and Singapore, South America, Islamic Iran and Turkey, the US South, etc.

Democracy or capitalism operates as the necessary political or economic condition and complement of modern free society because the latter is necessarily democratic politically and free economically, and holistic societal liberty, choice and right invariably comprises particular political and economic freedoms, choices and rights as its integral ingredient. On the other hand, democracy or capitalism does not constitute the sufficient political or economic condition and complement of a free society because the latter as a total social system is more than democratic and free economically in formal or substantive terms, but also free in its subsystems of culture and civil society. Equally, holistic societal liberty contains political and economic, but also cultural and individual freedoms, choices, and rights.[8] Hence, a free culture and civil society represent the necessary cultural and civic/individual prerequisites of modern

---

that 'the concept of free society held in the modern West is rooted in the right of the people to change the laws' versus Hayek suggesting that the latter denies that right in favor of immutable 'sacred' law, tradition, and other rules.

8 If one wishes, democracy becomes from the necessary into the sufficient condition of modern free society only insofar as its exists and functions in a kind of synergy with the other three conditions in that it invariably blends or simultaneously coexists with a free economy, civil society, and culture, as an ideal constellation that determines and typifies only truly free, liberal societies. In fact, such a synergic constellation and operation makes not only democracy, but also a free economy, civil society, and culture each—within but not outside and separate from it—both the necessary and sufficient condition of modern free society. But this may amount to a tautology that the synergic complex of democracy and a free economy, civil society, and culture represents the necessary and sufficient condition of modern free society as precisely such a total social system of these subsystems. Hence, the point is rather whether each of these subsystems in itself, in particular democracy or capitalism, constitutes

TABLE 1.1   *Modern free society as a total social system according to the sociological holistic approach.*

Democracy—Free polity	Capitalism—Free economy
Free Culture	Free Civil Society

free society, in addition to and conjunction with democracy and capitalism as the political and economic. In turn, none of them is sufficient if considered separately and in isolation from the others, a fallacy that is preempted by sociological holism or structuralism emphasizing the interconnection and interactions between all these parts or structures within the whole or structure.

The preceding yields a classification of the conditions, as well as elements and indicators, of modern free society into four categories. The first is formal-procedural and especially substantive-effective democracy, simply a democratic polity, as the necessary political condition, the second capitalism or generally a free economy as the economic, the third a free culture as the cultural, and the fourth a free civil society in the sense of an autonomous private life sphere as the civic or individual. Such a set of multiple conditions or elements suggests that democracy and capitalism represents each approximately just one quarter of the 'equation' of modern free society as the total social system, and political or economic freedoms separately form such a share of societal liberty as a holistic category. This is instructive to emphasize because it casts doubt on the supposed equivalence between (formal) democracy and a free society in political and everyday discourse, and the latter and capitalism according to 'libertarian' economics, expressing politics and economy reductionism or determinism remedied by a sociological holistic approach outlined above. 'Modern free society' is precisely what it says: *society* as a whole of freedom, not just any one of its parts taken separately and in isolation from the others, be it its political or economic system—i.e., paraphrasing classical economist J.B. Say, the polity and 'economy of society'—and only this holistic sociological approach does justice to it (Table 1.1).

Liberty, Equality, and Justice in Modern Free Society

As noted, modern free society is characterized with liberty as its basis and prime value that is typically conjoined and complemented with social equality

---

a sufficient condition of modern free society, and such a multidimensionality and complexity of the latter rules out an affirmative answer.

and justice, as what Mannheim and other sociologists, philosophers and economists connote its complements, along with human reason, happiness, dignity, hope, humanism, and progress according to the project of liberal, democratic and rationalistic modernity rooted in the Enlightenment. Mannheim and other theorists hence suggest that modern free society or modernity completely realizes its potential and promise, and holistic liberty attains or approximates its full value and meaning solely when conjoined with social equality, justice, reason, and other complements. Alternatively, they hold that equality, justice, and reason crucially help realize the potential of modern free society, and attain the full value and meaning of liberty by enhancing its worth and significance, just as being enhanced by it, resulting in equal, universal or inclusive, just, and reasonable freedom.

For instance, Adam Smith suggests this with his 'liberal plan of liberty, equality and justice'—also, implied in his precursor Hume and what Keynes calls the French 'political philosophers' like Condorcet, Voltaire, Montesquieu, etc.—and Thomas Jefferson with his principles of 'liberty and justice for all,' 'all men are created equal,' and the 'pursuit of happiness.' They both express the Enlightenment as the age and project of intertwined and mutually reinforced freedom, equality, justice, reason and rationalism, happiness and joy of life, dignity, hope, optimism, humanism, progress, and related values also present or anticipated in classical Greek-Roman democracy or republic and civilization and its revival by the libertine and humanistic Italian Renaissance.[9] Evidently, they consider liberty, equality and justice to exist in a

---

9 Manent (1998, p. 222) observes that the 'iron law of human obedience and inequality had been very rarely broken, only, and most eminently, by Greek cities and the Roman republic but also by such Italian cities as Venice and Florence. The Greeks, the Romans, and the Florentines proved that men could live in liberty and equality—that is, that they could rule and be ruled in turn—but only by belonging to the same body politic.' In particular, Manent (1998, p. 221) recognizes this: 'Even Athens—the most democratic body politic ever, (was) but at the same time the most exclusive club of white males.' Generally, the possible objection that mentioning classical Greek (Athens) democracy in this connection overlooks or downplays its slavery is valid. Yet, it is equivalent to objecting that Tocqueville's celebrated 'democracy in America' also featured such a system at approximately half of its space until almost a century after the American Revolution and Constitution, and even longer its (Jim Crow) sequel of segregation, discrimination and oppression, as Acemoglu and Robinson (2006, 2008) suggest. The similar objection that during the period of the Italian Renaissance the feudal bondage or master-servant socioeconomic regime persisted is also correct but analogous to noting that a 'master-servant' economy based on common law was perpetuated in the UK and the US until the later part of the 19th century, as Naidu and Yuchtman (2012), Steinberg (2003), Steinfeld (2001), and Orren (1994) report.

complementary and mutually reinforcing relationship, simply to be complements, as distinct from mutual exclusion, opposition and substitutes. They
thus suggest the principle of equal, universal or inclusive, just, and reasonable
freedom, as do later economists and sociologists.

These include Ricardo, Mill and others stressing universal economic and intellectual freedoms, including the 'law of equal competition,' Comte freedom
or 'right of every man,' Spencer the 'law of equal freedom,' Durkheim 'just liberty,' etc. They prefigure contemporary economic and sociological theories of
liberty-equality and justice complementarity, mutual reinforcement and synergy, and anticipate their historical-empirical conjunction in contemporary
free societies, the freest among them being the most equal or egalitarian and
just or equitable. For instance, Smith treats justice and so its basis or correlate
equality as more 'essential' than 'beneficence' and 'generosity' to the 'existence'
of society, thus predicting contemporary free societies' unique conjunction of
freedom with egalitarianism and equity or fairness, as exemplified by Scandinavia (as Samuelson in the opening citation suggests) and Western Europe,
Canada, etc.

Conversely, like Mannheim, Smith, Jefferson and other Enlightenment figures imply that modern free society fails to entirely realize its potential, and
holistic liberty to reach or approach its full value if instead disjointed from
social equality, justice, reason, and its other complements. After all, Smith's
'liberal plan' is not 'liberty or equality and justice' and Jefferson's principle not
'liberty or justice for all,' and generally neither is the Enlightenment the age
and project of either freedom or else equality, justice, reason, rationalism, happiness, joy of life, and progress. This hence rules out unequal, non-universal or
exclusionary, unjust and unreasonable 'freedom' or 'liberty' as an ersatz substitute or inner contradiction. Evidently, Smith, Jefferson and the Enlightenment
in general do not consider liberty and equality and justice to exist in a relationship of substitution, mutual exclusion and opposition, as substitutes and
opposites. They contradict 'libertarian' economics' (Mises-Hayek-Friedman's)
contrary claim to mutual exclusion ('trade-off') between liberty and equality
or justice—which is ironic given that Smith is deemed its putative founder
and hero, and the Enlightenment its philosophical root—and refute ideological and political efforts to create or sustain an arbitrary opposition between
these constitutive values or bases of a free or 'open,' 'good' society.

Moreover, Smith implies that illiberty is linked with and liberty ultimately eliminated by inequality or injustice in what can be denoted an obverse
'illiberal plan,' by admonishing that the 'prevalence of injustice must utterly
destroy' a free and any society. He thus anticipates the fatal destiny of the
many societies listed above precisely or primarily because of such injustice and

inequality compounded with un-freedom, including 19th-century England's vanishing of master-servant economy and exclusionary 'democracy' (and the British empire), Nazi Germany and fascist Europe, the Soviet Union, slavery in the US, and the petrification of Islamic Iran and Turkey, Singapore, South America, the Southern and related states of America, etc. At any rate, Smith, Jefferson, other Enlightenment figures, and later sociologists like Mannheim help define and specify the relationship between liberty and equality, justice, reason, happiness, progress, and related values within the framework of modern free society or modernity.

This yields the inference that modern free society involves liberty that exists essentially in conjunction with equality, justice, reason and related values as its complements, consistent with the Enlightenment philosophical project of modernity and its political outcomes the French and American Revolutions, and contrary to the 'libertarian' spurious or arbitrary opposition between them construed as supposed substitutes. By virtue of such conjunction, it constitutes a free, equal, just, open, rational, and thus truly or completely 'good' society precisely defined by the combination of these and related attributes. It is so in a long sequence and continuity of defining and conceiving this societal ideal from classical Greece through the Renaissance and the Enlightenment and the French ('liberty, equality and fraternity') and American ('liberty and justice for all') Revolutions to their contemporary variations and legacies. Modern free society therefore integrates and realizes humans' perennial quest for both liberty *and* equality, justice, reason, happiness, progress, and the like as its bases and primary values (summarized in Table 1.2). In accordance with the holistic sociological approach and in reality, it does so as the total social system encompassing a democratic polity, capitalism or a free economy in general, a free culture, and a free civil society, as elaborated and specified below.

Still, the holistic sociological argument that modern free society is the total social system of these elements and the complex of holistic liberty does not hinge—i.e., stand or fall—on the assumption that the latter is in this society typically conjoined with social equality, justice, reason, happiness, progress and related values as its complements, as Mannheim, Smith, Jefferson, the Enlightenment, and the French/American Revolutions indicate, and classical democracy and the Renaissance imply. Such an assumption or finding is secondary or subsidiary and does not substantially affect the above argument as primary that stands in its own right. Thus, even if somehow finding or assuming that freedom is not conjoined and complemented with but disassociated from and substituted by social equality or justice, as 'libertarianism' asserts by conceiving the two as substitutes, this does not change the fact or conception that modern society is such a complex of holistic, integral (called 'indivisible'

TABLE 1.2 *Modern free society's bases and primary values.*

Holistic, integral liberty	↔	Equality, egalitarianism, inclusion,
	↔	Justice, Equity, Fairness
	↔	Reason, Rationalism
	↔	Happiness, Joy of Life, Wellbeing
	↔	Dignity, Hope, Optimism, Humanism
	↔	Social Progress

Modern Manifestations

The Age of Reason, Liberty, Equality, Justice, Reason, Joy of Life, Hope, Progress (The Enlightenment)

The 'Liberal Plan of Liberty, Equality and Justice' (Smith)

'Liberty and Justice for All,' 'All Men Are Created Equal,' 'Pursuit of Happiness' (Jefferson, the American Revolution)

'Liberty, Equality and Fraternity' (the French Revolution)

Equal liberty and rights (Voltaire, Comte, Mill, Spencer)

Historical Precursors

Classical concept and practice of liberty, equality, justice, reason, democracy and republic (ancient Greece/Athens, Rome)

Human liberty, autonomy, equality, justice, dignity, artistic and scientific creativity, activity, i.e., humanism (the Italian Renaissance) ↔ Conjunction, complementarity, mutual reinforcement

---

by 'libertarian' economists like Mises) liberty, regardless of whether it is positively or negatively related to egalitarianism and equity. Relatedly, such a 'libertarian' assertion disjointing and 'defending' liberty from social equality and justice—and despite Smith's classical political economy's liberal plan including all the three—does not affect the definition and conception of modern free society as a total social system of a democratic polity, a free economy, a free culture, and a free civil society. Moreover, this is a definition that 'libertarian' economists would accept and propose as their own if adopted a holistic approach, but they usually do not adopt it and therefore are unable or unwilling to define modern free society holistically and thus realistically.

Either embracing Mannheim-Smith-Jefferson's premise of liberty and equality/justice as complements, or its 'libertarian' alternative construing them as substitutes, the above definition and conception of modern free society stands on its own basically unaffected. In sum, the relationship between freedom and

equality/justice is in itself inconsequential and neutral to defining and analyzing modern free society as a complex of holistic liberty and a system of free
political, economic, cultural and civil systems, which thus preempts 'libertarian' objections against treating these values as complements rather than substitutes within it, as supposedly prejudicial to a proper definition and analysis
of the matter. It can be theoretically plausible and empirically grounded to
posit that freedom is integrated or complemented with equality, justice, reason, happiness, progress and related values especially within modern free society, but not absolutely necessary to define, analyze and specify the latter as
such a complex, as done next.

Definition and Specification of Modern Free Society

Defining and conceptualizing modern free society as the social system of a
democratic polity and a free economy, free culture and free civil society, however, does not suffice, because it opens the question as to what these latter actually are or tend to become in the framework of the first. The question arises
what is specifically a democratic polity, i.e., genuine democracy, a truly free
economy, culture, and civil society within such a social system, i.e., one wonders what precisely the latter is in its integral political, economic, cultural, and
civic components, and the following addresses this question by redefining and
specifying them. Thus, modern free society constitutes a multiple totality of
democracy, economy, culture, and civil society only if these are in their definite
types rather than others. Only certain types of democracy, economy, culture,
and civil society—and not others—form political, economic, cultural, and
civic conditions or elements of modern free society, as specified next.

Modern Free Society and the Type of Democracy
First, as a total social system of freedom modern free society inherently incorporates as its political subsystem democracy only in its definite, solely genuine
and viable type. This is liberal, secular, and consequently universalistic and
egalitarian democracy. Liberal-secular and universalistic-egalitarian democracy hence forms the intrinsic, 'natural' political principle and constitutive,
'built-in' system of modern free society. In essence and in reality, modern free
society in its political dimension only develops and exists with liberal-secular
and universalistic-egalitarian democracy as the sole truly free, rational, inclusive, equal, non-discriminatory political system, simply a democratic polity.
This yields a proxy Michels-like 'iron' sociological law or historical pattern (but
opposite to that of oligarchy): in his words appropriately modified, 'who says

modern free society politically, says only liberal-secular and universalistic-egalitarian democracy.'

Of course, what has been stated for democracy in general also holds for its liberal-secular and universalistic-egalitarian type. This is that the latter as a solely free, democratic polity does not exhaust or subsume completely modern free society as more comprehensive incorporating, in addition, a free economy/culture/civil society, but constitutes its political core, essence, and face. As noted for democracy overall, its liberal-secular and universalistic-egalitarian type approximately represents one quarter of the 'equation' or whole of modern free society, in conjunction with a free economy/culture/civil society representing the remainder. Liberal-secular and universalistic-egalitarian democracy may well be the crucial component of modern free society for most social scientists—except for most economists preferring capitalism—and peoples in contemporary societies, but still needs to be specified as 'just' such a proportion of its whole to keep a measure of balance in respect of its four constitutive components.

Conversely, modern free society does not incorporate democracy in its opposite, spurious and unviable type such as anti-liberal, anti-secular and consequently anti-universalistic, anti-egalitarian 'democracy.' The latter is a political principle and system inherently adverse and ultimately destructive to this free societal system and thus human liberty, equality, justice, wellbeing, happiness, progress, and life. Simply, there is no such thing as modern free society politically with anti-liberal, anti-secular and anti-universalistic, anti-egalitarian 'democracy,' even if disguised or embellished formally and procedurally by 'constitutions,' 'rule of law,' 'elections,' etc. Theoretically, such 'democracy' is what Weber would call an inner 'impossible contradiction' and economists an 'impossibility theorem,' actually anti- or non-democracy, and thus the political antithesis and nemesis of this societal system of liberty. Hence, this, if one wishes to be consistent, results in Michels' inverse 'iron' sociological law, 'who says modern free society politically, never says anti-liberal, anti-secular, anti-universalistic, anti-egalitarian democracy as anti or non-democracy.'

In its liberal dimension, democracy is defined by universal, equal, and comprehensive political liberties, choices, and rights, as well as equality, justice, inclusion or non-exclusion, non-discrimination, influence and representation ('voice') in the polity. It is liberal democracy because of being the ideal, domain and practice of political freedom for all individuals and groups within a society, as well as all societies in the global societal context. Like liberty in general, universal political freedom is conjoined and complemented with such individual and group equality and justice as Smith-Jefferson-Mannheim's complements that help realize or approach its full value or worth for the polity.

Hence, as in modern free society as a whole, in this type of democracy liberty and equality/justice arise, exist and persist in a relationship of conjunction, complementarity, and mutual reinforcement, simply synergy. This is indicated by the widespread observation or expectation that the freest modern societies are also the most egalitarian and equitable (e.g., Scandinavian countries). Conversely, liberty and equality/justice do not function in relations of substitution, opposition and mutual exclusion, contrary to what 'libertarian' economists (Mises, Hayek, Friedman et al.) allege oblivious of or denying this reality and constructing a 'parallel universe' in which these freest societies are 'unfree,' as some leading representatives from contemporary mainstream economics (Samuelson[10]) object.

Liberal democracy uniquely endows and entitles everyone with a capacity, quest and exercise of liberty essentially defined and identified by freedom of choice—just as with that of happiness or joy of life in the sense of the Enlightenment as its philosophical foundation—so long as this does not dispense or interfere with such equal liberties/choices/joys of others. In addition, liberal democracy is unique in its all-encompassing or comprehensive and principled, consistent liberty in the polity. Such liberty involves both individual and group or micro- and macroscopic, elite and mass, insider and outsider, native and non-native, religious and non-religious, formal and substantive political and civil liberties and rights, including those of consent and dissent, stability and change, institutionalized conflict, reform and peaceful revolution, 'voice and exit,' and so on. In short, individual and group liberty in liberal democracy is universal in its subjects and comprehensive in its scope, and only constrained or tempered by such equal liberties of others.

In turn, such constraints mean that liberal democracy is not a Hobbesian anarchy governed by the 'law of the jungle' and of the 'strongest.' This contradicts both the 'libertarian' anarchic utopia of literal or figurative 'license to kill'—yet for aristocrats, oligarchs, theocrats or plutocrats against the populace, labor, masses or 'godless'—with impunity given a 'minimal' government controlled by oligarchy or plutocracy, and the conservative accusation of liberal democracy for 'anarchism.' The simple principle and message is 'you and everyone else are truly free and notably in the entire or comprehensive range of political relations and activities only in liberal democracy as long as you and anyone else do not do away with or intrude into others' liberty as freedom of choice,' as classical liberalism since the Enlightenment postulates and emphasizes, and its contemporary version elaborates and expands.

---

10   As seen in the opening citation, Samuelson (1964, p. 1983) effectively disposes of 'libertarian' economics as an ideological dogma disproved by reality, in particular of Hayek as a false prophet of freedom.

As a consequence, by virtue of its ideal, institution and practice of universal, equal liberty, freedom of choice, only limited by such liberties and choices of others, liberal democracy is intrinsically or ultimately tends to become universalistic and egalitarian, and thus a truly free, democratic, open, fair, inclusive, non-discriminatory, and representative political system. Relatedly, on account of its principle and reality of comprehensive and coherent political liberty, including both individual and collective, formal and substantive liberties, etc., liberal democracy constitutes a completely and coherently free, democratic, open polity. Like modern free society as a whole, by definition democracy is either universalistic, egalitarian, inclusive, open, as well as comprehensive and coherent in its holders and range of political liberties and rights—or not democracy, but its own contradiction such as non-universalistic, non-egalitarian, exclusionary, closed, partial and incoherent 'democracies' as its ersatz substitute or non sequitur. It is only liberal democracy that entirely fulfils this democratic imperative of universalism, egalitarianism, inclusion, openness, comprehensiveness and coherence in politics, notably political liberties and rights, just as modern free society does so within the total social system and human life overall.

In sum, liberal democracy is the only democratic type inhering to, compatible with and constitutive of modern free society because of being the sole consistent postulate and structure of political freedom, as well as equality and justice as its complementary postulates, in accordance with liberalism as the foremost ideal and institution of human liberty. On this account, liberal democracy is the necessary and sufficient condition of a free, open, democratic political system and in extension of modern free society in political terms. This leads to a variation on Michels' style 'iron' sociological law, historical pattern or empirical tendency—'who says liberal democracy, always says a free, open, democratic political system and free society politically.'

In its secular facet, democracy is defined by the structural-functional differentiation between politics and religion as different social structures with varying functions in society, notably political and religious powers, expressed in the legal and effective separation of church and state. It is secular democracy because of being the principle, realm and exercise of political liberties, rights, and autonomy especially from religious power, notably theocratic or theocentric coercion, oppression, intrusion, interference, exclusion, discrimination, punishment or sanction characterizing anti-secular 'godly democracies' as its opposites or bogus substitutes.

Like its liberal form, secular democracy is universalistic and egalitarian, and thus inclusive and open by its principle and system of universal and equal political freedoms and rights for individuals and groups—which are only constrained by those of others—regardless of whether or not they form or belong to organized religions like churches, sects, etc. This indicates its stark contrast and opposition to (and by) its anti-secular antithesis and nemesis such as non-universalistic and non-egalitarian, exclusionary and closed 'democracies.' These are effective theocracies privileging and dominated by the 'godly' against the 'godless' subject to systematic, severe and permanent oppression, exclusion, discrimination and severe punishment, including imprisonment, torture and death, for their religious, moral and political 'crimes' of heresy, blasphemy, pleasures-sins, dissent, etc.

Hence, if modern democracy is either universalistic and egalitarian, i.e., inclusive and open, or not really and fully one, then only the secular, like liberal, type completely satisfies this requirement, while its anti-secular, just as anti-liberal, antithesis or ersatz substitute totally fails this essential democratic test. In addition to political freedoms and rights, secular democracy is universalistic and egalitarian by its idea and practice of universal and equal religious liberties for all individuals, groups, regions and societies. This is in opposition to (and by) its anti-secular antipode allowing 'religious liberty' only for a certain group, region or society ('us,' 'true believers,' insiders, natives) and denying or violating it for others ('them,' 'infidels,' outsiders, foreigners). Relatedly, like its liberal twin, secular democracy is inherently all-inclusive or comprehensive and principled or consistent in its scope of religious liberty by involving both freedom of religion and freedom from religion. It is again in stark contrast to its anti-secular nemesis solely allowing and promoting freedom of religion—and only for 'us' versus 'them'—but denying and suppressing freedom from religion, thus exerting a theocratic form of anti-democratic coercion, oppression, and discrimination.

In this respect, secular democracy represents the necessary—but, unlike its liberal form, not sufficient—condition of a free, open, democratic polity and modern free society politically. This is consistent with that secularism or secularization, understood as the postulate of or trend to functional differentiation and autonomy of politics from religion, state from church, is observed or assumed to be an indispensable, yet not invariant, prerequisite of freedom in the political and social system. In turn, liberalism and the process of liberalization, as the principle of universal and comprehensive liberty and the process of liberation in society, intrinsically represents both. Evidently, not all secular democracies in formal-procedural or substantive terms or republics are liberal, as shown by the historical and present experience of 'popular democracies' or 'republics' in the Soviet Union, Eastern Europe during communism, China and North Korea, etc. Yet, virtually every liberal democracy is secular in the two meanings, as witnessed by contemporary composite liberal-secular democracies in Western Europe and elsewhere (Canada, etc.).

Furthermore, the preceding indicates and predicts whether and how secular democracy and secularism generally does and will become the sufficient condition of a free, open, democratic polity and thus of modern free society in political terms. Secular democracy and secularism overall tends to become the sufficient condition when it develops in or fuses with liberal democracy and liberalism as a whole to form composite liberal-secular democracy. This tendency is typically observed or expected in contemporary democracies and free societies during the entwined apparently irreversible or steady process of secularization and liberalization within modernity as a whole since the secularizing and liberalizing triad of the Enlightenment, the Industrial Revolution, and the French/American Revolutions through these days, especially in Western Europe and Canada, and to some extent the US. In this respect, whereas not invariably identical and linked, liberal and secular democracy manifest a strong tendency to ultimately reach an identity or synthesis in contemporary democracies and free societies through the process of secularization becoming entwined with that of liberalization and democratization in the Western world from Scandinavia to Canada (thus exempting China, North Korea, etc.).

In sum, a democratic political system in the context of modern free society tends to be invariably equivalent to and established, sustained, and predicted by liberal-secular and universalistic-egalitarian democracy. In turn, this type of democracy is profoundly opposite to and vehemently negated and persistently eliminated or subverted by its anti- and pre-liberal alternatives negating and eliminating or subverting universal and comprehensive political liberties and rights in the name of 'democracy' and 'freedom,' as exemplified by conservative, including fascist and false 'libertarian,' and other spurious illiberal 'democracies' or 'republics.' Liberal-secular democracy is also antithetical to and attacked and extinguished by its anti- and pre-secular counterparts that suppress and sacrifice such liberties, rights and even humans to 'higher' superhuman Divine causes and agents, as witnessed in theocracies, theocentric, and other ersatz religiously grounded, 'faith-based' 'democracies' or 'republics.'

As a consequence, societies from Western Europe to Canada having a political system of liberal-secular democracy are observed or expected to be invariably and drastically freer than those with its anti- and pre-liberal and anti- and pre-secular opposites such as conservative—in particular, religious and fascist—and related 'democracies' or 'republics.' Conversely, it is found or predicted that societies with a regime of anti-liberal conservative and anti-secular religious 'democracies' or 'republics' are or will be not only substantially less free than those with liberal-secular democracy, as exemplified by Turkey under Islamic governance, Catholic-dominated Poland, in part Ireland, South America and Mexico, the US South, Islamic Republic of Iran, etc.

Further, they are witnessed or anticipated to degenerate into absolutely un-free societies in which universal and comprehensive political and all societal liberty is vanquished or perverted beyond recognition into the unrestricted 'freedom' and absolute power and corruption of exclusionary aristocracy, oligarchy, or theocracy as the 'master-caste' in Michels' words. They thus end up in descending or petrifying into what Simmel connotes as medieval despotism during the Christian and Islamic Dark Middle Ages, and Comte primeval barbarism in Biblical and similar primitive times. They do so owing to anti-liberal and anti-secular, in particular conservative-religious, political regimes' intrinsic pattern of degenerating into totalitarian or authoritarian dictatorship. The latter is couched in and justified as a righteous defense, revolt and 'holy' total war (jihad and crusade) against 'Western,' 'anti-Islamic,' 'un-American,' 'anti-German' (during Nazism), 'anti-Christian,' 'godless' liberal democracy and liberalism condemned as 'unmitigated evil' ('Satan' in Islamic and Christian descriptions) and the supreme 'enemy,' viz., the 'European anti-Christ' for US theocratic evangelicalism. This is done because of liberal democracy's and liberalism's imputed mortal sin-crime of being the sole or foremost principle, system and practice of universal, comprehensive and holistic political and all societal liberty, equality, justice, inclusion, wellbeing, reason and progress, human valuation, dignity, happiness, and humane life.

And anti-liberal, anti-secular unfree society stipulates and punishes the sin-crime of human liberty, choice, respect and value, happiness and autonomous, dignified life devaluated by and sacrificed to what J.S. Mill and Weber connote (referring to Calvinism) the 'alleged will and glory of God,' including contemporary sociologists' reference to 'terror in the mind of God.' On the other hand, this same set of values and behaviors constitutes the defining and constitutive element or indicator of modern free society, including its liberal-secular democracy, simply a foremost virtue or merit. And displaying duplicity or delusion, even the most anti-liberal, anti-secular and consequently, other things equal, unfree contemporary societies do not claim or admit to be the most or less free than others, but instead claiming to be the freer and freest. This is shown by a range of what Sorokin would denote (and prefer to liberal-secular democracy) pure or diluted theocracies spanning from Islamic Republic of Iran to Catholic-dominated Poland to Dahrendorf's 'Southern Unites States' (commonly self-described and depicted by outsiders as the 'Bible Belt') precisely making such duplicitous or delusionary 'freedom' claims.

The book aims to assess especially contemporary Western and related societies' claims to being the 'free, freer, freest' modern society, with virtually all of them, including both those observed or expected to be the least free and the freest, indulging in such collective narcissism. At this point suffice it to say that the book assumes and expects that not all contemporary Western and related (plus non-Western) societies are 'created equal' in a sociological, non-theological sense in respect of modern free society, but instead more or less unequal in societal liberty, and thus their common narcissistic superior-freedom claims are probably not equally true or credible. Specifically, the preceding suggests that some societies such as those with a political system of liberal-secular and universalistic-egalitarian democracy are 'more equal' in freedom, simply freer, than others, thus the freest among them.

In extension, Western and related societies that are ideologically and politically more liberal and secular, or less conservative and religious, tend to be consistently and substantially freer in political terms (and 'happier') than do others, above all anti-liberal and anti-secular or 'godly' theocratic and theocentric and thus exclusionary and anti-egalitarian social systems. Liberal-secular societies are actually or likely the freest politically and otherwise (just as the 'happiest' judging by various surveys) and their opposites the least so, among Western and related countries. This is dramatically exemplified by the stark contrast and opposition between liberal-secular Western Europe, above all Scandinavia, or Canada and anti-liberal and anti-secular Catholic Poland and Islamic Turkey and in part the US (the fundamentalist South), and within the latter between the 'two Americas,' liberal and conservative America.

The aforesaid therefore specifies what a democratic polity, i.e., genuine democracy intrinsically is or actually becomes in the context of modern free society. In view of persistent and even intensifying anti-liberal and anti-secular denials, detractors and attacks, especially in Islamic states, including Turkey recently, Catholic Poland and Latin America, and evangelical parts of the US (the 'Bible Belt,' etc.), it is precisely liberal-secular democracy that is observed or expected to constitute what Durkheim would call the freest (and happiest) type of 'political society' among all contemporary Western and related societies. Conversely, the above specifies what a democratic polity, true democracy as an integral element of modern free society is not. It is not anti- and pre-liberal conservative, and anti- and pre-secular religious, including fascist and false 'libertarian,' and similar 'democracies' or 'republics' as actually anti- or non-democracies[11] and thus unfree, totalitarian or authoritarian political systems. The preceding suggests that it is insufficient or imprecise to propose that democracy represents a necessary political condition, integral element and relevant indicator of modern free society without specifying what the former

---

11   Acemoglu, Egorov, and Sonin (2009) use the term non-democracies in reference to such and related political systems, as do Kurzman and Leahey (2004), and Mulligan, Gil, and Sala-i-Martin (2004).

invariably represents within the latter—a liberal-secular and universalistic polity.

In sum, liberal-secular and universalistic democracy constitutes the invariant political proof and face of modern free society, rather than anti- and pre-liberal conservative, including fascist, neo-conservative and false 'libertarian,' and anti- and pre-secular religious spurious 'democracies' or 'republics' as invariably the polar opposite. One can conclude and predict that modern free society either comprises liberal-secular democracy as its political subsystem within its total social system of holistic liberty—or is not really or fully free politically.

Modern Free Society and the Type of Economy

Second, modern free society as a total social system typically comprises only a definite, truly free and most viable type of economy, specifically capitalism, as its economic subsystem. This is a rationally coordinated or regulated[12] and relatively egalitarian or equitable, simply rational and welfare capitalism, also connoted 'democratic capitalism,' 'capitalism with a human face,' the 'welfare state,' 'social democracy,' 'social market economy,' and the like. Negatively specified, the only type of economy/capitalism consistent with and comprised in modern free society is non-anarchic—in the sense opposite to Hobbesian anarchy—and non-aristocratic, non-oligarchic and non-plutocratic capitalism. This holds on the ground that anarchy ruled by what Durkheim calls the 'law of the strongest' and even staunch 'libertarian' economist Mises[13] refers to as the 'law of the jungle,' and aristocracy, oligarchy and plutocracy as anarchic systems and ruling classes of unrestrained force, power and domination are profoundly antithetical and destructive to economic and all freedom in society.

Hence, rational and welfare, i.e., non-anarchic and non-aristocratic or non-plutocratic, capitalism constitutes the most appropriate principle, integral

---

12   Almost a century ago, precisely one year or so before the Great Depression, the economist Gustav Cassel (1928) proposes a 'rationally regulated social economy' and generally a 'rationally organized society.' In particular, he suggests that the 'cyclical movement of trade, with all its pernicious effects on social economy (is) an evil which ought to be prevented in a rationally organized society,' thus converging with or anticipating his contemporary Keynes. In turn, Davis (1945, p. 136) insists that the 'liberal ethic is not at all incompatible with state regulation of economic affairs.'

13   Even the hardline 'libertarian' economist Mises (1962, p. 93) admits that 'man alone among all living beings consciously aims at substituting social cooperation for what philosophers have called the state of nature or *bellum omnium contra omnes* (war of all against all) or the law of the jungle.'

subsystem and effective method in economic terms of modern free society. In the complex of 'rational and welfare,' rational capitalism is defined by rationalistic coordination or reasonable regulation of the economy by society through effective or sensible government intervention in the latter for what even Adam Smith acknowledge as the social good or the public interest as against private economic agents' 'conspiracy against the public,' thus neutralizing the glorified 'invisible hand' of the market. Negatively, rational capitalism is characterized with such economic regulation or intervention for the non-aristocratic, non-oligarchic, non-plutocratic and related non-elite and non-private good and interest, thus differing from Hobbesian anarchy involving non-regulation or no rules—except the 'law of the strongest' and of the 'jungle'—and from aristocracy, oligarchy and plutocracy regulating or rather ruling the economy for anti-social, anti-public interests. At this juncture, this type of capitalism is rational and efficient even in Smith's terms of furthering or protecting the social good or public interest from private 'conspiracy,' including that of aristocracy, oligarchy, and plutocracy, against society. This hence contradicts 'libertarian' economists' (Mises-Hayek-Friedman's) accusations against this economic system as 'irrational' and 'inefficient' (and 'socialism,' 'statism,' 'collectivism,' etc.) and their allegations that only its anarchic, laissez-faire opposite is 'rational,' 'efficient' and 'free.'

In the composite 'rational and welfare,' welfare and generally egalitarian capitalism is defined by universal and equal or symmetrical and comprehensive economic freedoms, rights, life chances and wellbeing of individual and collective agents in the economy, notably the factors of production such as capital and labor and other non-capitalist elements. This is also what Smith implies in acknowledging the need for improving the condition of the 'lowest ranks of the populace,' as do Ricardo, J.S. Mill, Marshall, and other early economists. Alternatively, this type of capitalism is characterized with non-particularistic, non-hierarchical and non-fragmented, including non-aristocratic, non-oligarchic, non-plutocratic and related non-exclusionary, economic freedoms, rights, life chances, and wellbeing. It thus differs both from anti-egalitarian slavery, feudalism or the master-servant economy ruled by aristocracy and from non-welfare, non-egalitarian and non-democratic capitalism controlled by plutocracy as the 'new aristocracy' of wealth.

In this connection, welfare-egalitarian capitalism effectively manifests itself as liberal or democratic and so truly free even in respect of what Smith and other orthodox economists imply as the law of universal, equal freedom in the economy. This disproves 'libertarian' economists' claims to the contrary and their assertions that only non-welfare, non-egalitarian, specifically oligarchic or plutocratic, capitalism is a 'free' economic system as an ideological delusion or deceptive myth. And by definition, the first type of capitalism/economy represents the only capitalist/economic system of approximately universal welfare in the sense of widespread wellbeing and shared material prosperity, thus the 'greatest happiness to the greatest number,' by Smith's criterion of including also the 'lowest ranks of the populace,' and not only the 'rich and the powerful' like aristocracy, oligarchy and plutocracy, so the perverse 'greatest happiness to the smallest number.' In this respect, welfare-egalitarian capitalism provides and furthers not only what neoclassical economist Marshall connotes the 'material requisites of well-being' widespread and shared among most strata of society, including Smith's 'lowest ranks,' as axiomatic in its definition. It also establishes and sustains the economic prerequisites of universal, equal or symmetrical freedoms of the factors of production, including both capitalists and non-capitalists, contrary to 'libertarianism' denying both outcomes, especially the second.

Thus, contemporary societies with welfare capitalism, for example Scandinavian welfare states, are observed or expected to report or display the highest degrees of both wellbeing or 'happiness' and freedom 'second to none,' as economist Samuelson observes in the opening quote, among all others in the Western world and beyond. This exposes 'libertarian' economics as discredited by and blind to reality, residing in the fantasy 'parallel universe' in which this type of economy is both 'unprosperous' or 'unhappy' and 'unfree,' for example, Mises' 'socialism,' 'despotism,' Hayek's 'road to serfdom' and 'fatal conceit,' Friedman's European 'statism,' etc.

In aggregate, rationally regulated and welfare capitalism is solely inherent, linked and belongs to modern free society as its economic subsystem. It is by virtue of being the sole type of economy with universal, equal freedom of the factors of production, including both capital and labor, conjoined and mutually reinforced with comparatively the most widespread wellbeing or the 'greatest happiness of the greatest number' in Marshall-Bentham's sense. In particular, this type of capitalism is rational or efficient and welfare-enhancing or egalitarian alike by uniquely solving or preventing what Keynes prophetically diagnoses as the 'two outstanding faults' of anarchic, laissez-faire capitalism whose 'end' he effectively predicted on the eve and diagnosed in the wake of the Great Depression. And Keynes' diagnosis of capitalism, just as his general economic theory, has proven to be incomparably more empirically grounded, valid, realistic and predictive, and thus can be trusted far more than that of his dogmatic opponents, pro-capital ideologues and plutocratic apologists (e.g., Mises, Hayek, Friedman, Buchanan, etc.) writing instead of—and as if in—a laissez-faire fantasy, utopia or nirvana. As known, Keynes' explanation and solution of economic crises, specifically the Great Depression, defeated

Mises-Hayek's and related laissez-faire dogmas and 'crying fire in flood' solutions during the 1930s, just as President Roosevelt's New Deal did the Hoover Administration's economic policy dogma against government intervention and spending in the economy.

Of these two failures of laissez-faire capitalism the first can be deemed irrational and even self-destructive, what Keynes identifies as its 'failure to provide for full employment' because of its generating or succumbing to endemic catastrophic economic crises like the Great Depression and the Great Recession. The second failure is anti- or non-egalitarian in the form, in Keynes' words, of its 'arbitrary and inequitable distribution of wealth and incomes' as its intrinsic, constant or long-term outcome. First, rationally regulated capitalism efficiently solves and effectively prevents the laissez-faire 'failure to provide for full employment' because of recurring economic catastrophes, as through rational or sensible regulation of and intervention in the economy as necessary. Hence, it is truly rational or efficient by solving or preventing such ultimate macroeconomic irrationality or inefficiency like depressions, as it has done since the 1930s. Second, welfare-egalitarian capitalism efficiently solves and effectively prevents or at least considerably mitigates the laissez-faire 'arbitrary and inequitable distribution of wealth and incomes' through its universal, equal and comprehensive freedoms, rights, life chances and wellbeing in the economy, and is thus a genuinely welfare-improving, in the sense of Marshall, Pigou and welfare economics overall, and to that extent happiness-enhancing economic system.

Thus defined, this definite type of capitalism represents a substantive economic equivalent or complement of liberal democracy by virtue of both representing ideals, systems and practices of universal, equal and comprehensive liberties and rights in the economy and the polity, respectively. Consequently, rational and welfare capitalism manifests itself as the sole type of capitalism and economy generally that inheres and belongs to modern free society in economic terms, just as does liberal and secular democracy in political respect. In short, what liberal-secular democracy is to a free society politically rational-welfare capitalism—i.e. the welfare state or social democracy with capital-labor compromise—is to the latter economically.

In turn, such an economic system inhering and belonging to modern free society deeply differs from and transcends irrational and even self-destructive, unregulated, and extremely anti-egalitarian, in particular aristocratic, oligarchic or plutocratic, capitalism. The latter is effectively capitalist dictatorship in the form of Anarchy as absolute liberty/license for capital or plutocracy and Leviathan through systematic oppression of labor and other non-capitalists. Consequently, Western and related societies having an economic system of rationally regulated and egalitarian welfare capitalism are observed or expected to be substantially freer than those with unregulated and anti-egalitarian capitalism and all other capitalist or non-capitalist systems.

Moreover, societies with proxy-anarchic and oligarchic or plutocratic capitalism, in the sense of Hobbesian anarchy in the economy governed by the 'law of the jungle' and the 'law of the strongest,' tend, to be not only relatively less free as a whole—taking account of the degrees of freedom of all production factors like capital and labor, and not just capitalists or plutocrats—compared to those considered economically welfare capitalisms. They are also diagnosed or predicted to ultimately become unfree in absolute terms on their own right such that universal, equal and comprehensive economic liberty is eliminated or subverted beyond recognition into the absolute unlimited 'freedom' and power exclusively of the capitalist class as the new narrow aristocracy or oligarchy. They therefore descend to or evoke slavery, a master-servant economy, feudalism and patrimonialism or patrimonial capitalism.[14] This holds because of the inner logic of such a type of capitalism to mutate into capitalist dictatorship in the form of what even US President Theodore Roosevelt condemns as the 'tyranny' of plutocracy/wealth and so plutocratic, aristocratic or oligarchic anti-egalitarian capitalism with an unfree and even 'inhuman face.'[15]

Such an outcome is conjoined and aggravated by the persistent tendency of the unfree type of capitalism to self-destruction or chaos and thus utter economic irrationality through its recurring catastrophic crises and their mass resource destruction, misery, suffering, panic, and despair. This is epitomized by the Great Depression and the Great Recession both caused by the anarchic laissez-faire dogma, more precisely that of American 'unfettered capitalism'

---

14   Some economists and sociologists describe contemporary unregulated and anti-egalitarian plutocratic capitalism as the new 'patrimonial capitalism' defined by the absolute power and control of capital or plutocracy—including both capital owners and high-level managers like CEOs yet with growing ownership-over labor and other non-capitalists. Cohen (2003, p. 53) remarks that managerial capitalism 'has been replaced by a new 'patrimonial capitalism' that marks the revenge of the shareholders on the wage earners.' Similarly, Piketty (2014, p. 125) suggests that the 'general evolution is clear: bubbles aside, what we are witnessing is a strong comeback of private capital in the rich countries since 1970, or, to put it another way, the emergence of a new patrimonial capitalism.' In particular, Goldstein (2012, p. 288) detects the 'revenge' of US managers on workers, thus finding support for the 'fat and mean thesis' of corporate management-or rather mismanagement—above all of CEOs as the patrimonial caste or clique, in America.

15   Pryor (2002, p. 367) uses the expression 'capitalism with an inhuman face' in reference to such a capitalist system in the US especially since the 1980s and plutocratic, anti-labor Reaganism.

in the 1920s and the 2000s. Then, American 'unfettered capitalism' generously diffuses beyond the US economy as if by social contagion the Great Depression and the Great Recession and their misery and suffering as the fruit of its 'exceptional,' 'superior' economic values and institutions to the world, particularly Europe, including interwar Germany resulting in the rise of Nazism. Such a diffusion of the catastrophic economic crises and thus extreme irrationality of 'unfettered capitalism' hence causes the laissez-faire dogma to come full circle from the new world claiming its invention behind the 'veil of ignorance' to its home Europe—France, as Keynes suggests—with vengeance and catastrophe, as shown by the Great Depression and the Great Recession.

Also, those modern societies characterized with the following pattern are freer than others with the opposite, just as 'happier' and more egalitarian in wealth and income distribution. This pattern consists in conducting rational societal coordination through sensible, necessary ('common sense') government regulation of and intervention in capitalism to prevent, solve or mitigate—as Keynes[16] diagnoses and predicts them during the Great Depression—its extremely anti-egalitarian and self-destructive outcomes, and valuing and providing a high and equitable level of economic-social welfare.[17] In essence, this type of society is the freest and the happiest in economic and general terms, and the opposite the least free and happy among Western societies. This is epitomized by, as US leading economist Samuelson observes, Scandinavia enjoying freedom and life satisfaction (as confirmed consistently by surveys) 'second to none' precisely because of its welfare state—misconstrued as 'un-freedom' and 'tyranny' by Mises, Hayek, Friedman, and other 'libertarian' fanatics[18] and detractors—and notably being 'freer than my America' under

---

16   Keynes (1960, p. 381) identified both before and during the Great Depression that 'two outstanding faults' of unregulated, laissez-faire and plutocratic capitalism are its 'failure to provide for full employment and its arbitrary and inequitable distribution of wealth and incomes,' the first also observed during its previous severe crises and the second in its typical functioning, as also suggested by Piketty (2014). In view of such recurring and chronic failures, he diagnosed or predicted the 'end of laissez-faire' (Keynes 1972, pp. 275, 126) in 1926, even before the Great Depression (the 'Great Slump') described in 1930 as 'one of the greatest economic catastrophes of modern history,' and the consequent fall from grace of this doctrine during inter- and post-war times, as Baumol (2000) registers.

17   Alfred Pigou (1960, p. 11) treats economic welfare as a constitutive component of societal welfare stating that 'economic welfare is that part of social (or total) welfare which can be brought in relation to the measuring rod of money.' Overall, Pigou is regarded the 'founder' of welfare economics (Baumol 2000, p. 16).

18   In a notorious episode, this 'unfettered capitalism' and anti-labor 'libertarian' fanaticism reached the point of its advocates Hayek and Friedman personally visiting, in a show

unfettered capitalism, above all its ultra-conservative growingly influential segment like the South. What Samuelson observes for Scandinavia compared to the US with respect to economic and political freedom (plus 'happiness') appears to apply to Canada by comparison to its neighbor, at least the 'Southern United States,' as examined in this work.

The preceding therefore specifies what a free economy, specifically capitalism, inherently constitutes within the framework of modern free society. As with liberal-secular democracy, one cannot emphasize and reiterate sufficiently that such an economy is rationally regulated and egalitarian welfare capitalism to—as Keynes suggests—address catastrophic economic crises and extreme wealth/income inequalities as destructive or harmful to society in short and long-terms. This needs to be emphasized especially in view of the old and new growing anarchic laissez-faire 'libertarian' anti-regulation, anti-intervention and anti-egalitarian attacks and detractors in the US and the UK even after the near-catastrophe of the Great Recession and exploding economic inequality both caused or aggravated by such economic dogmas or orthodoxy. Alternatively, the above implicitly specifies what a free economy does not represent in modern free society: irrational/anarchic, unregulated, and anti-egalitarian oligarchic or plutocratic capitalism as effective capitalist dictatorship and thus an unfree economic system. As before, the preceding infers that it is not sufficient or precise enough just to state that a free economy, specifically capitalism, operates as a necessary economic condition, integral

---

of support, the fascist dictator Pinochet in Chile in spite or rather precisely because of the fact that the dictator's first acts in power—just as those of Hitler—involved outlawing unions and persecuting and murdering labor activists. Conversely, these visits to and support for a 'free-market,' anti-labor murderous fascist dictator revealed such 'libertarian' fanaticism, dogmatism, or partisanship, notably the sheer delusion and lunacy that even fascism is a 'free society' if has an economic system of 'unfettered capitalism,' as had Pinochet's regime, as well as interwar (Italian and other) fascism in Europe, including to an important degree Nazism that also abolished and persecuted labor unions and allied with large capitalists (Krupp, Thyssen, etc.). Cynics or critics may comment that by doing so, just as in other occasions, these economists precisely indicated what their pro-capital, anti-labor 'libertarianism' inherently represents or eventually amounts to—economic and political authoritarianism, as Tilman (2001) objects, and in that sense slightly modified or disguised fascism as the best kept secret of this economic ideology of anarchism and glorification of the 'law of the strongest' and the power of plutocracy and oligarchy, as Pryor (2002) suggests, masked as 'libertarian economics.' Counterfactually, cynics may wonder if Hitler would have merited these economists' visit and support because once in power he immediately outlawed unions and murdered labor activists—as part of the dream or nirvana of 'libertarian' economics—thus perhaps inspiring Pinochet and other later fascists in accordance with the pattern of continuity in fascism.

element or relevant indicator of modern free society with no specification of what the first inherently represents in the second—a rationally regulated, welfare type.

In sum, rational-regulated and egalitarian-welfare capitalism manifests the economic proof or face of modern free society rather than its irrational-anarchic and anti-egalitarian-plutocratic opposite as Hobbesian anarchy governed by the 'law of the jungle' and the 'license to kill' and the unrestrained 'tyranny' of wealth defining plutocracy in President Roosevelt's sense. One infers that modern free society either encompasses rationally regulated, egalitarian welfare capitalism as its economic subsystem within its total social system of freedom—or is not truly or entirely free economically.

Modern Free Society and the Type of Culture

Third, modern free society as a total social system of freedom invariably encompasses culture as a cultural subsystem only in its specific, genuinely free and most viable type. This constitutes rationalistic and liberal culture. It follows that solely rationalistic-liberal culture represents the inherent and constitutive cultural pattern and component of modern free society. Rationalistic-liberal culture is defined by cultural rationalism expressed in science and scientific knowledge, education, and technology and by intellectual freedom, in particular independence and autonomy from coercive and intrusive politics and religion, as well as economic compulsion and interests. In short, this type of culture is characterized with both reason and liberty, scientific rationalism (scientism) and cultural liberalism.

Specifically, cultural rationalism, in particular science and scientific knowledge, education, and technology, i.e., reason and scientism, define rationalistic culture. Intellectual freedom, including independence and autonomy from political and religious coercion and intrusion and economic compulsion, so cultural liberty or liberalism, defines liberal culture. On this account, the rationalistic-liberal represents a unique composite type of culture conjoining humans' two perennial faculties, quests, goals or outcomes—human, notably scientific and related, rationality and liberty, reason and freedom, and thus rationalism and liberalism. The rationalistic-liberal is the only cultural type inhering and belonging to modern free society by virtue of being the sole culture of reason and freedom, rationality and liberty in one complex.

In turn, such a unique composite type of culture profoundly differs from and supersedes the compound of cultural irrationalism and anti-rationalism, in particular religious and other superstition and fanaticism and anti-scientism, and the denial and suppression of intellectual liberty, including autonomy from coercive politics and religion and economic compulsion. Consequently,

Western and related societies characterized with a rationalistic-liberal culture, in particular scientific rationalism and academic freedom, are observed or expected to be invariably and drastically freer than those pervaded with mixed cultural irrationalism and anti-rationalism, especially the mix of religious superstitions and anti-science as a poison to both human reason and liberty. Furthermore, the second societies are not only or ultimately tend to become less free compared to the first. They are absolutely unfree apart from such comparisons and beyond any doubt in their own right as the invariant domains of intellectual and other cultural un-freedom especially with respect to science, education, philosophy, and art.

This is because cultural irrationalism and anti-rationalism manifesting unreason and manifested in superstition and anti-scientism intrinsically operate as or mutate into the typically religiously based and sanctified denial and suppression, or constraint and control of scientific rationalism, knowledge, education, technology, medicine, and academic and other intellectual freedom, activity and creativity. Hence, the compound of religious irrationalism and anti-rationalism subdues such cultural achievements and freedoms, like everything else and humans, to the 'higher Divine cause,' and ultimately—literally or figuratively—burns and buries them, from books, libraries, art, heretics, witches to dissenters, as 'ungodly' and 'infidels.' This is witnessed during the Christian and Islamic Middle Dark Ages,[19] in Germany under Nazism, America under Puritanism and during evangelicalism and conservatism, most Muslim countries, and so on.

In extension, Western and related societies that are more rationalistic-liberal culturally, notably value, trust and rely on reason, science, scientific knowledge and education, and academic freedom, and less superstitious and religious overall tend to be freer than those dominated by cultural irrationalism and anti-rationalism, particularly valuing, trusting and relying on superstition and religion, and espousing anti-scientism. The former are observed or expected to be the freest culturally, and the latter the most unfree in this sense among modern societies. This is exemplified by the deep and even deepening divide and divergence of Western Europe, in particular Scandinavia, and Canada from Catholic dominated Poland, the conservative half of America, Islamic-ruled Turkey and other Islamic countries.

---

19   Mueller (2009) refers to the Christian as well as Islamic Dark Ages as antagonistic and destructive to science, knowledge, intellectual freedom, and liberty, reason, and rationality in general to be valued and promoted most consistently and fully by the subsequent liberal, secular, and rationalistic Enlightenment seen as the intellectual foundation of modern liberal democracy and free society as whole.

The preceding specifies what a free culture exactly represents and means as a subsystem within modern free society as a total social system of freedom. It is the unique composite of rationalistic-liberal culture typified by scientific rationalism, knowledge, education, technology and intellectual freedom, in particular independence and autonomy from political and religious coercion and economic compulsion. This may need to be emphasized and re-iterated in light of various persistent and even intensifying anti-rationalistic, anti-scientific, anti-education, and anti-intellectual revolts and detractors from anti-evolutionists through anti-vaccination groups to climate change deniers, above all in the conservative regions of America within Western civilization and Islamic countries in the non-Western world. Conversely, the above implicitly specifies what a free culture precisely is not in the context of modern free society. It is not the compound of cultural irrationalism and anti-rationalism expressing unreason and expressed in religious superstition, ignorance and fanaticism and anti-scientism, anti-knowledge and anti-education as the lethal mix to reason and intellectual freedom alike. Hence, stating that a free culture forms the cultural condition or component of modern free society is not sufficient or precise without specifying what the first represents within the second—a rationalistic-liberal one.

In sum, the cultural proof and dimension of modern free society is invariably rationalistic-liberal culture expressed in scientific rationalism and liberty, and not cultural irrationalism and anti-rationalism epitomized by religious superstition, fanaticism, and anti-science reflecting unreason and producing un-freedom and ultimately societal perdition or petrification. This is witnessed by various religious or superstitious and tyrannical and eventually perished societies or groups in history—for example, medieval Europe, Puritan New England with 'witches,' US and other suicidal cults and sects—and petrified presently or until recently, viz., Iran, Saudi Arabia, Taliban, the post-bellum Southern United States, Utah, etc. In short, modern free society either incorporates rationalistic-liberal culture as its cultural subsystem within its total social system of freedom—or is not actually or completely free culturally.

Modern Free Society and the Type of Civil Society
Fourth, modern free society understood as a whole of elements encompasses civil society among these only in its definite, truly free and most viable type. And this type is liberal-secular civil society. This means that liberal-secular civil society represents the civic ideal and subsystem of modern free society as a total social system of freedom also incorporating its political, economic and cultural ideals and subsystems. Liberal-secular civil society constitutes a uniquely free, i.e., independent and autonomous, sphere of social life—also

called or related to everyday and private life, the life world, societal community, etc.—defined by universal, equal and comprehensive individual, personal liberties, choices, rights, and privacy. The liberal-secular type is hence the only really and fully free civil society in the larger context of modern free society as a whole thereby not to be confused with or reduced to its particular civic component.

In terms of relations with the other elements of modern free society, this type of civil society forms a substantive identity or functional equivalent of liberal-secular democracy in the non-political, private sphere of social life. In addition, it typically constitutes a complement of rational-welfare capitalism in the non-economic domain. In this respect, liberal-secular civil society is logically and empirically entwined and mutually reinforced invariably with its political equivalent of democracy. Additionally, it is positively related usually (though not necessarily) with its economic complement of rational-welfare capitalism. Alternatively, liberal-secular democracy represents the necessary and sufficient political, public condition for an equivalent type of civil society, i.e., private sphere. In turn, rational-welfare capitalism is the economic condition of civil society, with some qualifications, namely indispensable but to a lesser degree sufficing in this regard.

In essence, liberal-secular civil society and so a free private sphere of life can emerge, function and expand only where and when liberal-secular democracy exists and operates as its political and legal framework and protection, and primarily with rational-welfare capitalism as its economic setting and resource base. This is epitomized by most Western societies, especially Scandinavia and to some extent Canada, which feature the first component because of featuring the other two components of modern free society. Above all, Scandinavia is widely observed (as Samuelson suggests in the above observation) or expected to have the freest as well as the happiest, most elaborate and participatory civil society among Western and related societies, while also reaching the highest level of development of both liberal-secular democracy and rational-welfare capitalism. Conversely, it follows that essentially there is no such thing as a truly or fully free civil society in private life without liberal-secular democracy in the polity and, with some qualifications, rational-welfare capitalism in the economy. This is exemplified by the anti-liberal part of the US such as Dahrendorf's 'Southern United States,' and Islamic countries, including Turkey under Islamic rule, in the Western and non-Western world, which lack or simulate the first component because of lacking or simulating the other two components of modern free society, especially liberal-secular democracy.

In turn, the liberal-secular type of civil society drastically differs from and transcends that involving all-embracing control, moralistic repression, non-privacy, and severe punishment of sins-as-crimes and in that sense 'moral fascism' that is in anti- and pre-secular societies as a rule religiously grounded, enforced and sanctified. Thus, it is observed or expected that Western and related societies characterized with a liberal-secular civil society as an autonomous private sphere tend to be invariably and dramatically freer than those with its anti-liberal and anti-secular opposite. Moreover, societies with all-encompassing moralistic, religiously driven control, repression, non-privacy, and severe punishment of sins-as-crimes are not just less free in terms of individual liberties, choices, rights, and privacy than those with a liberal-secular civil society, i.e., a private life sphere separate and autonomous from coercive and intrusive politics and religion, as well as economic compulsion and pressure.

Furthermore, the first societies ultimately become unfree in absolute terms because of the inherent mode of anti-liberal and anti-secular civic societies to function as or develop into tyrannical suppression of personal liberty, choice, rights, and privacy and to that extent 'moral fascism.' This is shown by the Islamic Republic of Iran, Taliban regions, Turkey under Islamic rule, the post-bellum 'Southern United States' perpetuated or turned into Weber calls 'Biblical theocracy' (the 'Bible Belt') and Mormon-ruled Utah, Catholic-dominated Poland and Latin America, etc. In the Western world, 'moral fascism' is prototypically created or anticipated by Weber's diagnosed moralistic 'unexampled tyranny of Puritanism,' especially its proto-totalitarian 'theocracy of New England' modeled after Calvin's Geneva as the prototype, both being called the 'Biblical Commonwealth' and 'Christian Sparta.' Comparatively, moralistic 'Puritan tyranny' (as also termed by US early sociologist Edward Ross) is solely exampled or rivaled by Islam deemed the Puritan-Calvinist functional equivalent on account of theocratic religious revolution and war in Weber's comparative sociology of religion. The first moralistic 'tyranny' and thus elimination or perversion of free civil society is witnessed or expected, in an updated evangelical form, especially in the 'Southern United States' as Weber's Bibliocracy. And the second is, via Islamic fundamentalism, in Turkey and other Muslim societies under theocratic rule, along with a milder (in Weber's classic account) Catholic version, as established in post-communist Poland and retained in Latin America, in part Ireland, and other countries.

In extension, Western and related societies that are more liberal, secular and tolerant, or less religious and moralistic, with respect to individual liberties, choices, rights and privacy, so the private sphere of life, tend to be invariably and drastically freer than those anti-liberal and non-secular, or more theocentric and moralizing cum puritanical. Briefly, the first are certainly or likely the freest (and 'happiest') in personal, private and all other terms, and the second the most unfree (and 'unhappy'), among Western and related societies. This is shown by the dramatic contrast between secular 'post-Christian' Scandinavia and mots Western Europe overall and to some extent Canada on the one hand and Catholic-dominated Poland and Latin America, anti-secular 'Christian America' (above all, the evangelical South) and Islamic-ruled Turkey.

The foregoing specifies what a free civil society/private sphere of life does and does not constitute in the framework of modern free society. It does constitute a liberal-secular civil society as the realm of individual liberty, choice, rights, and privacy, and does not 'moral fascism' in the sense of totalitarian or authoritarian anti-liberal and non-secular moralistic, religiously driven, control, repression, and Draconian punishment for sins-crimes. Likewise, the above suggests that it is not enough to posit that a free civil society, an autonomous private life sphere represents a necessary civic condition and integral element of modern free society unless specifying what the first as a rule is and is not within the second—the liberal-secular vs. the anti-liberal, anti-secular.

In sum, liberal-secular civil society as the free private life sphere of individual liberty, choice, rights, and privacy autonomous from political-religious coercion and intrusion and economic compulsion and pressure provides the civic proof and face of modern free society. Conversely, such a proof of an unfree society consists of the overarching moralistic, religiously induced control and suppression of individual liberties, choices, rights, and privacies, and cruel punishment to the point of the death penalty for sins-crimes, and in that sense 'moral fascism.'

Modern Free Society in Aggregate

In aggregate, modern free society as a rule constitutes a total social system of, first, liberal-secular and universalistic-egalitarian democracy as the political condition and component, second, rationally regulated and egalitarian welfare capitalism as the economic, third, a rationalistic-liberal culture as the cultural, and fourth, a liberal-secular civil society as the civic. More precisely, modern free society exists and functions as the complex and integral of these conditions and components so long as they are integrated, exist, and function in interconnection, interaction, and mutual reinforcement. Thus, liberal-secular and universalistic-egalitarian democracy tends to invariably coexist, co-function and be integrated with a liberal-secular civil society as its substantive identity in the private sphere, typically with a rationalistic-liberal culture as its logical cultural equivalent or complement, and to an high or growing degree with rationally regulated and egalitarian welfare capitalism as complementary or mutually non-exclusive in the economy.

To that extent, Western and related societies that epitomize liberal-secular and universalistic-egalitarian democracy are more likely, almost invariably, to exemplify liberal-secular civil society and rationalistic-liberal culture, and to an important degree rational-welfare capitalism—and conversely—than those characterized with anti- and pre-liberal, specifically conservative, including religious and fascist, 'democracies' or 'republics.' On this account, modern free society exhibits an inner logic and intrinsic pattern and method of universal and holistic liberty, plus equality, justice, inclusion, reason, rationality, prosperity, wellbeing, happiness, and progress as its complements helping attain or increasing the full societal value of freedom for humans in typical conjunction and mutual reinforcement, thus being self-consistent.

To return to the initial theme, democracy and a free economy—i.e., capitalism with both capital and labor freedom—each forms one quarter of the modern free-society equation. The other two necessary and complementary parts are a free culture with artistic, intellectual, scientific, and educational freedoms, and a free civil society involving individual liberties, rights, choices, and privacy. Moreover, as a variation on that theme, formal democracy in the sense of the legal procedure of free elections forms just one fifth of the equation by forming a second part of a democratic polity, the other being substantive democracy in the form of effective democratic rule and political and civil liberties and rights.

In a similar variation, laissez-faire and plutocratic capitalism represents at most only one fifth or, considering the share of formal democracy, one sixth and even no part of the free society equation due to its dual formula of anarchy/license for capital and Leviathan/oppression of labor expressing disfigured, fragmented economic freedom. This exposes the 'libertarian' (Mises-Hayek-Friedman) fallacy or 'cheap trick' of conflating or presenting the approximately one-fifth or one-sixth, in the best of all scenarios, relative share of 'unfettered' capitalism in the equation or complex modern free society as if it were the sum total of the latter, an egregious variant of the general error committed by orthodox economics by mistaking economic freedom with societal liberty due to its built-in economic reductionism. (The preceding is represented in Table 1.3).

Modern Free Society versus Unfree and Pseudo-Free Societies

Negatively, modern free society does not constitute a social system and integration of the polar opposites of liberal-secular and universalistic-egalitarian democracy, rationally coordinated and egalitarian welfare capitalism, rationalistic-liberal culture, and liberal-civil society. It is not one of anti-liberal, anti-secular and exclusionary, inegalitarian 'democracy' or 'republic' as the old and

TABLE 1.3   *Modern free society and its specific elements.*

Polity	Economy
Liberal, secular, universalistic democracy	Rationally regulated, egalitarian welfare capitalism
CULTURE Rationalistic-liberal culture	CIVIL SOCIETY Liberal-secular civil society/private life sphere

TABLE 1.4   *Modern unfree society and its specific elements.*

Polity	Economy
Anti-liberal, anti-secular, exclusionary 'democracy'	Unregulated, inegalitarian plutocratic capitalism
CULTURE Cultural irrationalism and anti-rationalism	CIVIL SOCIETY Moralistic-religious repression—'moral fascism'

new regime of totalitarian oppression, particularly theocracy, of irrational-anarchic and anti-egalitarian, aristocratic, oligarchic or plutocratic capitalism as capitalist dictatorship, of cultural irrationalism and anti-rationalism as destructive to reason, science, and intellectual freedom, and of moralistic, religiously driven coercion, repression and punishment as 'moral fascism.'

Conversely, modern unfree society forms a complex and combination of these conditions or components also intertwined and mutually reinforcing in causing or forming and perpetuating such a total—rather totalitarian—societal system of un-freedom. In this respect, it exhibits a negative inner logic and intrinsic pattern and method of integral illiberty, as well as inequality, injustice, exclusion, unreason, irrationality, unhappiness, and non-progress as complements sustaining and sustained by un-freedom. Therefore, it is self-consistent in its own perverse, destructive way for holistic societal liberty and its complementary values and institutions of equality, justice, and the like (Table 1.4).

An intermediate category denoted modern pseudo-, quasi- or semi-free society represents some eclectic and typically inconsistent mixture of the preceding main conditions, components, and indicators of free and unfree societies. While usually claiming to belong to the first societies, this represents a halfway-free but not genuinely or completely free society. Specifically, it mixes in varying proportions the opposite elements of liberal-secular universalistic democracy and illiberal theocentric exclusionary 'democracy,' of rationally regulated welfare and anarchic plutocratic capitalism, of rational-liberal culture and cultural irrationalism and anti-rationalism, and of liberal-secular civil society and moralistic-religious repression. In this respect, pseudo-free societies reveal a high degree of 'sociological ambivalence'[20] and discontinuity with respect to the necessary conditions and defining elements of modern free society and its holistic liberty, in contrast to their free and unfree counterparts revealing positive and negative consistency and continuity. Free and unfree-societies tend to be and strive to persist as non-ambiguously and consistently social systems of holistic liberty and illiberty, and their pseudo-free alternatives do both in varying degrees or neither solely.

At first sight quasi-free societies as eclectic mixtures of contradictory components appear to be more complicated than their free or unfree alternatives, and perhaps even prevailing in societal reality, but this may not be necessarily the case within the Western and related settings. On the one hand, what are commonly regarded as fully and even exemplarily free societies may turn out on a closer examination to belong to the category of a pseudo- and even unfree society. This is apparently exemplified by the approximately conservative pole of the US, above all Dahrendorf's 'Southern United States,' and to an extent the UK since the 1980s through the 2010s, as well as Catholic-dominated post-communist Poland, Islamic-ruled Turkey from the 2000s, South Korea during recent decades, etc. In the first two cases, this appears to be mostly due to the insurgence and dominance of anti-liberalism, anti-secularism, anti-rationalism and anti-modernism in the form of conservatism since Reaganism and Thatcherism, including theocratic fundamentalism, totalitarian neo-fascism, and plutocratic 'libertarianism.'

On the other hand, some Western and related societies or regions that especially by US conservatives and 'libertarians' dismiss and despise as pseudo- or semi-free do or may prove upon inspection to be truly and completely free during the same period because of the opposite trends. These trends consist the process of reaffirmation, acceleration and extension of liberalism, secularism, rationalism, and modernism in most Western and related societies. This is evidently epitomized by Western Europe, especially Samuelson's Scandinavia, as well as Canada, Australia, New Zealand, the liberal pole of the US, etc. In

---

20   Merton (1976) coins and applies the concept of 'sociological ambivalence' by analogy to 'psychological ambivalence.' Bauman (2001) observes and emphasizes growing and pervasive 'ambivalence' in late 'liquid' modernity or post-modernity.

TABLE 1.5   *Conditions and components/subsystems of modern free, unfree, and quasi-free society.*

Modern free society	Modern unfree society
I Political condition and component/subsystem	
Liberal, secular, universalistic democracy	Illiberal theocentric exclusionary 'democracies' or 'republics'
II Economic condition and component/subsystem	
Rationally regulated, egalitarian welfare capitalism	Irrational unregulated, inegalitarian plutocratic capitalism
III Cultural condition and component/subsystem	
Rational-liberal culture-- scientific rationalism/liberty	Irrationalism, anti-rationalism-- superstition, anti-science
IV Civic condition and component/subsystem	
Liberal-secular civil society/ private life sphere	Moralistic-religious oppression--'moral fascism'

Modern quasi-free society

I   Eclectic inconsistent mix of liberal-secular democracy and illiberal theocentric 'democracy'

II   Eclectic inconsistent mix of regulated welfare and unfettered plutocratic capitalism

III Eclectic inconsistent mix of liberal-secular civil society and moralistic-religious control and repression

IV   Eclectic inconsistent mix of rational-liberal culture and cultural irrationalism and anti-rationalism

sum, quasi-free societies are neither completely free nor entirely unfree but both in varying proportions depending on certain social conditions and historical conjunctures, thus equivalent to a 'semi-free' society. (The aforesaid is condensed in Table 1.5).

Classification of Modern Societies

This section classifies contemporary Western and related societies, such as OECD countries, in the following manner for the purpose of the present work. First, it classifies into liberal society as a societal (ideal, pure) type the following countries within OECD: Australia, Austria, Belgium, Canada, Denmark, Finland, France, Germany, Iceland, Luxembourg, the Netherlands, New Zealand, Norway, Sweden, Switzerland, as well as the US. The latter is thus classified in its liberal rendition or vision (yet mostly weak, transient or exceptional) and regions (largely minority or decreasing), as distinct from its opposite, thus expressing the 'two Americas' in societal terms. In light of the observed growing and intensifying polarization between liberalism and anti-liberalism in the US, this can be considered and described as the 'liberal pole of America' or simply 'liberal America.' Dahrendorf by distinguishing the 'Southern United States' on account of their violations of 'fundamental human rights' from the others implies the idea of 'two Americas,'[21] liberal and the opposite, in societal, historical and geographical terms, as do other sociological insights and also American political and ordinary discourse where this is explicit, as in the widespread notion of 'culture wars' between America's opposing visions or parts.

Generally, the preceding countries or regions, as within the US, tend to be fundamentally and/or increasingly liberal, liberalized, and liberalizing societies, consequently epitomizing the equivalent type of society within the Western and related framework such as OECD. On this ground, they are deemed and classified as essentially 'liberal societies,' and observed and predicted or expected as a whole to attain the highest rank overall (rank I) on 'free society/liberty' among Western and all other countries.

Second, the present classification includes into anti- or non-liberal society as an opposite societal type these countries also within OECD: Mexico, Poland, South Korea, Turkey, as well as the US. Analogously, the latter is so classified in its anti- or non-liberal, specifically conservative, version or vision (mainly enduring, prevalent or resurgent) and regions (largely majority or growing), as shown by the 'Southern United States,' in both coexistence and perpetual conflict with 'liberal America' within the 'two Americas' in sociological or geographic terms. In general, these countries or regions like 'Southern United States' tend to be deeply or growingly anti- or non-liberal, non-liberalized, and non-liberalizing, specifically conservative, thus primarily exemplify the respective type of society in the Western framework, such as the US in this

---

21   The concept of the 'two Americas,' liberal and conservative, is justified by that, as Mueller (2009, p. 375) observes, the 'struggle between progressivism (liberalism) and traditionalism (conservatism) has gone on for much of the US's history, and continues today at an intensity unmatched in other rich, developed countries,' thus evidently continuing to divide ideologically and politically the country virtually into two 'countries' or parts. As noted, its justification also consists in that Dahrendorf (1979, p. 100) differentiates the 'Southern United States' because of its violation of 'fundamental human rights' and generally ultra-conservatism from the other parts of the US as not committing such violations and being more liberal or less conservative overall.

specification, and beyond, viz., the other non-Western countries within OECD. On this account, these are considered and classified as 'anti- and non-liberal societies,' and observed or expected as a whole to reach the lowest rank overall (rank III) on 'free society/liberty' among Western and other countries.

Third, this classification incorporates into intermediate, eclectic or mixed society as a hybrid social type such other OECD countries as Chile, Czech Republic, Greece, Hungary, Estonia, Ireland, Italy, Japan, Portugal, Slovakia, Slovenia, Spain, and the UK. Generally, these countries tend to, though in different proportions, mix, reconcile and mediate liberal and anti- or non-liberal societies' elements and tendencies, and thus manifest the corresponding type of society in the Western and related framework, with some of them approaching more the first and others the second of these societal poles. This provides the justification for considering and classifying them as 'intermediate, eclectic or mixed societies' along liberal-illiberal lines, and they are observed or expected as a whole to be ranked overall lower than liberal societies and higher than the anti-liberal (rank II) on 'free society/liberty' among Western and other countries.

In sum, out of thirty three Western and other countries within OECD,[22] fifteen, and in addition 'liberal America' of the 'two Americas,' are classified and denoted as liberal societies, six, plus 'conservative America' such as the 'Southern United States' and the like included, as anti- and non-liberal societies, and eleven as intermediate, eclectic or mixed societies. In turn, 'liberal societies' are as a whole predicted or expected to be the freest, 'anti-liberal societies' as a group the least free/most unfree, and 'mixed societies' generally in a middle position in this sense. The rest of this book examines whether and what degree these predictions or expectations are fulfilled. (The preceding is summarized in Table 1.6.)

Organization of the Work

Following this introductory chapter, the remainder of the present study is organized according to the classification of conditions, elements, and indicators of modern free society and their aggregation in a composite estimate. Chapter

---

22   During the later stages of completing this study, Israel was also admitted into OECD, so it was too late to include this country in the analysis. Also, the data on and/or rankings of Israel on dimensions of democracy and free society overall seem less available than those of most other OECD countries, so its omission is not likely to greatly affect the results and conclusions of this study.

TABLE 1.6   *Classification of western and related societies (OECD countries) in terms of free society/liberty.*

I   *Liberal, liberalized, liberalizing societies* (15 cases and 1/2)
     Australia, Austria, Belgium, Canada, Denmark, Finland, France,
     Germany, Iceland, Luxembourg, Netherlands, New Zealand, Norway,
     Sweden, Switzerland, the US in liberal weak, transient and exceptional
     rendition or vision and minority or decreasing regions (e.g., the Coast,
     parts of the North, etc.).

Expected free society/liberty	highest I—completely or largely free,
overall ranking	freest as a whole

II   *Anti- and non-liberal (conservative) societies* (4 cases and 1/2)
     Mexico, Poland, South Korea, Turkey, the US in anti- or non-liberal, con-
     servative strong, enduring or prevalent version or vision and majority
     or growing regions (e.g., the evangelical South, the Middle West, etc.).

Expected free society/liberty	
overall ranking	lowest III—unfree or pseudo-free,
	most unfree as a whole

III *Intermediate, eclectic, mixed societies* (13 cases)
     Chile, Czech Republic, Greece, Hungary, Estonia, Ireland, Italy, Japan,
     Portugal, Slovakia, Slovenia, Spain, the UK

Expected free society/liberty	
overall ranking	intermediate II—pseudo-free, largely
	free, unfree

---

2 focuses on the free polity in the sense of formal and substantive democracy and its own particular conditions, elements and indicators. Chapter 3 provides comparative estimates of democracy, i.e., political freedom for contemporary Western and related societies. Chapter 4 centers on the free economy and its specific conditions, elements and indicators. Chapter 5 makes comparative estimates of the free economy, i.e., economic freedom, for these societies. Chapter 6 examines free culture and its conditions, elements, and indicators. Chapter 7 yields comparative estimates of free culture, i.e., cultural liberties and rights, for these societies. Chapter 8 considers a free civil society and its conditions, elements and indicators. Chapter 9 renders comparative estimates of free civil society, i.e., individual liberties, choices, rights, and privacy for Western and related societies. Chapter 10 provides a summary of and conclusion about the comparative aggregate estimates and factors of modern free society for Western and related societies.

The Political Condition and Indicator of Modern Free Society—Democracy

Conditions and Indicators of Democracy

As indicated and commonly agreed, the aggregate political condition, component, and indicator of modern free society is a democratic polity, simply democracy. This leads to the question as to the particular conditions, components, and indicators of democracy itself considered both in its formal-procedural and substantive-effective types or dimensions. Hence, they can be categorized into the conditions, components, and indicators of formal-procedural and those of substantive-effective democracy.[1] At this point, the analysis is provisionally agnostic about what specifically democracy constitutes within modern free society, as it 'does not know' whether a democratic polity represents a liberal-secular ideological-political system or its opposites, anti- or non-liberal, particularly conservative, and anti or non-secular, including theocentric, 'democracies.'

---

1   These elements of democracy are similar but not identical to the Bollen indicators of liberal democracy. The latter are divided into, first, 'indicators of popular sovereignty' such as fairness of election, method of executive selection, and method of legislative selection and effectiveness, viz., free election, wide voting rights (franchise), equal weighting of votes, and a fair electoral process, and second, 'measures of political liberties' including press freedom; freedom of group opposition; government sanctions (i.e.) free speech/press, extent of government negative sanctions (Bollen 1980; 1990, 1998; Bollen and Grandjean 1981; Bollen and Jackman 1985, 1989). More recently, they are codified into 'democratic rule' involving political rights, competitiveness in the nomination process, chief executive elected, effectiveness of the elective legislative body, and 'political liberties' such as freedom of (broadcast and print) media, civil liberties, and freedom of group opposition (Bollen and Paxton 1998, p. 470). Also, the present indicators of democracy resemble but are not the same as those composing the POLITY IV democracy index involving the 'extent to which government executives are chosen through competitive elections, plus the presence of rules for political participation and the transfer of executive power' (Mulligan, Gil and Sala-I-Martin 2004, p. 55), etc. As also stated by the Polity IV Project, the 'Polity scheme consists of six component measures that record key qualities of executive recruitment, constraints on executive authority and political competition. It also records changes in the institutionalized qualities of governing authority.' (http://www.systemicpeace.org/polityproject.html).

The conditions, elements, and indicators of formal-procedural democracy comprise nominal-legal, in particular constitutional, political and civil liberties and rights, and institutionalized democratic means and procedures, as distinct from the extent of their actual realization, effectiveness, and application.[2] In the optimal case, nominal political and civil liberties and rights and democratic procedures are completely and consistently realized, effective, and applied. This expresses the fusion or strong congruence between formal-procedural and substantive-effective, simply nominal and real,[3] democracy into a whole, thus a fully democratic polity defined by universal and holistic political and civil liberty. Hence, an osmosis or harmony between formal-procedural and substantive-effective democratic variants and dimensions would define and typify a genuine, complete, consistent, or ideal democracy, thus providing the aggregate political condition, element, and indicator of modern free society.

In the opposite scenario, these nominal liberties and procedures are not implemented, effective, and applied, and instead exist and remain as pure formalities or 'technicalities' without substance to the point of not being worth the paper on which they are proclaimed and printed. This is epitomized by nominally the most 'democratic' constitutions, particular laws and legal procedures, yet not implemented and effective, but violated in political reality, and thus made 'dead' words and promises, 'cheap talk,' and simulation or 'placebo' of democracy and liberty. Such a situation consequently generates or reflects the fission or drastic incongruence between formal-procedural and

---

2   Eisenstadt (1998, p. 233) refers to the observation and possibility of 'a growth in the formal aspects and a weakening of the participatory (substantive) aspects of democracy' (as observed in South America since its democratization during the 1980s). Habermas (2001, p. 79) warns that 'to the degree that the social presuppositions for broad-based political participation are destroyed, even formally correct democratic decisions come to lose their credibility.' In particular, he predicts that 'procedurally correct majority decisions that merely reflect the fears and self-defensive reactions of social classes threatened by downward social mobility (i.e., reflect the sentiments of right-wing populism) will end up eroding the legitimacy of democratic procedures and institutions themselves' (Habermas 2001, pp. 50–1). Beck (2000, p. 115) asks and answers negatively 'whether a democracy with a 30 percent turnout at elections is still a democracy,' citing Congressional elections in the US. For example, the national turnout at the US 2014 congressional elections was estimated to be 36 percent (later revised somewhat upwards), which the *New York Times* (11/11/2014) described as the 'worst voter turnout' since 1942, 'bad for (some politicians), but it was even worse for democracy.' Centeno (1994, p. 135) cautions that a formal democracy, especially its exclusionary form, often 'disguises effective exclusion.'

3   Piketty (2014, p. 298) suggests that 'real democracy and social justice require specific institutions of their own, not just those of the market, and not just parliaments and other formal democratic institutions.'

substantive-effective democracy. Thus, formal-procedural democracy is solemnly proclaimed and extolled as the 'only' and the 'best' in legal, notably constitutional, rules and papers and political decisions and declarations, including 'constitutional guarantees for civil liberties,'[4] but substantive-effective democracy is essentially either non-existent or minimal.

Among classical sociologists and economists even Durkheim and Smith with their shared moral concerns, let alone Marx, Weber, Pareto, Simmel, and other conflict-oriented theorists, acknowledge and generalize the preceding. This is that societal norms and procedures, thus including the most 'democratic' constitutions and laws, do not necessarily and completely correspond and always translate to actual social activities in accordance with them, including substantive-effective democracy and liberty. Instead, they recognize a certain, even if minimal, margin of discrepancy and tension between the formal rules of 'social games,'[5] including those and procedures of democracy, and real conduct and life in society, in particular their effective realization in the polity, under certain structural conditions and historical circumstances. These theorists have no illusions and great expectations about the invariant fusion or complete harmony between social rules and institutions and real-life behaviors and processes, including the forms and procedures of formal-procedural democracy and the content and reality of substantive-effective democracy. They either—to paraphrase a book of master sociological-economic novelist Balzac[6]—lost illusions or tempered their expectations in the face of frequent real-life divergences between rule/norm and conduct/action in society, in particular nominal freedoms and rights, rules and procedures and their effective realization effectiveness, and promotion in the polity.

---

4   Fearon (2011, p. 1696) refers to 'constitutional guarantees for civil liberties' but these may or may not be sufficient for the actual existence and realization or to prevent violation of such and other liberties and human rights, and thus effective-substantive democracy, and sometimes even not being worth the paper on which they are written and printed, as witnessed in many countries from, as Dahrendorf (1979) implies, Nazi Germany and Stalinist Russia to the US South and Chile under Pinochet.

5   Dahrendorf (1979, p. 23) remarks that 'traditional liberalism is as insistent on formal rules for all sorts of social games as it is silent on the social condition of man.'

6   Piketty (2014, p. 22) mentions the greatest French sociologically-minded novelist Honoré de Balzac multiple times noting that 'now as in the past, moreover, inequalities of wealth exist primarily within age cohorts, and inherited wealth comes close to being as decisive at the beginning of the twenty-first century as it was in the age of Balzac's (book) Père (Father) Goriot' during the 1810–20s (also, Milanovic 2014).

For illustration, Weber portrays, based on his first-hand experience, what he considers formally or procedurally—in the sense of legal-rational authority—American democracy as substantively and effectively 'naked plutocracy' defined by that wealth, i.e., 'mere money, literally "purchases power" in the US political system. Also, he describes colonial New England's Puritan official "republic" as effectively "theocracy" and moralistic "tyranny" (Ross' term as well). Moreover, Pareto generally characterizes nominal Western democracies as actually 'demagogic plutocracies' and/or 'oligarchies.' This realization of actual or possible divergence provides an extant sociological ground and justification for distinguishing formal-procedural and substantive-effective (types or dimensions of) democracy.

Formal-Procedural Democracy

The conditions, elements, and indicators or dimensions of formal-procedural democracy thus understood are classified and specified as follows (Table 2.1).

The first condition, component and indicator of formal-procedural democracy involves free, fair, regular, inclusive, and non-discriminatory political elections. These elections are premised on and decided by the legal-constitutional majority rule as the democratic decision principle for determining electoral and other public outcomes, such as elected and non-elected individual and collective political agents, simply candidates and parties, 'winners and losers.'[7]

TABLE 2.1   *Conditions, elements and indicators of formal-procedural democracy.*

---

(1) Free, fair, regular, inclusive, non-discriminatory elections with the legal majority rule as the decision principle

(2) Legal freedoms, rights and opportunities to political participation and equality as inalienable citizenship rights—voting rights

(3) Freedom, right, openness, and opportunity for political position, open, free competition for power

(4) Legal-constitutional ideological-political pluralism and choice

(5) Legal-constitutional procedure of open, free competition in polity, multi-party competitive political systems

---

7 This does not mean that the political system should necessarily be majoritarian but can also be proportional, with both adopting the majority rule to decide the outcome of elections, though in the first case 'the winner takes all' and in the second winners and losers share in legislative power such as parliamentary seats and commissions and to a lesser extent in executive and judicial powers like ministerial posts and court appointments.

On the side of power-holders, executive and legislative state powers are mandated by legal-constitutional rules and regularly subjected to—and either elected and reelected or unelected in—free, fair, inclusive elections whose outcomes are determined by the majority rule.[8] On the side of power-subjects, citizens constituting the electorate have the legal-constitutional freedom, right, and choice to subject these powers to regular, free, fair, and inclusive elections (re)electing them or not, thus rendering or approximating formal democracy as 'self-enforcing.'[9]

The condition and indicator of formal-procedural democracy is hence that the people choose, (re)elect, and legitimate their political rulers through the mandatory rules and procedures of free, fair and inclusive elections. Conversely, in democracy rulers do not choose, select the people (re)electing them through 'natural selection,' distinction and discrimination[10] between 'good' and 'bad' citizens, for example, 'true' and 'untrue,' 'friends' and 'enemies,' 'proper' and 'improper,' 'patriotic' and 'unpatriotic,' 'godly' and 'godless,' 'moral' and 'immoral,' 'insiders' and 'outsiders,' simply 'us' and 'them.' If this happens, as through suppression of voting rights and distortion of electoral configurations or regions and processes, then it is the strong indicator or predictor of a profoundly undemocratic, exclusionary, and discriminatory political system in formal-procedural and also substantive-effective terms, such as aristocracy,

---

8   Ellman and Wantchekon (2000, p. 499) caution that 'in a democracy where the majority winner sets policy, dissatisfied groups, including groups outside the electoral process, may still be able to interfere with that policy. A losing party may organize a coup; voters may riot; unions may go on strike; investors may take their capital abroad; terrorists and foreign powers may threaten disruption and loss of life; foreign powers may withdraw aid or even impose a trade embargo.'

9   Fearon (2011, p. 1662) proposes that the 'institution of commonly understood electoral rules and procedures thus allows the citizens to credibly threaten mass protest if the ruler does not provide them with the means of aggregating their diverse observations (which explains) how electoral democracy can be self-enforcing.'

10   An example is the frequent distinction by, above all, conservative, politicians and others in America between 'all-American' and 'un-American' persons and groups, 'deserving' versus 'non-deserving' classes, including the '47 percent' low-class Americans during the 2012 Presidential election. Another example of rulers 'choosing' people to (re)elect them is the notorious anti-democratic practice of Congressional redistricting as Machiavellian partisan 'gerrymandering' (Besley and Preston 2007; Coate and Knight 2007). This is an illegal—as judged by various court decisions—tactic to gain and retain individual or party position in Congress such as the House of Representatives through creating 'all-American' electoral districts purged from 'un-American' persons and conversely, as persistently used by ruling anti-liberal conservatives in the South (particularly in Texas since the 2000s) and elsewhere in the US.

a master-servant or caste system, oligarchy, theocracy or a theocentric state, fascism and other totalitarianism.

The second, corollary condition, element and indicator of formal-procedural democracy comprises the legal freedom and right to political participation, inclusion, and equality as part of the sum of inalienable constitutional citizenship liberties and rights.[11] In particular, this condition incorporates equal voting freedoms, rights, and chances in the form of universal and maximal franchise for the legally eligible population regardless of its differential societal attributes such as property or wealth and income, political power and influence, social status and networks, race, ethnicity and national origin, gender, life style, religion, morality, penal confinement, education, ideology, etc. It also entails full and unrestricted opportunities to exercise the freedom and right to vote in elections, including a solemn special election day (typically Sunday) undisturbed or undistracted by competing considerations, obligations, and constraints like work, school, legal duties, church, religion, etc., expressing the societal evaluation and celebration of democracy. In addition, it contains legal, including constitutional, freedoms, rights, and opportunities for other forms of political participation, inclusion, and equality such as seeking and holding power or public office, in conjunction with and conditional on the established universal and equal right and opportunity to vote as the basis and necessary condition for all others.

Negatively, voting and other freedoms, rights, and opportunities for political participation in democracy are not legally restricted to a privileged 'proper' subset of the population or made impossible and difficult for the other parts on various justificatory grounds and in diverse ways. Such democratic rights and freedoms cannot be either privileged or denied because of economic factors such as property or wealth and income, political grounds like power and ideology, cultural determinants involving religion, morality, and education, and others, including race, ethnicity, nationality, and gender, as well as arbitrary or burdensome formalities (taxes, tests, and related stringent or onerous requirements). In sum, both rich and poor, aristocrats/plutocrats and the populace ('lords and commoners'), elites and masses, believers and infidels, saints and sinners, conformists and deviants (including current and especially former prisoners) have the same legal freedoms, rights, and opportunities to political participation and inclusion, including voting and other more active forms of participatory democracy.

---

11   Bruch, Ferree, and Soss (2010), Goldberg (2001), and Korpi (1989) emphasize constitutional citizenship liberties and rights in contemporary democracies.

The third correlative condition and indicator of formal-procedural democracy constitutes the freedom, right, openness, and opportunity to the pursuit and attainment of power and political position generally. This holds true in the sense of Schumpeter's definition[12] of democracy as the system and process of formally and effectively open, free competition for state power or political leadership by analogy—but not equation, as in 'public choice theory'—to the freely competitive market. Hence, this condition encompasses legal-constitutional universal and equal freedoms, rights, and opportunities to seeking and holding political power[13] through free competition for positions in government, with no economic, ideological-political, racial-ethnic, gender, religious, and any other formal grounds and types of inequality, restriction, discrimination, and exclusion. In particular, it involves the constitutional and other legal stipulation against and sanctioning of religiously grounded restriction, discrimination, and exclusion enforced on the equal freedom and right to open, free and fair contest for power or political leadership in Schumpeter's sense.

This means that democracy involves no establishing of religion in politics in the sense of the US Constitution prohibiting such 'establishment' by Congress and state legislatures—though many states, especially in the South, violate this constitutional stipulation—and no religious tests, also constitutionally prohibited since Jefferson, for political position and any public office, including government administration, judiciary, public education and health systems, and so on. Instead, such establishment and imposition of religion and religious tests for seeking and holding state power define theocracy as exclusionary religious tranny, 'godly' dictatorship profoundly antithetical and ultimately destructive to formal-procedural and substantive-effective democracy. What Jefferson denotes the constitutional 'eternal wall of separation of church and state' as a legal ideal in the US polity legally permits the equal freedom, right and opportunity to pursuing and holding power 'for all' regardless of their religious and any arbitrary (dis) qualifications inconsequential for the functioning and outcomes of formal-procedural as well as substantive-effective democracy, including free political competition, democratic rule, or state effectiveness.

---

12   Schumpeter (1950, p. 271) states that 'free competition for leadership defines democracy' and represents the 'free competition for a free vote.' He deduces 'thence the opposition between political monopoly and democracy' (Schumpeter 1950, p. 301).

13   Wright (2013, p. 5) proposes that 'in a deeply democratic society everyone actually participates equally in the exercise of power, but everyone needs to have equal access to participation.'

Generally, this condition consists in the freedom, openness, and inclusiveness of the nomination and election process[14] to all potential aspirants seeking political position regardless of their varying social, including racial-ethnic, gender, ideological, religious, moral, economic and other backgrounds, conditions, and public pronouncements. Conversely, this signifies that the existing ruling group is not closed and exclusive through Weber's 'monopolistic closure' of legal and actual opportunities for pursuing and holding power to insiders and against outsiders denied such an opportunity, freedom, and right on political, economic, and cultural, especially religious-moralistic, grounds, simply 'not born' into wealth, power, status, and 'divine' rights. Relatedly, the condition of formal-procedural democracy is that rulers or leaders do not form an oligarchy of the '(good) old boy networks,'[15] including estate and money aristocracy as actual plutocracy monopolizing the freedom, right and opportunity to seek and hold political power, just as franchise, for the few select 'best' and wealthy, i.e., oligarchs, aristocrats, and plutocrats.

Another condition is that they do not become or establish theocracy attaining 'monopolistic closure' of power for the 'godly' endowed with 'divine rights' to rule, oppress and ultimately eliminate the 'godless' denied any freedoms, rights and opportunities to power and politics, and even to exist as human beings in theocratic states driven by religious anti-democratic extremism. For illustration, paradigmatic exemplars include Puritan-evangelical and Islamic theocracies driven by anti-liberal and anti-democratic extremism such as fundamentalism and perpetrating constant, systematic and unrepentant 'holy' oppression and terror against 'infidels'[16] through a permanent religious revolution and war (crusade and jihad) that Weber identifies as the shared property of Calvinist Puritanism and Islam seen as theocratic and warlike functional equivalents.

---

14   Bollen and Paxton (1998, p. 470) include 'competitiveness in the nomination process' among the four dimensions of 'democratic rule,' which is also included in the Polity IV Project.

15   Mailath, Samuelson, and Shaked (2000, p. 48) refer to anecdotes concerning the importance of the 'old boy networks' in the US.

16   Mueller (2009, p. ix) states that 'wherever extremist religious beliefs exist, liberalism is at peril, alerting to the 'growing importance of religious extremism in the United States, South America, the Middle East,' thus primarily referring to American Puritan-rooted evangelicalism (exported to Latin American countries) and Islamic fundamentalism as theocratic anti-democratic functional equivalents, simply 'brothers in arms.' Mueller (2009, p. 392) points to those 'US evangelical Christians' whose 'Puritanical beliefs cause hardship, suffering, and often death' by denying and suppressing various political and individual liberties and rights, for example, the right to abortion.

The fourth condition/element/indicator of formal-procedural democracy represents the legal, particularly constitutional, provision and protection of ideological and political pluralism and diversity, thus freedom and possibility of choice between alternative contesting, including mutually exclusive, contradictory, and opposed, ideologies and political programs and policies. Negatively, it does not represent monism or uniformity and to some degree pseudo-pluralism legally, including constitutionally, enacted as (to be) uncontested in ideological and political terms, as the antithesis and simulation of pluralism and choice in the polity, respectively. In short, legal ideological and political pluralism and choice typifies formal-procedural democracy in terms of ideology and political programs, just as monism characterizes totalitarianism[17] and pseudo-pluralism a quasi-democratic polity. Formal ideological-political pluralism and choice also involves or results in potentially or actually free competition for power in Schumpeter's sense between alternative ideologies, programs and policies, in contrast to monism and quasi-pluralism involving or resulting in monopoly and duopoly in the polity, which are the antithesis and simulation of democracy, respectively.[18]

To that extent, the condition of formal-procedural democracy constitutes the legal freedom, choice, and right of alternative ideologies, programs, and policies in free, open competition both presupposing and implicit in ideological and political pluralism legally formulated and protected. Like the competitive market typified by what Weber calls peaceful exchange transactions due to 'pacification' in society, ideological-political competition and pluralism is premised on the maxim of 'live and let live' (used by Schumpeter and other economists to describe economic oligopoly) in politics as a condition of the operation and existence of formal-procedural, just as substantive-effective, democracy. By contrast, like a monopolistic market, ideological-political monopoly and monism is driven by the opposite maxim after the model of Machiavellianism and the image of the Hobbesian 'war of everyone against everyone' and the 'law of the jungle'[19] and of the 'strongest,' thus being destructive to democracy.

---

17   Dahrendorf 1959, p. 318) observes that 'totalitarian monism is founded on the idea that conflict can and should be eliminated. The pluralism of free societies is based on the recognition and acceptance of social conflict. For freedom in society means, above all, that we recognize the justice and the creativity of diversity, difference, and conflict.'

18   The analogy between the competitive market and formally democratic politics, however, is just that—no more than the use of a metaphor—so should not be taken too far as an equation, as in reductive economistic 'public choice theory' cum the 'economics of politics.'

19   As noted, even hardline laissez-faire, 'libertarian' economist Mises (1962, p. 97) admits, deviating from or mitigating economic 'libertarianism' cum plutocratic anarchism conjoined

Conversely, this condition consists in that the political system does not legally enact and judicially decide that 'there is no alternative,'[20] thus no choice in ideological and political terms as the path of imposition of monism and monopoly in politics, and thus totalitarianism. Simply, it means that there is no such thing as 'there is no alternative and choice' ideologically and politically in democracy and modern free society as a whole, and that such negative claims reveal or produce anti-democratic projects or outcomes.

As a corollary, the fifth condition/element/indicator of formal-procedural democracy contains the legal-constitutional rule and procedure of open, free and fair competition in the polity in Schumpeter's sense. Alternatively, this involves no political 'monopolistic closure' in Weber's sense such as pure monopoly and to some extent duopoly in politics analogously (but not equated) to their economic forms in the market. In addition to competing individual aspirants for state power or public office, this condition specifically entails the formal stipulation or existence of a multi-party and thus competitive polity through the legal recognition, protection, and equal treatment of multiple, including opposing, political parties and related groups. Such a political system supersedes one- and to some extent two-party and in that sense monopolistic and duopolistic regimes denying universal legitimacy to all (peaceful) political parties or structurally generating and sustaining party monopoly and duopoly.

Like that between firms in the market, competition between parties, just as individual candidates, and related associations in the polity is regulated by the process of 'equal competition'[21] as a variation on the Enlightenment Voltaire-Hume-Kant-Jefferson's principle of universal and holistic liberty and its corollary Comte's, Spencer's and Durkheim's sociological principle of 'equal freedom' and 'just liberty' in society. It means that all political parties as power-seeking and holding groups and related organizations, like individual aspirants, have the universal, equal legal freedom, right, and opportunity for open, free competition in a democratic polity, as do competing firms in a freely competitive market.

---

with labor oppression, that only humans living in society substitute social cooperation for 'the state of nature' governed by 'war of everyone against all' and the 'law of the jungle.'

20   Giddens (2000a, p. 39) observes that the 'side that is more powerful has an interest, as Margaret Thatcher proclaimed, in declaring that "there is no alternative" to its ideology and policy. Also, Bauman (2001, p. 7) apparently referring to Thatcher's proclamation, notes that 'when people say "there is no alternative to X" ("nothing to be done"), X moves from the territory of action to that of the action's conditions' (nothing can be done).'

21   The early English economist William Senior (1951) uses the term 'perfectly equal competition' in the market.

Just as ideological-political pluralism and competition, free competition between party organizations and individuals in the polity through a multi-party
system is premised on the maxim 'live and let live' in relation to other parties
and individual candidates. This is in stark contrast to political monopoly and
to some extent duopoly through one- and two-party regimes driven, especially
the first, by the 'live and let die' opposite or its variations, sometimes literally
via various acts of official 'political terror,'[22] including executions, imprisonment, prohibition, and generally suppression of actual or potential competing
groups and individuals in politics. Conversely, a condition of formal-procedural
democracy is that a polity does not legally, including constitutionally, stipulate
and enforce that 'there is no alternative and choice' with respect to parties and
related groups seeking power, like ideology and religion, and does not establish
and favor one or two of them, thus a one- and two-party system as the form of
political monopoly and duopoly. Simply, to deny or restrict potential alternatives and choices in respect of power-seeking parties and related groups, like
individual pretenders, is a flagrant non sequitur and negation of democracy in
its formal-procedural as well as substantive-effective dimension.

Substantive-Effective Democracy

The conditions, elements, and indicators of substantive-effective democracy
comprise actual, realized political and civil liberties, choices, and rights in
reality, as distinct from nominal and potential ones on the legal 'paper' of constitutions and laws defining its formal-procedural type. When effective political and civil liberties and rights completely or reasonably correspond to and
implement their formal statements, this indicates complete, consistent, genuine democracy, thus a truly free polity. Conversely, when the first fail to reach
or reasonably approximate their legal ideals such a divergence makes the latter, including their constitutional declarations, almost not worth the paper on
which they are written and printed from the stance of effective democracy and
generally the real political life of citizens. The following classifies the conditions, elements, and indicators of substantive-effective democracy (Table 2.2).

---

22   Besley and Persson (2009, p. 292) use a 'political terror scale ranked from 1 to 5,' with 'a
     cutoff of 3 and above' indicating that 'civil and political rights violations such as execu-
     tion, imprisonment and political murders/ brutality are widespread. In the worst cases,
     leaders of society place no limit on the means or thoroughness with which they pursue
     personal or ideological goals (such as through) purges: systematic murders and elimina-
     tions of political opponents within regimes.'

TABLE 2.2   *Conditions, elements and indicators of substantive-effective democracy.*

---

(1) Effective, realized universal and equal political and civil liberties and rights—universalism and egalitarianism

> Effective political and civil liberties and rights for racial-ethnic minorities and immigrants
>
> Effective political and civil liberties and rights for religious minorities (non-believers, with no-religion, agnostics, secularists, progressives, etc.)
>
> Effective political and civil liberties and rights for ideological-legal minorities (dissenters, dissidents, current and former prisoners, moral sinners, etc.)
>
> Effective political and civil liberties and rights for economic-class minorities (lower classes and underclass).

(2) Democratic, egalitarian, and just rule or governance of elected rulers or representatives

(3) Effective, realized freedom of opinion, speech, and dissent, collective association and opposition

(4) Effective universalism, equality, and justice in government positive and negative sanctions

(5) Degree of effective pacifism or peace, non-militarism, non-imperialism, and no wars

---

The first condition, element and indicator of substantive-effective democracy represents factual universal and equal political and civil liberties and rights. Hence, this involves real-life, implemented political universalism and egalitarianism in the sense and prototypical form of the Enlightenment and its 'comprehensive liberalism.'[23] Such universalism and egalitarianism are epitomized

---

23   Dombrowski (2001, p. 9) identifies the 'comprehensive liberalism of the Enlightenment,' as do Habermas (2001), Mannheim (1986), Mokyr (2009, 2014), Mueller (2009), and others. Buchanan and Tullock (1962, p. 21) state that 'both the theory of democracy and the theory of the market economy are products of the Enlightenment, and, for the eighteenth-century philosophers, these two orders of human activity were not to be discussed separately.' Schumpeter (1954, p. 372) states that 'Political Liberalism, which must be distinguished from economic liberalism, (involves) sponsorship of parliamentary government, freedom to vote and extension of the right to vote, freedom of the press, divorce of secular from spiritual government, trial by jury, and so on, including retrenchment and pacific, though not necessarily pacifist, foreign policy. This was the program of the first phase of the French Revolution. A tendency to carry it out eventually asserted itself everywhere.'

in the Enlightenment Voltaire-Kant-Hume-Jefferson's principle and realization of universal liberty, equality, and justice in the polity and all society, including equal treatment before the law and related political institutions. Its logical corollary is what Comte and Spencer state as the law of equal right and freedom and Durkheim as that of 'just liberty' in society, including the polity and the economy, and generally Smith's 'liberal plan of liberty, equality and justice' in their interconnection and mutual reinforcement. The Enlightenment justification of this principle is that liberty, like justice, in the polity and society is either universal and equal 'for all,' as in Voltaire-Jefferson's formulations—or not really 'liberty' but what Simmel[24] calls its 'compensatory substitute' and Germans ersatz, simulation or placebo 'faking' liberties, rights, and democracy.[25]

Consequently, genuine substantive-effective democracy is invariably defined, typified, and identified by the principle and realization of universal political and civil liberty, equality, and justice. This is in sharp contrast and contradiction to particularistic, exclusionary 'democracies' or 'republics' characterized with non-universal, exclusive 'liberty' monopolized by ruling groups or persons. These include what Mosca and Pareto call the narrow ruling class/ elite and Michels the closed 'old master-caste' particularly in slavery, master-servant, caste and similar societies. This is exemplified by aristocracy in feudalism, self-proclaimed 'God's agents'—for example, the 'elect' in Calvinism and its 'pure' sect Puritanism and its own successor revived evangelicalism—in theocracy, oligarchy and autocracy in other non-democratic regimes such as conservatism, fascism and communism, oligarchic plutocracy in 'unfettered' capitalism, etc. In this respect, genuine, self-consistent democracy is either universalistic and egalitarian in terms of political liberties, rights and choices or not truly 'democracy' but instead its perversion or simulation such as exclusionary 'democracies'[26] and societies overall, as an inner contradiction

---

He adds that the 'adherents of the Spanish Constitution of 1811 were the first to call themselves *liberales*,' and the 'French *libéraux* of the 1820's' (Schumpeter (1954, p. 372).

24   According to Simmel (1955, p. 166), tyranny can involve an 'expedient distribution of collective coercion and individual arbitrariness (as a) compensatory substitute.' This is epitomized or approximated in modern societies, above all the US since Reaganism and the UK under Thatcherism, by the 'libertarian' neo-conservative 'distribution' of collective compulsion and repression in polity, civil society, and culture and of individualistic 'arbitrariness' and 'free enterprise' in the economy, primarily in the form of plutocratic license against the non-wealthy.

25   Spiegler (2013, p. 1491) uses the expression 'placebo reforms' to describe policy reforms with 'no real impact' allowing that it may be 'possible to "fake" a reform.'

26   Centeno (1994, p. 135) notes that 'none of the revolutions that produced the developed states of Western Europe and of North America originally established what today would

and empirical impossibility from the prism of modern democratic ideals, values, and institutions. In sum, real-life universalism and egalitarianism in respect of realized political and civil liberties, rights, choices and opportunities constitute the first and overarching condition and dimension of substantive-effective democracy.

For example, this incorporates effective political and civil liberties and rights for racial-ethnic and related minorities as well as immigrants (or legally resident foreigners[27]), just as for the majority group, consistent with the principle and realization of universal liberty for all individuals and groups regardless of race, ethnicity, national origins, etc. It entails real-life universalism and egalitarianism through inclusion and equal, fair treatment in terms of race, ethnicity, national origins, and the like within the polity. Conversely, it eliminates or minimizes particularism and inequality in liberties and rights on racial, ethnic, national, and related grounds, specifically the institutional monopoly, closure, or favoritism of the majority group as race or ethnicity, and political repression, exclusion, and discrimination against corresponding minority groups. Such a duality of 'superior' majority-group monopoly on liberty and rights and their systematic denial and suppression for 'inferior' minority groups is a relic of the pre-democratic, aristocratic, and racial 'dead past,' for example, the slave or master-servant regime during the European Dark Middle Ages, slavery, discrimination, and oppression in the US Southern States, Nazism and interwar fascism in Europe, etc. Consequently, this duality represents a non sequitur and self-denial for modern and related Western substantive-effective democracy.

The present condition also encompasses effective political and civil liberties and rights for religious minorities or outsiders, as for the religiously majority insider group, self-consistent with the principle and realization of universal liberty for all individuals and groups irrespective of their type, degree, or lack of religion. It involves effective political and civil liberties, rights, choices and

---

be called a democracy. Even into the twentieth century large segments of these populations were excluded from voting for reasons of sex, class, or race. (For example) a state (can) only to consider the wishes of 8% of the population, as was the case in Britain in 1867 (which shows) an 'exclusionary democracy.' The idea of exclusionary 'democracies' is also implicit in Glenn (2011) and Somerville (2000) and that of exclusionary societies generally in Edgell, Gerteis, and Hartmann (2006), who identify religious non-belief (atheism) as the persistent and major basis for cultural and overall societal exclusion in contemporary America.

27   Beck (2000, p. 128) proposes 'tell me how the rights of minorities, outcasts and foreigners are handled in your country (officially and informally) and I will tell you how democracy is faring in your country!'

opportunities for non-believers, those believing in 'false' religions or belonging to no organized religion, agnostics, skeptics, secularists, progressives, and 'godless' liberals, just as for their opposites, 'true believers' and the 'godly,' simply both 'us' and 'them'[28] religiously considered. In short, this is universalism and egalitarianism through inclusion and equal, fair treatment in the polity in respect, or rather regardless, of religious belief, affiliation, and activity.

Conversely, this condition consists in delegitimizing and transcending political anti-universalism and inequality, exclusion and discrimination on a religious 'sacred' basis. The latter involves the institutionalized monopoly or dominance of the majority 'godly' group claiming to be 'Divinely ordained'[29]— for example, the 'Divine rights' of kings, the Calvinist-Puritan 'elect,' the evangelical 'only saved,' etc.—and the systematic oppression, exclusion, and elimination of minority 'godless' and dissenting 'heretic' out-groups[30] in the 'glory, name and mind of God.' Such a dualism of 'godly' majority-group monopoly on liberty and rights, and negating and eliminating them for minority 'godless' or dissenting out-groups forms a vestige of the pre-democratic theocratic 'dead past' from the viewpoint of the project and reality of modern democracy. For example, the dualism spans from what Pareto considers the

---

28   Lichterman (2008, p. 84) finds that in the US church members 'used religious terms to argue over the maps of "people like us" and "people not like us" that ultimately oriented their group action (and so) use religion in situation-specific ways to include or exclude others in civil society.'

29   Bendix (1974, p. 149) observes that in 'our world, inequality among men is considered an aspect of social organization, not a divinely ordained attribute of the human condition.' Hodgson (1999, p. 210) notes that 'in the history of capitalism, managerial authority has been legitimated by various ideological appeals, including divine right, natural law, the survival of the fittest and meritocratic entitlement.' Wright (2013, p. 7) remarks that 'human suffering and deficits in human flourishing are not simply the result of human nature, acts of God, or variations in people's attributes, but are the result of social causes.'

30   Juergensmeyer (2003) analyzed contemporary religiously induced and justified terrorism in a book titled 'Terror in the Mind of God.' Merton (1939, p. 437) comments that 'American nativism, in the form of anti-Catholic and later of anti-foreign sentiment, was partly rooted in this same *Puritanism (which)* finds its analogue in the various Nazi primers (viz.) the displacement of aggression against a convenient out-group (especially) marked in periods of economic strain (plus) the impugning of out-group morality (etc.).' Mueller (2013, p. 9) referring to 'evangelical Americans' notes that 'those with strong religious beliefs are often able to pass laws, which limit the freedoms of individuals in the community thereby harming those who would undertake the forbidden actions.'

mutation of the 'religion of Christ' for the 'poor and humble into the 'Roman theocracy' and the Christian and Islamic Dark Middle Ages through Calvin's 'holy' Geneva autocracy and Weber's 'Puritan theocracy of New England' to his 'Bibliocracy' in the Southern and other US (the 'Bible Belt'). As a consequence, this theocratic or oligarchic dualism of monopoly and closure of political as well as religious liberty by the 'godly' and its negation and elimination to 'infidels' represents a flagrant non sequitur, self-negation, and perversion in modern substantive-effective democracy.

In sum, substantive-effective democracy develops and functions as an opposite to and supersedes theocracy exactly defined by such an anti-democratic dualism. And if, as US early sociologist Ross states, religious 'Puritan tyranny' forms an 'antidote' to democracy, then the latter acts as a cure for the theocratic sacred 'poison' to universal, equal political and civil liberty. This holds as a rule or pattern, despite many theocracies claiming to be 'democracies' or 'republics' spanning from Calvin's *Christiana respublica* in Geneva through its heirs England's and New England's Puritan 'Holy Commonwealth' (described as *mixt aristocracie* by its rulers Winthrop et al.) to its attempted revival as 'paradise lost and found' by the 'Bibliocracy' in the US South, plus Catholic 'republics' in Europe and South America, 'Islamic republics,' etc.

Relatedly, the current condition contains effective political and civil liberties and rights for ideological and legal-moral minorities, as for their majority counterpart, compatible with the principle and realization of universal liberty for all individuals and groups regardless of their ideology and other ideas and their non-political activities or punishments such as imprisonment. Specifically, this involves effective equal political and civil liberties and rights for ideological dissenters, renegades, dissidents, apostates, heretics, etc., and deviants like current and former prisoners, especially those imprisoned due to sins-as-crimes such as nonviolent drug and other moral offenses, as for their ideologically conformist and morally non-deviant counterparts.

Therefore, a condition of substantive-effective democracy consists of political universalism and egalitarianism through inclusion and equal, fair treatment within politics in terms of ideology and other ideas, as well as the criminal justice status such as prior and present incarceration for sins-crimes. Negatively formulated, this overcomes or minimizes political anti-universalism and inequality on grounds of ideology and all ideas and on prior and current penal status. It thus supersedes the institutional monopolistic closure by the majority ideological group and its repression and exclusion of and discrimination against minority groups like ideological dissenters and non-political deviants like former or present prisoners punished for sins-crimes. The duality of ideological majority-group monopoly on liberty and rights and their negation for minority groups on the basis of 'false' ideology and other 'wrong' ideas and present or prior penal status is a remnant of the pre-democratic 'dead past' from the Christian Dark Middle Ages through slavery and discrimination in the US South to Nazism and fascism in interwar Europe, and thus a non sequitur and self-subversion for modern substantive-effective democracy.

Similarly, the current condition incorporates effective political and civil liberties and rights for economic minorities, just as for the majority, also consistent with the principle and realization of universal liberty for all individuals and groups regardless of their level of material resources grounding social classes. Specifically, this means effective and equal political and civil liberties and rights for low classes sociologically—not necessarily demographically—considered economic minorities on account of their lower material resources and thus 'economic power,' as for the upper class treated as the majority in the sociological sense of wealth-power and often in the demographic one when combined with middle classes, as in Western and related societies. In Weber's words, what he calls the Southern 'poor white trash' and generally the 'underclass' encompassing also other racial groups in America is institutionally entitled with and effectively exercises equal effective political and civil liberties and rights as does the US 'naked plutocracy' as the aristocracy of money—yet wanting to 'live like European landlords'—within substantive-effective democracy. Hence, this condition means political universalism and egalitarianism in the form of inclusion and equal, fair treatment of all groups and persons in politics in respect or rather regardless of their social class determined by the differential level of economic resources.

Negatively, it consists in dispensing with or minimizing political anti-universalism and inequality premised on sharp class stratification, namely the institutional closure and domination of the upper and upper-middle class as the sociological majority, and repression, exclusion, and discrimination targeting other classes as economic minorities. Such a duality of the wealthy class monopoly on political and civil liberties and rights and their denial or violation to non-wealthy classes is the pre-democratic 'ghost' of Michels' 'master-caste,' Pareto's feudal aristocracy, and Weber's capitalist plutocracy as rich oligarchies, thus a non sequitur and self-elimination for substantive-effective democracy. In sum, substantive-effective democracy is antithetical to and overcomes plutocracy in which, as Weber observes for its American version, money literally 'purchases power,' thus exerting President Roosevelt's diagnosed 'tyranny' of wealth held by the rich oligarchy over society despite Pareto's 'demagogic plutocracies' claiming or appearing to be 'democracies.' On this account, genuine substantive-effective democracy is not and cannot be plutocracy despite the latter's democratic pretensions, masks, and appearances, and relatedly aristocracy or oligarchy as essentially plutocratic equivalents,[31] as Aristotle and others recognize long ago (plutocrats being invariably the 'best' few, so aristocrats or oligarchs).

The second related condition, element, and indicator of substantive-effective democracy constitutes the democratic, egalitarian, and just rule and decision making by elected rulers and representatives, including executive, legislative, and judicial powers, or public officials. Such democratic governance consists of political structures and rulers effectively protecting and promoting political, civil and citizenship, as well as economic, individual and cultural liberties, rights, choices and opportunities. Alternatively, it involves no or minimal government coercion and repression, such as removing or minimizing control, surveillance, intrusion, and severe punishment of citizens' autonomous political and private activities.

Notably, democratic governance is negatively defined by *no* actions and agents on what analysts and others denote the government 'political terror scale' committing systematic violent repression and severe punishment. For example, such a scale includes arbitrary executions[32] and mass incarceration of 'enemies' and dissenters and moral sinners, all redefined and treated as criminals, as exemplified by prisoners of political and ethical conscience. Hence, a democratic government is distinguished and distanced from a violent, repressive, punitive, and police state exerting in various degrees and ways political terror and typifying non-democracy, and also found in religiously grounded nominal democracies or republics such as the conservative part of America, Catholic-dominated Poland, Turkey under Islamic rule, Islamic Republic of Iran, etc. The present condition also incorporates government effectiveness in promoting, protecting, and expanding economic and social welfare and life chances in society, including material wellbeing, prosperity, progress, security, happiness or life satisfaction, knowledge and education, health care, healthy life-styles and natural environments, and so on.

The third condition, element and indicator of substantive-effective democracy represents the factual enjoyment and exercise of freedom and right of

---

31   Acemoglu and Robinson (2008, p. 3298) indicate that 'before the French Revolution, much of Europe was dominated by two kinds of oligarchies: the landed nobility in agriculture and the urban-based oligarchy controlling commerce and various occupations.' Pryor (2002, p. 364) finds a tendency toward a 'greater oligarchical control of both the state and the economy' in the US during recent times.

32   Knight (1967, p. 792) implicitly presents a compelling argument against the death penalty in a free society by stating that 'social action does reduce freedom, but only killing people can destroy it.'

opinion and dissent, and of collective association and non-violent opposition toward prevailing ideologies, policies, and groups. This involves what Durkheim denotes the effective, unrestricted, and unpunished 'independence of thought' traced to heretics as 'precursors of liberal ideology,' and the freedom of public and private opinion and speech, including press and other media freedoms and rights, alternatively the absence of press and related censorship. It also incorporates the effective freedom of non-violent collective organization in the form of group assembly and of organized or unorganized institutional and non-institutional peaceful opposition to and of critique of ruling powers and prevalent ideologies, policies, and institutions.

At this juncture, the premise and outcome of substantive-effective democracy is that, as the Enlightenment emphasizes through Voltaire, Condorcet, Diderot, Montesquieu, Kant, Jefferson, Hume, etc., human thoughts, opinions, words, and speech, including disagreement, dissent, doubt and skepticism, are intrinsically independent, free, unconstrained, and not sanctioned negatively. This is in contrast to acts and deeds if these are violent and otherwise antidemocratic and antisocial. By implication, this also holds true for the peaceful collective association and opposition to and the criticism of the existing political system and its agents, as distinct from their violent, including terrorist, and coercive forms deemed inconsistent with and eventually destructive to substantive-effective as well as formal-procedural democracy.

The fourth condition and indicator of substantive-effective democracy represents realized universalism, equality, and justice in connection with the state's positive and negative sanctions such as rewards and punishments of individuals and social groups. The first type of government sanctions includes the universalism, egalitarianism, and relative generosity and quality of public goods and benefits such as health care, education, economic welfare and security, unemployment compensation, infrastructure, etc. through certain mechanisms like taxation and redistribution and subject to financial constraints in state budgets, etc. Hence, a universalistic and egalitarian welfare state in the broadest sense of a political system providing public goods defined by inclusion and thus non-excludable forms of wellbeing to all (eligible) citizens in society appears at this juncture as the indicator or proxy and covariate of substantive-effective democracy.

Such a state deeply differs from its non-universalistic, non-egalitarian variant or proxy doing so only for a certain narrow exclusionary group, typically the ruling class like aristocracy in feudalism and its equivalents plutocracy ('corporate welfare') or oligarchy in authoritarian, illiberal and oligarchic capitalism. What is common to all these classes is their attaining what Weber calls the 'monopolistic closure' and enjoyment of economic and non-economic, private and public welfare and privilege in the sense of his triple composite of superior wealth, power, and status. At least, a universalistic and egalitarian welfare state is compatible with substantive-effective democracy because of the latter's universalism and egalitarianism in liberties, rights and opportunities, as is its non-universalistic and anti-egalitarian variant with aristocracy, plutocracy, and oligarchy instead characterized with anti-universalism and anti-egalitarianism, particularism and exclusion.

The second type of government sanctions encompasses equal legal and other institutional treatment in the sense of equality before the law of all citizens and social groups regardless of their ascribed or attained attributes. In particular, this involves the government administration of effective criminal justice, including fair, non-Draconian, non-cruel punishments for criminal acts such as imprisonment, executions, etc., while moral sins as a rule not being punished, at least not harshly, in substantive-effective democracy, unlike theocracy and moralistic states defining and severely punishing them, including with death, as grave crimes. At the minimum, a fair and non-Draconian—the second usually being the first—relatively mild legal-penal system characterized with a crime-punishment balance, and minimizing the punishment of moral sins, is compatible with substantive-effective democracy. By contrast, an unfair and Draconian criminal justice system—the latter inherently being or eventually becoming the former—is incompatible with and destructive to substantive-effective democracy and instead typical for or consistent with non-democratic, especially theocratic, political systems. It is so by denying and reducing the effective exercise of political liberties and rights and participation in politics through mass incarceration for sins-cum-crimes and denying the voting right to present and former prisoners, as observed for some Western societies such as the UK and the conservative pole of the US during recent times.

The fifth condition and indicator of substantive-effective democracy is considered the degree of pacifism in the sense of sustained peace within the polity and society overall, as well as peaceful conflict avoidance and resolution in relation to other societies. Negatively, it is the absence or the minimal degree of militarism and imperialism, and notably no aggressive wars. This is on the ground that, as commonly observed and predicted, the first casualty of offensive war are political as well as civil and individual liberties and rights, consequently democracy and liberty and a free society in general, alongside human lives, family dissolution or disruptions, and societal resources. Alternatively, this condition involves enduring peace or peaceful conflict resolution in inter-state relations and tensions, as opposed to permanent and offensive imperial wars as false peace in the service of promoting bogus 'democracy' and 'freedom.'

The rationale for pacifism thus understood is the widespread observation or assumption that true, effective democracies do not fight wars with each other, and also do not militarily attack other societies, although the latter moment is neglected or deemphasized in the academic literature and political statements (perhaps because some 'democratic' governments launch military aggressions on 'undemocratic' regimes, as in Cuba, Vietnam, Grenada, Yugoslavia, Iraq, etc.). In sum, this condition of substantive-effective democracy is premised on the hard lesson from the past and present that no effective and viable democracy as the system of universal political and civil liberties and rights can endure and prosper without continual peace within society and in relation to other societies. In retrospect, this is what the American founders like Jefferson and *Madison*[33] admonished and predicted for the US and any government, while repudiating the Puritan theocratic-moralistic and militarist vision of America as 'Christian Sparta' after the model of Calvin's Geneva autocracy.[34]

---

33   Recall that James Madison warns (in *Political Observations* from 1795): 'Of all the enemies to public liberty war is, perhaps, the most to be dreaded because it comprises and develops the germ of every other. War is the parent of armies; from these proceed debts and taxes (as) known instruments for bringing the many under the domination of the few. No nation could preserve its freedom in the midst of continual warfare.'

34   Kloppenberg (1998, p. 32) notices that 'Madison and his allies repudiated the (Puritan) ideal of (America as) a 'Christian Sparta.' Garrard (2003, p. 24) refers to the ideal of post-Calvin and Calvin's Geneva as 'austere (Christian) Sparta' and the 'anti-Paris,' as extoled by Calvinist Rousseau versus Paris as epitomizing everything that Calvinists abhorred and detested, i.e., the center, civil society, and expression of Enlightenment liberalism, secularisms, and rationalism—and they, especially US evangelicals, seemingly still do up to the present time (as implied in Mueller 2009). It is just a slight flight of imagination to predict that if today's and future Euro-Calvinists or US Puritanical evangelicals had a 'rational choice' which single city in the Western and entire world to destroy, their first choice would probably be Paris that they redefine from the 'city of lights (liberties and knowledge)' into the 'city of darkness, sin, and Satan,' a sort of modern version of Babylon, thus likely perpetrating what even the Nazis did not. Like their Islamic dual enemies-brothers in arms did in pre-Islamic Alexandria, and their medieval ancestors against classical 'pagan' civilization, they would likely first burn and burry 'ungodly,' 'un-Christian' books and libraries and related objects and sites in the 'city of lights.' That this seemingly fantastic scenario is an ever-present, even if not imminent, danger under certain conditions and circumstances such as evangelical revolutions and wars, is implied in Mueller's (2009) detection and prediction of 'Puritanical' American evangelicalism as the single gravest adversary and treat to Western liberal democracy, literally together with Islamic fundamentalism.

Comparative Estimates and Types of Democracy

The preceding opens the question of what is the relationship between the conditions and the types of democracy or political system. One wonders which of these types fulfils the conditions of and thus constitutes democracy proper in the framework of modern free society—liberal, secular and universalistic or egalitarian democracies or their antitheses.[35] At this juncture, the provisional agnostic position of not knowing whether democracy within modern free society consists of the liberal, secular and universalistic type or the opposite and other types is abandoned. As implied in the previous chapter, this is done by observing or expecting that only liberal, secular and universalistic democracies intrinsically, systematically, and completely satisfy, comprise and exhibit these conditions, elements and indicators of democracy and thus of modern free society in political terms. Conversely, opposite sociopolitical systems such as anti-liberal, anti-secular and exclusionary or inegalitarian 'democracies' or 'republics' are observed or expected to fail to do so, and instead to inherently, systematically, and totally negate and eliminate or subvert them and hence democracy and modern free society as a whole.

Therefore, the liberal, secular and universalistic democratic type epitomizes a free polity in the shape of formal-procedural and substantive-effective democracy, while its opposite types exemplifying an unfree, totalitarian or authoritarian political system formally and effectively. In essence, liberal, secular and universalistic democracies have proven or are expected to prove to be the

---

35 Edgell et al. (2006, pp. 228–9) think that 'recent developments in Africa, Asia, and Latin America suggest that a covenantal (religious) model—rather than the secular vision of state-society relations that grows out of the Western enlightenment—may be more the rule than the exception, at least for the development of democracy on a global scale.' This is a peculiar statement because it expressly does not apply to the developed world but instead to Third-World non- or pre-liberal and non-secular 'democracies' as effectively theocratic or theocentric political regimes compared to Western liberal-secular democracies, as well as to hyper-religious 'American exceptionalism.' According to Mueller (2009, p. 1), however, today's Western and other developed societies represent as a rule ('with very few exceptions') liberal and secular democracies. Moreover, Mueller (2009, p. 17) remarks that such non-liberal and non-secular 'democracies,' citing the 'examples of India and Turkey,' are 'no guarantee of liberalism' defined following J.S. Mill as the 'liberty to do, think and say what one wants so long as the exercise of such liberty does not do undue harm to other,' and thus political and individual liberties and rights. In this sense, 'covenantal 'democracies' are no democracies or free polities at all from the stance of such liberties and rights defining liberal-secular, genuine democracy.

only genuine, consistent, and viable[36] (type of) modern democracy, thus a free political system in long terms. Conversely, anti-liberal, anti-secular, notably theocentric 'godly' (Islamic, Christian, etc.), and exclusionary 'democracies' represent a logical contradiction and empirical perversion and ultimately the lethal poison of a free polity and society, a bogus 'democracy.'

Consequently, liberal, secular and all-inclusive democracies are observed or predicted to be invariably and drastically more democratic—i.e., politically freer and more open, equal and fair—than their anti-liberal, anti-secular and exclusionary ersatz substitutes, such as conservative, including religion-based[37] and fascist, 'democracies' or 'republics.' From the stance of a free polity, the latter actually represent species of totalitarianism or authoritarianism, so anti- or non-democratic political systems—totalitarian or authoritarian 'democracies' as a non sequitur—thus being as distant and different from and opposed to liberal, secular and universalistic democracies as 'heaven and earth.' They are literally 'heaven' for their rulers and subjects (the 'grassroots') experiencing illiberal, non-secular and exclusionary 'democracy' or 'republic' as 'paradise lost and found' cum the 'Kingdom of God on the Earth.' This is among OECD countries shown by Catholic, evangelical and Islamic 'democracies' or 'republics' in post-communist Poland, Latin America and in part Ireland, the American South, Turkey, and beyond (Iran, Saudi Arabia, etc.). Conversely, ersatz 'democracies' condemn and destroy their liberal, secular and universalistic

---

36 Mueller (2009, p. 1) observes that the 'rich countries today, with very few exceptions, are liberal democracies. They are liberal in the sense that their citizens have freedoms to go and to do as they wish. They are democracies in that their citizens exercise a significant control over the state. In the poorest countries, one or both attributes of liberal democracy are often missing.' He elaborates that in a 'liberal democracy citizens not only participate in a democratic process but also get great freedoms to think and do as they please. Thus, liberal democracy requires two sets of institutions, voting rules and electoral laws that enable the state to provide goods and services that benefit the citizen, and constitutional rights and a judiciary that protects certain individual freedoms from the state' (Mueller 2009, p. 13). However, Mueller (2009, p. 400) warns that the religious and other extremist 'enemies of progress have proved to be stronger than Condorcet (Enlightenment philosopher) might have ever imagined; the triumph of reason and (liberal) democracy is still incomplete.' He concludes that 'it is religious extremists therefore that deserve the closest attention today from those who defend liberal democracy' (Mueller 2009, p. 417).

37 Mueller (2009, p. 397) warns that 'by circumscribing domains in which individuals can use their powers of reasoning, religions reduce the potential for people to make individual and collective decisions that advance their welfare on the earth. In this respect religion and democracy are incompatible. A well-functioning liberal democracy requires a great of tolerance from its citizens. Here we have another potential tension between religion and liberal democracy. All religions are inherently intolerant of one another and of secularism (e.g., "I am the Lord, your God, you shall have no other gods").'

antidote (or poison for Ross' Puritan tyranny') as 'hell' and the 'enemy of God,' in particular the Western 'European anti-Christ' for US theocratic evangelicals (and Polish Catholic would-be theocrats) perpetuating Weber's 'Bibliocracy' in the 'Southern United States' (the 'Bible Belt'), and 'anti-Islamic' and 'Satan' for their enemies yet 'brothers in arms,' Islamic fundamentalists.

Specifically, the question arises as to whether and to what extent modern Western and related societies fulfill, entail, and reveal the conditions, elements, and indicators of democracy. One wonders how politically free as well as open, equal, and just are these societies in relation to each other and so rank in democratic, free-polity terms. As a rule, Western and related societies characterized with a liberal, secular and universalistic democracy are observed or expected to more completely, consistently, and enduringly fulfill, possess, and display the prerequisites, components, and indications of democracy than those with opposite political systems such as anti-liberal, anti-secular and exclusionary conservative, religious 'democracies' or 'republics.' Consequently, the first societies tend to be invariably and drastically freer and more open, equal, and fair in political terms than the second, as well as more so than intermediate, eclectic cases. Observations indicate and expectations anticipate the pattern that, in essence, the first are the politically freest, most open, equal, and fair modern societies, and the second least so among all, with mixed political systems ranked between the two. These observations and expectations are essentially reaffirmed and confirmed, as shown in the rest of this and next chapter.

Classification of Modern Political Systems

For the present purpose, contemporary Western and related societies, more specifically OECD countries as the focus of this analysis, are classified in terms of types of democracy or political system as follows (Table 2.3.)

First, in the context of OECD certain countries are politically classified in liberal, secular and universalistic or egalitarian democracy, just as are sociologically in 'liberal society' in the previous chapter. They are specifically Australia, Austria, Belgium, Canada, Denmark, France, Germany, Iceland, Luxembourg, the Netherlands, New Zealand, Norway, Sweden, Switzerland, and the US, thus all the countries previously classified in 'liberal society.' As a variation of its general societal classification, the US is classified in this type of democracy specifically in its liberal, secular and universalistic or egalitarian ideology and/or governance (essentially weak, transient or exceptional) and regions (basically minority or decreasing), as distinct from the anti-liberal, anti-secular and exclusionary or inegalitarian polar opposite. In light of the political and

TABLE 2.3   *Classification of western and related societies (OECD countries) in democracy/ political freedom.*

I   Liberal, secular, universalistic, egalitarian democracies (15 cases and 1/2)

Australia, Austria, Belgium, Canada, Denmark, Finland, France, Germany, Iceland, Luxembourg, Netherlands, New Zealand, Norway, Sweden, Switzerland, the US in weak, transient and exceptional liberal, secular and inclusive ideology and governance and minority or decreasing regions (e.g., the Coast, parts of the North, etc.).

Expected democracy/political freedom   highest, I—completely or largely free
overall ranking

II   Anti-liberal, anti-secular, exclusionary, inegalitarian 'democracies' (4 cases and 1/2)

Mexico, Poland, South Korea, Turkey, the US in strong, enduring or prevalent conservative, religious (theocratic and theocentric), and particularistic or inegalitarian ideology and governance and majority or growing regions (e.g., the ultra-conservative, evangelical, exclusionary, anti-egalitarian South, the Middle West, etc.).

Expected democracy/political freedom   lowest, III—unfree or quasi-free
overall ranking

III   Intermediate, eclectic, mixed democracies (13 cases)

Chile, Czech Republic, Greece, Hungary, Estonia, Ireland, Italy, Japan, Portugal, Slovakia, Slovenia, Spain, the UK

Expected democracy/political   intermediate, II--quasi-or largely free
freedom ranking

---

ideological polarization and opposition with its opposite, this facet of American ideology and politics is specified and designated as the 'liberal-secular pole or half' of the US, simply 'liberal and secular America.' Such specification hence observes or assumes the co-existence and yet deep and growing polarization and intense opposition to the point of proxy or metaphorical (civil, culture) war between the 'two Americas' in political and ideological terms particularly, just as in sociological ones generally. As noted, the notion of the 'two Americas' ideologically and politically, as well as historically, geographically and sociologically, is implicit in Dahrendorf differentiating the 'Southern United States' from the rest owing to violations of 'fundamental human rights,' and also in other sociological, economic and related observations and analyses, just as in American political and ordinary discourse.

In general, all these countries or regions are essentially or growingly liberal, secular, and universalistic or egalitarian in political terms, and thus primarily epitomize the corresponding type of democracy in the Western world and beyond, as within OECD. Hence, these are considered and connoted 'liberal, secular and universalistic democracies,' and observed or expected to rank overall the highest (rank I) in terms of democracy/political freedom among OECD and all countries.

Second, the following countries are classified in anti- or non-liberal, anti- or non-secular, and exclusionary or inegalitarian 'democracy' or rather politics within OECD: Mexico, Poland, South Korea, Turkey, and the US, again all the countries classified in 'anti-liberal society' before. The US is so classified specifically in its conservative, religious or theocentric, and particularistic or inegalitarian ideology or governance (mostly enduring or prevalent) and regions (largely majority or growing). As noted, this coexists with and yet intensely polarizes from and opposes, by conducting a proxy civil or culture war especially since Reaganism in the 1980s on, 'liberal, secular and universalistic America' within the context of the 'two Americas' along ideological-political and geographical and historical lines. Given such intense polarization and opposition between the two, this second facet of American ideology or politics is specified and designated as the 'conservative, theocentric pole or half' of the US, simply 'conservative, theocratic America' as epitomized by Dahrendorf's 'Southern United States.'

Generally, all these countries or regions are profoundly or increasingly anti- or non-liberal, anti- or non-secular, including theocratic or theocentric, exclusionary and inegalitarian in the political sense, and thus prime instances of the equivalent type of 'democracy' or rather political system in the Western world (conservative America) and OECD overall (Mexico, Poland, South Korea, and Turkey). They are hence deemed and denoted 'anti-liberal, anti-secular and exclusionary democracies,' and witnessed or predicted to rank the lowest overall (rank III) in terms of democracy/political freedom among OECD countries.

Third, the following OECD countries are classified in intermediate, eclectic, or mixed democracy or political system: Chile, Czech Republic, Greece, Hungary, Estonia, Ireland, Italy, Japan, Portugal, Slovakia, Slovenia, Spain, and the UK, which thus includes the same countries classified in the corresponding type of society. This peculiar group of countries generally combines in varying degrees the liberal and non-liberal, secular and non-secular, universalistic and particularistic, egalitarian and inegalitarian attributes of the previous two groups. They thus exemplify the intermediate, mixed type of democracy in the Western world and beyond, although some of them are or tend to move closer to the first group and others to the second. On this account, they are regarded and described as 'mixed democracies,' and found or expected to rank overall lower than the first and higher than the second (rank II) in terms of democracy/political freedom among OECD countries.

In sum, fourteen societies, and additionally the 'liberal, secular' half of the us, are politically classified in liberal-secular democracy, six, plus the 'conservative, theocratic' pole of America (such as 'Southern United States,' etc.) in the opposite type of 'democracy,' and eleven as mixed democracies out of the total of 33 OECD countries. As a rule/whole, liberal-secular democracies are predicted or expected to be the most democratic, freest political systems, anti-liberal, anti-secular conservative 'democracies' the least democratic, most unfree politically, and mixed democracies placed between the two in this respect. The remainder of this and next chapter considers whether and what degree such predictions or expectations are fulfilled.

Comparative Estimates of Democracy for Western and Related Societies

Using the preceding conditions and indicators yields the comparative estimates of democracy, i.e., political freedom, for Western and related societies, specifically OECD countries (Table 2.4).

Evidently, these societies vary greatly[38] in terms of their average democracy/political freedom estimates ranging from below 6 to close to 10 on the 0–10 scale derived from fifteen rankings on particular dimensions of democracy. On the basis of such estimates these societies are categorized into the following categories. The highest, first category encompasses fully democratic, politically free societies that have democracy scores of 8 or higher. The second category comprises largely democratic, politically free societies with scores ranging from 7 to 7.99. The third category contains quasi- or half-democratic, politically pseudo- or semi-free societies having scores in the 6–6.99 range. The lowest, fourth category includes anti- or non-democratic, politically unfree societies whose democracy scores fall below 6. Consequently, all OECD countries are classified into corresponding comparative political systems: first, completely democratic, free; second, largely democratic, free; third, pseudo-democratic, semi-free, and fourth, undemocratic, unfree ones (Table 2.5). In short, these

---

38   This reveals what Brooks (2006, p. 192) describes as the 'remarkable diversity of developed democracies,' specifically in their degrees of political freedoms and rights. Specifically, Brooks (2006, p. 200) registers that 'cross-national variation in patterns of support for 'self-expressive' values accounts for major political differences between the United States (and also developing nations) and the less-traditional policy regimes found throughout much of Western Europe,' which implies that in this respect conservative America is closer to the non-West than the West.

TABLE 2.4   *Comparative estimates of political democracy, OECD countries.*

	Bollen index /10	Democ-racy quality index /10	Democ-racy index	Vot-ing 1	Vot-ing 2	Vot-ing 3	Partici-pation	Pluralism competi-tion	Civil liberties	State terror	Impris-onment	Execu-tions	Press freedom	Univer-salism	Peace	Paci-fism	TOTAL	Rank-ings	Av-er-age
Australia	9.99	7.97	9.01	9.45	8.42	9.32	7.78	9.58	10	7	7	10	7	5	8	6	131.52	16	8.22
Austria	9.7	8.01	8.54	9.13	8.44	7.49	8.33	9.58	9.41	9	9	10	8	8	10	9	141.63	16	8.85
Belgium	9.99	8.15	7.93	9.25	8.48	8.94	5.56	9.58	9.41	8	8	10	8	7	7	9	134.29	16	8.39
Canada	9.95	7.91	9.08	7.39	8.26	6.83	7.78	9.58	10	8	8	10	8	4	9	8	131.78	16	8.24
Chile	9.7	7.28	7.84	7.89	4.59	4.93	4.44	9.58	9.71	6	6	10	7	NA	6	6	106.96	15	7.13
Czech Republic	2.1	7.13	7.94	8.28	8.28	5.95	6.67	9.58	9.41	8	7	10	7	NA	8	8	113.34	15	7.56
Denmark	9.99	8.52	9.11	8.59	8.36	8.59	8.33	9.17	9.41	8	9	10	9	9	10	7	142.07	16	8.88
Estonia	1.82	7.45	7.85	6.81	5.35	6.42	6.11	9.58	8.82	7	6	10	8	NA	6	5	102.21	15	6.81
Finland	9.73	8.6	9.03	7.6	7.81	6.69	7.78	10	9.71	8	9	10	9	7	9	7	135.95	16	8.5
France	9.08	7.93	7.92	7.38	6.73	5.54	7.78	9.58	8.82	6	9	10	6	5	6	5	117.76	16	7.36
Germany	8.86	8.2	8.64	8.54	8.02	7.15	7.78	9.58	9.12	8	9	10	8	7	7	7	131.89	16	8.24
Greece	8.28	6.6	7.45	7.99	8.08	6.36	6.67	9.58	9.41	5	8	10	5	NA	5	4	107.42	15	7.16
Hungary	1.16	6.76	6.84	6.7	6.81	6.18	4.44	9.17	7.65	9	7	10	5	NA	7	9	102.71	15	6.85
Iceland	10	NA	9.58	8.95	8.93	8.14	8.89	10	9.71	10	10	10	8	NA	10	10	132.20	14	9.44
Ireland	9.72	8.17	8.85	7.33	7.49	6.99	7.78	9.58	10	9	9	10	8	5	7	9	132.91	16	8.31
Italy	9.68	7.16	7.98	8.98	9.2	7.52	7.22	9.58	8.53	7	9	10	5	5	6	7	124.85	16	7.8
Japan	9.98	7.53	7.96	6.95	6.87	5.27	6.11	9.17	8.82	9	10	5	5	6	8	8	119.66	16	7.48
Korea, South	5.3	7.06	7.97	7.29	7.29	5.8	7.22	8.75	8.53	5	8	8	5	NA	6	4	101.21	15	6.75
Luxem-bourg	9.77	NA	8.88	8.97	6.35	9.12	6.67	10	9.71	9	8	10	8	NA	7	9	120.47	14	8.61

TABLE 2.4　*Comparative estimates of political democracy, OECD countries.* (cont.)

	Bollen index /10	Democracy quality index	Democracy index	Voting 1	Voting 2	Voting 3	Participation	Pluralism competition	Civil liberties	State terror	Imprisonment	Executions	Press freedom	Universalism	Peace	Pacifism	TOTAL	Rankings	Average
Mexico	7.45	5.79	6.55	6.52	4.81	4.77	7.22	8.33	6.76	9	6	10	1	NA	1	9	94.20	15	6.28
Netherlands	9.97	8.36	8.92	8.75	8.38	7.46	8.89	9.58	9.41	8	9	10	9	8	7	7	137.72	16	8.61
New Zealand	10	8.18	9.26	9.08	8.6	7.7	8.89	10	10	8	7	10	9	5	10	7	137.71	16	8.61
Norway	9.99	8.81	9.93	8.04	7.92	7.82	10	10	10	8	9	10	9	10	7	7	142.51	16	8.91
Poland	2.21	7.13	7.09	5.03	5.14	5.09	6.67	9.58	9.12	7	7	10	6	NA	7	5	99.06	15	6.6
Portugal	3.9	7.61	7.79	7.7	8.82	5.58	6.67	9.58	9.41	7	7	10	7	NA	8	6	112.06	15	7.47
Slovakia	2.1	6.83	7.29	8.52	8.29	5.98	5.56	9.58	8.82	8	7	10	8	NA	7	8	110.97	15	7.4
Slovenia	5.08	7.61	7.57	7.66	7.79	5.17	6.67	9.58	8.82	8	9	10	6	NA	7	8	113.95	15	7.6
Spain	1.04	7.59	8.3	7.36	7.64	7.32	7.22	9.58	9.41	9	8	10	7	NA	7	7	113.46	15	7.56
Sweden	9.99	8.66	9.45	8.71	8.41	8.58	8.33	9.58	9.71	9	9	10	8	9	7	8	141.42	16	8.84
Switzerland	9.97	8.7	9.09	5.65	5.19	4.84	7.78	9.58	9.41	9	9	10	8	8	9	9	132.21	16	8.26
Turkey	7.64	5.51	5.12	8.13	7.42	8.52	5	7.92	2.94	6	6	10	0	NA	2	5	87.20	15	5.81
UK	9.91	8	8.31	7.52	7.38	6.61	6.67	6.67	9.41	6	8	10	6	5	6	5	116.48	16	7.28
US	9.24	7.76	8.05	6.65	4.77	4.25	7.22	9.17	8.24	2	0	0	6	3	4	2	82.35	16	5.15

I Average democracy score 8 or higher—Completely democratic, free political systems

II Average democracy score 7–7.99—Largely democratic, free political systems

III Average democracy score 6–6.99—Pseudo-democratic, semi-free political systems

IV Average democracy score under 6—Undemocratic, un-free political systems

TABLE 2.5 *Average democracy/political freedom estimates and classification, OECD countries.*

I	Average scores of 8 or higher—Completely democratic/free political systems (15 cases)
	Australia, Austria, Belgium, Canada, Denmark, Finland, Germany, Iceland, Ireland, Luxembourg, Netherlands, New Zealand, Norway, Sweden, Switzerland
II	Average scores 7–7.99—Largely democratic/free political systems (11 cases)
	Chile, Czech Republic, France, Greece, Italy, Japan, Portugal, Slovakia, Slovenia, Spain, the UK
III	Average scores 6–6.99—Pseudo-democratic/semi-free political systems (5 cases)
	Hungary, Estonia, South Korea, Mexico, Poland
IV	Average scores below 6—Undemocratic/unfree political systems (2 cases)
	Turkey, the US ('conservative America')

represent polities or states of approximately complete freedom, substantial freedom, quasi-freedom, and un-freedom.

First, the highest fully democratic, free polity category (scores of 8 or higher) comprises virtually exclusively liberal, secular and universalistic or egalitarian democracies, with a single exception of another, mixed political system. Specifically, the following fifteen countries exemplifying liberal, secular and universalistic or egalitarian democracy are 'completely democratic, free political systems' in a descending order (Table 2.6).

They are Iceland (9.44 out of maximum 10), Norway (8.91), Denmark (8.88), Austria (8.85), Sweden (8.84), the Netherlands (8.61), New Zealand (8.61), Luxembourg (8.61), Finland (8.50), Belgium (8.39), Ireland (8.31), Switzerland (8.26), Germany (8.24), Canada (8.24), and Australia (8.22). In particular, the five highest ranked societies in democracy/political freedom are all liberal, secular and universalistic democracies, of which four are Scandinavian countries in regional terms. Notably, the single most democratic, politically freest society, Norway, is a paradigmatic, probably most liberal, secular and universalistic democracy in the Western and thus entire world, and regionally a Scandinavian country. The results hence clearly reaffirm most previous observations in the sociological and related literature, and strongly fulfil the present predictions or expectations. In this respect, if there is such thing as an 'exclusive club' of approximately complete democracy/political freedom, minimally a kind of

TABLE 2.6   *Political democracy ranking, OECD countries.*

Rank	Country	Index (0–10)	Category of polity	Classification
1	Iceland	9.44	Completely Democratic	Liberal
2	Norway	8.91	Completely Democratic	Liberal
3	Denmark	8.88	Completely Democratic	Liberal
4	Austria	8.85	Completely Democratic	Liberal
5	Sweden	8.84	Completely Democratic	Liberal
6	Netherlands	8.61	Completely Democratic	Liberal
7	New Zealand	8.61	Completely Democratic	Liberal
8	Luxembourg	8.61	Completely Democratic	Liberal
9	Finland	8.50	Completely Democratic	Liberal
10	Belgium	8.39	Completely Democratic	Liberal
11	Ireland	8.31	Completely Democratic	Intermediate
12	Switzerland	8.26	Completely Democratic	Liberal
13	Germany	8.24	Completely Democratic	Liberal
14	Canada	8.24	Completely Democratic	Liberal
15	Australia	8.22	Completely Democratic	Liberal
16	Italy	7.80	Largely Democratic	Intermediate
17	Slovenia	7.60	Largely Democratic	Intermediate
18	Spain	7.56	Largely Democratic	Intermediate
19	Czech Republic	7.56	Largely Democratic	Intermediate
20	Japan	7.48	Largely Democratic	Intermediate
21	Portugal	7.47	Largely Democratic	Intermediate
22	Slovakia	7.40	Largely Democratic	Intermediate
23	France	7.36	Largely Democratic	Liberal
24	UK	7.28	Largely Democratic	Intermediate
25	Greece	7.16	Largely Democratic	Intermediate
26	Chile	7.13	Largely Democratic	Intermediate
27	Hungary	6.85	Pseudo-Democratic	Intermediate
28	Estonia	6.81	Pseudo-Democratic	Intermediate
29	South Korea	6.75	Pseudo-Democratic	Anti-Liberal
30	Poland	6.60	Pseudo-Democratic	Anti-Liberal
31	Mexico	6.28	Pseudo-Democratic	Anti-Liberal
32	Turkey	5.81	Undemocratic	Anti-Liberal
33	US	5.15	Undemocratic	Anti-Liberal[a]

a Conservative governance and regions.

'club convergence'[39] in democratic terms, within OECD and in extension the world, then it is populated almost entirely by liberal, secular, and universalistic democracies among Western and related societies.

More precisely, only two liberal, secular and universalistic democracies are not comprised in completely democratic, free political systems, France and the US in liberal-secular and inclusive governance and regions, which only seemingly or partially disconfirms the expectations but not really or entirely. This is because France[40] is found in the category of largely democratic, free political systems, which is consistent with the general expectations that these democracies are minimally such and typically fully so. Also, the missing link of the US in fact confirms the observation or prediction that its liberal, secular and inclusive ideology and governance is indeed weak, transient and exceptional and such regions really a minority or dramatically decreasing. For instance, one or two branches of the federal legislature and even almost two-third of state legislatures are seized and controlled by anti-liberal, anti-secular, including theocratic or theocentric, and anti-universalistic forces since 2010 and especially 2014 since the anti-democratic, in design or outcome, 'Tea Party' counter-revolution and dominance especially, as Dahrendorf and other analysts would expect, in the ultra-conservative South.

In short, the case of France highlights that liberal, secular and universalistic democracy is at the minimum largely free, and that of the US that such a political system is replaced by its opposite, or remains temporary and weak in the latter. In turn, the only country not belonging to liberal, secular and universalistic democracies that is comprised in the fully democratic, free category is Ireland classified in mixed political systems, while none of anti-liberal, anti-secular and anti-universalistic 'democracies' being included in it. To that extent, the first only seemingly disconfirms and the second entirely confirms the expectations. Thus, the presence of Ireland in this category may indirectly confirm these expectations if taking into account this country's most recent movement toward liberal, secular or non-theocentric and universalistic democracy or civil society (the recognition of partial abortion rights and same-sex marriage despite theocentric or religious intrusions, etc.), even if not becoming fully one yet, and not so classified.

The absence of bogus anti-liberal, anti-secular and anti-universalistic 'democracies' is entirely expected and intrinsic to their spurious nature. At the end, what the category of full democracy/political and civil liberties does or

---

39   Aghion, Howitt, and Mayer-Foulkes (2005, p. 175) use the term 'club convergence' in the context of economic growth such that certain countries tend to converge to the same rate.

40   More on contemporary France's political system see Prasad (2005).

will comprise are therefore exclusively liberal, secular and universalistic democracies either in existence and functioning, such as fourteen out of fifteen completely democratic, free political systems, or in tendency and prospect like Ireland and, judging by similar tendencies or potentials, possibly some others, for example, Spain, Czech Republic, etc., in the foreseeable future.

As seen, these existing democracies are epitomized by most Western European societies, especially Scandinavia, alongside non-European countries like Australia, Canada, and New Zealand. Generally, these societies exhibit a picture of the highest level or the fastest and most coherent rate of advance of political and civil liberties, rights, choices, opportunities, openness, equality, and justice in terms of both formal recognition and effective realization. They attain or approach the point of near-complete integration or congruence between the conditions, elements, and indicators of formal-procedural and those of substantive-effective democracy, thus political and civil liberties, rights, openness, equality, and justice de jure on constitutional and other legal paper and de facto in the polity's reality. Alternatively, they succeed or attempt to remove or mitigate certain contradictions and discrepancies between these dimensions of democracy and forms of political liberty, specifically the divergences of the substantive from the formal.

In general, within this category of societies, the relative degree of liberalism, secularism, and universalism or egalitarianism in the polity decisively determines and predicts the level of political and civil liberties, rights, and choices, as well as openness, inclusion, equality, and justice. The most liberal, secular, and universalistic or egalitarian democracies as a rule and group are observed or expected to have the strongest political and civil liberties, rights and choices, alongside openness, inclusion, equality, and justice, simply to be the most democratic, freest politically. This is demonstrated by Scandinavian and related societies such as Austria, the Netherlands, Belgium, Switzerland, Luxembourg, and Germany, plus some non-European countries like New Zealand, Canada, and Australia, with the only exception of Ireland. In particular, the single most liberal, secular, and universalistic or egalitarian region of societies or society invariably tends to be the most democratic, the freest in political and related terms.

If one does not know what is the most democratic, politically freest region of societies and society, one knows and predict it with virtual certainty or high probability when observing the most liberal, secular, and universalistic or egalitarian such as Western and Northern Europe, particularly Scandinavia, in regional terms and within it Norway as a major exemplar (thus not counting Iceland as a minor example). This link appears so strong that it exists and functions as an osmosis and to that extent as a proxy 'iron law' of democracy and political and civil liberty such that—paraphrasing Michels' 'iron law of oligarchy'—'who says the (most) liberal, secular, and universalistic society or societies, says the (most) democratic, politically free (freest).' Needless or perhaps needed to say, this represents a statement of fact and empirical generalization doing justice to the presented rankings or a plausible expectation rather than a favorable ideological value judgment, as the above scores indicate and demonstrated below.

Second, the aforesaid generally applies, though to a lesser extent, to the category of 'largely democratic, politically free societies' (scores 7–7.99). For instance, these countries are shown to be largely democratic, politically free in a descending order: Italy (7.80), Slovenia (7.60), Spain (7.56), Czech Republic (7.56), Japan (7.48), Portugal (7.47), Slovakia (7.40), France (7.36), UK (7.28), Greece (7.16), and Chile (7.13). As the previous, this category is composed of some liberal, secular and universalistic democracies (France) and mostly mixed political systems, thus at least in part fulfilling the expectations. Conversely, just as the first, this category contains no opposites to liberal, secular and universalistic democracy, i.e., anti-liberal, anti-secular and anti-universalistic 'democracies,' which hence also reaffirms the previous observations and confirms the present expectations. It indicates that liberal, secular and universalistic democracies, while typically being (most) fully democratic/free, tend to be at the minimum largely so—as exemplified by France—which is essentially consistent with the expectations. By contrast, it indicates that mixed political systems as a whole tend to be largely— rather than completely—democratic/ free at the maximum or on average, with certain rare exceptions noted earlier (Ireland), thus also confirming the expectations. On the contrary, anti-liberal, anti-secular and anti-universalistic 'democracies' prove to be neither fully nor largely democratic/politically free and to that extent never really democracies but ersatz substitutes of democracy, thus strongly fulfilling the opposite expectations.

Third, the category of pseudo-democratic societies, semi-free polities (scores 6–6.99) consists of certain mixed political systems, alongside some non-liberal, non-secular and non-universalistic 'democracies.' More specifically, this category comprises in a descending order these countries: Hungary (6.85), Estonia (6.81), South Korea (6.75), Poland (6.60), and Mexico (6.28). All these countries are deemed non-liberal, non-secular, and non-universalistic or mixed political systems, which hence largely fulfills the expectations that especially the first are typically unfree or at most quasi-free, but never fully or largely free. In turn, none of liberal, secular and universalistic democracies are comprised in this category of pseudo-democracy and semi-freedom, thus fulfilling the expectations that they are either as a rule fully or at the minimum largely democratic, politically free. In respect of their rank, these pseudo-democratic societies look more different from the highest than the lowest category involving undemocratic, unfree political systems identified next.

Fourth, the category of undemocratic, unfree political systems (score under 6) contains exclusively non-liberal, non-secular, and non-universalistic 'democracies,' which is entirely consistent with most prior observations and the current expectations. Conversely, it does not contain any liberal, secular, and universalistic democracies, as well as mixed political systems, also wholly compatible with the expectations. As the observe of the first category, if there is what Weber might call a 'pariah club' of undemocratic, unfree polities, simply of non-democracy and political un-freedom and civil illiberty among Western and related societies grouped in OECD, then it is composed exclusively of non-liberal, non-secular, and non-universalistic 'democracies,' which strongly and unambiguously fulfills the expectations. More specifically, this category includes in an ascending order of un-freedom only two countries, Turkey (5.81) and the US (5.15) classified into these 'democracies' in its conservative, religious, or theocratic, and exclusionary ideology and governance and regions, as since 2010–14 in the federal legislature and most Southern and similar states as the internal exemplar of this bogus type of 'democracy.'

While geographically involving only either non-European (the US) or non-Western (Turkey) societies, this category involves in sociological terms exclusively those classified as anti-liberal, anti-secular, and anti-universalistic 'democracies'—giving meaning to the 'exclusive club' of non-democracy and un-freedom—just as expected. These are the two societies with the lowest scores and rankings on democracy/political freedom among all OECD countries, for example, Turkey ranks 32, and (the 'conservative-theocratic' half of) America 33 on the 1–33 ranking order. The last rank is seemingly most unexpected, yet generally consistent with the observations and expectations that anti-liberal, anti-secular, and non-universalistic 'democracies' due to being ersatz substitutes or simulations of democracy tend to rank the lowest overall. Hence, the rankings of these two countries are to be placed in the context of the overall rank of such spurious 'democracies.' For example, Turkey is forced to move from a secular democracy to these 'democracies' under Islamic rule, and the US belongs to them in its pole of conservative, theocratic or theocentric, and exclusionary governance and regions recently, from the federal legislature to the vast majority of state governments since 2010–14. The lowest rankings of these two countries simply reflect or exemplify the predicted lowest overall rank of anti-liberal, anti-secular, and anti-universalistic 'democracies,' and thus are hardly a surprise in this context. And this applies to those of Islamic-ruled Turkey and 'conservative-theocratic America' such as the

'Southern United States': if they both move to this bogus type of democracy, then their ranks (32 and 33) are exactly what to be expected and predicted in such a framework.

Alternatively, their low ranks and generally being part of this undemocratic, politically unfree category indicate that such spurious 'democracy' invariably eliminates or overwhelms liberal, secular, and universalistic democracy established or attempted previously, temporarily and partially in the US (e.g., the 1930–40s, 1960s, 2008–10, the non-Southern states) and to some extent Turkey (since Ataturk's secular state until the Islamic rule of the 2000–10s). This confirms the co-existence, polarization and tension of the 'two Americas' and so the double, Janus-face of America in this sense, and perhaps of the 'two Turkeys' in ideological-political, geographic and historical terms. In particular, it reaffirms that the conservative, theocratic, and exclusionary pole of the US paradigmatically and persistently epitomized by the 'Southern United States' tends to prevail over liberal, secular and universalistic Jefferson's America, and theocentric Islamic-ruled Turkey over secular (Ataturk's) Turkey in recent times.

At this juncture, perhaps all Western and related countries within OECD display a 'Janus-face' of democracy and non-democracy, political and civil liberty and illiberty, human rights and their violations, peace and militarism, etc., and the West overall reportedly shows 'two faces.'[41] Still, probably the US does most manifestly, saliently and persistently than these other countries, judging by historical trends and events and recent tendencies. This is indicated by the continuing proxy civil, ideological and culture wars between liberal, secular, and inclusive America and its opposite represented by, as Dahrendorf suggests, the 'Southern United States,' a battle without parallel in intensity, duration and drama in the Western world, and beyond the latter paralleled only by Turkey during Islamic rule, plus post-communist Catholic-dominated Poland, in OECD. At any rate, such evident prevalence of this opposite in America and Turkey essentially explains and predicts their scores and ranks on democracy/ political freedom, including the shocking US lowest score and rank. Evidently, one cannot escape or 'cheat' on Michels' style 'iron law' of having non-liberal, non-secular, and non-universalistic 'democracies' inescapably yields the lowest degree of democracy and political freedom, as Turkey under Islamic rule and the US in conservative, theocentric, and exclusionary governance and regions prove by their lowest ranks. If Islamic Turkey and 'conservative America' like the 'Southern United States' are or become such ersatz 'democracies,' they

---

41   This cites Duverger's (1972) *Janus: The Two Faces of the West* (book title).

are or will be inevitably ranked on democracy or political freedom precisely as above, so this means no surprise, let alone shock, at their lowest rankings.

Generally, in stark contrast to those belonging to the first category, these societies in the fourth as a rule present a portrait of the lowest degree, or the most rapid and obstinate negation, decline and suppression, of political and civil liberties, rights, choices, opportunities, openness, equality, and justice in form and especially substance. Consequently, they reveal comparatively low levels of formal-procedural and particularly substantive-effective democracy and thus 'integrate' the two in a manner adverse and ultimately destructive to political and civil liberties and rights, and thus opposite to the integration typical of liberal, secular, and universalistic democracies. At most, they contain or sustain various aberrations or discrepancies of substantive-effective from formal-procedural democracy, thus indicating their failure or reluctance to de facto implement or honor political and civil liberties and rights de jure in the constitutional and other laws making these latter hardly worth the paper on which they are written or printed.

Thus, the countries with the lowest ranking on democracy/political freedom appear as substantively Islamic and Christian anti-liberal, anti-secular and anti-universalistic theocratic or theocentric regimes suppressing or excluding liberal and secular groups in politics and society. Thus, this is manifest in Turkey under Islamic theocentric government and the US in its pole of conservative, theocratic, and exclusionary governance and regions termed 'evangelical America,' specifically its Southern 'Bibliocracy' in Weber's sense of Biblical theocracy (plus Catholic-dominated Poland during post-communist times). In conjunction, they represent exclusionary oligarchic political regimes and restrictive monistic or duopolistic ideological and party systems, as exemplified by Turkey during Islamic rule, and the Southern and other conservative regions of America persistently (and Poland under Catholic dominance). In addition, they are or seek to become pre-liberal mono-ethnic political systems negating or violating the modern concept of a multi-ethnic, multi-cultural and multi-linguistic society by nationalist and racist suppression and exclusion of ethnic-national, racial and linguistic minorities denied basic liberties and rights and even official existence or dignity by the majority group. Cases in point include Turkey with the brutal oppression of some ethnic minorities (Kurds)—encouraged by the Western governments within NATO by their disgraceful silence and blank support of their loyal military 'ally'—under extreme religious-nationalistic government favoring the dominant ethnicity, and the US South constantly, although the racial-ethnic target for political repression, exclusion and discrimination may be variable or moving over time. (For instance, the target has apparently varied or moved from Native, African Americans and

Southern and Eastern Europeans before the 1960s to Hispanics, immigrants, and others in Southern and other anti-liberal states today.)

As the obverse of the pattern observed in the first, in the fourth category of societies the relative level of anti-liberalism, anti-secularism, and anti-universalism or anti-egalitarianism crucially determines and predicts the degree of political un-freedom and civil illiberty and the lack of rights, choices and opportunities, as well as closure, exclusion, discrimination, inequality, and injustice in the polity. The most anti-liberal, anti-secular, and anti-universalistic or anti-egalitarian 'democracies' almost invariably tend to display the lowest or no political freedoms and civil liberties, rights, choices and opportunities, as well as openness, inclusion equality, and justice, simply to be the least democratic, the most unfree in political respect. This is evidently shown by Islamic-ruled Turkey during the 2000–10s and 'evangelical America' such as the 'Southern United States' pervaded and dominated by theocratic, exclusionary fundamentalism for long since postbellum times (and before) through these days.

And the single most anti-liberal, anti-secular, and anti-universalistic country or region within it is virtually certain to be the least democratic, the most unfree politically, for example Turkey under Islamic governance or even, judging by the rankings, 'conservative-theocratic' America among OECD countries, and the US South persistently among regions. As the obverse of the first category, if one does not know what is the most undemocratic, politically unfree society or region, one knows it when seeing the most anti-liberal, anti-secular, and anti-universalistic, Islamic Turkey as a country or 'conservative America' as one of the 'two Americas.' Like the opposite link, this connection seems so strong becoming a fusion and operating as a negative 'iron law' of non-democracy and political un-freedom and civil illiberty so that 'who says the (most) anti-liberal, anti-secular, and anti-universalistic society or region within it or societies, says the (least) democratic, politically free.' As before, this is a statement of fact or prediction, not an adverse ideological value judgment, as further demonstrated in the next chapter.

In general, these comparative estimates of democracy/political freedom for OECD countries indicate that not all Western and other actual or putative democracies are 'created equal,' equally democratic, politically free societies.[42] In sum, they indicate an overall pattern that societies politically classified as liberal, secular, and universalistic democracies virtually exclusively form the

---

42   Sutton (2013, p. 742) observes that 'so far, modern Western democracies continue to display considerable variety in institutional forms and the distribution of political power (for example), with manifest implications for incarceration practices.'

most democratic, politically free, 'green' societal space and pole, and those as their opposites represent the most non-democratic, politically unfree 'red zone' and pole, with some secondary variations in both directions. The sources and grounds for the above democracy estimates are presented and discussed in the next chapter.

A Note on Liberal Democracies and Welfare States

Some sociologists[43] classify 'developed democracies'—i.e., welfare-state regimes—into 'liberal democracies' represented by Australia, Canada, Ireland, New Zealand, the UK, and the US, 'Christian democracies' exemplified by Austria, France, Germany, Italy, the Netherlands, Switzerland, and similar countries in continental Europe, and 'social democracies' including Norway, Sweden, and Scandinavia overall. Such classification apparently conflates types of democracy with welfare-state regimes as if they were identical, while since the latter's inception in late 19th-century Germany through the US New Deal and postwar Scandinavia both democracies and non-democracies have been welfare states, and conversely. As a corollary, it uses a criterion for classification—i.e., public welfare provision—that is not intrinsic to and not defining of liberal democracy instead defined by the degree and scope of political and civil liberties and rights, simply liberty in the polity, which may or may not be related to such government provisions. Consequently, what are termed 'liberal democracies' are defined not, as done in this work and generally, by the high degree of political and civil liberties and rights but instead by a minimal or diminishing level of public welfare provision and thus actually minimalist and diluted, even non-existent or dissolving welfare states, as exemplified by the US and to a lesser extent the UK.

In economic terms, these 'liberal democracies' are (conflated with) 'liberal' laissez-faire capitalism, which is not necessarily identical with and even, in its ultimate form of capitalist dictatorship or plutocracy, destructive or subversive to liberal democracy defined by universal political and civil liberty, as demonstrated by the US and the UK since Reaganism and Thatcherism. Therefore, such an equation falls into the discredited 'libertarian' Hayekian trap that economic freedom as the essence of capitalism, more precisely unrestricted 'free enterprise' for capital against labor, invariably generates or corresponds to political and civil liberty defining liberal democracy, an evident empirical fallacy, for example, the Singapore/Chile syndrome.

Hence, these 'liberal democracies,' for example the US, may be 'liberal' in the sense of minimal public welfare provision and unfettered capitalism

---

43   See Brooks and Manza (2006, pp. 478–81).

cum market 'neo-liberalism'—which is a contradiction because of applying a democratically neutral or an extra-democratic, economic criterion to define *political* democracy—but not in that of universal and civil liberties and rights in the polity axiomatically and factually defining liberal democracies. Second, 'Christian democracies' seem a non sequitur so long as religion and modern democracy tend to be mutually exclusive or functionally differentiated, and consequently the latter is typically a liberal-secular political system precisely, above all, in Europe, just as are 'Islamic democracies.' Christian or Islamic 'democracies' are as self-contradictory and impossible in political terms as is Christian or Islamic 'science' in scientific respect. For example, to include France as a paradigmatic exemplar of a secular polity into 'Christian democracies' is a flagrant error, and this is true to a lesser extent of Austria, Germany, Italy, the Netherlands, and Switzerland (despite various 'Christian-democratic,' mostly Catholic political parties often misleading observers in this direction). In turn, the US appears to belong to 'Christian democracies' rather than to 'liberal democracies' in the sense of this analysis on the account of the historical and persistent fusion of religion and politics, at least in the 'Bible Belt.' In short, there is no such thing as Christian—and for that matter, Islamic and any religious— 'democracies' so long as religion and democracy are substitutes rather than complements, as abundantly shown for long, just as neither is there 'Christian or Islamic science.' And if there is such thing, they are effectively theocracies and thus anti-democracies from the standpoint of liberal-secular democracy that is differentiated from and neutral to religious, including Christian, Islamic, and other, doctrines, just as 'Christian or Islamic science' is invariably anti-science, as exemplified by their shared 'creationism' and anti-evolutionism.

Third, 'social democracies' represent a conventional and appropriate description of Scandinavian societies on account of their 'universal distribution of benefits and services' and thus universalistic and comprehensive welfare states, as well as regulated, yet capitalist economies. On account of their also universal political and civil liberties and rights, however, they are to be, as done in this analysis, classified into 'liberal democracies,' actually the strongest instances of liberal democracy. Hence, they are better designated as social-liberal democracies in respect of equally universal public-welfare provision *and* political-civil liberty, respectively. In the present context, the main point is that democracy is liberal primarily because of its universal political liberties and civil and rights as a whole, and *not* its minimal public welfare provision and unfettered capitalism, as exemplified in the US and to some extent the UK. Capitalism may well be 'liberal' because of minimal public welfare provision and laissez-faire but this is another matter of an economic structure not to be conflated with liberal democracy as a political system. Moreover, 'liberal' or 'neo-liberal' capitalism has often shown to be different from and even opposite to liberal democracy and civil society, as demonstrated by various past and present capitalist dictatorships or plutocracies characterized by capital's unrestricted 'free enterprise.' They span from Chile under Pinochet's proto-fascist dictatorship[44]—notoriously supported by Hayek, Friedman and other 'libertarian' economists personally visiting, advising and encouraging the 'free market' dictator, especially about the superior efficiency and prudence of suppressing labor unions and killing their activists—through Singapore and to Reagan's America and Thatcher's Britain.

---

44   Kerrissey (2015, pp. 647–8) reports that 'upon seizing power, Pinochet immediately sought to eradicate worker organizations, as they were his main political opposition. When Pinochet seized power, he immediately outlawed unions and severely repressed activists.' He thus apparently implemented or carrying to the logical extreme the 'libertarian' ideal and paradise of anarchy reserved for capital and Leviathan/oppression inflicted on labor, as Hayek and Friedman probably expounded and elaborated it in person to their 'free-market' dictator when they visited the latter in show of advice and support. Cynics may comment that, after secretly supporting McCarthy in the 1950s and fervently endorsing a conservative ideological extremist, Goldwater, for President in 1964, over a liberal (Tilman 2001), 'libertarian' economists like Friedman and the other 'Chicago boys' could not descend lower, but they apparently did by flirting and befriending a fascist dictator, which is counterfactually identical to, say, Keynes doing so with Stalin. Yet, such episodes at least proved and exposed what economic 'libertarianism' a la Hayek and Friedman really is beneath its imposing rhetoric of 'liberty' and 'free enterprise'—an authoritarian, plutocratic ideology and policy, as noted in Dahrendorf 1979; Tilman 2001; Van Dyke 1995), with ultimately fascist, totalitarian tendencies, outcomes, and sympathies. So, Pinochet's proto-fascist dictatorship is the paradise where 'libertarianism' logically culminates and 'libertarians' like Hayek and Friedman and the Chicago School overall make a pilgrimage, as is the US Southern anti-labor slave-style economy identified by Acemoglu and Robinson (2008); for example, there is the 'Ludwig Mises Institute' precisely in the heart of the anti-labor, anti-liberal, anti-secular theocratic 'deep' South.

Sources and Grounds for Democracy Estimates

Aggregate Estimates of Democracy

The following presents the sources and grounds for the comparative estimates of democracy, i.e., political freedom, and the resulting classification of Western and related societies into the preceding categories. In general, the present aggregate democracy estimates and ranks—aggregated from sixteen objective rankings taken from various sources or derived from available data—are grounded in or consistent with certain relevant indicators and rankings such as the indexes of liberal democracy in political sociology, as well as others in the non-academic literature.

For example, these estimates are convergent with the Bollen[1] indexes of liberal democracy (Table 3.1) that are probably best known in the sociological and related academic literature. Thus, Western and related societies with the highest and to some degree lowest Bollen indexes of liberal democracy are almost identical to those in the present aggregate estimates. On the one hand, countries with the maximal (around 100 or so), highest Bollen indexes include Iceland (100), New Zealand (100), Australia (99.9), Belgium (99.9), Denmark (99.9), Norway (99.9), Sweden (99.9), Japan (99.8), the Netherlands (99.7), Switzerland (99.7), and Canada (99.5). As seen, all these countries (with a single exception of Japan) also have the highest aggregate democracy estimates in the present ranking and belong to the 'completely democratic' category, along with a few additional cases such as Austria, Luxembourg, Finland, Ireland, and Germany. Strikingly, both the past countries with the maximal Bollen indexes and those presently with the highest democracy estimates are virtually all liberal, secular, and universalistic democracies, with just a single exception in each ranking, Japan in the first, and Ireland in the second, which entirely and dramatically fulfills the expectations. Notably, Scandinavian countries, except for Finland, feature the maximal Bollen indexes, just as all of them are included in the ten societies with the highest democracy estimates and the 'completely democratic' category, with the striking identity that the same country is shown

---

1 Bollen (1990) notes that each index represents the average of six closely interrelated indicators or dimensions of liberal democracy (noted previously) and ranges from 0 to 100. The Bollen indexes of liberal democracy are also used by Smits, Ultee and Lammers (1998) and other sociologists and political scientists.

TABLE 3.1   *Liberal democracy indexes, OECD countries, various years.*

Country	Year	Liberal democracy index	Point (Index/10)
Australia	1965	99.9	9.99
Austria	1965	97.1	9.70
Belgium	1965	99.9	9.99
Canada	1965	99.5	9.95
Chile	1965	97	9.70
Czech Republic[a]	1965	21[b]	2.10
Denmark	1965	99.9	9.99
Estonia[a]	1965	18.2[c]	1.82
Finland	1965	97.3	9.73
France	1965	90.8	9.08
Germany West	1965	88.6	8.86
Greece	1965	82.8	8.28
Hungary[a]	1965	11.6	1.16
Iceland	1965	100	10.00
Ireland	1965	97.2	9.72
Italy	1965	96.8	9.68
Japan	1965	99.8	9.98
Korea South	1965	53	5.30
Luxembourg	1965	97.7	9.77
Mexico	1965	74.5	7.45
Netherlands	1965	99.7	9.97
New Zealand	1965	100	10.00
Norway	1965	99.9	99.9
Poland[a]	1965	22.1	2.21
Portugal[a]	1965	39	3.90
Slovak Republic[a]	1965	21[b]	2.10[a]
Slovenia[a]	1965	50.8[d]	5.08
Spain[a]	1965	10.4	1.04
Sweden	1965	99.9	9.99
Switzerland	1965	99.7	9.97
Turkey	1965	76.4	7.64
UK	1965	99.1	9.91
US	1965	92.4	9.24

a Change of political system since 1965, index retained for long-term perspective.
b The same as Czech Republic (united as Czechoslovakia).
c Based on USSR's democracy index.
d Based on Yugoslavia's democracy index.
Source: Bollen (1990); Smits et al. (1998).

to be the most democratic in both rankings, Iceland (with New Zealand in the first). The above shows a remarkable convergence or continuity between the two rankings at different points of time in terms of most democratic countries.

On the other hand, ten or so countries with the lowest Bollen indexes of liberal democracy are Spain (10.4), Hungary (11.6), Estonia (18.2), Czech Republic (21), Slovak Republic (21), Poland (22.1), Portugal (39), Slovenia (50.8), South Korea (53), Mexico (74.5), and Turkey (76.4). As seen, some of these countries such as Poland, South Korea, Mexico, and Turkey remain among those with the lowest democracy estimates presently, which indicates their continuity in or path-dependence in this respect in spite of a formal change of their political system[2] since the Bollen indexes—for example, the end of communism and military dictatorship in the first two and of one-party rule in the third, as well as partial convergence between the two rankings. By contrast, most others, notably Spain and Czech Republic, as well as Portugal and the other former Communist states, rank higher in the present ranking, reflecting a substantive change of their political system toward liberalization, secularization, and democratization since then, thus consistent with the expectations.

It is also striking that the countries with the minimal Bollen indexes and those with the lowest democracy estimates alike are all the opposites of liberal, secular, and universalistic democracy, viz., proto-fascist (Spain), communist (Poland, etc.), and other authoritarian (South Korea, Mexico) states in the first ranking, and anti-liberal, theocentric ones in the second—the last three plus Turkey and the US in the conservative pole—thus both rankings fulfilling the expectations. An apparent difference between the two rankings is that Turkey and the US have higher Bollen indexes than current estimates, yet, the first's index is the eleventh lowest overall (i.e., lower than those of 22 other countries) and that of the US the third lowest among Western societies in particular (viz., lower than 18 others), thus both being less different in this sense than it appears. Now, if the difference between the two rankings is still deemed substantial, it indicates that Turkey under Islamic rule and the US during conservative resurgence and dominance have become more anti-liberal, anti-secular, anti-universalistic, and consequently less democratic since the Bollen indexes,

---

2 Countries such as Czech Republic, Estonia, Poland, Slovak Republic, and Slovenia, as well as Portugal, Spain, and to some degree South Korea have experienced a radical change of their political system to democratization since the 1960s, but their Bollen indexes are taken into account for the aim of a long- or medium-term perspective encompassing half a century or so, and on the ground of observed path-dependence (Inglehart and Baker 2000; Inglehart 2004) in this and related respects. Conversely, discounting the Bollen democracy indexes for these countries would be more arbitrary than counting them, as well as it neglects such a perspective and overlooks this path-dependence.

which is reflected in the present estimates and thus fully confirms the expectations. If it is not, then it indicates that both Turkey and the US in the conservative pole involve some degree of continuity in or path-dependence on anti-liberal, anti-secular, anti-universalistic 'democracy,' though this seems to apply less to the first given its long-standing official secularism only recently reversed during Islamic rule.

Some additional differences between the two rankings are Japan, Italy, the UK, and even Chile and Greece being ranked higher, and Germany lower, on the Bollen index than in the present estimation. They are probably explained by that the first five countries have become less liberal, secular, universalistic and thus democratic, and the last somewhat more so since the Bollen indexes. While Japan and Italy are seemingly more puzzling or complex cases, this particularly holds for Greece due to a sequel of military dictatorship and exclusionary ethno nationalism, the UK because of conservative revolt and repression (Thatcherism), and Chile owing to proto-fascist dictatorship (by Pinochet supported by Thatcher) compounded with theocentric influence. Lastly, it is to be noted that Bollen indexes of liberal democracy were calculated for the period of the 1960s, and the present democracy estimates mostly for that of the 2000–10s, which both highlights the general convergence and explains the particular differences between the two.

In the non-sociological literature, the 'Democracy Ranking of the Quality of Democracy' combines 'freedom and other characteristics of the political system' with 'performance of the non-political dimensions.'[3] In this ranking, ten societies with the highest scores and ranks described as the 'best democracies in the world' are presently classified into the category of liberal, secular and universalistic democracy (Table 3.2), with the single exception of a mixed case.

These 'best democracies' are in particular Scandinavian[4] societies, including Norway ranked 1, Sweden 3, Finland 4, Denmark 5, other North-Western European countries such as Switzerland 2, the Netherlands 6, Germany 7, Belgium 10, as well as New Zealand 8, alongside Ireland 9 as a mixed case, almost exactly just as in the present estimates. Conversely, among ten countries with

---

3   The 'Democracy Ranking model refers to one political dimension and five non-political dimensions, which are: (1) gender (socio-economic and educational gender equality); (2) economy (economic system); (3) knowledge (knowledge-based information society, research and education); (4) health (health status and health system); (5) environment (environmental sustainability)' (see http://democracyranking.org).

4   Paxton (2002, p. 259) cites Sweden and by implication Scandinavia overall as a society of 'high within-group trust and networks' that have 'a strong positive influence on democracy' (also, Putnam 2000).

the comparatively lowest scores and ranks in this ranking of democracy, for example, Turkey ranked 69, Mexico 60, Greece 41, Hungary 38, Slovakia 35, Italy 27, South Korea 32, Czech Republic 29, Chile 25, and Japan 20, all of them belong to opposite or intermediate political systems, thus entirely corresponding to those in the present estimation. In particular, the 'quality of democracy'

TABLE 3.2   *The democracy ranking of the quality of democracy 2015, OECD countries.*

Rank	Country	Total score	Total score	Rank change	Point (2013–14 Score/10)
		2010–2011	2013–2014	loss/gain	
1	Norway	87.7	88.1	0	8.81
2	Switzerland	86.1	87.0	0	8.70
3	Sweden	85.9	86.6	0	8.66
4	Finland	85.7	86.0	0	8.60
5	Denmark	84.2	85.2	0	8.52
6	Netherlands	82.6	83.6	0	8.36
7	Germany	80.9	82.0	+1	8.20
8	New Zealand	81.7	81.8	−1	8.18
9	Ireland	79.5	81.7	+2	8.17
10	Belgium	80.1	81.5	−1	8.15
11	Austria	79.7	80.1	−1	8.01
12	United Kingdom	79.2	80.0	0	8.00
13	Australia	79.1	79.7	0	7.97
14	France	76.0	79.3	+4	7.93
15	Canada	79.1	79.1	−1	7.91
16	United States	77.5	77.6	−1	7.76
17	Portugal	76.1	76.1	0	7.61
18	Slovenia	74.2	76.1	+1	7.61
19	Spain	77.3	75.9	−3	7.59
20	Japan	73.6	75.3	+1	7.53
21	Estonia	71.9	74.5	+3	7.45
22	Chile	71.7	72.8	0	7.28
23	Italy	70.6	71.6	+2	7.16
24	Czech Republic	70.7	71.3	−1	7.13
25	Poland	70.3	71.3	0	7.13
26	Korea, Rep.	70.1	70.6	0	7.06

TABLE 3.2   *The democracy ranking of the quality of democracy 2015, oecd countries.* (cont.)

Rank	Country	Total score	Total score	Rank change	Point (2013–14 Score/10)
		2010–2011	2013–2014	loss/gain	
27	Slovak Republic	67.9	68.3	+2	6.83
28	Hungary	68.1	67.6	−2	6.76
29	Greece	68.7	66.0	−7	6.60
30	Mexico	56.7	57.9	0	5.79
31	Turkey	55.3	55.1	−7	5.51
	Iceland	NA	NA	NA	NA
	Luxembourg	NA	NA	NA	NA

Source: http://democracyranking.org/ Quality of Democracy = freedom & other characteristics of the political system & performance of the non-political dimensions (1) socio-economic and educational gender equality; (2) economy; (3) knowledge-based information society, research and education; (4) health status and health system; (5) environmental sustainability.

does not rank the UK (ranked 12) and the US (16) in top ten Western and related democracies, and in that sense is generally similar with the present estimates, although with some particular differences (for example, *Democracy Ranking* assigns a slightly higher rank to Ireland and a lower one to Austria, etc.).

In addition, according to 'Democracy Index' (by the Economist Intelligence Unit[5]), among top ten Western and other societies with the highest rank and overall score (Table 3.3) are Norway ranked 1 overall, Iceland 2, Sweden 3, New Zealand 4, Denmark 5, Switzerland 6, Canada 7, Finland 8, Australia 9, and the Netherlands 10. This Index is computed by combining what are considered particular dimensions of democracy such as electoral process/pluralism, functioning of government, political participation, political culture, and civil liberties.

As known, all these countries ranked the highest overall on the 'Democracy Index' are politically classified as liberal, secular and universalistic democracies, which makes the ranking almost identical with the present estimation,

---

5   The *Economist Intelligence Unit* for its Democracy Index uses the following indicators: I Electoral process and pluralism, II Functioning of government, III Political participation, IV Political culture, and v Civil liberties.

TABLE 3.3 *Democracy index, OECD countries, 2015.*

Country	Rank	Overall score/point
Norway	1	9.93
Iceland	2	9.58
Sweden	3	9.45
New Zealand	4	9.26
Denmark	5	9.11
Switzerland	6	9.09
Canada	7	9.08
Finland	8	9.03
Australia	9	9.01
Netherlands	10	8.92
Luxembourg	11	8.88
Ireland	12	8.85
Germany	13	8.64
Austria	14	8.54
UK	15	8.31
Spain	16	8.30
USA	17	8.05
Italy	18	7.98
Korea	19	7.97
Japan	20	7.96
Czech Republic	21	7.94
Belgium	22	7.93
France	23	7.92
Estonia	24	7.85
Chile	25	7.84
Portugal	26	7.79
Slovenia	27	7.57
Greece	28	7.45
Slovakia	29	7.29
Poland	30	7.09
Hungary	31	6.84
Mexico	32	6.55
Turkey	33	5.12

Note: Democracy Indexes combine electoral process/pluralism, functioning of government, political participation, political culture, and civil liberties.
Source: The Economist Intelligence Unit 2015.

in which they also occupy the highest positions. Notably, all five Scandinavian countries are ranked among the ten most democratic societies in the Western and entire world, just are in the present ranking. Hence, both rankings completely confirm the observation or expectation that Scandinavia is the most democratic, politically free region of societies precisely by virtue of being the most liberal, secular and universalistic democracy. In particular, the country ranked 1 on democracy/political freedom, including civil liberties, Norway can be considered the single most liberal, secular and universalistic democracy, perhaps alongside Iceland with such a rank in the present estimation.

Conversely, none of the countries classified in non-liberal, non-secular and non-universalistic bogus 'democracies' as well as mixed political systems is ranked among these ten most democratic societies in the world in the above Index. This is hence also entirely consistent with the expectations and reaffirms that liberal, secular and universalistic democracies form an 'exclusive club' of the greatest level of democracy and the highest degree of political freedom and civil liberties and rights.

They are followed by countries ranked from 11 to 20 such as Luxembourg, Germany, Austria, Ireland, the UK, and Spain, some non-members of OECD, and the US ranked 20 overall in the world and the last among what are called 'full democracies,' notably with the lowest degree of 'civil liberties'[6] (8.24 versus 10 for Norway, etc.) As seen, the first three of these countries are also classified as liberal, secular, and universalistic democracies, the other three as mixed political systems, and the US both in the first category in liberal, secular, universalistic governance and regions and the opposite in the conservative, religious, and exclusionary. This thereby makes this second-highest tier, except for the last case, generally similar with that in the present estimation. Alternatively, ten OECD countries with the lowest rank and overall score on democracy are in a descending order Estonia, Chile, Portugal, Slovenia, Greece, Slovakia, Poland, Hungary, Mexico, and Turkey, which is similar to their ranks or scores in the present estimation. Recall that all these countries are classified either as non-liberal, non-secular, and non-universalistic ersatz 'democracies' or mixed political systems, and none as liberal, secular, and universalistic democracy. This thus confirms the adverse expectation and 'selection' that the first are

---

6   Brooks (2000, p. 500) finds in respect of political-civil liberties in the US during 1972–96 'highly consistent partisan preferences, with support for civil rights disposing voters to favor Democratic over Republican candidates.' Brooks and Manza (1997, p. 945) report that 'rather than displacing the old cleavages, newer ideological conflicts have developed alongside persistent social-group cleavages in the US electorate. The electoral divisions between major social groups generally remain as large as were prior to the pivotal shifts of the 1960s.'

drastically and the second significantly less democratic, politically free than the third category of the present classification. Particularly, the two countries with the lowest democracy rank and score, Mexico and Turkey classified in the first category are also among the three—along with the conservative half of America—ranked and estimated so in the present estimation.

Of course, some differences are that 'Democracy Index' ranks higher Anglo-Saxon or English-speaking countries like Australia, New Zealand, Canada, Ireland, the UK, and the US (plus South Korea, Chile, and Greece), but slightly or appreciably lower those of Continental Europe such as Germany, France, Belgium, etc., than does the present estimation. Whether or not such ranking expresses and is thus distorted by the bias, inertia or stereotype of 'superior' Anglo-Saxon or English-speaking democracy/political freedom, it is not greatly different from the present estimation, and does not disconfirm the expectations. For example, the UK rank is not dramatically higher (15) than presently (23), while that of the US (17) is so compared with the latter (33).

Yet, it essentially confirms the expectation by indicating that the latter in liberal, secular, and universalistic governance (e.g., the Presidency and in part Congress since 2009) and regions (California, etc.) temporarily supersedes or counters its opposite (the 2001–08 Federal government and the South), and yet not entirely, as the second revolts and resurges, as since 2010 and this region. And this is just as expected and indicated by that this country's ranking is the last among 'full democracies,' as the net effect of these countervailing political systems and processes, simply the 'two Americas.' Counterfactually, if the UK and the US overall under the above specification were factually more democratic/politically freer, they would rank much higher in this ranking, say, in top ten or two rather than just in the second tier of 'full democracies.' This generally confirms the observation and expectation that liberal, secular and universalistic democracies—as enduring and consistent wholes like in Scandinavia, and not just transient, inconsistent parts, as in the liberal half of the 'two Americas'—exclusively occupy the highest level of democracy/political freedom.

Generally, there are various and often different rankings and indexes of democracy[7] or political freedom in the academic and especially non-academic literature, which may differ from and even contradict the present ranking and estimation. As seen, the present ranking is generally congruent with or not greatly different from those mentioned, thus not as surprising as it might seem, especially with respect to democracy estimates for some countries such as the

---

7   The probably best known of other democracy indexes and ranking in the political science literature is the Polity IV Project by the Center for Systemic Peace.

TABLE 3.4   *Voter turnout by country, vote to registration ratio, parliamentary elections, OECD, 1945–2001.*

Country (Elections)	Percentage	Point (Percentage/10)
Australia (22)	94.5	9.45
Belgium (18)	92.5	9.25
Austria (17)	91.3	9.13
New Zealand (19)	90.8	9.08
Italy (15)	89.8	8.98
Luxembourg (12)	89.7	8.97
Iceland (17)	89.5	8.95
Netherlands (16)	87.5	8.75
Sweden (17)	87.1	8.71
Denmark (22)	85.9	8.59
Germany (14)	85.4	8.54
Slovakia (4)	85.2	8.52
Czech Republic (4)	82.8	8.28
Turkey (10)	81.3	8.13
Norway (15)	80.4	8.04
Greece (16)	79.9	7.99
Chile (11)	78.9	7.89
Portugal (10)	77.0	7.70
Slovenia (3)	76.6	7.66
Finland (16)	76.0	7.60
United Kingdom (16)	75.2	7.52
Canada (18)	73.9	7.39
France (15)	73.8	7.38
Spain (8)	73.6	7.36
Ireland (16)	73.3	7.33
Republic of Korea (10)	72.9	7.29
Japan (22)	69.5	6.95
Estonia (4)	68.1	6.81
Hungary (3)	67.0	6.70
United States (17)	66.5	6.65
Mexico (19)	65.2	6.52
Switzerland (14)	56.5	5.65
Poland (5)	50.3	5.03

Source: Voter Turnout since 1945. A Global Report. The International Institute for Democracy and Electoral Assistance.

US and in part the UK compared with others like continental Europe,[8] above all Scandinavia, Canada, Australia, etc. though such congruence is not consequential for its validity or relevance for it has its own basis. Still, as an exercise for the sake of greater completeness or congruence and preempting possible objections, the above three general rankings[9] of democracy are incorporated into the present ranking (as in the previous chapter), which yields almost identical estimates or ranks for these societies.

The above confirms that the present ranking is highly congruent and correlated with these and similar rankings, and alternatively their inclusion does not contradict but essentially reaffirms it. Notably, with this inclusion, the estimates and ranks of both the most and the least democratic societies are mostly kept intact or subject to minor variations. In this respect, the present ranking can be taken to have a reasonably high degree of validity, plausibility or congruence with the previous ones, although no single ranking or estimation of democracy and modern free society is absolutely valid or non-controversial and is bound to be controversial no matter what are its sources and grounds. In turn, the sources and grounds for the particular quantitative estimates of the conditions, elements and indicators of democracy/political freedom (aggregated in Table 3.4) are presented and elaborated next, according to the preceding classification. In addition, some qualitative considerations of certain political freedoms with missing or insufficient data, reports, or rankings are provided (Appendix 3.1)

Freedoms, Rights, and Opportunities to Political Participation

Generally, the observed pattern is that liberal, secular and universalistic democracies as a whole tend to demonstrate a stronger freedom, right, and opportunity to political participation, inclusion, and equality such as voting freedoms, rights, and turnouts than opposite and intermediate political systems, with secondary variations. Particularly, these estimates are based on the data on comparative election turnout rates taken as, other things equal, indicators or proxies for the freedom, right, and opportunity to political, specifically

---

8   Giddens (2000a, p. 33) notes that the US and the UK 'have public institutions and infrastructures inferior to those in many Continental countries.' Brooks and Manza (2006, pp. 481–90) register that 'preferences for public social provision are, for instance, generally higher in Western European societies in comparison to the United States, and highest in Scandinavia' an find that 'mass policy preferences exert a significant influence over welfare state spending, particularly' in European democracies compared to the US, the UK, and others.

9   The Bollen Liberal Democracy Indexes from the 1960–80s are useful for a longer perspective on modern democracy and complementary to those more recent.

electoral, participation for Western and other democracies. Higher election turnout rates hence express or predict, all else equal, the higher freedom, right, and opportunity to electoral participation, and conversely. To that extent, countries with the highest voter turnout rates tend to have the highest freedom, right, and opportunity to electoral participation, simply voting, just as the other way round, with certain variations. Thus, countries with the highest voter turnout are generally liberal, secular and universalistic democracies, and conversely, albeit with some particular exceptions.

For example, the estimates of voter turnout are derived from the 'Global Report' of the International Institute for Democracy and Electoral Assistance (Table 3.5).

TABLE 3.5   *Voter turnout by vote to voting age population ratio. Parliamentary elections, 1945–2001, OECD.*

Country (Elections)	Percentage	Point (Percentage/10)
Italy (15)	92.0	9.20
Iceland (17)	89.3	8.93
Portugal (10)	88.2	8.82
New Zealand (19)	86.0	8.60
Belgium (18)	84.8	8.48
Austria (17)	84.4	8.44
Australia (22)	84.2	8.42
Sweden (17)	84.1	8.41
Netherlands (16)	83.8	8.38
Denmark (22)	83.6	8.36
Slovakia (4)	82.9	8.29
Czech Republic (4)	82.8	8.28
Canada (18)	82.6	8.26
Greece (18)	80.8	8.08
Germany (14)	80.2	8.02
Norway (15)	79.2	7.92
Finland (16)	78.1	7.81
Slovenia (3)	77.9	7.79
Spain (8)	76.4	7.64
Ireland (16)	74.9	7.49
Turkey (10)	74.2	7.42
United Kingdom (16)	73.8	7.38
Republic of Korea (10)	72.9	7.29

Country (Elections)	Percentage	Point (Percentage/10)
Japan (22)	68.7	6.87
Hungary (3)	68.1	6.81
France (15)	67.3	6.73
Luxembourg (13)	63.5	6.35
Estonia (4)	53.5	5.35
Switzerland (14)	51.9	5.19
Poland (5)	51.4	5.14
Mexico (19)	48.1	4.81
United States (28)	47.7	4.77
Chile (11)	45.9	4.59

Source: Voter Turnout since 1945. A Global Report. The International
Institute for Democracy and Electoral Assistance.

According to this Report, top ten or so Western and related OECD countries having the highest turnout in elections, taking vote to registration ratios (from 1945 to 2001) include Australia (95%), Belgium (93%), Austria (91%), New Zealand (91%), Italy (90%), Luxembourg (90%), Iceland (90%), the Netherlands (88%), Sweden (87%), Denmark (86%), and Germany (85%). This strongly fulfills the expectations since virtually all of these countries (with a single exception of Italy) are considered liberal, secular, and universalistic democracies[10]

10   Among OECD countries, Australia, Belgium, and (parts of) Austria, alongside Chile, Greece, Italy, Luxembourg, Mexico, Switzerland (some cantons), and Turkey have compulsory voting laws, with variations in sanctions and level of enforcement. For example, level of enforcement is strict in Australia, Belgium, Luxembourg, and Switzerland, weak in Austria, Chile, Greece, Mexico, and Turkey, and sanctions are not enforced in Italy. The source is International IDEA's 2002 Voter Turnout Since 1945 A Global Report. By contrast, while these countries aim to encourage, allow, or expand voting as much as possible, others such as the US, above all the South, do the opposing by maximally suppressing or limiting and making difficult and onerous this basic democratic freedom, right, and act. Thus, while people are somewhat forced or induced to vote in Australia, for example, they, at least certain targeted 'un-American' groups, are forced *not* to do so, and thus denied the basic democratic freedom and right, in the US South. This manifests a striking difference, displaying another primarily Southern-driven anti-liberal and non-democratic 'American exceptionalism' drastically contrary to what is usually claimed by the latter (viz., 'unique' and 'superior' voting and all democratic freedoms and rights). In turn, one should distinguish compulsory voting laws in democracies like Australia from those in non-democracies such as some Islamic states, North Korea, etc., so that these laws have opposite aims or effects in these two political systems. This preempts the simplistic objection that Iran

in the present classification. Conversely, among bottom ten countries having the lowest electoral turnout are Poland (50%), Switzerland (57%), Mexico (65%), the US (67%), Hungary (67%), Estonia (68%), Japan (70%), South Korea (73%), Ireland (73%), and Spain (74%). This is generally consistent with the expectations, as most of these countries (except for Switzerland as an apparent outlier) are classified presently as either anti-liberal, anti-secular, and non-universalistic 'democracies,' including the US in the conservative rendition, or mixed political systems. For example, the US has the lowest voter turnout among Western societies (minus Switzerland as a curious outlier) and is ranked 120 out of 169 countries in the world, which means only 49 other countries occupy lower ranks. An identical or comparable trend is observed in comparative voter turnout rates, taking vote to voting age population ratios as probably the more indicative or meaningful indicator of the freedom and/or level of political participation (Table 3.6).

TABLE 3.6   *Recent voter turnout, selected OECD countries.*

Country	Election type	Voter turnout	Point (Turnout/10)
Australia	Parliamentary	93.23% (2013)	9.32
Austria	Parliamentary	74.91% (2013)	7.49
	Presidential	53.57% (2010)	
Belgium	Parliamentary	89.37% (2014)	8.94
Canada	Parliamentary	68.28% (2015)	6.83
Chile	Parliamentary	49.25% (2013)	4.93
	Presidential	41.98% (2013)	
Czech Republic	Parliamentary	59.48% (2013)	5.95
	Presidential	59.08% (2013)	
Denmark	Parliamentary	85.89% (2015)	8.59
Estonia	Parliamentary	64.23% (2015)	6.42
Finland	Parliamentary	66.85% (2015)	6.69
	Presidential	68.86% (2012)	
France	Parliamentary	55.40% (2012)	5.54

and North Korea, for example, have compulsory voting laws and yet, or rather because of this, they are non-democracies, which fails to account for such laws and their positive democratic effects in Australia and many other representative democracies. Similarly, the 'rule of law' is to be distinguished and has opposite purposes or outcomes in democracies and non-democracies, for example, in Scandinavia and Canada versus Iran and North Korea and to an important degree the US South as or if closer to third-world anti-liberal and anti-secular states than Western liberal-secular democracies.

Country	Election type	Voter turnout	Point (Turnout/10)
	Presidential	80.35% (2012)	
Germany	Parliamentary	71.53% (2013)	7.15
Greece	Parliamentary	63.60% (2015)	6.36
Hungary	Parliamentary	61.84% (2014)	6.18
Iceland	Parliamentary	81.44% (2013)	8.14
	Presidential	69.32% (2012)	
Ireland	Parliamentary	69.90% (2011)	6.99
	Presidential	56.11% (2011)	
Italy	Parliamentary	75.19% (2013)	7.52
Japan	Parliamentary	52.66% (2014)	5.27
Korea	Parliamentary	58.03% (2016)	5.80
	Presidential	75.84% (2012)	
Luxembourg	Parliamentary	91.15% (2013)	9.12
Mexico	Parliamentary	47.72% (2015)	4.77
	Presidential	63.14% (2012)	
Netherlands	Parliamentary	74.56% (2012)	7.46
New Zealand	Parliamentary	76.95% (2014)	7.70
Norway	Parliamentary	78.23% (2013)	7.82
Poland	Parliamentary	50.92% (2015)	5.09
	Presidential	55.34% (2015)	
Portugal	Parliamentary	55.84% (2015)	5.58
	Presidential	48.70% (2016)	
Slovakia	Parliamentary	59.82% (2016)	5.98
	Presidential	50.48% (2014)	
Slovenia	Parliamentary	51.73% (2014)	5.17
	Presidential	42.41% (2012)	
Spain	Parliamentary	73.20% (2015)	7.32
Sweden	Parliamentary	85.81% (2014)	8.58
Switzerland	Parliamentary	48.40% (2015)	4.84
Turkey	Parliamentary	85.18% (2015)	8.52
	Presidential	74.13% (2014)	
United Kingdom	Parliamentary	66.12% (2015)	6.61
United States	Parliamentary	42.50% (2014)	4.25
	Presidential	66.66% (2012)	

Source: The International Institute for Democracy and Electoral Assistance.

For example, ten OECD countries with the highest turnout ratios during 1945–2001 are Italy (92%), Iceland (89%), Portugal (88%), New Zealand (86%), Belgium (85%), Austria (84%), Australia (84%), Sweden (84%), the Netherlands (84%), and Denmark (84%). Since most of them are liberal, secular, and universalistic democracies, along with two mixed cases, but none being an anti-liberal instance, this largely fulfills the expectations. Conversely, ten OECD countries with the lowest electoral turnouts are Chile (46%), the US (48%), Mexico (48%), Poland (51%), Switzerland (52%), Estonia (54%), Luxembourg (64%), France (67%), Hungary (68%), Japan (69%), and South Korea (73%). With three exceptions, most of these countries are classified either as anti-liberal, anti-secular, and non-universalistic 'democracies,' including the US in the conservative rendition, or mixed political systems, which at least in part support the expectations. For instance, the US exhibits the lowest voter turnout (48%) among all Western societies (considering Chile part of South America) and merely almost half of that of the first ranking country, Italy (92%), around 30 percent lower than that of France (67%), and overall ranked 138 of 169 countries, so only 30 or so countries in the entire world have lower turnouts.

And the most recent elections confirm and continue the long-term pattern of differences in electoral turnout (Table 3.7) between most Western democracies and American democracy. Thus, all the Western countries listed have substantially (often doubly) higher voter turnouts especially in parliamentary elections than the US during the 2000s. (Most OECD countries, 18 out of 33,

TABLE 3.7   *Political participation indexes, OECD countries, 2015.*

Country	Index/point
Norway	10
Iceland	8.89
Netherlands	8.89
New Zealand	8.89
Austria	8.33
Denmark	8.33
Sweden	8.33
Australia	7.78
Canada	7.78
Finland	7.78
France	7.78
Germany	7.78

Country	Index/point
Ireland	7.78
Switzerland	7.78
Italy	7.22
Korea	7.22
Mexico	7.22
Spain	7.22
United States of America	7.22
Czech Republic	6.67
Greece	6.67
Luxembourg	6.67
Poland	6.67
Portugal	6.67
Slovenia	6.67
United Kingdom	6.67
Estonia	6.11
Japan	6.11
Belgium	5.56
Slovakia	5.56
Turkey	5.00
Chile	4.44
Hungary	4.44

Source: The Economist Intelligence Unit 2015.

do not hold presidential elections, while all holding the parliamentary that hence provide more complete voter turnout data for comparative purposes.) For illustration, ten or so countries with the highest voter turnouts (higher than 70%) in the most recent parliamentary elections include Australia (93%), Luxembourg (91%), Belgium (89%), Denmark (86%), Sweden (86%), Turkey (85%), Iceland (81%), Norway (78%), New Zealand (77%), Austria (75%), the Netherlands (75%), Spain (73%), and Germany (72%). This largely fulfills the expectations, for most of these countries belong to liberal, secular, universalistic democracy, with only two exceptions, one belonging to the opposite and the other to the mixed political system.

Conversely, among ten or so countries with the lowest voter turnouts (under 60%) in the most recent parliamentary elections are the US (43%), Mexico (48%), Switzerland (48%), Chile (49%), Poland (51%), Slovenia (51%), Japan

(53%), France (55%), Portugal (56%), South Korea (58%), and Czech Republic (59%), and Slovakia (less than 60%). While seemingly inconclusive, this finding is generally consistent with the expectations in that most of these countries, including the US in the conservative pole, belong to anti-liberal, anti-secular, anti-universalistic or mixed political systems, and only two to liberal, secular, universalistic democracy—and especially that four out of five cases belonging to the first system (except for Turkey) are cited. In particular, the exceptionally low US voter turnout is usually explained by persistent and even growing voter suppression (including 'gerrymandering') in 'conservative America,' such as the South, mixed with political apathy, and mostly explains the victories of anti-liberal, anti-secular forces (particularly the 'Tea Party') in the Congressional and state elections of 2010/2014.

In addition, the estimates of political participation are taken from the above 'Democracy Index' as its third element (Table 3.8).

TABLE 3.8   *Indexes of political pluralism, OECD countries, 2015.*

Country	Index/point
Finland	10
Iceland	10
Luxembourg	10
New Zealand	10
Norway	10
Australia	9.58
Austria	9.58
Belgium	9.58
Canada	9.58
Chile	9.58
Czech Republic	9.58
France	9.58
Estonia	9.58
France	9.58
Germany	9.58
Greece	9.58
Ireland	9.58
Italy	9.58
Netherlands	9.58
Portugal	9.58

Country	Index/point
Poland	9.58
Portugal	9.58
Slovakia	9.58
Slovenia	9.58
Spain	9.58
Sweden	9.58
Switzerland	9.58
United Kingdom	9.58
Denmark	9.17
Hungary	9.17
Japan	9.17
United States of America	9.17
Korea	8.75
Mexico	8.33
Turkey	6.67

SOURCE: THE ECONOMIST INTELLIGENCE UNIT 2015.

For instance, ten or so countries with the highest indexes of political participation include Norway (10), Iceland (8.89), the Netherlands (8.89), New Zealand (8.89), Austria (8.33), Denmark (8.33), Sweden (8.33), Australia (7.78), Canada (7.78), Finland (7.78), France (7.78), Germany (7.78), Ireland (7.78), and Switzerland (7.78). Since these countries (except for Ireland) are all considered and presently classified as liberal, secular and universalistic democracies, this ranking fully confirms the expectations. Conversely, ten or so countries with the lowest indexes of political participation are Chile (4.44), Hungary (4.44), Turkey (5.00), Slovakia (5.56), Belgium (5.56), Japan (6.11), Estonia (6.11), Czech Republic (6.67), Greece (6.67), Luxembourg (6.67), Poland (6.67), Portugal (6.67), Slovenia (6.67), and UK (6.67). Most of these countries are classified either as anti-liberal, anti-secular, anti-universalistic or mixed political systems, with only two exceptions, which largely confirms the expectations. In light of these data, a comparatively high voter turnout appears as the necessary and basic, though not sufficient and full, condition of universalistic or representative democracy at least in its formal dimension, with certain variations. Conversely, a relatively low voter turnout manifests itself as contradicting or weakening universalistic or representative democracy in its formal dimension, with variations.

In comparative terms, some Western democracies such as Australia, Belgium, Italy, and Switzerland force or motivate their electorate to vote in elections and make voting as universal and easy as possible. By stark contrast, anti-democratic conservative forces in the US at the federal and state level, especially the Southern and related states, effectively force or induce eligible voters, above all the poor and various 'un-American' minorities, *not* to vote, instead making this basic democratic right and act maximally exclusive and hard for these targeted groups. While the first passing and enacting compulsory voting laws providing legal incentives or duties for democracy, the second continue with an ever-growing intensity and 'productivity' to pass and enforce coercive anti-voting rules that provide legal—or rather illegal, as usually judged by federal courts—disincentives or prohibitions and Machiavellian tactics against such political participation. Consequently, the first universalize or expand voting freedoms, rights, and opportunities to virtually all eligible populations, whereas the second minimize or contract them to a subset of the population, resulting in the respective expansion and contraction of democracy.

While by such practices Western democracies implement the democratic principle of people choosing their leaders or representatives, Southern and related states and conservative leaders at the US federal level by their opposite actions reach or asymptotically approximate the perverse anti-democratic point at which anti-liberal masters (including fundamentalist 'Bible Belt' theocrats) choose their 'people' through unlawful or anti-democratic strategies such as voter suppression by the old and new means and selection (redistricting cum 'gerrymandering'). Thus, the first are or become truly representative democracies by representing virtually all populations, while the second become petrified as and petrify an unrepresentative, exclusionary 'democracy' generously providing full representation only for a subset of the population and severely inflicting others with under- or complete non-representation, above all, the poor, religious non-believers, ideological dissenters, and sinners-prisoners. For instance, US Congress looks as the most unrepresentative political body, alongside the UK House of Lords as an aristocratic feudal 'anachronism,'[11] in particular the Senate described as the 'good olds boys' network and the 'millionaires' (and godly) club' in which non-millionaires and the 'godless' need not apply, as an extreme exemplar or correlate of 'incumbency veto power,'[12] among Western parliamentary institutions.

---

11   Giddens (2000a, p. 74) writes that 'as it stands, the House of Lords is an anachronism in a democratic society.' In turn, Hill (2002, pp. 280–1) thinks that the US Senate 'is perhaps the most unrepresentative body in the world outside Britain's House of Lords.'

12   Acemoglu et al. (2010, pp. 1512–3) suggest that 'perfect' democracy is a 'situation in which there is no incumbency veto power and no such consent is necessary' and use

No doubt, as done in some Western democracies, forcing or inducing people to vote and thus choose their leaders through compulsory voting laws, though often with weak enforcement, is no optimal solution in liberal democracy but instead the second best option. Yet, what is witnessed in the US South and similar regions and at the federal level under anti-liberal, anti-secular, and anti-universalistic governance—i.e., the conservative half of the 'two Americas'— is the worst option in this respect. For the opposite practice of forcing or inducing people, at least certain targeted populations, *not* to vote and thus not to choose their representatives through compulsory anti-voting laws and tactics yet strongly enforced is destructive to liberal and universalistic democracy. From the perspective of liberal, universalistic, and representative democracy, hence compulsory voting laws in some Western democracies obligating or motivating people to vote and choose their representatives seem a 'lesser evil' than their anti-voting opposites and Machiavellian tactics in the US South and by the conservative federal government or legislature forcing or inducing them not to do so. The second practice results in voter suppression and the perverse (s)election of voters by leaders (by 'gerrymandering') and thus in drastic and growing anti-democratic distortion and contraction typical of conservative regimes[13] and yet unparalleled in the democratic world. This holds true only within the context of Western and related liberal democracies and multi-party political systems, including the US, as the focus of this analysis, and not for non-Western and illiberal Third-World (e.g., Islamic, Christian, popular) 'democracies' and one-party regimes not of present interest, so distinguishing compulsory voting laws in democratic and non-democratic societies is important.

Ideological-Political Pluralism and Competition

The comparative estimates of ideological-political pluralism, choice, and competition are grounded in or congruent with some observations and estimations of this indicator of democracy in Western and other societies. More precisely, the estimates are taken from the indexes of political pluralism and by implication competition in the electoral process, as the first element of the above aggregate 'Democracy Index' (Table 3.9).

---

incumbency veto power as an 'inverse measure of democracy, though it only captures one stylized dimension of how democratic a regime is.'

13   Llavador and Oxoby (2005, p. 1186) report that democratic, 'franchise contractions are mostly fostered by conservative governments.'

TABLE 3.9   *Civil liberties indexes 2015, OECD countries, 2015.*

Country	Civil liberties index/point
Australia	10
Canada	10
Ireland	10
Norway	10
New Zealand	10
Chile	9.71
Finland	9.71
Iceland	9.71
Luxembourg	9.71
Sweden	9.71
Austria	9.41
Belgium	9.41
Czech Republic	9.41
Denmark	9.41
Greece	9.41
Netherlands	9.41
Portugal	9.41
Switzerland	9.41
Spain	9.41
United Kingdom	9.41
Germany	9.12
Poland	9.12
Estonia	8.82
France	8.82
Japan	8.82
Slovakia	8.82
Slovenia	8.82
Italy	8.53
Korea	8.53
United States of America	8.24
Hungary	7.65
Mexico	6.76
Turkey	2.94

Source: The Economist Intelligence Unit 2015.

Thus, political systems with the maximal index of 'electoral process and pluralism' (10) are exclusively liberal, secular and universalistic democracies, for example Scandinavian countries and Finland, Iceland, Norway, joined with Luxembourg and New Zealand. This finding therefore clearly and strongly reaffirms the expectation that liberal, secular and universalistic democracies are the most pluralistic and in that sense the most competitive and open electoral and political systems. Alternatively, no single case of non-liberal, non-secular and non-universalistic 'democracies' as well as mixed political systems has such a maximal index, which also confirms the opposite expectation that these are less pluralistic, competitive and open than the first. As also expected, the group with the second highest index of 'electoral process and pluralism' (9.58) includes the remaining liberal, secular and universalistic democracies such as Australia, Austria, Belgium, Canada, France, Germany, the Netherlands, Sweden, and Switzerland, joined by most eclectic political systems like Chile, Czech Republic, Estonia, Greece, Ireland, Italy, Portugal, Slovenia, Slovakia, Spain, and the UK, with only one country, Poland not belonging to the first and second categories.

Conversely, political systems with the lowest indexes of political pluralism and electoral competition involve four non-liberal, non-secular, and non-universalistic 'democracies' such as Turkey under the Islamic government (6.67), Mexico (8.33), South Korea (8.75), and the US (9.17) in the conservative rendition, along with two intermediate systems Hungary (9.17) and Japan (9.17), and only one case Denmark (9.17) not belonging to either. Consequently, this finding confirms the negative expectation that such 'democracies' as a group are the least pluralistic, competitive, and open electoral and political systems, and thus 'ersatz' forms of democracy on this, just as any, particular dimension, as well as that mixed cases are more so than these, but less than liberal, secular, and universalistic democracies. Alternatively, it reaffirms (even after taking account of an unexpected outlier like Denmark) the expectations that the latter as a whole have the highest degree of political pluralism and electoral competition as a particular manifestation of their forming the 'exclusive club' of true, full democracy, freedom in the polity among contemporary Western and all societies.

As implied, the aforesaid of ideological-political pluralism and choice holds true for the comparative estimates of free competition in the polity in Schumpeter's sense of individuals or groups feely competing for power or leadership and in the typical form of a multi-party system. Insofar as free competition through a multi-party system in politics dynamically exemplifies or manifests the existence or potential of political pluralism and choice, the estimates of the former tend to be, other things equal, generally identical to and mostly predicted by those of the latter. In this respect, pluralism estimates and those of political competition form an identity or composite in which the first predict the second, at the minimum being highly correlated with each other. For instance, the indexes of political pluralism and electoral processes in the 'Democracy Index' can be taken to also represent or approximate those of free competition in politics via a multi-party system, simply of a competitive, open polity.

Effective Universal Political and Civil Liberties

In general, the estimates of effective universal and equal political and civil liberties and rights in Western and related societies are based on or compatible with various studies and observations, including those pertaining to national human rights institutions.[14] Specifically, they are taken from the indexes of effective civil—and by association political—liberties as part of the above 'Democracy Index 2015' (Table 3.10).

Thus, five countries with the maximal index on civil liberties (10) include Australia, Canada, Ireland, New Zealand, and Norway, and the other five with the

TABLE 3.10   *Level of political repression/state terror, OECD countries, 2009–12.*

Country	2009	2010	2011	2012	Point[a]
Australia	1.9	2.0	1.8	1.7	7
Austria	0.9	0.9	0.8	0.8	9
Belgium	1.2	1.1	1.1	1.1	8
Canada	1.4	1.3	1.3	1.2	8
Chile	2.2	2.2	2.2	2.0	6
Czech Republic	1.4	1.3	1.1	1.1	8
Denmark	1.4	1.4	1.4	1.4	8
Estonia	2.2	1.7	1.7	1.9	7
Finland	1.5	1.4	1.4	1.5	8
France	2.6	2.4	2.3	2.3	6
Germany	1.4	1.4	1.3	1.3	8
Greece	3.3	2.8	2.3	2.6	5
Hungary	1.2	1.1	1.0	0.8	9
Iceland	0.2	0.2	0.1	0.1	10
Ireland	0.6	0.6	0.6	0.6	9

---

14   Cole (2005) and Cole and Ramirez (2013) focus on national human rights institutions.

Country	2009	2010	2011	2012	Point[a]
Italy	1.8	1.8	1.7	1.7	7
Japan	1.0	1.0	1.0	1.0	9
Korea	2.9	2.7	2.8	2.8	5
Luxembourg	0.6	0.6	0.6	0.6	9
Mexico	0.5	0.6	0.6	0.6	9
Netherlands	1.5	1.4	1.4	1.3	8
New Zealand	1.1	1.1	1.1	1.1	8
Norway	1.6	1.5	1.5	1.4	8
Poland	1.8	1.9	1.8	1.9	7
Portugal	2.1	2.1	2.0	1.8	7
Slovakia	1.5	1.3	1.1	1.1	8
Slovenia	1.6	1.6	1.3	1.2	8
Spain	1.2	1.1	1.0	0.9	9
Sweden	1.2	1.3	1.2	1.2	9
Switzerland	0.8	0.7	0.8	0.8	9
Turkey	2.6	2.4	2.3	2.3	6
United Kingdom	2.6	2.5	2.4	2.5	6
United States	4.6	4.7	4.6	4.2	2

a 2012 Level 0–0.5 = 10 points, level 0.6–1 = 9 points, level 1.1–1.5 = 8 points, level 1.6–2 = 7 points, level 2.1–2.5 = 6 points, level 2.6–3 = 5 points, level 3.1–3.5 = 4 points, level 3.6–4 = 3 points, level 4.1–4.5 = 2 points, level 4.6 or higher 1 point.

Note: the higher score, the higher level of political repression/state terror.

Source: The political terror scale http://www.politicalterrorscale.org.

second highest (9.71) are Chile, Finland, Iceland, Luxembourg, and Sweden. Consequently, eight of these ten countries belong to the category of liberal, secular, and universalistic democracy, two to its mixed counterpart, and none to its opposite. This hence largely confirms the expectations that such democracies as a whole implement the highest level of effective civil liberties. In particular, of the five countries with the maximum indexes four belong to the first category, only one (Ireland) belongs to its mixed counterpart, and none to its opposite, which reaffirms that it is these democracies as a whole that, above all, reach maximal effective civil-political liberties. Regionally, except for one (Denmark), all Scandinavian countries as paradigmatic instances of liberal, secular and universalistic democracy are ranked among top ten on this dimension, thus reaffirming the observations and predictions that they as a region implement civil and political liberty 'second to none' in the Western and entire world and perhaps history.

On the other hand, ten or so countries with the lowest scores on civil liberties represent Turkey (2.94), Mexico (6.76), Hungary (7.65), the US (8.24), Italy (8.53), South Korea (8.53), Estonia (8.82), France (8.82), Japan (8.82), Slovenia (8.82), and Slovenia (8.82). Hence, virtually all of these countries belong to the categories of anti-liberal, anti-secular, and anti-universalistic 'democracies,' including the conservative pole of America, or mixed political systems, with one single exception like France belonging to the first category. This therefore generally fulfills the expectation that the first two tend to implement the lower level of effective political and civil liberties. Notably, out of the four countries with the lowest scores three are classified as such bogus 'democracies,' Turkey under Islamic government, Catholic-influenced Mexico, the US in conservative-religious governance or regions, thus fully confirming the expectations that they as a whole attain the lowest level of such liberties. For instance, Turkey has the lowest score overall and the conservative section of America among Western societies. This strongly confirms that anti-liberal and anti-secular theocratic or theocentric political systems epitomized by the two are the most adverse and destructive to effective civil and political liberties and rights in general and in particular within the West, respectively.

In addition, a qualitative estimation considers sociological and other studies and observations that indicate that liberal, secular and universalistic democracies are as a rule or pattern observed and predicted to comprise the most effective universal political liberties and rights, including national human rights institutions, which hence fully confirms the expectations. Thus, in these political systems racial-ethnic, religious, ideological-legal, and any minorities manifestly enjoy the most numerous, secure, and strongest political and civil liberties and rights, just as do majority groups, thus demonstrating consistency in universal and equal liberty. Alternatively, anti-liberal, anti-secular and anti-universalistic 'democracies' are found to have the least—and often non-existent—and weakest effective and universal political and civil liberties and rights, as entirely expected. In such political regimes, racial-ethnic, religious, ideological-legal, and other minorities are evidently deprived of elemental effective political-civil liberties and rights are monopolized for/by majority groups, displaying closure, exclusion, and duality in this respect that makes them spurious, closed and exclusionary bogus 'democracies.' As typical, eclectic political systems show intermediate effective universal political-civil liberties and rights.

First, a qualitative estimation takes account of sociological and other observations and studies of effective universal political liberties and human rights for racial-ethnic minorities as well as immigrants in Western and related societies. These observations show that the most effective and universal political liberties and human rights for racial-ethnic and related minorities are found in liberal, secular and universalistic democracies, while converse is true for their anti-liberal, anti-secular and anti-universalistic alternatives, with their eclectic counterparts being at an intermediate level in this regard. Observations also indicate that liberal, secular and universalistic democracies permit immigrants to exercise more actual political liberties and human rights than do their opposites, as well as their eclectic counterparts.[15] For example, most of Western Europe and such nations of immigration as Canada and New Zealand are found to endow legal immigrants ('resident foreigners') with voting rights for local elections, while New Zealand doing so for all elections.[16] In this

---

15   Collins (2010, p. 13) observes that 'undocumented immigrants have become 'socially constructed as criminals by recent immigration policies' in the US. King, Massoglia, and Uggen (2012, p. 1787) register that 'over 44 million noncitizens have been ordered to leave the US since 1925.' Menjívar and Abrego (2012, p. 1388) identify 'legal violence' against immigrants in America in that the US legal system 'has increasingly linked immigrants with terrorists and criminals, helping to move immigration matters from the civil to the realm of criminal law. This process has fashioned a violent context for immigrants already in the country, where social suffering becomes commonplace, normalized, and familiar.' In general, Klandermans, Toorn, and Stekelenburg (2008, p. 992) note that 'regulations for immigrants have become more restrictive, resulting in more limiting thresholds for immigration' in the Western world since the 2000s.

16   According to The International IDEA Handbook for Electoral Justice (2010, p. 17) 'some countries grant electoral rights to resident foreigners. New Zealand does so for all elections. Other countries, for example, Argentina, Canada and Uruguay, do so for local elections, as do the countries of the European Union under the terms of the European Convention on the Participation of Foreigners in Public Life at Local Level of 1992.' Also, Bloemraad, Korteweg, and Yurdakul (2008, p. 165) report 'countries such as the Netherlands, Sweden, and New Zealand allow noncitizens local voting rights.' In turn, Ceobanu and Escandell (2010, p. 310) find that 'North Americans have become more supportive of immigration as time has passed, but the attitudinal gap between the two national populations (Canada and the United States) persists. The publics of Australia and New Zealand, another pair of settler societies, have also favored less restrictive immigration over time. Whereas Australians' opinions have shifted toward steady levels of immigration, those of New Zealanders have continued to denote a preference for reduced levels.' Frank, Akresh, and Lu (2010, p. 394) present evidence that 'Latino immigrants experience skin-color-based discrimination in the workplace' in the US. Koopmans (2013, p. 153) finds that indices like the Multiculturalism Policy Index and Indicators of Citizenship Rights for Immigrants 'indicate Australia, Canada, and Sweden as countries with strong multicultural policies

respect, the salient exceptions are such immigrant societies as Australia and the US as the supposed exemplary and legendary 'nation of immigrants' depriving this minority group from such an elemental political freedom and right and excluding it from the political process, thus resulting in the exclusionary subversion or contraction of democracy.[17] This hence confirms the existence of the 'two Americas,' in which the xenophobic, anti-immigrant pole probably has become or always been, as in conservatism and the South, stronger than the opposite. These findings provide the first sources and grounds for an additional comparative qualitative estimation of this crucial dimension of substantive democracy.

Second, consideration is given to findings or estimates of effective political freedoms and rights for religious and non-religious minorities, including those with minority or no religion, atheists, agnostics, secularists, liberals, progressives, humanists, rationalists, and the like.[18] Thus, it considers some reports[19] of the adverse treatment by some states of such minorities especially through

and Denmark, Switzerland, France, and Germany as countries with weak multicultural policies. The United States, New Zealand, Norway, and Belgium occupy intermediary positions on both indexes.' Also, Koopmans (2013, p. 160) registers that Canada's naturalization policies are 'more inviting, more proactive, and less constrained by security concerns (than the US).' Koopmans (2013, p. 163) adds that 'naturalization rates are substantially higher in Canada compared with the United States' and 'trust in government is also higher among immigrants in Canada compared with the United States, even after controlling for the fact that native Canadians also trust their government more.'

17   Plotke (2002, p. lvi) notes that in the US 'nondemocratic projects' spring from 'many sources' such as 'anti-immigrant agitation on the right,' compounded with the 'rigorous antiunion efforts of large corporations.' As an indicative instance replicated or evoked many times since, King, Massoglia, and Uggen (2012, p. 1821) comment that 'after a 1948 plane crash in California's Los Gatos Canyon killed 28 deportees, folksinger Woody Guthrie offered poignant commentary on their anonymity (and treatment). When press accounts reported only the names of the US guard and flight crew, he wrote, "You won't have your names when you ride the big airplane/All they will call you will be 'deportees.'"' Reskin (2003, p. 12) suggests that some US employers tend to 'forbid workers from speaking any language but English while on the job,' as well as to 'reserve jobs for co-religionists.'

18   Acemoglu et al. (2012, p. 1464) remark that 'those worried about the slippery slope of giving more rights to religious groups in Turkey fear that any constitutional guarantees can be changed in the future,' as he Islamic-based government precisely attempts to do at the time of writing these lines. Bruce (2002) states 'God Is Dead' in the sense of the accelerating process of secularization in the Western world. Gorski and Türkmen-Dervişoğlu (2013, p. 197) alert to 'modern episodes of sacrificial violence, such as the (Puritan) New England witch craze (and) the violent cults of the 1980s, such as those in Jamestown and Waco.'

19   Other sources on the discrimination and exclusion of non-believers in general include International Humanist and Ethical Union (http://freethoughtreport.com) and the

suppression, exclusion, and punishment of and discrimination against non-believers and related groups, and studies of 'godly' polities as effective or proxy theocracies.[20] These reports indicate that the maximal or most substantial effective political and civil liberties and rights for religious and non-religious minorities alike are invariably observed in liberal, secular and universalistic democracies such as Western/Northern Europe, above all Scandinavia, which completely reaffirms the expectations.

Conversely, they reveal that such freedoms and rights for religious and non-religious minorities are minimal and even non-existent in countries classified as anti-liberal, anti-secular and anti-universalistic, particularly ethnic-nationalistic or theocentric, 'democracies,' as well as mixed systems. These include Mexico, Poland, South Korea, Turkey, and the conservative government and regions of the US, as well as Greece,[21] thus rendering them effective theocracies (Poland, Turkey, the American South), as fully expected. As usual, medium liberties and rights for religious and non-religious minorities are found in eclectic political systems, including Eastern Europe, Ireland, the UK, and others. The above furnishes the second ground for the qualitative estimation of these liberties and rights as the highest for liberal, secular, and universalistic Western democracies, particularly Scandinavia and Canada, the lowest for their opposites, especially Poland, Turkey, and the US in conservative rule and regions, and medium for their intermediate counterparts such as the UK[22] and others.

American Humanist (http://americanhumanist.org), while a source on modern theocracies is Theocracy Watch (http://www.theocracywatch.org).

20   Mueller (2013, p. 12) registers 'widespread constraints on individual freedoms across the world, as a result of religious influence on legislation.' For example, he notes that 'a quarter of the Western democracies put prohibitive restrictions on women's freedom to have an abortion' (Mueller 2013, p. 12).

21   Bloemraad et al. (2008, p. 158) include Greece (together with Germany pre-2000, Austria, and Switzerland) into the category of 'ethnic nationalism' and a 'descent principle of citizenship.'

22   According to 'Freedom of Thought 2014: A Global Report on Discrimination Against Humanists, Atheists, and the Non-religious; Their Human Rights and Legal Status,' presently the UK government 'is consulting on new qualifications for 14–18 year olds (in state schools), and these almost entirely exclude non-religious beliefs from study. In England, Wales and Northern Ireland, every state-funded school (which are 100% or virtually 100% funded by public monies) is legally required to hold a daily act of collective worship. In the schools that are not designated with a religious character, this worship must be wholly or mainly of a broadly Christian character. Schools can apply to have this changed to another faith for some or all of their students, but they cannot have this changed to be secular.'

Third, a qualitative estimation pays attention to observations or estimations of effective political freedoms and rights for ideological-legal minorities such as dissenters, dissidents, and prisoners in Western and related societies.[23] As previously, these observations indicate that liberal, secular and universalistic democracies such as Western European countries maximize effective political freedoms and rights for these ideological-legal minorities, including former and current prisoners, which is completely consistent with the predictions. Conversely, they show that anti-liberal, anti-secular and anti-universalistic 'democracies,' particularly Islamic-ruled Turkey and the conservative political-regional half of the US (the federal legislature and most state legislatures and governors since 2010–14 and the South and like regions constantly), minimize or deny such political freedoms and rights, as fully expected, with eclectic political systems like Eastern Europe, the UK, etc. at an intermediate point in this respect.

Effective Democratic Rule

State Terror

A specific ground for the comparative estimates of state repression or terror represents the 'political terror scale' for Western and non-Western societies. Initially intended to test for violations of 'international human rights standards' by countries receiving US foreign aid, this scale is taken as an indicator or proxy of government severe coercion, violent repression and arbitrary Draconian punishment. The 'political terror scale' includes widespread arbitrary executions and mass imprisonment not only for ordinary violent and other crimes but also for political dissent and opposition. Certain regimes, though in various ways and degrees, initially reproduce and then punish political or ideological prisoners of conscience, simply 'enemies,' including the 'associates of Satan' and 'witches' by theocracies among them, above all Islamic-ruled Turkey, Catholic-dominated Poland, and 'evangelical America.' Such punishments also involve criminalizing and severely punishing moral sins and vices like drugs, alcohol, consensual sex, prostitution, etc., especially in conservative, evangelical, and puritanical America (the South, Utah, etc.) as the undisputed 'leader' among these and all other OECD countries, followed by Turkey

---

23   Sutton (2013, pp. 715–23) registers the 'unprecedented growth in rates of criminal incarceration beginning in the 1970s—most conspicuously in the United States but to some degree in other countries as well,' displaying the 'American model of mass incarceration' and thus 'intensified penal repression.'

during Islamic rule (still failing to criminalize adultery and alcohol) and in part the once Puritan Britain. To that extent, the 'political terror scale' is considered to indicate or approximate undemocratic, illiberal rule contradicting and perverting substantive democracy into political oppression, and thus effective dictatorship.

Thus, largely fulfilling the expectations, countries with the lowest scores (lower than or around 1) on the 'political terror scale' include those that are presently classified as liberal, secular and universalistic democracies (Table 3.11).

TABLE 3.11   *Penal repression/imprisonment, OECD countries, 2015.*

Country	Prisoners	Date	Population	Prisoner rate	Point[a]
Australia	35,949	4.15–6.15	23.75 m	151	7
Austria	8,188	1.1.15	8.58 m	95	9
Belgium	11,769	1.3.14	11.24 m	105	8
Canada	37,864	2013–14	35.68 m	106	8
Czech Republic	20,628	30.10.15	10.56 m	195	7
Chile	44,238	30.9.15	17.90 m	247	6
Denmark	3,481	1.5.15	5.67 m	61	9
Estonia	2,830	26.10.15	1.31 m	216	6
Finland	3,105	16.5.15	5.47 m	57	9
France	60,896	1.9.15	64.39 m	95	9
Germany	63,628	31.3.15	81.29 m	78	9
Greece	11,798	1.1.15	10.81 m	109	8
Hungary	18,424	13.10.15	9.83 m	187	7
Iceland	147	1.1.14	325,700	45	10
Ireland	3,733	30.10.15	4.64 m	80	9
Italy	52,434	31.10.15	60.81 m	86	9
Japan	60,486	31.12.14	127.02 m	48	10
Korea (Rep of)	50,800	31.7.14	50.09 m	101	8
Luxembourg	631	1.1.15	562,400	112	8
Mexico	255,138	30.6.15	120.20 m	212	6
Netherlands	11,603	30.9.14	16.88 m	69	9
New Zealand	8,906	29.6.15	4.60 m	194	7
Norway	3,710	13.5.15	5.19 m	71	9
Poland	72,609	30.9.15	37.99 m	191	7
Portugal	14,238	15.10.15	10.33 m	138	7

TABLE 3.11   *Penal repression/imprisonment, oecd countries, 2015.* (cont.)

Country	Prisoners	Date	Population	Prisoner rate	Point[a]
Slovakia	9,991	1.10.15	5.43 m	184	7
Slovenia	1,511	25.5.15	2.06 m	73	9
Spain	63,025	30.10.15	46.38 m	136	8
Switzerland	6,923	3.9.14	8.20 m	84	9
Sweden	5,400	1.1.15	9.75 m	55	9
Turkey	172,562	5.10.15	78.47 m	220	6
UK: England	85,843	30.10.15	58.02 m	148	8
USA	2,217,000	.13	317.76 m	698	0

a   Prisoner rate (per 100,000) under 50 = 10 points, rate 50–100 = 9 points, rate 101–150 = 8 points, rate 151–200 = 7 points, rate 201–250 = 6 points, rate 251–300 = 5 points, rate 301–350 = 4 points, rate 351–400 = 3 points, rate 401–450 = 2 points, rate 451–500 = 1 point, rate 500 or higher = 0 points.

Source: International Centre for *Prison* Studies http://www.prisonstudies.org Roy Walmsley. World Prison Population List (eleventh edition) 2015.

They are, for example, Austria, Belgium, Canada, Iceland, Luxembourg, the Netherlands, New Zealand, Sweden, and Switzerland, along with their eclectic counterparts like Czech Republic, Hungary, Ireland, Japan, Slovakia, Slovenia, Spain, and only one of their opposites such as Mexico.[24] Conversely, as also expected, most of the countries with the highest scores (around 2 and higher) on the 'political terror scale' are classified as anti-liberal, anti-secular and exclusionary democracies such as Poland, South Korea, Turkey, and the conservative section of the US, along with intermediate political systems like Chile, Greece, and the UK, and with only one of them belonging to the first category in the present classification, namely France. Notably, among Western democracies, 'conservative America' and the UK consistently rank the first and second on the 'political terror scale,' thus self-contradicting the claim to be the most and even only democratic and free societies in the world, such clams being further contradicted by various related practices (e.g., the revelations of government massive secret spying on citizens in these two counties, especially the first).

---

24   The likely reason for Mexico's surprisingly low score on 'political terror scale' is that, as Fearon (2011, p. 1693) observes, "Ballots rather than bullets' can then be cheaper for political elites. Mexico's transition to democracy may illustrate this mechanism.'

Imprisonment and Executions as Elements of State Terror

As noted, state repression or 'political terror' especially resorts to penal coercion and severe punishment through imprisonment and executions, which hence can be estimated separately based on readily available and relatively known data. Thus, the comparative estimates of imprisonment and executions are derived from the global data on these forms of legal repression (Table 3.12).

TABLE 3.12   *Number of death sentences and executions, OECD countries, 2015.*

Country	Reported executions	Death sentences and executions	Point[a]
Australia	0	0	10
Austria	0	0	10
Belgium	0	0	10
Canada	0	0	10
Chile	0	0	10
Czech Republic	0	0	10
Denmark	0	0	10
Estonia	0	0	10
Finland	0	0	10
France	0	0	10
Germany	0	0	10
Greece	0	0	10
Hungary	0	0	10
Iceland	0	0	10
Ireland	0	0	10
Italy	0	0	10
Japan	3	4	5
Korea South	0	1	8
Luxembourg	0	0	10
Mexico	0	0	10
Netherlands	0	0	10
New Zealand	0	0	10
Norway	0	0	10
Poland	0	0	10
Portugal	0	0	10
Slovakia	0	0	10
Slovenia	0	0	10
Spain	0	0	10

TABLE 3.12   *Number of death sentences and executions, oecd countries, 2015.* (cont.)

Country	Reported executions	Death sentences and executions	Point[a]
Sweden	0	0	10
Switzerland	0	0	10
Turkey	0	0	10
United Kingdom	0	0	10
United States	28	80	0

a Death Sentences and Executions 0 = 10 points, 1–10 = 5 points, more than 10 = 0 points.
Source: 2015 Global Report Death Sentences and Executions 2015, Amnesty International April 2016.

And fully consistent with the expectations, of ten or so countries with the lowest imprisonment rates most of them are mostly classified as liberal, secular and universalistic democracies such as Austria (98), Denmark (73), Finland (58), France (98), Germany (79), Iceland (47), the Netherlands (82), Norway (72), Sweden (67), and Switzerland (82), alongside some of their intermediate counterparts like Ireland (88), Japan (51), and Slovenia (66), and only one of their opposites (South Korea 99).

Conversely and mostly confirming the expectations, ten countries with the highest imprisonment rates are largely classified as anti-liberal, anti-secular and exclusionary bogus 'democracies' such as, first and foremost, the conservative governance or region of the US (716), followed by Poland (217), Mexico (210), and Turkey (179). They are joined with intermediate political systems, including Chile (266), Hungary (186), Estonia (238), Slovakia (187) and the UK (148), and with only one country not belonging to these two categories, New Zealand (192). In particular, the US imprisonment rate is by far the highest among these and all societies,[25] almost three times higher than the second overall, Chile and five times that of the next Western country, the UK. The above indicates the unrivaled magnitude of penal repression and Draconian intensity of punishment in the conservative pole of America compared to any other country in the West and beyond. This is especially dramatic when taking into account that the vast majority of those imprisoned in 'conservative America' are non-violent moral offenders like drug users, so sinners as prisoners of

25   Moreover, as the Economist (10/13/2016) commented that 'America, with less than 5% of the world's population, accounts for almost 25% of the world's prisoners.'

ethical conscience, as distinct from violent criminals, and even many (after-the fact proven) innocent persons incarcerated especially for false sexual allegations, as sacrifices to the enduring ghost of Weber's moralistic 'unexampled tyranny of Puritanism.'

Also, fulfilling the expectations, liberal, secular and universalistic democracies invariably do not resort to death sentences and executions as the ultimate, irreversible form of penal compulsion and Draconian punishment, while the only mixed political regime that does so being Japan. Alternatively, anti-liberal, anti-secular and exclusionary democracies tend to do so more. This is epitomized by 'conservative America' as the outlier in death sentences and executions in the Western world and even the leader in this respect among all OECD countries, followed by South Korea, thus largely confirming the expectations, while Poland and Turkey as well as perhaps Greece not doing so mostly because of the European Union's death-penalty prohibition.

For example, the conservative part of the US, above all the South, accounts for all (39) reported executions and (80) combined death sentences and executions within the Western world, if not counting Asian countries like Japan and South Korea (Table 3.13).

TABLE 3.13 *World press freedom indexes, OECD countries, 2014.*

Rank	Country	Index	Point[a]
1	Finland	8.59	9
2	Netherlands	8.76	9
3	Norway	8.79	9
4	Denmark	8.89	9
5	New Zealand	10.01	9
7	Switzerland	11.76	8
8	Sweden	12.33	8
9	Ireland	12.40	8
11	Austria	13.18	8
12	Slovakia	13.26	8
13	Belgium	14.18	8
14	Estonia	14.31	8
15	Luxembourg	14.43	8
16	Germany	14.80	8
18	Canada	15.26	8
19	Iceland	15.30	8
21	Czech Republic	16.66	7

TABLE 3.13 *World press freedom indexes, oecd countries, 2014.* (cont.)

Rank	Country	Index	Point[a]
23	Portugal	17.27	7
25	Australia	17.84	7
31	Chile	19.23	7
34	Spain	19.92	7
38	United Kingdom	21.70	6
40	Slovenia	22.26	6
41	United States	22.49	6
45	France	23.83	6
47	Poland	23.89	6
67	Hungary	28.17	5
70	Korea	28.58	5
72	Japan	28.67	5
77	Italy	28.93	5
89	Greece	30.35	5
149	Mexico	49.33	1
151	Turkey	50.76	0

a Index 0–5 = 10 points, index 6–10 = 9 points, index 11–15 = 8 points, index 16–20 = 7 points, index 21–25 = 6 points, index 26–30 = 5 points, index 31–35 = 4 points, index 36–40 = 3 points, index 41–45 = 2 points, index 46–50 = 1 point, 51 and more = 0 points.
Source: 2016 World Press Freedom Index, Reporters without Borders.

The above indicates lethal Puritan-rooted unparalleled penal coercion and repression and Draconian cruelty and primeval vengeance justified by the Biblical 'eye for eye' retribution in the 'Bible Belt.' Moreover, 'conservative America' ranks the fifth in executions in the entire world, being surpassed in this regard only by dictatorships and theocracies such as China, Iran, Saudi Arabia, and Iraq, and in the company of others like Yemen, Pakistan, Sudan, North Korea, etc., which seemingly shows that it is closer to these theocratic and other undemocratic regimes than to Western liberal-secular democracies.

Evidently, true, liberal-secular democracies such as Western Europe, Canada, etc. as a whole do not execute, just as imprison dramatically less, while ersatz, anti-liberal and anti-secular 'democracies' do on a mass scale, as shown by China, Iran, North Korea, Saudi Arabia, etc., or persistently and unapologetically driven by religious fanaticism and cruelty, as witnessed in 'evangelical America.'

Effective Freedom of Opinion and Dissent

The specific source and ground for estimating or approximating the effective freedom and right of opinion and dissent are the comparative indexes of press freedoms taken as the indicator or proxy in this respect in Western and related societies, as well as some observations about the absence or presence of censorship.[26] In turn, the effective freedom of collective organization or group association and opposition, while not quantitatively estimated because of the lack of similar indexes, is implied in respective studies, including those of political extremism or radicalism threatening democracy and political liberties and rights in these societies.[27]

---

26   Mulligan et al. (2004, p. 65) suggest that 'press censorship, prohibition of various public gatherings and other suppression of civil liberties can be used to block entry and/or allow the political leader to gain a public support advantage over the competition.' In turn, they find that 'richer and democratic countries have more civil liberties.' (Mulligan et al. 2004, p. 65).

27   Banerjee and Rohini (2001, p. 189) register that 'many recent writers on the nature of the public discourse in America have complained about the lack of a moderate voice on many important and politically charged issues-whatever little debate one sees seems to be dominated by ideological extremists.' Specifically, Brooks and Manza (2013, p. 740) observe that 'on the eve of the (Great Recession), a common expectation among many social scientists and political commentators was that an economic calamity of this magnitude would stimulate greater support for public provision and government regulation of the economy. (Yet) between 2008 and 2010, Americans tended to move away from support for government responsibility for addressing social problems. What specific mechanisms account for apparent departures from economic rationality in the current era?' They identify conservative 'ideological extremism' or 'partisanship' in the US as the 'key' in that 'strong Democratic identifiers, for instance, moved toward slightly higher levels of support for government responsibility, and strong Republican identifiers moved much faster in the opposite direction (i.e.) individuals who more strongly identified with the Republican Party moved away from government faster than Democratic Party identifiers moved toward government.' Baldassarri and Bearman (2007, p. 787) note that in American conservatism, a 'soft ideological realignment of the party elite, initiated under Reagan as a consequence of his economic and social programs, was radically accelerated by a new cohort of strongly conservative Republicans from the South who replaced the moderate wing of the Republican Party,' thus by Southern extremists. Also, Hicks (2006, p. 505) comments that 'a large Southern impact on the Republican's Congressional ascendance of the past half century is broadly apparent (and) a white, Southern evangelical impact in particular' typically in the direction of political and economic extremism in the form of religious and market fundamentalism. Similarly, Fischer and Mattson (2009, p. 438) suggest that the 'most sizeable and oft-noted shift toward ideology-party consistency—and thus toward partisan polarization—was the defection of Southern whites to the Republican

Global Press Freedoms

Taken as an indicator or approximation of the freedom and right of opinion and dissent, global press freedom's estimates are derived from its indexes calculated by professional associations (Table 3.14).

Largely consistent with the expectations, countries with the highest degrees of press freedoms (in inverse relation to their indexes) are as a rule those

TABLE 3.14   *Universalism and egalitarianism (collectivism) scores in 18 nations, 1953 to 1992.*

Nation	Collectivism score	Point[a]
Australia	−1.0	5
Austria	.83	8
Belgium	.23	7
Canada	−1.23	4
Denmark	1.17	9
Finland	.53	7
France	−.84	5
Germany	.06	7
Ireland	−.55	5
Italy	−.65	5
Japan	−.32	6
Netherlands	1.02	8
New Zealand	−.83	5
Norway	1.68	10
Sweden	1.51	9
Switzerland	.71	8
UK	−.76	5
USA	−1.62	3

a Score 1.6–2 = 10 points, score 1.1–1.5 = 9 points, score 0.6–1 = 8 points, score 0.1.-0.5 = 7 points, score -0.5–0 = 6 points, score -0.6—1 = 5 points, score -1.1–1.5 = 4 points, score -1.6–2 = 3 points. Collectivism: (1) corporatism, (2) consensus government, (3) years of leftist rule, (4) universalism in public benefits, (5) absence of violent political conflict. (750).
Source: Pampel (1998:755).

---

party as a result of the Democrats' embrace of the Civil Rights movement.' Generally, Baldassarri and Bearman (2008, p. 413) observe that 'exiting moderate Republican members of Congress were replaced by a new cohort of socially conservative Republicans' and in that sense more extreme members, as continued and even escalated with the formation of the 'Tea Party' during the 2010s.

classified as liberal, secular, and universalistic democracies, with secondary variations. For example, of twenty countries with the highest levels of press freedom, the vast majority are liberal, secular, and universalistic democracies, namely Finland, the Netherlands, Norway, Luxembourg, Denmark, New Zealand, Iceland, Sweden, Austria, Switzerland, Germany, Canada, Belgium, and Australia, alongside mixed cases like Czech Republic, Estonia, Ireland, Portugal, and Slovakia, and only one opposite case, Poland. Conversely, among those with the lowest degree of press freedom are anti-liberal, anti-secular, and anti-universalistic 'democracies' such as Mexico, South Korea, Turkey, and the conservative pole of the US, along with intermediate cases like Chile, Greece, Hungary, Italy, Japan, Slovenia, Spain, and the UK, and only one instance classified in the first category, France.

With such rare exceptions among them, liberal, secular, and universalistic democracies as a whole tend to exhibit a higher level of press freedom than do either their opposites or mixed counterparts, including the conservative pole of the US and the UK. Thus, virtually all European and other countries (except for one) classified into this category of political systems have higher degrees of press freedom than those of conservative America and the UK belonging to the other two categories in the present classification. Alternatively, the UK and the US are ranked 21st and 22nd respectively in terms of press freedom among 33 OECD countries, indicating that only 11 or 12 among these are placed lower in this ranking. Notably, ten countries from the first category display degrees of press freedom between three times, namely Finland, the Netherlands, Norway, Luxembourg and twice or so, including Denmark, New Zealand, Iceland, Sweden, Austria, Switzerland, higher than those of the UK and especially the US, thus contradicting the claims that the two have the freest -and even the only free mass media in the Western and entire world.

Effective Universalism, Equality, and Justice of Government Goods and Sanctions

Universalism and Egalitarianism in Public Goods

These estimates are derived from the indexes of political universalism and by implication equality and justice ('collectivism scores'), including universalism in public goods like government benefits, corporate capital-labor coordination, consensus governance, and non-violence, for most Western democracies (Table 3.15).

Thus, countries with the highest and positive indexes of political universalism and thus egalitarianism are Scandinavian and other European welfare

TABLE 3.15 *Global peace index, OECD countries, 2015.*

Rank	Country	Score	Points[a]
1	Iceland	1.148	10
2	Denmark	1.150	10
3	Austria	1.198	10
4	New Zealand	1.221	10
5	Switzerland	1.275	9
6	Finland	1.277	9
7	Canada	1.287	9
8	Japan	1.322	8
9	Australia	1.329	8
10	Czech Republic	1.341	8
11	Portugal	1.344	8
12	Ireland	1.354	7
13	Sweden	1.360	7
14	Belgium	1.368	7
15	Slovenia	1.378	7
16	Germany	1.379	7
17	Norway	1.393	7
18	Poland	1.430	7
19	Netherlands	1.432	7
20	Spain	1.451	7
21	Hungary	1.463	7
22	Slovakia	1.478	7
23	Chile	1.563	6
24	Italy	1.669	6
25	Estonia	1.677	6
26	United Kingdom	1.685	6
27	South Korea	1.701	6
28	France	1.742	6
29	Greece	1.878	5
30	United States	2.038	4
31	Turkey	2.363	2
32	Mexico	2.530	1

a Score 1–1 = 10 points, Score 1.2–1.3 = 8 points, Score 1.4–1.5 = 7 points, Score 1.6–1.7 = 6 points, Score 1.8–1.9 = 5 points, Score 2.0–2.1 = 4 points, Score 2.2–2.3 = 3 points, Score 2.4–2.5 = 2 points, Score higher than 2.5 = 1 point.

Source: Institute for Economics and Peace 2015.

states, for example, Norway (1.68), Sweden (1.51), Denmark (1.17), Holland (1.02) Austria (0.83), Finland (0.53), Switzerland (0.71), Belgium (0.23), and Germany (0.06). Since all these states are presently classified as universalistic, liberal and secular democracies, such indexes confirm the expectations that the latter as a rule tend to have a higher level of the political universalism and equality in the provision of public goods and justice in government sanctions than do their opposites and mixed counterparts, allowing for secondary variations.

In turn, the lowest and negative indexes of political universalism charac-terize so-called Anglo-Saxon countries such as the US (-1.62), Canada (-1.23), Australia (-1.0), New Zealand (-.83), the UK (-.76), along with France (-.84), Italy (-.65), Ireland (-.55), and Japan (-.32). Since these countries are variously clas-sified into all the three types of political systems, such scores seemingly do not support fully the expectations, but they are not as unexpected as it seems. Thus, 'Anglo-Saxon' countries, including even those such as Canada, Australia, and New Zealand, classified as universalistic, liberal and secular democracies typically are not observed and considered to be as 'universalistic' as their Euro-pean versions, especially Scandinavian and related welfare states, with respect to the provision of public goods. This holds true, with some qualifications, of Japan and Italy in relation to Northern European welfare states. Consequently, the lower indexes of political universalism of the Anglo-Saxon as compared with the European sub-group of universalistic, liberal and secular democracies is not totally surprising, but predictable, as are neither those of Japan and Italy as mixed political systems. To that extent, the only truly unexpected case or outlier within this category of political systems remains France whose index of political universalism is expected to be higher by virtue of being classified into universalistic, liberal and secular democracies, but still being so than that of the US, for example.

In turn, the low or rather negative political universalism indexes of the US, the UK and Ireland are completely consistent with the expectations. This is be-cause the first, namely its prevailing conservative, theocentric and exclusion-ary governance, ideology or region, is classified into exclusionary, anti-liberal and anti-secular 'democracies' and the last two into mixed political systems. In particular, the conservative US polity is estimated to have by far the lowest index of political universalism and egalitarianism among 18 Western societies, which fully confirms the negative expectations about exclusionary, anti-liberal and anti-secular spurious 'democracies.' Overall, with some exceptions such as the Anglo-Saxon sub-group and France, universalistic, liberal and secular democracies, notably Scandinavian and other European welfare states, as a whole exhibit a higher level of political universalism and egalitarianism, par-ticularly of universal public goods, than do their opposites epitomized by the

US conservative political system or region, above all the exclusionary, anti-liberal, anti-welfare Southern states, and their mixed counterparts exemplified by that of the UK.

Justice of Government Sanctions

Since government negative sanctions especially incorporate imprisonment and the death penalty, the estimates of the equality and justice of such sanctions are implied in those of these punitive measures in Western and other societies,[28] such as data on prisoners and executions as elements on the 'political terror scale' and indicators of penal repression[29] considered earlier. As noted, universalistic, liberal and secular democracies such as Scandinavian and other Western European countries overall show the lowest level of penal repression in the sense of the smallest numbers of prisoners and the lowest prisoner rate among developed societies. Conversely, as also seen, the conservative part of the US has by far the greatest numbers of prisoners and the highest prisoner rate and to that extent the most intense level of penal repression[30] among Western and other societies within OECD, followed by Chile and Mexico as the distant second and third, all these countries being classified in anti-liberal or intermediate political systems.

---

28   Skrentny (2006, p. 229) registers that modern states 'engage in trade-offs when they lower welfare spending, as declines in this area are associated with increases in imprisonment rates. In addition, right-party rule is associated with higher imprisonment rates, an effect that trumps labor market factors.' In particular, Skrentny (2006, p. 229) refers to the 'evidence of American exceptionalism, as these political effects are stronger in the United States than elsewhere. The dispersed nature of policymaking, the local control of police, and the politicization of the judiciary and prosecutorial state functions (judges and prosecutors are often elected) make the American polity vulnerable to moral panics.' In short, Skrentny (2006, p. 229) notes 'the great rise in incarceration rates and the larger, reactionary culture of control in the United States and the United Kingdom.' Skrentny (2006, p. 237) concludes that the 'growing (US) state role in punitive criminal law illuminate(s) a chilling development with great political implications' of mostly non-democratic character.

29   The source is Prison Studies http://www.prisonstudies.org. In addition, Mulligan et al. (2004, p. 63) find that 'nondemocracies are much more likely to use the death penalty' as well as that 'large and British legal origin countries are more likely to have the death penalty,' 'British' apparently expressing the legacy of common master-servant law as well as the Draconian 'ghost' of Puritanism. Overall, they report that 'authoritarian regimes are more likely to torture, execute, regulate religion, censor the press and spend a lot of money on the military' (Mulligan et al. 2004, p. 73).

30   Other sources on crime and punishment in the US are https://www.hrw.org and http://www.sentencingproject.org.

In addition to incarceration rates, the equality and justice of government negative sanctions can be estimated or approximated by taking account of the use of the death penalty, or alternatively its abolition in Western and other societies. As known, all universalistic, liberal and secular democracies—just as European societies, including theocentric Poland and Islamic-ruled Turkey under the impetus of the first by belonging or aspiring to the European Union—have abolished the death penalty. In turn, the only Western country applying capital punishment remains the US in its conservative governance (the Federal government under conservatism) and regions (Southern and related states) conducting by far the highest number of executions and death sentences followed by Japan and South Korea as mixed systems with considerably smaller numbers of these acts.

A more general source and ground for estimating or approximating the equality and justice of government negative sanctions, as of effective democratic rule, pertains to the rankings on the 'political terror scale' as the indicator of government violent repression and coercion. As seen, Scandinavia and Western Europe as a whole displays a lower index of political repression than do all other societies, thus fully confirming the expectations in this respect about liberal, secular and universalistic democracy into which the former is classified. Conversely, polities like the conservative governance or region of the US and the UK exhibit higher indexes of political repression, with the first's index on the 'political terror scale' even being the highest among all Western and other societies. This is also consistent with the expectations about the opposite kind of 'democracy' and mixed political systems into which the two are classified respectively.

Peace in the Polity and Pacifism

Peace Estimates
The comparative estimates of peace are derived from the 2015 Global Peace Index, as computed by Institute for Economics and Peace (Table 3.16).

Thus, out of the ten highest ranked countries on this index eight—Iceland, Denmark, Austria, New Zealand, Switzerland, Finland, Canada, and Australia—are classified into liberal, secular, and universalistic democracy, none as its opposite, and only two, Czech Republic and Japan as a mixed political system. This fulfills the expectations that the first are essentially peaceful both internally within the polity and externally in relation to other states. In particular, two countries with the highest ranks are Scandinavian societies like Iceland and Denmark, which reaffirms that such a type of democracy tends to be most peaceful and least violent.

Conversely, the ten lowest ranked countries on the peace index include almost all of those (except for one) classified as illiberal 'democracies'—Mexico,
South Korea, Turkey, and the conservative US—along with others belonging to
mixed systems such as Chile, Estonia, Greece, Italy, and the UK, and only one
to liberal democracy, France. This confirms the expectations that the first are
basically non-peaceful and violent internally or externally or both. Notably,

TABLE 3.16 *Military spending as percentage of GDP, OECD countries, 2015.*

Country	Percentage	Point[a]
Australia	1.9	6
Austria	0.7	9
Belgium	0.9	9
Canada	1.0	8
Czech Republic	1.0	8
Chile	1.9	6
Denmark	1.2	7
Estonia	2.0	5
Finland	1.3	7
France	2.1	5
Germany	1.2	7
Greece	2.6	4
Hungary	0.8	9
Iceland	0.1	10
Ireland	0.4	9
Italy	1.3	7
Japan	1.0	8
Korea, South	2.6	4
Luxembourg	0.5	9
Mexico	0.7	9
Netherlands	1.2	7
New Zealand	1.2	7
Norway	1.5	7
Poland	2.2	5
Portugal	1.9	6
Slovak Republic	1.1	8
Slovenia	1.0	8
Spain	1.2	7

Country	Percentage	Point[a]
Sweden	1.1	8
Switzerland	0.7	9
Turkey	2.1	5
United Kingdom	2.0	5
United States	3.3	2

a Percentage 0–0.3 = 10 points, percent 0.4–0.7 = 9 points, percent 0.8–1.1 = 8 points, percent 1.2–1.5 = 7 points, percent 1.6–1.9 = 6 points, percent 2.0–2.3 = 5 points, percent 2.4–2.7 = 4 points, percent 2.8- 3.1 = 3 points, percent 3.2–3.5 = 2 points, percent 3.6–3.9 = 1 points, percent 4 and higher = 0 points.
Source: Stockholm International Peace Research Institute http://www.sipri.org.

the three countries ranked the lowest are Mexico (32), Turkey (31), and the US (30) in conservative governance or regions. This thus strongly confirms the expectations that anti-liberal, anti-secular or theocentric and anti-universalistic political systems tend to be least peaceful and most violent either within the polity or in relation to other states. In particular, among Western societies the society with the lowest rank on the Global Peace Index is 'conservative America' in political or regional terms, with only non-Western states like Mexico and Turkey being ranked lower overall within OECD.

Some other 'global peace' indexes (such as that computed by the *Economist*) reveal an essentially identical pattern. Thus, liberal, secular universalistic democracies such as those in Scandinavia and beyond have higher 'global peace' indexes than other countries,[31] with, for example, Norway, New Zealand, and Denmark being ranked number 1, 2 and 3 respectively, which completely confirms the expectations. Conversely, opposite 'democracies' have lower 'global

---

31   *The Economist* reports that the global peace index 'takes note of internal factors—crime rates, prison population, trust between citizens—and external ones, like relations with neighbours, arms sales, foreign troop deployments. Norway's top place reflects its calm domestic atmosphere and good relations with nearby states. In the case of Israel (119th), high military spending, a huge army and unresolved local conflicts are deemed to outweigh its low level of ordinary crime. Canada comes eighth; its American neighbour a dismal 96th, strangely just above Iran. America, at a lowly 96th position (only one above Iran), is dragged down by factors such as its involvement in Iraq and heavy military spending' (http://www.economist.com).

peace' indexes, with, for example, 'conservative America' described as ranking 'dismal' 96 (and 'only one above Iran') among all countries, thus fully confirming the expectations.

Pacifism versus Militarism Estimates

The comparative estimates of pacifism or militarism as the obverse and opposite, simply anti-pacifism, are derived from the level of military spending as a percentage of GNP (Table 3.17).

Military spending is taken as, if it is comparatively low or decreasing, either a pacifist, peace-promoting or, if it is high or increasing, a militaristic, anti-pacifist and ultimately war indicator, predictor or proxy. Thus, countries classified as liberal, secular and universalistic democracies[32] as a whole show the lower level of military spending and to that extent of militarism, anti-pacifism and war, and alternatively the higher degree of peace, peaceful conflict resolution or pacifism in relation to other societies, than do their opposites. This is hence fully consistent with the predictions in this respect, with some rare exceptions. For example, countries with the lowest military spending as a percentage of national income (lower than or around 1 percent) and thus the most pacifistic include liberal, secular and universalistic democracies Austria (0.8), Belgium (1.1), Iceland (0.1), Luxembourg (0.6), New Zealand (1.1), Sweden (1.2), and Switzerland (0.8), along with their mixed counterparts Czech Republic (1.1), Hungary (0.8), Ireland (0.6), Japan (1.0), Slovakia (1.1), Slovenia (1.2), and Spain (0.9), and only one opposite case, Mexico (0.6). In turn, the sole major exception or outlier in these terms among the countries classified as such democracies appears to be France, but its military expenditure as a percentage of GNP (2.3) is almost half of that of the US (4.2), for example, which hence generally supports the expectations.

By stark contrast, those countries classified as anti-liberal, anti-secular, and anti-universalistic 'democracies' display a significantly higher level of military spending as a percentage of national income and thus militarism, anti-pacifism and war, with minor variations. Countries with the highest military expenditure as a percentage of national income (around and higher than

---

32   Mulligan et al. (2004, p. 57) find that 'democracies (spend) about 3 percentage points of GDP less (than non-democracies) on the military (which) implies that democracies are spending somewhat more on nonmilitary government consumption.' Alternatively, they suggest the reason 'why nondemocracies might be more prone to international conflict' is that they 'spend a couple of percentage points more of their GDP on the military,' thus inferring 'some connection between democracy and peaceful foreign policy, at least vis-a-vis other democratic countries.' (Mulligan et al. 2004, p. 65).

2 percent) and thus the most militaristic or anti-pacifistic encompass all of those (except for Mexico) classified as such 'democracies,' for example, the US in conservative governance (the Federal legislature or administration under conservatism), South Korea (2.8), Turkey (2.3), Poland (1.9), joined with mixed systems like Greece (2.6), the UK (2.5), and Chile (2.0), plus France as the only case not classified into these two categories. In particular, the US in conservative governance and the UK rank first and second in military spending and to that extent militarism and anti-pacifism—and as a consequence imperialism and 'imperial wars'—among advanced Western democracies, thus excluding Greece and South Korea. Moreover, the US conservative-reproduced military-industrial complex accounts for almost half of world military expenditure—i.e., about ten times more than the population share—and in that sense global militarism, anti-pacifism, imperialism and effective or potential war, other things equal.[33]

The above cases highlight the common observation or prediction that the expanded military-industrial complex involving exorbitant 'defense spending' exerts an actually or potentially negative and eventually destructive effect on democracy and freedom overall in these and other countries from the 1950s to these days. This is because the higher level of military expenditure or a stronger military-industrial complex predicts or expresses the equivalent degree of nationalism, militarism, potential imperialism, and the likelihood of offensive wars—i.e., zero or minimal pacifism and peace—and consequently the lower or decreasing index of democracy and liberty. As well-known, this is what even a US prominent military figure-become President admonished and predicted at the height of the Cold War during the 1950s.

In sum, relatively high or growing military expenditure and generally a strong military-industrial complex indicates a corresponding degree of (in factor-analytic terms, 'loads on') militarism and indirectly imperialism, bellicosity, the likelihood of offensive war, and aggressive nationalism, and thus, other thing equal, subverts or threatens democracy and political freedom both within society and in other societies. This is exemplified by the conservative part of the US and to some extent the UK among Western societies, plus China, Russia, and Islamic countries in the non-Western world. The reverse holds true of a comparatively low or diminishing military expenditure, and a weak military-industrial complex, by indicating manifest or latent pacifism and

---

33   Steinmetz (2005) points to the 'new American imperialism' during the early 2000s and Abbot (2005) to its 'imperial wars.' Acemoglu and Yared (2010, p. 83) observe that 'nationalism and militarism are strong around the world, in countries ranging from the United States to China, Russia, and India.'

peaceful inter-state conflict revolution, thus, with some qualifications, enhancing democracy and freedom at home and abroad. This is witnessed in most of Western Europe, in particular least Scandinavia (plus Costa Rica, for example, among Latin American countries). Overall, the above sources demonstrate that liberal, secular, and universalistic democracies as a rule have the highest index of peace and in that sense pacifism, and the lowest military expenditure and thus militarism, potential imperialism, bellicosity, the likelihood of offensive war, and aggressive nationalism, while their antitheses being characterized with an opposite pattern. This provides strong evidence for a positive interconnection and mutual reinforcement of democracy and freedom with peace or pacifism, low military spending, a small military-industrial complex and weak militarism, and no imperialism and offensive wars, just as conversely, which thus confirms classical sociological and other predictions in this respect.

Militarism versus Democracy—The Persistent 'Janus Face of the West'?

At the end a disclaimer or qualification and even warning may be needed in the light—or rather darkness—of the serious and potentially grave nature and effects of militarism as indicated or approximated by the level of military spending. Generally, militarism with its complements and reciprocal intensifiers of aggressive nationalism, imperialism or neo-colonialism, and offensive wars historically has been and remains the darkest and most lethal side of what often appears as the Janus-face, two faces of modern Western society.[34] It does so by threatening and subverting democracy and political and other freedoms both in Western societies and those that are victims or targets of their militarism, imperialism, and aggressive wars—in flagrant violation of the UN prohibition of such wars—such as non-Western countries, for example, Latin America, Asia, and Africa during the 1950–70s, the former Yugoslavia, Iraq, and others more recently.

Hence, while the complex of liberalism, secularism, universalism, egalitarianism, and rationalism creates and sustains democracy and its political and civil liberties and rights within Western societies, the anti-liberal compound of nationalism, militarism, imperialism, neo-colonialism, and offensive war destroys or perverts and undermines these ingredients of a free society both in these and non-Western attacked or targeted countries. In short, what the first complex gives in democracy and liberty, the second compound takes away both in the West and beyond. Evidently, the 'Janus-faced' West has not or could

---

34   As noted, in 1972 the French sociologist Duverger wrote a book titled *Janus: The Two Faces of the West*.

not have 'forgotten' or abandoned yet completely its 'good old' nationalist, militarist, imperialist, colonial, bellicose, and warlike instincts, ways, and means, as indicated by the persistence and expansion of NATO after the demise of its Cold War enemy and reason for its existence. This is recently manifested in its various illegal wars (against Yugoslavia, Iraq, Libya, etc.)—by the standard of international law such as the above UN prohibition of offensive war—defining or approximating inter-state terror. These habits and acts contradict the West's liberal, secular, universalistic, and rationalistic face, and pervert democracy and modern free society both in Western countries and those they attack or target to impose their 'superior' interests, values and way of life. This contradicts the liberal principle of individual and collective autonomy, including the 'live and let live' existential minimum of coexistence between both individuals and collectivities, including nations or states.

Ultimately, the resolution of the internal contradiction between the bright face of the West in the form of Enlightenment-based lightness of liberalism, secularism, universalism, and rationalism and its dark side in the way of aggressive nationalism, militarism, imperialism, neo-colonialism, and offensive wars determines and predicts the condition of democracy and political liberty and generally modern free society both in Western and non-Western settings. When/if the first face prevails or reasserts and the second weakens or recedes, as in parts of Western Europe—in spite of NATO and its continuing expansion and growing bellicosity and near-suicidal tendencies[35] manifesting the absolute corruption of absolute military power—this does and will reaffirm, promote, and sustain democracy and political liberty and modern free society in both of these settings. Conversely, when/if the Western liberal face is continuously contradicted and overwhelmed—as during the Cold War, the aggressive wars against Vietnam, Yugoslavia, Iraq, etc.—by its dark militarist, imperialist, and warlike side, the effect is and will be adverse and ultimately destructive at home and beyond.

---

35   NATO manifests near-suicidal tendencies in that since the dissolution of the Warsaw Pact it, acts—as by building 'missile shields,' preparing for 'star wars,' expanding into Eastern Europe and parts of the former Soviet Union—as if it would win a total nuclear war against its defined 'enemy,' thus conceivably causing mutually assured destruction, so a truly MAD outcome (Habermas 2001; Schelling 2006). For example, most American conservative politicians since Goldwater, Reagan, and other 'Cold Warriors' through their today's proxies seem convinced that the US military and NATO overall could easily be a 'winner takes all' in a nuclear or other war against 'enemies' like Russia and China, thus denying or overlooking the likelihood of MAD, which appears as a textbook definition of collective suicidal or at least irresponsible and risky behavior.

In particular, the relationship between the Western face of latent pacifism or peaceful inter-state conflict resolution and its dark side of a bellicose military-industrial complex, including exorbitant, threatening military spending of societal material and human resources, as in the conservative US and the UK, determines and predicts the state and trend of democracy and political and civil liberty and modern free society overall in Western and non-Western counties. More specifically, so long as such pacifism continues to be negated and overwhelmed by a warlike military-industrial complex and virtually unlimited military spending, as in the US in conservative governance, this does and will pose a grave threat to democracy and freedom in both societies, as even the American President admonished half a century ago. If this admonition is correct, the Western military-industrial complex may mutate in the lethal weapon destroying or subverting democracy and freedom in the West itself, just as in its victims or targets, rather than obliterating the 'enemy,' and in that sense become virtually suicidal from the stance of liberalism and rationalism as the principle of liberty and reason in society and the sole basis and predictor of modern free society.

In short, the aforesaid cautions against totally idealizing the West and its political system insofar as it is 'Janus-faced,' with 'two faces' contradicting and opposing each other. The one involves the dark side of aggressive nationalism, militarism, imperialism, neo-colonialism, and offensive wars,[36] including a military-industrial complex and extravagant military spending, negating and neutralizing, as non-Western observers object and emphasize, its Enlightenment lightness of liberalism, secularism, universalism rationalism, and pacifism, as especially witnessed during the Cold War. In contrast to non-Western cynicism or skepticism toward the West, however, this also suggests against underestimating or downplaying its Enlightenment liberal, secular, universalistic, rationalistic, and pacifist legacy and 'face' and the latter's capacity to ultimately override or counterbalance the nationalistic, militarist, imperialist, colonial, and warlike past, 'instinct,' and side, and thus to

---

36   However, Hess and Orphanides (2001, p. 780) propose that the classical Kantian 'hypothesis that a perpetual peace would necessarily prevail only if all states were democratic is false, as is the hypothesis that a more democratic world would necessarily be more peaceful.' In their view, this is because of the 'relative propensity for democratic countries to generate diversionary wars and the frequency with which opportunities for appropriative war are exploited by democratic and nondemocratic leaders' (Hess and Orphanides 2001, p. 804). Prima facie, the US/NATO 1999 attack on Yugoslavia qualifies as a case of 'diversionary wars' in light of the American President's impeachment in the late 1990s and the 2003 US/UK invasion of Iraq as an instance of 'appropriative (oil) war.'

sustain democracy and freedom, as growingly observed in Western Europe, above all Scandinavia.

While this probably (and hopefully) holds true in the long run, some persistent, salient, and threatening deviations from this relatively pacifist trend or the classical ideal of pacifism threaten to reverse it, as within NATO recklessly expanding beyond its original and natural boundaries and acting increasingly bellicose and irrational to the suicidal no-return point of MAD (mutually assured destruction). These anti-pacifist aberrations primarily include the conservative US and UK government continuing to have the first and second highest military expenditure and thus display the most severe degree of militarism, imperialism, and the proclivity for what Spencer ironically ruled out as 'offensive wars,' driven by aggressive nationalism mixed with militant religion, among Western societies.

Appendix 3.1 Qualitative Considerations of Political Freedoms

Freedom, Fairness, and Inclusiveness of Elections
In general, observations suggest that among Western and related societies the highest degree of freedom and fairness of elections is demonstrated, first and foremost, by liberal, secular and universalistic democracies in Western/ Northern Europe and beyond, including Australia, Canada, and New Zealand. These democracies are observed to invariably hold the freest, fairest, the most inclusive, non-discriminatory elections among all contemporary societies, with virtually no serious contestations, complaints, and disputes—for example, by non-winning political candidates, parties or constituencies— concerning the degree of electoral freedom, fairness, inclusiveness, and non-discrimination. Alternatively, the lowest or decreasing degree of freedom and fairness of elections is manifested by non-liberal, non-secular theocentric, and non-universalistic 'democracies' in non-Western Europe like Turkey and elsewhere such as Mexico and the US in anti-liberal, anti-secular or hyper-religious[37] exclusionary governance and regions (the South, etc.), just as observed and expected.

These bogus 'democracies' tend to hold the least free, fair, and inclusive elections among Western and related societies, and instead approach or resemble more Third-World countries like theocracies, kleptocracies, plutocracies,

---

37   Mueller (2009, p. x) emphasizes the 'dangers traditionalism (conservatism) and religion pose for liberal democracy.'

oligarchies, dynasties, 'banana republics,'[38] etc. They are constantly plagued with various and continuing major contestations of and complaints about electoral un-freedom, un-fairness, exclusion or discrimination by harmed persons and groups. This is dramatically epitomized by the 2000 US Presidential (un) Election[39] decided by an extra-democratic judicial decision as an exemplar of an irregular or dubious political outcome, along with the House of Representatives since 2010, the Senate from 2014 and the South through both undemocratic voter selection and suppression, various irregularities in Turkey's elections during Islamic government, etc. In turn, intermediate, mixed political systems feature a medium degree of freedom and fairness of elections, although most of them appear closer in this respect to liberal, secular and universalistic democracies than to their opposites. They are not, however, fully equal to liberal, secular and universalistic democracies because of some limitations on electoral freedom and fairness induced by a variety of factors, including majority-group nationalism (Greece, Hungary, Estonia, Japan, Slovenia, and Spain), religious intrusion even if tempered or contested (Chile, Ireland), aristocratic vestiges, as embodied in the House of Lords in the UK, and so on.

More specifically, the estimates of the freedom and fairness of elections are grounded in some comparative reports on these matters for modern Western and related democracies,[40] for example, the 2010 International IDEA Handbook of Electoral Justice. This report cites selected countries as apparently failing short or casting doubt on 'electoral justice' due to 'some critical rulings by electoral justice systems,' thus implying that most of other democracies succeed to

---

38   In passing, recurring government closures, 'shutdowns' mostly caused by hardline conservatives in US Congress (e.g., that in 2013 deliberately provoked by what is widely perceived as a Texas conservative extremist called because of such destructive or Machiavellian actions by some of his party colleges 'Lucifer in the flesh' and the like), and generally the constant drama, mixing elements of fiscal tragedy or madness and grotesque, about the federal budget qualify as Third-World or 'banana-republics' practices unknown or unparalleled in most Western democracies.

39   The International IDEA Handbook on Electoral Justice (2010, p. 58) reports that 'some stable and mature democracies with fewer preventive measures and a simple and straightforward regime for bringing challenges and assigning liabilities have seen practically no electoral disputes, for example, the Scandinavian countries where the political culture abhors excessive regulation. Others have faced disputes arising from very close election results but, despite the tensions and difficulties at a particular point in time, have been able to overcome the crisis – the most notable recent case being the 2000 presidential election in the United States.'

40   For example, see Electoral Justice: The International IDEA Handbook 2010.

fulfill this condition of democracy. Among the cited countries is included the US because of the Supreme Court 2000 'final suspension of manual recount of votes' in Florida. The others are Spain for the Constitutional Court declaring that 'certain political parties illegal due to possible ties with terrorism' in 2003, the UK in light of the 2005 European Court of Human Rights judgment that the prohibition of prisoner voting in parliamentary and local elections was 'in violation of the European Convention on Human Rights,' Mexico owing to the Electoral Court ordering 'recount of votes' in the 2006 presidential election, Turkey due to the 2007 Constitutional Court 'annulment of the presidential election results,' and Germany in view of the 2008 Constitutional Court declaration that 'some provisions of the Federal Electoral Act' were unconstitutional (Table 3.17).

TABLE 3.17   *Electoral justice—Some critical rulings by electoral justice systems/decision ruling.*

United States 2000	Supreme court: Final suspension of manual recount of votes in some districts of the state of florida
Spain 2003	Constitutional Court: Declared certain political parties illegal due to possible ties with terrorism
United Kingdom 2005	European Court of Human Rights: General prohibition preventing persons serving prison sentences from voting in parliamentary and local elections in the UK was in violation of the European Convention on Human Rights
Mexico 2006	Electoral Court of the Judicial Branch of the Federation of Mexico: Recount of votes ordered in presidential election for more than half of the polling stations for which it was requested
Turkey 2007	Constitutional Court: Annulment of the presidential election results
Germany 2008	Constitutional Court: Declared some provisions of the Federal Electoral Act establishing the effect of 'negative voting weight' in the electoral system unconstitutional, obliging the legislature to formulate a new constitutional provision by June 2011 at the latest.

source: electoral justice: the international Idea handbook 2010, pp. 2 3. http://www.idea.int/.

The preceding provides grounds for assigning medium scores on this dimension of democracy to these countries[41] cited as offending the freedom and fairness of elections, although not minimum ones on the charitable assumption that such offenses are exceptional rather than regular in these Western and related societies. Conversely, it serves as the basis of imputation of the highest scores to countries absent from this list, applying a variation of Hobbes' principle of what is not prohibited is permitted, namely those not cited as offenders are presumed innocent of violations ('good' governments) and thus to respect the freedom and fairness of elections, although this is not an optimal method of estimation. At this juncture, the 'news' of 'critical rulings by electoral justice systems' is taken, all else equal, as the 'bad news' for 'electoral justice,' as exemplified by the cited government for violations, which, alongside the other countries cited, are consequently assigned lower scores than others.

Conversely, 'no news' of such 'critical rulings by electoral justice systems' is taken, other things equal, as the 'good news' for 'electoral justice,' as epitomized by the notable yet expected absence of most Western Europe, in particular Scandinavia, and other democracies, for example, Australia and Canada, from the citations list, which explains the highest scores for these non-cited countries. In turn, three out of the six countries cited for electoral offenses are presently classified as anti-liberal, anti-secular and anti-universalistic spurious 'democracies,' for example, Mexico, Turkey, and the US in conservative governance and regions, two as mixed political systems such as Spain and the UK, and only one in the category of liberal, secular and universalistic democracy like Germany. This is at least in part consistent with the expectations, as evidently the first political systems tend to offend this dimension of democracy more than do the second and especially the third, as precisely expected.

Freedom and Right of the Pursuit of Political Position

Quantitative estimates of the freedom, right, and opportunity to the pursuit and holding of political position or public office are not provided because of the lack of cross-national rankings and indexes on this element of democracy. Still, a qualitative estimation or approximation is perhaps possible by considering

---

41   Admittedly, one may object that Germany's, Mexico's and Turkey's Courts' decisions apparently fostered rather than undermined, as by those of the US and Spain's Courts and the UK government, 'electoral justice.' If so, then, the only the last three countries should have mixed estimates and medium scores on this dimension of democracy. Still, such estimates and scores are assigned to all the six countries because even in the first three cases such 'critical' judicial rulings expressed and tried to redress some prior lack or violation of 'electoral justice.'

common observations and relatively established patterns among Western and related societies. It thus takes into account observations and reports especially on the legal and effective discrimination against and suppression and exclusion of non-believers and related social groups in politics, especially government or public office, among contemporary societies, in particular Catholic Poland, Islamic Turkey, and the conservative half of the US.[42]

These observations indicate that liberal, secular and universalistic democracies such as Western and Northern European and related countries, particularly Scandinavia and Canada, feature the strongest and most encompassing freedom, right, and opportunity in this respect, thus fully confirming the expectations. These democracies endow with such freedom and right all prospective individuals or groups seeking state power or public office regardless of their religious beliefs or non-beliefs and political ideologies, notably including both believers and non-believers, with some variations. On this and other accounts, they are truly and solely universalistic, open, and competitive democracies among contemporary political systems. Simply, all individual and group aspirants for power or office 'may and need apply' no matter how 'godly' or 'godless,' ideologically 'proper' or 'improper,' 'patriotic' or 'unpatriotic' they are. In short, these democracies truly attain or greatly approach what Jefferson would call 'liberty and justice (and equality) for all' in the pursuit of or competition for and holding of political power and public office, thus realizing democratic ideals. In this sense, they can be denoted 'Jeffersonian'[43] and generally Enlightenment-based democracies implementing the Age of Reason ideals of universalism, egalitarianism, liberalism, secularism, and rationalism. In an ironic twist, Jefferson's America[44] does not appear among or perhaps has

---

42   The sources are http://freethoughtreport.com and http://americanhumanist.org.

43   Mueller (2009, p. 415) proposes that the 'intensity to which religious beliefs are incompatible with liberal democracy and more generally with rational thought depends on both the nature of these beliefs and the intensity to with which they are held. The religious beliefs of a Thomas Jefferson (are not).'

44   Mueller (2009, pp. ix-x) suggests that in particular 'the growing importance of religious extremism in the United States' (alongside South America and the Middle East) illustrates the 'dangers' of conservatism and religion to liberal democracy. In his view, as noted, the 'struggle' between liberalism ('progressivism') and religious-political conservatism ('traditionalism') 'has gone on for much of the US's history, and continues today at an intensity unmatched in other rich, developed countries' (Mueller 2009, p. 375). Mueller (2009, p. 403) notes that US 'religious extremists' such as white Southern and other evangelicals in the 2004 Presidential election 'gave Bush more than 16 million votes than they gave Kerry, more than 5 times the difference separating the candidates' and that the failures of the former's presidency 'reveal potential costs to a democracy from the bias that religion can

exited from them since his time indicating that its liberal, secular and universalistic face is weaker than the opposite.

Conversely, observations and studies suggest that the above freedom and right is the weakest and least encompassing in Catholic dominated Poland,[45] fervently nationalistic and theocratic Turkey under Islamic government, persistently authoritarian South Korea (similar to Singapore and Taiwan as also substantively dictatorships), and the conservative half of the US in anti-liberal, anti-secular, exclusionary governance such as Congress and most state governments since 2014 and regions like the South, etc. Recall that all these are classified as anti-liberal, anti-secular and anti-universalistic or mixed political systems, which confirms the expectation. Contrary to their opposites, these political systems permit this freedom and right only to certain individuals and groups and deny or violate it to others, especially on grounds of religion (Poland, Turkey, and the conservative pat of America) and ethnicity (Turkey, plus Greece among the mixed systems) and nativism [the US South]. They do so by favoring believers and majority ethnic groups and discriminating against and excluding non-believers or secularists and minority ethnicities in seeking, competing for, and holding power or office.

On account of such monopoly of religious believers and dominant ethnicities, they represent the most exclusionary and monopolistic or closed, particularly theocratic or theocentric, 'democracies' among Western and related political systems. In such bogus 'democracies' others than the 'godly' and ethnic majority simply 'may not and need not apply' for power or office despite the other, possibly superior, attributes and qualifications of the 'ungodly' or secularists and minorities. Briefly, such ersatz 'democracies' negate and abolish Jefferson's 'liberty and justice (and equality) for all' in pursuing or competing for and holding power or office, and thus fail to implement democratic ideals. Analogously, they can be described as 'anti-Jeffersonian,' anti-Enlightenment

---

introduce into citizen choices,' while religion being 'much less of a factor of how people vote in Europe than in the US.'

45   Mueller (2009, p. 378) observes that in 'some of the poorest EU countries, like Poland traditional and religion still have a strong hold on a large segment of the population. In rich EU countries, traditionalism (with some exceptions) is largely a spent force. Religious fundamentalism of the kind so often found in the US is almost non-existent in Europe—unless one counts (Islamic) immigrants,' which indicates anti-liberal and so anti-democratic fundamentalist-theocratic 'American exceptionalism.' Also, Mueller (2013, p. 10) notes that 'most blasphemy laws have been repealed in the Western democracies, but as of 2002, Ireland and Great Britain still had them on the books. (The British Parliament repealed its law in 2008, however.) The Greek constitution authorizes the seizure of newspapers that perpetrate "an offense against the Christian or any other known religion."'

'democracies' opposing and reversing the Age of Reason ideals of universalism, egalitarianism, liberalism, secularism, and rationalism into their opposites. Ironically, Jefferson's America appears among or entering them since his days, which indicates that its anti-liberal, anti-secular and anti-universalistic face in governance (e.g., federal and state legislatures since 2010–14) and most regions (the South and the like) is stronger.

As usual, intermediate, eclectic political systems, exemplified by most of Eastern Europe, Ireland, Japan, Portugal, Spain, the UK, etc., evince a mixed level of the freedom, right, and opportunity to the pursuit of political position between liberal, secular and universalistic democracies and their theocentric and nationalistic opposites. For example, they are located on this dimension of democracy between Scandinavia and Canada on the one side and Poland, South Korea, Turkey, and the conservative pole of the US on the other.

Notes on US Estimates of Democracy

This section summarizes the grounds for the specific US estimates of democracy and thus provides a rationale for them to American readers and makes non-American readers more familiar with America's political system.

Free and Fair Elections

The US estimate for free and fair elections may require an additional explanation insofar as it is deemed dubious or surprising and the American political system is supposed to be a model of electoral freedom and fairness. In addition to the Supreme Court 2000 'final suspension' of the electoral process, generally the US political system is assigned such a score on this dimension of democracy, first, because of the frequent negation or violation of its freedom, fairness, and inclusiveness. At the minimum, this holds especially for the South where national and state elections are hardly ever fully free, fair, and inclusive because of the control and manipulation of the electoral and entire political process by anti-liberal conservatives, including 'born again' theocratic evangelicals, for the sake of perpetuating their power and wealth. No wonder, UN and other outside observers have attempted to monitor Presidential and other elections for their freedom and fairness in the South for many years, but always physically prevented or harassed as 'foreign interference' (e.g., Texas in the 2000–10s). In a way, the degree of electoral freedom, fairness, and inclusion in the US South is almost equal or comparable to that in Third-World dictatorships, theocracies, oligarchies, kleptocracies or 'banana republics'—i.e., minimal and further diminishing recently. This was paradigmatically exemplified by the Presidential Southern (perhaps rigged) Un-Election[46] of 2000, as well as various precedents and sequels in this region until these days, including the 2010 and 2014 midterm elections.

The second additional reason for the US estimate consists of the 'electoral college' in view of its observed tendency to a 'more unequal distribution of resources and less efficient provision of global public goods'[47] as a non- or pseudo-democratic and non-egalitarian outcome, let alone its actual or possible discrepancy from democratic outcomes like popular votes, as witnessed in the 2000 Presidential election. Comparatively, such an electoral mechanism is an anomaly or rarity among modern Western and other democracies[48]—for example, Finland in the past—specifically for presidential elections through voting by the electorate, not by a parliament vote, as in Germany and Italy.

Yet another reason involves the persistent periodic practice of Congressional redistricting degenerating into a largely anti-liberal conservative Machiavellian and partisan, often tragi-comic operation notoriously known as 'gerrymandering'[49] reproducing, jointly with voter suppression, illegitimate institutions or

---

46   Hill (2002, p. viii) use the term 'un-election' to describe the 2000 Presidential election whose vote counting was suspended and thus the outcome was decided by the (divided) Supreme Court.

47   Lizzeri and Persico (2001, p. 227) find that the US 'electoral college generates a more unequal distribution of resources and less efficient provision of global public goods.' They infer that the 'electoral college system is always less efficient than a system with a nationwide district' (Lizzeri and Persico 2001, p. 238).

48   According to the Administration and Cost of Elections (ACE) Electoral Knowledge Network only 15 (6 percent) states of 235 in the world use 'electoral college or committee' to elect the 'head of the state,' for example, the US, Germany, and Italy, plus India, Pakistan, and some other Asian countries.

49   Friedman and Holden (2008, p. 113) note that conservative forces in the South and elsewhere 'have used the redistricting process to achieve partisan political ends. Most recently, the much publicized Republican redistricting in Texas in 2003 caused four Democratic congressmen to lose their seats and would have been even more extreme but for the Voting Rights Act, which effectively protected nine Democratic incumbents.' In particular, Friedman and Holden (2008, p. 135) find that 'partisan gerrymandering (when practiced by Republicans) and racial gerrymandering are basically synonymous *in effect*' (also, Brooks and Manza 2013) As an indicator of US conservatives' persistence in illegal partisan gerrymandering in the South, media reported that in 2014 a federal judge 'ruled that two of (Florida) 27 congressional districts must be revised because (its) leaders improperly conspired to rig the boundaries to protect the party's majority in Washington. Although Democrats outnumber Republican voters in Florida, the congressional map produced by the legislature resulted in the election of a congressional delegation with 17 Republicans and 10 Democrats.' The International IDEA Handbook on Electoral Justice (2010, p. 151)

undemocratic outcomes to the point of electoral manipulation and conspiracy (e.g., the House of Representatives[50] since 2010). This procedure thus operates as a typically anti-democratic and frequently illegal procedure effectively reversing the democratic rule of people choosing leaders into the opposite, with especially conservative rulers, including 'godly' evangelical elites or networks,[51]

---

notes that the US Supreme Court requirement is that electoral 'districts be 'as mathematically equal as reasonably possible'; and in 1983 it held that congressional districting with a deviation of over 0.7 per cent from the target figure was unconstitutional.'

50   For example, in the 2012 elections the Democratic candidates gained about 1 million votes more than the Republican ones, and yet the latter achieved majority in the House of Representatives mainly because of conservative redistricting cum 'gerrymandering,' voter suppression, and related anti-democratic conspiracies especially in the Southern and other states ruled by hard-core 'Tea Party' and similar conservatives since 2010 and before. On this account, the power configuration of the House of Representatives can be deemed, in part, a result of electoral fraud or conspiracy through gerrymandering, voter suppression, and related unlawful or Machiavellian tactics by US conservatives since their capturing and controlling these states in 2010. This indicate or intimates that they would probably not achieve that amount of victories in these and other recent elections (e.g., 2014) without such systematic violations of democratic rules and procedures or Machiavellianism, simply by 'playing' legal and fair electoral games. Washington Post (from March 2016) comments that in the 2013 decision, the 'Supreme Court conservatives said that key parts of the Voting Rights Act are no longer needed because discrimination in voting is a thing of the past. As soon as the decision came down, Republican state legislatures moved swiftly to pass new voting hurdles that previously would have required Justice Department approval before. Here's a summary of the Republican voting program: Impose voter ID requirements. Shorten early voting periods. Eliminate early voting on Sundays, when many African-American churches organize 'souls to the polls' voting drives after services. Eliminate same-day registration. Restrict the ability of citizen groups to conduct voter registration drives. Reduce the number of polling places. Especially since the GOP sweep of 2010, Republican-controlled states have selected from this menu to restrict voting rights in any way they could.'

51   Manza and Brooks (1997, p. 39) observe that the US 'has long appeared exceptional in the degree to which religion has influenced social and political life.' They note that 'the common European pattern of a secular left coalition contesting for power against a conservative coalition rooted in religious groups made little headway in the United States. Despite expectations that the New Deal political realignment in the 1930s would lead to a pattern of electoral alignments dominated by class, the political significance of religious cleavages has proved to be resilient throughout the 20th century' (Manza and Brooks 1997, p. 39). Brooks (2002, pp. 206–7) identifies the 'disproportionate influence of evangelical clergy,' through the 'network position of religious leaders,' in contemporary American politics, particularly on the 'politics of family decline concern' as manifested in the 'growing association between level of family decline concern and presidential vote choice (as) a new cleavage in US politics.' Overall, Brooks (2002, p. 193) observes that 'compared with

in the South and similar regions selecting voters to (re)elect and entrench them in power permanently or uncontested. Comparatively, 'gerrymandering,' at least on its scale and in its collusive unconstitutional—as usually declared by the Supreme and other courts—form in the US South, is unknown or unparalleled among most Western democracies, and to that extent represents another instance of conservative anti-democratic, anti-liberal, anti-secular, and exclusionary or discriminatory Southern-driven 'American exceptionalism.' In sum, it is the anti-liberal, anti-secular, and anti-universalistic South and generally 'conservative America' that provides the prime reason for the US seemingly surprising estimate of free, fair, and inclusive elections.[52]

Equal Freedom and Right to Political Participation

As before, the US estimate for the equal freedom and right to political participation such as voting requires an additional explanation[53] since it is seemingly surprising and, as noted, generally America has been (self) defined as the prime and often sole model of political democracy and modern free society

---

other Western democracies, the US continues to be characterized by exceptionally high levels of religious commitment and religious-organizational strength.'

52   Brooks (2006, p. 191) remarks that 'if anything defines democracies, it is elections,' and to that extent a country or region with low electoral freedom, fairness, and inclusiveness does not qualify as democracy, as exemplified by the South and thus at least half of the US. Relatedly, Berezin (1997, p. 376) registers the 'weakening of political engagement and growing social inequality in the US.'

53   Blee and Creasap (2010, p. 269) remark that the 'disavowal of democratic processes, strategies of violence and terrorism, conspiratorial belief, intense nationalism, and/or support for criminal action' define extreme neo-conservatism or the 'new right' (NR) in the US. In this view, 'two historical shifts were instrumental in the rapid rise of the NR in the US. One was the alliance of free market advocates and social conservatives, traditionally separate wings of US conservatism. The other was the entry of large numbers of conservative Protestant evangelicals into secular political life (i.e.) the politicization of religious conservatives, especially evangelical Protestants. Ironically foreshadowing a later move by Islamic fundamentalists across the globe, this New Christian Right (NCR) decried the secularization of the West and urged a repoliticization of religion. NCR fought to wield moral authority through the state, bring Christian evangelical believers into positions of state power, and curb the actions and expressions of nonbelievers' (Blee and Creasap 2010, p. 273). They add that 'new enemies were needed to replace those that had become less relevant to conservatives, such as Soviet-era communists. Immigrants, liberals, working women, counterculturists, abortion providers, welfare recipients, secular humanists (etc.) became its new targets' (Blee and Creasap 2010, p. 2743). They also note 'new efforts by the US Christian Right to develop transnational religious alliances (e.g., with Haider's neo-Nazi 'Freedom Party' in Austria)' (Blee and Creasap 2010, p. 280).

overall. Generally, the US estimate on this dimension of democracy is justified by sociological and other findings indicating that such freedoms and rights are often denied or restricted, simply voter suppression or restrictions especially since the victory of extreme conservative ('Tea Party') forces in the 2010–14 midterm elections.[54]

As typical, the pattern of suppression of voting freedoms and rights and thus of democracy especially (though not solely) holds for the South observed to persist and escalate as an anti-liberal, anti-secular, anti-universalistic, and consequently non-democratic or 'under-democratized' region in this and related respects.[55] The South and generally the conservative half of America therefore

---

54 The Brennan Center for Justice reports 'New Voting Restrictions in Place for 2016 Presidential Election.' It elaborates that in 2016, '14 states will have new voting restrictions in place for the first time in a presidential election. The new laws range from strict photo ID requirements to early voting cutbacks to registration restrictions. Those 14 states are: Alabama, Arizona, Indiana, Kansas, Mississippi, Nebraska, New Hampshire, Ohio, Rhode Island, South Carolina, Tennessee, Texas, Virginia, and Wisconsin. (This number decreased from 15 to 14 when the D.C. Circuit blocked a voter registration requirement in Alabama, Georgia, and Kansas on September 9, 2016. Georgia was removed, but Alabama and Kansas remain on the map because certain restrictions remain in place. Other recent court rulings have impacted the map: North Carolina and North Dakota were removed after courts blocked restrictive laws. Despite a recent court victory mitigating the impact of Texas's photo ID law, it is still included because the requirement is more restrictive than what was in place for the 2012 presidential election.) This is part of a broader movement to curtail voting rights, which began after the 2010 election, when state lawmakers nationwide started introducing hundreds of harsh measures making it harder to vote. Overall, 20 states have new restrictions in effect since the 2010 midterm election.'

55 Acemoglu and Robinson (2006, p. 326) note that 'despite losing the Civil War, antebellum political elites managed to sustain their political control of the South, particularly after reconstruction ended in 1877 and the last Northern troops left (as they) derailed political reforms they opposed, and freed slaves were quickly disenfranchised through the use of literacy tests and poll taxes.' Acemoglu and Robinson (2008, p. 269) in particular note anti-democratic 'political disenfranchisement, intimidation, violence and lynching' in the US South after the Civil War. Hicks (2006, p. 506–67) emphasizes the persistent and even growing influence on contemporary US politics (in particular welfare policy) of the 'elites of politically active white Southern evangelicalism' with their 'fusion of economic (market) and religious fundamentalism.' Amenta et al. (2001, p. 226) characterize the contemporary South as an 'underdemocratized polity' in which 'political leaders are chosen by way of elections, but in which there are great restrictions on political participation, political assembly and discussion, voting, and choices among leadership groups.' Lloyd (2012, p. 483) observes that the South today 'remains a relative stronghold of conservatism (yet) stubbornly still lagging on a host of social indicators such as education and health outcomes.' Moreover, Lloyd (2012, p. 490) suggests that the 'once outlying South has

drastically reduces the US estimate for the freedom and right of voting, just as virtually all political and other liberties and rights.

A specific reason for the US estimate on this democratic indicator is the comparatively low—for example, the four or second lowest from 1945–2001—turnout in elections among Western and related democracies, as commonly noted and lamented. And the main (though not sole) explanation of such a low turnout in American elections is the persistent negation or violation of the freedoms, rights, and opportunities to political participation, inclusion, and equality such as voting suppression as a persisting and even escalating practice especially (but not only) in the ultra-conservative South, as well as the Federal legislature, administration and judiciary under the control of conservatism. At least, this region anti-liberal elites continue and even intensify their suppression of voter freedoms, rights, and opportunities, in conspiracy with or complicity by Federal governance under conservatism, through inventing a myriad of devices spanning from 'good old' literacy tests and poll taxes to the ever-new creative ones, for example, eliminating or reducing early voting, long lines for voting, onerous identification requirements, purging voters from voting lists immediately before elections and otherwise, etc., to the point of outright or subtle electoral fraud, Third-world or banana-republic style, as in the 2000 Presidential Election.

Through such never-ending voting suppression or restriction tactics these elites aim and succeed to make this basic political participation, inclusion, and equality as difficult, onerous, inconvenient, and costly in time and effort and to deter or discourage from voting as many people as possible. This voting suppression especially targets certain groups, above all the poor and politically powerless, including both what Weber called the 'poor white trash' and racial-ethnic minorities, as well as 'un-American' religious non-believers, ideological dissenters, and moral sinners-as-criminals like prisoners of ethical conscience such as drug offenders, etc. No wonder, primarily because of such anti-liberal and anti-democratic continuing and exacerbating voter suppression making this basic political participation as hard as possible for some

---

assumed a lead role in shaping national conservative politics,' by implication invariably in an anti-democratic or anti-liberal direction. In his view, the recent 'Southernization' of American politics (and culture) especially includes the 'diffusion of evangelical religion' and the 'rise of Tea Party conservatism as a national movement' (also, Madestam et al. 2013), plus the 'mainstreaming of country music' of what Weber called the Southern 'poor white trash' or, as proudly self-described, 'rednecks' (Lloyd 2012, p. 499). Also, Lloyd (2012, pp. 494–8) cites the 'growth of xenophobic organizations and restrictive legislation' and comments that 'for many, this is further evidence of the persistently insular and reactionary nature of the American South' and its 'primitivism and violence.'

targeted populations, the South has historically had and continues to have—as witnessed during the 2000s elections, including 2014—the lowest electoral turnout in the US and in extension among virtually all Western societies, especially by vote to voting age population ratios as seen before. Within this region, voter suppression and manipulation seems particularly systematic and severe in Texas judging by electoral turnout rates in general and of those of minorities in particular, but not solely, as this is a shared Southern, 'Bible Belt' anti-democratic, anti-secular and anti-liberal syndrome and 'pride' spanning from Mississippi, Alabama, and Tennessee to Oklahoma and Texas.

As also noted, voting suppression and, other things equal, the consequent lower voter turnout in the South and similar conservative parts in America reflect anti-democratic attempts to reverse the democratic principle of people electing their leaders or representatives into the opposite practice of the latter seeking to select and elect the former. This also applies to the related activity of Congressional redistricting cum notorious gerrymandering especially persistent and pervasive in this region, resulting in ultra-conservative, in particular 'born again' theocratic, elites effectively selecting and 'electing' their voters. To that extent, various new ways and means of voting suppression through conservative state laws and Machiavellian tactics in the US South and beyond in conservative America are not just 'formalities' or 'technicalities,' as neither were the old ones that, far from being 'gone with the wind,' are covertly perpetuated or retrieved by such anti-voting legal or rather illegal Southern 'innovations.' They function as the anti-liberal, anti-democratic lethal weapons denying or restricting elemental political participation, at least for certain targeted populations, and thus subverting or contracting universalistic or representative democracy, by causing or contributing to at least two non-democratic outcomes.

The first outcome represents the lowest electoral turnout, expressing or predicting, all else equal, the corresponding level of voting freedoms and rights, among modern Western and related democracies. The second and corollary outcome is reaching or approximating—conjoined and mutually reinforced with conservative gerrymandering—the perverse Orwellian scenario of rulers 'electing' people rather than conversely. Given its persistence and even escalation in historical time and its systemic, methodical character and pervasiveness in social space, voting suppression in the South and similar US regions, conspired with or complicit by Federal governance under conservatism, is not a random transient act. It rather constitutes an intrinsic pattern of activity, displaying a 'method to the madness' of conservative anti-liberalism and consequently anti-democracy, illiberty, anti-universalism, and exclusion.

In sum, the comparatively low election turnout in conservative America provides a sort of 'proof in the pudding' for the suppression or limitation of voting freedoms and rights, above all in the South and related hyper-conservative regions in conspiracy or complicity with Federal governance under conservatism, and thus a rationale for the US estimate on this dimension of democracy. Notably, the fact that the electoral turnout as a vote to voting age population ratio in the US has been since at least 1945 about half of that of the first ranked Western country indicates that, to paraphrase Shakespeare, something is deeply 'rotten' or wrong—i.e., undemocratic, unfair, non-universalistic, unrepresentative, and un-free—in conservative America as the presumed best and 'only' Western democracy and free society, cum the 'leader of the free world.' That less than half of eligible Americans are able or induced and tend to vote in elections, compared to dramatically higher proportions for other Western democracies, proves, other thing equal, that the suppression or restriction of voting freedoms, rights, and opportunities is comparatively more severe and persistent in the 'land of freedom,' more precisely the conservative half of the US, such as the South, etc.

This figure is so low by comparison with other Western democracies that it appears as if political leaders in the US, especially anti-liberal, theocratic rulers in the South and 'conservative America' overall, attempted and succeeded to 'elect' the people/electorate, as they do through the Machiavellian and illegal tactic of gerrymandering, rather than conversely. In doing so, they pervert the basic premise and procedure of representative democracy. They thus threaten to extinguish or subvert the latter beyond recognition into exclusionary, unrepresentative 'democracy' excluding and denying representation to targeted groups, for example, the 'poor white trash' constantly, racial minorities historically, and the religious-moral minority of secularists (not to mention nonbelievers) and sinners-cum-criminals recently or growingly. And to add insult to injury, the then conservative-dominated Supreme Court in 2013 invalidated the Civil Voting Rights of the 1960s on the ground that the long-standing electoral discrimination against minorities in the Southern states no longer exists, while the above shows that instead such a suppression of the basic political freedom and right persists, intensifies and escalates, as seen after the extremist 'Tea Party' resurgence and dominance in the South and beyond since 2010–14.

In addition, the estimate of participation is derived from *the Economist Intelligence Unit*'s ranking in which the US political participation index is lower, mostly due to the Southern and similar conservative states' persistent and recently escalating suppression and violation of voting freedoms, rights, and acts, than that of ten other Western democracies. And this is what Southern and conservative states essentially mean by 'states rights'—their rights to commit above and various related anti-democratic and anti-liberal acts, just as slavery and legalized discrimination in the past. Since a substantial and growing part of the US population lives and thus is expected to vote and otherwise politically participate in the South and related conservative regions, this is not just a regional but also a national matter, the more so given the observation of American democracy 'heading south' and being subverted under the anti-liberal, anti-secular, undemocratic, and exclusionary 'shadow of Dixie.'[56]

Still another reason for the US estimate is that even the presumed model of democracy lacks a special election non-working day unlike virtually all major Western and related democracies. While seemingly a trivial or inconsequential and hardly noticed detail, it represents a salient non- or pseudo-democratic exception in that it may express the consequential absence of appreciation, respect, or opportunity for equal voting freedoms and rights. This holds true because of actual or potential problems with the full realization of such freedoms and rights during working days ('too busy' or 'couldn't get time off to vote')—as a rule the first Tuesday in November—as compared with an official non-working election day like Sunday or Saturday. For example, reports show that no less than 69% of those not voting in the 2014 congressional elections did not do so 'because of schedule conflicts with work or school' or were 'too busy,' etc.[57] Despite or perhaps because of such strong negative effects of working-day voting in elections on the voter turnout, including Presidential elections, its supposedly foremost democratic institution and protector of democracy, Congress controlled or obstructed by conservatives refuses to address this serious problem (incidentally not remedied by early voting that is itself curtailed and obstructed by conservative forces). This includes its refusal of passing the 'Weekend Voting Act' the intent of which, as an apparently simple and effective 'fix,' being to precisely remedy this chronic and serious problem in the American electoral and political system, and dramatically more so than most other Western democracies.

In turn, such an electoral 'working day' exception is probably grounded in or compounded with apparent traditional Puritan-rooted theocratic or theocentric, anti-secular considerations, for example, observance of 'Sabbath,' obligatory or expected Sunday church attendance, 'blue laws' prohibiting various non-religious activities, etc. These Puritan and related religious vestiges apparently aim at or succeed in overcoming or devaluating the basic liberty, right, and act of democracy and thus effectively the latter itself. And a superficially

---

56   These are the observations Cochran (2001) makes in his analysis of the recent trends in American democracy. Cochran (2001) suggests that contemporary American politics has been placed under the anti-liberal, ant-democratic 'shadow of Dixie' resulting in 'democracy heading south.'

57   The source is Pew Research Center.

irrelevant moment of sacrificing Sunday as a near-universal day of voting and formal exercise and celebration of democracy in Western and other democracies to the theocratic 'godly' Sabbath legacy of Puritanism in America—i.e., 'dead Sunday' after the image of graveyard[58]—reaffirms what sociologists and other analysts from Hume and Comte through Weber and Pareto and many contemporary observers diagnose and predict. This is that a historically Puritan, generally Calvinist society never has been and will be completely democratic and free both in formal and substantive terms, notably a liberal, secular, universalistic, egalitarian, and representative democracy and modern free society as a whole. It is because Puritanism and all Calvinism has invariably been and evidently remains, either as a legacy and ghost revived through theocratic evangelicalism, the design and system of theocracy as religious dictatorship and so anti-democracy and thus an antithesis, grave treat, and deadly poison of liberal, secular, universalistic, and representative democracy as the sole genuine, functioning and sustainable democratic and free political system.[59]

---

58   Referring to Prohibition, Pegram (1998, p. 99) observes that 'many immigrants saw no reason to adopt the stern Puritan tradition of "a dead Sunday, with the silence of a graveyard and bare of any joys of life"' (also, Andrews and Seguin 2015). In passing, 'libertarian' economists Mises (1950) uses the phrase 'peace of cemetery' attributed to 'socialism' (conflated with communism), but overlooks this Puritan-conservative model and precedent, as well as its own evangelical sequel in the 'Bible Belt' where, in an ironic twist, an institute bearing his name is located.

59   That Puritanism and its heir evangelicalism represents the anti-liberal, anti-democratic design and system of theocracy or sectarianism is suggested or implied by many analysts. Zaret (1989, pp. 168–9) notes that 'Puritanism had only fortuitous links with democratic developments, as it had strongly authoritarian tendencies that opposed any liberalizing withdrawal of religion form the political arena (such that) a coercive, intolerant politics of moral reform lay at the heart of Puritanism.' Archer (2001, p. 276) proposes that the 'founders of New England colonies were the Ayatollah Khomeneis of the early 17th century. The Puritan state was a minority 'dictatorship of the holy' (and) an authoritarian theocracy. The idea that there should be a separation of church and state was completely alien to (Puritanism) (but) the unity of religion and politics was axiomatic (and) central to the very rationale for founding these new societies.' Munch (2001, p. 242) observes that American 'religious fundamentalism demonstrates that open access to policy-making and in this sense democracy is in itself no safeguard against the intrusion of moral absolutism in the exercising of individual rights.' Munch (2001, p. 269) infers that US 'fundamentalist Protestant movements (arise) against the reality of a liberal and pluralist society.' Kaufman (2008, pp. 410–16) remarks that 'religious dissenters looking to escape persecution in Puritan Massachusetts founded Rhode Island (and) a decision in the state legislature (Massachusetts) regarding mandatory taxes for support of Congregationalist churches (indicated) a desire to control, rather than liberate, religious congregations.' Fischer and Mattson (2009, p. 446) describe Puritanism as 'religious sectarianism' that

Alternatively, these and other analysts posit that if such a country becomes democratic and free in the sense of liberal, secular, and universalistic democracy and society it does or will in spite and opposition of Puritanism and Calvinism in general, and because of the opposite complex of liberalism, secularism, universalism, and rationalism, as shown by Geneva after Calvin, post-Calvinist Holland, post-Puritan England, New England, and Jeffersonian America. In this framework, the striking and exceptional taboo on Sunday voting day in America, in stark contrast to most Western and other democracies, is not accidental and trivial. It is determined and predicted by the theocratic and generally anti-democratic, repressive legacy of Puritanism which has reportedly over-determined American politics, economy, culture, and civil society.[60] In passing, this holds true of a variety of other bizarre taboos or prohibitions infringing on basic political, individual, and economic liberties, rights, and activities, including various 'blue—and other, as many Americans call them, 'dumb'—laws,' including the prohibition of selling and buying alcohol and other practices on Sunday, as vestiges of the theocratic and hypocritical

---

is 'embedded in American nationalism' and colonial New England as the theocratic 'tight-knit 'community of saints.' Mueller (2009, p. 382) invokes Hobbes' observation that the 'goading of Presbyterian (Puritan) preachers' produced a 'civil war over religion' in England.

60 Moreover, McLaughlin (1996, p. 249) suggests that through Puritanism 'Calvinism served the same sociological function for Anglo-Saxon countries' as fascism in being not only 'linked with political freedoms and economic progress (but also) to Nazism.' Archer (2001, pp. 277–81) notes that the 'Puritan idea that the Bible revealed the will of God, and that government should act to reorganize society in accordance with that will remained a central element of American culture to this day (as) inheritors of the Puritan tradition had accepted the formal separation of church and state, but they remained committed to the task of moral regeneration and of establishing a Godly society in America (and) rallied together to force the government to use its authority to uphold their notion of righteousness, and to enforce what they deemed to be a Godly way of life.' Munch (2001, pp. 223–4) observes that American politics and all society is 'religiously (Puritan) determined' in that 'in no other country did Puritanism attain significance comparable to (that) in the (us) as the carrier of modern normative culture.' As a result of Puritanism, Munch (2001, p. 228) notes that 'the characteristic feature of the relationship between religion and political order in (the us) is that the two are not purely differentiated, nor is politics released from "religious tutelage."' Kaufman (2008, p. 422) suggests that the 'modern American corporate system has adopted an incarnation of this (Puritan) institutional frame (ruled by large property-owners): profitsharing with employees is rare, and corporate governance is run in the interest of management and shareholders rather than employees or society as a whole.' Mueller (2009, p. 392) observes that today in the us 'Puritanical beliefs cause hardship, suffering, and often death.'

moralistic revolt and ghost[61] of Puritanism from England to New England and America.

Another reason for the estimate is that the US political system in conservative governance and regions solidifies and even reinforces—in view of the growing exorbitant monetary spending, the Supreme Court's removal of limits to corporate financing of political campaigns,[62] etc.—its long-standing position as the only or main one among Western societies where, as Weber notes a century ago, wealth or money 'purchases' political power, both in the federal government[63] and state and local governments. This plutocratic, monetary path to political power therefore causes a perversion of democracy into, in his words, a 'naked plutocracy' and thus ultimately its vanishing act into what US President Roosevelt deplores as the 'tyranny' of wealth. In this sense, not much has essentially changed since Weber's diagnosis and Roosevelt's warning.

And if something has changed, it has been actually in the direction of money purchasing power and influence in US politics, above in conservative governance and regions like the South, evermore historically during post-Tocqueville times and comparatively in relation to Western democracies, as observed by many sociological and other studies and lamented by the general public in America. On this account, Tocqueville's early celebrated 'democracy

---

61   Zaret (1989, p. 170) remarks that the 'Puritan vision of godly politics' represented a 'coercive theocracy,' and Juergensmeyer (1994, p. 45) notes that the 'Puritans, with their theocratic revolt against the increasing secularism of seventeenth-century English politics, may be regarded as precursors of modern antisecular radicals' such as US 'born again' evangelicals and similar religious extremists and Islamic fundamentalists, including terrorists in both groups.

62   Wright (2013, p. 7) observes that in the US the capitalist 'assault on democracy intensified after the Supreme Court's recent decision on the (unlimited) use of corporate funds in political campaigns.' In retrospect, such plutocratic anti-democratic assaults confirm Weber's classic observation, based on first-hand experience, of plutocracy in America. Weber (1946, p. 310), who visited the US in 1904, observes that 'in America mere 'money' in itself also purchases power, but not social honor' and thereby renders American politics into being (ruled by) what he calls the 'naked plutocracy' as the 'all-American' moneyed aristocracy or oligarchy.

63   Evoking Weber's observation that 'mere money purchases power' in American politics, Bertrand, Bombardini, and Trebbi (2014, p. 3885) observe that 'trillions of dollars of public policy intervention, government procurement, and budgetary items are constantly, thoroughly, scrutinized, advocated, or opposed by representatives of special interests. The sheer relevance of the $4 billion federal lobbying industry has become evident in any aspect of the 2008–2009 financial crisis, including emergency financial market intervention (the TARP), financial regulation, countercyclical fiscal policy intervention, and health care reform.'

in America' in which, as he puts it, people are 'more equal in wealth and power' than ever before and in any other societies at the time looks like a distant past and memory or realized egalitarian utopia, if not a fantasy and dream for those Americans growingly being unequal, specifically inferior, on these interrelated accounts to the new aristocracy of money and dominance. Since then Tocqueville's 'democracy' has evidently degenerated into what Weber and Pareto as well as US President Roosevelt diagnose as 'naked' and 'demagogic' plutocracy, oligarchy, or kleptocracy embodied by the various species of robber barons, all primarily thanks to conservative anti-liberal and anti-universalistic ideology, governance and regions.

Freedom and Right to the Pursuit of Political Position

With respect to this freedom and right in the US political system, the Jeffersonian constitutional prohibition of government 'establishment of religion' and of using a religious test for seeking and holding power or public office is often subverted, violated, or suspended by various laws and/or policies at both national and state levels[64] exclusively by conservative, theocratic and exclusionary forces, during their control of Federal institutions and the South and related regions. First, at the federal level, paradigmatic instances of such constitutional violations or contradictions include 'one nation invisible under God,' 'in God we trust' and similar proclamations non-existent in the original document since Jefferson and Madison, yet inserted in the Constitution during the collective hysteria—in a sequence of such hysterias since Puritanism—of the Cold War against the 'godless' enemy under the immediate influence or as

---

64 Bell (2002, p. 483) observes that during the 2000 Presidential elections, 'George W. Bush proclaimed himself to be a born-again Protestant, whose life has been changed directly by Jesus Christ. Al Gore asserted that he was a born-again Protestant who frequently asked himself 'W.W.J.D' (What Would Jesus Do?). Nothing like this has ever been seen in an American presidential political campaign.' One can add that, in fact, something like this has always been seen in American Presidential political campaigns and politics overall at least since Reagan in 1980 and even before (Goldwater in 1964, etc.). Dayton (1999, p. 41) remarks that 'disestablishment (of Puritanism) would not occur in Massachusetts until 1815, and religious tests for office-holding would persist in the United States long after the passage of Thomas Jefferson's landmark 1786 Act for Establishing Religious Freedom.' Edgell et al. (2006, p. 214; also, Edgell 2012) register that the 'gap in willingness to vote for atheists (presidential candidates) versus other religious minorities (Catholic or Jewish) is large and persistent' in American politics and generally find that 'atheists continue to be the least accepted group, despite their small numbers' in the US.

the enduring anti-democratic legacy ('ugly scars'[65]) of McCarthyism and its parent theocentric conservatism. For illustration, if not knowing the country in question the following report[66] may be mistaken as a depiction of contemporary Islamic theocracies like Iran, Saudi Arabia and Taliban, or the past Puritan theocracy in colonial America, than of a Jeffersonian and Western liberal, secular and universalistic democracy, the 'first America' of freedom.

Thus, a reports find that 'the US has a range of laws and practices that equate being religious with being an American, and vice versa. Sometimes these are dismissed as mere 'Ceremonial Deism.' But when every court and every dollar has 'In God We Trust' prominently displayed, and when children start their day in the state school by pledging their allegiance to 'One Nation under God,' it inculcates a conviction that to be American is to believe in God. The only mention of religion in the US constitution is the statement that 'no religious test shall ever be required as a qualification to any office'; yet the idea that only religious Americans can be good Americans is so powerful that not one out of the 535 members of the US Congress publicly admits to being non-religious. In America, you might have the right to be an atheist, but being public about it can have debilitating consequences for your chances of success in life, especially in certain states. For example, there are several Congress members who refuse to list their religious affiliation, but exactly zero of the 535 members of Congress claim to be non-religious. In 2011 the House of Representatives approved a resolution reaffirming 'In God We Trust' as the nation's motto and

---

65   Smelser and Mitchell (2002, p. 47) recognize that McCarthyism and the 'red scare' 'seriously compromised the civil liberties and livelihood of some citizens, and both left ugly scars on the body politic.' Pontikes, Negro, and Rao (2010, pp. 456–7) note that during the "Red Scare" from 1945 to 1960, 'Congress held hearings and film artists named as suspected communists were blacklisted by studios and deprived of work' and analyze Hollywood's Red Scare as 'an instance of moral panic, where activists stigmatize a group as abnormal and deviant.'

66   The source is 'Freedom of Thought 2013: A Global Report on the Rights, Legal Status, and Discrimination Against Humanists, Atheists, and the Non-religious' by the International Humanist and Ethical Union (IHEU). Also, 'Freedom of Thought 2014: A Global Report on Discrimination Against Humanists, Atheists, and the Non-religious; Their Human Rights and Legal Status' reports that 'For example, the US has a range of laws and practices that equate being religious with being an American, and vice versa. Sometimes these are dismissed as mere 'Ceremonial Deism.' But when every court and every dollar has 'In God We Trust' prominently displayed, and when children start their day in the state school by pledging their allegiance to 'One Nation under God,' it inculcates a conviction that to be American is to believe in God. The only mention of religion in the US constitution is the statement that 'no religious test shall ever be required as a qualification to any office'; yet the idea that only religious Americans can be good Americans is so powerful that not one out of the 535 members of the US Congress publicly admits to being non-religious.'

encouraging its placement in all public buildings by a vote of 396–9 (with two abstentions).' Note that 'encouraging its placement in all public buildings' is a clear and unequivocal syndrome of deterring and excluding anyone who does abide by 'In God We Trust' from applying for or holding public office and political power, and generally of theocratic coercion and theocentric indoctrination. The report concludes that the '1954 addition of the phrase 'under God' to the Pledge of Allegiance, the recitation of which is widely required by law in most states at the start of each school day; In 1956, Congress adopted 'In God We Trust' as the country's official motto, which is now posted on US money and in courthouses at every level of government.'

As known, both 'in God We Trust' and 'under God' proclamations were enacted during the hysteria of McCarthyism and the Cold War, and were not (as most Americans seem to think) in the original Constitution and its subsequent amendments, as evidently for Jefferson et al. such and related theocratic or 'godly' elements did not belong to it, and contravened its principle against the government 'establishment of religion' and for the 'wall of eternal separation of church and state.' In terms of this Constitutional principle and Jeffersonian secular democracy, these proclamations hence were intentionally unconstitutional and anti-democratic, exclusionary, and coercive, as well as manifesting irrational crowd sentiments in Le Bon-Pareto's sense, and in that sense 'smuggled' through conservative-controlled Congress driven by or immersed in the paranoid climate of McCarthyism and the Cold War that was used an excuse for such and other attacks on political and civil liberties and rights. And most disturbingly for both the Constitutional principle and Jeffersonian democracy, this supreme legislative body and the presumed guardian of them in America evidently desists in such unconstitutional and anti-democratic actions by persistently reaffirming them until these days, as by Congress' repeated reaffirmation of 'In God We Trust' and 'under God'—to the point of what Weber calls an 'annoying ceremonial' of congressmen holding hands like children in its recitation in front of Capitol Hill—during recent years, as if it had no better things to do in terms of political and civil liberties and rights.

Yet such unconstitutional and irrational and undemocratic practices from a Jeffersonian standpoint reveal the logic and 'method to the madness' of the 'godless need not to apply to political power or public office' at the federal level in the 'land of freedom' and 'best democracy' to be enjoyed and monopolized by the 'godly' like those in conservative-controlled Congress—for most years since 1994 through 2016—and their state variants. Also, if not knowing the military in question, for instance, one may easily mistake this report[67] as depicting

---

67   The source is 'Freedom of Thought 2013: A Global Report on the Rights, Legal Status, and Discrimination Against Humanists, Atheists, and the Non-religious.'

a crusading or 'evangelical army' and 'Christian soldiers' rather than a modern one(s): the 'US Air Force Deputy Chief of Chaplains stated 'We reserve the right to evangelize the unchurched.' And 80 soldiers at US Army's Ft. Eustis were punished with punitive maintenance work for refusing to attend the base-endorsed 'Commanding General's Spiritual Fitness' Christian rock concert.'

At the state level, a myriad of laws and/or practices requiring the public acknowledgment of the 'existence of Divinity' and the like by candidates for government positions subvert or violate the Constitutional prohibition of 'establishment of religion' and the Jeffersonian 'wall of eternal separation of church and state,' as done systematically and for long, above all in the ultra-conservative 'under-democratic,' including theocentric evangelical-dominated, 'insular and reactionary' South. On this account, this region becomes or rather continuous to exist as what Weber calls 'Bibliocracy' (the 'Bible Belt') in the sense of 'Biblical theocracy,' especially in its Puritan variant considered and in-stituted as 'Divinely ordained' by Calvinism, consequently drastically lowering the US qualitative estimate on this dimension of democracy and virtually all the other estimates for America's polity as well as economy, civil society, and culture.

The following report[68] again may be mistaken to describe the resurrected colonial Puritan theocracy or Islamic theocracies rather than Jeffersonian and Western liberal, secular, and universalistic democracy in the 'first America,' if not knowing the US states in question. As reported, 'despite being ruled uncon-stitutional and effectively struck down by the Supreme Court (in 1961); at least seven states–Arkansas, Maryland, Mississippi, North Carolina, South Carolina, Tennessee, and Texas–still have in place constitutional provisions that bar atheists from holding public office; The state of Arkansas even has a law that bars an atheist from testifying as a witness at a trial. A 2006 law in Kentucky requires the state Office of Homeland Security to post plaques acknowledging that Almighty God has been integral to keeping the state safe on penalty of up to 12 months in prison (but) the Supreme Court has refused to review the constitutionality of the law.' The report cites the following US states as indica-tive: 'Arkansas: 'No person who denies the being of a God shall hold any office in the civil departments of this State, nor be competent to testify as a witness in any Court.' Maryland: 'That no religious test ought ever to be required as a qualification for any office of profit or trust in this State, other than a declara-tion of belief in the existence of God; nor shall the Legislature prescribe any other oath of office than the oath prescribed by this Constitution.' Mississippi:

---

68   The source is also 'Freedom of Thought 2013: A Global Report on the Rights, Legal Status, and Discrimination against Humanists, Atheists, and the Non-religious.'

'No person who denies the existence of a Supreme Being shall hold any office in this state.' North Carolina: 'The following persons shall be disqualified for office: First, any person who shall deny the being of Almighty God.' South Carolina: 'No person who denies the existence of a Supreme Being shall hold any office under this Constitution.' Tennessee:[69] 'No person who denies the being of God, or a future state of rewards and punishments, shall hold any office in the civil department of this state.' Texas: 'No religious test shall ever be required as a qualification to any office, or public trust, in this State; nor shall any one be excluded from holding office on account of his religious sentiments, provided he acknowledge the existence of a Supreme Being (sic).'

What is striking is that these ultra-conservative, mostly Southern, states claim that the obligation to acknowledge, as the last state stipulates, the 'existence of a Supreme Being (God)' is 'no religious test'—what test is then?—thus unapologetically violating the Constitution, intentionally contradicting Jefferson, and cynically attacking or insulting reason and intelligence by an Orwellian 'double-speak' anti-logic and 'depraved' mental gymnastics. Simply, 'there is no religious test whatsoever, only you must believe in God, otherwise

---

69   *Tennessean* commented in March 2016 that '*Tennessee* lawmakers who back Bible bill are theocrats.' It elaborated that 'this is Tennessee, not Tehran. We are governed by the people, not the religious authorities. If legislators truly care about religious liberty, they would vote against an ill-advised effort to endorse the Holy Bible as the official state book. However, the theocrats in the Tennessee General Assembly have a good shot at getting their way. This, despite Attorney General Herbert Slatery's warning last year that such a bill could be ruled to be unconstitutional. Aside from the potential constitutional issues this presents, the bill, if passed by the Senate, should invalidate the false narrative that there is an attack on Christians' religious liberty. The Bible bill is clearly an attack on religious minorities, and secular, agnostic or atheistic people, who are also protected by the state and federal constitutions. It is also an attack on religious people who have a strong interest in ensuring that government does not endorse one way to worship God over another. Lawmakers who support it are acting like the ayatollahs of the Legislature, dictating what beliefs are acceptable and making Tennessee a laughingstock.' This lengthy citation is instructive because it effectively describes the 'Bible Belt' as a whole, i.e., most Southern and related US states. Notably, the lament that 'this is Tennessee, not Tehran' indicates that theocratic conservatives aim to make this and other Southern states like Iran's Islamic theocracy, and evidently succeed as shown by the follow-up report. Thus, *Tennessean* reported in April of 2016 that 'having already made a .50-caliber sniper gun the official state rifle, Tennessee lawmakers on Monday gave final approval to making the Holy Bible the state's official book. The state Senate voted 19-8 in favor of the bill despite arguments by the state attorney general that the measure conflicts with a provision in the Tennessee Constitution stating that 'no preference shall ever be given, by law, to any religious establishment or mode of worship.'

need not apply for state position or office'—that is the theocratic 'logic' and method to the 'madness' of US Southern ('Bible Belt') and related conservative states as 'governments of God,' 'Biblical gardens' of the 'Dominion of God,' and the like, as is that of their Islamic enemies and 'brothers in arms' alike. That acknowledging the 'existence' of God is no religious test for power in these states not only exemplifies Orwellian anti-logic, delusion and deception but evokes what Hume diagnoses as the Puritan 'madness with religious ecstasies' and Pareto as the theological 'cage for the insane.'

Additionally and ironically, these very religious groups that were suppressed, excluded, and discriminated against when in minority (e.g., Catholics in Maryland by Puritans or their heirs, neo-Puritan evangelicals in Texas under Mexico, etc.) once in power perpetrate the same acts against 'ungodly' minorities. They therefore reveal the totalitarian pattern of denying to others what one righteously demanded for oneself—liberty, freedom of conscience, equality, inclusion, justice, rights, and the like, yet another tendency shared with Islamic fundamentalists and theocracies, as well as fascists and neo-fascists.

Political Pluralism and Competition

The general basis for the US estimate is the widespread observation and finding that American democracy features a relatively low degree of ideological-political pluralism or diversity and so choice/freedom and competition, typically lower than that of most other Western democracies. In particular, according in the above Economist Intelligence Unit's ranking, the US index of political pluralism and electoral process is the lowest among advanced Western societies, including Western Europe, plus Canada, Australia, and New Zealand, as well as lower than some Eastern European countries like Czech Republic. Furthermore, it is the fourth lowest, along with Hungary, and Japan, among all OECD countries, with only Mexico, South Korea, and Turkey having the lower indexes, and ranked overall 28–31 out of 33. Like the exceptionally low electoral turnout, the striking and seemingly surprising fact that the US political system features the exceptional, lowest degree of ideological-political pluralism and consequently choice/freedom among advanced Western democracies indicates that probably something crucial is deeply 'defective' or 'wrong' in 'American democracy' in its conservative ideology, governance and region, thus revealing the adverse/reverse kind of 'American exceptionalism' in this respect.

And that non-Western countries like Mexico and Turkey feature such lower indexes may or may not be a 'consolation prize' for the supposed model of and even 'sole' Western democracy in time and social space. While the US political system—as its politicians claim and most Americans think—appears as the champion of ideological pluralism and so choice/freedom compared to what they love to hate or disdain and deride its neighbor Mexico, as well as China and the Third-World overall (plus the former Soviet Union during the Cold War), it reveals itself, above all in its conservative ideology, governance and region, in the less glorious light, if not monistic darkness, by comparison to also neighboring Canada and virtually all Western European democracies. In particular, an exceptionally lower degree of ideological-political diversity and choice has been particularly observed for Congress for long time.[70] In addition, ideological pluralism and choice during, for instance, the Presidential elections of 2016 was reduced to that between proto-fascism[71] (including irrationalism) produced by and reproducing conservatism as an anti-liberal authoritarian ideology and regime of repression and militant feminism (joined with militarism) perverting and compromising liberalism as the ideal and system of universal liberty, equality, and justice.

As for ideological pluralism and choice, the evaluation of political competition is based on the widespread observation and experience that American politics, especially its conservative ideology, governance and region, constitutes in these terms a political or party duopoly and an oligarchic, plutocratic

---

70   Jacobs and Tope (2007, p. 1471–2) remark that during the 2000s the Vermont representative in the House 'was the only member of Congress who claimed to be a socialist in the post–civil rights period,' just as there has been only one self-declared atheist in Congress overall. Generally, they identify the 'conservative political resurgence' and even the 'dominance of conservatism' in Congress and US politics overall after the 1960s through the 'enduring alliances between social and economic conservatives' against the 'dispossessed' (Jacobs and Tope 2007, p. 1460, 1487).

71   This is in the sense of Putnam's (2000, p. 350) observation of 'proto-fascist' America during the 1950s. During the 2016 Presidential elections one candidate appeared to play the proto-fascist and plutocratic 'card' of nativism and wealth as if entitled to become President solely because of being a 'real American' and rich, and the other that of feminism (compounded with militarism) as if entitled to this only or mostly because of being of a certain gender. To that extent, the victory of the one will be that of proto-fascism (including irrationalism) and plutocracy, and of the other that of radical feminism (and militarism), consequently resulting in the proxy totalitarian and plutocratic elimination of liberal democracy in the first scenario, and the perverse 'liberal' deformation of it in the second. This book was completed before the 2016 elections, but their outcome probably will not greatly affect the main premise and findings, i.e., the coexistence and opposition between the 'two Americas,' in particular that 'conservative America' has been stronger politically than 'liberal America' since the 1980s, as Mueller (2009) observes, and even perhaps, as Lipset (1996) and Munch (2001) suggest, in American history beginning with theocratic Puritanism.

system[72] with its proverbial 'good old boys' networks, and comparatively more so than most other Western democracies. For instance, this is especially (but not solely) indicated by the smaller number of competing or relevant political parties—in particular, the conspicuous absence of a major worker-based or socialist party as formed in Europe and the UK—in the former representing a relatively rigid two-party system than in the latter instead being truly multi-party systems. In this respect, the first appears more duopolistic and less competitive—in the sense of what economists calls pure, perfect competition involving multiple, theoretically infinite competitors—than the second, though this market analogy should not be taken literally or carried too far, as done in the economics of politics cum 'public choice theory.' Also, like for other democracies, the index of political pluralism and choice indicates or predicts an equivalent US estimate for free competition in politics through a multi-party system.

Effective Universal Political Liberties

In particular, like those for Catholic dominated Chile and especially Poland and Islamic-ruled Turkey, the US qualitative estimation[73] considers various ob-

---

72   Hill (2002, p. xii) describes American politics as a political duopoly and thus quasi-monopoly, and Pryor (2002, p. 364) registers the growing tendency 'toward a greater oligarchical control of both the state and the economy' in America. In general, Esteban and Ray (2008, pp. 275–6) register find a 'positive association between political and economic power (such that) higher wealth obscures true productive merit in the quest for public support of economic projects. The wealthy fuel corrupt behavior in their attempt to corner public resources (as) wealthy agents may confound the resource allocation process because of their greater ability to corner resources'—i.e., oligarchic plutocracy, by implication, above all, in the US within the Western world, as well as third-world countries.

73   Pichardo (1997, pp. 426–7) observes that 'many conservative mobilizations in USA (are) attempts by religious groups to coerce the state to enforce behavioral and moral codes consistent with their beliefs.' Mueller (2009, p. 375) observes that the 'struggle between progressivism (liberalism) and traditionalism (conservatism) has gone on for much of the US's history, and continues today at an intensity unmatched in other rich, developed countries,' citing President 'Bush's religious zeal.' Mueller (2009, p. 378) adds that the 'conflict between progressivism and traditionalism is somewhat different in Europe than in the US. In some of the poorest EU countries, like Poland traditional and religion still have a strong hold on a large segment of the population. In rich EU countries, traditionalism (with some exceptions) is largely a spent force. Religious fundamentalism of the kind so often found in the US is almost non-existent in Europe.' He infers that 'it is (US and Islamic) religious extremists therefore that deserve the closest attention today from those who defend liberal democracy' (Mueller 2009, p. 417).

servations of the virtually non-existent or minimal effective political freedoms and rights of religious minorities like non-believers and moral sinners, above all, but not solely, in the hyper-religious, evangelical South[74] and related conservative regions. A crucial overarching observation identifies and emphasizes the intensifying and expanding tendency to genuine or proxy 'American theocracy,'[75] climaxing in the Southern 'Bible Belt' (plus Mormon-ruled Utah) and escalating beyond to 'Middle' and eventually most America, with minor or shrinking oases in the theocratic or theocentric 'desert' like Vermont and other within 'liberal and secular America.'

Particular observations point to state subsidies and various other support to religion in the US by both the federal government under conservatism and conservative states. They also detect religious intrusion, coercion, and repression in the polity and society via conservative anti-liberal and anti-secular ideological, culture and temperance wars—launched by Reaganism's attack on liberalism as 'anti-American' and 'ungodly,' so a proxy civil war against liberals as 'un-American' using McCarthyism's formula—in violation of the Constitutional provision against the government 'establishment of religion' and the

---

74   DiPrete et al. (2011, p. 1236) observe that 'political conflict between proponents of secular and religiously orthodox values has been especially prominent since the Reagan presidency.' Hout and Fischer (2002, pp. 165–6) find that the 'political part of the increase in 'nones' (with 'no religion') can be viewed as a symbolic statement against the Religious Right. In the 1990s many people who had weak attachments to religion and either moderate or liberal political views found themselves at odds with the conservative (theocratic) political agenda of the Christian Right and reacted by renouncing their weak attachment to organized religion.' Glaeser, Ponzetto, and Shapiro (2005, p. 1313) find a 'nonmonotonic relationship between religious extremism and religious attendance' in the US (and other countries) such that 'religious attendance predicts Republicanism.' Rydgren (2007, p. 241) refers to 'Interwar fascism in Europe and early postwar right-wing radicalism in the US' as the American equivalent or analogue. Owens, Robinson, and Smith-Lovin (2010, p. 492) single out US 'sectarian evangelical Protestants whose efforts animated the first wave of a Christian Right movement.' Bailey and Snedker (2011, p. 848) observe that in the US South 'Christianity was used to support slavery on the basis of biblical and evangelistic reasons. Southern religious groups voiced unanimous, enthusiastic support for maintaining racial segregation.'

75   Phillips (2006) explicitly uses the term 'American theocracy' seen as arising in recent times, as does Hedges (2006), and Archer (2001), Friedland (2001), Turner (2002), and Van Dyke (1995), imply. Also, US Representative Christopher Shays (R-CT) reportedly stated that the 'Republican Party of Lincoln has become a party of theocracy' (*New York Times* 3/23/2005). In particular, Weisbrod (1999, pp. 146–7) register the 'reconstitution of a theocracy' through the 'church overlapping and penetrating the state' in Utah under near-total Mormon rule.

'religious test' for public office, and the formal separation of church and state. For example, only one US declared non-believer, atheist has ever been member of Congress,[76] indicating the long-standing and persisting theocentric nature, composition, and operation of the federal legislature in post-Jeffersonian times. As also noted, the same pattern of 'non-believers need not apply' for political position or public office is observed in most conservative-controlled state legislatures, most absolutely and rigidly in the South, with minor variations.

Most of these observations portray the US conservative government at both federal and state levels as an effective or proxy theocracy, and yet unconstitutional by self-contravening the constitutional principle that 'no religious test shall ever be required as a qualification to any office,' through the 'only religious Americans-are-good Americans' exclusionary and discriminatory equation. Thus, reportedly of all the (535) members of the US Congress in recent times virtually not a single one (1) of the two major political parties is publicly 'non-believer' or even 'non-religious' and 'secularist,' except for some atypical independents. In addition, as noted, reports suggest that such theocentric elements as the belated and Machiavellian insertion of 'Under God' into the Pledge of Allegiance and belatedly making 'In God We Trust'[77] a national credo, as largely the vestiges of the hysteria of McCarthyism and the Cold War, flagrantly violate the Constitutional principle against government 'establishment of religion' and the legal separation of church and state.

Other reported violations at the federal level include what Weber called 'annoying'[78] religious ceremonials like ubiquitous prayers in major governmental institutions, including Congress and the Supreme Court—plus the

---

76   For instance, Pete Stark of California is reportedly the first and only open non-believer (atheist) to be a member of US Congress. This dramatically epitomizes the underlying theocratic substance—despite and contravening the constitutional secular form—at least the 'theocentric' (Wall 1998) pro-religious and anti-secular bias of the US political system such as the federal legislature, as well as state legislatures, above all, but not solely, in the South (plus Mormon-controlled Utah) as effectively the region of theocracy in content and even informally in name cum the 'Bible Belt' since the end of the Civil War through these days. To that extent, this anti-democratic outcome can be described as the Southern 'empire (confederacy) strikes back' or the 'revenge of the South' by substituting evangelical as in essence a religiously sanctified master-slave political system or 'holy' totalitarianism, for racially based slavery as well as segregation.

77   This observation is based on International Humanist and Ethical Union's freethoughtreport.

78   Weber (1946, p. 303) remarks that the 'opening by prayer of not only every session of the US Supreme Court but also of every Party Convention has been an annoying ceremonial for quite some time.'

Presidential participation in the 'National Prayer Breakfast'[79] and the 'White House Christian Fellowship'—precisely supposed to abide by and uphold that constitutional principle. Still more involve Presidents taking oath of office with the Bible in their hands as if they were 'pastors in chief' and their prime duty to enforce the Biblical 'law of the land,' 'charitable choice' giving public financial resources (taxpayers' money) to private religious congregations and thus violating or blurring the separation of church and state,[80] etc. On the basis of such reports and observations, analysts may wonder if these acts and many others are not the government 'establishment of religion,' the unconstitutional application of a religious test for political position, the tearing down of the 'wall of separation of church and state,' then what it is. Moreover, observers depict US theocrats and evangelicals as 'American fascists,' in particular the 'Bible Belt' seen as the anti-liberal 'protototalitarian' equivalent of Islamic Iran and Taliban.[81]

---

79 Lindsay (2008, p. 77) notes that 'for instance, President George H.W. Bush may not be an evangelical, but his participation in gatherings administered by evangelical groups (like the National Prayer Breakfast) provided portals through which evangelicals have gained entry into the higher circles of American society.' And virtually all US Presidents in modern times have participated in such, in Weber's words, 'annoying' and apparently unconstitutional religious ceremonials, and historically only Jefferson reportedly abstained. Also, Lindsay (2008, p. 78) characterizes the Bush son administration as the 'most evangelical in modern history.' Upon reading such observations, including that about the 'White House Christian Fellowship' (Lindsay 2008, p. 69), the question arises as to what happened to the Constitutional principle against the government establishment or promotion of religion and the separation of church and state, including Presidency and the answer is evident—it is grossly and routinely violated, such violations becoming effectively the norm, and upholding it a rare exception a la Jefferson.

80 Chaves (1999, pp. 836–7) registers that the 1996 welfare reform established 'by statute that organizations whose main activity is religion (such as congregations) may receive public money to support social service activity.' Chaves (1999, p. 843) adds that 'generally it is political and religious conservatives who have been the strongest advocates of these initiatives, and political and religious liberals who have been most strongly against them. The Charitable Choice section of the welfare reform legislation was sponsored by Senator John Ashcroft, Republican of Missouri, and initiatives inspired by this legislation have been actively promoted by prominent conservative religious organizations such as the Christian Coalition and the Family Research Council. Many nationally prominent liberal religious organizations, in contrast, have been strongly opposed to charitable-choice legislation and initiatives. Americans United for the Separation of Church and State has assembled a coalition of 46 organizations opposed to Charitable Choice.'

81 Mansbach (2006), Moulitsas (2010), Phillips (2006) use or imply the term 'Christian Taliban' or 'American Taliban' in reference to rising and ruling, as in the 'Bible Belt,' theocratic anti-liberal and anti-democratic Puritan-rooted evangelicalism. Bauman (1997,

Particularly, the US estimation on this important dimension of substantive democracy can be based on observations that the effective political freedoms and rights of ideological minorities are virtually non-existent since McCarthyism and the 'red scare'[82] defining conservative America as 'proto-fascist'[83] during the 1950s according to some observations through these days. A specific ground for such an estimation is the reported[84] virtually zero-degree of

p. 184) suggest that the 'evangelist churches of the Bible Belt,' alongside the 'Islamic integrisme of ayatollahs,' 'belong to a wider family of (proto) totalitarian solutions offered to all those who find the burden of individual freedom excessive and unbearable.' Hedges (2006) describes US Puritan-inspired evangelicals or fundamentalists as 'American fascists.' Lindsay (2008, p. 67) reports that US 'evangelicals have become more prominent within the power elite over the last 30 years,' especially becoming 'more prominent in national politics,' notably that the 'sense of embracing an evangelical faith and then using it in one's leadership motivated nearly all (91 percent) of the leaders (thus) bringing their evangelical convictions with them on their rise to the top.' Lindsay (2008, p. 75) suggests, however, 'little support for the hypothesis that evangelicals are colluding to take over America.' Yet, the above ('using (evangelicalism) in one's leadership,' 'bringing their evangelical convictions with them on their rise to the top') and the reported tendency 'to steer large bureaucracies or powerful institutions toward their evangelical aims' and their cohesion emerging 'from the shared religious identity of evangelical elites' imply the opposite. So does even more the reported 'prevalence of faith in the exercise of their public leadership' (Lindsay 2008, p. 68), contaminating politics with religion and subverting democracy into theocracy, For example, Lindsay (2008, p. 78) observes that the Bush II administration was the 'most evangelical in modern history,' which precisely indicates that evangelicals are not only 'colluding' but even to some extent succeeding to 'take over America,' not to mention the South subjected to the total(tarian) rule of evangelicalism and so turned into the theocratic 'Bible Belt.'

82   Lipset (1955) identifies the early post-war 'radical right' as the major threat to American Democracy. Furthermore, Plotke (2002, pp. xxxi–lvi) finds that the overall (US) political spectrum has shifted notably to the right. (So) a range of radical right ideas (opposition to virtually all government regulation, rejection of the entire welfare state) has grown in significance and now appears across a large part of the political spectrum. Many of the substantive positions of the postwar radical right now extend much further toward the political center than (before 1964). The center of American politics has moved notably to the right.'

83   Putnam (2000, p. 350) suggests that America during the 1950s was 'provincial, misogynist, racist, protofascist (sic) and (worst of all) boring compared with the enlightened, liberated (1960s-1990s).'

84   Becky and Western (2004, p. 152) report that in the US 'between 1925 and 1975, the prison incarceration rate hovered around 100 per 100,000 of the resident population. By 2001, the imprisonment rate, at 472 per 100,000, approached 5 times its historic average. In (1997) more than 60 percent of Federal prisoners were serving time for drug crimes.' Notably, they find that the 'lifetime risks of imprisonment roughly doubled from 1979 to 1999'

effective political freedoms and rights of prisoners in the US compared with their extensive degrees in most other Western democracies,[85] with expected exceptions like the UK. For example, in 2005 the European Court of Human Rights judged that the UK 'General prohibition preventing persons serving prison sentences from voting in parliamentary and local elections in the UK was in violation of the European Convention on Human Rights.'[86] To that extent, this applies to the even more severe and extensive prohibition of prisoner voting to encompass both current and former prisoners in the US, above all in its conservative states in the South and beyond. While formally the US is not under jurisdiction of the European Court of Human Rights and thus not obligated by the European Convention on Human Rights, this indicates that the presumed 'model' of democracy and free society falls short even of the standards of political and civil liberties and rights in the despised 'old world' primarily thanks to its prevailing or resurgent conservative ideology, governance and regions.

Becky and Western (2004, p. 164). Mueller (2013, p. 9) suggests that 'many of those in jail in the US are guilty of drug-related crimes, and so this latter statistic can be attributed to the draconian nature of US policies with respect to drugs in comparison to other rich democracies. But these draconian policies can also be traced to the much stronger religious beliefs in the United States,' above all 'Evangelical Americans.' Uggen and Manza (2002, p. 778) find that among Western and other democracies, the US 'is virtually the only nation to permanently disenfranchise ex-felons as a class in many jurisdictions, and the only country to limit the rights of individuals convicted of offenses other than very rare treason or election-related crimes.' Notably, they suggest that the findings 'signal a true democratic contraction in the US' such that there is 'considerable evidence that ballot restrictions for felons and ex-felons have had a demonstrable impact on national elections, and in this sense rising levels of felon disenfranchisement constitute a reversal of the universalization of the right to vote (placing) felon disenfranchisement within a broader model of social control of dispossessed groups' (Uggen and Manza 2002, pp. 794–6). In particular, Wakefield and Uggen (2010, p. 399) indicate that 'disenfranchisement of current and former felons has altered the outcome of numerous national elections, most notably the 2000 presidential race.' Kohler-Hausmann (2013, pp. 351–2) registers '2.3 million people in prisons and jails, over 5 million people on probation or parole supervision at risk of imprisonment' in America during the 2010s., and comments that 'these numbers are—from both a historical and international perspective—staggering (yet) both understate the reach of the criminal justice system and, in some sense, misrepresent the modal criminal justice encounter (misdemeanor and its punishment).'

85   Other sources on non-existent or minimal prisoner political rights in the US include *Fairvote* (http://www.fairvote.org) and *Sentencing Project* (http://www.sentencingproject.org) and for political prisoners of conscience in the US Amnesty International.

86   The source is *Electoral Justice: The International IDEA Handbook* (2010, 2).

In sum, the above suggests three grounds for the US qualitative estimation of effective universal or equal political liberties and human rights. These are, first, the complete exclusion of legal (let alone illegal) immigrants and in part some racial-ethnic minorities from the political system, second, the near-total suppression, exclusion, and discrimination against religious minorities such as non-believers from power or public office, and third, the denial of basic voting and other rights to ideological-legal minorities like prisoners. On this account, American politics in its Federal governance (Congress, Presidency, Supreme Court) under conservatism and its ultra-conservative Southern and other regions aims and succeeds to maximize suppression, exclusion and discrimination in politics by suppressing, excluding, disenfranchising, and discriminating against as many 'un-American' groups as possible, especially immigrants, in part racial-ethnic minorities, the 'godless,' and prisoners. In this respect, it appears to effectively function as an anti-liberal, anti-secular, and exclusionary 'democracy.' This long-standing anti-democratic pattern of conservatism has further expanded and intensified during recent times with various conservative insurgencies and electoral victories since 1980s through the 2010s, as exemplified by the 'Tea Party' proto-fascist, authoritarian reactionary rebellion and dominance in the South and related regions. To indicate how anti-democratic and anachronistic 'conservative America' is in comparative terms, instead Western societies, including neighboring Canada, aim and succeed in maximizing political liberation, inclusion, and equality by emancipating, enfranchising and including as many minority groups as feasible, including immigrants, racial-ethnic minorities, the 'godless,' and prisoners, thus revealing themselves as true, i.e., liberal, secular and universalistic democracies.

The 'Political Terror Scale'

Strikingly, the US in its conservative ideology, governance and regions manifests itself as a salient exception, conspicuous outlier by having by far the highest 'political terror scale' score (the only country having 4 or higher than 3) among not just Western democracies but all countries within OECD. This hence manifests conservative supremacist 'American exceptionalism' perversely in the form of exceptional, unique 'best' repression and undemocratic, illiberal rule, and self-contradicts conservatism's standard claims to an 'exceptional nation' in superior and even only democracy and freedom. Consequently, the US polity in its conservative ideology, governance and regions consistently occupies the highest level (3) on the 'political terror scale' and thus of government violent repression and undemocratic rule by formally elected power elites among Western and related societies. This holds for the period of 2007–12[87] and evidently after, as since 2010–14, with the Federal legislature and most states again ruled by conservatism in its invariant violent, repressive manner, including mass imprisonment for sins-crimes and widespread executions discussed next.

Imprisonment and Executions

Within the US, the vast majority of states (31 at the present), above those in the South and related conservative regions, apply the death penalty, in addition to the Federal Government applying it both to nonmilitary crimes and the military.[88] The data on imprisonment and executions hence provide the ground for the US estimate on this aspect of effective democratic rule as a crucial component of substantive democracy. Generally, such an estimate considers various observations showing the relatively low level of democratic rule and the high degree of oppression and compulsion in the US polity specifically in its conservative ideology, governance and regions compared to most Western democracies.

The regional rationale for the US estimate is the common observation and experience that formally elected—or self-selected through gerrymandering and other Machiavellian tactics—conservative Southern and other elites cum 'good (and godly) old boys' persist in undemocratic, illiberal rule and oppression. This includes penal repression through mass incarceration[89] of

---

87   The source is http://www.politicalterrorscale.org which defines Level 3 of the 'political terror scale' as follows: 'There is extensive political imprisonment, or a recent history of such imprisonment. Execution or other political murders and brutality may be common. Unlimited detention, with or without a trial, for political views is accepted,' with the highest level being 5 and the lowest 1. As reported, Amnesty International has consistently placed the US government on level 3 of the political terror scale during 2007–12, notably as the only such case among Western democracies.

88   Alesina and La Ferrara (2014, p. 3402) note that 'today, 34 states in the United States allow capital punishment' and the Federal Government has two death penalty statutes, one for the military and the other for nonmilitary crimes.' Since then some US states have abolished the death penalty so that 31 of them still use it at the time of writing these lines.

89   Aizer and Doyle (2015, p. 759–60) observe that 'The United States has the highest incarceration rate of any OECD country—with rates triple that of the next highest country. The high rate of incarceration in the United States cannot be explained by higher rates of crime. Since 1990, US crime rates have fallen each year, while incarceration rates have doubled to the point where over 2.2 million adults were incarcerated and an additional 4.8 million were under supervision 759 of correctional systems in 2011,' inferring that 'what distinguishes the United States is the punitiveness of its criminal justice policies: the ratio of those incarcerated to those convicted is 70% higher in the United States than

sinners-as-criminals and widespread executions—including DNA-proven innocent persons or not deserving the death penalty due to various biases or errors[90]—in the anti-liberal, undemocratic South and related regions, in which about half of the American population lives and growingly migrates. Moreover, since the Presidential election of 2008 and the consequent 'Tea Party' anti-democratic rebellion and influence, theocratic Southern and related states have intensified and expanded their undemocratic, anti-liberal rule and oppression, including penal repression, by comparison and opposition to the 'liberal,' 'big' federal government. It follows that they are being primarily responsible for the US's 'exceptional' ranking on the comparative 'political terror scale' during that period. Hence, the Southern and related regional anti-liberal, anti-democratic, above all theocratic ('Bible Belt') 'revenge' mostly explains, together with federal governance (Congress, Presidency, Supreme Court) under conservatism, why the US score on the 'political terror scale' is much higher (4.2) than that of its neighbors Canada (1.2) and even of Mexico (0.6) since 2008–10 and before.

Effective Universalism, Equality, and Justice of Government Goods and Sanctions

The US estimate is supported by the reported lowest degree of political universalism, notably of universal public goods and benefits, in 'conservative America' among major Western democracies. The estimate is also grounded in various observations of Draconian laws and sanctions through excessive, unfair punishment policies in the US, above all in federal governance under conservatism and the South and other ultra-conservative regions, as epitomized by irrational and harsh 'three strikes' laws in most states. The ground for the estimate is thus what analysts diagnose as an Orwellian 'normal pathology' or

---

the next highest country.' This disjuncture indicate an Orwellian repressive and thus anti-democratic trend of no or less crime and (yet), invariably Draconian, more punishment (as also suggested by Cooney and Burt 2008).

90   Alesina and La Ferrara (2014, p. 3402) refer to the striking finding that in the US 'between 1973 and 1995, the proportion of fully reviewed capital judgments (4,578 state capital appeals, 248 state post conviction reversals, and 599 capital sentences reviewed by federal habeas corpus courts) in which serious error was found and which were overturned at one of the three stages was 68 percent. (For example) 7 percent were found to be innocent, 75 percent were resentenced to less than death, and 18 percent were resentenced to death.' In general, Boudon (2011, pp. 44–5) observes that the 'death penalty tends to disappear from modern democratic societies notably because it has been repeatedly shown to have no dissuasive power. Moreover, it renders judicial error irreparable and is obviously cruel.'

'pathological normalcy' in the form of 'less crime, more punishment'[91] for effectively non-crimes like moral sins in the US. This includes the observed link between politics such as reelection and harsh punishment, as exemplified by the greater degree of 'sentencing harshness of elected judges'[92] in the South and beyond. A related ground consists in the observations of the resulting unparalleled mass incarceration and thus the exploding probability of imprisonment in the 'expanding carceral archipelago (Gulag) of disciplinary control.'[93] Yet another related ground for the estimate is, in addition to the observed use of torture and indefinite detention,[94] the continuous exceptional use of the death penalty in the US on mostly religious—traced to Puritanism as Tocqueville suggests—and thus dogmatic irrational grounds,[95] especially the South and other conservative states, as reportedly an instrument of 'terror,' especially 'terrorizing' the poor and powerless underclass.[96] The estimate is

---

91 Cooney and Burt (2008) find 'less crime, more punishment' in conservative America during the 'war on crime,' specifically the 'war on drugs,' and alcohol and other sins-crimes, an outcome apparently ushering in or reminiscent of an Orwellian totalitarian or Draconian dystopia.

92 Lim (2013, p. 1361) suggests that the greater 'sentencing harshness of elected judges is strongly related to the (conservative) political ideology of the voters in their districts, while that of appointed judges is not.'

93 This and similar expressions are used by King et al. (2012) and Wacquant (2002).

94 The US government use of torture and indefinite detention during the 'war on terror' is registered in Einolf (2007) and Turk (2004).

95 Mueller (2009, p. 385) proposes that 'if the seculars' position on capital punishment is based on their judgment about its efficacy as a deterrent, then the (US) evangelicals (use) an alternative criterion—most likely some version of an eye for an eye. From the perspective of a utilitarian morality, their position is difficult to defend.'

96 Jacobs, Carmichael, and Kent (2005, p. 656) note the description of the use of the death penalty in the US, above all the South, as an instrument of perpetuating 'privilege' and 'selective terror.' Bauman (1997, p. 43) notes that the spectacle of execution is 'cynically used by (US) politicians to terrorize a growing underclass' of poor and powerless—with neither decent legal nor basic political representation—as in the South and similar regions ruled by conservatism, including evangelicalism, applying and sanctifying such punishment on religious grounds of 'Biblical law,' just as Islamic fundamentalism does on the basis of 'Sharia law.' This indicates that in respect of the death penalty, imprisonment and Draconian punishment overall religious conservatism in South and beyond effectively renders 'Biblical law' equivalent to 'Sharia law' that thus becomes redundant to 'establish.' US conservatives accuse Islamists seeking to impose 'Sharia law' in America, concealing the fact or impression that they act as allies ('brothers in arms') in this and many other anti-liberal, anti-secular and exclusionary aspects, as Mueller (2009) shows, even if fighting crusade and jihad for dominance, thus both engaging, as Turner (2002) observes, in 'jihadic politics.'

thus grounded on the US conservative government and region being the only one applying—Puritan-inspired, sanctified and style—and so the leader in executions among Western democracies and in the entire world, alongside dictatorships like China and North Korea and Islamic theocracies Iran, Saudi Arabia, Taliban, etc. Critics may add that the company of these dictatorships and theocracies in respect of executions, mass imprisonment for sins-crimes and the 'political terror scale' demonstrates the true, though usually disguised, nature and effects of the conservative ideology, governance and regions of the US, simply 'conservative America' as the petrified and even expanded— as through the population and political expansion of the South—anti-liberal, anti-secular, and anti-universalistic part of the 'two Americas.' In general, the estimate is supported by observations documenting the rise and expansion of the police/punitive and Orwellian-like security and surveillance state in the US climaxing in the 2000–10s but starting during the Cold War and McCarthyism, and comparatively more so than in most Western societies, except for the UK, as shown by similar scandals of violations of privacy.

The Economic Condition and Indicator of Modern Free Society—A Free Economy

Conditions and Indicators of a Free Economy

By assumption, the general economic condition, subsystem, and indicator of modern free society represents a free economy as an economic system of universal and equal or symmetrical liberties, choices, and rights. Since such an economic system constitutes within modern free society as a rule a market economy primarily in the form of capitalism (and secondarily non-capitalism), this signifies such economic liberties, choices, and rights for its two major collective agents or factors of production like capital and labor, entrepreneurs and workers, as well as producers and consumers intersecting with them. Such universality and equality or symmetry of economic liberties, choices, and rights of capital and labor define and typify the free market capitalist (or non-capitalist) economy, just as that of their political forms defining and typifying democracy.

This pattern of economic liberty accords with, does justice to, and historically derives from the Enlightenment postulate of universalism and egalitarianism in respect of liberties, choices, and rights,[1] and consequently Comte-Spencer-Mill's principle of universal, equal freedom for all agents in the economy and society as a whole, including Senior's 'law of equal competition' in the market. As with regard to democracy, at this juncture a provisionally agnostic position is taken on the question of what a free economy specifically constitutes within modern free society, as one 'does not know' whether it is a rationally coordinated and egalitarian welfare, or uncoordinated and inegalitarian plutocratic, capitalism. The preceding hence raises the specific question of conditions, elements, and indicators of a free economy (Table 4.1).

---

1 Dombrowski (2001), Habermas (2001), Hodgson (1999), Hoff and Stiglitz (2010), Mokyr (2009), Mueller (2009), Phelps (2007), and Piketty (2014) register the Enlightenment's comprehensive liberalism, universalism, and egalitarianism in respect of liberties, choices, and rights, notably its principle of universal, equal individual liberty, as well as its scientific rationalism and its technological and economic ramifications.

TABLE 4.1   *Conditions and indicators of a free economy.*

Capital, entrepreneurial freedom and choice
Universal, equal, secure, and protected property liberties and rights
High degree of permanent or sustained market-economic competition
Free foreign trade
Freedom and right of foreign investment of capital
Freedom and right of consumption
Labor freedom and agency
Labor rights, fair rewards, and basic benefits
Economic democracy
Freedom and right of movement of labor within and beyond the economy

---

The first condition, element, and indicator of a free economy—i.e., of universal and equal economic liberty—consists of capital, entrepreneurial freedoms,
choices, and rights. This is the freedom, choice, and right of capitalist activity
and/or entrepreneurship in the economy within the framework of the institutional 'rules of social games,' including legal, conventional, or moral norms.[2]
It specifically involves the freedom of economic adventure, risk-taking, and
founding of enterprises, profit making, investment, business management,
production, distribution and consumption, invention and innovation, and
other entrepreneurial and related activities while playing by the legal and related 'rules of the social game.' In this sense, it represents free enterprise in the
function of preserving and promoting universal economic freedom, thus equal
and complementary capital-labor collective liberties and rights, as well as free
competition in the market.

Negatively, entrepreneurial freedom is not 'free enterprise' for destroying or
subverting these, notably labor, liberties and market competition by anti-labor
actions and anti-competitive practices of monopolization and industrial concentration and control, as the subversion of the 'rules of the social game.' The aggregate outcome of such practices is creating or sustaining Hobbesian anarchy
for capitalists according to the 'law of the strongest' and the 'law of the jungle'
in the 'state of nature' and Leviathan for labor and other non-capitalists[3] in the

---

2   Dahrendorf (1979) as well as Bruni and Sugden (2013) refer to liberalism's emphasis on the
    institutional, in particular legal, 'rules' of 'social games,' and Bhagwati (2011), Etzioni (1999),
    Sandel (2013) stress the role of moral norms in the economy.
3   The capital anarchy and Leviathan-over-labor formula is suggested or implied by economists
    and sociologists. Alvaredo et al. (2013, p. 10) find that the increases of capitalist incomes and
    by implication power and freedom ('top 1 percent') 'come at the expense' of those of labor

form of control and tyranny over the latter. This duality represents the asymmetrical mix of unrestrained freedom through near-absolute and arbitrary power—the literal or figurative 'license to kill'—by capitalist agents, and of severe restraint and persistent oppression of workers, including corporate and government anti-labor or anti-union actions, in the economy.[4] Such a mixture

('the remaining 99 percent'). Similarly, Bivens and Mishel (2013, p. 72) remark that in the US 'as long as the shift to the top 1 percent is not associated with *improved* growth, then the rest of the income distribution is harmed by this increase in top 1 percent shares,' in terms of living standards and in consequence freedom and collective bargaining power. Bourdieu (1998,27,42) notes the anarchic-like, unrestrained freedom and domination of the capitalist class and identifies the 'verdict of the new Leviathan' in capital markets, suggesting that the opposition between capitalists and workers 'is rather like that between masters and slaves.' Cohen (2003, p. 54) detects 'a new 'patrimonial capitalism' characterized with the unlimited freedom and power as well as 'revenge' of capital (shareholders} on labor (wage earners), and Piketty (2014, p. 399) also points to the 'patrimonial capitalism of the twenty-first century' similarly described. In particular, Fligstein (2001, pp. 56–7) observes that the 'US is the purest case of a society in which capitalist firms are able to use the policy domains of the state for their own interest (so that) the US system of rules or exchange is a victory for capitalist firms 'inferring that the 'US federal government always acts to preserve and enhance firms, while other governments may pursue policies oriented toward protecting other social groups,' such as workers. McMurtry (1999, p. 255) suggests that what he names the cancer stage of capitalism' involves 'fascisms of all kinds,' namely the imperative of 'succeed or perish in the brutal global competition' is not far off *Mein Kampf's*, 'humanity as a whole must flourish. Only the weak and cowardly will perish.'" Prior (2002, p. 364) observes that American capitalism tends to move toward 'Hobbesian anarchy' for the capitalist class (or 'mafia capitalism'), combined with that the 'repression of the population will be harsher,' i.e., an 'oligarchic' economic and political system. Schutz (2001, p. 162) remarks that 'capitalist market systems constitute societies that are just as hierarchical as those based on other economic systems (e.g.) Soviet-style central planning, feudalism, and ancient slave-based systems '. Wright (2013, p. 7) suggests that the 'inherent' problem of capitalism is the 'structural power of capital'—plus its 'inequalities of wealth'—versus labor that is 'not in a position to freely choose between democratically organized workplaces and authoritarian firms (and so) the employment relation cannot really be considered 'capitalism between consenting adults.'

4   Acemoglu and Robinson (2008, pp. 268–9) remark that 'even though former slaves were enfranchised and slavery was abolished at the end of the Civil War, the South largely maintained its pre–Civil War agricultural system based on large plantations, low-wage uneducated labor, and labor repression, and it remained relatively poor until the middle of the twentieth century' and later. Bebchuk and Fried (2003l, pp. 74, 89) find that 'executives have substantial influence over their own pay,' indicating that 'managerial power substantially affects the design of executive compensation in companies with a separation of ownership and control.' Also, Piketty (2014, p. 24) observes that 'top managers by and large have the power to set their own remuneration, in some cases without limit and in many cases without any clear relation to their individual productivity, which in any case is very difficult to estimate in a large organization. This phenomenon is seen mainly in the United States and to a lesser degree in Britain,

is antithetical and leads to the destruction or perversion of a free economy perished or perverted in 'libertarian' anarchism as substantively an equivalent or proxy of slavery and a master servant system, and thus of the overarching economic condition, subsystem, and indicator of modern free society.

In sum, the first condition, element, and indicator of a modern free economy represents capitalist entrepreneurial freedom, 'free enterprise' that operates, first, respecting the 'rules of the social game,' and second, preserves or promotes rather than eliminates or undermines equal or symmetrical capital-labor liberties and free market competition. Conversely, capitalist 'free enterprise' that eliminates or restricts collective labor liberties, choices, and rights through anti-labor or anti-union actions, as well as free market competition via monopolization and concentration is its own contradiction and negation—i.e., equivalent to aristocratic absolute, unlimited freedom in feudalism—and thus a grave violation of universal and equal economic liberty defining a free economy. In short, it degenerates into aristocratic, plutocratic capitalism, simply, as US President Theodore Roosevelt warned, the 'tyranny of plutocracy' by its wealth.

The second condition, element, and indicator of a free economy is the security and protection of the universal and equal freedom and right to acquire, accumulate, and use economic resources or property for production, consumption, and other purposes. In short, it comprises universal, equal, secure, and protected material property liberties and rights. This condition hence involves the legal security and protection of personal, private productive property[5] such as physical/industrial and financial/money capital, thus wealth used

---

and it may be possible to explain it in terms of the history of social and fiscal norms in those two countries over the past century.' Bivens and Mishel (2013, p. 71) registers policy changes in the US economy shifting 'bargaining power' to 'those at the top of income distribution' and subverting the 'bargaining power of those at the bottom and middle,' and thus damaging the 'wage prospects of low- and moderate-wage workers, including the declining real value of the minimum wage and the failure to update labor law to provide a level playing field in the face of growing employer hostility to union organizing efforts.' Desai (2005, p. 189) observes that a 'system that allows managers to characterize income differently depending on the audience legitimizes earnings manipulation and permits managers a certain license.'

5   Replicating or evoking Weber, Mises (1951, p. 37) emphasizes that private material property or ownership as a 'sociological category' expresses the 'power to use economic goods' by their owners in relation to, specifically legal and/or effective exclusion of others within society from using them. Yet, Mises, like his colleague Hayek and US followers a la Freidman et al., harbors the 'libertarian' capitalist fallacy or illusion that only laisser-faire capitalism consistently and fully protects and promotes private property rights, and any other economic and political systems do not, and instead eliminate or suppress them, lumping together in a remarkable confusion Soviet 'socialism' with Scandinavian and other Western European welfare capitalisms or social democracies and the US New Deal. In retrospect, Mises, Hayek,

in the function of production, saving, and investment. It also entails the legal security and protection of private non-productive property—for example, residential houses, cars, home electronics and appliances, monetary savings, social security benefits, retirement funds and state pensions, etc.—so wealth used in the service of consumption, leisure, and generally life support, quality, and pleasure or enjoyment.[6] It indicates that actual or prospective owners of production and consumption wealth are legally secure and protected in exercising their property freedoms, choices, and rights regardless of their particular ideological, political and other, especially moral-religious, attributes and actions.

Negatively, this condition signifies that private property liberties, choices, and rights in a free economy are not distributed in an unequal or asymmetrical manner among economic agents or production factors, such as permitted and promoted to capital, and denied or restricted for labor and other non-capitalists on various grounds, including legal punishment like incarceration, political dissent, ideological divergence, moral 'sins,' religious 'heresy' and non-belief,

---

and US 'libertarian' economists both refuse to acknowledge and fail to predict that it is in fact their ideal, 'dream system'—American unfettered, plutocratic capitalism and its political regime—that has proved to be the worst offender of private property rights among Western economies. This specifically applies to the property rights of moral sinners-criminals like nonviolent drug and sexual offenders, through the federal government and states seizing their properties, including houses, financial resources and even pensions, for moralistic Puritan reasons of their illicit pleasures, sins-crimes like drug, sexual and related offenses, with (e.g., Congress' Act from the 1980s) or usually without and simulated valid legal grounds and procedures, as in the South (Texas, etc.). Apparently, such a pattern is the historical legacy or residue of Puritanism which never truly respected and enhanced individual liberty and privacy, as neither does its declared hair revived evangelicalism, including the private property and related economic liberties and rights of sinners and religious dissenters (as noted for Puritan-ruled New England in Kauffman 2008) cum 'witches.' Consequently, so long as American unfettered, plutocratic capitalism, like 'godly,' puritanical politics, continues to be pervaded by the moralistic and theocratic ghost and vestige of Puritanism—for example, what Munch (2001, p. 225) identifies as Winthrop's theocracy glorified by Reagan et al.—the systematic and unapologetic, Puritan-style violation and disrespect of these private property and other economic liberties and rights, generally individual liberty and privacy, likely will persist in the foreseeable future contradicting 'libertarian' laissez-faire illusions. No doubt, this is a sober and pessimistic prediction or expectation. Yet, it is fully consistent with what Weber calls the 'iron consistency' of Puritanism, like its parent Calvinism, and its sequel evangelicalism as a 'gloom and doom' religion in denying, suppressing, and violating individual liberty and privacy, including the private property and other economic liberties and rights of 'witches' such as sinners-criminals making more than half of the total US prison population of almost 2.4 million today, the largest in the Western and entre world.

6 Akerlof (2007), Phelps (2007), Scitovsky (1972), and Steckel (2008) acknowledge or imply the consumption and hedonistic aspect of property rights.

etc. In short, the negative condition of a free economy is *no* inequality, exclusion, and discrimination with respect to private property rights, specifically their maximal permission for capitalists and their negation or restriction for non-capitalists. In pragmatic terms, no capitalists and non-capitalist are in a free economy denied and deprived of personal property either for production or consumption purposes because of non-economic reasons, especially government actions on the 'political terror scale' such as mass imprisonment for nonviolent sins-crimes—mostly not formally or mildly punished in modern free society—on moralistic and religious grounds invoked by theocracies or theocentric societies.

For example, it is a flagrant denial or violation of equal secure property rights as the condition of a free economy expropriating the property, including houses, monetary resources, and pensions, of prisoners, especially those of political and ethical conscience such as ideological dissenters, religious 'heretics,' and nonviolent moral offenders (e.g., imprisoned drug users and traders, sexual deviants, etc.), not to mention innocent persons incarcerated and even executed. It is briefly an act of illegitimate predation, usurpation of private property, especially of non-capitalists, without or dubious legal but strong moralistic-religious grounds driving such actions, thus belonging to the 'political terror scale' noted before and defining a predatory state. And a truly free economy, as well as democracy, does not or would not commit these actions, which is its negative condition of restraint such that inaction in this case is, as Weber would put it, the best course of action ('just do not do it') in economic terms.

The third condition, element, and indicator of a free economy involves a high degree of permanent or sustained market and generally economic competition, simply highly competitive markets and economies. This specifically signifies the existence and operation of free, open, and effective competition in the market. However, this condition is not necessarily identical to the theoretical model of what the neoclassical economist Leon Walras calls the 'hypothetical regime of absolutely free competition' posited by orthodox economics and disputed or relaxed in its later developments, especially since the 1930s with the appearance of the theories of monopolistic and imperfect competition.[7] Simply, the condition consists in that market competition is substantially free, open, or effective, and not necessarily pure or perfect in the sense of orthodox

---

7   Walras (1926) does this in his main theoretical work *Elements of Pure Political Economy*. The early exponents of the theories of monopolistic and imperfect competition are Chamberlin (1948) and Robinson (1933), followed by Dixit and Stiglitz (1979), Hart (1985), Spence (2002), Stiglitz (2002), etc.

economics a la Walras et al.[8] Alternatively, it stipulates that competition is conceptually distinguished from and empirically not eliminated by monopoly as its poison, and subverted by what Schumpeter calls monopoloids such as duopoly and oligopoly as its perversions or simulations, including monopolization and market concentration and consolidation through mergers, takeovers, and acquisitions as typically anti-competitive and anti-consumer processes in design or outcome.[9]

This condition also entails the institutional, in particular legal and political, effective protection and promotion of free, open, and effective market competition against its opposites and subversions, such as monopoly, monopoloids, and monopolization or concentration through anti-competitive and anti-consumer mergers and related activities. It particularly includes anti-monopoly, 'anti-trust' laws and policies[10] and their consistent implementation by corresponding government institutions. To the extent that, as even Adam Smith classically admonishes, individual capitalist entrepreneurs ('traders') invariably, though secretively, tend to eliminate or restrict free competition for their private gains through 'conspiracy against the public,'[11] this necessitates that such a market structure is legally and otherwise institutionally protected and promoted against capitalists inherently seeking to become what his successor Cairnes calls 'non-competing industrial groups,' simply monopolists and oligopolists in the economy.

The above implies that if Smith's individual capitalists completely succeed in their 'conspiracy against the public,' free competition will degenerate into private, usually government-approved monopoly and monopoloids. Consequently, competitive will degenerate into monopolistic capitalism as an economic system that is ultimately its own nemesis and a regression into

---

8   Elaborations, discussions, and critiques of the Walrasian model of perfect competition and general market equilibrium are found in Arrow and Debreu (1954), Blaug (2001), Hicks (1961), Makowski and Ostroy (2001), Phelps (2007), Samuelson (1983a), Schumpeter (1954), Stiglitz (1979), etc.

9   Moreover, Schumpeter (1949, pp. 105–6) argues that the 'bulk of economic progress is incompatible' with perfect competition which is 'inferior to (the 'monopoloid' species of capitalism) and has no title to being set up as a model of efficiency.' In turn, Baker (2003) Pryor (2002), Stiglitz (2002) and Waldman (2003) note the anti-competitive effects of oligopoly and market concentration through mergers, etc.

10   The importance of anti-monopoly 'anti-trust' laws and policies for sustaining market competition and freedom overall is stressed in Acemoglu and Autor (2012), Baker (2003), Carlton (2007), Dobbin and Dowd (2000), Fligstein (2001), etc.

11   Bruni and Sugden (2013) and Eggertsson (2012) cite Smith's statement about capitalists' constant 'conspiracy against the public.'

feudalism and aristocracy typified by what Weber calls the 'monopoly of status groups,' and a mutation or equivalence to state socialism characterized by
public monopolies. At this point, the sole relevant difference of monopolistic
capitalism from feudalism and state socialism or communism is that this is
an economic system of, as Weber puts it, private 'capitalist monopolies' and
these are systems of status and public monopolies.[12] Thus, all of them are
anti- or non-competitive by the standard of free, open, and effective competition in the market, contrary to the glorification or apologetics of the first 'free
enterprise' forms of monopoly by hardline plutocratic 'libertarian' economists
like Mises, Hayek, and Friedman et al. who either deny these monopolies as
non-existent or justify them as 'competitive,' thus denying reality or resorting

---

12   Yet, this is an equivalence or approximation that pretended 'libertarian' economists like
      Mises, Hayek, Friedman, etc. are either unable to detect or unwilling to acknowledged
      due to their laissez-faire dogma or myth that, if totally followed with no government regu-
      lation of market monopolization and concentration like mergers, evidently generates or
      sustains monopolistic and thus anti-capitalistic outcomes in capitalism itself. Following
      their dogma of 'free enterprise' private capitalist monopolies being more efficient than
      and superior to any public state monopoly, Hayek (1960), Friedman (1982), and other bo-
      gus 'libertarians' claim or imply that, for example, AT&T during its monopolistic posi-
      tion in the phone market was 'better' for American consumers' welfare in terms of price,
      quality, and service than the US post office—which they or 'libertarian' politicians want
      to abolish as 'big government'—or Amtrak (public rail service). This applies to various
      notorious private monopolies in the US pharmaceutical industry with even more sinis-
      ter and graver consequences for consumer welfare and health to the no-return point of,
      directly or indirectly, endangering human life and inflicting death by their monopolistic
      practices (e.g., exorbitant price increases making their medicines prohibitively expen-
      sive for most people with or without insurance coverage), compared to any public mo-
      nopoly. Of course, Friedman and other pretended 'libertarian' economists would defend
      and rationalize such economically monopolistic and ethically abhorrent practices in the
      pharmaceutical and most other US industries as 'free enterprise'—cynics may add the
      'free enterprise' in drastically reducing consumer welfare and even inflicting harm and
      endangering human health and life. (In passing, since monopoly is commonly defined
      as plunder, extortion, depredation, predation, spoliation, theft, and the like even in clas-
      sical/neoclassical economics from Smith and Mill to Walras, Pareto, and Marshall, eco-
      nomically monopolistic 'rational' actions are hence also ethically abhorrent or immoral,
      contradicting Friedman's and other 'libertarian' fallacy of separating profit-making 'busi-
      ness' from ethics or morality). Yet, for most Americans experiencing and remembering
      the predatory and effectively criminal conduct of this and most other private US monopo-
      lies and oligopolies past and present, such assertions are uninformed and naïve at best,
      apologetic and malicious at worst, as Van Dyke (1995) suggests. For example, Dahrendorf
      (1979, p. 38) describes Hayek's and other 'libertarian' assertions as no more than the ideo-
      logical justification of capitalist plutocracy, simply the 'haves' and equally ideologically
      driven attacks on the non-capitalist 'have-nots.'

to what Samuelson calls a 'mental gymnastics' of a 'depraved kind' that deliberately conflates competition with private monopoly or monopoloids like oligopoly.

In this respect, the imperative of free market competition requires actually protecting competitive capitalism from capitalists themselves as Smith's intrinsic 'natural born' would-be-monopolists and oligopolists or Cairnes' 'non-competing' groups through legal and other institutional mechanisms such as anti-monopoly and related competition-protective laws and government institutions and sanctions.[13] Consequently, free competition, like most other conditions and indicators of a free economy, represents in the long-run—i.e., in order to be sustained in the face of anti-competitive tendencies—an institutionalized condition established or preserved by legal instruments and state institutions rather than a 'natural state' spontaneously emerging from the interactions of individual capitalists. In fact, what would emerge from their interactions and 'free enterprise' is instead, as Smith admonishes and effectively predicts, monopoly, at best monopoloids like duopoly and oligopoly, through ever-growing market concentration and consolidation eliminating or perverting free competition. In sum, a major condition of a free economy constitutes free, open, and effective market competition that, while deviating from the theoretical model of perfect, pure competition, profoundly differs from and is promoted and protected from elimination or subversion by monopoly and monopolization via institutional mechanisms such as anti-monopoly laws, policies, and sanctions.

The fourth, corollary condition, element, and indicator of a free economy represents free trade. Free foreign trade is typically considered a logical, ultimate extension and 'dramatic exemplification' of free competition beyond a national market and economy and into world markets and global economies, while as a rule enhancing both productive efficiency, productivity, and innovation and consumer welfare and choice as entwined 'gains of trade.'[14] Free trade is theoretically distinguished from and practically opposed and sub-

---

13   On this account, Smith implies, just as Keynes suggests later, that it is private capitalists that tend to become the crucial problem and to that extent 'enemy,' and the liberal-democratic state the main solution or protector, of competitive 'free market' capitalism. This is contrary to the pro-capitalist glorifications and assertions and anti-labor postures of 'libertarian' economists a la Mises, Hayek, Friedman, et al. as the staunch defenders of capitalist dictatorship, plutocracy, and oligarchy against non-capitalists and non-plutocrats, following or evoking what Samuelson (1994, p. 628) calls 'classical apologists' explaining the 'interest and profit earned by capitalists' as a 'reward for their "abstinence" and "waiting."'

14   Samuelson (1983a, p. 203) denotes free foreign trade 'but one dramatic exemplification' of free competition, and Melitz and Redding (2014, p. 317) reassert 'welfare gains from trade.'

verted by market protectionism, industrial closure, and economic nationalism overall on a variety of grounds from purely economic to ideological-political and cultural, including religious, ones. This condition of a free economy can be negatively restated as no or minimal market protectionism and economic nationalism as destructive to free trade and eventually free competition in the national market, as well as adverse to the efficiency of the economy, including business innovation and consumer welfare as estimated in product price, quality, and service. Industrial protectionism functions and persists as the functional equivalent of monopoly and oligopoly by monopolizing the domestic market for domestic 'our' agents and closing or restricting it to their global competitors, 'foreigners,' operating as an economic form of nationalism, in particular political and cultural xenophobia as a form of collective madness or hysteria. In short, like monopoly and oligopoly, protectionism violates the laws of equal competition and freedom in the market and economy by favoring nationals ('us') and discriminating against non-nationals ('them') in markets.

Free trade particularly includes the freedom of exports of goods and services to and their imports from other competing economies in the world regardless of the ideological, political, and religious differences, national animosities or divergences, and even military tensions between them. Alternatively, it involves no or low degree of protection and favoring of domestic agents and of discrimination against foreign economic ones, including both companies and individuals, through various ways and means—for example, legal prohibitions and restrictions, government subsidies, preferential tariffs, quotas, etc.—expressing economic nationalism, including politically and culturally driven xenophobia. In sum, a condition and indicator of economic freedom is free trade that extends and exemplifies free competition to the world market, and consequently no or minimal degree of protectionism and economic nationalism and xenophobia as an adverse force to competitive markets and producer inventions and to consumer wellbeing. Simply, the economy is freely competitive and open not only with respect to 'native' agents such as 'our' firms, workers and consumers but also to 'foreigners' by permitting equal freedom and competition to both.

The fifth related condition and indicator of a free economy encompasses the freedom and right of foreign investment of capital. First, this condition entails the freedom and right of capital investment by national agents, both firms and individuals, in other economies, including direct foreign investments in industrial facilities and production and in stock-market and other financial investments. Second, it comprises the freedom and right of foreign corporate and individual entities to invest capital in the domestic economy, including industrial and financial investments and transactions. In addition, the condition of free foreign investment contains the freedom and right of non-nationals to acquire, hold, and use productive and non-productive property—for example, land, factories, office buildings, houses, etc.—in the national economy and of nationals to do the same in other economies. Negatively stated, this condition consists in no favoritism, preferential treatment of the domestic investment of capital by national companies, and of the acquisition and holding of property by nationals, and no prohibition of or discrimination against their investments in other economies ('exporting jobs,' 'outsourcing,' etc.) and against non-nationals investing or acquiring and holding assets in ('buying out') 'our' economy. In sum, a condition of a free economy is that both national and non-national economic agents have the freedom and right to foreign investment of capital, and to acquire and hold production and consumption assets in other economies.

The sixth condition, element, and indicator of a free economy constitutes the freedom and right of consumption and thus the satisfaction of various material and non-material human needs, wants, and aspirations, including extrinsic and intrinsic motivations. In short, it is the condition of consumer freedom, choice, and rights. This involves the consumer freedom of choice between alternative products and services, and among competing producers and service providers in the market. It means that consumers, subject to the resource constraint of their effective demand by income constraints, are free to choose between various, ideally unlimited or multiple numbers of marketed products and services and their producers and providers, including both domestic and foreign ones. The condition also incorporates legal, institutionalized consumer protection from unlawful and unethical market activities and transactions by sellers or producers, including cheating, fraud, low quality, dangerous or unhealthy products, marketing disinformation and misrepresentation, in particular advertising deception and harassment, extortion, predation, etc. In short, it signifies that consumers are legally and effectively protected from variations of predatory 'mafia capitalism,' 'gangster capitalism,' 'kleptocracy,' and the like.[15]

Negatively defined, consumer freedom ideally consists in that consumers are not prohibited, prevented, or restricted from choosing, purchasing, and consuming some products and services, or in certain quantifies and at specific times, on various non-economic grounds, including political coercion in free foreign trade ('no trading with the enemy'), moral and religious condemnations or restrictions such as 'sins' (e.g., prohibitions for selling and buying alcohol and other 'sinful' goods on Sunday or other days), and the like. In sum,

---

15 Pryor (2002, p. 364) predicts that American 'liberal capitalism might be slowly replaced by Hobbesian anarchy or mafia capitalism,' Giddens (2000b, p. 35) refers to 'gangster capitalism' in which 'rent-seeking is backed by the use of violence,' and Acemoglu (2005, p. 1046) uses the term 'kleptocratic regimes' that 'impoverish their citizens.'

a condition of a free economy is what most economists extoll as consumer sovereignty in respect of the choice and consumption of products and services offered in the market, and consequently no or minimal prohibition and restriction of what goods they should or should not choose and consume and which contribute to or reduce their welfare, health, and happiness.

The seventh condition, element, and indicator of a free economy consists of labor liberty and agency. In accordance with the principle of universal and equal freedom and competition, a major prerequisite and expression of a free economy is that labor as one factor of production, aggregate economic agent possesses and exercises symmetrical and complementary liberties, choices, and rights, and autonomous actions, just as capital as another enjoys and exerts 'free enterprise.[16] Negatively stated, the condition of a free economy is that labor freedom and agency is not systematically denied, depreciated, suppressed, or violated, while that of capital being recognized, glorified, promoted, and expanded in equally systematic ways and means. Instead, this represent a pattern defining capitalist dictatorships as the 'tyranny' of plutocracy, thus authoritarian capitalism, past and present, just as pre-capitalism such as feudalism, a master servant economy and slavery defined by an extreme asymmetry between the working masses as servants or slaves and landed and merchant aristocracy as the master class. Simply, theory and evidence both suggest that there is or can be no such a thing as a modern free economy without comprehensive and effective labor freedom, choice, and agency symmetrical and

---

16   'Libertarian' economists Mises, Hayek, Friedman, et al. glorify Smith-Spencer's law of universal, equal freedom and agency in the economy and society but invariably limit its application to their darling capital and deny or restrict it for labor condemned as the enemy of 'free enterprise.' Thus, they somehow miraculously overlook or forget that universal, equal freedom and agency in the economy logically and actually applies to all economic agents, factors of production, thus including labor, and not only to capital. For 'libertarian' economics, 'equal freedom' signifies equal freedom and agency for all capitalists and plutocrats or oligarchs only, thus being substantively equivalent to that of aristocrats in feudalism and slave-owners in slavery, with labor substantively—and often legally through anti-union laws as in the US South—reduced to the status of servants and in part slaves. In short, 'libertarian' economics' 'equal freedom' is, as noted of Hayek's version, equal and permitted for the 'haves' exclusively, and not for the 'have-nots.' Libertarian' economics therefore perpetuates and rationalizes aristocratic, plutocratic, oligarchic capitalism as effectively capitalist dictatorship and thus an unfree economic system and an adverse condition and element of modern free society. What 'libertarian' economics celebrates and defends as capitalist 'free enterprise' plutocrats or oligarchs monopolizing equal freedom and agency and denying it to labor are basically contemporary equivalents of pre-capitalist aristocrats enjoying the same asymmetry in liberty and action over servants in feudalism, simply the aristocracy of capital/money continuing that of land/war.

complementary as well as countervailing to capital and entrepreneurial liberties, choices, and actions.

In terms of the two main factors of production—i.e., what economists call total factor productivity—symmetrical and complementary labor freedom and agency is the half of the equation of a free and productive economy, and thus of the economic conditions of modern free society, the other half being that of capital and entrepreneurs. This condition, first, encompasses individual labor freedom and agency, as distinguished from and overcoming its slave and master-servant condition and treatment and other physical coercion and oppression of laborers. Simply, individuals are legally free to choose whether or not, for which employer, where to work, etc., and negatively, not coerced physically to do so by employers, as by extant slave and master-servant laws and their legacies,[17] or by government, as exemplified by coerced unpaid or poorly paid state prison labor widespread in capitalist and other dictatorships as well as theocracies, etc.

Second, this condition comprises the freedom of labor collective organization, action, and complementary or countervailing power and influence, as through free associations like unions, peaceful industrial protests and strikes, etc., in relation to capital and its own organizations and interest groups. Thus, in a fully free economy labor is institutionally and effectively free to organize, act, and have and exert relative power or influence as a collective agent, just as is capital as a collectivity in the sense of economic organization and its association with other organizations. Negatively formulated, labor is not physically coerced or constrained to relinquish or disavow such collective freedom and agency, notably unionization, by capitalist employers and/or the state through anti-union activities and laws, while capital enjoying and exerting unlimited liberties and actions, a pattern defining capitalist dictatorships as unfree economic systems when considering both factors of production.[18] The overarching

---

17   Acemoglu and Robinson (2008, p. 286) note the 'continuation of the pre–Civil War economic order (slavery) after the Northern troops left the South,' Naidu and Yuchtman (2012, p. 107) that until the late 19th century 'Master and Servant law gave employers the ability to criminally (as opposed to civilly) prosecute and severely punish a majority of employees across industries for breach of contract in Great Britain,' and Steinberg (2003, p. 451) that 'the 'law drawn on by English capitalists was not a mere remnant of feudalism but was a particular development of the 18th and 19th centuries and championed by them. Master and servant should be seen as a historical form of advanced formal subsumption of labor in the absence of other institutional or technical forms of control in the workplace.'

18   Wright 2013, p. 7) remarks that unregulated plutocratic capitalism 'generates severe deficits in realizing democratic values for three reasons: by excluding crucial decisions from

and strong ground for this is that labor constitutes an essential factor of production and consequently its productive operation presupposes its freedom and agency symmetrical and complementary to that of capital. In sum, a condition of a free economy is that labor institutionally has and effectively realizes symmetrical and complementary individual and collective freedom and agency, just as does capital, while inequality at the expense of the first factor of production and in favor of the second indicates capitalist dictatorship such as plutocratic capitalism and its variations.

The eighth closely related condition, element, and indicator of a free economy comprises labor rights, fair rewards, and basic benefits. The principle of universal, equal economic rights stipulates that a free economy is also conditional on that labor as the second essential factor of production is entitled with and exercises comprehensive institutionalized and effective rights that are equivalent or symmetrical and complementary to those of capital, as well as fair material compensation for its productive contribution and other benefits necessary to its functioning and preservation. Negatively stated, an important condition of a free economy is that labor rights are not denied, suppressed, devaluated, and violated, its material rewards not unfair or exploitative, and its benefits not eliminated or minimized below the basic level, while those of capital being affirmed, promoted, appreciated, and maximized, a pattern typifying capitalist dictatorship[19] such as plutocratic capitalism as an essentially unfree economic system.

---

public deliberation, by allowing private wealth to affect access to political power, and by allowing workplace dictatorships.'

19   In a way, if one does not know what capitalist dictatorship in the sense of Theodore Roosevelt's 'tyranny of plutocracy' in the US is one knows it when seeing it or its element and predictors, as the following. The media reported in November of 2014 that 'seven of the 30 largest US corporations paid more money to their chief executive officers last year than they paid in US federal income taxes (according to a study). Amid talk in Washington about corporate tax reform, the study said the seven companies, which in 2013 reported more than $74 billion in combined US pre-tax profits, came out ahead on their taxes, gaining $1.9 billion more than they owed. At the same time, the CEOs at each of the seven companies last year was paid an average of $17.3 million, said the study, compiled by two Washington think tanks. The seven companies cited were Boeing Co, Ford Motor Co, Chevron Corp, Citigroup Inc, Verizon Communications Inc, JPMorgan Chase & Co and General Motors Co. The Institute for Policy Studies and the Center for Effective Government, the study's co-authors, said its findings reflected "deep flaws in (the US) corporate tax system." Such flaws probably indicate that, paraphrasing Shakespeare, something is deeply rotten in the kingdom' of the US, presumably exceptional cum superior, plutocratic and oligarchic economic-political system reproduced by conservatism.

Specifically, this condition, first, includes the institutional provision and effective exercise of the labor rights to collective bargaining with capital or management about wages, salaries, and non-wage benefits, as well as some level of employment protection, work safety, minimal labor standards, a degree of flexibility in work hours and schedule (including paid overtime), and related conditions of its employment such as hiring and firing practices. Second, it involves the labor rights to a just, fair distribution of wages and salaries in relation to its productivity and to that of capital, thus distributive justice, as well as the right and opportunity for profit sharing with capitalist owners and management whenever economically founded and justified by workers' productive contribution to firm profits. Negatively stated, it consists in the labor right to *no* exploitation and discrimination on any grounds, no unfair wages and benefits and so unjust income and wealth inequality in relation to capital, and to lack of or minimal material deprivation and hardship while operating as a factor of production—i.e., no or low poverty in work a la the 'working poor'—and the like.

Third, the condition contains the labor rights to material and non-material benefits necessary for its wellbeing and survival, work performance, and life functioning, and provided by employers and/or government, including health care, preschool care, education, paid vacation and parental leave, unemployment and welfare assistance, retirement benefit and pensions, etc. As noted, the compelling rationale for labor's rights, fair rewards, and basic benefits is that it represents just as an indispensable factor of production as does capital, and consequently its productivity or efficiency necessitates them—including 'efficiency wages'[20] versus subsistence and starvation pay—equally or symmetrically to those of capitalists. In sum, a crucial condition and element of a free economy is that labor as an indispensable factor of production formally has and effectively exercises comprehensive rights, fair rewards, and basic benefits in symmetry and as a necessary complement to those of capital and/or entrepreneurship as another such aggregate productive agent.

The ninth corollary condition, element, and indicator of a free economy consists of economic, industrial democracy.[21] By assumption, the latter represents an economic analogue or complement of political democracy, and is

---

20   Akerlof (2002, p. 414) defines 'efficiency wages' as being 'above rock bottom' or market-rates and suggests that 'psychological and sociological explanations for efficiency wages are empirically most convincing.'

21   Piketty (2014, p. 397) suggests that 'without real accounting and financial transparency and sharing of information, there can be no economic democracy,' and Wright (2013, p. 7) alerts that 'so long as workers are not in a position to freely choose between democratically

typically mutually linked and reinforced with the latter. In the context of the relationship between the polity and the economy, the presence and level of political democracy to some extent determines and predicts the existence and degree of its economic variant, and conversely the second positively influencing or complementing the first. On this account, despite its different structure and functioning, setting, and scope, economic democracy cannot be considered completely separate and independent from its political type.

This also holds true because both indicators condition and indicate—in factor-analytic terms 'load on'—modern free society and its holistic liberty as the overarching variable. At this juncture, economic democracy particularly indicates ('loads on') a free economy and thus merits to be included in the latter's conditions and indicators, just as political democracy does a free polity. Just as political democracy forms the institutional system of liberties and rights in the polity, economic democracy represents a kind of institutionalization of symmetrical and complementary or countervailing labor and capital freedoms, powers, and actions, including their conflict resolution, within the economy, specifically inside of firms. While political democracy overcomes or reduces strict hierarchy and oligarchy in politics, economic democracy supersedes or mitigates rigid master–slave or servant hierarchies and the absolute power of plutocracy in an economy, specifically within firms. Just as political democracy is freedom-enhancing and socially efficient and progressive alike in the long-run, economic democracy enhances both symmetrical and complementary or countervailing labor and capital freedoms and improves organizational efficiency, especially total factor productivity, and thus industrial or technical progress. This contradicts the opposite assertions of anti-labor 'libertarian' economists attacking economic democracy as its being 'inefficient' and obstructing 'free enterprise.'[22]

---

organized workplaces and authoritarian firms, the employment relation cannot really be considered 'capitalism between consenting adults.'

22   On logical grounds, the statements or implications of anti-labor 'libertarian' economists a la Mises, Hayek, Friedman, et al. that economic democracy is economically 'inefficient' and obstructs 'free enterprise' in economy seem as dubious as the conservative, in particular fascist-theocratic, allegations that liberal democracy is ineffective politically and impedes 'freedom'—as conservatism, including fascism or theocracy, understands it—in the polity. More importantly, just as the negative claims of conservatism about the freedom and effectiveness of liberal democracy, these 'libertarian' assertions have been disproved or contradicted by empirical studies and observations that economic democracy or its proxy actually enhances both labor-capital liberties and powers/actions *and* also economic efficiency and productivity, including firm profitability, as Giddens (2000a), Hodgson (1999), Kenworthy (2002), Putterman, Roemer, and Silvestre (1998), and Wright (2001) suggest. This is exemplified by the superior economic performance of German and

Economic democracy involves, first, capital-labor industrial cooperation and democratic partnership within firms and beyond in the function of en-hancing the firm's and the economy's productivity, efficiency, performance, and innovation, as well as cohesion and peaceful conflict resolution. This is distinct from and supersedes their mutual hostility, opposition, and conflicts, notably capitalist absolute power and domination over workers after the master–slave or servant pattern in slavery, feudalism and aristocracy, and early aristocratic, plutocratic capitalism. Second, as the particular form of the first, economic democracy includes labor co-participation and co-determination in company decision-making and management through proximate power-sharing and cooperative democratic institutions within firms such as work councils with symmetrical or complementary representation of both factors of production, and the like.

Negatively stated, economic democracy implies the condition of no arbitrary dictatorship and oppression by capital over labor in the economy, specifically firms, just as political democracy is conditional on the lack of dictatorial and oppressive power by rulers over subjects in the polity. This holds good despite or rather because of considerations of economic efficiency, including produc-tivity and profitability, as shown by the superior performance of European, particularly German, and other companies with such democratic mechanisms as work councils.[23] As before, the fact that labor represents a necessary factor

other European companies with work councils, for example, Volkswagen, etc., strong unions, and related forms and exercises of economic democracy that is virtually non-existent or negligible in most of their American counterparts.

23   Dustmann et al. (2014, p. 177) observe that the 'model of industrial relations has been very successful in Germany, where negotiation with unions and participation of work councils in decision-making processes are widely regarded as an important cornerstone in further-ing common interests and even improving productivity.' They add that 'Germany's culture of common interest is dissimilar to the view about worker representations commonly held in the United States. A recent US example is the attempt of the management of the Ger-man company Volkswagen to introduce a works council at its Chattanooga plant in Ten-nessee. While the participation of works councils in management decisions is considered by Volkswagen as a cornerstone of successful firm policy that helps furthering common in-terests, Tennessee Governor (and conservative senators) ha(ve) been outspoken in oppos-ing any union formation at the plant, fearing that it endangers the state's effort to attract investment' (Dustmann et al. 2014, p. 177), on an evidently false pretext masking typical Southern conservative anti-union ideas and policies. In addition, reportedly in September 2014 the 'head labor official on Daimler AG's supervisory board says he considers it "unac-ceptable" that the German automaker's Mercedes plant in Alabama stands alone among the company's factories around the world without union representation for its workers (stating) it should be normal that we have a union at each of our plants. We have very dif-ferent behavior on the part of the company in some cases. In India we are in the process

of production coexisting and co-functioning with capital provides a compelling rationale for economic democracy as the system of symmetrical and complementary or countervailing labor-capital liberties, powers, and actions. This holds on grounds of both the imperative of efficiency such as improving labor and total-factor productivity, plus profitability in the long-run, and the principle of equal freedom for the factors of production.

Conversely, the 'libertarian' or conservative economic and political opposition to economic democracy on both grounds face the burden of proof to demonstrate that it is economically inefficient and freedom-limiting alike, thus running contrary to most empirical evidence, especially that on the positive effects of work councils on efficiency and symmetrical freedoms through shared decision-making in European, especially German, firms. In sum, an important, though often overlooked or downplayed—as in the US literature and public—condition of a free economy is the existence and functioning of economic democracy as the positive factor both of complementary freedom and agency and of productivity and efficiency within firms.

The tenth condition, element, and indicator of a free economy constitutes the freedom and right of movement of labor within and beyond the national economy. Such freedom of labor mobility represents the equivalent or complement of the free movement of capital like capitalist investors, entrepreneurs, and managers inside and outside of an economy. To that extent, a fully and consistently free economy embraces and promotes the freedom of movement for labor and capital alike as the major factors of production. Consequently, the justification for the free movement of labor is both on grounds of the principle of symmetrical, complementary freedom and the imperative of economic efficiency such as total factor productivity.

First, the labor freedom of movement within and beyond the economy is symmetrical, complementary, and consistent with that of capital, and thus with the principle of equal economic freedoms, rights, and agency. Second, such freedom is necessary for and instrumental in improving labor's economic productivity and overall efficiency, as a factor of production whose productive and otherwise efficient operation, like that of capital, presupposes a high degree of free movement theoretically or ideally equivalent, even if actually and realistically seldom equal, to that of the latter. In this respect, prohibitions or restrictions of the freedom of labor movement within and especially beyond the national economy cannot be persuasively defended on grounds either of

---

of founding a union for our plant there, and we have the support of the company that will happen. But in the USA, in the South, it is being resisted.' If so, it seems that basic labor liberties, rights, and collective actions are more denied in the US South as part of the 'free' developed First World than in India belonging to the 'unfree,' backward Third World.

the freedom and right or the efficiency and productivity of the factors of production or aggregate economic agents. Instead, such prohibitions are justified
commonly and spuriously in economic terms by considerations like 'protecting' domestic workers or jobs against 'foreigners,' 'national security,' racial-
ethnic factors, ideological, religious and cultural differences, etc.

The first dimension of this condition comprises the high and even maximal
degree of freedom of labor mobility within the national economy, simply internal migration such as geographic mobility across the regions, states, and lo-
calities of a country. This dimension as a sociologically horizontal movement,
while sometimes overlapping, is not necessarily identical and cannot be equated with social mobility as vertical upward or downward movements within the
system of social stratification, specifically class structure. Internal migration
thus involves the freedom of mobility within geographical, physical space, and
social mobility such freedom in institutional space as an intersecting but distinct environment, although labor, like capital, may view free movement in the
former setting as the means to move freely upwards within the latter.

The second dimension is represented by the degree of freedom of labor
movement beyond the national economy, including that of permanent or
temporary immigration to the country in question and of emigration to other
countries. In sum, the freedom of labor movement within and beyond the national economy is an equivalent or complement to that of capital and goods
and services through free competition in the domestic market and free trade
and foreign investment in global markets, respectively.

Conditions and Indicators of a Free Economy
and Types of Capitalism

At this juncture, the analysis suspends the provisional agnostic stance on
the problem of which economic system, specifically type of capitalism, most
completely and consistently fulfills and displays the conditions, elements, and
indicators of a free economy. This is done by observing or expecting that rationally regulated and egalitarian welfare capitalism tends to inherently, coherently, and fully realize and display them rather than other economic systems,
specifically anarchic or unregulated and anti-egalitarian plutocratic capitalisms. Alternatively, all or most of the above parameters of a free economy are
observed or expected to be found in the first rather than in the second type of
capitalism and economic system generally.

Consequently, rationally regulated and egalitarian welfare capitalism as a
rule epitomizes a modern free economy rather than its antipodes such as irrational, even self-destructive—i.e., catastrophic crisis-prone—unregulated and

anti-egalitarian, specifically plutocratic, oligarchic and in that sense aristocrat-ic, capitalism. Like liberal, secular, and universalistic democracy with respect to a free political system, coordinated and welfare capitalism demonstrates or is expected to be the only genuine and viable or sustainable (type of) a free economy in the long run. By contrast, its alternative, anarchic and plutocratic, laissez-faire capitalism proves or is likely to be the exact opposite, substan-tively an unfree economy through its capital-Anarchy, labor-Leviathan pluto-cratic formula and unviable ultimately in that, as Pareto observes and predicts, capitalist and any aristocracies, oligarchies or plutocracies as forms of dictator-ship 'do not last' indefinitely. Such an adverse outcome is due to laissez-faire capitalism's inner tendency to self-destruction in its self-generated economic catastrophes like the Great Depression and the Great Recession, as well as the slave or feudal-style inequality between the new money aristocracy or oligar-chy as plutocracy—notably, the 'top heavy' 1 percent in the US—perpetuating or evoking what Michels calls the aristocratic 'master-caste' and non-capitalist classes.[24]

On this account, the economic system of rationally regulated and welfare capitalism tends to be genuinely free by virtue of its universalistic and egali-tarian Enlightenment-rooted principle of universal and equal freedom and agency for capital and labor as the two main coexisting and co-functioning production factors. By stark contrast and vehement opposition, the econom-ic system of anarchic and plutocratic, capitalism operates and appears as an ersatz 'free economy,' bogus 'free enterprise.' This is traced to its pre- and anti-Enlightenment, specifically feudal and slavery, anti-universalistic, anti-egalitarian perverse law of unequal freedom and agency in favor of plutocracy or oligarchy as the novel aristocracy of capital against the non-wealthy and non-capitalists—as Tönnies suggests—as the proxy new slaves or servants substantively, even if not legally, in relation to the latter exercising the 'tyranny' of wealth in the sense of Roosevelt. As a consequence, rationally regulated and welfare capitalism tends to be typically and substantially a freer economy than its unrestrained and plutocratic opposite,[25] and even attains—as observed for

---

24   Akerlof and Shiller (2009), Piketty (2014), and Stiglitz (2010) compare the Great Depres-sion and the Great Recession as catastrophic economic crises. Wolff (2002) describes the highest 1 percent of the wealthy in the US as 'top heavy,' Lenski (1966) remarks that 1 or 2 percent receives at least half of total income in feudal, agrarian society, while Mankiw (2013) 'defending the (top) one percent' the wealthy in America and Welch (1999) stand-ing 'in defense' of economic inequality generally.

25   In fact, unregulated aristocratic or oligarchic capitalism's most ardent advocates from 'libertarian' economists Mises, Hayek, and Friedman positing the Anarchy-for-capital, Leviathan-for-labor formula to neo-conservative 'revolutionaries' Thatcher and Reagan

its variant or social democracy in Scandinavia by Samuelson—economic as well as political and individual freedom 'second to none' in modern society and societal history.

The question specifically opens as to whether and to what degree modern Western and related societies fulfill and reveal the preceding conditions, elements, and indicators of a free economy—i.e., how they rank on the dimension of economic freedom? Societies with rationally regulated and welfare capitalism are observed or expected to more substantially and coherently satisfy and display these parameters of a free economy by ranking higher on economic freedom than those of its unregulated and plutocratic or oligarchic opposite and other alternative systems. As in liberal, secular, and universalistic democracy versus illiberal 'democracies' and other political regimes, such observations and expectations of the higher degrees of freedom—in conjunction and mutual reinforcement with equality, inclusion, justice, and shared wellbeing and prosperity—in the first economic system than the second and any intermediate systems are empirically validated, as demonstrated in the remainder of this and following chapter.

Classification of Modern Economic Systems

As with regard to those of democracy or the polity, one can classify contemporary Western and related societies such as OECD countries with respect to types of capitalism or economic system in the following way (Table 4.2).

First, classified in rationally regulated and egalitarian welfare capitalism are the following countries: Australia, Austria, Belgium, Canada, Denmark, France, Germany, Iceland, Luxembourg, the Netherlands, New Zealand, Norway, Sweden, Switzerland, and the US. The latter is so classified in regulatory and egalitarian ideology and governance (weak, transient or exceptional) and regions (minority or decreasing), as distinct from the anti-regulatory and anti-egalitarian opposite, thus observing or assuming the 'two Americas' in economic terms co-existing in opposition and conflict. These countries and regions tend to be comparatively the most regulatory and egalitarian societies or regions in economic terms, and consequently form the main instances of rationally regulated and welfare capitalism among Western and other economies. As such, they are regarded and described as 'rationally regulated and egalitarian welfare

---

implementing that alchemy claim that 'there is no alternative' to this capitalist type, as Bauman (2001), Beck (2000), Bourdieu (1998), Giddens (2000a), Hodgson (1999), and Piketty (2014) note.

TABLE 4.2   *Classification of western and related societies (OECD countries) in a free economy/economic freedom.*

I   Rationally regulated, egalitarian welfare capitalisms (15 and ½ cases)
       Australia, Austria, Belgium, Canada, Denmark, Finland, France, Germany, Iceland,
       Luxembourg, Netherlands, New Zealand, Norway, Sweden, Switzerland, the US in in
       regulatory and egalitarian ideology and governance (weak, transient or exceptional)
       and regions (minority or decreasing, e.g., the Coast, parts of the North, etc.).
     Expected free economy/economic freedom   highest, I—completely or largely free
     overall ranking

II   Unregulated, inegalitarian plutocratic/oligarchic capitalisms (4 and ½ cases)
       Mexico, Poland, South Korea, Turkey, the US in anti-regulatory and anti-egalitarian or
       anti-welfare strong, enduring or prevalent ideology and governance (Reaganomics,
       etc.) and majority or growing regions (e.g., the anti-labor South, the Middle West).
     Expected free economy/economic freedom   lowest, III—unfree or quasi-free
     overall ranking

III Intermediate, eclectic, mixed capitalisms (13 cases)
       Chile, Czech Republic, Greece, Hungary, Estonia, Ireland, Italy, Japan, Portugal, Slova-
       kia, Slovenia, Spain, the UK
     Expected free economy/economic freedom   intermediate, II—quasi-, largely free
     overall ranking   or unfree

---

capitalisms,' and proved or predicted to attain the highest overall rank (I) on
the dimension of a free economy/economic freedom among OECD and other
countries. As seen, all these countries or regions belonging to rationally regulated and welfare capitalism are also politically classified in liberal, secular, and
universalistic democracy, indicating or predicting a strong association between
these economic and political systems.

   Second, these OECD countries are classified in unregulated and plutocratic
or oligarchic capitalism: Mexico, Poland, South Korea, Turkey, and the US. The
latter is classified in anti-regulatory and anti-egalitarian or anti-welfare ideology and governance (strong, enduring or prevalent) and regions (majority or
growing) coexisting and conflicting with and launching an all-out assault, especially since Reaganomics,[26] on the rationally regulated, egalitarian economy

---

26   A leading contemporary US economist, Solow (1987, p. 182) observed that what the 'Rea-
      gan Administration' cares about is the 'distribution of wealth and power and its program
      is and has always been in favour of the redistribution of wealth in favour of the wealthy
      and of power in favour of the powerful.'

and the welfare state within the 'two Americas' in economic ideology/policy and regional terms. These countries and regions are in comparative terms the most persistently or growingly anarchic or unregulated and plutocratic or oligarchic capitalist economies overall, and hence epitomize the corresponding type of capitalism within OECD. They are therefore considered and termed 'unregulated and inegalitarian plutocratic or oligarchic capitalisms,' and observed or predicted to reach the lowest rank overall (III) with respect to a free economy/economic freedom within the OECD. As seen, these countries or regions are also politically classified into an anti-liberal, anti-secular, and anti-universalistic political system, which indicates or predicts that the latter and unregulated and plutocratic or oligarchic capitalism are associated.

Third, the rest of OECD countries are consequently classified into eclectic, intermediate, mixed capitalism and generally economy, such as Chile, Czech Republic, Greece, Hungary, Estonia, Ireland, Italy, Japan, Portugal, Slovakia, Slovenia, Spain, and the UK.[27] These countries exemplify this type of capitalism within the OECD by virtue of mixing or reconciling in varying ways and proportions rationally regulated and egalitarian welfare and of unregulated and plutocratic capitalisms, with some coming closer to the first and others to the second. Thus, the term 'mixed capitalisms' is used to describe them, and these are ascertained or anticipated to have an intermediate overall rank (II) on a free economy/economic freedom within the OECD. Lastly, these countries thus economically classified are also politically grouped in 'mixed democracies,' which implies that that the latter are linked to 'mixed capitalisms,' subject to some variations.

Comparative Estimates of a Free Economy for Western and Related Societies

The conditions and indicators of a free economy provide criteria for generating its corresponding comparative indexes, or estimates of economic freedom for Western and related societies such as OECD countries (Table 4.3).

Despite being considered capitalist and thus 'free' economies, these societies display significant variations in their free-economy estimates, i.e., degrees of economic freedom, with varying scores on a 0–10 scale (derived from ten particular rankings), just as do in democracy or levels of political liberty.

---

27   The UK perhaps seems closer to unregulated and plutocratic or oligarchic capitalism especially during Thatcherism, but still is not probably 'unregulated' in the sense or degree of the US and 'plutocratic or oligarchic' of that of (also) Chile, Greece, Mexico, Poland, South Korea, and Turkey.

TABLE 4.3   *Comparative estimates of a free economy/economic freedom.*

Country	Property rights	Free trade	Global-ization	Labor rights	Union density	Work rights	Earnings	Work hours	Pros-perity	Immi-gration	TOTAL	Rankings	Average
Australia	8	3.29	7	4	3	3	2	3	8	10	51.29	10	5.13
Austria	8	8.24	7	8	5	5	3	4	6	7	61.24	10	6.12
Belgium	7	10	9	8	10	10	4	6	5	6	75	10	7.5
Canada	9	5.32	8	4	5	5	3	3	10	8	60.32	10	6.03
Chile	7	5.73	7	4	3	3	NA	0	0	2	31.73	9	3.53
Czech Republic	5	10	7	6	3	3	4	1	3	3	45	10	4.5
Denmark	9	6.14	8	8	10	10	3	7	9	5	75.14	10	7.51
Estonia	7	10	NA	8	1	1	NA	1	0	7	35	8	4.38
Finland	10	5.55	7	8	10	10	3	4	8	3	68.55	10	6.86
France	7	4.45	8	8	1	1	3	9	4	6	51.45	10	5.15
Germany	8	7.04	8	8	3	3	4	10	6	7	64.04	10	6.4
Greece	3	4.23	6	0	5	4	NA	0	0	5	27.23	9	3.03
Hungary	5	10	8	6	3	3	10	1	0	2	48	10	4.8
Iceland	9	6.12	7	8	10	10	10	3	6	4	73.12	10	7.31
Ireland	8	7.52	10	6	6	6	1	7	7	5	63.52	10	6.35
Italy	4	4.67	7	8	7	7	3	2	0	5	47.67	10	4.77
Japan	7	3.27	5	6	3	3	1	2	4	NA	34.27	9	3.81
Korea, South	6	7.79	6	0	1	1	6	0	2	NA	29.79	9	3.31
Luxembourg	9	7.08	NA	NA	7	7	1	5	7	10	53.08	8	6.64

Mexico	2	6.25	6	2	2	2	NA	0	0	1	21.25	9	2.36
Netherlands	9	10	9	8	3	3	2	10	8	5	67	10	6.7
New Zealand	10	4.21	7	6	4	4	5	3	9	10	62.21	10	6.22
Norway	10	4.66	7	8	10	10	6	9	10	5	79.66	10	7.97
Poland	5	8.01	7	4	3	2	6	1	0	1	37.01	10	3.7
Portugal	6	6.18	7	4	3	3	0	4	2	4	39.18	10	3.92
Slovakia	4	10	8	8	3	3	6	2	3	1	48	10	4.8
Slovenia	5	10	NA	NA	4	4	4	4	3	5	39	8	4.88
Spain	6	4.95	7	6	3	3	3	4	3	7	46.95	10	4.7
Sweden	9	5.73	8	8	10	10	4	5	9	7	75.73	10	7.57
Switzerland	10	8.37	9	6	3	3	NA	5	10	10	64.37	9	7.15
Turkey	3	5.01	5	0	1	1	10	1	0	2	28.01	10	2.8
UK	8	3.98	8	4	5	5	3	4	5	6	51.98	10	5.2
US	6	2.32	7	2	2	2	2	2	7	6	38.32	10	3.83

I   Average free-economy score 7 or higher—Completely free economic systems
II Average free-economy score 5–6.99—Largely free economic systems
III Average free-economy score 4–4.99—Quasi-free, semi-free economic systems
IV Average free-economy score under 4—Unfree economic systems

For instance, societies like the US and the UK usually deemed or claimed to be 'freer' and paradigmatic 'capitalistic' economies, thus with the higher degrees of economic freedom, turn out to be less so than many others such as Scandinavia and other parts of Western Europe construed as the opposite, especially by 'libertarian' American economists and conservative politicians. These comparative estimates of economic freedom supply the rationale for classifying Western and related economies into four categories. They are, first, 'completely free' (average scores[28] 7 or higher), second, 'largely free' (6–6.99), third, 'quasi-free' (5–4.99), and fourth, 'unfree' (under 5) economies, specifically capitalisms. Consequently, Western and related societies are classified in these categories of capitalisms with their respective levels of a free economy, i.e., degrees of economic freedom (Table 4.4).

The first category of 'completely free' economies entirely encompasses rationally regulated and egalitarian welfare capitalisms, thus reaffirming previous observations and confirming the present expectation but contradicting 'libertarian' economists' contrary assertions as ungrounded. Such instances of this type of capitalism as those in Western/Northern Europe, in particular Scandinavia, classified into it prove to be the freest economies and so capitalisms, having the highest aggregate index of economic freedom. These societies with regulated and welfare capitalism, in particular Scandinavian countries, rank consistently the highest on almost all the specific conditions and indicators of a free economy, i.e., economic freedom, among all Western and other capitalist economies, including the presumably 'freest' and 'purest' American and

TABLE 4.4   *Average free economy/economic freedom estimates and classification,*
OECD countries.

I	Average scores 7 or higher—Completely free economies/capitalisms (6 cases)
	Belgium, Denmark, Iceland. Norway, Sweden, Switzerland
II	Average scores 5–6.99—Largely free economies/capitalisms (11 cases)
	Australia, Austria, Canada, Finland, France, Germany, Ireland, Luxembourg, Netherlands, New Zealand, UK
III	Average scores 4–4.99—Quasi-free economies/capitalisms (7 cases)
	Czech Republic, Estonia, Hungary, Italy, Slovenia, Slovakia, Spain
IV	Average scores under 4—Unfree economies/capitalisms (9 cases)
	Chile, Greece, Japan, South Korea, Mexico, Poland, Portugal, Turkey, US

---

28   Curiously, using the threshold of 8 or higher, no economy would qualify as 'completely free' due to relatively low scores in particular rankings, which required its adjustment to 7 and so on.

British types of capitalism. More precisely, 'completely free' economies and the six highest ranked on economic freedom are in a descending order: Norway (7.97), Sweden (7.57), Denmark (7.51), Belgium (7.50), Iceland (7.31), and Switzerland (7.15) (Table 4.5).

Just as in democracy ranking, four of these six economies are Scandinavian countries, joined with two adjacent or related instances (Belgium and Switzerland), which strongly confirms the linkage between liberal, secular, and

TABLE 4.5   *Free economy ranking, OECD countries.*

Rank	Country	Index (0–10)	Category of economy	Classification
1	Norway	7.97	Completely Free	Welfare Capitalism
2	Sweden	7.57	Completely Free	Welfare Capitalism
3	Denmark	7.51	Completely Free	Welfare Capitalism
4	Belgium	7.50	Completely Free	Welfare Capitalism
5	Iceland	7.31	Completely Free	Welfare Capitalism
6	Switzerland	7.15	Completely Free	Welfare Capitalism
7	Finland	6.86	Largely Free	Welfare Capitalism
8	Netherlands	6.70	Largely Free	Welfare Capitalism
9	Luxembourg	6.64	Largely Free	Welfare Capitalism
10	Germany	6.40	Largely Free	Welfare Capitalism
11	Ireland	6.35	Largely Free	Mixed Capitalism
12	New Zealand	6.22	Largely Free	Welfare Capitalism
13	Austria	6.12	Largely Free	Welfare Capitalism
14	Canada	6.03	Largely Free	Welfare Capitalism
15	UK	5.20	Largely Free	Mixed Capitalism
16	France	5.15	Largely Free	Welfare Capitalism
17	Australia	5.13	Largely Free	Welfare Capitalism
18	Slovenia	4.88	Quasi-Free	Mixed Capitalism
19–20	Hungary	4.80	Quasi-Free	Mixed Capitalism
19–20	Slovakia	4.80	Quasi-Free	Mixed Capitalism
21	Italy	4.77	Quasi-Free	Mixed Capitalism
22	Spain	4.70	Quasi-Free	Mixed Capitalism
23	Czech Republic	4.50	Quasi-Free	Mixed Capitalism
24	Estonia	4.38	Quasi-Free	Mixed Capitalism
25	Portugal	3.92	Unfree	Mixed Capitalism
26	US	3.83	Unfree	Plutocratic Capitalism[a]
27	Japan	3.81	Unfree	Mixed Capitalism
28	Poland	3.70	Unfree	Plutocratic Capitalism
29	Chile	3.53	Unfree	Mixed Capitalism

TABLE 4.5   *Free economy ranking, OECD countries.*

Rank	Country	Index (0–10)	Category of economy	Classification
30	Korea	3.31	Unfree	Plutocratic Capitalism
31	Greece	3.03	Unfree	Mixed Capitalism
32	Turkey	2.80	Unfree	Plutocratic Capitalism
33	Mexico	2.36	Unfree	Plutocratic Capitalism

a Conservative America

universalistic democracies and free economies in the form of regulated, welfare capitalism, so political and economic freedom. Thus, the region of the most rationally regulated and egalitarian welfare capitalism, Scandinavia, shows to be also the freest economy in regional terms. Notably, the single country with the most rationally regulated and egalitarian welfare capitalism, Norway, proves to be the freest national economy as well.

In retrospect, while unexpected at first glance, such ranking reaffirms a US leading economist's realization that 'egalitarian and (putatively) regimented' Scandinavia was 'freer'[29] than America in economic as well as political terms during postwar times especially because of more comprehensive, generous, and symmetrical and complementary—in relation to capital—labor liberties, actions, rights, rewards, and benefits in the first than in the second economy. Conversely, forms if unregulated and inegalitarian[30] plutocratic or oligarchic

---

29   Recall that Samuelson (1964, p. 226) states that 'by most Millian criteria (of liberty), (economically) regimented Scandinavia was freer than my America' (cited in Tilman 2001, p. 39) during postwar times. Moreover, Samuelson (1983b, p. 59) proposes that, for example, 'forty years after Friedrich Hayek wrote down his nightmare of the welfare state leading remorselessly to the totalitarian murder of freedom, Scandinavians enjoy freedom second to none that the world has ever seen.' On this account, Hayek's 'nightmare of the welfare state' turns out to be a kind of 'libertarian' blindness and fantasy, an unrestrained Anarchy-for-capital, oppressive Leviathan-for-labor ideology couched as 'economic theory' blind to rather than analyzing reality—unlike his nemesis Keynes's realistic analyses, as Akerlof (2007) emphasizes—and prone to fantastic predictions, thus revealing, as Bourdieu (1998, p. 101) puts it, the 'ultra-conservative utopia' as a form of 'lunacy.' In turn, Bhagwati (2011, p. 164) remarks that the 'Scandinavians have an approach to capitalism that differs from that in the United States, for example: the former is more egalitarian in outcomes whereas the latter is more focused on ensuring equal opportunity.'

30   Benabou (2003, p. 329) characterizes the US economic as well as political system as 'more inegalitarian' than those of other Western countries.

capitalism are the conspicuously missing link in the category of complete economic freedom, and its mixed variant only isolated presence.

The second category of 'largely free economies/capitalisms' also incorporates mostly instances of rationally regulated and egalitarian welfare capitalism, as well as a single mixed counterpart, but none of its opposite, which generally fulfills the expectations than the former economic system is freer than the latter. Specifically, the following economies are shown to be 'largely free' in a descending order: Finland (6.86), the Netherlands (6.70), Luxembourg (6.64), Germany (6.40), Ireland (6.35), New Zealand (6.22), Austria (6.12), Canada (6.03), the UK (5.20), France (5.15), and Australia (5.13). Nine of these eleven countries exemplify regulated and egalitarian welfare capitalism, and only two, Ireland and the UK, mixed economic systems. Conversely, countries with unregulated and inegalitarian plutocratic or oligarchic capitalism are once again conspicuously missing from the category of 'largely free economies,' thus confirming the expectation that this capitalist type is neither completely nor mostly free economy, and invariably less free than rationally regulated and egalitarian welfare capitalisms.

The third category of 'quasi-free economies' comprises exclusively mixed economic systems, and no of rationally regulated and egalitarian welfare capitalism and its opposite, thus generally confirming the expectations. For illustration, 'quasi-free economies' are in a descending order these countries: Slovenia (4.88), Hungary (4.80), Slovakia (4.80), Italy (4.77), Spain (4.70), Czech Republic (4.50), and Estonia (4.38), all of which being mixed economic systems in the present classification. This confirms that they are less free than regulated and egalitarian welfare capitalism but more than its opposite. They thus show to be neither entirely free nor unfree economies by exhibiting aggregate degrees of economic freedom that are ranked between those of welfare and plutocratic capitalism, just as previously observed and presented anticipated. In particular, they display the degrees of labor liberties and rights that are invariably lower than those of welfare capitalisms but mostly higher than those of plutocratic or oligarchic capitalism. In turn, the fact that unfettered and inegalitarian plutocratic capitalism is not comprised even in this category and instead relegated to the last 'unfree' zone, as seen next, partly confirms the expectation that regulated and egalitarian welfare and 'mixed' capitalist economies are as a whole freer than this capitalist type. Conversely, its absence from this intermediate category of economic freedom, just as from the previous two, and its relegation to the 'unfree' zone reaffirms that it is typically less free than these other types of capitalism.

The fourth and last category of 'unfree economies' largely comprises unregulated and/or anti-egalitarian plutocratic, oligarchic capitalism, along with its mixed counterpart but no regulated and egalitarian welfare capitalisms. This hence validates both prior observations and current anticipations, while disconfirming 'libertarian' economists' opposite assertions and their political counterparts' uniformed claims. For illustration, this last category includes in an ascending order of un-freedom the following economies: Portugal (3.92), the US (3.83), Japan (3.81), Poland (3.70), Chile (3.53), Korea (3.31), Greece (3.03), Turkey (2.80) and Mexico (2.36), of which five are unregulated and anti-egalitarian plutocratic capitalisms and four mixed economies in the present classification. These six countries, along with the other three, hence turn out to be the least free economies and particularly capitalisms among Western and related societies exhibiting the lowest aggregate index of economic freedom. Strikingly, all the countries, including Mexico and the US, economically classified as unregulated and inegalitarian plutocratic or oligarchic capitalisms are comprised in the category of 'unfree economies,' as precisely anticipated.

Conversely, this category of the lowest economic freedom involves no single instance of rationally regulated and egalitarian welfare capitalism, which fully supports the anticipations and clearly contradicts 'libertarianism.' Also, contradicting 'libertarianism,' some proxy laissez-faire cases appear less free than regulated and welfare capitalisms, for example Chile under Pinochet's fascist dictatorship (supported and celebrated by 'libertarian' economists Hayek and Friedman et al. from the Chicago School) and the US in antiregulatory and anti-egalitarian governance and policy (Reaganomics) and regions like the South than Western Europe, particularly Scandinavia. This reaffirms Samuelson's and other observations of the higher degrees of economic and other freedom in Scandinavian 'regimented' and welfare than in American and any unfettered and plutocratic capitalism. Thus, as the obverse of the ranking of Scandinavia and Western Europe, unregulated and plutocratic capitalisms[31] consistently rank lower than the first on most indicators of economic freedom, especially labor liberties and rights, among OECD countries.

---

31   Moreover, the minimal degree of labor liberties and rights to the point of a proxy slave condition, including non-existent industrial democracy, represents the single strongest factor of oligarchic anti-labor capitalism in conservative America and Mexico to exemplify unfree economies by comparison to Western European regulated and egalitarian welfare capitalisms. In short, such a type of capitalism a cause and exemplar of an unfree economy, and a modern proxy of master-servant economies, and even modified slavery, as the post-bellum US South, as Acemoglu and Robinson (2008) suggest. Conversely, it represents no factor and instance of a free economy contrary to 'libertarian' economists' ungrounded, discredited, and outdated claims to 'free enterprise' in such an economic system in which labor is forced by anti-labor ideology, politics, and laws to a slave-like position of powerlessness, disorganization, and extreme existential insecurity. US and Mexican economies ranking similarly on many aspects of economic freedom may seem 'shocking' at first sight, but this shock is not unprecedented if one remembers that, for example, the US children poverty rate is 'shockingly' almost identical to that of Mexico, at any rate the second highest among OECD countries, as Smeeding (2006) notes.

CHAPTER 5

Sources and Grounds for Free Economy Estimates

General Considerations

This chapter presents the grounds and sources for the comparative estimates of a free economy and the ensuing ranking of Western and related societies in the preceding four categories. Generally, these aggregate estimates and categories are grounded in or consistent with a variety of sociological, economic, and other academic studies, empirical data (especially from OECD) and other sources such as non-academic estimations and rankings of countries on economic freedom and the like.

First and foremost, the estimation or expectation that rationally regulated and relatively egalitarian welfare capitalism tends to be invariably and substantially freer—i.e., rank higher as a whole on economic freedom—than its unregulated and anti-egalitarian plutocratic or oligarchic alternative accords with scientific studies, empirical data, and other sources. They demonstrate that welfare capitalism, as prevalent in Western Europe and beyond (e.g., Canada), is superior both in economic freedom and efficiency, as well as equality, justice, social mobility, wellbeing, and happiness or life satisfaction, compared to plutocratic or oligarchic capitalism as especially dominant in some countries like South Korea, Mexico, Poland, Turkey, and the US in the preceding specification of anti-regulatory and anti-egalitarian ideology and governance and regions such as Reaganomics and the Southern states. Notably, Scandinavian and related countries are universally observed or estimated to have the highest degree of economic freedom, widespread shared prosperity, physical wellbeing, including health, stature, etc., relative wealth and income equality, social mobility, and happiness or life satisfaction in the Western and entire world.[1] This is primarily because, as found by studies and surveys, of their economic

---

1 Kleven (2014, p. 77) remarks that 'American visitors to Scandinavian countries are often puzzled by what they observe: despite large income redistribution through distortionary taxes and transfers, these are very high-income countries. They rank among the highest in the world in terms of income per capita, as well as most other economic and social outcomes.' He adds that 'the economic and social success of Scandinavia poses important questions for economics and for those arguing against large redistribution based on its supposedly detrimental effect on economic growth and welfare.'

system of rationally coordinated and egalitarian welfare capitalism, simply being developed welfare states and comprehensive social democracies.[2]

No wonder, these welfare states, from Denmark, Sweden, Norway, and Finland to the Netherlands and Belgium to Austria, Germany, Switzerland, and Canada are with a monotonic regularity observed to be the 'happiest,' featuring the highest level of life satisfaction, among Western and other societies, being typically 'happier' or their people more 'satisfied with life' than other economic systems. Evidently, the welfare state or model of capitalism has consistently and unambiguously proven to be the most effective and secure means and path to attaining Bentham's ideal of the 'greatest happiness to the greatest number' in the sense of what Alfred Pigou calls 'economic welfare' and 'social welfare,' material and non-material wellbeing, including health and life expectancy. Notably, this model has proven superior in this respect to its alternative, non-welfare plutocratic or oligarchic capitalism, as found or approximated primarily non-Western economies like South Korea, Mexico, Poland and Turkey, plus the US in the above specification and to some degree the UK as the vestige of Thatcherism.

On this account, the welfare model of capitalism constitutes a genuine economy of wellbeing and in that sense happiness, life satisfaction, joy of life, and the like. The welfare state probably for the first time in social history fully realizes the premise of the Enlightenment and its product classical political economy, including Smith, that the only societal goal of the economy (and government) is to provide and increase human happiness in society, more precisely what Alfred Marshall[3] calls the 'material requisites' for it in the form of 'wellbeing' as a blend of 'economic and social welfare.'

Conversely, by ranking typically lower in terms of happiness or wellbeing, non-welfare, unregulated, and plutocratic capitalism shows to be a failure in attaining this end, thus denying its own social justification and legitimacy, and falling in the same category as slavery, feudalism, a master-servant economy, fascism, communism, and other failed economic systems. To that extent, the welfare model of capitalism has demonstrated to the best instrument to implement Jefferson's ideal and legal right of 'pursuit of happiness' into an actual condition in the economy and society.

---

2 La Porta et al. (2008, p. 312) observe that 'we see social democracies in Continental Europe but not in the United States.'

3 Alfred Marshall (1961, p. 3) states that 'Political Economy or Economics is a study of mankind in the ordinary business of life; it examines that part of individual and social action which is most closely connected with the attainment and with the use of the material requisites of wellbeing.'

Comparative data and reports like surveys make it abundantly evident and clear that welfare capitalisms, from Scandinavia and Western Europe to Canada, simply make people 'happy' or 'satisfied with life,' in the sense of both economic and social wellbeing, notably 'happier' than do non-welfare and plutocratic or oligarchic alternatives, spanning from Turkey to Mexico and the US in the above regional specification such as Southern and related states. In macro-economic and social terms, welfare capitalisms evidently represent or lead to 'happy' societies in this sense, in contrast to non-welfare and plutocratic capitalism representing or leading to an 'unhappy or less happy society and thus joining slavery, feudalism, a master-servant economy, fascism, communism, and related economic systems in this respect. And evidently it is easier for individuals, with some exceptions, to realize the ideal or right of 'pursuit of happiness' in a 'happy' or 'happier' than in an 'unhappy' or 'less happy' society, as indicated by comparing the reported degrees of happiness in Scandinavia and most Western Europe to others, including the US and the UK, which are in all surveys higher in the first societies. Simply, individuals are more likely to be 'happy' in the first than the second societies, just as they are observed to be more non-religious or non-superstitious in a secular and rationalistic than in a religious or irrational society, and conversely, their showing a higher degree of religiosity or anti-science superstition in the latter social system.

Hence, to the degree that a 'happy,' 'happier' society determines and predicts, with certain variations, its constituent individuals reaching more happiness than otherwise, and conversely, the welfare model of capitalism appears as the best solution, and its non-welfare, plutocratic opposite, the worst recipe, for attaining the sole or main end of the economy (and the polity). Recall that this end is Bentham's desideratum of the 'greatest happiness to the greatest numbers' and Smith's variation, Jefferson's ideal and legal right of 'pursuit of happiness,' Marshall's notion of 'material requisites of wellbeing,' Pigou's composite of 'economic and social welfare,' and the like.

In sum, observations indicate that rationally regulated and egalitarian welfare capitalism in Scandinavian and other Western European and related societies tends to generate superior, most favorable outcomes for economic freedom and wellbeing, just as for their non-economic forms. In retrospect, these findings reaffirm Samuelson's striking admission that during the postwar period regulated and egalitarian Scandinavia was economically as well as politically 'freer' than America presumably in spite—or rather because—of the latter's exceptional irrationally 'unfettered' and/or anti-egalitarian plutocratic-oligarchic capitalism.

Conversely, because, as documented by observations, of their economic system of irrational, unregulated and/or anti-egalitarian plutocratic capitalism societies like non-Western countries South Korea, Mexico, Poland and Turkey, plus the US in the above specification and to some degree the UK as the relic of Thatcherism reveal comparatively inferior or suboptimal economic and related outcomes. These outcomes involve the lower degrees of economic freedom, of shared and widespread, as distinct from exclusive and narrow, prosperity and wellbeing, including health and life expectancy—this applies more to the US than the UK—wealth and income equality, social mobility, and happiness or life satisfaction in the Western setting.[4] As seen, these countries with a mono-tonic regularity turn out to be the least 'happy' or 'satisfied with life,' with some variations, among advanced Western and related societies, invariably less so than Scandinavia and most of Western Europe, thus situated at the opposite pole on the comparative scale of happiness or life satisfaction and wellbeing. In light of to such low rankings of these countries on this scale, one cannot emphasize and reiterate enough that, as Smith implies and Jefferson explicitly states, the ultimate purpose and rationale of an economy, consequently capi-talism, is to generate and increase human happiness in society, notably a proxy of Bentham's 'greatest happiness to the greatest number.' More specifically, the supreme end and justification of capitalism, like any economy, is to create and distribute within society Marshall's 'material requisites' for happiness under-stood as wellbeing, a combination of Pigou's economic and social welfare.

On this account, while welfare capitalism exemplified in Scandinavian and related Western societies successfully passes an economy's ultimate test of re-producing maximal or widespread happiness in the sense of wellbeing, plu-tocratic capitalism, as represented by the above countries, exposes itself as a dismal failure in this respect—just as does its historical analog and precursor aristocratic feudalism—and thus falls on its own grounds of economic effi-ciency, prosperity, etc. Observations and other sources presented show that irrationally unregulated, anti-egalitarian, plutocratic capitalism almost invari-ably reproduces inferior and adverse outcomes for economic freedom, equality, mobility, wellbeing, and in that sense happiness in those societies with such an economy. Furthermore, this model of capitalism is often treated or described as 'belated feudalism', a master-servant economy—as in conservative America and Great Britain for long—'neo-feudalism,' the 'new patrimonial capitalism,' a near- slave system (in the post-bellum US South), and economic fascism in the sense of ultra-conservative 'right totalitarianism,' thus as the opposite and destructive force to economic freedom and wellbeing, even if couched in the discourse of 'free enterprise' and the like.

---

4 Benjamin et al. (2012, p. 2108) refer to the 'finding that average SWB (subjective well-being) has remained flat in the United States over the past decades.'

Generally, plutocratic capitalism is considered and depicted as an oppressive oligarchic economic and political system, thus a far cry and deviation from a free economy. Particularly, some analysts portray this capitalist economy as the 'new patrimonial' capitalism characterized with the anarchic freedom, near-absolute power and 'revenge' of capital and higher management over labor and other non-capitalists through coercion, repression, depredation, and degradation of the latter, as particularly observed in the US in the above specification since Reaganomics and the South and similar regions and in part the UK during Thatcherism and its sequels during last several decades.[5] On this account, the new 'patrimonial capitalism' is equivalent or consistent with aristocratic, plutocratic or oligarchic capitalism, just as the old patrimonialism and its ruling class involved feudalism as its special case and aristocracy. The sources and grounds for the specific quantitative estimates of a free economy/economic freedom (as aggregated in Table 4.3) are presented next. In addition, qualitative considerations are offered about some economic freedoms for which data, rankings or reports are missing or insufficient (Appendix 5.1).

Property Freedoms and Rights

The comparative estimates/points of private property freedoms and rights are derived from some global rankings of countries on this dimension of economic freedom as well as academic and other observations. For example, in a global rating on private property rights and legal systems[6] (Table 5.1), the most highly rated (with scores 8 or higher) are such instances of rationally regulated and egalitarian welfare capitalism as Western European societies, including Finland, Norway, Switzerland, Sweden, the Netherlands, Luxembourg, Iceland, Denmark, Austria, and Ireland together with New Zealand and Canada, with no cases of its mixed counterpart or its opposite. Notably, not a single example of unregulated and inegalitarian plutocratic or oligarchic capitalism, including the US in the above specification is found in this top rating on property rights. To that extent, this rating strongly confirms the expectation and observation that regulated and welfare capitalism constitutes and epitomizes a free modern economy, featuring the highest degree of economic freedom, including even private property freedoms and rights, contradicting opposite 'libertarian' assertions as ideological dogmas or delusions.

---

5   Cohen (2003) and Piketty (2014) use the term the 'new patrimonial' capitalism primarily with reference to plutocratic anti-egalitarian capitalism.

6   The source is http://www.freetheworld.com.

TABLE 5.1   *Economic freedom ratings—legal system/property rights, OECD countries 2013.*

Country	Score/world rank	Point[a]
Australia	7.9 (15)	8
Austria	8.0 (10)	8
Belgium	7.1 (24)	7
Canada	8.0 (11)	9
Chile	7.0 (27)	6
Czech Republic	6.1 (51)	5
Denmark	8.1 (8)	9
Estonia	7.3 (22)	7
Finland	8.8 (1)	10
France	7.0 (26)	6
Germany	7.8 (18)	8
Greece	5.8 (62)	4
Hungary	6.2 (50)	5
Iceland	8.2 (7)	9
Ireland	8.0 (12)	8
Italy	5.7 (65)	4
Japan	7.6 (20)	8
Korea, South	6.2 (47)	6
Luxembourg	8.3 (5)	9
Mexico	4.4 (112)	2
Netherlands	8.0 (9)	8
New Zealand	8.8 (2)	10
Norway	8.6 (3)	10
Poland	6.4 (42)	5
Portugal	7.0 (28)	6
Slovak Republic	5.6 (72)	4
Slovenia	6.0 (55)	4
Spain	6.4 (39)	5
Sweden	7.9 (16)	8
Switzerland	8.3 (4)	9
Turkey	5.3 (82)	3
United Kingdom	7.8 (17)	8
United States	7.0 (29)	6

a   Score 8.6 or higher =10 points, Score 8.1–8.5 = 9 points, Score 7.6–8 = 8 points, Score 7.1–7.5 = 7 points, Score 6.6–7 = 6 points, Score 6.1–6.5 = 5 points, Score 5.6–6= 4 points, Score 5.1–5.5 = 3 points, Score 4.6–5 = 2 points, Score 4.1–4.5 = 1 point, Score 4 or lower = 0 points
SOURCE: HTTP://WWW.FREETHEWORLD.COM

Conversely, countries with the lowest rating on property rights (7 or lower) include all the cases of unregulated and inegalitarian plutocratic or oligarchic capitalism, for example, South Korea, Mexico, Poland, Turkey, and the US in the preceding specification, along with many of its mixed counterpart like Chile, Greece, Hungary, Italy, Portugal, Slovakia, Slovenia, and Spain, but only one case of its opposite, France. If so, the rating reaffirms that plutocratic or oligarchic capitalism represents and exemplifies an unfree economy, having as a whole the lowest degree of economic freedom, including property freedoms and rights, contradicting the 'libertarian' claims to the contrary. Moreover, the paradigmatic exemplar of such a model of capitalism, the US economy since Reaganomics and primarily in the South has the lowest score—for example, lower than Japan's and equal to France's—among the most advanced Western economies, including Northern Europe, and excluding its Southern parts. Overall, only 12 largely less developed economies—for example, Chile, Czech Republic, Greece, Hungary, Italy, South Korea, Mexico, Poland, Slovakia, Slovenia, Spain, and Turkey—out of 32 OECD members have the lower scores on this economic freedom and right than or the same as the US economy. At first glance, this finding is unexpected and shocking, but fully expected in and consistent with the present framework that predicts unfettered and plutocratic capitalism to have the lowest rank overall and so be in the category of 'unfree economies' versus regulated and welfare capitalism predicted to attain the highest ranking and thus to belong to that of 'completely free economies.'

Free Trade and Freedom of Foreign Investment

The comparative estimates of free global trade for Western and related economies are corroborated by observations of the freedom of exports to and imports from other economies. For example, they are derived from the comparative data on the proportion share of foreign trade in GDP, calculated as the sum of merchandise exports and imports divided by the value of GDP and taken as the indicator or proxy of free global trade (Table 5.2).

The data show that ten or so OECD countries with the highest share of foreign trade in GDP (60 percent and higher) in 2014 are Belgium (173.8), the Netherlands (143.3), Switzerland (83.7), Austria (82.4), South Korea (77.9), Ireland (75.2), Luxembourg (70.8), Germany (70.4), Mexico (62.5), Portugal (61.8), Denmark (61.4), and Iceland (61.2), alongside the former communist countries Slovakia (170.8), Czech Republic (159.0), Hungary (155.9), Slovenia (141.9), Estonia (129.7), and Poland (80.1). Thus, excepting the last group undergoing exceptional, dramatic liberalization of foreign trade since the demise of communism, nine of these countries are classified in regulated and welfare capitalism, one in the mixed category (Ireland), and only two in plutocratic, oligarchic capitalism (Mexico, South Korea), which hence to an important degree confirms the expectations. Adding the former communist countries, out of 16 countries with the highest percentage of foreign trade in GDP nine belong to the first category, four to the second, and only three to the third (plus Poland), thus at least in part confirming the expectation that welfare capitalism as a whole

TABLE 5.2   *Foreign trade as a percentage of GDP, OECD countries, 2014 (Current US Dollars).*

Country	Percentage	Point[a] (Percentage/10)
Australia	32.9	3.29
Austria	82.4	8.24
Belgium	173.8	10
Canada	53.2	5.32
Chile	57.3	5.73
Czech Republic	159.0	10
Denmark	61.4	6.14
Estonia	129.6	10
Finland	55.5	5.55
France	44.5	4.45
Germany	70.4	7.04
Greece	42.3	4.23
Hungary	155.9	10
Iceland	61.2	6.12
Ireland	75.2	7.52
Italy	46.7	4.67
Japan	32.7	3.27
Korea, Rep.	77.9	7.79
Luxembourg	70.8	7.08
Mexico	62.5	6.25
Netherlands	143.3	10
New Zealand	42.1	4.21
Norway	46.6	4.66
Poland	80.1	8.01
Portugal	61.8	6.18
Slovak Republic	168.3	10
Slovenia	141.9	10
Spain	49.5	4.95

Country	Percentage	Point[a] (Percentage/10)
Sweden	57.3	5.73
Switzerland	83.7	8.37
Turkey	50.1	5.01
United Kingdom	39.8	3.98
United States	23.2	2.32

a Percentage 100+ = 10 points, Percentage 90–99 = 9 points, Percentage 80–89 = 8 points, Percentage 70–79 = 7 points, Percentage 60–69 = 6 points, Percentage 50–59 = 5 points, Percentage 40–49 = 4 points, Percentage 30–39 = 3 points, Percentage 20–29 = 2 points, Percentage 10–19 = 1 point, Percentage 0–9 = 0 points

SOURCE: WORLD BANK, MERCHANDISE TRADE (% OF GDP).

tends to have a greater degree of freedom of foreign trade than other economic systems.

Conversely, OECD countries with the ten lowest shares of foreign trade in GDP (below or around 50 percent) in 2014 are the US (23.2), Japan (32.7), Australia (32.9), the UK (39.8), New Zealand (42.1), Greece (42.3), France (44.5), Norway (46.6), Italy (46.7), Spain (49.5), and Turkey (50.1). This yields a more ambiguous, complicated picture, involving four countries classified into welfare capitalism, and six [including the US in the second rendition] into plutocratic and mixed categories, which apparently confounds the expectation. It may not really or entirely confound them, however, because many of the countries classified into plutocratic or oligarchic capitalism rank in the group with the lowest shares of foreign trade in GDP (the conservative pole of the US, Turkey), which is in part consistent with or at least does not contradict the expectation.

Alternatively, most of the countries classified into welfare capitalism belong to the group with the highest shares of foreign trade in GDP, which also partly confirms or at least does not disconfirm the expectation. In addition, the country with by far the lowest share of foreign trade in GDP, the US (in the dual specification) is classified into plutocratic capitalism, and thus strongly confirms the expectation that such an economic system tends to evince a lower degree of free trade than welfare capitalism. Moreover, the US share (23), besides being significantly lower than that of the presumably 'most closed' advanced economy Japan (33), is half of those of France (44) presumed as welfare 'statism' to be less open to global trade than 'unfettered' American capitalism but evidently is not, and of Norway (47), Italy (47), and Spain (49) also described and dismissed by US 'libertarian' economists as 'statist,' 'socialist,' or 'welfarist.'

Another striking result is that the UK, the classic bastion and champion of 'free trade' and laissez-faire overall since the Industrial Revolution and classical political economy represented by Smith and Ricardo has the fourth lowest free-trade-to-GDP ratio among OECD countries. Also strikingly, out of the five countries with the lowest free-trade-to-GDP ratios, four are Anglo-Saxon or English-speaking ones, the US, Australia, the UK, and New Zealand—only excluding Canada—usually invoked or claimed as paragons of 'free trade' and 'open economies,' but data show that they are hardly so by comparison to their counterparts in Europe and beyond.

No doubt, geographic distance or isolation from Europe probably accounts for the strikingly low US share as well as the relatively lower shares of such other English-speaking immigrant countries as Australia and New Zealand (plus Japan), but does not provide a complete explanation. For example, with an approximately equal distance from Europe, Canada's share of foreign trade in GDP (53) is more than twice higher than that of the US, while those of New Zealand and Australia even more distant in this sense being significantly higher, as is that of Mexico (62) almost three times greater. Also, the US low share may be explained in part and thus 'rationalized' by that bigger economies often exhibit lower shares of foreign trade in GDP than do their smaller counterparts, but again this is not the entire story or explanation. Thus, the US share is more than three times (and not just 3 or even 30 percent as supposedly insignificant differences) lower than that of the biggest European economy Germany (70), while being half or so of those of the other big economies or countries in Europe such as Spain (47), Italy (46), France (44), the UK (40), just as significantly smaller than Japan's (33), the world's third largest economy. (Also, the foreign trade percentage of China as the world's second biggest economy and largest country is 45, which is almost twice as that of the US.) Hence, if neither geographic distance nor 'bigness' completely explains and rationalizes the US economy's strikingly low share of foreign trade in GDP, it may well be that it is plutocratic capitalism (as specified above) that is primarily responsible for such an inferior outcome with respect to this economic freedom. At any rate, such exceptionally low figure for the US economy reveals a peculiar and neglected kind of reverse non-superior 'American exceptionalism' and justifies the estimate of free trade.

In addition, the comparative estimates for free global trade are supported by some computations of economic globalization indexes[7] for Western and other societies in 2016 (Table 5.3).

---

7   The source is the KOF Index of Globalization 2016 http://globalization.kof.ethz.ch/media/filer_public/2016/03/03/rankings_2016.pdf.

TABLE 5.3 *Indexes of economic globalization, OECD countries, 2016.*

Country	Index	Point (Index/10)
1. Ireland	93.08	9.31
2. Luxembourg	91.80	9.18
3. Netherlands	90.89	9.09
4. Hungary	86.85	8.69
5. Estonia	86.11	8.61
6. Belgium	85.95	8.60
7. Slovakia	83.63	8.36
8. Austria	83.25	8.33
9. Czech Rep.	82.89	8.29
10. Finland	82.23	8.22
11. Portugal	81.35	8.14
12. Denmark	81.17	8.12
13. New Zealand	81.05	8.11
14. Sweden	80.56	8.06
15. Switzerland	77.78	7.78
16. Chile	77.42	7.74
17. Norway	76.76	7.68
18. Canada	76.12	7.61
19. Poland	75.72	7.57
20. Spain	74.80	7.48
21. Iceland	74.56	7.46
22. Slovenia	74.37	7.44
23. Australia	73.64	7.36
24. Greece	71.39	7.14
25. UK	67.62	6.76
26. Italy	67.02	7.70
27. France	66.53	6.65
28. Mexico	64.06	6.41
29. Germany	61.08	6.11
30. Korea, Rep.	59.83	5.98
31. US	59.40	5.94
32. Turkey	55.42	5.54
33. Japan	50.77	5.08

KOF Index of Globalization 2016
http://globalization.kof.ethz.ch/media/filer_public/2016/03/03/rankings_2016.pdf

Thus, most OECD countries with the highest economic globalization indexes (80 or higher) exemplify or approximate regulated and welfare capitalism, thus mostly confirming the expectations. These countries are Ireland (93.08), Luxembourg (91.80), the Netherlands (90.89), Belgium (85.95), Austria (83.25), Finland (82.23), Denmark (81.17), New Zealand (81.05) and Sweden (80.56), along with some mixed or transitional cases closer to this than unregulated and plutocratic capitalism like Hungary (86.85), Estonia (86.11), Slovakia (83.63), and Portugal (81.35).

Conversely, those economies with the lowest economic globalization indexes (below 70) mostly represent or approach unregulated and plutocratic or oligarchic capitalism, largely consistent with the expectations. These economies include Turkey (55.42), the US (59.40) in the above specification, South Korea (59.83), and Mexico (64.06), joined with mixed cases like Japan (50.77), Italy (67.02) and the UK (67.62), and only two opposite instances such as Germany (61.08) and France (66.53) as apparent 'outliers' within the category of regulated and egalitarian capitalism. Notably, all Western European economies, including not only Scandinavian and other Northern welfare capitalisms but also Germany, France, Spain and Italy, alongside Australia, Canada, and New Zealand, are ranked higher on economic globalization and consequently free global trade than the US economy that features the third lowest index among all OECD countries, with only Japan and Turkey having the lower ones.

This ranking confirms the observation that Western European, especially Scandinavian, economies are both regulated and egalitarian welfare capitalisms/states *and* more globalized in terms of free trade than the US economy as the exemplar of unfettered and plutocratic capitalism in the above economic ideology/policy and regional specification. In this sense, it indicates that the first economies are comparatively the most open and competitive globally, notably more so than the US economy as reportedly 'relatively closed'[8] and to some extent uncompetitive; a perennial example is car manufacturing and related industries,[9] along with various protectionist and nationalist restrictions

---

8 Leijonhufvud (2004) and Obstfeld (2012) indicate that the US is a 'relatively closed' rather than the most and only open—as ethnocentric 'libertarian' economists and conservative politicians allege—economy, thus a mockery of glorified American 'free market' capitalism.

9 Hendel and Lizzeri (1999, p. 1098) find that 'unreliable' American car brands—and most being such—'suffer a more severe lemon problem' of poor quality and thus low competitiveness by experiencing 'stepper price declines' than their Japanese counterparts. Baily and Solow (2001, p. 156) observe that 'Germany is the greatest manufacturing power in Europe and runs a substantial trade surplus in manufactured goods with the United States (as) German companies exported in segments of the market where they had unique or high quality

of free trade and foreign investment. Alternatively, the above indexes refute and reveal as a dogma or myth orthodox and 'libertarian' economics' assertion that the second type of capitalism promotes and engages more in free global trade and generally globalization and less in protectionism, thus being a more open and competitive economic system, than the first dismissed as protectionist and closed ('socialist,' 'statist').

The preceding about those of free global trade applies, with necessary qualifications, to the comparative estimates of the freedom of foreign investment in Western and related economies. The indexes of economic globalization can be taken also as estimates or proxies for the comparative freedom of foreign investment given that the former encompasses the latter as its major facet and process, alongside and mutually related and reinforced with free global trade. Consequently, the aforesaid of comparative free-global trade estimates inferred from economic globalization indexes can be applied, other things equal, to those of the freedom of foreign investment. The indexes of economic globalization comprise and free global-trade estimates closely relate to those of the freedom of foreign investment, including that of investments in the national economy by foreigners and in competing economies by nationals.

The highest economic globalization indexes of economies exemplifying regulated and welfare capitalism such as most of Western Europe, notably Scandinavia, can be plausibly taken to incorporate equivalent estimates of their freedom of foreign investment, just as global free trade. Conversely, the lower indexes of the economies epitomizing plutocratic capitalism entail corresponding estimates of their freedom of foreign investment, like of global free trade. While seemingly simplistic, this inferring of the particular from general estimates has compelling theoretical and substantive grounds in that any estimation of the level of economic globalization involves that of the freedom of investment globally, just as free global trade. Alternatively, the estimates of the freedom of foreign investment as well as free global trade are typically aggregated and in that sense vanish in the aggregate indexes of economic globalization. At the minimum, it is plausibly and realistic to assume that the indexes of globalization imply or relate to those of the freedom of foreign investment, and conversely, dubious and unrealistic to posit no relationship between the two as one of the general and the particular.

---

products, like specialized machine tools or luxury automobiles,' alongside the 'productivity leader in these industries (Japan).' Goolsbee and Krueger (2015, p.7) refer to the Congress' 'Committee on Foreign Investment in the United States' that is apparently nationalistic or protectionist, simply redundant in a free market economy.

Labor Freedom and Agency

In general, a variety of data and observations provide support for the comparative estimates of labor freedom and agency for Western and related economies. In particular, the estimates are based on the data on labor union density in the sense of relative membership in unions for OECD countries during the last decade or so (Table 5.4).

TABLE 5.4   *Labor union density, OECD countries, 2013–14.*

Country	Percentage	Point[a]
Australia	15.5	3
Austria	27.8	5
Belgium	55.1	10
Canada	26.4	5
Chile	15.5	3
Czech Republic	12.7	2
Denmark	66.8	10
Estonia	5.7	1
Finland	69.0	10
France	7.7	1
Germany	18.1	3
Greece	21.5	4
Hungary	10.5	2
Iceland	86.4	10
Ireland	27.4	5
Italy	37.3	7
Japan	17.6	3
Korea	10.1	2
Luxembourg	32.8	6
Mexico	13.5	2
Netherlands	17.8	3
New Zealand	18.7	3
Norway	52.1	10
Poland	12.7	2
Portugal	18.9	3
Slovak Republic	13.3	2
Slovenia	21.2	4
Spain	16.9	3

Country	Percentage	Point[a]
Sweden	67.3	10
Switzerland	15.7	3
Turkey	6.3	1
United Kingdom	25.1	5
United States	10.7	2
OECD Average	16.7	

a Percentage 50 or higher = 10 points, Percentage 45–49 = 9 points,
Percentage 40–44 = 8 pounds, Percentage 35–39 = 7 points, Percent-
age 30–34 = 6 points, Percentage 25–29 = 5 points, Percentage 20–24
= 4 points, Percentage 15–19 = 3 points, Percentage 10–14 = 2 points,
Percentage 5–9 = 1 points, Percentage under 5 = 0 points
SOURCE: OECD HTTP://WWW.OECD-ILIBRARY.ORG/EMPLOYMENT/
DATA/TRADE-UNIONS/TRADE-UNION-DENSITY_DATA-00371-EN

Such density and generally institutionalized unionization is taken as the indicator or predictor, at least proxy, of labor freedom and agency. Notably, it
is considered the economic, more precisely labor-market, equivalent or analogue of the freedom of organization or assembly in the polity and society. The
higher labor union density and the presence of institutionalized unionization
overall, other things equal, indicates or predicts, minimally approximates, an
equivalent degree of labor liberty and agency in the sense of complementary
or countervailing power and influence versus capital, just as conversely. This
constitutes an indicator or predictor of the freedom of organization and assembly as applied to the economy such as the labor market, by analogy to that
in the polity and society. As expected, the highest labor union density and to
that extent the degree of labor liberty and agency is observed in the countries
characterized by the economic system of regulated and welfare capitalism
such as Western Europe, notably Scandinavia, with minor variations. During
the 2007–2014 period top five countries in terms of labor union density, indicated by the percentage of unionized workers out of the total work force, are
Iceland (between 85–86), Finland (69–70), Denmark (66–68), Sweden (67–71),
and Norway (52–54), followed by Belgium (54–55).

Conversely, also largely consistent with the expectations, the lowest labor
union density and thus degree of labor liberty, agency, and power is found in
the economies of unregulated and plutocratic or oligarchic capitalism, though
with salient exceptions. For example, during that period the US economy
consistently displays the lowest labor union density (11–12) of all the most

advanced Western economies, except for France, while among all OECD countries only Turkey (6–12), Estonia (6–8), and South Korea (10–11) usually having lower densities, with even Mexico (14–17) having the slightly higher. Strikingly, US labor union density is between five and almost eight times lower than those of Scandinavian and some other Western European economies (e.g., Belgium), thus dramatically confirming and exemplifying the differences between repressive, anti-labor plutocratic and welfare, social-democratic capitalism in terms of labor liberty and agency. In turn, the UK economy as a case of mixed capitalism also confirms the expectations by virtue of having a labor union density figure (26–30) that is intermediate between these two types of capitalism, namely more than twice high as that of the US but half (or more) lower than those of these Western European economies.

Labor Rights, Rewards, and Benefits

An almost identical pattern is observed with respect to the comparative estimates of labor rights, rewards, and benefits for Western and related economies. In essence, the degree of labor liberty and agency in the sense of complementary or countervailing power and influence versus capital determines and predicts the level and amount of its rights, rewards, and benefits. Consequently, economies featuring the highest degree of the first are also observed and expected to feature the greatest level of the second, and conversely. Specifically, Scandinavian and other Western European egalitarian, welfare capitalisms, with minor variations, rank the highest on the first dimension of economic freedom and on the second alike. Conversely, unfettered, plutocratic capitalism tends to rank the lowest on both dimensions, with rare exceptions.

Global Labor Rights

For illustration, the present estimates are derived from the Global Labor Rights Index for OECD Countries in 2015 (Table 5.5).

TABLE 5.5   *Global labor rights indexes, OECD countries, 2015.*

	Index	Point[a]
Rating 5	No guarantee of rights.	
Greece	5	0
Korea, Republic of	5	0
Turkey	5	0

	Index	Point[a]
Rating 4	Systematic violation of rights.	
Mexico	4	2
Poland	4	2
Unites States	4	2
Rating 3	Regular violation of rights.	
Australia	3	4
Canada	3	4
Chile	3	4
Hungary	3	4
Portugal	3	4
Spain	3	4
United Kingdom	3	4
Rating 2	Repeated violation of rights.	
Czech Republic	2	6
Ireland	2	6
Japan	2	6
New Zealand	2	6
Switzerland	2	6
Rating 1	Irregular violation of rights.	
Austria	1	10
Belgium	1	10
Denmark	1	10
Estonia	1	10
Finland	1	10
France	1	10
Germany	1	10
Iceland	1	10
Italy	1	10
Netherlands	1	10
Norway	1	10
Slovakia	1	10
Sweden	1	10

a Index 1 = 10 points, Index 2= 6 points, Index 3= 4 points, Index 4= 2 points, Index 5= 0 points

SOURCE: INTERNATIONAL TRADE UNION CONFEDERATION 2015 GLOBAL LABOR RIGHTS INDEX, THE *WORLD'S WORST COUNTRIES FOR WORKERS*.

As shown, economies with the strongest labor rights or their weakest violations indicated by a corresponding index or rank of (1—'Irregular Violation of Rights') include Austria, Belgium, Denmark, Estonia, Finland, France, Germany, Iceland, Italy, the Netherlands, Norway, Slovakia, and Sweden. The vast majority of these economies (with the exception of Estonia, Italy, and Slovakia) are presently classified into regulated and welfare capitalism, which largely fulfills the expectation that this economic system permits and protects labor rights more than do other systems. In short, these economies form the world's best 'countries for workers.' In addition, countries with the second highest labor rights index or second weakest violations (2—'Repeated violation of rights') comprise Czech Republic, Ireland, Japan, New Zealand, and Switzerland, which are classified into welfare or mixed capitalisms, but none into plutocratic capitalism, which is thus generally consistent with the expectations.

Conversely, economies with the weakest and even no labor rights or their most intense violations indicated by a corresponding index or rank (4—'Systematic violation of rights,' and 5—'No guarantee of rights') are Greece (5), Republic of Korea (5), Turkey (5), Mexico (4), Poland (4), and the US (4). Analogously, except for Greece, all of these economies, including the US in the above specification, are classified into oligarchic or plutocratic capitalism, which clearly supports the expectation that the latter tends to have least or even no labor rights, being essentially an anti-labor and thus, from the stance of labor as a factor of production, unfree economic system.

Curiously, Mexico and the US are assigned the same index or rank of labor rights (4), the second lowest, which may seem at first glance surprising or shocking. Still, this identical low rank of Mexico and the US on labor rights is actually expected, as it confirms or expresses (in factor-analytic terms 'loads on') their common or convergent anti-labor economy of oligarchic or plutocratic capitalism. This is thus partial proof of such commonality or convergence, which casts doubt on US 'libertarian' economists' and conservative nativist politicians' claims to unique and superior American 'free enterprise' capitalism glorified as having the most labor rights in relation to the Mexican 'unfree,' 'inferior' economy construed as the opposite.

The same index indicates that Mexico and America in the anti-regulatory and anti-welfare pole share or converge on the same type of plutocratic anti-labor capitalism, and conversely, their indexes would be greatly different, namely that of the US economy drastically higher, if they had diverse economic systems, i.e., if the latter was really distinct from the Mexican in terms of labor rights and conditions.

Especially, labor rights and conditions in Mexico (e.g., border regions) and the South (Texas, etc.) appear virtually identical, basically non-existent or minimal and severe, with most workers, from agriculture and construction to manufacturing and services, on both sides of the border reduced substantially (even if not legally) to a new proxy slave status, as witnessed in the second region during post-bellum times. It may be distressing or disconcerting to US, notably Southern, 'blue collar' and other workers and 'shocking' or 'impossible' to other Americans that they have basically the same, second weakest labor rights in the Western world and beyond as their Mexican counterparts, but that is evidently a hard reality indicated by the above index. Notably, the labor rights index or rank for the US economy is the fourth lowest, along with Mexico, among all OECD counties, with only those of Greece, Republic of Korea, and Turkey being lower. In sum, these five are identified as the 'world's worst countries for workers,' but by implication the best for plutocrats or capitalists, fully consistent with the expectation that anarchic and plutocratic or oligarchic capitalism as the shared economic system of most of them has nonexistent or minimal labor rights compared to regulated and welfare capitalism.

Generally, the present comparative estimates of labor rights, rewards, and benefits for Western and related economies are corroborated by a number of economic and sociological observations and statistical data (OECD, World Bank). In particular, the additional grounds for the highest estimates of labor rights, rewards, and benefits in welfare capitalism consist of many such studies and findings of the superior performance of Western European, above Scandinavian, welfare states and fiscal systems.[10] For example, recall that the economic systems of welfare capitalism are estimated to have the highest degree of public benefits universalism, and those of unfettered capitalism the lowest, above all the US and the UK, thus supporting their respective higher and lower estimates on the above dimension.

Also, these estimates are supported by sociological and economics studies documenting that Scandinavian and related welfare capitalisms have both the higher degree of economic equality and (probably), as a consequence, labor social mobility than the American and British variants of unfettered capitalism. These studies indicate that the first type of capitalism is more egalitarian and consequently mobile or open to a greater degree than the second as

---

10   For example, despite the apparent laissez-faire glorification and value-laden terminology (government taxation of capital cum 'distortionary taxation' implying that only such 'zero-taxation' is non-distortionary as the perennial dream and claim of capitalist plutocrats), Alesina and Perotti (1997, p. 930) admit that at 'very high levels of centralization of the labor market (as in Scandinavia) the mechanism by which labor taxation is transmitted to labor costs changes. In an economy-wide bargaining, the unions are able to internalize the positive link between higher taxation and social security and welfare benefits. This induces the union to moderate its wage claims.'

instead more economically unequal and, as a result, more closed in the sense of upward mobility. These findings therefore ground the differential estimates for these economies.[11] Relatedly, these estimates take account of analyses and findings of differential degrees of economic equality, fairness and redistribution, income and wealth inequality, distributive injustice and labor exploitation in Western and other economies. In general, most studies find or imply that economies characterized with regulated, welfare capitalism are typified with the higher degrees of economic equality/fairness and redistribution, and the lower levels of distributive injustice and labor exploitation than those of unregulated, plutocratic capitalism.

Additional grounds and sources for the present estimates include data and observations of annual work hours in these economies, including vacation time and facilities in the US and Europe, poverty rates, and the like. The general pattern of their findings or implications is identical. This is that welfare-capitalist economies feature, with some variations, shorter annual work hours, plus more and higher-quality vacation facilities, and most notably, substantially lower poverty rates than those of unfettered plutocratic capitalism, above all the US in the above specification and to some degree the UK. For example, the rate of poverty in general and of children in particular in the first economies is typically half or more of those of the second, especially the US and to a lesser degree the UK, plus Mexico among OECD countries.[12]

In particular, the estimates of employment protection as a form of labor rights are derived from the data on the strength or strictness of employment protection (Table 5.6).

TABLE 5.6   *Work rights—strictness of employment protection legislation, OECD countries, 2013–15.*

Country	Index	Point[a]
Australia	1.67	5
Austria	2.37	6

11   Alesina and Angeletos (2005, p. 975) register that 'Americans overestimate social mobility (actually lower), while Europeans underestimate it, and that some of the welfare programs in Europe, such as in public education or public health, may actually help reduce the effect of luck.'

12   The US child poverty rate (21.9%) is more than twice than that (10% or lower) in most other Western European counties Smeeding (2006) and almost equivalent to that (22%) of Mexico.

Country	Index	Point[a]
Belgium	1.89	5
Canada	0.92	3
Chile	2.63	7
Czech Republic	2.92	7
Denmark	2.20	6
Estonia	1.81	5
Finland	2.17	6
France	2.38	6
Germany	2.68	7
Greece	2.12	6
Hungary	1.59	5
Iceland	1.73	5
Ireland	1.40	5
Italy	2.68	7
Japan	1.37	4
Korea	2.37	6
Luxembourg	2.25	6
Mexico	2.03	6
Netherlands	2.82	7
New Zealand	1.39	4
Norway	2.33	6
Poland	2.23	6
Portugal	3.18	8
Slovak Republic	1.84	5
Slovenia	2.16	6
Spain	2.05	6
Sweden	2.61	7
Switzerland	1.60	5
Turkey	2.31	6
United Kingdom	1.10	4
United States	0.26	2
OECD Average	2.04	

a Index 4 and higher = 10 points, 3.5–3.9 = 9 points, 3–3.4 = 8 points,
2.5–2.9 = 7 points, 2–2.4 = 6 points, 1.5–1.9 = 5 points, 1–1.4 = 4 points,
0.5–0.9 = 3 points, 0.4–0.2 = 2 points, 0.2–0.1 = 1 point
SOURCE: OECD HTTP://WWW.OECD-ILIBRARY.ORG/

Specifically, economies with the highest indexes on this dimension are typically those of Western European, particularly Scandinavian, regulated and welfare capitalism, and those with lowest ones belong to its unfettered, plutocratic variant. Thus, ten economies with the strongest employment protection and in extension unemployment compensation,[13] just as the highest labor union density as the probable factor, are Portugal (index 3.18), Czech Republic (2.92), the Netherlands (2.82), Germany (2.68), Italy (2.68), Chile (2.63), Sweden (2.61), Slovenia (2.60), Austria (2.37), and Korea (2.37). As known, with two exceptions, these economies are classified into regulated and welfare capitalism or its mixed counterpart, which generally supports the expectations. Conversely, ten economies with the weakest employment protection and unemployment compensation, just as the lowest labor union density as the likely reason, include the US (index 0.26), Canada (0.92), the UK (1.10), Japan (1.37), New Zealand (1.39), Ireland (1.40), Switzerland (1.60), Australia (1.67), Estonia (1.81) and Slovak Republic (1.84). This yields a mixed picture involving instance of all the three types of economic system, and thus inconclusive evidence.

Labor Rewards and Benefits

The estimates of labor rewards take account of the latest available data on real minimum wages for OECD countries (Table 5.7), as their indicators or proxies.

TABLE 5.7   *Real minimum wages, OECD countries, 2015 (in 2014 constant prices at 2014 USD Ppps).*

Country	Real minimum wages	Point[a]
Australia	21 464.5	10
Austria	NA	NA
Belgium	20 922.0	10
Canada	16 995.1	8
Chile	6 308.4	3
Czech Republic	7 667.1	3
Denmark	NA	NA

---

13   Eriksson and Rooth (2014, p. 1036) remark that the 'Swedish social safety net is more generous than the US system. In Sweden, unemployed workers get unemployment benefits for 300 days at a replacement rate of up to 80 percent.'

Country	Real minimum wages	Point[a]
Estonia	7 601.8	3
Finland	NA	NA
France	19 841.5	9
Germany[b]	21,216[a]	10
Greece	11 593.0	5
Hungary	8 675.7	4
Iceland	NA	NA
Ireland	18 036.7	9
Italy	NA	NA
Japan	14 347.5[c]	7
Korea	13 668.1	6
Luxembourg	23 307.9	10
Mexico	1 911.7	0
Netherlands	21 522.0	10
New Zealand	18 889.1	9
Norway	NA	NA
Poland	11 081.9	5
Portugal	10 517.1	5
Slovak Republic	8 245.5	4
Slovenia	14 281.5	7
Spain	12 082.7	6
Sweden	NA	NA
Switzerland	NA	NA
Turkey	9 979.2	4
United Kingdom	16 994.1	8
United States	15 062.0	7

a $20,000 and higher = 10 points, $18,000 and higher = 9 points, $16,000 and higher = 8 points, $14,000 and higher = 7 points, $12,000 and higher = 6 points, $10,000 and higher = 5 points, $8,000 and higher = 4 points, $6,000 and higher = 3 points, $4,000 and higher = 2 points, $2,000 and higher = 1 point, under $2,000 = 0 points
b Germany's annual minimum wage is calculated by converting euros in dollars (at an exchange rate of 1.20) for 40 hours a week for 52 weeks. (According to Federal Statistical Office of Germany 'there has been a statutory minimum wage of 8.50 euros for all employees in the whole of Germany since 1 January 2015').
c 2014
SOURCE: HTTP://WWW.OECD-ILIBRARY.ORG

These data show that ten countries with the highest real minimum wages, among those with such a legal mandate of minimal labor incomes, include Luxembourg, Australia, Germany, Belgium, France, the Netherlands, New Zealand, Ireland, Canada, and the UK. Most of these countries, with two exceptions (Ireland and the UK), are classified in rationally regulated and egalitarian welfare capitalism. This hence almost completely confirms the expectations that labor rewards and benefits are higher in this capitalist type and generally economic system than in others. Conversely, ten countries with the lowest real minimum wages are Mexico, Chile, Czech Republic, Estonia, Hungary, Slovak Republic, Turkey, Portugal, Poland, and Greece. All these economies are classified either in unregulated and inegalitarian capitalism or its mixed type, and none into its regulated and egalitarian opposite, thus generally consistent with the expectations. As a particular curiosity, the US economy ranks neither among top nor bottom ten economies in this respect, which perhaps reflects the duality of regulated-egalitarian welfare versus unregulated-plutocratic capitalism, although the second is apparently stronger or in regional majority, which is indicated by that the real minimum wage is substantially lower than predicted by the level of development, notably among the highest GNP per capita. This is also indicated or approximated by that the US real minimum wage is only 37 percent of median income,[14] the lowest among OECD countries, together with that of Chile—and even lower than Mexico's 38—compared with 61 percent for France, 60 for New Zealand, 57 for Luxembourg, 53 for Australia, 51 for Belgium, 48 for the Netherlands and the UK, 45 for Canada etc.

In addition, the estimates of labor benefits and rights take into account the data on average annual work hours in Western and related economies (Table 5.8).

TABLE 5.8   *Average annual hours actually worked per worker, OECD countries 2014.*

Country	Annual Work Hours	Point[a]
I		
Australia	1664	4
Austria	1629	5
Belgium	1576[b]	6
Canada	1704	3
Denmark	1436	9

---

14   The source is http://www.oecd-ilibrary.org (minimum wages relative to median wages).

Country	Annual Work Hours	Point[a]
Finland	1645	5
France	1473	8
Germany	1371	10
Iceland	1864	1
Luxembourg	1643	5
Netherlands	1425	9
New Zealand	1 762	2
Norway	1427	9
Sweden	1609	5
Switzerland	1568	6
II		
Czech Republic	1776	2
Estonia	1859	1
Hungary	1858	1
Ireland	1821	1
Italy	1734	3
Japan	1729	3
Portugal	1857	1
Slovak Republic	1763	3
Slovenia	1561	6
Spain	1689	4
United Kingdom	1677	4
III		
Chile	1990	1
Greece	2042	0
Korea	2124	0
Mexico	2228	0
Poland	1923	1
Turkey	1832[b]	1
United States	1789	2

a Hours under 1,400 = 10 points, hours 1,400–1,450 = 9 points, hours 1,450–1,500 = 8 points, hours 1,500–1,550 = 7 points, hours 1,550–1,600 = 6 points, hours 1,600–1,650 = 5 points, hours 1,650–1,700 = 4 points, hours 1,700–1,750 = 3 points, hours 1,750–1,800 = 2 points, hours 1,800–2,000 = 1 point, more than 2,000 = 0 points

b 2013

SOURCE: OECD HTTP://WWW.OECD-ILIBRARY.ORG

Consistent with the expectations, Western European, above all Scandinavian, and similar regulated and egalitarian welfare-capitalist economies have lower 'average annual hours actually worked per worker' than those exemplifying or approximating unfettered and inegalitarian plutocratic capitalism, especially the US in the above ideological and regional specification. For example, average annual work hours are lower in all Western European countries, including the Netherlands (1,381 hours), Germany (1,397), Norway (1,420), France (1,479), Ireland (1,529), Denmark (1,546), Belgium (1,574), Sweden (1,621), Switzerland (1,636), Finland (1,672), and Austria (1,699), plus the UK (1,654), Canada (1,710) and Australia (1,728), than in the US (1,790). In turn, the US economy features the longest annual work hours among most advanced Western capitalist economies,[15] as has during last several decades, while within OECD only six

---

15   Samuelson (2004, p. 145) observes that 'French or German per-hour productivity does surpass the US per-hour productivity' and then predicts that 'If only the French and Germans would match US weekly and monthly average number of total hours of work, their bicycles would be running ahead of the US frontrunner.' Also, McDaniel (2011, p. 27) notes that 'there are dramatic differences in the evolution of market work in Organisation for Economic Co-operation and Development (OECD) countries from 1960 onward. For example, in France and Germany the number of market hours worked per adult in 1960 was greater than in the United States. Over the period 1960–2004, hours declined more than 30 percent in France and Germany. In contrast, hours per adult in the United States remained relatively flat over the same period.' In the manner of 'pure' economists, this difference is explained by purely economic factors such as the higher 'effective tax rate on labor income' and 'productivity catch-up' (McDaniel 2011, p. 28) with the US economy in these European economies, overlooking other forces, notably greater labor liberties, rights, and rewards in the second leading to lower work hours. This includes union strength or support (Acemoglu 2001), the 'role of works councils in Germany' (Acemoglu and Jorn-Steffen 1998), and workers' successful demands to work less, for example, 35 or so hours a week regardless of the level of taxation or productivity, as Beck (2000) suggests. 'Pure' US economists seem to overlook that shorter or decreasing work hours may well be associated with a higher degree of freedom for labor either irrespective of taxes and productivity, and the longer or increasing ones with a low or non-existent one, such as the slave-like status of workers, as in the American South historically (Acemoglu and Robinson 2008), or suppression and decline of unions, as in the US economy overall. Lastly, that comparatively high taxes are often irrelevant for work hours is indicated by that Scandinavians 'work more in the market and less at home than would be predicted given the large tax distortions they face' (Ragan 2013, p. 168). In passing, most economists harbor a bizarre predilection to label virtually all taxes as larger or smaller 'distortions' hence to be somehow removed to increase 'efficiency' as if the only efficient economy were, and modern society or civilization could exist and function, without any taxation, thus residing in an Ivory tower in the face of the reality that 'mass taxation (is) now considered normal throughout much of the developed world' (Besley, Ilzetzki, and Persson 2013, pp. 205–6).

countries having higher figures, two former communist economies experiencing abrupt tradition to capitalism, such as Estonia (1,889), Czech Republic (1,800), two exemplars or proxies of oligarchic or anti-labor feudalized capitalism like Mexico (2,226), Turkey (1,855), along with two mixed cases Greece (2,034), Chile (2,029), which generally affirms the anticipations.

Additionally, the above comparative estimates include prosperity rankings of Western and other countries by some non-academic organizations.[16] Thus, during 2015 ten countries with the highest prosperity index are mostly either instances or proxies of regulated and egalitarian welfare capitalism (Table 5.9), just as anticipated.

TABLE 5.9 *Prosperity index, OECD countries, 2015.*

Overall rank	Country	Point[a]
1	Norway	10
2	Switzerland	10
3	Denmark	10
4	New Zealand	9
5	Sweden	9
6	Canada	9
7	Australia	8
8	Netherlands	8
9	Finland	8
10	Ireland	7
11	United States	7
12	Iceland	7
13	Luxembourg	6
14	Germany	6
15	United Kingdom	6
16	Austria	5
17	Belgium	5
18	Japan	5
19	France	4
20	Spain	4
21	Slovenia	4
22	Czech Republic	3
23	Portugal	3

16 This is the Legatum prosperity index (http://www.prosperity.com).

TABLE 5.9   *Prosperity index, OECD countries, 2015.* (cont.)

Overall rank	Country	Point[a]
24	Korea, Rep.	3
25	Poland	2
26	Estonia	2
27	Chile	2
28	Slovakia	1
29	Italy	1
30	Hungary	1
31	Greece	0
32	Mexico	0
33	Turkey	0

a Rank 1–3 = 10 points, Rank 4–6 = 9 points, Rank 7–9 = 8 points,
Rank 10–12 = 7 points, Rank 13–15 = 6 points, Rank 16–18 = 5 points,
Rank 19–21 = 4 points, Rank 22–24 = 3 points, Rank 25–27 = 2 points,
Rank 28–30 = 1 point, 31 or higher = 0 points
Prosperity Index include sub-indices for economy, entrepreneurship
& opportunity, governance, education, health, safety & security,
personal freedom and social capital
SOURCE: LEGATUM HTTP://WWW.PROSPERITY.COM

Notably, the county consistently ranked number 1 on this index, Norway is universally considered a paradigmatic exemplar of welfare capitalism/state followed by such other instances or proxies as Switzerland (rank 2), Denmark (3), New Zealand with some qualifications (4), Sweden (5), Canada (6), Australia (7), the Netherlands (8), Finland (9), plus Ireland (10) deemed an intermediate type. Conversely, none of the presumed paragons of unregulated and/or plutocratic capitalism (unless counting New Zealand and Ireland in this category, which is dubious), notably the US economy (ranked 11), belong to the top 10 economies in terms of prosperity, just as nether does the UK economic system (15) classified in the intermediate capitalist category. As a consequence, this prosperity ranking provides the rationale for deriving the comparative estimates of the degree of economic and related prosperity closely related to labor rewards, benefits, and rights.

Generally, the ranking confirms that egalitarian, welfare capitalism tends to significantly more promote labor wellbeing and economic prosperity and to that extent happiness than does its unfettered and plutocratic opposite. At this juncture, the prosperity ranking largely corresponds or coincides with most rankings and surveys of comparative happiness in Western and other countries such that typically Scandinavian and other Western European welfare states such as Denmark, Norway, Sweden, Finland, Austria, the Netherlands, Belgium, etc. are found to be the happiest among these and in the world as a whole. Evidently, their welfare capitalism/state generates superior economic prosperity in particular and happiness in general compared with its unregulated, plutocratic opposite. To reiterate, it is commonly known since Bentham and Smith, but obscured or hidden by US and other 'libertarian' economists, that the only or main societal function and end of capitalism and any economy is to generate and promote human happiness for the feasibly maximal quantity of individuals—not just aristocracy, plutocracy, oligarchy—more precisely to provide Marshall's 'material requisites' for pursuing and attaining happiness in Jefferson's sense. And evidently, Scandinavian and other Western welfare capitalism precisely and more effectively does so than any other economic system, including American and in part British laissez-faire plutocratic, let alone South American oligarchic semi-feudal, capitalism.

On this ground, it is welfare capitalism that fulfills and triumphantly passes Smith-Bentham's test of the 'greatest prosperity/happiness for the greatest numbers' of persons/groups in society—though perhaps contrary to their expectations—notably Jefferson's principle of the universal 'pursuit of happiness' and Marshall's 'material requisites' for the purpose of wellbeing. Conversely, unfettered and plutocratic capitalism, especially in its American version, by virtue of its 'inhuman face'[17] objectively and dismally fails the same test, perhaps contrary to Smith-Bentham's and especially 'libertarian' expectations. Moreover, welfare capitalism's success in wellbeing and happiness is intrinsic and predicted by universal or shared societal 'welfare,' as is unfettered plutocratic capitalism's failure by 'plutocratic.' For capitalist plutocracy, like pre-capitalist aristocracy or oligarchy, is inherently adverse and ultimately destructive to widespread prosperity and to that extent happiness, but maximally efficient in reproducing 'prosperity' and 'happiness' for plutocrats cum oligarchs as the top '1 percent.'[18]

---

17   Pryor (2002, p. 367) predicts that 'as a result the US economic system will evolve in many different ways toward a capitalism with an inhuman face.'

18   Lenski (1966, p. 308) estimates that in pre-modern agrarian societies the governing class, i.e., 'the top 1 or 2 percent of the population usually received not less than half of the total income of the nation' and suggests that in industrial societies the 'comparable figure is substantially less (around 10 percent).' Wolff (1998, p. 131) reports that 'distribution of wealth in the United States became much more unequal in the 1980s and that trend continued, albeit at a slower pace, in the 1990s. The only households that saw their mean net worth rise in absolute terms between 1983 and 1995 were those in the top 20 percent and the gains were particularly strong for the top one percent. All other groups suffered real wealth losses, including the median household, and declines were particularly

Freedom of Movement of Labor

In general, the qualitative comparative evaluation of the freedom of movement of labor within and beyond the economy takes into consideration observations of and data on internal migration and immigration. First, it considers
the observations that the degree of freedom and scope of movement of labor
within the national economy, i.e., internal economic and related migration,
is common and unrestricted in Western and related economies, though partially denied or restricted for ethnic minorities in some countries like Greece
(non-Greek ethnicities), and Turkey (Kurds). It is particularly widespread and
historically legendary in the US through inter-state and other regional movements of labor, though such high geographic or demographic mobility in this
economy, like other Western economies, does not necessarily represent or
even correspond to equivalent social mobility within the stratification system.

A case in point for such a disjuncture between geographic and social mobility is the recently growing internal migration in the US from the North to
the South because of the latter's persistently low wages and associated benefits like health insurance, unemployment compensation, and pensions,
and generally the continuing systematic repression of labor maintained in a
slave-like condition through the brutal plutocratic suppression of union organization, collective bargaining, industrial democracy (work councils, etc.),
and other anti-labor practices since the end of the Civil War through these
days. This indicates that high geographic or demographic mobility expressing

---

precipitous at the bottom.' Alvaredo et al. (2013, pp. 4–5) find that in the US the 'share of
total annual income received by the top 1 percent has more than doubled from 9 percent
in 1976 to 20 percent in 2011. There was then a sharp reversal such that the top share is
today back in the same range as in the 1920s. The experience is markedly different in continental Europe and Japan (as) the top 1 percent shares are not far today from their levels
in the late 1940s, whereas in the US the share of the top 1 percent is higher by more than
a half.' They also note that wealth concentration 'is significantly greater in the US, where
the top 1 percent owns about 35 percent of aggregate wealth (for comparison, the share
is about 20–25 percent in Europe)' (Alvaredo et al. 2013, p. 16). Bivens and Mishel (2013,
p. 57) suggest that in the US the 'increase in the incomes and wages of the top 1 percent
over the last three decades (is) driven largely by the creation and/or redistribution of
economic rents, and not simply as the outcome of well-functioning competitive markets
rewarding skills or productivity based on marginal differences.' Generally, Corak (2013,
pp. 98–9) proposes that the US 'top 1 percent are also different in the way advantages are
passed on to the next generation, which certainly involves much higher-quality schooling
and other investments of human capital from the early years onward, but may well also
involve nepotism in the allocation of jobs.'

the unrestricted freedom of movement of labor within a national economy is neither a necessary nor sufficient condition of such social mobility in the stratification system, as most of those Americans migrating from the North to the South have realized or probably will realize, and conversely, the second type of movement does not necessarily presupposing and requiring the first. Generally, geographic and social mobility have moved in somewhat different directions in the US during last several decades, with the first increasing or continuing, especially in a new direction from the North to the South (e.g., Florida, Texas) and similar regions (Arizona, etc.), and the second largely declining in historical terms or compared to many other Western countries such as Scandinavia.

Second, the evaluation also takes into account of the observations of the freedom of movement of labor transcending the boundaries of a national economy, simply that of emigration from and immigration to other economies. Generally, all Western and related countries, with some minor or partial exceptions (perhaps Turkey), permit, if not 'voice,' the fully free 'exit' of domestic labor from their national economies, but none of them allows the completely free entry of foreign labor, and relatively less so than that of foreign capital. This reveals an asymmetry between these two aspects of the freedom of labor movement, reflecting the persistence of economic nationalism and closure, including political and cultural xenophobia, even in the 'most open' economies, notably the First, 'free World' invidiously self-distinguished from the 'closed' and 'unfree' Third World until recently at least. In other words, while that of emigration has become virtually unproblematic and unlimited in Western and related economies, freedom of immigration continues and even becomes more problematic and restricted such that none of them exhibits a degree of the second that is equivalent to that of the first. In light of this duality, the present evaluation takes account primarily of the data on freedom of immigration as evidently more consequential for the present purpose.

More specifically, the estimates of the freedom of immigration are inferred from the proportion of foreign-born people in the total population of a country, which is taken as an indicator or proxy in this respect (Table 5.10).

TABLE 5.10   *Foreign-Born population as percentage of total population OECD countries, 2015.*

Country	Percentage	Point[a]
Australia	27.6	9
Austria	16.7	7
Belgium	15.5	7

TABLE 5.10   *Foreign-Born population as percentage of total population OECD countries, 2015.* (cont.)

Country	Percentage	Point[a]
Canada	20.0	8
Chile	1.9[a]	2
Czech Republic	7.1	4
Denmark	8.5	5
Estonia	10.1	5
Finland	5.6	4
France	12.6[b]	6
Germany	12.8	6
Greece	8.7[a]	5
Hungary	4.5	3
Iceland	11.5	6
Ireland	16.4	7
Italy	8.8[a]	5
Japan	NA	NA
Korea	NA	NA
Luxembourg	43.7	10
Mexico	0.8	1
Netherlands	11.6	6
New Zealand	28.2	9
Norway	13.9	6
Poland	0.9[a]	1
Portugal	7.3[a]	4
Slovak Republic	3.2	3
Slovenia	16.1	7
Spain	13.4	6
Sweden	16.0	7
Switzerland	28.3	9
Turkey	1.9[a]	2
United Kingdom	12.3	6
United States	13.1	6

a Percentage 30 or higher = 10 points, Percentage 25–29 = 9 points, Percentage 20–24 = 8 points, Percentage 15–19 = 7 points, Percentage 12–14 = 6 points, Percentage 9–11 = 5 points, Percentage 6–8 = 4 points, Percentage 3–5 = 3 points, Percentage 1–2 = 2 points, Percentage under 1 = 1 point
b 2010

SOURCE: OECD HTTPS://DATA.OECD.ORG

As the data show, ten Western and related countries with the highest percentage of foreign-born population are Luxembourg (43.7), Switzerland (28.3), New Zealand (28.2), Australia (27.6), Canada (20), Austria (16.7), Ireland (16.4), Slovenia (16.1), Sweden (16), and Belgium (15.5). They hence include not only classic nations of immigration like Australia, Canada, and New Zealand, as in a way by definition, though another such nation, the US, is conspicuously missing from this top ten ranking. They also involve many Western and other European countries, including Switzerland, Austria, Sweden and Belgium, that are usually not considered immigrant societies but presently classified into regulated and egalitarian welfare capitalism, as well as liberal, secular and universalistic democracy, just as are the above three nations of immigration. It follows that virtually all of the countries with the highest percentage of foreign-born population largely belong To this economic and political system, with two exceptions (Ireland, Slovenia) as mixed systems. This strongly confirms the expectation that welfare capitalism, just as liberal democracy, tends to achieve the greatest degree of freedom of immigration and related freedoms in comparative terms.

In turn, ten countries with the lowest percentage of foreign-born population are Mexico (0.8), Poland (0.9), Chile (1.9), Turkey (1.9), Slovakia (3.2), Hungary (4.5), Finland (5.6), Czech Republic (7.1), Portugal (7.3) and Greece (8.7). They thus include instances of plutocratic or oligarchic capitalism, as well as anti-liberal, anti-secular and anti-universalistic democracy, such as Mexico, Poland, and Turkey, and only one of the opposite economic and political system like Finland, as well as several mixed cases, Chile, Czech Republic, Greece, Hungary, Portugal, and Slovakia. On this account, the first three cases fully confirm the expectation that plutocratic capitalism joined with anti-liberal polity attains the lowest degree of freedom of immigration and related economic as well as political freedoms. The second two instances, however, seemingly disconfirm the opposite expectation about egalitarian welfare capitalism, as well as liberal democracy, in relation to freedom of immigration, as do to a lesser extent the six mixed cases.

A closer look may reveal that this is not necessarily so insofar as their relatively low percentage of foreign-born population is explained mostly by exogenous non-societal impediments such as geographic distance and isolation and harsh weather in the case of Finland, as well as the relatively recent reconstitution as independent nation-states and relative economic backwardness in those of Chile, Czech Republic, Greece, Hungary, Portugal, and Slovakia, both factors evidently precluding these countries from becoming destinations or targets of immigration so far. To that extent, one can anticipate that so long as such geographic distance and isolation are mitigated or redefined as lesser

impediments by potential immigrants, countries classified in egalitarian welfare capitalism and liberal democracy such as Finland will experience growing
immigration—as has Iceland in recent years—and thus reach a higher percentage of foreign-born population historically and compared to those belonging to the opposite economic and political system. Also, one can expect that
as they will do also in the long run as they become 'older,' more established
independent nation-states and economically more developed, namely former
communist countries, especially Czech Republic and to some extent Slovak
Republic and in part Hungary, as well as perhaps Portugal, all classified in
eclectic economic and political systems.

Another level of comparison is comparing the classic or traditional English-
speaking nations of immigration among themselves in terms of percentage
of foreign-born population in the total population. This comparison reveals a
striking, surprising difference between Australia, Canada, and New Zealand on
one hand and the US on the other. The percentage of foreign-born population
is more than twice as high in New Zealand and Australia, and substantially
higher in Canada compared to that of the US, showing a striking divergence. At
this juncture, it appears that even all the nations of immigration 'are not created equal' or rather have not remained such in this respect, with the first three
revealing themselves as significantly more open societies than the fourth. Conversely, the US, widely regarded as the most immigrant and thus open country
in modern history, surprisingly reveals itself as a relatively closed society compared to these other nations of immigration, including neighboring Canada.

Moreover, the divergence in the percentage of foreign-born population
seems so substantial that Canada and even more Australia make the US para-
doxically appear as if it were not really a 'nation of immigration' by comparison, just as their higher percentages convert supposedly non-immigrant European societies like Switzerland, Austria, Sweden, and Germany into immigrant
nations. Yet, these dramatic and probably surprising differences even between
the traditional nations of immigration become less so in the present context
in which Australia, Canada, and New Zealand are classified into egalitarian
welfare capitalism, as well as liberal-secular democracy and the US into the
opposite economic and political system in the inegalitarian and anti-liberal
specification. Essentially, they are explained and predicted by the differing
economic and political systems of the first three versus the fourth. They thus
confirm the expectation that egalitarian welfare capitalism, in conjunction
with liberal-secular democracy, tends to attain a higher degree of freedom of
immigration as indicated or approximated by the percentage of foreign-born
population,' just as all other economic and political freedoms, compared with
its alternative economic-political systems.

Furthermore, such an economic and political system also explains why—even seemingly more surprisingly—no less than nine European countries, while conventionally not regarded as immigrant nations, have higher percentages of foreign-born population and in that sense freedom of immigration than does the US. Namely, most of them are classified into egalitarian welfare capitalism, as well as liberal democracy, for example, Austria, Belgium, Germany, Luxembourg, Sweden, and Switzerland, along with a few eclectic instances like Estonia, Ireland, and Spain, even if usually not considered countries of immigration in the sense of the US, Australia, and Canada. This factor largely explains the apparent paradox or 'surprise' that even if America is commonly viewed as the classic, quintessential 'nation of immigration' more than any other in modern history, dozens of countries have higher or similar percentages of foreign-born population, such as Europe, including also France, the Netherlands, and the UK. Overall, egalitarian welfare capitalism, joined with liberal democracy, mostly explains why 12 Western societies, i.e., the three other immigrant nations plus nine European societies, have higher percentages of foreign-born population than the US, which so ranks 13 among OECD countries in this respect.

Appendix 5.1 Qualitative Considerations of Economic Freedoms

Capital-Entrepreneurial Freedom
No comparative quantitative estimates of capital-entrepreneurial freedom are given because of the lack of appropriate data and rankings but a qualitative estimation or approximation is premised on the observation that this element of a free economy exists and operates within and observes the rules and institutional settings of various 'social games,' notably the norms and expectations of universal liberty, equality, and justice in society. In the first scenario, capital and entrepreneurship by virtue of respecting these rules sustains and enhances a free economy, notably the principle of universal, equal freedom for all the factors of production, thus including labor and other non-capitalists, alongside capitalists and/or entrepreneurs. In the second scenario, capitalist 'free enterprise' by violating such rules ushers in and maintains 'Hobbesian anarchy' through unlimited freedom for capital in the economy, combined with Leviathan-like oppression of labor and all non-capitalists, thus eliminating or perverting a free economy into its antithesis. Such an antithesis comprises substantively continuing slavery or reestablishing a slave-like economic system through such a mix of capitalist anarchy and labor oppression—as in the post-bellum fiercely pro-capital or plutocratic and anti-labor or anti-union US

South—a master-servant economy, feudalism or neo-feudalism, the new patrimonialism, the new patrimonial capitalism, and the like. All these are extremely unfree economic systems in which the principle of universal freedom for all productive agents, particularly capital and labor, is eliminated or perverted into the literal or figurative 'license to kill' for capitalists and entrepreneurs and zero or minimal liberties and rights for workers and other non-capitalists.

Consequently, societies in which capitalist-entrepreneurial activity plays by the 'rules of the social game,' notably those of universal liberty, equality, and justice in society, have higher degrees of capital freedom than those in which it degenerates into license for this factor of production mixed with oppression of labor and all non-capitalists. Typically, societies with an economic system of rationally coordinated and egalitarian welfare capitalism exemplify the situation in which capital and entrepreneurship tends to play by the 'rules of the social game' such as those of universal liberty, equality, and justice in society by recognizing and allowing them also to labor and non-capitalists overall as another factor of production. Conversely, societies with unrestrained and anti-egalitarian plutocratic capitalism epitomize the opposite pattern of capital and entrepreneurship not playing by these 'rules' of universal liberty, equality, and justice in society by monopolizing them for itself and denying them to labor and other non-capitalists. As a result, welfare capitalism is typified by the proximate equality or symmetry between capital/entrepreneurship and labor liberties and rights, thus implementing the principle of universal, equal economic freedom.

By contrast, plutocratic capitalism is characterized with an extreme inequality or asymmetry between capital and labor freedoms and rights privileging the first to the point of becoming the absolute master over the second reduced to a proxy slave or servant status, which flagrantly negates the principle of universal, equal freedom in the economy. Such inequality[19] precisely defines and identities plutocracy, like aristocracy, thus plutocratic capitalism as capitalist dictatorship, just as aristocratic feudalism, master-servant economies, and patrimonialism as despotic pre-capitalist economic systems. This indicates that

---

19   None other than US investor Carl Icahn laments that the 'average (US) worker makes approximately $50,000 per year. The average annual compensation of the thirty highest paid CEOs is approximately $47 million per year (i.e., nearly 1,000 times higher). (I don't believe this disparity was ever this great even in most dictatorships!) You will hear many politicians argue that government should not interfere with the 'business judgment,' of our companies and, therefore they cannot pass laws to encourage 'income equality.' This is completely untrue—the sad fact is that the government has actually passed many laws that have brought about 'income inequality.' (www.carlicahn.com).

plutocracy represents a variant of aristocracy, and thus plutocratic capitalism substantively perpetuates or reinvents aristocratic feudalism, master-servant economies, and patrimonialism, as exemplified by capitalist neo-feudalism and the new patrimonial capitalism.

In sum, the point is that capital-entrepreneurial freedom is truly 'freedom' from the viewpoint of the economy as a whole insofar as it also recognizes the equal or symmetrical freedom of the other factors of production such as labor and other non-capitalist agents, and thus the principle of equality or symmetry in this respect; and it does so playing by the 'rules of the social game' such as universal liberty, equality, and justice in society. Conversely, it is not really freedom from this holistic viewpoint if it degenerates into anarchy[20] as the proxy 'license to kill' and does not recognize equal freedom for labor and other non-capitalist agents and thus the principle of equality, by violating the 'rules' of universal liberty, equality, and justice in society.

The preceding provides grounds for inferring or assuming the maximal degrees of capital-entrepreneurial freedom for the Western and other societies characterized with the economic system of regulated and welfare capitalism. This hence holds true of most of Western and other Europe, especially Scandinavia, as well as countries like Australia, Canada, and New Zealand. Alternatively, the above also justifies the inference of a mixed degree of capital-entrepreneurial freedom for those societies with the economic system of anarchic and plutocratic or oligarchic capitalism, which thus applies to such non-Western OECD countries as Mexico, Poland, South Korea, Turkey, and the US in the above specification, along with some mixed cases like Chile and Greece.

Free Market Competition

Like those for capital-entrepreneurial freedom, the comparative quantitative estimates of the degree of market competition in Western and related economies are not provided due to the lack of data or rankings, but a qualitative evaluation considers various observations and findings. In general, these observations indicate that economies typified by welfare capitalism such as those in most of Western Europe, notably Scandinavia, tend to exhibit the highest degree of market competition, as well as free trade and global openness, contrary to 'libertarian' assertions and preconceptions. Alternatively, they as

---

20   Even some staunch pro-capital, anti-labor cum 'libertarian' economists distinguish
      capitalist-entrepreneurial and generally economic freedom from anarchy in the economy
      and society. Thus, Mises (1951, p. 56) complains that 'people often fail to perceive the fun-
      damental difference between the liberal and the anarchistic idea.'

a rule are characterized with the lowest level of monopoly and monopolization through concentration and monopolistic or oligopolistic dominance in
the market, including mergers, acquisitions, and other monopolizing, anti-
competitive practices, as well as with strict and fully enforced anti-monopoly
laws and regulations.

In essence, both the inner logic and prevalent reality of welfare capitalism
in most of Western Europe, including Scandinavia, is to be free competition,
yet rationally coordinated and regulated, and non-monopoly through anti-
monopoly laws in the domestic economy, just as free trade and global openness in relation to other economies. Its inner logic is that free competition
promotes economic welfare, notably the wellbeing of consumers and workers,
thus most of agents in the economy, and monopoly, including market concentration through oligopoly and mergers, eliminates or reduces it. And its prevalent reality is that free competition is observed to the rule within welfare capitalism, as in most of Western Europe, particularly Scandinavia, and monopoly
or oligopoly, including anti-competitive mergers, an exception.

By contrast, observations suggest that economies with plutocratic or oligarchic capitalism display overall a lower degree of market competition, as well
as free trade and global openness—again contradicting 'libertarian' assertions
and preconceptions—as exemplified by non-Western countries like Mexico,
Poland, South Korea, Turkey, and the US in the above specification, along with
Chile and Greece as mixed cases. In turn, these economies feature a higher
level of monopoly and monopolization in the form of monopolistic or oligopolistic dominance and concentration in the market, including competition-
destroying mergers, acquisitions, and related practices, as well as non-existent
or lax and not or weakly enforced anti-monopoly laws and regulations.

By analogy, the inner logic and prevalent reality of plutocratic, oligarchic
capitalism in these economies is observed to be monopoly or oligopoly, monopolization and market concentration though mergers and other monopolizing, activities, and no or lax anti-monopoly rules, just as relatively limited
free trade and comparative closure toward other economies. Its inner logic is
that monopoly or oligopoly, including monopolizing merger activity, maxi-
mizes the profits and wealth of capitalist plutocracy or oligarchy, and minimizes the welfare of non-capitalists, including most consumers and workers.
After all, plutocratic or oligarchic capitalism can logically only be and actually
is an economic system of monopoly or oligopoly as the market equivalent of
plutocracy or oligarchy. Alternatively, only monopoly or oligopoly as a market
structure is logically consistent and actually corresponds with plutocratic or
oligarchic capitalism as an economic and political system. In this sense, there
is an equivalence or correspondence between plutocracy and monopoly as

the market mechanism of plutocratic closure and dominance, and a virtual identity of oligarchy in economic-political systems and oligopoly in markets. Hence, the prevalent reality of plutocratic, oligarchic capitalism, as in South Korea, Mexico, Poland, Turkey, and the US during Reaganomics and especially in the South is observed to be monopoly or oligopoly, including monopolizing merger activities, and free competition mostly a transient exception.

For instance, the number of domestic car producers in the American economy is only two (General Motors, Ford) or at most three (plus Fiat-Chrysler), excluding foreign European and Japanese companies. This therefore effectively makes the US automotive market a duopoly or oligopoly when considering only domestic manufacturers and sellers which would solely remain either in a hypothetical autarchic long envisioned by Hamilton and other nativists, or in what Parsons calls an actual 'self-subsistent' economic-social system in the scenario of global war, trade wars, and even more likely protectionist-nativist 'America first' closure against 'foreign' competitors.[21] By stark contrast, the number of domestic car producers in Western Europe is around dozen (e.g., VW, BMW, Mercedes-Benz, Porsche, Opel; Volvo; Jaguar/Land Rover; Citroen/ Peugeot, Renault; Seat, Fiat, Skoda, etc.) and in Japan even ten or so (Toyota, Nissan, Honda, Mazda, Suzuki, Isuzu, Hino, Mitsubishi, Subaru, Daihatsu, Fuji Heavy Ind.). To that extent, this indicates or approximates free market competition in European and Japanese car markets even if considering only their domestic producers and sellers by comparison to the US duology or oligopoly in this respect by using the same consideration.

The car market is a particularly important indicator or proxy of the presence or absence of free market competition in modern economies. It is particularly

---

21 The US government effectively imposed Japan's car 'Voluntary Export Restraints' on America from the 1980s, which represents an instance or proxy of an actual or potential protectionist and nativist closure of this sector of American 'free market capitalism' to supposedly 'unfair' foreign competition, the standard justification of domestic cars' lower quality, especially unreliability, compared to Japanese and European imports. Such a nativist distortion or simulation of free competition has forced Japanese car manufacturers to significantly reduce their exports from Japan and to open production facilities in the US, but has not attained its stated or implicit goal, increasing or preserving the market share of domestic manufacturers, i.e., 'the 'big three,' which has steadily decreased since. At any rate, without Japanese, European and other foreign companies, the US car market would be hypothetically duopoly or oligopoly, and effectively could become so if such economic nativism persists or intensifies, as witnessed in the rise and prominence of the nativist, xenophobic, and proto-fascist 'Tea Party' in the South (above all Texas) and beyond, as well as nationalistic and anti-free-trade demagogic Presidential pretenders and other politicians.

indicative of the US economy especially since Reaganomics widely observed to represent a set of oligopolies—i.e., most of its sectors controlled by a few large firms—and in that sense a generalization of the automotive industry, as exemplified by the government's investigation of anti-competitive practices like collusion in various industries as 'abusive' oligopolies'[22] (major airlines, cable and phone companies, health care providers, national banks, etc.) and proxy monopolies (some pharmaceutical firms). The preceding helps infer the highest degrees of market competition in welfare capitalism such as most of Western Europe, in particular Scandinavia, and the lower in plutocratic or oligarchic capitalisms Mexico, South Korea, Poland, Turkey, and the US in the above specification.

Consumer Freedom, Choice, and Rights

While the comparative quantitative estimates of consumer freedom, choice, and rights for Western and related economies are not provided due to the lack of proper data, a qualitative evaluation is perhaps possible whose justification consists of a blend of academic studies and findings with related non-academic estimations and rankings. Generally, economic and sociological observations indicate that consumer freedom and choice between alternative products and services in the market is common, widespread, and further increasing, above all because of the expansion of economic globalization, notably free global trade, in virtually all of these economies. Still, these observations indicate or imply that the degree of consumer freedom and choice is to some extent, perhaps surprisingly, greater in Western European than in the US, Japanese and in part the UK economies primarily because the first are observed to be more open and globalized and the second 'relatively closed' and less globalized. Consequently, they suggest that the degrees and numbers of consumer freedoms, choices, and rights in an economy is enhanced and sustained by the level and process of globalization, including free global trade and openness, while being reduced or distorted by economic closure and protectionism, and not only determined by the structure and internal competitiveness of the domestic

---

22   In another notorious exemplar, Gowrisankaran, Nevo, and Town (2015, p. 201) observe that the US health care market is substantially and growingly concentrated in its being dominated by 'oligopoly firms' such as large managed care organizations and hospitals. For example, in their estimate the 'proposed merger between Inova hospital system and Prince William Hospital (in Northern Virginia), which the FTC challenged, would have significantly raised prices' and add that this market is 'more concentrated than the average market but not an outlier, implying that hospital mergers in other (markets) may also cause price increases and hence be cause for antitrust concern' (Gowrisankaran et al. 2015, pp. 201–202).

market. In particular, observations indicate that expanded free global trade dramatically expands consumer freedoms, choices, and rights in an economy, as much as and perhaps even more than domestic commerce in the time of globalization, just as exemplifying free competition in the market.

To that extent, the above requires taking account of the indexes of economic globalization, including free global trade, in constructing the comparative estimates of consumer freedom, choice, and rights. And the higher indexes of economic globalization, notably free global trade, predict or contribute to the higher comparative estimates of consumer freedom, choice, and rights in an economy, other things equal such as the structure and competitiveness of the domestic market and commerce, etc. As a consequence, those economies with the highest economic globalization indexes are observed or expected to have the equivalent estimates of consumer freedoms, choices, and rights at least in the long run, and conversely. This is based on the observation or expectation that the process of globalization, above all free global trade, operates to dramatically expand such attributes in the domain of consumption, just as to exemplify competition in consumer markets. As a result, consumer freedom/choice comparative estimates would be largely equivalent or similar to such globalization indexes. Thus, the Western European economies of welfare globalized capitalism would rank the highest on this economic freedom, and comparatively higher than the US, Japanese and in part the UK economic systems of non-welfare and/or relatively closed capitalism.

Industrial Democracy
The comparative estimates of modern industrial democracy for Western and related economies are not available in a quantitative form, and instead a qualitative evaluation maybe is possible. This takes into consideration sociological and economic studies and observations that this element of economic freedom is developed in most of Europe, as within the European Union, and other countries such as Canada, and yet virtually non-existent or suppressed in the US economy. In particular, such an evaluation considers the observations that work councils as an aspect and exercise of economic democracy are relatively common in Western and especially Northern Europe, especially Germany.[23] Notably, the European Commission since 1995 through 2009 has issued several directives for establishing 'European Works Councils' defined as 'bodies

---

23 Hodgson (1999, p. 208) observes that 'worker involvement in some management decisions may become a matter of employment law, as already in Germany. These extensions of worker participation and codetermination may yield substantial benefits in terms of enhanced productivity and profitability for the firms involved.'

representing the European employees of a company' at the level of the European Union,[24] i.e., involving two or more member states. Also, work council in certain forms are found in some other countries like Canada.[25] By stark typical contrast, work councils are observed to have become effectively non-entities, taboos, or rare and diminishing occurrences in the US economy.[26] This observation hence would justify the minimal qualitative estimation on economic democracy for the US economy.

In addition, the evaluation takes account of some comparative findings of 'bureaucratic burden' in the sense of the relative proportion and thus positional power or influence of 'administrative and managerial' personnel among total employees within organizations. According to these findings, Western, especially Scandinavian, welfare-capitalist economies have a lower 'bureaucratic burden'[27] and to that degree a higher degree or proxy of industrial democracy

---

24   The European Commission elaborates that through European Works Councils 'workers are informed and consulted by management on the progress of the business and any significant decision at European level that could affect their employment or working conditions.' It adds that 'member States are to provide for the right to establish European Works Councils in companies or groups of companies with at least 1000 employees in the EU and the other countries of the European Economic Area (Norway, Iceland and Liechtenstein), when there are at least 150 employees in each of two Member States. A request by 100 employees from two countries or an initiative by the employer triggers the process of creating a new European Works Council. The composition and functioning of each European Works Council is adapted to the company's specific situation by a signed agreement between management and workers' representatives of the different countries involved.' (http://ec.europa.eu).

25   Rogers and Streeck (1995, p. 22) invoke 'joint health and safety councils in Canada, as an example of a council-like structure in a North American country.'

26   Dustmann et al. (2014, p. 177) remarks that 'Germany's culture of common interest is dissimilar to the view about worker representations commonly held in the United States. A recent US example is the attempt of the management of the German company Volkswagen to introduce a works council at its Chattanooga plant in Tennessee. While the participation of works councils in management decisions is considered by Volkswagen as a cornerstone of successful firm policy that helps furthering common interests, Tennessee Governor has been outspoken in opposing any union formation at the plant (by the claim to) attract investment.' Yet, Volkswagen effectively repudiated such claims as false by proceeding to introduce a works council and allowing union formation in the plant.

27   Sen (1994, p. 388) refers to the finding that among the OECD 16 advanced economies, the 'bureaucratic burden,' defined as the 'relative proportion of 'administrative and managerial workers' among total employees in nonfarm occupations,' is (in 1980) between '2.5 percent in Sweden to 11.5 percent in the United States, which is the highest in the list,' followed by the UK, Canada and Australia.

than does American capitalism in which workers are found to be over-controlled, over-regulated, and 'over-managed' by such administrative and managerial staff and thus denied and deprived of autonomy and democratic or shared governance, such as participation in organizational decision-making. Notably, the 'bureaucratic burden' as measured and thus the repression or control of workers is reportedly no less than almost five times lower in Sweden's economy than in the US economy, which to that extent reveals itself as the Western leader (or 'mother') of all labor-repressive or controlling bureaucracies.

These dramatic differences in labor autonomy and participation epitomize coordinated, welfare capitalism's superior outcomes both for economic freedom and efficiency by comparison to its unrestrained, plutocratic opposite, and yet again affirm and evoke Samuelson's admission that seemingly 'regimented' Sweden is economically and otherwise 'freer' than 'my America.' They would provide an additional basis for the maximum and minimum estimates of economic democracy for the Swedish and US economy, respectively. These finding thus contradict US 'libertarian' economists in their dogmatic and ethnocentric dismissals of the first and related economies as inefficient European 'bureaucracies,' 'socialism,' 'statism,' and the like, and their glorifying of the second as the supreme model of economic efficiency and free of bureaucracy,[28] exposing them as blinded by their dogma or ethnocentrism to the reality of welfare capitalism's best performance in this and virtually all freedoms compared to plutocratic capitalism. Given that Samuelson's observation is from half a century ago, US 'libertarian' economists and politicians, just as conservatives overall, appear to deny any economic and political reality, instead living in a kind of fantasy world or parallel universe,[29] in which unregulated, plutocratic capitalism mixed with anti-liberal and anti-secular 'democracy is 'freer' and 'better' than regulated and welfare capitalism joined with liberal-secular democracy, simply the best.'

---

28   Myles and Turegun (1994, p. 115) note that after ww II the 'American labor force was indeed overmanaged' largely because 'American employers hire more labor to supervise and regulate the activity of other workers.' By contrast, they suggest that 'employers in all sectors of the Swedish economy employ disproportionately more "knowledge workers," and such employees are less likely to be involved in exercising authority over other employees' (Myles and Turegun 1994, p. 115).

29   As known, the 'libertarian' and generally conservative denial of societal reality has escalated to denying that even some physical realities or processes, such as climate change through global warming, are real, not to mention biological evolution for long denied as 'just a godless theory' by US conservatives.

Notes on US Estimates of a Free Economy

Aggregate Estimates

In particular, some economists[30] register and analyze the 'repressive' capitalist and agricultural economy, pervaded by severe and systematic 'repression' of labor increasingly regardless of race, in the US South as the effective 'continuation of the pre-Civil War economic order' of slavery during post-bellum and recent times. At this juncture, the Southern slave and post-slave anti-labor repressive economy represents the paradigmatic instance of unfettered, anti-egalitarian, and aristocratic or plutocratic and oligarchic capitalism in America and the Western world. Such an economy dramatically documents on a regional level that this type of capitalism constitutes intrinsically or ultimately becomes an unfree as well as inefficient economic system. This holds true especially by comparison with egalitarian, welfare capitalism established and consolidated in most of Western Europe, just as neighboring Canada epitomized by its universal health care system, while the South was and remains under a new proxy slavery transcending racial boundaries to encompass also what Weber calls the 'poor white trash' with its 'ethnic honor'[31] as the sole 'honor' of the dis-privileged masses in an ethnically heterogeneous society. The Southern and other 'hillbilly' economy evidently persists as an extreme, slave-style case of unfettered and anti-egalitarian oligarchic 'good old boys' and 'red neck' capitalism through the lack of and vehement opposition to rational regulation of its operation and adverse outcomes. Notably, this economic system features virtually no legal protection of labor from capital repression and exploitation such as anti-union laws and low wages persisting in the South and related regions for long, which substantially lowers the US estimate on a free-economy.

Capital-Entrepreneurial Freedom

As usual, the US qualitative estimation of this element of economic liberty may need to be explained so long as it seems dubious or surprising and because it is claimed, as by 'libertarian' economists and conservative politicians

---

30   Samuelson (2004, p. 142) observes that US 'textiles, shoes and manufacturers moved from New England to the low-wage South early in the last century.' Acemoglu and Robinson (2008, pp. 268–9) note that 'even though former slaves were enfranchised and slavery was abolished at the end of the Civil War, the South largely maintained its pre–Civil War agricultural system based on large plantations, low-wage uneducated labor, and labor repression, and it remained relatively poor until the middle of the twentieth century.'

31   Baxter and Margavio (2000, p. 406) comment that Weber 'cites as an example of ethnic group honor the way 'poor white trash' in the US act as aggressive bearers of racial antipathy.'

in America, that American 'unfettered' capitalism forms the exceptional, main, and even sole space of capital-entrepreneurial freedom in the Western and entire world, as well as in history. Various observations indicate that 'exceptional' anti-labor and anti-competitive American 'free enterprise' seeks to and usually succeeds to subjugate, repress, and control labor, as well as to eliminate or limit and subvert competition in the US economy comparatively more so than in most other Western and related capitalist economies such as those in Europe and Canada, minus the UK and Mexico. Especially, they identify the Southern version of anti-labor capitalist 'freedom' as anarchy or the 'license to kill' through the systematic subjugation and repression of labor substantively reduced to a slave- or servant-style condition deprived of collective organization and action via unions during post-bellum times.

In addition, the estimate for capital-entrepreneurial freedom in the US economy is based on the reported pattern of abuses of innovations by many American companies for anti-competitive monopolistic aims. It also take into account the observed comparative backwardness of some US industries in terms of applied technologies and production processes, including quality control, compared to their competitors in many other advanced economies. For example, such backwardness has been salient and persistent by comparison to Japan and Germany observed to be more technologically advanced and efficient, especially having higher productivity and superior quality control, in car manufacturing and related industries, and most of Western Europe in environmental and related inventions.[32]

---

32   As an illustration of US manufacturing companies' long-standing tendency to anti-competitive inventions, Baker (2003, pp. 29–30) observes that the US car manufacturers colluded to 'share information and intellectual property on ways to reduce emissions had suppressed industry research and development into air pollution control equipment by undermining each firm's individual incentive to innovate. The challenged agreement was in force during an era in which the Big Three automakers likely had only a limited incentive to innovate relative to that of their fringe rivals.' Baker (2003, p. 30) points to 'another celebrated conspiracy' in that General Electric, Westinghouse and others colluded 'during the late 1950s to rotate the low bid for procurement of various electrical equipment among firms according to the phases of the moon (sic).' In particular, Nicholas (2008, p. 1378) registers that 'General Electric was well known for its "defensive" patents in the electrical lamp market, while the leading players in the chemicals industry, especially DuPont, used strategic patenting to deter entry.' Baily and Solow (2001, p. 156) observe that 'Germany is the greatest manufacturing power in Europe and runs a substantial trade surplus in manufactured goods with the United States,' while noting that Japan is the 'productivity leader' in industries producing luxury automobiles and specialized machine tools. Overall, Triglia (2002, p. 247) suggests that the 'competitiveness of industry' in the US economy (generally 'Anglo-Saxon capitalism') is lower to that of most European and

Property Freedoms and Rights

As before, the US estimate is to be explained in more detail, the more so that American capitalism is widely regarded as or claimed, as by 'libertarian' economists and conservative politicians, to the only, exceptional realm and protector of private property freedoms and rights. Against this background, the US estimate (6) for private property freedoms and rights is supported by historical and empirical evidence. For example, during the 1980s US Congress dramatically expanded and reinforced ('amended') the existing laws for asset seizure or forfeiture by allowing state and local authorities to confiscate and retain most (up to 80% of the value) of assets of various moral sinners cum criminals such as drug offenders and pornography distributors. This has been and continues to be done on the apparent assumption that drug use and trade, distributing and even consuming adult content, and similar sins are so grave crimes that necessitate almost completely dispossessing these offenders and thus denying or violating constitutional private property freedoms and rights for this group of sinners-cum-criminals. And the latter have become a continuously growing category, as indicated by the literally exploding prison population (around 2.3 million today) of which such and other moral sinners make the overwhelming majority (more than half overall, around two third or so of federal prisoners).

At this juncture, for these American sinners-criminals the constitutional celebrated right to 'liberty, property, and life' is hardly worth the paper on which it is written and printed, although fully applied and thus 'priceless' to capitalists-plutocrats and their even faster-growing wealth and income. Moreover, incredibly but true, civil asset forfeiture law allows the police in the US to size the monetary and all assets of suspicious persons even without ever being convicted or charged for any sin-crime in a fantastic Orwellian-like disregard of constitutional 'sacred' private property freedoms and rights.[33]

---

other economies ('Rhine-Japanese capitalism.' Exemplifying US companies' relative technological and organizational, for example, quality-control, backwardness, Grossman and Maggi (2000, p. 1271) note that 'Japanese firms are reputed to have uniformly competent personnel, which contributes to a high standard of quality control' compared to that of their American counterparts.

33 Consider the following report by the New York Times (November 09, 2014). 'The seminars offered police officers some useful tips on seizing property from suspected criminals. Don't bother with jewelry (too hard to dispose of) and computers ('everybody's got one already'), the experts counseled. Do go after flat screen TVs, cash and cars. Especially nice cars. In one seminar, captured on video in September, Harry S. Connelly Jr., the city attorney of Las Cruces, N.M., called them 'little goodies.' And then Mr. Connelly described how officers in his jurisdiction could not wait to seize one man's 'exotic vehicle' outside a local bar. 'A guy drives up in a 2008 Mercedes, brand new,' he explained. 'Just so beautiful,

In this connection, a historical instance and precedent for such exceptional negations of the private property freedoms and rights of certain groups, especially sinners-criminals and 'enemies,' in the US seems the Protestant Reformation's violent seizure of the assets of political opponents and Catholic monasteries. Reportedly, the Reformation seized Catholic monasteries and the property of opponents in Germany,[34] as did Calvinism in parts of France, Geneva, Holland, and through Puritanism in England and New England and Presbyterianism in Scotland. Such violent actions, especially by Puritan theocratic rulers dispossessing and exterminating 'witches,' non-Puritans, and Native Americans in New England, provides a model or historical precedent for the US government, including 'Bible-Belt' states, confiscating the properties (e.g., houses, savings, pensions, etc.) of sinners-criminals, 'deviants,' 'enemies,' foreigners, and other 'un-American' groups for 'anti-American' (i.e., sinful and 'godless') activities. These activities—as most others in American 'unfettered' capitalism and 'godly democracy—are evidently moralistic and religiously driven and sanctified, but they self-contradict and violate what are rhetorically celebrated as sacred constitutional and comparatively exceptional private property freedoms and rights. As typical, this confirms that Puritan-rooted morality and religion poisons[35] or contaminates virtually everything in American 'pure,' 'free enterprise' capitalism, including evidently

---

I mean, the cops were undercover and they were just like 'Ahhhh.' And he gets out and he's just reeking of alcohol. And it's like, 'Oh, my goodness, we can hardly wait.' Mr. Connelly was talking about a practice known as civil asset forfeiture, which allows the government, without ever securing a conviction or even filing a criminal charge, to seize property suspected of having ties to crime. The practice, expanded during the war on drugs in the 1980s, has become a staple of law enforcement agencies because it helps finance their work. It is difficult to tell how much has been seized by state and local law enforcement, but under a Justice Department program, the value of assets seized has ballooned to $4.3 billion in the 2012 fiscal year from $407 million in 2001. Much of that money is shared with local police forces.' If so, then the Constitutional protection and the political celebration of private property—'most protected' and celebrated among Western and all societies—are not worth the paper on which they are printed for most Americans, especially moral sinners like drug offenders made criminals by the conservative Puritan sin-crime equation, except for plutocracy or oligarchy.

34   Kim and Pfaff (2012, p. 210) note that early Protestant 'Evangelicals' in Germany and elsewhere 'attacked priests and monks, smashed icons, and looted monasteries and the property of prominent loyalists.'

35   In retrospect, this also confirms Edward Ross observing that 'Puritan tyranny' acts as the (reverse) 'antidote' to democracy and by implication economic freedom in America regarded as the 'lineal descendant' of Puritanism.

the nominally inviolable freedom and right of private property, just as even more within democracy and civil society, including political and individual liberties and rights.

The US comparatively modest score on property rights needed to be explained in more detail because it is likely surprising given the constitutional 'liberty, property, and life' principle and its political glorification. Yet, its denial or violation to moral sinners-criminals such as non-violent drug and sexual offenders is not unexpected, but prefigured by the historical precedent of theocratic and moralistic Puritanism's violent dispossession and elimination of 'witches' and the 'godless.' In this context, the expanded federal asset forfeiture federal laws and their state/local enforcement through confiscating and retaining most of the private assets of moral sinners-cum-criminals in America appears déjà vu in that it reenacts or evokes the Puritan dispossession of 'witches' and 'heathen.' Comparatively, this reveals obverse (non-superior) 'American exceptionalism' with respect to private property freedoms and rights among Western and related economies. This is because none of these denies or violates these freedoms and rights to moral sinners-criminals, at least not on the scale and with Puritan-style zealotry, intensity, and consistency that the US government does, especially the 'Bible Belt.' Thus, in conjunction with the theocratic and moralistic legacy of Puritanism, the South depresses the US score on private property freedoms and rights, just as does on all dimensions of economic, political, individual, and cultural freedom.

Free Market Competition
In particular, the US qualitative estimation is grounded in and supported by observations and findings of the lower or diminishing degree of free competition in relation to the growing scale of monopoly, oligopoly, and market concentration in the American economy as compared to most other advanced economies, especially those within the European Union. In addition, the rationale for such an estimate is the comparative lower level of legal and effective protection and promotion of free competition against monopolization, as epitomized by lax and non- or weakly enforced anti-monopoly laws, in the US in relation to the European Union.

As an indicative additional example, in 2015–16 the Congress hearings about admitted 'scandals' like exorbitant prices increases of life-saving medications (e.g. anti-allergy drugs, etc.) revealed the anti-competitive monopolistic pattern of the US pharmaceutical industry and the economy as a whole, with some exceptions. These products are often produced by a single pharmaceutical company, and thus monopolized in the US market, while ten or so such companies produce them and so compete in Europe such as the European

Union. Consequently, the prices of these medications are multiple, almost ten times higher in the US market (e.g., $600 for an anti-allergy medicine) than the European ($75–100), demonstrating what Smith detected and condemned as the 'evil of monopoly' in the matters of health, life and death. Relatedly, owing to such monopoly of a single producer, their prices have sky-rocketed in the US market (from around $50–60 in 2007 to $600 in 2016, etc.), while staying stable or slightly increasing in the European subject to such competition of multiple producers. Then thanks to such monopoly and its abuse through exorbitant prices, the CEO of the company is awarded—or rather self-determines with the 'little help' of the hand-picked board of directors, as in most US corporations—an also extravagant pay (almost $20 million per year), nearly 400 times higher than the average wage, while lying about the size of its profits (understating them by 60%) accruing from its monopolistic abuse, and overcharging the government (by almost half a billion dollars). And to add insult to injury, the executives of such monopolistic or oligopolistic pharmaceutical and other companies reportedly, as Weber put it, by their money 'purchase' political power by influencing Congress and state legislatures to enact laws in favor of their marketing campaigns (e.g., the 2013 law allowing sale of an anti-allergy medication to US schools, etc.).

During these scandals, it is often commented that each shows 'what is wrong' with the pharmaceutical industry as a monopoly or oligopoly—and the health care system driven by profit above all maximized on life and death—in the US, but this inference can be generalized to the market or industry as a whole given that they are indicate a pattern, and not exceptions, in the economy. (In another symptomatic instance noted in the *Economist* some time ago, virtually all US major cities from New York to Los Angeles are reduced to a single, dominant newspaper and thus monopoly in this sector, while those in Europe have multiple or several competing newspapers and so effective competition in this respect.)

Free Trade and Freedom of Foreign Investment
The ranking on economic globalization provides another rationale for the relatively low estimate of free global trade for the US economy. The latter is ranked on economic globalization lower than virtually all other major Western and related economies (excepting only Italy and Japan), and 20 out of 31 OECD members (overall 25 among all countries), thus only 11 of these having lower indexes. Consequently, this justifies the medium estimate of free global trade for the US economy, and conversely, not having the same score as most other Western and related economies from Scandinavia through Germany and France to Canada and Australia.

A 'consolation prize' is that the American economy is not ranked the lowest on this dimension of economic freedom, with Italy and especially Japan having even lower free global trade scores. Yet, this is far cry from its being, as asserted and celebrated by US 'libertarian ' economists and nationalist politicians, the most or even only open, globalized, competitive, and 'free' economic system in the world precisely because of being the sole or major paragon of 'unfettered' capitalism. To the extent that free global trade and economic globalization overall represents the extension and 'exemplification' of free market competition within an economy, then the US comparatively low score on the first may well exemplify the lower degree of the latter as compared to most other Western economies. If in an age of accelerating and pervasive economic globalization the degree of market competition within a national economy tends to be exemplified by the scope of free global trade, the US economy's low index of the second may express the equivalent estimate of the first. Simply, it may reveal itself as less competitive internally than most Western economies precisely because of its being relatively more 'closed' to foreign economic and non-economic relations. If so, this objectively justifies the perhaps surprisingly low estimate of free global trade for the US economy as compared to most Western and related economies.

The specific grounds for the US score on free global trade involve more numerous or restrictive import–export prohibitions and restrictions, subsidies, quotas, tariffs, etc., usually for ideological or political reasons, compared to most other advanced economies. This is exemplified by 'no trade with the enemy' distortions of free global trade and markets during and after the Cold War and subsequent 'imperial wars' (e.g., Cuba, Iran, and various other trade blockades, etc.). Such grounds also involve many US corporations persistently acting or attempting, by influencing government, to restrict or distort foreign competition by spurious 'fair trade' claims and 'protectionist lobbies,' as well as mixed military and commercial imperialism[36] expanded to South America under dictatorial regimes, as exemplified by Chile during Pinochet's 'free enterprise' (Chicago-style economics) neo-fascist dictatorship. As seen, the

---

36 Dreiling and Darves 2011, p. 1519) suggest that US 'corporate involvement in trade policy' is a 'force for protectionism,' as through 'protectionist lobbies,' and not just for 'greater trade liberalization.' Dube, Kaplan, and Naidu (2011, p. 1376) report that coups and 'regime changes led to significant economic gains for corporations that stood to benefit from US interventions in developing countries.' Berger et al. (2013, pp. 863–4) find that 'US covert services engaged in interventions that installed and/or supported political leaders in other countries' and that 'US influence raised the share of total imports that the intervened country purchased from the US' such that the 'new goods that were shipped from the US to the intervened country were products that US firms were less competitive in producing (bad cars?).'

overall ground also consists of the lower level of globalization and thus openness of the American economy than most Western European economies,[37] notably Scandinavia.

The above thus provides a plausible rationale for constructing the comparative estimates of the freedom of foreign investment for Western and related economies in general and for the relatively lower estimate of this dimension of economic freedom for the US economy. An additional more specific rationale is that the freedom of foreign investment in its two components, just as free global trade, has historically been more restricted and suppressed on economic or ideological, political, and cultural grounds in the US economy than in most other Western economies, including Europe and Canada. This is exemplified by the past and current prohibitions or restrictions of investments in the US economy by foreign entities (including Russia and China) and in other economies (Cuba, Iran, North Korea, Russia, etc.) by American companies and individuals, including being prohibited from touristic transactions. These anti-foreign measures are enacted and maintained because of either 'rational' economic and especially irrational reasons such as ideology, politics, nationalism, xenophobia, and culture closure, related or corresponding to trading blockades and wars on 'no trade with the enemy' grounds. In particular, the freedom of foreign entities (e.g., from Russia before, in part China now, Japan until recently) to acquire productive as well consumption assets in the US economy seems more suppressed or restricted, at least condemned or disproved as 'selling and buying out America' by xenophobic politicians and the public, than in most other Western economies.

Above all, various foreign investment and free-trade blockades and embargoes, including 'commercial imperialism' by the US government in Latin America like Chile by installing neo-fascist military dictatorships,[38] display the

---

37   Brady, Beckfield, and Zhao (2007, p. 315) observe that 'trade openness' in the US economy is 'far below West European levels,' for example, 26.3% versus 162.7% in 2000. They suggest that the level of globalization in the US economy is 'too low to be the main cause of deindustrialization. (Thus) foreign markets remain a small part of most US firms' revenues' (Brady et al. 2007, p. 321). In particular, Brady et al. (2007, p. 324) find that the 'small, highly globalized countries of Scandinavia remain far more highly unionized than less globalized countries like the US.' Also, Brady, Beckfield, and Seeleib-Kaiser (2005, p. 925) observe that 'Sweden has a generous welfare state and is highly globalized, while the United States is less globalized and has a minimal welfare state.'

38   Berger et al. (2013, pp. 867–8) notice that the 'CIA intervened most heavily in Latin America,' citing the 'famous CIA orchestrated coup of 1973.' Notably, Berger et al. (2013, p. 889) find that 'covert CIA interventions increased the influence of the US over foreign governments, and that this was used to increase US exports to the intervened countries' like Chile and other Latin America. In turn, they find that the 'increase in imports from

self-contradiction and comparative 'exceptionalism' of American 'unfettered capitalism' in relation to most Western economies. This holds true so long as most of these latter, with the predictable and partial exception of the UK, do not resort to such hostile and aggressive actions, at least not on that scale and with such an intensity, duration, and ideological stringency, as exemplified by the Cuba[39] economically irrational trade, investment, and tourist blockade (including even prohibiting and punishing imports of the famed Cuba cigars) and many others since the Cold War through the 'war on terror.' Consequently, such practices objectively depress the US index or estimate of the freedom of investment, just as free global trade, compared with those for most other Western economies.

Consumer Freedom, Choice, and Rights

The preceding thus provides an explanation and basis for the qualitative estimation of consumer freedoms, choices, and rights in the US economy as compared with most Western European economies—the lower level of globalization and openness, including free global trade, and the higher degree of protectionism[40]

---

the US was greatest for goods which the US had a comparative *dis*advantage in producing. That is, the new goods that were shipped from the US to the intervened country were products that US firms were less competitive in producing' (Berger et al. 2013, p. 864).

39   What Spencer observed for the UK government in the 19th century applies, with prudent modifications, to the Cuba trade blockade by the US government: it is the 'astounding belief that an act of parliament can abrogate one of Nature's decrees—can, for instance, render it criminal in a trader to buy goods in France (add cigars and rum in Cuba), and bring them here to sell, whilst the moral law says it is criminal to prevent him! As though conduct could be made right or wrong by the votes of some men sitting in a room in Westminster (replace with Congress)!'

40   Persson and Tabellini (2006, p. 323) imply than the US economy features more protectionism than most other Western economies predicting that the latter, i.e., 'parliamentary and proportional democracies seek consensus among broader coalitions of voters, they should have not only larger government spending, but also less protectionist trade policies. Parliamentary or proportional democracy each raise the probability of a subsequent liberalization by about 10 percentage points, compared to majoritarian and presidential democracy,' such as the US. They infer that a 'new parliamentary democracy is more prone to pursue economic liberalization than a new presidential democracy' (Persson and Tabellini 2006, p. 323) as commonly epitomized by the US. Also, Alesina, Spolaore, and Wacziarg (2000, p. 1292) suggest such an implication or interpretation finding that 'trade liberalization and average country size are inversely related,' with the US as the largest among OECD countries.

and economic nationalism in the first than the second.[41] The rationale is that evidently the low (high) level of globalization and openness, particularly free global trade, matters negatively (positively) for the degree and amount of consumer freedoms, choices, and rights in the US (and any) economy, equally, if not more in a globalizing setting and time, just as do domestic markets and trades.

An additional reason for the US estimate is that studies and casual observations indicate that the level of consumer rights and protection is comparatively low, even if to some extent increasing recently, for example, in banking and other financial services following the Great Recession. Thus, consumers, as well as workers, seem less protected from corporate fraud and crime, corruption, collusion, poor product quality such as the fast physical depreciation (breaking down) of durable goods like cars, consumer electronics, home appliances, homes, etc., false and aggressive advertising, etc., in the US economy, while legal sanctions for such 'white-collar' crimes being mild (figuratively, 'slap on the wrist'), as compared with most other advanced economies. And this is essentially an outcome of and compatible with the inner logic and operation of plutocratic capitalism, insofar as plutocrats are by definition or in reality unwilling to punish themselves fairly (unless being a kind of masochists) through a government controlled by plutocracy, just as being incapable of their claimed and demanded 'self-regulation,' as even Adam Smith acknowledges by detecting capitalists' persistent 'conspiracy against the public.'

Labor Freedom and Agency

That US labor union density is between five and almost eight times lower, therefore provide the rationale for the estimate (2) on labor liberty and agency for the US economy, only joined on this dimension of economic freedom with France among advanced Western economies, and Turkey, Estonia, and South Korea within the OECD setting.

---

41 For example, an accurate statistical count or even casual look would disclose that most department stores in Western European and related societies, plus other parts of Europe, Southern America, etc., have a far higher percentage of foreign, imported products than those in the US in which such goods remain, despite increasing imports during recent times, a tiny minority, except for consumer electronics like televisions for the simple reason that their domestic brands are non-existent or of inferior quality. As a result, consumers in the first societies seem or are likely in the long run to have more freedoms, choices, and eventually rights and protection from company fraud, crime, poor quality, etc. than those in the second, which demonstrates or exemplifies that the higher level of globalization through free global trade tends to enhance these attributes of consumers and consumption, and conversely.

An addition reason for such an estimate consists in that various economic and sociological studies document that labor repression, control, and coercion in the US economy tends to be more severe, pervasive, and persistent than in most other Western economies and even OECD countries, except for Turkey, South Korea, Chile, Mexico, etc. Thus, many analysts register and emphasize that pro-capital and anti-labor ideology and policy prevails in the US economy and polity, consequently considered and depicted as an oligarchic economic and political system, especially since the 1980s (and before) with the resurgence of repressive plutocratic, anti-union conservatism such as Reaganomics and its sequels. Some studies suggest that the critical historical point in terms of providing the institutional basis for growing labor coercion and repression in the US during postwar times was the anti-labor Taft-Hartley Act, conjoined with McCarthyism, and related acts and policies.[42] In particular, many analysts note both the declining incidence and the increasingly violent suppression of labor strikes and related collective actions in the US economy during last several decades, though with various historical precedents, especially during the period prior to the New Deal and its first true legalization of unions. Moreover, some observers[43] regard labor as descending into a slave-like status in modern American and generally plutocratic and anti-egalitarian capitalism, just as others find that its servant-style condition in the latter as well as its British variant has a long tradition, with its legacy or vestige of 'serf-like American underclass.'

In particular, economic and sociological analyses indicate that labor oppression and union suppression continues to be most pervasive, intense, and

---

42   Stepan-Norris and Southworth (2010, p. 231) remark that in the US during the 1950s the 'anti-labor Taft-Hartley Act (Labor Management Relations Act) passed and McCarthyism took hold' in an apparent association. Blau and Kahn (2000, p. 93) note that 'among the OECD nations, the US stands at an extreme with an especially low rate of collective bargaining coverage, pay setting which is often determined at the plant level even within the union sector, and an absence of formal or informal mechanisms to extend union-negotiated pay rates to nonunion workers.' Flanagan (1999, p. 1151) observes that 'labor unions and collective bargaining are among the institutional constants of economic life. Even among industrialized countries, unionization varies widely, with the highest density rates (in Scandinavian countries) reaching several times the lowest density rates (in the US and France). The percent of wage and salary workers *covered* by the terms of collective bargaining agreements typically exceeds union membership. This distinction is crucial in continental European countries. France, with the lowest density rate but the highest coverage rate among the countries is an extreme example, but North American countries, where membership and coverage are virtually synonymous, are at the other extreme.'

43   Bourdieu (1998, p. 42) suggest that the 'opposition' between capital and labor in modern plutocratic and anti-egalitarian capitalism 'is rather like that between masters and slaves.' Perrucci and Wysong (2007, p. 57) point to the 'serf-like American underclass.'

persistent in the historically and fiercely anti-union post-bellum US South, as the apparent legacy and even continuation of its slave economy. For example, some analysts observe that a slave-like 'repressive economy' characterized with 'labor repression' by capital has persisted in the South for long during post-bellum times after the official abolition of slavery.[44] Furthermore, they imply that actually the latter has been expanded in the form of near-universal labor coercion and oppression through anti-union laws and practices transcending the old racial boundaries to include also what Weber himself witnessed and called the Southern 'poor white trash.' As in all dimensions of economic and political freedom, the Southern syndrome of long-standing and further intensifying labor coercion and oppression,[45] as the evident heritage and indirect sequel and even trans-racial effective expansion of slavery, depresses the US estimate of labor liberty, agency, and power among Western and related economies. Counterfactually, otherwise the estimate for the US economy would be likely positive and substantially higher, for example, comparable with that for

---

44   Acemoglu and Robinson (2006, p. 326) observe that 'after the Civil War, with the abolition of slavery and the enfranchisement of the freed slaves, one might have anticipated a dramatic change in economic institutions. Instead, what emerged was a labor-intensive, low-wage, low-education, and repressive economy that in many ways looked remarkably like that of the antebellum South. Slavery was gone, but in its place were the Ku Klux Klan and Jim Crow.' They infer that the 'persistence of labor repression in the US South is consistent with changes in political institutions because they were offset by the exercise of de facto power (and) the result was the continuation of the pre–Civil War economic order after the Northern troops left the South. It took almost another 100 years until more effective reforms were implemented in the US South' (Acemoglu and Robinson (2008, pp. 269–87). Brady, Baker, and Finnigan (2013, p. 880) note that Southern US states have 'low unionization and high working poverty,' for example, 'nearly a fifth of individuals in employed households were poor in Mississippi and Texas.' Kimeldorf (2013, p. 1056) observes that 'replacement workers, having previously operated on the fringes of US labor relations in the Deep South and other nonunion strongholds, began rapidly moving into the mainstream' as another instance of Southernization of the American economy and politics.

45   Rogers and Streeck (1995, p. 22) present the 'story of futile attempts in the United States to institute union-independent workforce representation.' For example, in 2014 reportedly the head labor official on Daimler AG's supervisory board stated that it was 'unacceptable' that the 'German automaker's Mercedes plant in Alabama stands alone among the company's factories around the world without union representation for its workers (saying) it's should be normal that we have a union at each of our plants. We have very different behavior on the part of the company in some cases. In India we are in the process of founding a union for our plant there, and we have the support of the company that will happen. But in the USA, in the South, it is being resisted.'

Canada whose labor union density (27–28) is more than twice as high comparatively only when counting the anti-union South in this comparison and similar to those of many Northern states.

Labor Rights, Rewards, and Benefits

In addition to the data on real minimum wages, other observations and studies support the estimate on this dimension of economic freedom for the US economy. Generally, they indicate that comparatively labor rights and benefits are minimal or diminishing in the US economy, above all the South. They also find American welfare-state backwardness and negative exceptionalism[46] such as non-existent or low and short welfare assistance compared to most other advanced societies, especially Western Europe, above all Scandinavia, as well as Canada, etc. In addition, economic research documents the divergent trends of declining or stagnating labor wages and dramatically growing capital profits, just as executive compensation, in the US economy during the last several decades.[47] These tendencies have no parallels or such intensity in most other Western, above all welfare-capitalist, economies, with the partial yet expected exception of Great Britain. This trend hence confirms the expectations that unfettered, plutocratic capitalism invariably generates or perpetuates greater capital-labor income and wealth differentials in favor of the first than its welfare alternative, and justifies the lower estimate of labor rewards for the US and UK economy than for Western European economies.

Yet another rationale for such an estimate consists in that the US rates of general and children poverty are the highest among these economies, in particular dramatically higher than those of Scandinavian and other welfare-capitalist economies, as is dramatic the pervasiveness and persistence of homelessness in the first compared to the second in which it is unknown or not at the scale and severity observed in America during recent times, above all since the resurgence of neo-conservatism and its Reaganomics. Another ground for the US estimate include the comparatively low level of pensions and to some extent threatened and challenged retirement, social security benefits. This includes,

---

46   In general, Pryor (2002, p. 13) notes that 'in almost all cases (of comparison with OECD countries) the US appears almost alone at one extreme (which indicates) 'American (negative) exceptionalism.'

47   Pencavel (2011, p. 565) finds labor in US manufacturing industry has experienced 'a fall in real wages by about 40 percent since 1960' and infers that 'workers' distributional position in US manufacturing has deteriorated considerably.' Notably, Pencavel (2011, p. 569) asks 'if per worker compensation in 2008 is only about 60 percent of what manufacturing firms could have paid each worker, where has the real income of these firms gone?' and his answer is 'to profits.'

with some partial exceptions (e.g., Medicare for the elderly), non-existent or weak and inferior health care rights and outcomes compared to most Western economies, above all, those with universalistic and comprehensive welfare states, including Northern Europe and Canada, with universal health care systems. This holds true of us health care system at least until the recent health reform aiming to establish universal coverage, and yet constantly threatened to be repealed, though seemingly not replaced by a viable alternative program, by its staunch opponents.

In particular, the data support the estimate for the us economy in which employment protection seems, for all intents and purposes, virtually non-existent or a rapidly disappearing act, compared to most other Western economies primarily because of the low and further diminishing labor union density and thus complementary agency and power. A proxy consolation prize for us workers is that their level of employment protection is not the last in the Western world, with their French counterparts even having a lower one, and also among OECD countries, as those in Turkey, Estonia, and South Korea have the lowest levels.

The preceding therefore justifies the estimate of labor rewards, benefits, and rights for the us economy. Generally, the dramatic difference in annual works hours between European economies such as the Netherlands, Germany, Norway, and France versus the us economy as well as South America and Southern Europe like Mexico and Chile, Greece and Turkey demonstrates that egalitarian, welfare capitalism promotes labor wellbeing through reducing work duration and increasing leisure dramatically[48] more than its opposites or mixed counterparts, namely American unfettered plutocratic and Mexican and other oligarchic capitalisms. This holds true unless one claims seriously or cynically that 'working to death'[49] or excessively, as observed or approximated in the us

---

48   Giddens (2000a, p. 110) observes that a 'society too dominated by the work ethic would be a thoroughly unattractive place in which to live. An inclusive society must provide for the basic needs of those who can't work, and must recognize the wider diversity of goals life has to offer.' In turn, us economist Samuelson (2004, p. 145) admits that 'French or German per-hour productivity does surpass the us per-hour productivity' and predicts that 'if only the French and Germans would match us weekly and monthly average number of total hours of work, their bicycles would be running ahead of the us frontrunner,' yet a prediction not fulfilled yet and unlikely to be in the foreseeable future given the opposite trend toward less work and more leisure in these and most European economies by contrast to the us economy.

49   Manent (1998, p. 220) notices that 'Europeans tend to think that Americans overwork themselves if not exactly to death, at least to a degree where there is not much point in continuing to live.'

economy during recent times but not before (e.g., the 1950–60s), instead promotes labor wellbeing, 'dignity,' and 'happiness.' Yet, the observed relationship
of the latter to long work, just as to the market and consumption,[50] is invariably or typically negative in most Western economies.

Freedom of Movement of Labor

The US percentage of foreign-born population and thus of degree of freedom
of immigration or movement of labor is high enough to justify the estimate
(6) of this dimension, but is lower than those of other traditional and emerging immigrant countries such as Australia, Canada, New Zealand, and even
Switzerland, Austria, Belgium, Ireland, and Sweden hence assigned higher estimates on this dimension of economic freedom.

---

50   Lane (2000, p. 3) finds that 'amidst the satisfaction people feel with their material prog-
      ress, there is a spirit of unhappiness and depression haunting advanced market democ-
      racies (which) mocks the idea that markets maximize well-being.' Lyness et al. (2012,
      p. 1024) observe that 'Europe has been a trendsetter in the development of innovative
      approaches to working time. By the mid-1990s, all European Union (EU) countries were
      required to establish maximum weekly work hours, minimum paid days off, and parity
      between part-time and full-time workers in wages and occupational benefits. In addition,
      several European countries have reduced full-time work weeks to fewer than 40 hours.
      US legislation, in contrast, continues to set the standard fulltime work week at 40 hours
      (a level established seven decades ago) and is silent on maximum weekly hours and part-
      time parity.' Specifically, they find that 'Nordic countries are most supportive of working
      parents, followed by the Continental countries (while) the least public support provided
      in Anglophone countries, especially the United States, where work hours are especially
      long and relatively unregulated' Lyness et al. (2012, p. 1026). For example, Lyness et al.
      (2012, p. 1027) report that 'part-time status tends to be associated with a desire for more
      work hours, especially in the United States, and full-time employment is generally linked
      to a desire for fewer hours, although the United States is distinctive in that a relatively
      high proportion of its full-time workers want to work *more* hours,' whole observing that
      'institutions that strengthen employees' bargaining capacity, especially unions, increase
      workers' control over their working time, specifically their capacity to negotiate work
      schedules that benefit employees.' They conclude that 'Nordic countries stand out as hav-
      ing, on average, the highest per capita GDP, public social expenditure, and women's labor
      force participation rates, and a comparatively large service sector, a relatively high union
      coverage rate, and relatively short standard work weeks—and, in general, more favorable
      outcomes with respect to workers' control over their working time. In contrast, Eastern
      European countries (alongside the US) have quite different macroeconomic and labor
      market features (including comparatively long standard work weeks) and, overall, less
      favorable worker control outcomes' (Lyness et al. 2012, p. 1043).

CHAPTER 6

The Cultural Condition and Indicator of Modern Free Society—A Free Culture

Conditions and Indicators of a Free Culture

The general cultural condition, element, and indicator of modern free society by definition and in reality consists of a free culture. Consequently, the specific cultural prerequisites, ingredients, and dimensions of modern free society represent universal and comprehensive liberties, choices, and rights in the domain of culture. In turn, they are intertwined and mutually reinforcing with the previous two sets of conditions, components, and indicators—political and economic ones—of modern free society.

Such a set of cultural liberties, choices, and rights by assumption defines a free culture as an integral field or subsystem of modern free society, typically in conjunction and mutual reinforcement with political democracy, a free economy, as well as a free civil society, as its other fields or subsystems. Historically, Enlightenment universalism, egalitarianism, rationalism, and 'comprehensive liberalism,' including its corollary the principle of universal, equal freedom, concerning culture, especially scientific and other intellectual liberty, constitute the basis and inspiration for the universality, equality, and comprehensiveness of cultural liberties, choices and rights, just as their political, economic, and civil-individual versions considered in this analysis. Hence, as a cultural revolution inspiring and leading to both the Industrial Revolution and the French and American Revolutions, the 18th century Enlightenment grounds and epitomizes or generates a free culture, just as a free polity, economy, and civil society.

Comparatively, such cultural liberties, choices, and rights are solely or primarily realized, and thus a free culture found, in a certain category of contemporary Western and related societies assumed earlier and to be confirmed later. As with a free polity and economy, as well as a free civil society considered later, at this juncture a kind of provisional agnosticism is assumed on the issue of what a free culture exactly constitutes or becomes within modern free society. Thus, one 'does not (want to) know' whether it constitutes rationalistic, liberal, and secular culture or instead alternative cultures. In turn, the conditions, elements, and indicators of a free culture are mutually related with and reinforcing each other, and are classified and specified as follows (Table 6.1).

TABLE 6.1   *Conditions and Indicators of modern free culture.*

Artistic freedom
    Freedom of apolitical and politically dissenting/critical art
    Freedom of 'immoral' art
    Freedom of irreligious art

Academic and other intellectual freedom
    Scientific freedom and right of research and theorizing, scientific rationalism
    Freedom and right of 'immoral,' irreligious, politically dissenting scientific
    research and theory (e.g., evolution theory, stem-cell research, global warming
    theory, etc.)
    Freedom and right of theoretical dissent and criticism, critical science and theory
    Freedom from superstition, irrationalism, anti-rationalism, including
    anti-scientism

Educational freedom
    Freedom to teach and study 'immoral,' irreligious, or politically dissenting educa-
    tional subjects
    Freedom to teach and study evolution theory/evolutionary biological science
    Freedom to teach and study global warming theory/climate science
    Freedom to teach and study other irreligious or politically dissenting theories/
    sciences

Ideological freedom
    Freedom from coercive, orthodox, dominant ideology, world-view, philosophy, and
    ideas, ideological orthodoxy
    Freedom for alternative ideologies, world-views, philosophies, and ideas, ideologi-
    cal heterodoxy and dissent

Religious freedom
    Freedom of religion
    Equal freedom and right of all religions, churches, believers vs. the 'only true'
    religion/church/believers
        Religious choice, openness, and pluralism vs. religious closure, monopoly, and
        discrimination
            Freedom of non-theistic 'religion' or 'faith' (e.g., spiritualism, mysticism,
            magic, etc.)
    Freedom from religion
        Freedom from coercive, monopolistic, organized, orthodox, dominant religion/
        church, religious orthodoxy and dogma

Freedom from theocracy, i.e., religious totalitarianism and war

Freedom for non-belief, religious dissent, skepticism, and criticism, agnosticism, secularism, etc.

Cultural openness

Artistic, scientific, educational, ideological, religious and related cultural openness to the outside world

Open to foreign art and artists, science and scientists, education and educators, ideologies and ideologues, religions and believers, cultures and culture agents

No or minimal cultural closure, nationalism, and protectionism

Cultural-social globalization

The first condition, element, and indicator of a free culture comprises universal, equal, and comprehensive artistic freedoms, choices, and rights. This condition consists of the freedom and right to artistic imagination and creation, activity and creativity. It is thus the freedom of aesthetic art in the sense of its being autonomous and unconstrained from or uncensored by exogenous non-artistic forces and standards, in particular coercive, repressive, and intrusive politics and religion, as well as economy, ideology, nationalism, and moralism. In this sense, a free art is freed from the intrusion, coercion, and repression of both state and church and their respective legal and moral codes suppressing or restricting, censoring artistic and related freedom on various extraneous non- and anti-artistic grounds like 'morality,' 'moral purity,' 'decency,' 'obscenity,' 'public,' 'national security,' 'patriotism,' 'one nation indivisible under God,' 'community,' 'family values,' 'faith,' 'godliness,' 'in God we trust,' 'sacred tradition,' etc. If a free culture and modern free society as a whole possesses and enjoys a special oasis of virtually unrestrained individual liberty, initiative, activity, and creativity, then it is probably aesthetic art as the realm, exercise, and product of human imagination that knows no boundaries and constraints, together and closely connected with the civil sphere of privacy and intimacy.

Hence, negatively stated, a condition, dimension, and indicator of a free culture is no censorship, overt or covert, and consequently self-censorship of artistic and related freedom, activity, and creativity or innovation[1] by political,

---

1   Becker (1974,767; also, DiMaggio 1987) suggests that innovation in art—conceived as a 'collective action' and art works as the 'product of the cooperative activity of many people'— is only constrained by internal forces such as 'artistic conventions, whose existence both makes the production of work easier and innovation more difficult,' and thus not by external,

religious, economic, ideological, nationalistic, moralistic, and other extra-artistic and thus spurious or dubious justifications. Alternatively, any form or degree and justification of suppression or censorship of artistic and other intellectual freedom, activity, and creativity indicates or predicts an unfree culture on this dimension and in extension an un- or pseudo-free society as a whole. A free culture and society without artistic and related freedom, activity, and creativity—however trivial or insignificant might seem from a superficial stance and through the depreciation of art and other intellectual pursuits—represents logically a non sequitur and empirically an impossibility or rarity. At best, it is a partially and incoherently free culture and society, with its liberty fractured and lacking an artistic, aesthetic ingredient as (as Comte suggests) an original and inherent aspect of humans and social life.

Simply, there is no such thing as modern and any completely and consistently free society, in particular a free culture and an intellectual sphere, without the liberty of aesthetic art, activity, creation, and creators. This especially applies to art in relation to, specifically autonomy from, a coercive, repressive, and intrusive state attempting to suppress or censor artistic freedom, produces, and producers with varying anti- or non-artistic justifications. The same holds for art being autonomous from a theocratic and moralistic religion. The exemplars are Puritanism—and its theological parent Calvinism and its descendant revived evangelicalism—as pretended 'pure' church and anti-artistic morality within Christianity and Islam self-defined in the essentially same way among the world religions, both sharing vehement hostility and violent destructiveness to artistic liberty, creativity, and creators.

This is important to emphasize because some analysts and groups, above all spurious 'libertarian' economists and politicians in historically Puritan societies such as the UK and the US, tend to deny or minimize that artistic and related intellectual freedoms, activities, products, and producers are important at all for a free society to the point of their near-zero importance so that people can live without them still in 'freedom,' simply no 'great deal.' Such a 'libertarian' tendency, like virtually all anti-cultural as well as anti-liberal, anti-secular, and anti-rationalistic tendencies, perpetuates the vehemently anti-artistic, moralistic, and theocratic repressive pattern and heritage of

---

non-artistic factors. Caves (2003, pp. 73–74) notes that arts and entertainment as 'creative industries' in their production and consumption 'fiercely resist governance by anything approaching a complete contract' and thus extraneous legal or economic constraints, as distinguished from other industries, and artists typically have the *art for art's sake* attitude to their products expressing their deriving enjoyment ('utility') from 'creative work' contrary to the standard economic view that work engenders the opposite ('disutility').

Calvinist Puritanism with its irreconcilable antagonism and violent nihilism to secular sensual culture such as aesthetic art and amusements[2] in America[3] and England. For instance, Puritanism's hostility to and suppression of music and theatre since Shakespeare's days to later times is particularly intense, notorious and, via its heir evangelicalism, persistent. Thus, perpetuating the anti-artistic ghost of Puritanism, ersatz 'libertarians' downplay freedom of aesthetic art as a superfluous liberty, a luxury or nuisance puritanical descendants in these countries 'cannot afford' or 'don't like,' particularly as irrelevant compared to their glorifying individual market-economic freedoms a la 'free enterprise' ('all you need is free markets and nothing else') as supreme and absolute—yet primarily for capitalist plutocracy according to the plutocratic Anarchy, Leviathan over labor formula. A logical consequence of such a Puritan-style 'libertarian' devaluation of artistic freedom and activity as redundant in a free society is the minimal public expenditures on the aesthetic arts and the humanities in America and to some degree Britain as compared to most other Western and related societies, as shown later.

---

2   J.S. Mill identifies (1991, p. 77) the 'fanatical moral intolerance of the Puritans' in that 'wherever the Puritans have been sufficiently powerful, as in New England, and in Great Britain at the time of the Commonwealth, they have endeavored, with considerable success, to put down all public, and nearly all private, amusements: especially music, dancing, public games, or other assemblages for purposes of diversion, and the theatre,' adding that these activities are 'regulated by the religious and moral sentiments of the stricter Calvinists and Methodists (as) intrusively pious members of society. (For the Puritans) all persons must be ready to conform to the idea of a Christian commonwealth, as understood by the early settlers in New England, if a religious profession similar to theirs should ever succeed in regaining its lost ground.' Weber (1930, p. 105) also emphasizes the 'entirely negative attitude of Puritanism to all the sensuous and emotional elements in culture and in religion, because they are of no use toward salvation and promote sentimental illusions and idolatrous superstitions,' attributing such a 'fundamental antagonism to sensuous culture of all kinds' to the Calvinist 'harsh doctrines of the absolute transcendentality of God and the corruption of everything pertaining to the flesh,' joined with the 'inner isolation of the individual.'

3   Scitovsky (1972, pp. 64–66) observes that Americans 'smile condescendingly over the prejudices of 18th-Century America, which morally disapproved of the theatre and frowned on wasting time and money on sports and the arts. But this is no smiling matter, because our behavior is still governed by those prejudices (due to) society and its Puritan attitude,' in particular 'our Puritan rejection of pleasure as the ultimate aim of life.' Scitovsky (1972, p. 68) concludes that US 'government's cheerful sacrifice of the citizens' access to nature for the sake of illusory or insignificant increments of safety is part of the same philosophy that lies behind the neglect of the arts' and Americans' 'very modest enjoyment of the arts is part and parcel of our modest enjoyment of life; (notably) our government's miserly attitude toward the arts is (the) integral part of a larger (Puritan) collective preference system.'

More specifically, the artistic condition, component, and indicator of a free culture and in extension society involves, first, the freedom of apolitical and/or politically dissenting, diverging, and critical art and artists. Negatively formulated, this signifies *no* resort to political and legal suppression or restriction through censorship of such artistic freedoms, activities, and products, for example, burning, otherwise destroying, and proscribing products, activities, and producers of art that are denounced and disapproved for political, ideological, and similar non-artistic reasons. The underlying logic and rationale for this condition is that in a free culture and democracy politics and law have nothing to do—i.e., no legitimate basis to control, censor, or interfere—with artistic activity and freedom, simply art as the domain of relatively unconstrained liberty, creativity, and imagination, although often in tension with societal, including political, ideological, economic, nationalist, religious and moralistic, constraints.[4]

Second, the present condition entails the freedom of 'immoral' or amoral aesthetic art in the sense of artists being free to make a decision and choice between alternative 'right' and 'wrong' moral ideas and norms in their artistic activities and creations, just as do individuals between 'sins' and 'virtues' in their personal actions and private life within a free civil society. Negatively stated, this means *no* moralistic suppression or censorship of 'immoral,' 'indecent,' 'obscene' 'impure,' 'corrupt,' and 'depraved'—terms especially used by Puritanism/Calvinism and Islam among religions, and Nazism and fascism among political ideologies and systems—and related artistic activities, actors, and products, for instance, burning, destroying, and banning such works of art and artists on moralistic and related extra-artistic grounds.

Third and related, the artistic condition and indicator of a free culture and society overall incorporates the liberty of irreligious or non-religious art in that artists have the freedom of choice between belief and non-belief, 'godliness' and 'godlessness' in their practices, ideas, and works, just as do individuals in their real life in the context of a free civil society. Negatively stated, this signifies *no* religiously sanctified suppression or censorship of irreligious, non- religious, non-believing, 'heretic,' 'blasphemous,' 'godless' and related artistic activities, creators, and creations, particularly burning, destroying, and proscribing such

---

4 Johnson (2007, p. 99) suggests that the 'tension' between individual creativity in art, specifically founding artistic organizations, and societal or environmental constraints 'is captured in the idea of 'cultural entrepreneurship' (referring) to the creativity and initiative of the founder *and* to the constraint and opportunity represented by the specific cultural schemas that structure the historical context in which the founder is embedded,' as illustrated by the '17th-century founding of the Paris Opera.'

art products and artists on the basis of 'holy'—usually mixed with moralistic and often political, ideological, and other extra-artistic—justifications.

At this juncture, a pragmatic, unambiguous, and manifest negative condition, dimension, and indicator of a free culture and society as a whole is the absence of systematic or recurring practice of literal burning and otherwise destroying or of effective prohibition of artistic and related works, activities, and producers on political-legal, moralistic, religious, and other extra-artistic grounds. In a way, if one does not know to define what an unfree culture and society in general is in reality one knows it when seeing its act of burning, burying, otherwise destroying, and prohibiting—induced by undemocratic politics, rigid moralism, and theocratic religion—artistic and other intellectual activities, products, and producers, including their collections in libraries[5] burned and buried (as 'pagan') during the Christian (and Islamic) Dark Middle Ages. Consequently, any culture and society as a whole that does this is as far from a free type as burning, destroying, and banning such and other books and their authors are from building and augmenting a library. The latter is that original and continuing cultural hallmark of civilization and, through knowledge, of social progress and what Jefferson—who had the largest private library in revolutionary America consistent with and fulfilling his Enlightenment ideals—considers an educated and informed, minimally literate democracy and electorate.

It is important to reemphasize this seemingly trivial element of cultural and individual liberty because it is sometimes openly or covertly dismissed and depreciated in favor of more 'important' liberties. Thus, especially US pretended economic 'libertarians' tend to, as another legacy of Puritanism, explicitly or implicitly downplay the burning, burying, destroying, and banning politically, morally, and religiously condemned artistic and related works, activities, and producers, including libraries, as irrelevant or secondary for a free culture and society compared to the supreme importance that they impute to economic 'free enterprise' for capitalist plutocracy and its tyranny of wealth in Roosevelt' sense over non-capitalists or the non-wealthy. Moreover, from the standpoint

---

5   An historical exemplar is the burning of the library of Alexandria by invading Muslim forces. In passing, Rousseau, a Catholic-turned-Calvinist (and back), justified that act suggesting that, as Garrard (2003, p. 16) reports, 'had the library contained works opposed to the Gospels and had Pope Gregory been in the position of the Caliph Omar, "the Library would still have been burned, and it would be perhaps the finest deed in the life of that Illustrious Pontiff"' and in extension Christianity, thus expressing the affinity between Islam and the latter, above all, Calvinism in respect of destroying 'infidel' or 'pagan' artistic and other intellectual products and producers, as especially burned and buried during the Christian and Islamic Dark Middle Ages, Mueller (2009) suggests.

of cultural freedom and life and civilization no act is perhaps more anti-cultural and anti-civilizing, barbarian and primitive, than burning, destroying, and prohibiting artistic products, activities, and producers of imagination and related creations such as books, libraries, artists, and writers for whatever, including the most 'patriotic,' 'holiest,' and 'purest,' extra-artistic reasons. A truly free culture and society does not commit or justify such an activity literally destructive ('fire and burial') of artistic and other cultural freedom and creativity, human reason, knowledge and progress, and civilization, and resurrecting the Hobbesian primitive 'state of nature' in the form or image of the 'law of the jungle.'

The aforesaid holds true, with some variations, of scientific and related intellectual liberty as the second related condition, element, and indicator of a free culture and in extension the cultural prerequisite of modern free society overall. This condition consists of the freedom and right of scientific and other academic and intellectual activity, creativity, and productivity. This involves the liberty of science autonomous from and unconstrained by non-scientific and other non-intellectual forces and norms of evaluation, above all a coercive, repressive, and intrusive polity and a theocratic and irrational or anti-rational, i.e., superstitious and anti-science religion, as well as economic compulsion, agents, and interests, ideological dogmas, nationalism, etc.

Therefore, like aesthetic art, in a free culture and society science and related rationalistic intellectual activities, producers, and products are inherently and effectively autonomous from the control, interference, and surveillance of state and church, as well as reasonably independent of economic imperatives, organizations, and gains, for example, no conflict of scientific and material interest in research and other academic work. The above yields a negative formulation of the scientific condition and indicator of a free culture and society. This is no suppression or restriction of scientific and other academic freedom, activity, and creativity through censorship of its agents and products. For example, it involves no burning and burying, otherwise destroying and banning such works of science and philosophy as books and others on political, ideological, nationalistic, moralistic, religious and other anti- or non-scientific bases, as well as for economic reasons usually disguising narrow plutocratic or oligarchic interests.

Generally, this condition of a free culture consists of the freedom and right of continuous pursuit of research, theorizing, and debate in science as what Weber calls vocation or profession, thus of engaging in and contributing to scientific rationalism and progress involving the production, accumulation, codification, and diffusion of theoretical and empirical knowledge. Particularly, it encompasses the freedom and right of pursuing, proposing, and disseminating scientific research, knowledge, theory, and findings that may be characterized or perceived as 'inappropriate,' 'offensive,' 'outrageous,' and the like. Science and its theories, methods, and results can be construed and denounced as politically and ideologically dissenting, 'immoral' or 'amoral,' irreligious or non-religious, 'heretic' or 'blasphemous,' 'useless' or 'costly' by anti—or extra-scientific forces and standards such as repressive and intrusive government, theocratic, anti-scientific, and moralistic religion, and plutocratic and other economic vested interests. For illustration, instances of scientific liberties and rights in Western and related societies include the freedom and right to pursue and demonstrate evolutionism in biology versus its unscientific opposites—not to mention heliocentric versus geocentric 'flat earth' astronomy—researches and procedures (stem-cell research, vaccination, radiation, etc.) in medicine, global warming theory in climate science despite the opposition of business vested interests and the denials by non-scientists like ideological, political, religious, nationalist, and other anti-science extremists, etc.

Relatedly, the scientific condition and indicator of a free culture involves the freedom and right of theoretical dissent or divergence from and scientifically grounded criticism of existing societal institutions, conditions, ideas, and ruling groups, including state, nation, church, and the economy system. In short, this means a critical or autonomous science of society, in particular politics, ideology, religion, morality, the economy, etc. Negatively stated, this condition consists of the stipulation and expectation of freedom from anti- and pre-scientific religious superstition[6] and generally irrationalism and anti-rationalism, specifically anti-scientism, enforced and propagated by a repressive and intrusive political regime and theocratic and anti-rationalistic religion, as well as plutocratic and other economic groups. For instance, it comprises the freedom from coercive imposition of, besides the discredited 'flat earth' theory in astronomy, the belief in and the ritual of exorcism of 'Satan,' the associated 'witches,' and similar religious superstitions and theological dogmas, the pre-scientific dogma of 'creationism' and its variant anti-scientific

---

6 Mueller (2009, p. 415) remarks that in the 'absence of a scientific explanation, humans are likely to substitute a religious one. However, once a scientific explanation for a seemingly inexplicable even has been found, humans can—and many do—abandon the religious one. Once one understands the heart's role in blood circulation and the important of (the latter) for life, one can understand why person dies when his heart stops beating. One does not need to postulate the existence of evil spirits. Thus, many people can and do get quite well without assuming that evil spirit and gods are the causes of various events. Presumably, an entire society composed of such people could survive (but the opposite society could not). If a sudden bout of amnesia were to inflict all Europeans and block out their memory about religion life in Europe will go on more or less unchanged.'

'intelligent design'[7] politically enforced or religiously infiltrated, 'godly' unscientific medicine (prayer, holy-book reading, etc.) prescribed as a substitute for its scientific version, the imposed denial of global warming theory by political, ideological, religious, nationalistic, and other extreme anti-science forces, plus narrow economic interests, and so on.

The third corollary condition, element, and indicator of a free culture encompasses educational freedoms and rights. In a way, these freedoms and rights represent the logical extension of scientific and related academic freedom so long as education adopts, applies, and disseminates, just as do technology and medicine, science and its theories, concepts, and findings, and to some extent aesthetic art and its elements. On this account, the freedom of science represents the foundation and necessary, though perhaps not sufficient, prerequisite for that of education, just as, with some variations, of technology and medicine. Conversely, the freedom of education and to some degree of technology and medicine tends to be primarily (although not exclusively) conditioned and predicted by or closely linked to that of science, as well as in part of aesthetic art. Consequently, the aforesaid of scientific and artistic freedom and activity mostly applies to educational freedoms, rights, and activities, above all public and secular education. This is because secular, scientific—as distinct from religious,[8] non-scientific—education is typically considered a public good and thus non-exclusive societal benefit, just as are science and scientifically based technology and medicine.

Generally, these freedoms comprise the freedom and right to teach and study educational subject-matters that are characterized by extra-educational forces like governments, religions—as with respect to public secular education—and economic groups as politically dissenting or different, 'immoral' or 'indecent,' irreligious and non-religious, 'heretic' or 'blasphemous' economically 'useless' or 'impractical.' A recurring instance is the freedom and right to teach (for teachers) and study and learn (for students), as within the system of secular public education, scientific evolutionism in biology and thus evolutionary

---

7 Parkera and Hackettb (2012, p. 40) imply that 'intelligent design'—a pretended scientific proof or version of theological creationism—is an instance of 'collective scientific deviance' and 'scientific oddities' and in that sense of anti- or non-science.

8 Mueller (2013, p. 12) suggests that 'it is difficult to argue that religious education provides positive externalities to the community. To the extent that religious education displaces other subjects, such as math and history, it produces a negative externality by lowering the future productivity of adult workers, and making future adults less well-informed about issues that are important for good citizenship.'

biological science, negatively the freedom from forced teaching and learning its non- and anti-scientific opposites, 'creationism' and 'intelligent design' as taught and learned in private religious schools in the conservative, Southern US and to a lesser degree the UK, and other, especially Islamic, countries, including Turkey. A recent example is the freedom and right to teach and study global warming theory and climate science overall in secular public education, negatively the freedom from being forced to its unscientific alternatives and denials imposed or propagated by anti-science extremists and some industries, and in part taught and learned in private church-based schools. Additional examples comprise the freedom and right of teachers to teach and of students to study and learn any other politically and ideologically dissenting or 'correct,' including 'unpatriotic,' religiously 'unholy' and 'godless,' 'heretic' or 'blasphemous,' morally 'impure' and 'indecent,' and economically 'useless' or 'impractical' theories, concepts, and sciences.

In sum, the freedom of education represents a logical extension of that of science and the aesthetic arts and a necessary condition and integral element of a free culture and society. Within the latter, education, like science and art, is intrinsically free, i.e., independent and autonomous from extraneous, especially anti-educational, anti-scientific, and other anti-rationalistic, constraints and intrusions.

The fourth condition, element, and indicator of a free culture represents what can be termed ideological and similar freedom. This freedom is closely related to scientific and other intellectual and artistic freedoms, as well as political and civil liberties and rights that involve as their constitutive component ideological pluralism and choice. In the context of a free culture, ideological freedom consists of that of creating, holding, and disseminating theoretically 'all kinds' of ideologies, world-views, philosophies, and ideas, and not only political ones pertaining to democracy, but also their cultural and other non- and apolitical variations. In this sense, this condition can be stated as ideological and philosophical freedoms and rights in cultural and 'spiritual,' as actually related to but still analytically distinct from political and 'material,' terms.

A paradigmatic exemplar of such spiritual freedoms is the freedom of and from religion as a cultural phenomenon, which is considered separately because of its special and distinct salience for a free culture, democracy, and modern free society as a whole. Negatively formulated, they encompass the freedom, i.e., autonomy and independence from imposed, orthodox, and dominant ideologies, world-views, philosophies, and ideas, be they political or non-political, and in that sense from ideological imposition, orthodoxy, dominance or hegemony. In a positive formulation, they contain the freedom and right of inventing, holding, and diffusing alternative ideologies, world-views, philosophies, and ideas of political and non-political contents and implications, and thus multiple ideological options, heterodoxy, and dissent.

The fifth condition, element, and indicator of a free culture and society in general constitutes religious freedom. The latter represents a manifest and salient dimension of the freedom of ideology, world-views, ideas, and thought in the cultural sense, and practically related to, though conceptually distinguished from, political and civil liberties in democracy, as well as individual liberty, choice, and privacy within a free civil society.

On one hand, it encompasses the freedom of religion through free invention, acceptance and propagation of and engagement in its constitutive components such as religious dogma or belief, practice or ritual, and organization or church, as classically divided and analyzed in Durkheim's and Weber's sociology of religion. This involves the universal, equal freedom and right of all religions, churches, denomination, and believers, as different from the monopolizing liberty of conscience for the self-proclaimed 'only true' religion, church, denomination, and faithful. Relatedly, it entails religious choice, openness, inclusion, and pluralism, as opposed to religious closure, monopoly, exclusion, and discrimination. In addition, it encompasses the freedom of polytheistic, as distinct from monotheistic, and non- and pseudo-theistic, non-theocentric religion. This includes, for example, 'paganism,' deism with no anthropomorphic Divinity as found in Christianity and Islam, spiritualism without Divine elements, mysticism, magic, etc., simply religions, churches, and believers with 'no God' but with the general notion of 'sacred' in Durkheim's sense, with Buddhism and to some extent Confucianism being such examples. Thus, the liberty to believe, practice, and worship any religion and God or a 'holy' functional equivalent represents the essential, basic freedom of religion. Simply, to believe or worship whatever 'sacred' one wishes forms the minimum of the freedom of/for religion.

On the other hand, this condition of a free culture and society entails the freedom from religion in the sense and form of individual and group autonomy and independence from being forced or pressured to the triple composite of religious dogma, practice, and organization. In particular, such autonomy incorporates the liberty from theocratic—i.e., coercive, repressive, and monopolistic—as well as organized, dogmatic, and dominant religion or church, thus from religious coercion, repression, monopoly, and dogmatism. At this juncture, the individual and group liberty from theocracy as religious totalitarianism or 'holy' dictatorship constitutes the minimum of the freedom from religion. It does so because the liberty from theocracy thus understood is effectively the freedom from severe coercion, violent repression, 'holy' terror and war, and ultimately destruction, torture and death as theocratic intrinsic attributes and ultimate outcomes, as of any type of totalitarianism or tyranny.

In turn, any strident negation and elimination of the freedom from religion may hide or escalate in denying and eliminating the basic, minimal liberty from theocracy and thus 'holy' repression, terror, war, destruction, and death. This is exemplified historically by medieval Islam and orthodox Calvinism, particularly Puritanism, and recently by their revivals through Islamic fundamentalism and evangelicalism. In this sense, to paraphrase Clausewitz's classic definition of war, theocratic dictatorships and wars represent the natural 'continuation' or escalation of the politics of negation and elimination of the freedom from religion by 'other means' such as violence against the 'godless' and 'sinful' within society and 'evil' and 'ungodly' societies. In Michels' words, therefore 'who says there is no freedom from religion, eventually says there is no freedom from theocracy, so religious tyranny, terror, war, mass destruction, and death.' This is needed to emphasize because even centuries after such a defining pattern of medieval Islamic and Calvinist theocracies since Calvin's Geneva and Weber's noted 'unexampled tyranny of Puritanism' in North America, Islamic fundamentalism and Puritan-rooted evangelicalism, above all in 'conservative America,' deny and eliminate the freedom from religion and the liberty from theocracy, so repression, terror, war, suffering, and death in the name and for the 'glory of God.' Alternatively, recognizing and protecting the liberty from theocracy represents not only the minimal negative freedom from religion but also the positive minimum of human autonomy, choice, dignity, and agency in relation to super-human 'sacred' entities and causes.

Lastly, as an ultimate form or logical extension, the freedom from religion contains the liberty and right of non-belief and thus non-theism, religious dissent and divergence, skepticism and criticism, agnosticism, secularism, liberalism, progressivism, scientism, and the like. Simply, individuals and groups being free *not* to believe and worship any religion and god forms the logical and indispensable complement of their freedom of believing whatever religions and gods, both being integral elements of religious liberty. Therefore, liberty of conscience comprises not only the freedom to believe and worship whatever religion and god or a sacred' equivalent an individual or group wishes, as usually assumed and especially demanded by religious groups when *not* in political power, such as Islamic and Puritan-evangelical sects and cults. It also involves the freedom of believing and worshiping no religions[9] and gods at all,

---

9   The Pew Research Center's second US Religious Landscape Study in 2014 'finds that the percentage of adults (ages 18 and older) who describe themselves as Christians has dropped by nearly eight percentage points in just seven years, from 78.4% (in 2007) to 70.6% in 2014.

an individual and group liberty these religious groups typically deny to others and eliminate once capturing power such as an Islamic or Puritan-evangelical sect or party becoming a state-church—as in Iran and Turkey in recent times, New England and the US South—and instead solely recognized and preserved in a genuine free culture, as well as liberal-secular democracy.

In turn, the coercive imposition or pressure of religious faith and worship, like any belief and practice, on non-believers contradicts and eventually eliminates or perverts a free culture and society, and ultimately counterproductive. So does the prohibition or suppression of such beliefs and worships for believers and worshipers, though societies, like Islamic and Puritan-evangelical theocracies, denying or suppressing the freedom from religion dismiss the first contradiction and exclusively center on and complain about, when in sectarian opposition, the second. Simply, for a free culture and society it is as inadmissible, repressive, and futile to force or pressure non-believing or indifferent individuals and groups to believe a religion or practice a religious ritual as is preventing or prohibiting believers from doing so, but societies such as theocracies without the freedom of religion only acknowledge the latter possibility and disregard the former.

As Voltaire, Hume, Diderot, and other Enlightenment philosophers suggested, to impose religious and any belief is just as unnatural, useless, and undignified as is to prohibit it by virtue of religion or non-religion being a private matter.[10] This is by contrast to theocratic churches and sects complaining about such prohibition when not in power, yet engaging in the imposition or coercion of their beliefs and practices once capturing the state as their invariant political end justifying the means, including violence, terror, civil and holy wars, etc. The non sequitur of the imposition of belief therefore provides a rationale for the freedom from religion, just as that of its prohibition gives a justification to the freedom of religion. Alternatively, coercively suppressing or punishing religious and other non-belief condemned as 'ungodliness,' 'heresy,' 'blasphemy,' and the like is as incompatible with and inadmissible in a free culture and society as is the coercive enforcement of such non-beliefs, albeit those societies and groups that negate the freedom from religion disregard the first

---

Over the same period, the percentage of Americans who are religiously unaffiliated–describing themselves as atheist, agnostic or "nothing in particular"–has jumped more than six points, from 16.1% to 22.8% (56 million).'

10   Mueller (2013, p. 14) remarks that 'religion is largely a private consumption good.' Also, Fitzpatrick (1999, p. 47) remarks (referring to the Protestant Reformation) that religious liberty in the sense of freedom for religion 'begins with interior conviction that no amount of coercion can change,' but so does liberty of conscience in the form of freedom from religion.

incompatibility and only consider and complain about the second. Likewise, the non sequitur of the first practice furnishes the ground for the freedom from religion, just as that of the second supplies a reason for the freedom of religion.

And both the formal and substantive grounds for considering the freedom from religion an integral aspect of religious liberty and rights are as, if not more, compelling as those for the freedom of religion. First, it is logically consistent to do so insofar as religious freedom as the liberty of conscience is a subtle, complex, multidimensional rather than simple, unidimensional, one-sided category. Moreover, the freedom from religion by virtue of involving the choice between religion and non-religion, belief and non-belief in the 'sacred' versus the 'profane' in Durkheim's sense, including divine and non-divine, is perhaps logically prior to and more general than that of religion implying consequent and more specific choices between different religions or beliefs systems and gods, once the first choice is made or faced.

Second, it is substantively grounded to consider the freedom from religion an integral aspect of religious liberty in view of the long history and in part present reality of religious coercion, oppression, terror, war, and the resulting destruction, suffering, and mass death for 'higher' causes. Such religious processes and outcomes represent to a large extent both the cause and the effect precisely of the non-existent or suppressed freedom from religion, including dogma, practice, and organization separately or most often in conjunction, at least of the absence of the liberty from theocracy, as the minimum of human autonomy, dignity, and agency vis-à-vis the 'holy.'

In this respect, it is primarily (though not solely) the denial, absence, or violation of the freedom from religion that helps explain the seeming mystery ('why') of so much and intense religious oppression, terror, war, destruction, suffering, and death in the past and in part the present, especially innumerable and partly continuous 'holy' wars of 'true believers' against 'infidels,' as called in Islam and Calvinism, including Puritanism and revived evangelicalism. As noted, in Clausewitz's terms, religious wars represent the eventual 'continuation' or escalation of the politics or policy, ideology, and culture of *no* freedom from religion by 'other means' of mass violence, destruction, suffering, and death. On this account, the freedom from religion represents a necessary and even sufficient condition of no or minimal and diminishing religiously sanctified repression, violence, wars, destruction, and death construed as absolutely commanded by and in the name and 'mind of God' in contrast to their non-religious forms.[11]

---

11   Juergensmeyer (2003, p. 217) observes that the 'absolutism of religion has been revealed especially in the notion of cosmic war. Although left-wing movements subscribe to

The sixth condition, element, and indicator of a free culture consists of cultural openness to the world beyond its national boundaries. This condition forms a cultural analogue and typically relates to economic openness as expressed in free foreign trade and freedom of movement of labor beyond a national economy. Like an economy, a culture to be considered fully and consistently free necessitates to be open not only to cultural activities, works, and agents within its geographic boundary, but also to those from the rest of the world, thus simply opening both to insiders and outsiders, natives and foreigners in these terms. More specifically, this involves artistic, scientific and other intellectual, educational, ideological, religious and related forms of cultural openness to the outside world. A free culture is open and welcoming to artistic, scientific and other intellectual, educational, ideological, religious and related cultural activities, works, and agents originating beyond its national setting, and not just as to those within the latter. Simply, it represents an open cultural system to outside, foreign art and artists, science and scientists/academics, education and educators, ideas, ideologies and their holders, religions and believers, and generally cultures and culture actors, and not solely or primarily to their domestic, native counterparts.

Consequently, negative stated, a condition and indicator of a free culture is that it features no or minimal cultural, including artistic, scientific and other academic, educational, ideological, and religious, closure, nationalism, and protectionism analogous and typically related to their economic and political forms. A closed, nationalist, and protectionist culture forms the cultural equivalent of and usually linked with a corresponding economy and polity characterized with market and political closure, economic and state nationalism, and industrial and ideological protectionism. Hence, a culture characterized with closure, nationalism, and protectionism in relation to the world's cultures falls short of being fully free, just as does a closed, nationalistic, and protectionist economy and polity vis-à-vis other economies and political systems. A 'free' culture that is not substantially open to and involved in the outside world is

---

what may seem a similar idea—the concept of class conflict—ordinarily this contest is thought to take place only on a social plane and within the temporal limitations of history. Religious concepts of cosmic war, however, are ultimately beyond historical control, even though they are identified with this-worldly struggles. A satanic enemy cannot be transformed; it can only be destroyed. The vast time lines of religious struggles also set them apart from secular conflicts. Most social and political struggles have sought conclusion within the lifetimes of their participants. But religious struggles have taken generations to succeed.'

just as an inner contradiction or practical impossibility as is a 'free' market economy with low free foreign trade and to some degree a 'free' polity with lack of openness to other political systems or ideologies. In the globalizing age, just as that of an economy and polity, the openness of a culture is mostly indicated or approximated by the level of cultural-social globalization.

Types of Culture and Comparative Estimates of Cultural Liberty

At this juncture, the provisional agnostic position is abandoned by observing and/or expecting that rationalistic, liberal, and secular cultures inherently, systematically, and completely tend to fulfill and exhibit the conditions, elements, and indicators of a free culture. Conversely, their alternatives, notably its antithesis and nemesis cultural irrationalism and anti-rationalism through superstition anti-scientism, do not, and instead demonstrate the characteristics of a fundamentally unfree culture. Consequently, rationalistic, liberal, and secular culture most fully and consistently fulfills and reveals the general cultural condition and indicator of modern free society as a whole.

Defined and typified by the fusion of scientific rationalism with intellectual and other cultural liberty, rationalistic, liberal, and secular cultures are observed or expected to epitomize a free culture ranging from the freedoms of the aesthetic arts, science, education, and ideology to the freedom of and from religion. By stark contrast, irrationalism and anti-rationalism, in particular religious and related superstitions and anti-science, are witnessed or anticipated to exemplify an unfree culture and culturally typify an unfree society. As with the specific political and economic (and later civil) prerequisites, subsystems, and indices of modern free society, rationalistic, liberal, and secular culture constitutes the only genuine free and viable cultural type among Western and related (though not necessarily other) societies. By contrast, the compound of irrationalism and anti-rationalism, superstition and anti-science, is intrinsically antithetical and ultimately becomes destructive to cultural liberties, notably academic, educational, and related intellectual freedom, just as by definition to human reason, thinking, and knowledge, and thus reasonableness, rationality, and progress in culture and society.

Furthermore, irrationalism-anti-rationalism tends to be unviable and self-destructive because of its tendency for causing perdition, regression or petrification of society through religious superstition and anti-science vanquishing or degrading social life and humans to its primitive or barbarian pre-civilized stage, usually what Comte calls the theological, theocratic, and military state. As a consequence, rationalistic, liberal, and secular cultures are invariably and incomparably freer, more humanistic, reasonable, and progressive than any alternatives, notably their antithesis and poison, cultural irrationalism and anti-rationalism. In particular, scientific rationalism, simply scientism, including its applications and outcomes in education, technology, medicine, and other realms of culture and society, as a rule substantially enhances and sustains human freedom and emancipation, dignity and agency, prosperity and wellbeing, including health and longevity, knowledge and progress, hope and optimism, while superstition and anti-science negates and destroys or subverts all of them.

Specifically, the aforesaid opens the issue of whether and to what extent Western and related societies fulfill and manifest the preceding conditions and indicators of a free culture, how they rank on cultural liberties and rights. Those societies typified with rationalistic, liberal, and secular culture, particularly scientific rationalism and academic and related intellectual freedom, are observed or expected to fulfill and manifest these conditions and indicators more inherently, consistently, and completely than do others. They do so by ranking higher on cultural liberties and rights than do their opposites pervaded with the compound of cultural irrationalism and anti-rationalism, particularly religious superstition and anti-science. Such observations and expectations are strongly reaffirmed, as shown next.

Classification of Modern Cultures

In this connection, using types of culture as the basis yields the following classification of Western and related societies (Table 6.2)

First, rationalistic, liberal, and secular culture is used to describe and classify countries such as Australia, Austria, Belgium, Canada, Denmark, France, Germany, Iceland, Luxembourg, the Netherlands, New Zealand, Norway, Sweden, Switzerland, and the US. Predictably, the latter is so classified in its rationalistic, liberal, and secular cultural dimensions (transient or exceptional) and regions (minority or decreasing) versus its anti-rationalistic, anti-liberal and anti-secular or religiously over-determined counterpart, thus identifying or positing the co-existence of and conflict—often termed culture wars—between the 'two Americas' culturally. These countries and regions are continuously or increasingly rationalistic, liberal, and secular in all cultural, including artistic, scientific, educational and religious, respects, and consequently first and foremost exemplify this type of culture among Western and related societies within OECD and the world as a whole. On this account, these countries or regions (as within the US) are deemed and denoted 'rationalistic, liberal, and

TABLE 6.2   *Classification of Western and related societies (OECD Countries) in free culture.*

I	Rationalistic, liberal, secular cultures (15 and ½ cases)
	Australia, Austria, Belgium, Canada, Denmark, Finland, France, Germany, Iceland, Luxembourg, Netherlands, New Zealand, Norway, Sweden, Switzerland, the US in rationalistic, liberal, secular (transient or exceptional) cultural dimensions and minority or decreasing regions (e.g., the Coast, parts of the North, etc.).

Expected free culture/cultural freedom overall ranking   highest, I—completely or largely free

II Anti-rationalistic, anti-liberal, anti-secular, religiously over-determined cultures (4 and ½ cases)

    Mexico, Poland, South Korea, Turkey, the US in anti-rationalistic, anti-liberal, anti-secular cultural dimensions (enduring or prevalent) and majority or growing regions (e.g., the Southern and Middle US).

Expected free culture/cultural freedom overall ranking   lowest, III—unfree or quasi-free

III Intermediate, eclectic, mixed cultures (13 cases)

    Chile, Czech Republic, Greece, Hungary, Estonia, Ireland, Italy, Japan, Portugal, Slovakia, Slovenia, Spain, the UK

Expected free culture/cultural freedom overall ranking   intermediate, II—quasi- or largely free

secular cultures' and found or anticipated to be the most highly ranked overall (rank I) on the dimension of free culture/cultural freedom among these societies. As seen, all these societies are also classified into liberal, secular, and universalistic democracy, which indicates that rationalistic, liberal, and secular culture essentially corresponds or connects to this political system, as well as into rationally regulated and egalitarian welfare capitalism, thus indicating its corresponding or connecting to the latter as well, though this link is probably less manifest or direct.

Second, anti-rationalistic, anti-liberal, and anti-secular or religiously over-determined culture serves to describe and classify countries like Mexico, Poland, South Korea, Turkey, and the US. By analogy, the latter is thus classified in its anti-rationalistic, anti-liberal, and anti-secular cultural dimensions (enduring or prevalent) and regions (majority or growing) coexisting with and launching culture wars, especially since Reaganism, against the 'rationalistic, liberal, and secular America' within the 'two Americas' culturally. As the exact obverse of the first, these countries and regions are persistently or growingly anti-rationalistic, anti-liberal, and anti-secular in all or most cultural, including artistic, scientific, educational and religious, aspects primarily because of being religiously over-determined or path-dependent, and hence represent this type of culture among Western and other societies. In this respect, they are identified and depicted as 'anti-rationalistic, anti-liberal, and anti-secular cultures' and widely observed or plausibly predicted to be ranked the lowest overall (rank III) on the dimension of free culture/cultural freedom among these societies. As noted, these countries and regions are politically classified into anti-liberal, anti-secular, and anti-universalistic 'democracy' and economically into unregulated and inegalitarian plutocratic capitalism, which suggests that anti-rationalistic, anti-liberal, and anti-secular or religiously over-determined culture essentially corresponds or relates to such a political regime and to some extent to that economic system.

Third, the intermediate, eclectic or mixed type of culture describes and classifies the following countries within OECD: Chile, Czech Republic, Greece, Hungary, Estonia, Ireland, Italy, Portugal, Slovakia, Slovenia, Spain and the UK. As usual, these countries are characterized with certain mixtures of rationalistic, liberal, and secular and anti-rationalistic, anti-liberal, and anti-secular cultures, with some being closer to the first and others to the second, and so are representative of this type of culture among Western and related societies. In this sense, they are treated as and named 'mixed cultures,' and usually experienced or anticipated to be ranked overall higher than the second group and lower than the first (rank II) with regard to free culture/cultural freedom. As seen, these countries are classified into mixed political and economic systems as well, which implies that an equivalent type of culture generally corresponds or relates to these types of polity and economy, although such relations are probably less direct or strong than in the previous two cases.

Comparative Estimates of Free Culture for Western and Related Societies

Based on the above conditions and indicators, the comparative estimates of a free culture/cultural freedom for Western and related societies are generated (Table 6.3).

Like those of democracy, a free economy (and later a free civil society), they indicate (with scores on a 0–10 scale) that these societies to some extent differ with respect to a free culture, including particular cultural liberties and rights.

TABLE 6.3 Comparative estimates of a free culture, OECD countries.

Country	Artistic Freedom 80	Artistic Freedom 90	Free Research	Evolution	Out-Of-School	Primary Education	Political Culture	Freedom of Religion	Freedom from Religion	Culture Openness	TOTAL	Rank-ings	Average
Australia	5	5	10	NA	4	8	8.75	9	7	8	64.75	9	7.19
Austria	NA	NA	NA	5	NA	NA	7.5	5	4	10	31.5	5	6.30
Belgium	NA	NA	10	9	9	10	6.88	3	7	9	63.88	8	7.99
Canada	7	9	10	NA	10	NA	8.75	8	6	9	67.75	8	8.47
Chile	NA	NA	NA	NA	0	4	6.88	9	0	4	23.88	6	3.98
Czech Republic	NA	NA	10	6	NA	NA	6.88	8	8	8	46.88	6	7.81
Denmark	NA	NA	NA	9	4	NA	9.38	6	10	9	47.38	6	7.90
Estonia	NA	NA	NA	6	6	NA	6.88	9	9	6	42.88	6	7.15
Finland	NA	10	10	6	8	9	8.75	9	7	8	75.75	9	8.42
France	9	10	5	9	9	10	6.25	4	8	9	79.25	10	7.93
Germany	9	10	5	8	10	10	8.13	4	6	8	78.13	10	7.81
Greece	NA	NA	NA	4	10	NA	6.25	1	0	8	29.25	6	4.88
Hungary	NA	NA	NA	7	7	9	6.88	9	6	8	52.88	7	7.55
Iceland	NA	NA	NA	10	8	10	10	6	6	5	55	7	7.86
Ireland	NA	0	NA	7	9	10	9.38	8	4	10	58.38	9	6.49
Italy	NA	1	NA	7	10	10	8.13	6	0	6	47.13	7	6.73
Japan	NA	10	10	9	10	10	7.5	10	8	5	69.5	8	8.69
South Korea	NA	10	10	NA	9	10	7.5	7	4	1	48.5	7	6.93

TABLE 6.3   *Comparative estimates of a free culture, OECD countries.* (cont.)

Country	Artistic Freedom 80	Artistic Freedom 90	Free Research	Evolu-tion	Out-Of-School	Primary Education	Political Culture	Freedom of Religion	Freedom from Religion	Culture Openness	TOTAL	Rank-ings	Average
Luxembourg	NA	NA	NA	6	1	6	8.75	9	6	8	44.75	7	6.39
Mexico	NA	NA	0	NA	6	8	4.38	2	2	2	24.38	7	3.48
Netherlands	8	9	10	7	10	10	8.13	10	7	9	88.13	10	8.81
New Zealand	NA	NA	10	NA	10	10	8.13	10	7	6	61.13	7	8.73
Norway	NA	NA	10	9	10	10	10	8	9	8	74	8	9.25
Poland	NA	NA	0	5	5	7	4.38	8	0	7	36.38	8	4.55
Portugal	NA	NA	10	6	10	NA	6.88	9	0	8	49.88	7	7.13
Slovakia	NA	NA	NA	5	NA	NA	5	5	3	8	26	5	5.2
Slovenia	NA	NA	NA	7	7	8	5.63	9	4	6	46.63	7	6.66
Spain	NA	NA	10	8	10	10	8.13	7	5	8	66.13	8	8.27
Sweden	10	10	10	9	10	10	10	8	10	8	95	10	9.5
Switzerland	NA	NA	10	6	10	10	9.38	8	5	9	67.38	8	8.42
Turkey	NA	NA	0	0	4	7	5.63	0	0	4	20.63	8	2.58
UK	5	5	10	9	10	10	8.75	6	9	9	81.75	10	8.18
US	2	1	0	2	0	4	8.13	7	1	7	32.13	10	3.21

I Average free-culture score 8 and higher—Completely free cultures.
II Average free-culture score 7–7.99—Largely free cultures.
III Average free-culture score 6–6.99—Quasi-free, semi-free cultures.
IV Average free-culture score under 6—Un-free cultures.

TABLE 6.4   *Average free culture estimates and classification of cultures, OECD countries.*

I	Average free-culture scores 8 and higher—Completely free cultures (11 cases) Canada, Denmark, Finland, Japan, Netherlands, New Zealand, Norway, Spain, Sweden, Switzerland, UK
II	Average free-culture scores 7–7.99—Largely free cultures in a descending order (9 cases) Australia, Belgium, Czech Republic, France, Germany, Hungary, Estonia, Iceland, Portugal
III	Average free-culture scores 6–6.99—Quasi-free cultures (6 cases) Austria, South Korea, Ireland, Italy, Luxembourg, Slovenia
IV	Average free-culture scores under 6—Unfree cultures (7 cases) Chile, Greece, Mexico, Poland, Slovakia, Turkey, the (conservative) US

These estimates hence help to categorize Western and related societies into different cultural categories such as, first, 'completely free,' second, 'largely free,' third, 'quasi-free,' and fourth, 'unfree' cultures (Table 6.4).

The first category comprises 'completely free cultures' defined and typified by the highest degrees of cultural liberties and rights, as indicated by their estimates (8 and greater) being higher than those of all other societies. Specifically, 'completely free cultures' cultures are exemplified by these countries ranked in a descending order: Sweden (9.50), Norway (9.25), the Netherlands (8.81), New Zealand (8.73), Japan (8.69), Canada (8.47), Finland (8.42), Switzerland (8.42), Spain (8.27) and Denmark (8.20), and UK (8.18) (Table 6.5).

It is indicative that in the present classification most of these countries (7 out of 10) are classified into rationalistic, liberal, and secular culture, with only a few exceptional instances (Japan, Spain, and UK) of its mixed counterpart, but none of those belonging to its opposite. This therefore supports the prediction that rationalistic, liberal, and secular cultures entailing strong scientific rationalism and genuine intellectual freedom epitomize a free culture by exhibiting the highest degrees of cultural liberties and rights among all others comparatively and historically, for example, since classical Greek civilization or the artistic and humanistic Renaissance through these days. In short, it confirms that these cultures as a whole tend to be ranked the highest on cultural freedom. So, if simply one does not know what a free culture tends to be within modern free society, one knows it when seeing primarily rationalistic,

TABLE 6.5   *Free culture ranking, OECD countries.*

Rank	Country	Index (0–10)	Category of culture	Classification
1	Sweden	9.50	Completely Free	Rationalistic
2	Norway	9.25	Completely Free	Rationalistic
3	Netherlands	8.81	Completely Free	Rationalistic
4	New Zealand	8.73	Completely Free	Rationalistic
5	Japan	8.69	Completely Free	Eclectic
6	Canada	8.47	Completely Free	Rationalistic
7	Finland	8.42	Completely Free	Rationalistic
8	Switzerland	8.42	Completely Free	Rationalistic
9	Spain	8.27	Completely Free	Eclectic
10	UK	8.18	Completely Free	Eclectic
11	Belgium	7.99	Largely Free	Rationalistic
12	France	7.93	Largely Free	Rationalistic
13	Denmark	7.90	Largely Free	Rationalistic
14	Iceland	7.86	Largely Free	Rationalistic
15	Germany	7.81	Largely Free	Rationalistic
16	Czech Republic	7.81	Largely Free	Eclectic
17	Hungary	7.55	Largely Free	Eclectic
18	Australia	7.19	Largely Free	Rationalistic
19	Estonia	7.15	Largely Free	Eclectic
20	Portugal	7.13	Largely Free	Eclectic
21	South Korea	6.93	Quasi-Free	Anti-Rationalistic
22	Italy	6.73	Quasi-Free	Eclectic
23	Slovenia	6.66	Quasi-Free	Eclectic
24	Ireland	6.49	Quasi-Free	Eclectic
25	Luxembourg	6.39	Quasi-Free	Rationalistic
26	Austria	6.30	Quasi-Free	Rationalistic
27	Slovakia	5.20	Unfree	Eclectic
28	Greece	4.88	Unfree	Eclectic
29	Poland	4.55	Unfree	Anti-Rationalistic
30	Chile	3.98	Unfree	Eclectic
31	Mexico	3.48	Unfree	Anti-Rationalistic
32	US	3.21	Unfree	Anti-Rationalistic[a]
33	Turkey	2.58	Unfree	Anti-Rationalistic

a Conservative America.

liberal, and secular cultures in Western Europe and elsewhere, notably Scandinavia and Canada, and secondarily some of their mixed counterparts like Japan, Spain, and UK, but invariably not their opposites. With respect to these mixed cases, it seems that Japan, Spain, and UK move to overcoming or mitigating cultural traditionalism in the first case, Catholic and Puritan irrationalism, illiberalism, and cultural over-determination in the second and third, and consequently becoming or approaching rationalistic, liberal, and secular cultures.

The second category encompasses 'largely free cultures' characterized with the second highest degrees of cultural freedom indicated by their corresponding estimates (7–7.99) being lower than those of the first but higher than those of the other categories. For instance, these cultures include in a descending order of freedom: Belgium (7.99), France (7.93), Denmark (7.90), Iceland (7.86), Czech Republic (7.81), Germany (7.81), Hungary (7.55), Australia (7.19), Estonia (7.15) and Portugal (7.13). Presently, all these countries are classified into either rationalistic, liberal, and secular culture or its mixed counterparts, but none into its opposite, which therefore generally supports or at least does not disconfirm the anticipations. Notably, the fact that no single instance of anti-rationalistic, anti-liberal, and anti-secular or religiously over-determined culture is included in this, just as the first, category strongly supports the expectation that its rationalistic, liberal and secular opposite—though Iceland's score is lower than expected for a Scandinavian country, thus appearing as an anomaly within Scandinavia—as well as its mixed counterpart will rank overall higher on cultural freedom. In respect of such mixed cases, it appears that Czech Republic, Estonia, and Hungary tend to overcome Communist non-liberalism, and Portugal to moderate Catholic irrationalism, illiberalism, and cultural over-determination, thus probably moving toward or approaching rationalistic, liberal, and secular cultures.

The third category consists of 'quasi-free cultures' featuring the intermediate, medium degrees of cultural liberties and rights indicated by their lower estimates (6–6.99) than those of the first two categories but higher than those of the fourth. Included in these cultures are in an ascending order of pseudo-freedom: South Korea (6.93), Italy (6.73), Slovenia (6.66), Ireland (6.49) and Luxembourg (6.39) and Austria (6.30). Three of these countries belong to mixed culture, two to rationalistic, liberal, and secular culture and one to its opposite according to the above classification, which generally means inconclusive evidence. Still, it can be interpreted as partly supporting the expectations that anti-rationalistic, anti-liberal, and anti-secular or religiously over-determined cultures are not completely or even largely free but at best quasi- or half-free—and only one of them being in this category—as well as their mixed counterparts often involve 'mixed feelings' in respect of cultural freedom. In turn, the two apparently disconfirming cases like Austria and Luxembourg can be interpreted as rare anomalies ('outliers') from the rule or pattern of rationalistic, liberal, and secular cultures as a whole having the highest degree of cultural freedom. Or perhaps admittedly, they do not belong to this type of culture, in particular Austria so long as Catholicism continues to exert an adverse impact on cultural freedom in this and other Catholic countries, just as does Islam in Turkey and evangelical Protestantism in the Southern and related US.

The last, fourth category contains 'unfree cultures' is typified by the lowest degrees of cultural liberties and rights indicated by their estimates (under 6) being lower than those of all the previous categories. Such cultures include the remaining OECD countries in an ascending order of culture un-freedom, namely Slovakia (score 5.20), Greece (4.88), Poland (4.55), Chile (3.98), Mexico (3.48), the US (3.21), and Turkey (2.58). Four of these seven countries, including the US in the second specification, are presently classified as anti-rationalistic, anti-liberal, and anti-secular or religiously over-determined cultures, and three as mixed ones, but none as rationalistic, liberal, and secular ones, which confirms the predicted lowest overall rank of the first group of societies on cultural freedom.

These are mostly societies historically or currently religiously over-determined or path-dependent, for example, Mexico, Poland and in part Chile by Catholicism, Greece by the Orthodox Church even if to a lesser extent, Turkey by Islam recently—compounded in the last two cases by religious and ethnic nationalism—America by Puritanism since New England and its heir evangelicalism, as in Dahrendorf's post-bellum 'Southern United States'[12] and beyond.

---

12   At the minimum, within America this intrinsic and strong link of unfree with anti-rationalistic, anti-liberal, and anti-secular or religiously over-determined culture applies to the 'Southern United States,' namely the American South (the 'Bible Belt') as the regional 'leader' in religiously based irrationalism and anti-rationalism, in particular religious superstition and anti-science, among virtually all Western and related societies and regions. The culturally and otherwise anti-rationalistic, anti-liberal, and anti-secular South therefore dramatically decreases the estimate and ranking of the US as a whole on cultural liberty, just as does on political, economic, and civil liberties and rights. Counterfactually, if the evangelical South were not taken into account, the US would probably have a much higher estimate and ranking on this dimension of liberty, just as on its other dimensions, specifically belonging to the category of free cultures, as well as to liberal-secular democracies, free economies, and free civil societies, for example, closer to 'liberal Canada' (as condemned or disdained by Sothern and other anti-liberals) than to Catholic-dominated Mexico and Poland and Islamic-ruled Turkey in this respect. At least, the stark contrast between the US 'Bible Belt' pervaded by perennial religiously driven 'monkey trials' against science and academic freedom and rationalistic Western Europe—with

Notably, conservative America ranks 32 among 33 countries in terms of cultural freedom, which means the second least free/most unfree culture within OECD, with only Turkey ranking lower. Hence, it ranks the first, 'best,' 'exceptional' a la Reagan's inverted 'American exceptionalism' in this respect within the Western world—no other country from the latter comes even close to this dismal rank. To add insult to injury for conservative America and its extreme nationalists and supremacists, this half of the US, thus the South and the like, ranks even lower in free culture than its disdained and assaulted Southern neighbor, Mexico ranked 31, let alone its Northern also depreciated and maligned neighbor, Canada with a remarkably high ranking at 6 (so 25 ranks higher).

Consequently, other things equal, the countries and regions in this category are less rationalistic, liberal, and secular in cultural and related terms, notably with weaker scientific rationalism and lower degrees of academic, artistic, and other intellectual freedom, than most of Western Europe and its equivalents in this respect like Canada and others. As a consequence, their lowest rank dramatically both reaffirms the previous observations and validate the present expectations. This is that cultures with stronger, more persistent religiously rooted irrationalism and anti-rationalism, notably religious superstition ('witches,' 'Satan,' 'miracles,' etc.) and anti-science ('flat earth,' 'creationism,' 'intelligent design,' 'godly' medicine) exhibit a strong tendency to be unfree absolutely, and invariably less free relative to their rationalistic, liberal, and secular counterparts. So, if one does not know or doubts what an unfree culture initially represents or eventually becomes within modern free society, one knows and detects it when seeing the compound of religiously grounded irrationalism and anti-rationalism in especially Catholic Poland, Islamic Turkey, and 'evangelical America' to distinguish it from 'secular America' within the 'two Americas' in cultural and other terms to the point of perpetual and intense culture wars. (The US aggregate free-culture estimate is discussed more in the Appendix 7.1.)

These cases prove again, after the long history of such proofs, that irrationalism and anti-rationalism, notably religious superstition and ignorance and

---

which the first wants by no means/ways to be associated or compared—in cultural and all terms exemplifies this difference in substance or quality between alternative types of culture and their varying patterns and legacies. Exemplifying the noted invariant pattern, the anti-science and generally anti-rationalistic South, with some relatively rare and special exceptions as oases of scientific rationalism and intellectual freedom (universities, etc.) in the vast desert of illiberty and irrationalism, sharply depresses and primarily explains the seemingly implausible low US estimate of a free culture, and thus its lower ranking on cultural liberties and rights than all Western countries.

anti-science and anti-education, never have and likely will lead to a free culture and society overall, and thus to generate and sustain cultural and any liberties, choices, and rights. Instead, they tend toward eliminating or perverting these liberties and rights, and ultimately causing societal perdition or petrification and degradation. The paradigmatic exemplar involves the Christian and Islamic Dark Middle Ages, which are apparently perpetuated or resurrected, with some adaptations, in anti-rationalistic, anti-liberal and anti-secular cultures, above all Catholic-dominated Poland, Islamic-ruled Turkey and the evangelical, Southern US. To many observers they thus appear as the New Dark Ages in which all culture, including science, art, and education, becomes déjà vu subdued by and ultimately vanishes almost without trace in religion and theocracy.

A least, they appear such compared with rationalistic, liberal, and secular cultures in most of Western Europe, and the Southern US in relation to Canada, for example. Such rationalistic, liberal, and secular cultures instead embrace, continue, and realize the Enlightenment pattern and legacy of rationalism through reason and knowledge and liberalism as the principle of universal and comprehensive liberty, notably science and academic and other intellectual freedom, inspiring both the French and American Revolutions and the Industrial technological Revolution. On this account, the difference between the two categories is not just in their different statistical-like degrees of culture freedom. It is rather a difference in substance or kind between the respective irrational and pre-liberal and the rationalistic and liberal patterns and legacies of the Dark Middle Ages and of the Enlightenment as their opposite and overcoming in their religious component.

Sources and Grounds for Free Culture Estimates

Artistic Liberties and Rights

The evaluation of artistic liberties and rights takes into consideration various studies and observations of these and related issues such as the attributes, forms, tendencies, and the degree of salience and appreciation of aesthetic art in contemporary Western and other societies.[1] Unfortunately, explicit estimations or indexes of artistic liberties and rights, unlike their political, economic, as well as civil forms, for Western and other societies are mostly absent or neglected in the sociological and other academic literature, and hence have to be derived or inferred indirectly and by implication, as done presently.

For illustration, the present estimates take account of the statistical data about the level of public spending on the aesthetic arts in some modern Western societies (Table 7.1), taking them as indirect expressions or at least approximations and correlates of artistic liberties and rights, just as direct and explicit indicators of the societal salience and appreciation of art.

Thus, the data show that the highest public expenditure on and thus, other things equal, societal appreciation of the aesthetic arts is characteristic for Western European and related mostly rationalistic, liberal, and secular

---

1   Adorno (1991, pp. 101–04) identifies the 'perennial conflict between artists active in the culture industry and those who control it' among modern Western societies, above all the US, suggesting that the 'culture industry no longer has anything in common with (artistic) freedom. It proclaims: you shall conform, without instruction as to what; conform to that which exists anyway, and to that which everyone thinks anyway as a reflex of its power and omnipresence.' Gottdiener (1985, p. 998) suggests that while many semiotic aspects of mass culture 'are controlled by industry, important degrees of freedom remain for the production of meanings that are independent of either the logic of exchange value or the dominant cultural sensibility.' Blau, Blau and Golden (1985, p. 317) find that, unlike income inequality, inequality in education reduces the 'proportion of artists in a city (so that) for artistic and cultural endeavors and so freedoms) to flourish and expand requires fairly high levels of education that are widespread, which implies that there is little educational inequality.' In a case study, Fishman and Lizardo (2013, p. 213) report that 'whereas pedagogical practices in Portugal encourage young people to adopt the post-canonical, anti-hierarchical orientation toward aesthetics constitutive of the omnivorous orientation, corresponding practices in Spain restrict omnivorousness by instilling a hierarchical, largely canonical attitude toward cultural works.'

TABLE 7.1   *Public expenditure on arts and museums, OECD countries ($ Per Capita, 1987).*

Country	Art Spending	Point[a]
Australia	19.1	5
Austria	NA	NA
Belgium	NA	NA
Canada	28.3	7
Chile	NA	NA
Czech Republic	NA	NA
Denmark	NA	NA
Estonia	NA	NA
Finland	NA	NA
France	35.0	9
Germany	39.1	9
Greece	NA	NA
Hungary	NA	NA
Iceland	NA	NA
Ireland	NA	NA
Italy	NA	NA
Japan	NA	NA
Korea	NA	NA
Luxembourg	NA	NA
Mexico	NA	NA
Netherlands	33.5	8
New Zealand	NA	NA
Norway	NA	NA
Poland	NA	NA
Portugal	NA	NA
Slovak Republic	NA	NA
Slovenia	NA	NA
Spain	NA	NA
Sweden	45.2	10
Switzerland	NA	NA
Turkey	NA	NA
United Kingdom	16.0	5
United States	3.3	2

a $40 or more per head = 10 points, $35–39 per head = 9 points, $30–34 per head = 8 points, $25–29 per head = 7 points, $20–24 per head = 6 points, $15–19 per head = 5 points, $10–14 per head = 4 points, $5–9 per head = 3 points, $1–4 per head = 2 points, under $1 per head = 1 point. Source: Throsby (1994, p. 21).

cultures such as Germany, France, the Netherlands, and Sweden, as well as Canada and to a lesser extent Australia, plus Great Britain as a mixed instance. Conversely, it is the lowest in non-rationalistic, non-liberal, and non-secular or religiously over-determined cultures, more specifically the US, at the minimum 'evangelical America' such as the Southern and other 'Bible Belt.' Moreover, the government spending on the arts as a proportion of all public expenditure in Germany (0.79) and France (0.77) is more 15 times, and in the Netherlands (0.45), and Sweden (0.42) around 9 times higher than in the US (0.05). Similarly, as a percentage of GNP (Gross national product), the public expenditure on the arts in Sweden (0.24), the Netherlands (0.23), France (0.22) and Germany (0.21) is between 12 and 10 times, and in Canada (0.18), Great Britain (0.14), and Australia (0.11) from 9 to 5 times, higher than in the US (0.02). As a consequence, the total public expenditure (in dollars) on the arts per capita is higher in Sweden (45.2) almost 15 times, in Germany (39.1) 13 times, France (35) and the Netherlands (33.5) more than 10 times, as well as Canada (28.3), Australia (19.1), and Great Britain (16) about 9, 6, and 5 times respectively than in the US (3.3).

Most other Western European, particularly Scandinavian, and related rationalistic, liberal, and secular cultures exhibit the same pattern of high public spending on and/or societal salience and appreciation of the arts, and conversely their alternatives typified by religiously driven irrationalism or anti-rationalism showing the opposite. Still, hardly any of these latter cultures, including Catholic dominated Poland[2] and to a lesser extent Ireland as a mixed case, Turkey under Islamic government, can really emulate or surpass the US, more specifically 'conservative-evangelical America,' in respect of extremely lower public investment in and valuation or encouragement[3] of artistic activity and creativity and thus by implication liberty or agency.

---

2 Mueller (2009, p. 14) notes that the 'Polish constitution ensure(s) that the vast majority of Polish children receive instruction—even at state schools—in only Roman Catholicism.' He also observes that 'Ireland still has blasphemy laws on the books' (Mueller 2009, p. 104).

3 Throsby (1994, pp. 20–21) comments that the 'relatively low level of expenditure in the United States is explained in part by the smaller extent of direct provision (state ownership) of arts facilities in America compared with the European countries, and in part by the fact that the US places by far the greatest reliance on voluntary support to the arts through charitable giving.' Throsby (1994, p. 21) adds, however, that 'even after allowance is made for indirect support for the arts through the tax system (charitable giving), overall levels of public subvention in the US are still likely to come out lower than in the other countries,' and infers that the low 'ranking of the US relative to the rest of the world has apparently not changed greatly over the last few decades (citing Scitovsky's interpretation of) it as indicating differences in American and European tastes which would only be altered by education.'

The comparative data on government spending on and thus public appreciation of the arts for later periods reveal, confirm, and even reinforce the above pattern[4] (Table 7.2).

TABLE 7.2   *Government expenditure on the arts and museums, OECD countries ($ Per Capita, 1993–96).*

Country	Art Spending	Point[a]
Australia	25	5
Austria	NA	NA
Belgium	NA	NA
Canada	46	9
Chile	NA	NA
Czech Republic	NA	NA
Denmark	NA	NA
Estonia	NA	NA
Finland	91	10
France	57	10
Germany	85	10
Greece	NA	NA
Hungary	NA	NA
Iceland	NA	NA
Ireland	9	1
Italy	NA	NA
Japan	NA	NA
Korea	NA	NA
Luxembourg	NA	NA
Mexico	NA	NA
Netherlands	46	9
New Zealand	NA	NA
Norway	NA	NA
Poland	NA	NA

---

4   The 2000 US National Endowment for the Arts summary of International Data on Government Spending on the Arts during the 1990s concludes that 'direct per capita government spending on the arts was the lowest in the United States —$6 per person. By contrast, Finland and Germany had comparatively high per capita pubic arts spending of $91 and $85, respectively.' Furthermore, it notes that 'in the United States, for example, 1996 appropriations for the National Endowment for the Arts were down over 40 percent from its 1992 appropriation.'

Country	Art Spending	Point[a]
Portugal	NA	NA
Slovak Republic	NA	NA
Slovenia	NA	NA
Spain	NA	NA
Sweden	57	10
Switzerland	NA	NA
Turkey	NA	NA
United Kingdom	26	5
United States	6	1

a $50 or more per head = 10 points, $45–49 per head = 9 points, $40–44 per head = 8 points, $35–39 per head = 7 points, $30–34 per head = 6 points, $25–29 per head = 5 points, $20–24 per head = 4 points, $15–19 per head = 3 points, $10–14 per head = 2 points, $5–9 per head = 1 point, under $4 per head = 0 points.

Source: Research Division Note #74 January 2000, International Data on Government Spending On the Arts, National Endowment for the Arts.

Thus, during 1990s countries with the highest government spending on and public appreciation of the arts (per capita and as a percentage of GDP) are Finland, Germany, Sweden, the Netherlands, France, and Canada, followed by Australia as the sole exception and Great Britain, all of them, except for the last, being classified into rationalistic, liberal, and secular cultures. Conversely, countries with the lowest government arts expenditure are by far the conservative, Southern US classified into non-rationalistic, non-liberal, and religiously over-determined cultures and Ireland into their mixed counterparts. For illustration, the government arts spending per capita (in dollars) in Finland (91), Germany (85), Sweden (57), France (57), the Netherlands (46) and Canada (46) is between 8 and 15 times than that in the US (6), and from 5–10 times than that in Ireland (9). An identical picture emerges in this spending as a percentage of GDP (Gross Domestic Product)—for example, 10 times higher in Canada (0.21) and the Netherlands (0.21), 13 times in France (0.36), 15 times in Sweden (0.36), 18 times in Germany (0.36) and 23 times in Finland (0.47) than in the US (0.02) and somewhat less so compared to Ireland (0.07). In particular, the government arts expenditure in the US is not only dramatically lower, by double-digit ratios, than that in these countries but also multiple times so than in the others: for example, 7 times lower than in UK (0.14) and Australia (0.14) and even more than 3 times in Ireland as the sole 'competitor' in this respect among these societies.

Generally, the data strongly confirm the expectation that rationalistic, liberal, and secular cultures, as epitomized by most of Western Europe and Canada, as a rule promote artistic liberty, rights, and creativity directly or indirectly through their higher government spending on and thus greater public appreciation of the arts than do their non-rationalistic, non-liberal, and non-secular opposites, as primarily represented by Puritan-rooted evangelical America, viz., the Southern US, and in part Catholic-dominated Ireland, suppressing aesthetic liberties overtly or by minimizing artistic expenditures.

The above pattern evidently continues through the 2000s as date show (Table 7.3).

For example, during the 2000s even before the Great Recession, the total budget per capita of National Endowment for the Arts in the US (0.51) is from 9

TABLE 7.3   *Arts grants and total arts revenues, selected countries, 2003–2004.*

	Total arts grants per capita in Can$	Total budgets per capita in Can$	Data Year
Countries with arts councils with a similar mandate to Canada council for the arts			
Arts council England	$22.99	$24.36	2003–2004
Scottish arts council	$20.00	$22.37	2003–2004
Creative Wales (arts council of Wales)	$17.46	$19.46	2003–2004
The arts council (Ireland)	$16.28	$17.91	2003
Arts council of northern Ireland— National lottery fund	$13.62		2003–2004
Australia council	$6.19	$6.91	2003–2004
Creative New Zealand	$5.64	$7.01	2003–2004
Canada council for the arts	$4.15	$4.73	2003–2004
National endowment for the arts (US)	$0.44	$0.51	2003
Statens Kulturrad (Swedish National Council For Cultural Affairs)	$28.38		
Kunstradet And Kunststyrelsen (Danish Arts Foundation and the Danish Arts Council)	$19.39		
Norsk kulturrad (arts council Norway)		$10.97	
Pro Helvetica (Arts Council Switzerland)	$2.97	$4.45	

SOURCE: CANADA COUNCIL FOR THE ARTS OCTOBER 2005.

to 50 times lower than those of comparable agencies in other countries and regions such as Switzerland (4.45), Canada (4.73), Australia (6.91), New Zealand (7.01), Norway (10.97), Ireland (17.91), Denmark (19.39 total arts grants per capita vs. 0.44 of the US), Scotland (22.37), England (24.36), and Sweden (28.38). These data place the spending of National Endowment for the Arts in proper comparative perspective as strikingly and exceptionally low—contradicting conservative attacks on it as having 'too big' a budget and 'wasting taxpayers' money' on 'obscene,' 'godless' art, etc.—and thus as an indicator of the US government's (including, Congress') exceptional 'miserly' spending on and its Puritan-style depreciation and condemnation of the arts and so artistic activities, rights, and liberties.

The above data therefore implicitly corroborate the observations or expectations that rationalistic, liberal, and secular cultures tend to be characterized with a higher degree of artistic liberties, rights, activity, and creativity—if these are implied or approximated in the extent of public expenditure of material resources on and thus of societal salience and appreciation of the arts[5]—than do their opposites permeated by religiously based irrationalism or anti-rationalism. To the extent that the higher (lower) levels of public expenditure on and of societal salience and appreciation[6] of the aesthetic arts express or predict the greater (smaller) degrees of artistic liberty, agency, and creativity, the above data can be plausibly taken as proxies for the latter and thus to support the present comparative estimates of this element of a free culture.

---

5   Osborne (2002) observes that 'Germany's public arts funding, for example, allows the country to have 23 times more full-time symphony orchestras per capita than the United States, and approximately 28 times more full-time opera houses. In Europe, publicly funded cultural institutions are used to educate young people and this helps to maintain a high level of interest in the arts. In America, arts education faces constant cutbacks, which helps reduce interest.' For example, Osborne (2002) remarks that the US neo-conservative 'agenda of reducing government became part of the rationale for shutting down Mozart and Shakespeare along with Serrano.'

6   Ashenfelter and Graddy (2003, p. 763) suggest that artistic auctions are another means of public or rather private evaluation of the arts (e.g., masterpieces in painting) proposing that the 'value of most important works of art is established by public auction, either directly, by an actual sale, or indirectly, by reference to other sales. How the auction system works is thus a critical determinant of how the public's preferences are translated into the evaluation of artistic work. The auction system is central in the determination of the incentives for artistic work, and the efficiency of the auction system is a key determinant of the cost of creating and distributing works of art.' They conclude that 'although the market is surely not all that is important in the judgement of art and artists, it is certainly one of the key components of our understanding of what is good and bad' (Ashenfelter and Graddy 2003, p. 783).

Scientific/Academic Freedoms and Rights

The comparative evaluation of scientific/academic freedoms and rights for Western and related societies take into consideration various sociological and other studies and observations of these issues.[7] More specifically, the estimation takes account of the observed degrees of freedom of research in science, in particular that of stem-cell research as a recent exemplar and predictor or proxy of scientific freedoms and rights in general, in these societies.[8] Thus, the estimates of the freedom of stem-cell research are derived from the available information on this aspect of scientific liberty. As expected, rationalistic, liberal, and secular cultures as epitomized or approached in Western and Northern Europe and elsewhere exhibit the highest degree of freedom of stem-cell and by implication related scientific research, expressing their composite of scientism and liberalism. For illustration, countries that most fully permit and promote the freedom of stem-cell research include Australia, Belgium, Finland, Canada, Czech Republic, the Netherlands, New Zealand, Norway, Portugal, Spain, Sweden, Switzerland, and UK, alongside Japan and South Korea.

Most of these countries exemplify and thus are classified as rationalistic, liberal, and secular cultures, a few in their mixed counterparts (Czech Republic, Portugal, and Spain) and only one (South Korea) in their opposites, which generally supports the expectations. Alternatively, none of Western and Northern European rationalistic, liberal, and secular cultures fully deny and suppress the freedom of such research, but at most some of them, including France and Germany, apply certain regulations and limitations primarily because of humanistic and related secular non-religious reasons by stark contrast to their non-rationalistic, non-liberal, and non-secular alternatives.

Conversely and expected, non-rationalistic, non-liberal, non-secular or religiously over-determined cultures, as exemplified by Poland, Turkey, and the US in the second specification, alongside Ireland as the mixed case, display the lowest level of, actually non-existent, freedom of stem-cell and related scientific research reflecting religiously sanctified irrationalism and anti-rationalism, specifically 'godly' superstition and anti-scientism. Moreover, among Western and related societies these hyper-religious Catholic, Islamic, and

---

7   Kurzman and Leahey (2004, p. 974) find that during the 1980s-90s intellectuals defined by higher education, including scientists or academics and scientific associations, and thus intellectual liberties and rights 'are significantly more prevalent in democracies than in nondemocracies' as well as in the latter that 'democratized' than in those failing to do so.

8   The sources for the estimates of the freedom of stem-cell research in modern societies are http://www.eurostemcell.org and http://www.explorestemcells.co.uk.

Protestant-evangelical countries or regions (within the US) are the only ones almost totally and uncompromisingly prohibiting or suppressing stem-cell research exclusively for 'godly' superstitious and anti-scientific reasons. These reasons appear as superstitious because of the proven or potential medical and other benefits of such researches, and anti-scientific due to condemning and substituting science with non-science (prayer, Bible/Koran reading as placebo 'alternative medicine' and Islamic/Christian 'science' overall). Thus, just as none of rationalistic, liberal, and secular cultures denies the freedom of stem-cell and related research, so none of their non-rationalistic, non-liberal, and ultra-religious opposites permits it. At this juncture, the contrast and mutual incompatibility are strikingly conspicuous and strong between the two varieties of Western and related cultures with respect to this and related freedom of research, just as in all other dimensions of scientific and cultural liberty.

Since the explicit comparative data on or estimations of the freedom of scientific research in general for Western and related societies are missing or incomplete, for the present purpose this dimension of a free culture can be plausibly epitomized or approximated by the observations concerning free or unfree stem-cell research. Consequently, rationalistic, liberal, and secular cultures such as Western and Northern Europe and beyond by virtue of their greatest degree of freedom of stem-cell research are also likely, other things equal, to have the highest level of freedom of scientific research generally or relatedly, as in biology, medicine, and related sciences. If these cultures permit and promote a high degree of freedom of research in this specific and presumably extremely, from a moral-religious and other non-scientific standpoint, sensitive field or science, it is plausible to expect or assume they do so in all or most other fields and sciences on the assumption that true scientific liberty is intrinsically self-consistent, holistic, and indivisible. This assumption implies that the freedom of stem-cell research is not random and separate from but consistent with and reflects and exemplifies that of all research and scientific liberty in general within rationalistic, liberal, and secular cultures. For instance, it implies that this freedom is consistent and linked with such scientific and educational freedoms as that of researching and teaching biological evolution, global warming or climate change, and the like, revealing a self-reinforcing inner logic of scientific rationalism and liberty within these cultures.

Conversely, non-rationalistic, non-liberal, and hyper-religious cultures like Poland, Turkey, and the conservative US, together with the mixed instance of Catholic dominated Ireland, can be inferred or assumed from their lowest degree of freedom of stem-cell research to have, all else equal, the correspondingly low level of freedom of scientific research overall, at least in the concretely involved or related sciences like 'sensitive' biology, medicine, etc. Analogously, so long as such cultures deny and suppress freedom of this research on the ground of its being 'immoral' and 'ungodly,' they are plausibly expected, just as actually observed, to do so in most other, or at least related, fields assuming that, like scientific liberty, illiberty is self-consistent and self-propelling to an important degree. This signifies that the *un*-freedom of stem-cell research may not be an accident and isolated from, but compatible with and expressing, that in other or related fields and scientific/academic illiberty overall within non-rationalistic, non-liberal, and hyper-religious[9] cultures. For example, it means that this un-freedom is compatible and associated with other scientific and educational un-freedoms like prohibiting or suppressing biological evolutionism and global warming theory or climate science, indicating a kind of 'method to the madness' of anti-scientism and anti-liberalism within these cultures.

Educational Freedoms and Rights

Educational freedoms and rights are for the present purpose exemplified by the freedom and right of education in biological evolution, in global warming or climate science, and in school access or enrolment, and thus estimated by the comparative estimates of these three elements. For example, the comparative estimates of the freedom and right of education in biological evolution or evolutionary biology, as a paradigmatic instance and predictor of educational freedoms and rights, are based on the observations and data about the levels of 'acceptance of evolution' in modern societies (Table 7.4).

TABLE 7.4   *Public acceptance of evolution, OECD countries, 2005.*

Country	Percent	Point[a]
Australia	NA	NA
Austria	55–59	5
Belgium	75–79	9
Canada	NA	NA

---

9 According to Mueller (2009, p. 3), 'all religions contain dogmas and beliefs which either directly contradict scientific knowledge or rest on questionable evidence. By circumscribing domains in which individuals can use their powers of reasoning, religions reduce the potential for people to make individual and collective decisions that advance their welfare on the earth.'

Country	Percent	Point[a]
Chile	NA	NA
Czech Republic	60–64	6
Denmark	75–79	9
Estonia	60–64	6
Finland	60–64	6
France	75–79	9
Germany	70–74	8
Greece	50–54	4
Hungary	65–69	7
Iceland	80	10
Ireland	65–69	7
Italy	65–69	7
Japan	75–79	9
Korea	NA	NA
Luxembourg	60–64	6
Mexico	NA	NA
Netherlands	65–69	7
New Zealand	NA	NA
Norway	75–79	9
Poland	55–59	5
Portugal	60–64	6
Slovak Republic	55–59	5
Slovenia	65–69	7
Spain	70–74	8
Sweden	75–79	9
Switzerland	60–64	6
Turkey	25–29	0
United Kingdom	75–79	9
United States	40–44	2

a Percentage 80 or more = 10 points, percentage 75–79 = 9 points, percentage 70–74 = 8 points, percentage 65–69 = 7 points, percentage 60–64 = 6 points, percentage 55–59 = 5 points, percentage 50–54 = 4 points, percentage 45–49 = 3 points, percentage 40–44 = 2 points, percentage 35–39 = 1 point, percentage under 35 = 1 points.

Source: Jon D. Miller et al. (2006).

While the 'acceptance of evolution' does not solely or directly measure the freedom and right of education in biological evolution—but also possibly prior knowledge of biology and related science—it still can be taken as its predictor or expression, at least a proxy, to the effect that the higher or lower levels of the first predict or express, minimally approximate the equal degrees of the second. To that extent, cultures with the greatest 'acceptance of evolution' are, other thing equal, observed or predicted to have the highest educational freedom in this respect, and conversely.

The above data indicate that most of the countries with the highest levels of 'acceptance of evolution' and thus scientific biology and educational freedom in this respect belong to rationalistic, liberal, and secular cultures such as those in Western and Northern Europe, particularly Scandinavia, thus confirming the prior observations and the present expectations. For example, top ten countries on this dimension of educational freedom and rights include Scandinavian ones like Iceland, Denmark, Sweden and Norway, together with other Western and related rationalistic, liberal, and secular cultures, including France, Belgium, and Germany, plus some mixed cases like Japan, Spain, and UK. The highest level of 'acceptance of evolution' in these cultures probably both predict and reflect the greatest degree of freedom of education in scientific biology, as well as the knowledge of this and related sciences and the superior performance of their educational systems overall. Simply, in these countries educators, students, and others accept to the greatest extent evolution probably because they are the freest to teach and study and thus know the best evolution and in extension scientific biology and related science, and their educational systems are the most effective. Therefore, the greatest 'acceptance of evolution' in these cultures is the predictor or expression both of the highest degree of freedom of education in and of knowledge or basic literacy[10] in scientific biology and related sciences, and of the strongest scientific quality and performance of their educational systems in general.

Conversely, according to the data, countries with the lowest levels of 'acceptance of evolution' and so scientific biology and educational freedom in this respect are largely non-rationalistic, non-liberal, and ultra-religious cultures, consistent with what has been observed before and is expected presently. Notably, the two most religious and theocentric societies Turkey under Islamic government and the conservative, Southern US[11] during the revival

---

10   Gauchat (2012, p. 170) notes the general 'association between scientific literacy or education and public trust in science (so) that educated populations will evince greater overall trust in science, which cross-national studies confirm.'

11   Observations in Blee and Creasap (2010), Evans and Evans (2008), Gauchat (2012), Martin (2002), Mooney (2005), and Mueller (2007) indicate that the educational freedom of

of anti-scientific evangelicalism are also the two societies ranked the lowest on the 'acceptance of evolution' among all OECD countries. This hence completely and dramatically confirms the expectation that non-rationalistic, non-liberal, and ultra-religious cultures tend to have a drastically lower degree of freedom and right of education in—plus knowledge of—biological evolution and related scientific fields such as stem-cell research and the like than do their rationalistic, liberal, and secular types. Admittedly, the exceptions to the above expectation or the outliers are Ireland and Austria with their higher and lower, respectively, 'acceptance of evolution' than probably expected, while both being Catholic countries.

In turn, the lowest level of 'acceptance of evolution' in Turkey under Islamic rule, the conservative US, and similar cultures is both the predictor and the reflection of the lowest degree of freedom of education in scientific biology, as well as of lack of knowledge of this science and related sciences and the inferior or inadequate performance of their educational systems overall. Simply, educators, students, and others in these countries accept evolution the least, probably because they are least free to teach and study, thus being the most ignorant of, evolution and consequently scientific biology and related science, and their educational systems are the least effective as a whole. In this connection, ignorance, as generated by lack or low freedom to teach and study evolution and thus scientific biology, may be really 'bliss.' Yet, one can assume that only if educators and especially students and others in Turkey and the US under Islamic and evangelical fundamentalism were freer and knew better in terms of scientific biology and their educational systems more effective in promoting this and related science,[12] they would probably accept evolution more. Hence, the lowest 'acceptance of evolution' in these two countries predicts and/or reflects both the lowest degree of freedom of education in and the highest degree of ignorance of scientific biology and related science, and generally the weakest scientific quality and performance of their educational systems.

---

teaching and studying evolution theory and other 'ungodly' theories in the US, above all the 'Bible Belt,' has been more restricted or challenged since at least the latter's 1925 'Money Trial' than in most Western countries.

12   Mueller (2007, p. 50) suggests that a 'liberal democracy cannot ban the printing of horoscopes in newspapers, but at the same time it should not subsidize them or make astrology courses part of the science curriculum. The same holds true for religion,' including the 'Book of Genesis' and its creationism or the latter's derivative, anti-evolution 'intelligent design'. Thus, Mueller (2007, p. 51) specifically observes with reference to the US that 'teaching young children that Darwinian evolution is just a hypothesis about how humans came to be, and no more plausible than the Book of Genesis is not likely to create intelligent citizens.'

Another related instance consists of the comparative evaluation of the freedom and right of education in global warming or climate change as a more recent example and predictor of educational freedoms and rights in Western and related societies.[13] The freedom and right of education in global warming seems to be strongly correlated with the 'acceptance of evolution' such that countries with the high levels of the second also feature the corresponding degrees of the first, and conversely. This thus indicates that educational, like scientific, liberty has a self-consistent, holistic, and indivisible logic. Overall, rationalistic, liberal, and secular Western and related cultures tend to have the highest degree of the freedom and right of education in climate change in relation to anti- or non-scientific religious or political denials and opposing economic interests, confirming the expectation of their strongest educational freedoms and rights. For example, this freedom and right is the strongest and the most universal and undisputed in most Western-Northern European and related societies.

Conversely, non-rationalistic, non-liberal, and ultra-religious cultures have the lowest degree of the freedom and right of education in global warming because of vehement anti- or non-scientific religious and political denials and attacks, and the determined opposition of narrow economic interests, consistent with the expectation of their absent or weakest educational freedoms and rights. For example, among Western countries the lowest degree of agreement with the scientific finding that climate change such as global warming is caused by human activity is reported for conservative America,[14] thus fully confirming the expectation that educational freedoms and rights are lower in anti-rationalistic, illiberal, and religiously dominated cultures.

In addition, the comparative estimates of the freedom and right of school access take into consideration comparative data on the rates of enrolment in primary education as a proxy and indicator of educational freedom and opportunity respectively for Western and related societies (Table 7.5 and 7.6).

---

13   The comparative estimates of the freedom and right of education in global warming or climate change are also based on studies in (Acemoglu et al. 2012; Rudel, Roberts, and Carmin 2011; Stern 2008). In particular, Gauchat (2012, p. 184) notes the 'growing public skepticism toward the problem' of global climate change in the US by sharp contrast to other Western countries, because by implication of the lesser freedom of education or knowledge and basic scientific literacy (i.e., more ignorance) of this and related fields and sciences in the first than in the second.

14   The source is 'Global Trends 2014' report, Ipsos MORI.

TABLE 7.5   *Out-of-school rate for children of primary school age, OECD countries, 2008–2012.*

Country	2008	2009	2010	2011	2012	Point[a]
Australia	3.6	3.4	3.4	3.5	4	
Austria	NA					NA
Belgium	1.4	1.0	0.9	0.9	1.0	9
Canada	0.2	0.1	10			
Chile	4.6	6.5	5.9	6.9	7.3	0
Czech Republic	NA					NA
Denmark	3.4	2.9	3.5	3.6	3.8	4
Estonia	3.1	4.0	3.3	3.4	2.9	6
Finland	2.4	2.4	2.1	1.7	8	
France	0.8	0.8	0.8	1.0	1.1	9
Germany	0.2	0.3	0.4	0.3	0.2	10
Greece	0.1	0.2	0.4	0.4	10	
Hungary	3.4	2.1	1.4	1.5	2.2	7
Iceland	1.9	1.2	0.7	1.2	1.5	8
Ireland	0.1	0.3	0.3	0.2	1.2	9
Italy	0.7	0.7	0.7	0.6	0.9	10
Japan	0.0	0.0	0.0	0.0	0.1	10
Korea	0.6	0.4	1.1	1.0	9	
Luxembourg	1.8	2.7	5.1	5.4	1	
Mexico	5.4	4.6	3.6	2.8	6	
Netherlands	0.5	0.4	0.3	0.1	0.1	10
New Zealand	0.5	0.4	0.5	0.5	0.7	10
Norway	0.9	0.8	1.0	1.1	0.7	10
Poland	4.5	3.9	3.6	3.6	3.4	5
Portugal	0.8	0.9	0.7	10		
Slovakia	NA					NA
Slovenia	2.7	2.6	2.7	2.8	2.3	7
Spain	0.2	0.1	0.2	0.3	0.3	10
Sweden	3.7	1.6	0.7	0.6	0.5	10
Switzerland	2.2	1.5	1.0	1.0	0.7	10
Turkey	1.4	1.1	3.5	2.9	3.8	4
United Kingdom	1.5	0.2	0.3	0.4	0.3	10
United States	3.6	5.1	6.3	7.1	7.2	0

TABLE 7.5   *Out-of-school rate for children of primary school age, OECD countries, 2008–2012* (cont.)

Country	2008	2009	2010	2011	2012	Point[a]
World	9.2	9.3	9.1	8.8		
Developed	1.6	1.9	2.4	2.4		
Developing	10.7	10.1	10.2	9.9	9.6	

a 2012 Percentage 0–0.9 = 10 points, percentage 1.0–1.4 = 9 points, percentage 1.5–1.9 = 8 points, percentage 2.0–2.4 = 7 points, percentage 2.5–2.9 = 6 points, percentage 3.0–3.4 = 5 points, percentage 3.5–3.9 = 4 points, percentage 4.0–4.4 = 3 points, percentage 4.5–4.9 = 2 points, percentage 5.0–5.4 = 1 point, percentage higher than 5.4 = 0 points.
Source: UNESCO http://data.uis.unesco.org/.

TABLE 7.6   *Net enrolment rate in primary education, OECD countries, 2008–2012.*

Country	Percent	Point[a]
Japan	99.9	10
Netherlands	99.9	10
Germany	99.8	10
Spain	99.7	10
United Kingdom	99.7	10
Sweden	99.5	10
New Zealand	99.3	10
Switzerland	99.3	10
Norway	99.3	10
Italy	99.1	10
France	99	10
Korea Rep.	99	10
Belgium	99	10
Ireland	98.8	10
Iceland	98.5	10
Finland	98.3	9
Hungary	97.8	9
Mexico	97.2	8
Slovenia	97.2	8
Australia	96.5	8
Poland	96.4	7
Turkey	96.2	7

Country	Percent	Point[a]
Luxembourg	94.6	6
Chile	93.1	4
United States	92.9	4
Austria	NA	NA
Canada	NA	NA
Czech Republic	NA	NA
Denmark	NA	NA
Estonia	NA	NA
Greece	NA	NA
Portugal	NA	NA
Slovakia	NA	NA

a 2012 Percentage 99 or more = 10 points, percentage 98 = 9 points, percentage 97 = 8 points, percentage 96 = 7 points, percentage 95 = 6 points, percentage 94 = 5 points, percentage 93 = 4 points, percentage 92 = 3 points, percentage 91 = 2, percentage 90 = 1 point.

Source: UNESCO http://data.uis.unesco.org.

For example, countries with the highest rates of enrolment in primary education—or conversely the lowest ones of out-of-school children—are Japan (99.9), Netherlands (99.9), Germany (99.8), Spain (99.7), UK (99.7), Sweden (99.5), New Zealand (99.3), Norway (99.3), Switzerland (99.3), Italy (99.1), Belgium (99), France (99), and South Korea (99). As known, the vast majority of these countries (10 out of 15) are classified in rationalistic, liberal, and secular culture, several in its mixed counterpart, and only one in its opposite. To that extent, this reaffirms that rationalistic, liberal and secular cultures as a whole provide and promote both more educational freedoms *and* opportunities than do their opposite or mixed forms.

In turn, OECD countries with by far the lowest rates of enrolment in primary education, and conversely the highest one of out-of-school children, are found to be Chile (93.1) and the US (92.9), of which the first is classified in intermediate, and the second (in the conservative rendition) in non-rationalistic, non-liberal, and ultra-religious, cultures. Thus, the major underlying reason for this striking 'American exceptionalism' in the sense of exceptionally low enrolment in primary education in relation to the Western world is the religiously driven opposition to secular public education in favor of 'no education' as 'better'[15]

---

15   Darnell and Sherkat (1997, p. 307) observe that especially in America 'Protestant religions and secular education has always been high. The furor over teaching Darwin's theory of evolution in public schools was raised early in the 20th century, and Protestant skepticism

and the resulting expansion of private religious and home schooling[16] (especially the 'Bible Belt'), a phenomenon unparalleled in European countries (except, in part, for the UK). To that extent, the above confirms that religiously determined anti-rationalistic and anti-liberal cultures tend to diminish both freedom and opportunity in (public) educational systems. It may be shocking or scandalous to observe that the presumed paragon of educational freedom and equal opportunity exhibits the lowest rate of enrolment in primary education among OECD countries. Yet, this becomes perfectly understandable and predictable, a normal outcome, and not a random effect, if considering the anti-science pattern and 'method to the madness' of these cultures versus the positive impact of their rationalistic, liberal, and secular alternatives on both educational freedom and opportunity.

Ideological and Religious Freedoms and Rights

The comparative estimation of ideological freedoms, choices, and rights takes into account sociological and other observations of this indicator of a free culture. Ideological freedoms and rights are typically intertwined and mutually reinforced with their academic, as well as political and civil, forms. Because of this interconnection and mutual reinforcement what has been stated of the grounds and sources for the comparative estimates of academic freedom can be applied, with prudent modifications, to those for its ideological form.

In addition, ideological freedoms and rights, especially those with political content, may be to some extent estimated or approximated by the estimates of political culture that hence is taken as a correlate or proxy in this respect. In turn, these estimates are derived from the indexes of 'political culture' comprised in the 'Democracy Index 2015' (Table 7.7).

---

over the value and propriety of scientific investigation has continued unabated ever since. For many conservative Protestants, education serves to undermine both secular and divine authority by promoting "humanism" and denigrating faith.' Darnell and Sherkat (1997, pp. 308–09) find that in contemporary America 'conservative Protestant opposition to secular education stems primarily from conflicts over how children should be socialized and the desirability of secular humanist values (and) when confronted with a choice between affordable state-supported secular institutions or no higher education, advice from renowned fundamentalist authors is: No schooling is better than secular schooling.'

16   Mueller (2007, pp. 51–52) remarks that 'in the United States, parents are allowed to send their children to private schools rather than public schools and even to educate their children themselves. The overwhelming majority of parents who choose these options do so to ensure that their children receive a religious education.'

TABLE 7.7   *Political culture index, OECD countries, 2015.*

Country	Index/Point
Norway	10
Iceland	10
Sweden	10
New Zealand	8.13
Denmark	9.38
Switzerland	9.38
Canada	8.75
Finland	8.75
Australia	8.75
Netherlands	8.13
Luxembourg	8.75
Ireland	9.38
Germany	8.13
Austria	7.50
United Kingdom	8.75
Spain	8.13
United States of America	8.13
Italy	8.13
South Korea	7.50
Japan	7.50
Czech Republic	6.88
Belgium	6.88
France	6.25
Estonia	6.88
Chile	6.88
Portugal	6.88
Slovenia	5.63
Greece	6.25
Slovakia	5.00
Poland	4.38
Hungary	6.88
Mexico	4.38
Turkey	5.63

SOURCE: THE ECONOMIST INTELLIGENCE UNIT 2015.

First, within OECD countries with the maximal index of 'political culture' (10) and by approximation ideological freedom with political content are Iceland, Norway, and Sweden. All the three countries are categorized in the category of rationalistic, liberal and secular culture, which therefore strongly confirms the expectation that this cultural type features the comparatively highest and even sometimes the absolutely maximal degree of ideological freedom insofar as the latter is related to or approached by the level of 'political culture.' More generally, ten or so countries with the highest 'political culture' and approximately ideological freedom indexes include, along with the above three, Denmark (9.38), Ireland (9.38), Switzerland (9.38), then Australia (8.75), Canada (8.75), Finland (8.75), Luxembourg (8.75), and UK (8.75). As known, in the present categorization nine of these countries are categorized in rationalistic, liberal, and secular culture, while only two, Ireland and UK in its mixed counterpart, but none in its opposite. This ranking therefore strongly confirms the expectations that rationalistic and liberal cultures as a whole attain and cultivate the highest levels of ideological freedoms, choices, and rights through their (liberal) 'political culture' that is the most compatible with them and democracy in general.

Conversely, the following are ten or more countries with the lowest indexes on 'political culture' and by approximation ideological freedom: Mexico (4.38), Poland (4.38), Slovakia (5.00), Turkey (5.63), Slovenia (5.63), Greece (6.25), France (6.25), Belgium (6.88), Chile (6.88), the Czech Republic (6.88), Estonia (6.88), Hungary (6.88), and Portugal (6.88). Recall that most of these countries are presently categorized either in anti-rationalistic, anti-liberal, and anti-secular cultures or their mixed counterparts, and only two in their opposites, namely France and Belgium, that can be interpreted as rare exceptions to the pattern ('outliers'). This hence generally supports the expectations that the first two types of culture overall have the lower degrees of ideological freedom related to their non- or quasi-democratic 'political culture' than does the third type as a whole. Notably, the two cases with the lowest index of 'political culture' and thus, other things equal, ideological freedom and choice are Mexico and Poland widely regarded as anti-rationalistic, anti-liberal, and anti-secular, religiously (Catholic) over-determined cultures.

The comparative estimates of religious freedom in both forms take into consideration analyses and observations of this and related phenomena among Western and other countries. First, the comparative estimates of freedom of religion take into account, for example, Religious Restriction Index (GRI) Scores for these countries, as estimated by some research organizations (Table 7.8).

In general, these GRI scores are relatively low for most Western and other countries, thus indicating, other things equal, a high or important degree of

TABLE 7.8   *Government religious restriction index scores by region, OECD countries 2009.*

Country	Index (GRI)	Point[a]
Australia	0.9	9
Austria	2.7	5
Belgium	3.9	3
Canada	1.3	8
Chile	0.8	9
Czech Republic	1.1	8
Denmark	2.4	6
Estonia	0.7	9
Finland	0.8	9
France	3.4	4
Germany	3.2	4
Greece	4.6	1
Hungary	0.5	9
Iceland	2.2	6
Ireland	1.0	8
Italy	2.2	6
Japan	0.3	10
Korea South	1.5	7
Luxembourg	0.8	9
Mexico	4.1	2
Netherlands	0.4	10
New Zealand	0.4	10
Norway	1.2	8
Poland	1.0	8
Portugal	0.6	9
Slovakia	2.8	5
Slovenia	0.9	9
Spain	1.9	7
Sweden	1.0	8
Switzerland	1.0	8
Turkey	6.4	0
United Kingdom	2.2	6
United States	1.6	7

a Index 0–0.4 = 10 points, index 0.5–0.9 = 9 points, index 1.0–1.4 = 8 points, index 1.5–1.9 = 7 points, index 2.0–2.4 = 6 points, index 2.5–2.9 = 5 points, index 3.0–3.4 = 4 points, index 3.5–3.9 = 3 points, index 4.0–4.4 = 2 points, index 4.5–4.9 = 1 points, index 5 or higher = 0 points.

Source: http://www.pewforum.org.

freedom of religion, although with certain salient and unexpected variations. The lowest GRI scores (below 1) and hence the highest degrees of freedom of religion are estimated for Western and other European countries such as the Netherlands, Hungary, Portugal, Estonia, Finland, Luxembourg, and Slovenia, as well as some non-European ones like Japan, New Zealand, Chile, and Australia. Conversely, the highest GRI scores and in that sense the lowest degrees of freedom of religion are calculated for certain non-Western and non-European countries such as Turkey, Greece, and Mexico, as well as some Western European ones like Belgium, France, and Germany.

Apparently, these scores only in part confirm and even to some extent, namely the last three cases, disconfirm the expectations that rationalistic, liberal, and secular cultures such as those in Western and Northern Europe tend to exhibit a higher degree of freedom of (and from) religion than their non-rationalistic, non-liberal, and hyper-religious opposites. Still, in an alternative interpretation using the Enlightenment Jeffersonian stipulation of *no* government establishment, imposition, and promotion of religion as the condition and criterion of freedom of (and from) religion, these and other exceptions or outliers in the above scores may turn out to be not as unexpected or disconfirming as they appear at first glance. Thus, the comparatively high GRI scores (above 2) for some Western and other European countries exemplifying rationalistic, liberal, and secular or mixed cultures—for example, Belgium, France, Germany, Austria, Denmark, Italy, and UK—may be interpreted to reflect the underlying principle and practice of *no* or weak government establishment, imposition, and promotion of religion, just as the opposite idea and activity in conventional interpretations. At the minimum, this applies more to some of these countries such as Belgium, France, and Germany characterized with the strict separation of religion and politics, and less to the others like Austria, Denmark, Italy, and UK, etc., so long as these latter are regarded as having state religions or religious monopoly. Especially, US 'rational choice' theorists of religion insist on this in a counter-distinction from America's supposed lack of official or promoted and subsidized religion and its 'exceptional' religious pluralism and competition.

In turn, the relatively low GRI scores (under 2) for some European and other countries, including Poland, Chile, Ireland, the US, etc., that, including the latter in the second rendition, exemplify more or less non-rationalistic, non-liberal, and ultra-religious cultures may be interpreted to reflect precisely the tenet or policy of government establishment, imposition, and promotion of religion, just as the opposite, for example, the constitutional prohibition of such an activity in America, in conventional interpretations. This holds true for either of those countries like Poland and to a lesser extent Chile and Ireland typified with state or protected and favored religions, specifically, Catholicism, or the others such as conservative America officially without such a religion and yet effectively promoting and subsidizing it, mostly Protestantism, notably evangelicalism in the South,[17] in contravention to or suspension of the constitutional non-establishment stipulation and the Jeffersonian 'wall' of separation of church and state. On such alternative interpretations, the above exceptions or outliers in either direction may turn out to be largely consistent with the expectation that rationalistic, liberal, and secular cultures as a rule demonstrate the highest degree of freedom of religion precisely because they refrain from establishing or promoting a particular and any religion, by comparison to their alternatives instead doing the exact opposite. This pattern is even more clearly and drastically evidenced for freedom from religion next.

Generally, the comparative estimates of freedom from religion are also supported by studies and observations of this second component of religious liberty, especially in relation to state religions and its reduction or subversion through government financial and other support for churches and denominations. Particularly, they take account of the comparative data on the levels of importance of religion, specifically the percentages of 'religion no important' in a country (Table 7.9).

TABLE 7.9   *Freedom from religion, OECD countries, 2005–11.*

Country	Religion not important	Point[a]
Australia	67	7
Austria	51	4
Belgium	68	7
Canada	61	6
Chile	27	0
Czech Republic	72	8
Denmark	83	10
Estonia	78	9
Finland	69	7
France	74	8
Germany	62	6
Greece	24	0

---

17   Bailey and Snedker (2011, p. 855) note that 'during the late 19th century, Southern culture was increasingly dominated by conservative Protestantism' and, one can add, continues to be by the early 21st century.

TABLE 7.9   *Freedom from religion, OECD countries, 2005–11.* (cont.)

Country	Religion not important	Point[a]
Hungary	63	6
Iceland	60	6
Ireland	53	4
Italy	30	0
Japan	71	8
Korea South	52	4
Luxembourg	64	6
Mexico	44	2
Netherlands	65	7
New Zealand	67	7
Norway	78	9
Poland	24	0
Portugal	33	0
Slovakia	45	3
Slovenia	51	4
Spain	55	5
Sweden	88	10
Switzerland	57	5
Turkey	13	0
United Kingdom	76	9
United States	36	1

a   Percentage 80 or more = 10 points, percentage 75–79 = 9 points,
percentage 70–74 = 8 points, percentage 65–69 = 7 points, percentage
60–64 = 6 points, percentage 55–59 = 5 points, percentage 50–54 = 4
points, percentage 45–49 = 3 points, percentage 40–44 = 2 points,
percentage 35–39 = 1 point, under 35 = 0 points.
SOURCES: GALLUP 2005–11; ALSO, FREEDOM OF THOUGHT
2013: A GLOBAL REPORT ON THE RIGHTS, LEGAL STATUS, AND
DISCRIMINATION AGAINST HUMANISTS, ATHEISTS, AND THE
NON-RELIGIOUS.

This is regarded as an indirect indication or proxy of the degrees of freedom
from religion, notably in relation to its organized and official, orthodox form,
as well as a direct indicator or predictor of the process and level of secularization. Arguably, whether and the extent to which 'religion is no important'
in a society expresses or predicts, all else equal, if freedom from religion

exists and its degree, as well as the existence and level of secularization and rationalization overall. Conversely, the high importance of religion typically reflects or predicts lack or weakness of such and related liberties, and instead the presence or severity of religious and political coercion and repression, cultural constraints through irrationalism and anti-rationalism such as superstition and anti-science, and societal pressure, climate ('ambiance of fear'), and sanctions. To that extent, other things equal, the higher percentages of 'religion no important' in a country indirectly reflects or approximates the greater degrees of freedom from coercive, official, orthodox, or organized religion, as well as directly indicates the high level of secularization and rationalization, and reversely.

As the data show, countries with the highest percentages of 'religion no important' and thus degrees of freedom from religion and levels of secularization are those in Western, Northern, and Central Europe, notably Scandinavia, plus some others beyond. They all epitomize and are classified into liberal-rationalistic and secular cultures, thus strongly confirming the expectations. Conversely, those with the lowest percentages of 'religion no important' and so the equivalent degrees of freedom from religion and levels of secularization are some non-Western and non-European countries. Instead, they exemplify mostly non-liberal, non-rationalistic, and ultra-religious cultures, as also expected.

For instance, among the ten countries ranked the highest on 'religion no important' and so on freedom from religion and secularization nine are in Europe, including Sweden, Norway, Denmark, UK, Estonia, Czech Republic, France, Finland, and Belgium, and only one beyond, namely Japan. Notably, the top three countries are Sweden, Norway, and Denmark representing Scandinavia as the paradigmatic exemplar of a liberal, rationalistic, and secular modern culture, thus completely and even dramatically reaffirming the expectations. The preceding hence justifies the maximum estimate of freedom from religion for Scandinavian and other societies with the high rankings on 'religion no important' as an expression or predictor of the accelerated process and the high level of secularization and rationalization.

In turn, ten countries with the lowest ranking on 'religion no important' and so freedom from religion and secularization are mostly non-Western and non-European ones, for example, Turkey, Poland, Greece, Chile, Italy, the US, Portugal, Mexico, Slovakia, and Slovenia. Most of them, with a few exceptions, belong and are classified into non-liberal, non-rationalistic, and ultra-religious cultures, as expected. Notably, the bottom three in this ranking are Turkey, Poland, and Greece, closely followed by Chile, Italy, and the US. Most of these, including the US in the second specification, are largely, with minor variations, cases of a non-rationalistic, non-liberal, and ultra-religious (Islamic, Catholic,

Orthodox Christian, Protestant-evangelical) or eclectic culture, thus largely consistent with the expectations. The above therefore provides the rationale for the estimates of freedom from religion for Turkey, Poland, Greece, Chile, Italy, the us, and other countries with the comparatively low rankings on 'religion no important' as the indication or prediction of the reversed or slow process and low level of secularization and rationalization. In addition, the grounds for the us score on this indicator of a free culture include observations suggesting that the individual freedom from coercive, encompassing, intrusive, and organized religion, above all in 'conservative America' like the South[18] is relatively lower or decreasing;[19] by comparison with most other Western societies.

Overall, the comparative estimates of freedom from religion for these societies take into account studies and observations of their processes and levels of secularization—of which the percentage of 'religion no important' is a

---

18 The press reported the following in February 2016: 'We need a revolution at this point because corruption is so vast,' said Cheryl, a 43-year-old chief financial officer from Atlanta. She spoke on condition that her last name not be used because she said the stigma of being not religious in the South would harm her career and her child.' Evidently, 'being not religious' is still a proxy crime or serious violation in the us South, which is what makes it an effective theocracy, more precisely Weber's 'Bibliocracy' cum the 'Bible Belt,' and comparatively closer to Islamic theocratic countries or regions like Iran or Taliban, where this is also criminalized, than to the Western world, in fact laying outside of its sphere from Western Europe to neighboring Canada. This also justifies once again considering the 'Southern Unites States' as the 'other America,' following Dahrendorf (1979), and generally the 'two Americas'.

19 Edgell et al. (2006,214) find that 'atheists are at the top of the list of groups that Americans find problematic in both public and private life, and the gap between acceptance of atheists and acceptance of other racial and religious minorities is large and persistent. It is striking that the rejection of atheists is so much more common than rejection of other stigmatized groups. For example, while rejection of Muslims may have spiked in post-9/11 America, rejection of atheists was higher (and) concerns about atheists were stronger than concerns about homosexuals.' They conclude that the above reveals the 'symbolic logic of exclusion' (Edgell et al. 2006, p. 230) of atheists from 'cultural membership in American society,' just as from political and public positions. Krasa and Polborn (2014, p. 308) observe that 'Reagan's conservative revolution has created a cultural wedge between the parties that only widened in the 1990s and 2000s.' They comment that 'Ronald Reagan's election and the contemporaneous integration of evangelicals into the main stream of the Republican party is widely interpreted as the starting point of a clearer ideological differentiation between parties (i.e.) a cultural radicalization of the Republican party under Reagan, and similarly later under George W. Bush' (Krasa and Polborn 2014, p. 321).

particular dimension—as its predictor or correlate. Thus, the faster process or greater extent of secularization in general, just as of 'religion no important' in particular, in these societies is taken to predict or correlate with the higher degree of freedom from religion, and conversely. Specifically, the most secularized Western and related countries such as those in Western/Northern Europe, notably Scandinavia, and beyond tend to also exhibit the highest degrees of freedom from religion, while the reverse holds for their religious opposites or mixed counterparts, such as Turkey, Poland, Greece, Chile, Italy, the US in the second rendition, etc.

No doubt, this link between secularization and freedom from religion is axiomatic and so tautological from the stance of a rationalistic, liberal, and secular culture. Yet, it is still needed to emphasize and reiterate in the view of various, especially US 'rational choice' theorists' and conservative politicians,' denials of secularization as a 'myth' and notably its strong positive impact on this dimension of religious liberty they either deny or reluctantly admit as secondary to freedom of religion. Hence, to the extent that a certain high level of secularization, as exemplified in a corresponding percentage of 'religion no important,' constitutes the necessary and even, if conjoined with liberal democracy and rationalistic culture, sufficient condition of freedom from coercive, organized, or official religion, the comparative estimates of this religious liberty are compatible with and grounded in the observed levels of culture secularism.

Culture Openness

Lastly, the comparative estimates of culture openness to the world beyond national boundaries take into account the observations and estimations of the level of cultural and social globalization for modern societies (Table 7.10).

TABLE 7.10 *Index of social-cultural openness/globalization, OECD countries, 2012.*

Country	Index	Point[a]
1. Ireland	91.43	10
2. Austria	90.28	10
3. Belgium	89.75	9
4. Switzerland	89.43	9

TABLE 7.10   *Index of social-cultural openness/globalization, OECD countries, 2012.* (cont.)

Country	Index	Point[a]
5. Canada	88.72	9
6. Netherlands	87.87	9
7. Denmark	86.19	9
8. France	85.65	9
9. UK	85.50	9
10. Portugal	84.50	8
11. Czech Republic	83.33	8
12. Slovakia	82.33	8
13. Norway	82.28	8
14. Germany	82.16	8
15. Sweden	82.13	8
16. Spain	81.20	8
17. Luxembourg	81.14	8
18. Finland	80.78	8
19. Hungary	80.59	8
20. Greece	80.33	8
21. Australia	79.65	7
22. Poland	77.42	7
23. US	76.24	7
24. Italy	74.50	6
25. Slovenia	73.77	6
26. Estonia	73.69	6
27. New Zealand	72.77	6
28. Iceland	68.96	5
29. Japan	64.57	5
30. Turkey	64.16	4
31. Chile	51.75	2
32. Mexico	51.11	2
33. Korea, Rep.	45.75	1

a   Index 90 or higher = 10 points, index 85–89 = 9 points, index 80–84 = 8 points, index 75–79 = 7 points, index 70–74 = 6 points, index 65–69 = 5 points, index 60–64 = 4 points, index 55–59 = 3 points, index 50–54 = 2 points, index 45–49 = 1 point, index under 45 = 0 points.

Source: http://www.globalization-index.org/.

These estimations show that the highest level of cultural-social openness, as expressed by the 'index of social globalization,' is observed in most Western European societies and thus, with some exceptions, rationalistic, liberal, and secular cultures, consistent with the expectations. For instance, of the ten countries with the highest 'index of social globalization' and in that sense cultural openness to the outside world nine are in Western Europe—for example, Ireland, Austria, Belgium, Switzerland, the Netherlands, Denmark, France, UK, and Portugal—and only one outside this region, Canada. All of these represent instances of a rationalistic, liberal, and secular culture, except for Ireland and Portugal as rare exceptions to the expected pattern at this point.

Conversely, certain non-Western and non-European countries as largely non-rationalistic, non-liberal, and ultra-religious cultures evince a lower level of cultural-social openness, although with more variations and exceptions, thus in part confirming the expectations. For illustration, ten countries with the lowest highest 'index of social globalization' and thus cultural openness to the world include six usually deemed non-Western, for example, Estonia, Slovenia, Italy, Poland, Greece, and Hungary, three non-European such as New Zealand, the US, and Australia, and only one Western or Northern European country, Finland. No doubt, geographic distance or isolation from Western Europe as the perceived culture center may lower the level of cultural-social globalization, especially for Finland and Estonia at its periphery and more for New Zealand, the US, and Australia, yet evidently not for Canada, thus probably not being a complete explanation. Conversely, proximity to this center does not necessarily increase this level, as shown by Italy, Poland, etc. Moreover, a mostly non-rationalistic, non-liberal, and religiously over-determined or eclectic culture either compounds and overlays geographic isolation or distance from Western Europe, as with the US in the second specification (at the minimum, the South) and Greece, or overcomes spatial proximity, as in Poland and in part Italy.

Alternatively, a strong rationalistic, liberal, and secular culture weakens the negative effect of geographic distance or isolation on cultural openness, as in Finland and Australia, and even completely neutralizes it, as demonstrated by Canada. It does so by making their social globalization indexes higher than that of another major isolate, the US, and probably otherwise, i.e., if counterfactually they had instead opposite cultures. This justifies the US estimate[20] of

---

20   Janssen, Kuipers, and Verboord (2008, p. 728) report that the 'US pattern (of cultural globalization) differs markedly from that of the European countries,' including France, Germany, and the Netherlands, in its being less open or more national-oriented and thus nativist and closed—as exemplified by the 'strong national orientation' of the *New York*

culture openness, as does the observation of the 'sadistic intolerance to cultural otherness'[21] in 'conservative America' such as the South, and comparatively more than in most Western societies observed to be more tolerant of such differences, especially those between religious believers and non-believers. The above leaves New Zealand with its lower 'social globalization' index than expected—seemingly due to its geographic isolation and small size—as the sole or major exception to the expectation that non-rationalistic, non-liberal, and hyper-religious cultures have low culture openness, with Italy, Slovenia, Estonia, and Hungary as partial exceptions, just as is Ireland to the reverse pattern.

Generally, the comparative estimates of culture openness to the world largely correspond to the overall indexes of globalization, combining those of its economic, political, and cultural-social forms, for modern societies (Table 7.11).

As expected, rationalistic, liberal, and secular cultures such as Western European and related countries typically have the higher overall 'index of globalization' and to that extent of openness to the world than their opposites. For example, ten Western and other countries with the highest overall 'index of globalization' and thus openness are, in this order, Belgium, Ireland, the Netherlands, Austria, Sweden, Denmark, Hungary, Portugal Switzerland, Luxembourg, and Czech Republic, more or less epitomizing the first type of culture, except for Ireland as the sole or major exception to the expected pattern. Conversely, half of the ten countries with the lowest overall 'index of globalization' and so openness includes such instances of a non-rationalistic, non-liberal, and religious culture as Mexico, Turkey, the US in the second specification, and

---

Times—such that 'even in fields where US hegemony is less salient (e.g., literature, theater, and classical music), coverage is more national in focus than coverage in the European papers.' Thus, they detect a clear globalization or 'internationalization of arts and culture coverage in the European newspapers, but not in (the American),' specifically the *New York Times*, as during 1995–2005 (Janssen et al. 2008, p. 733). They conclude that the Western countries analyzed 'differ significantly in their levels of cultural protectionism' (Janssen et al. 2008, pp. 733–34), with the US exhibiting the highest level of the latter and thus the lowest degree of culture openness, as exemplified by the 'relatively limited coverage of foreign actors' in its best-known and presumably most globally open newspaper. So, if the supposedly cosmopolitan, non-parochial *New York Times* has the 'relatively limited coverage of foreign actors' compared to its European counterparts, then this applies even more to other major, mostly nativist or parochial, US newspapers probably approaching the zero or so coverage of non-Americans in art and culture.

21   Bauman (2000, p. 106; 1997, p. 184) observes that there is a 'sadistic intolerance to cultural otherness widespread in American society' and that 'sexual mores were no doubt exploited as one of the more important footholds for intolerance,' with such a tendency being especially perpetuated by the 'evangelist churches of the Bible Belt'.

TABLE 7.11 *Total index of globalization, OECD countries, 2012.*

Country	Index
1. Belgium	92.76
2. Ireland	91.95
3. Netherlands	90.94
4. Austria	90.55
5. Sweden	88.23
6. Denmark	88.11
7. Hungary	87.38
8. Portugal	86.73
9. Switzerland	86.64
10. Luxembourg	86.02
11. Czech Rep.	85.76
12. UK	85.54
13. Canada	85.53
14. Spain	84.36
15. Finland	84.34
16. France	84.12
17. Slovakia	83.83
18. Norway	83.19
19. Australia	81.60
20. Germany	81.53
21. Greece	81.30
22. Italy	81.02
23. Poland	80.81
24. Estonia	79.34
25. New Zealand	78.31
26. Slovenia	77.67
27. US	74.88
28. Chile	73.31
29. Iceland	72.96
30. Turkey	69.99
31. Japan	64.13
32. Korea, Rep.	62.39
33. Mexico	59.96

SOURCE: HTTP://WWW.GLOBALIZATION-INDEX.ORG/.

Poland, alongside mixed culture types such as Chile, Slovenia, Estonia, and South Korea, or seeming exceptions to the expected pattern like Iceland and New Zealand. Notably, the overall US 'index of globalization' is the sixth lowest among Western and related OECD (and 35th of all) countries, so only five of these having lower indexes. Of these three are mostly non-rationalistic, non-liberal, and over-religious cultures like Mexico, Turkey, and South Korea, one an intermediate culture, namely Chile, and only one the opposite culture type such as Iceland. To that extent, this provides another compelling rationale for the estimates of culture openness for these non-rationalistic, non-liberal, and over-religious cultures.

Appendix 7.1 Notes on Cultural Freedom Estimates for the US

Artistic Liberties and Rights
In particular, the preceding indirectly or implicitly provides grounds for the US estimate of this dimension of a free culture. In addition, the explicit rationale for this estimate consists of observations indicating that artistic freedoms, activities, and agents are subject to persistent, consistent, and severe suppression or restriction, as during most of American history since anti-artistic Puritanism until its evangelical revival these days.[22] Historical observations indicate that artistic and related intellectual liberties, activities, products, and producers are

---

22   For example, Bourdieu and Haacke (1995, p. 10) observe that ultra-conservative US sena-
      tors during the 1980–90s 'made us recognize that free expression, even though guaranteed
      by the Bill of Rights, is by no means secure without the vigilance of a public that is ready
      to fight for it. The political climate of the country had deteriorated to the point that Con-
      gress passed an amendment, introduced by Helms, which prohibited public funds from
      being spent on "materials which in the judgment of the National Endowment for the Arts
      may be considered obscene." It was the first time since the establishment of NEA that
      political criteria were imposed on the professional review panels (SO). Limitations on the
      freedom of speech. According to the updated law of October 1990, the chairmen of the
      NEA must insure that the agency's decisions on awarding grants are "sensitive to the gen-
      eral standards of decency and respect and diverse beliefs of the American public." This
      vague formula resembles the (healthy popular sentiment) that the Nazis invoked when
      they purged German museums of "degenerate art". Also, Blee and Creasap (2010, p. 273)
      observe that 'foreshadowing a later move by Islamic fundamentalists across the globe,'
      the New Christian Right (NCR) in America 'campaigns against secular and liberal influ-
      ence in politics and cultural life ignited culture wars that raged for decades over issues as
      diverse as (sexually explicit art and the like)' at the beginning of the 21st century.

suppressed or constrained through censorship and self-censorship[23] on moralistic grounds[24] a la 'obscenity,' 'indecency,' human 'depravity,' 'corruption,' 'sins' and 'original sin,' and similar terms that Puritanism—following its parent Calvinism—and its heir revived Protestant evangelicalism tend to use, as do Islam and fascism, including Nazism. Calvinist Puritanism and American evangelicalism share with Islam and fascism a vehement and violent anti-artistic, anti-aesthetic, just as an anti-intellectual, anti-rationalistic, anti-liberal, and anti-democratic common denominator frequently overriding or mitigating their theological and ideological differences, religious and political rivalries, and military conflicts. For example, the US Supreme Court often plays the role of a supreme Puritan-style censor of artistic freedom and creativity in America by deciding what is art and not ('obscenity') through non-artistic judicial

---

23   Bourdieu and Haacke (1995, p. 10) note that in the US 'in order to avoid censorship, artists and institutions applying for public funds are now driven to exercise self-censorship. It is well-known that self-censorship is often more effective than open censorship,' implying that this also holds true, with minor variations, of scientists and scientific institutions. As a case or proxy of the mix of artistic censorship and self-censorship in the US culture industry, Adorno (1991, p. 105) remarks that 'cynical American film producers are heard to say that their pictures must take into consideration the level of eleven-year-olds. In doing so they would very much like to make adults into eleven-year-olds.'

24   Hull (1999, p. 3) reports that 'like speech, obscenity has also been the target of censorship in the United States. Books containing sexual references, whether works of literature like James Joyce's *Ulysses* or manuals on reproduction, were banned under an 1873 federal anti-obscenity law. Sexually explicit books have long created controversy in the United States.' Moreover, Hull (1999, p. 3) notes that even 'in the 1960s, some of the most censored titles included *Lady Chatterley's Lover, Tropic of Cancer*, and *Lolita*—all of which contain sexually explicit material. In the 1980s, the most frequent objections to books and other printed materials were based on the claim that their content was sexually explicit, profane, or obscene. With the passage of time, anti-obscenity laws in the United States evolved to the point where books like *Ulysses* could no longer be deemed obscene based on a few passages; instead, to be ruled obscene, a book had to be proven to have absolutely no redeeming artistic or literary merit. Obscenity is not protected by the First Amendment, but the courts have struggled to define obscenity and to distinguish it from constitutionally protected forms of speech.' Hull (1999, pp. 3–4) cites a recent example: 'In 1996 obscenity law was given a boost when Congress adopted the Communications Decency Act (CDA), which outlawed the distribution of pornography on the Internet. One year later, however, the Supreme Court declared the CDA unconstitutional.' Hull (1999, p. 4) concludes that 'though attempts at censorship occur frequently in US history, they tend to be reversed with comparable frequency,' yet these reversals do not preempt renewed, almost never-ending attempts in this direction, as exemplified by continuing 'Communications Decency Acts' in various new forms and disguises even if after the initial form(s) being proved unconstitutional and thus unlawful.

examination[25] reminiscent of the Inquisition's investigation of 'heresy,' as if it had nothing more important to perform in its function to uphold the Constitution, or perhaps because, for some of its ultra-conservative members, the latter entails no right to privacy and so the private pleasure or enjoyment[26] of art, entertainment, and life overall.

The above anti-artistic pattern has often reached the no-return point of banning and burning[27] 'obscene,' irreligious, and ideologically 'un-American' books and other artistic and intellectual products and producers through recurring 'witch-hunts,' as exemplified by the 'red scare,' McCarthyism, the war on drugs, alcohol, and other temperance wars, thus perpetuating the Puritan reproduction of 'witches' and 'witch trials' and recreating 'Salem with witches.'[28] And as noted, the burning and otherwise suppressing of artistic and other intellectual books and other works, including their libraries, represent an ultimate act of barbarism and primitivism reversing civilization. In particular, by virtue of being driven and justified by moralistic panics and religious hysterias, it provides an exemplar or expression of what Hume calls the Puritan and other 'madness

---

25   DiMaggio (1987, p. 451) observes that 'for a time, the US Supreme Court used a "redeeming-social-importance" standard to identify pornography, rendering the distinction between literature and smut a matter of judicial review,' so of heteronomous non-artistic rather than autonomous artistic judgment.

26   Mandel (2009, p. 1653) proposes that 'art owners take pleasure in its intrinsic value (e.g., for aesthetic pleasure or as a "storehouse" of an artist's deftness), and to the extent that it is a luxury good, they derive additional enjoyment from the signal of wealth that owning a masterpiece transmits. It is the mixture of pecuniary and nonpecuniary payoffs to ownership that makes artworks both compelling to purchase and difficult to value.'

27   Hull (1999, p. 50) observes that 'Senator Joseph McCarthy, chairman of the Senate Permanent Subcommittee on Investigations of the Committee on Government Operations, launches a crusade against communism in the United States government; books suspected of containing communist propaganda are burned in US information libraries abroad, and many of these libraries are closed.' Also, Hull (1999, pp. 53–55) notes that in 1989 'US Senator Jesse Helms attacks the National Endowment for the Arts for its funding of obscene art' and that in 1997 'after one scene in the film Tin Drum is declared obscene by an Oklahoma judge, police in Oklahoma City, Oklahoma, confiscate copies of the film from video store owners, libraries, and a citizen's home (sic).' Largely due to such moralistic attacks, as Throsby (1994, p. 21) registers, 'appropriations for the National Endowment for the Arts, the principal vehicle for direct central government financing of the arts, fell by about 30 percent in real terms' during the 1980s (and later), even if 'appropriations for State arts agencies nearly doubled in real terms over the same period.'

28   Putnam (2000, p. 355) uses the phrase 'Salem with witches' as an exemplar of intolerant 'sectarian community' with 'little liberty' exemplified by Salem and generally Puritan-rule New England during the 17th century.

with religious ecstasies' and Pareto puritanical 'insanity,' and in that sense a 'method to the madness' of an anti-artistic, anti-intellectual, anti-rationalistic, and anti-liberal pattern.

As implied above, a related indirect ground for the US estimate on artistic freedom is the exceptionally low public appreciation of the aesthetic arts, as indicated by the lowest government spending on and 'miserly attitude'[29] toward the latter, in America among Western societies. This non-artistic 'American exceptionalism' is primarily the legacy of anti-artistic Puritanism with its private and public 'religious ecstasies' substituting for artistic enjoyment and its moralistic 'insanity' equating such and related pleasures with and punishing them as grave crimes to the no-return point of death in the past and long imprisonment in the present.

Scientific Liberty

Therefore, the religiously, above all 'Puritanical,' determined[30] low degree of freedom in a potential life-saving or promoting field of science like stem-cell research provides a specific, partial ground for the qualitative evaluation of US scientific liberty through free empirical and theoretical research. The overall ground for the estimate consists of studies and reports suggesting that the degree of scientific/academic freedom overall in the US has been relatively low during most of its history[31] and even declining during recent times, above all

---

29   Scitovsky (1972, p. 68) observes that the US 'government's miserly attitude toward the arts is (the) integral part of a larger collective preference system,' mostly molded and sustained by Puritan-based cultural conservatism and thus an enduring ghost of anti-artistic and ultra-moralistic Puritanism condemning and suppressing the human enjoyment of art and life overall.

30   Mueller (2009, p. 392) refers to US religious extremists 'whose Puritanical beliefs cause hardship, suffering, and often death by denying others the possibility of having safe and cheap abortions (plus) means of birth control' and by implication the freedom of stem-cell and related life-saving research (also, Evans and Evans 2008). Blee and Creasap (2010, p. 272) observe that in the US 'conservative traditionalism is found in movements to ban the teaching of evolution and sex education in schools as antithetical to Biblical teachings (plus) to limit access to abortion, pornography, gambling, and prostitution as violations of morality, and they support the death penalty and other forms of harsh punishment for criminals as essential for a moral social order.' Also, Gauchat (2012, p. 171) registers that US 'religious groups clash with science over moral, epistemological, and ontological issues, such as Darwinian evolution, stem cell research, and AIDS research.'

31   ACADEME's report on academic freedom in 2009 finds that 'US professors feel less powerful (relative to administration and politics) than their colleagues abroad.' Moreover, it reports that 'US academics are (or perceive themselves to be) among the least powerful, especially compared with academics in other countries with mature higher education

the war on terror, just as its precedent the Cold War,[32] compared with most Western societies.

Moreover, it is strongly grounded in some accounts indicating that scientific freedom and even science itself is undermined, threatened, and attacked to the point of becoming the casualty or permanent target of what is identified as the conservative politicization and distrust of and 'war on science' in America with the resurgence of anti-science neo-conservatism[33] since the 1980s.

systems, such as Japan, Germany Italy, and Norway.' Coats (1967, 724) remarks that academic freedom 'never been the rule' in the US, and scientists the 'principal victims of public attacks' through various trials against free science and thought, including not only evolutionary biology but virtually all the 'ungodly' and/or 'un-American' natural and social sciences and scientists. Among these attacks and trials, the probably most notorious is the 1894 Richard Ely 'socialist' heresy trial. Pak (2007, p. 87) notes: 'Perhaps no other academic freedom case of this or any other period has provoked as much indignation and sympathy among subsequent generations of American academics as the Ely trial. Imagine a professor at a Midwestern state university who has been summoned to defend himself before an investigative committee and an open audience against the accusation by a state official that he was a socialist.' Pak (2007, p. 87) comments that (though questions) the 'usual interpretation of the case of Ely, a leftist economist (accused as a socialist) at the University of Wisconsin, is that it may have been among the worst infringement of academic freedom in history—a modern equivalent of Galileo's trial'. Pak (2007, p. 83) elaborates that the 'dispute over faculty governance and autonomy had a long history in America, going all the way back to the 17th century. Unlike the medieval universities, which originated as autonomous guilds of teachers or students in populous urban centers, American colleges and universities were artificial creations transplanted in the "wilderness," on the initiative of local dignitaries, magistrates, and church leaders. From the beginning they remained under the control of external governing boards, which usually delegated most of the governing duties to the administration. Under this arrangement, the faculty was liable to be treated as a body of hirelings doing contract labor. The faculty couldn't claim to be the university, in the sense that the medieval faculty of the University of Paris could.' No wonder, Richard Ely recounted 'when I first went to Germany I seemed to breathe a new and exhilarating atmosphere of freedom (which) did not exist in (American universities)' (cited in King 2004, p. 1).

32 Piketty (2014, p. 17) notes the pernicious effect of the Cold War on academic freedom in social science, including economics, in the US citing some influential economies theories—for example, the 'theory of the Kuznets curve' of diminishing income inequality in modern capitalism—as a 'product of the Cold War' through 'optimistic predictions' intending 'quite simply to maintain the underdeveloped countries within the orbit of the free world.'

33 Mooney (2005, p. 5) detects the conservative 'war on science' in America since the resurgence of neo-conservatism (the New Right) and explains this attack by that American conservatism intrinsically and vehemently opposes the 'dynamism of scientific inquiry—its constant onslaught on old orthodoxies, its rapid generation of new technological

At the minimum, in light of these observations, this holds true of the US South depicted as a region with the persistently lowest degree of academic as well as educational freedom, just as economic, political, and civil liberty, in the US since ante- and post-bellum times through these days, and even within Western world as a whole. For example, in spite or perhaps because of—in accordance with the inhumane Puritan-evangelical logic—its life-saving and other health benefits, free stem-cell and related research remains an absolute, unquestioned taboo and prohibition in the 'Christian' South, just as in Islamic Turkey and Catholic Poland, for 'holy' reasons, as does freedom of research in many other fields of natural and social science. To the extent the hyper-religious and ultra-conservative South substantially reduces the US estimate of this dimension of cultural liberty, just as does on artistic and other cultural liberties.

For example, almost equally as freedom of stem-cell research, scientific freedom is non-existent or extremely low in the following sociological and economic fields of research as proxy taboos within the US South from Tennessee to Texas, as compared to the other states, as well as Western societies or regions. The first field-taboo with no or low freedom of research is capitalist dictatorship in the form of plutocratic, oligarchic capitalism as the 'tyranny of wealth' and the generalized functional equivalent of slavery in the post-bellum South, in particular the persistent and even growing and severe oppression of labor reduced to a slave-like condition through low wages and benefits, and the prohibition and repression of labor unions. For example, hardly any researchers or academics in the South are permitted or willing, in a mixture

---

possibilities.' Examining and finding strong support for this thesis, Gauchat (2012, p. 171) refers to the observation that in the US the 'political neutrality of science began to unravel in the 1970s with the emergence of the new right (NR)—a group skeptical of organized science and the intellectual establishment in colleges and universities (and) closely aligned with the religious right (which) gained considerable political power with the election of President Reagan (while) the election of President George W. Bush in 2000 (marking) the start of the conservative "war on science."' In particular, Gauchat (2012, p. 168) notes that the neo-conservative 'administration under George W. Bush was widely seen as unfriendly toward the scientific community. As a consequence, many scientific organizations and advocacy groups became concerned that political and ideological interests were threatening the cultural authority of science.' Generally, Gauchat (2012, p. 184) finds that US 'conservatives were far more likely to define science as knowledge that should conform to common sense and religious tradition (and their) unfavorable attitudes are most acute in relation to government funding of science and the use of scientific knowledge to influence social policy,' envisioning that 'not only could growing conservative distrust of science threaten funding, it may also fundamentally transform how science is organized.'

of censorship and self-censorship, to investigate or question the Southern 'formula' of persistent poverty through slave-like low wages and labor oppression and union suppression, most notably the outlawing of unions and collective bargaining in public educational institutions (including universities and colleges at which they work) in most Southern states, with some rare exceptions (Florida until recently).

The second field-taboo with such (un)freedom is fundamentalist theocracy as the tyranny of the 'godly' and therefore exclusionary democracy in the South hence become the 'Bible Belt,' in particular the systematic, unapologetic, and perpetual oppression, exclusion, and discrimination against the 'godless,' i.e., non-believers, agnostics, secularists, liberals, progressive and the like, who, as told by Southern ruling evangelicals, 'need not apply' in the polity such as for political position or public office. For instance, not many researchers or academics in the South are allowed or disposed, again due to a censorship and self-censorship mix, to investigate or cast doubt on Southern theocratic 'godly' and thus repressive and exclusionary politics—with religion replacing race as the basis for oppression, discrimination, and exclusion—notably the non-believers 'need not apply' for political power long-standing rule, either as a written state-constitutional injunction or common political pressure and expectation.

The third, corollary field-taboo with the relative low freedom of research is religiously driven moralistic control, coercion, repression, and Draconian punishment for sins-as-crimes, including mass imprisonment and executions of sinners-criminals, not rarely of innocent persons (as proven after-the-fact by DNA and other evidence), and in that sense Puritan-rooted moral fascism in the South. For illustration, again not many researchers or academics in especially the 'deep' South, due to censorship or self-censorship, are permitted or willing to examine or cast doubt on Southern and national temperance wars such as the war on drugs, persistent alcohol prohibitions ('dry' counties) and restrictions (the 21-year age limit), the partial criminalizing of adultery, and other instances ('dumb laws') of Puritan-style moralistic coercion, repression, and punishment.

The fourth field-taboo perhaps with also a low, though slightly higher than the above, freedom of research or opinion is the Southern unique or pervasive compound of irrationalism and anti-rationalism, specifically religious superstition and anti-scientism, and in that sense the 'New Dark Ages' of ignorance-as-bliss or virtue, unreason and anti-science. For example, only some researchers or academics in the South can brave censorship or overcome self-censorship and investigate or openly question the Southern suppression of stem-cell and related research, biological evolution in favor of its anti-scientific opposites 'creationism' or 'intelligent design' and global warming theory or climate science subjected to official political prohibitions or denials due to a mix of anti-scientific 'godly' and narrow economic interests, especially plutocratic attacks and subversions. Thus, plutocratic attacks on and subversions of science (and education) in general have intensified and escalated in the US South and similar regions during recent years (especially since the 2010–14 Tea Party insurgence, influence and regional Dominance), targeting both physical and social sciences (e.g., at universities[34] in Florida, Oklahoma, etc.) and generally academic freedom. Such ant-science and anti-freedom plutocratic tendencies indicate that plutocracy becomes through a logic or escalation (or cancer-like metastasis) a lethal weapon against both natural and social science and thus academic freedom, just as against economic, political, and civil liberties, in the South and beyond in the US.

In sum, due to a mix of censorship and self-censorship, in the South scientific freedom or dissent is non-existent or lower than in the other regions and beyond not only in stem-cell research but also in the Southern 'holy' trinity of labor oppression and union suppression as the (patho)logical sequel of slavery, evangelical theocracy as 'holy' tyranny, terror, discrimination, and war, Puritan moral fascism, conjoined with the New Dark Ages of religious superstition and anti-science. All these represent potential social-science fields of investigation to be objectively treated as facts or 'things' in Durkheim's' sense, yet turned into proxy taboos, nearly prohibited subjects.

As a consequence, the US comparatively low estimate on scientific/academic freedom, just as on virtually all cultural as well as political, economic, and civic liberties and rights, is attributed to the persistent and solidifying backwardness of the South on this and all other dimensions of a free culture and society, thus to the factual co-existence and persistence of the 'two Americas' that are different and even opposite not just geographically but also in sociological terms of liberty. Counterfactually, 'controlling for' the South, the US estimate on scientific (like artistic) liberty, including that of stem-cell research, would be likely the same or comparable to the highest estimates of other Western and

---

34   For instance, the media reported in 2015 that an oil plutocrat effectively ordered even a public—not just private—University in Oklahoma to fire researchers because of their studying the observed connection between the dramatically increasing number (by several hundred times) of earthquakes in this state and this plutocratic and related activity (fracking, etc.). In another instance, reportedly other 'Big Brother' plutocrats decide which faculty to hire or fire in a proxy Orwellian manner in the economics department also at a public University in Florida depending on whether or not these economists adhere or not to the plutocratic, anarchic ('no government regulation') ideology and agenda.

related societies, for example, Canada, while with this region being equivalent to those of other countries like Mexico, etc. On this account, this region acts as the regional nemesis of the US in terms of scientific and virtually all cultural and social freedom, thus exacting perhaps 'Southern revenge' or 'justice' during post-bellum times, as discerned or implied in what many analysts detect as the 'Southernization' of America in culture, as well as politics, economy, and civil society, with the observed overwhelmingly pernicious and even lethal effects on the 'land of freedom.'

Educational Freedoms and Rights

As typical, the lowest 'acceptance of evolution' in the US among Western societies is to be primarily, although not exclusively, attributed to and found in the South cum the fundamentalist[35] 'Bible Belt' where evolution has been subject to multiple and continuous 'Monkey trials' since 1925 to these very days in various ways and means, for example, being banned in private religious schools, taught (rather distorted) along with creationism in public education, dismissed as 'just as theory,' etc.

Relatedly, the freedom and right of education in global warming is the weakest and most tenaciously denied or disputed in the US, at the minimum the South where it is virtually non-existent or a taboo due to the standard mix of religious superstition and anti-science politics with vested old-energy interests, among all Western and related societies. If so, this displays a kind of peculiar new 'American exceptionalism,' at least 'Southern pride,' even if this uniqueness in denying and opposing rational societal action on global warming may eventuate into its complete or partial perdition (New York's and

---

35   Miller, Scott, and Okamoto (2006, p. 765) observe that the 'acceptance of evolution is lower in the United States than in Japan or Europe, largely because of widespread fundamentalism and the politicization of science in the United States.' In general, Glenn (2011, p. 10) notes that 'there is no federal right to education, and education is not discussed in the US Constitution. In this regard, the US diverges from the international community; for example, the UN Declaration of Human Rights and the European Union Declaration of Rights both assert that education is a fundamental right.' Also, Mueller (2013, p. 16) remarks that 'in a famous (rather infamous) case, the US Supreme Court even granted Amish parents the right to deny their children any education beyond the eighth grade, so as to protect the children from exposure to ideas that might undermine their faith in the Amish religion. In so doing, the Court not only restricted the children's freedom to choose other religions, but greatly restricted their freedom to choose lifestyles other than the conservative lifestyle of the Amish.'

Florida's coastal cities,[36] New Orleans, etc.) or irreversible damage and suffering (e.g., Texas long draughts and present or impending water shortages).

Political Culture

As regards the US index on this dimension, it is in neither in the top ten nor in the bottom dozen countries and so somewhere in the middle, which probably supports or highlights the frequent observations or expectations that the level of democratic 'political culture' and by implication ideological freedom is not uniform or congruent in this country, but typically higher in the liberal North/ Coast, and lower in the ultra-conservative South and similar regions, which exemplifies the 'two Americas' in this respect. Moreover, in respect of liberal-democratic 'political culture' as the cultural foundation of democracy and ideological freedoms that is virtually non-existent or historically limited and weak in this region, the conservative 'Southern United States' appears (as Dahrendorf and other observers suggest) as if it were almost a different country from most other regions of the US, and not just from neighboring Canada, as does in almost all other cultural as well as political, economic and civic respects.

36　As an instance of potential perdition by conservative anti-science superstition, in May 2015 the media reported—with a headline 'sea rise threatens Florida coast, but no state-wide plan'—that 'America's oldest city is slowly drowning. St. Augustine's centuries-old Spanish fortress sits feet from the encroaching Atlantic, whose waters already flood the city's narrow streets about 10 times a year—a problem worsening as sea levels rise.' Further, it is reported that 'St. Augustine is one of many chronically flooded communities along Florida's coast, and officials in these diverse places share a concern: They're afraid their buildings and economies will be further inundated by rising seas in just a couple of decades. The effects are a daily reality in much of Florida. Drinking water wells are fouled by seawater. Higher tides and storm surges make for more frequent road flooding from Jacksonville to Key West, and they're overburdening aging flood-control systems. But the state has yet to offer a clear plan or coordination to address what local officials across Florida's coast see as a slow-moving emergency. (The conservative Governor) is skeptical of man-made climate change and has put aside the task of preparing for sea level rise. Despite warnings from water experts and climate scientists, skepticism over sea level projections and climate change science has hampered planning efforts at all levels of government, the records showed. Florida's environmental agencies under (the Governor) have been downsized, making them less effective at coordinating sea level rise planning in the state, documents showed.' If this is not a paradigmatic exemplar of impending or prospective perdition of a region or city and perhaps in extension a state within a society due to anti-science mostly religious superstition, then one wonders what it is.

The Civic Condition and Indicator of Modern Free Society—A Free Civil Society

Conditions and Indicators of Free Civil Society

Axiomatically and actually, a free civil society constitutes yet another, more specifically civic condition, element, and indicator of modern free society in mutual connection and reinforcement with a free polity, economy, and culture. Despite their almost identical designations, a free civil society does not exhaust modern free society, just as neither do political democracy, a free economy, and a free culture taken separately and in isolation from the rest of the latter as a as a whole. It represents the civil subsystem, the privacy sphere of modern free society as the total social system defined by a societal complex of holistic liberty, just as these are its respective political, economic, and cultural subsystems and liberties. While self-evident and redundant to state for sociologists, this is important to emphasize to avoid methodological reductionism by reducing modern free society and so its complex of holistic liberty to only one of its conditions and components, though such a fallacy is committed less through its reduction to a free civil society or a free culture than to democracy by many political scientists and politicians and to a free economy, specifically capitalism, by most, especially 'libertarian,' economists.

The preceding leads to deciphering and considering the specific conditions, elements, and indicators of a free civil society thus understood. Generally, these conditions consist of a set of comprehensive, universal, and equal individual liberties, choices, rights, and privacy. Such a set of liberties defines and typifies a free civil society as an autonomous private sphere of life—usually called by sociologists and other analysts the 'life-world'[1]—in relation to the public domain, coercion, and control of the political system and the economic existential compulsion and imperatives of the economy, simply, independent

---

1 Especially Habermas (2001) uses and elaborates on the concept of a 'life-world'—a term implicit in earlier sociologists like Tönnies, Simmel, Weber and his followers Husserl and Schutz, etc.—to characterize civil society in the sense of everyday private or individual activities and experiences. Garcelon (2010, p. 342) comments that a life world is a 'phenomenological concept postulated by Alfred Schutz and developed by Jürgen Habermas to trace a "horizon of relevance" orienting everyday practices in a given social group at a given time.'

from both state repression and intrusion and excessive market/money influence and interference.[2]

Like their political and economic variants, the comprehensiveness, universality, and equality of individual liberties, choice and rights, thus free civil society, derives from and realizes Enlightenment all-encompassing liberalism, universalism, and egalitarianism in respect of personal liberty, choice, and privacy, and its resultant, the principle of universal, equal liberty for all individuals and groups. On this account, notably its concept of individual liberty and choice independent from both an oppressive state and a theocratic church, the Enlightenment can be considered the main philosophical source and justification of modern free civil society, just as of liberal democracy, a free economy, and a free culture, and modernity overall commonly regarded as its offspring.[3] Moreover, the Enlightenment movement constituted a sort of free micro-civil society in itself, as exemplified in Paris' salons as 'the civil working spaces of the project of Enlightenment.'[4]

As with respect to democracy and a free economy, at this point the analysis remains provisionally agnostic concerning what a free civil society in the sense of a private-life sphere separate and autonomous from politics, religion, and the economy precisely represents or becomes within modern free society. One 'does not know' yet whether it is a liberal-secular civil society or instead

---

2 In particular, Habermas (2001, pp. 87, 153) registers the tendency to the invasion (or colonization) of the life-world by the capitalist economy and the state as 'self-regulating systems steered by money and administrative power.' Moreover, Habermas (2001, pp. 87, 153) proposes that 'social pathologies arise only as a consequence of an invasion of exchange relations and bureaucratic regulation' of the life-world, i.e., the 'reckless monetarization of the lifeworld' and the spilling-over of 'administrative power.'

3 Dombrowski (2001, p. 9) describes 'Enlightenment liberalism' as 'comprehensive' by encompassing all the domains of society, thus including its civil sphere. Habermas (2001, p. 132) regards liberal modernity as a 'child of the Enlightenment.' Mannheim (1986, p. 55) observes that liberalism as the theory of 'principle of liberty' is premised on the Enlightenment, by contrast to conservatism resting 'primarily on romanticism' and medievalism generally. Mueller (2013, p. 4) observes that 'out of the Enlightenment came, therefore, a movement for a separation of Church and State, and a weakened role for the Church.' Also, he notes that 'with the help of the Enlightenment thinkers, Europeans came to the realization during the eighteenth century that religious differences were not worth killing and dying for' (Mueller 2013, p. 17).

4 Garrard (2003, p. 23) notes that 'of the many voluntary associations that made up eighteenth-century French civil society, the preferred habitat of the Enlightenment société de penser were the salons, "the civil working spaces of the project of Enlightenment."' The most prominent of these in Paris after 1750 was that of the Baron d'Holbach, whose biweekly dinners at his home earned him the title of 'maître d'Hotel de la Philosophie.'

its anti-liberal and religiously determined or theocentric alternatives. The conditions, elements, and indicators of a free civil society are classified and considered next (Table 8.1).

The first and overarching, almost axiomatic condition and indicator of a free civil society represents comprehensive private liberty and personal choice in social-moral and related relations, as distinct from, though often related to, political and economic matters. Therefore, this condition encompasses social-moral liberties, choices, rights, and responsibilities of individuals, the degree of freedom and scope of choice in their private life sphere. In the limiting case, it reaches the point of personal freedom of choice between 'sainthood' and 'sin'—being a 'saint or sinner'—'virtue' and 'vice' in terms of morality, thus morally 'right' and 'wrong' actions.[5] In this sense, a critical condition and indicator of free civil society is the comprehensive, universal, and unrestricted individual freedom of choice between alternative courses of moral action, more specifically 'moral' action proper and its alternatives. This is consistent with the fact and on the ground that in a free civil society morality regulates and sanctions individual conduct only according to its inner freedom, logic, and sanction of conscience.[6]

---

5 While like his colleague Mises and all 'libertarian' economists extolling economic freedom as primary and determining of all others, Hayek (1960, p. 79) proposes that 'moral esteem would be meaningless without freedom' and the 'freedom of action that is the condition of moral merit includes the freedom to act wrongly,' though he incorrectly attributes such freedom only to unregulated capitalism and denies it exists in its regulated welfare counterpart, which is contradicted by what Samuelson (1964, 1983) observes as the highest degree of his freedom in Scandinavian and other welfare states.

6 Simmel (1955, p. 95) suggests that 'morality has no other sanction than the individual's conscience' and thus nothing to do with forces outside the latter, in particular with religion and politics, church and state sanctions or laws. If so, this exposes what Pareto (1935, p. 1608) detects as the Puritan-rooted US government practice of enforcing 'morality by law' through criminalizing various sins (from Prohibition to the war on drugs) as effectively violating the essence of morality—and in that sense being immoral as well as futile in the long run—just as such enforcement of religious belief violates the nature of religion as voluntary and individual. In Simmel's terms, the enforcement of morality as well as faith by law violates the freedom of the 'individual's conscience,' which Puritanism/Calvinism self-righteously and vehemently demanded for itself when not in power (as in France, pre-Calvinist Holland, Anglican England, etc.), but systematically and unapologetically denied to others after capturing the state and instituting theocracy, as in New England and through evangelicalism the 'Bible Belt' and 'evangelical America.' Kaplan (2002, p. 18) observes that Calvinism's 'love' for freedom of conscience 'did not necessarily translate into "liberality," a willingness to grant others the freedom you demand for yourself.' The identical or similar pattern of demanding for itself and denying to others freedom of individual conscience is observed in Islam,

TABLE 8.1   *Conditions and indicators of free civil society.*

Comprehensive private liberty, personal choice, and privacy in social/moral matters
    Freedom of choice between ('saint and sinner') 'virtue' and 'vice'

Personal bodily liberties, choices, and rights
    Freedom of birth control
    Freedom of abortion

Personal freedom, choice, and right of alcohol production, distribution and consumption
    Unrestricted freedom of alcohol consumption after a certain age
    Low, reasonable age limits for alcohol consumption

Freedom of production, distribution, and consumption of drugs and related substances
    Freedom of consumption and possession of non-medical and medical drugs
    Partial 'free enterprise' in the production and distribution of non-medical drugs

Individual sexual freedoms
    Personal freedom of premarital sex
    Personal freedom of extramarital sex
    Personal freedom of homosexuality
    Personal freedom of adult entertainment
    Personal freedom of the 'oldest profession'

Freedom from personal violence and death, the right to life, property, and happiness
    Freedom from the aggressive use or threat of weapons and other means of personal violence
    The state of civilized society vs. the 'state of nature,' the law of civility and non-violence
    Freedom from random death, the right to life, property, and happiness
    The civil freedom and right to 'live and let live'

Hence, it is self-sufficient and autonomous or growingly separating and diverging from religion or church with its characteristic fears or hopes of 'Divine' punishment or reward[7] and from politics or the state and its legal norms and punishments, including its criminalizing and harshly punishing moral sins, as done in moralistic and theocratic states. In this sense, in free civil society individual moral action is intrinsically self-determined and self-regulated by conscience (including remorse) as its own reward or punishment rather than being determined by religion or Divine punishment and reward and enforced and sanctioned by laws. The latter precisely defines its unfree opposites, above all moralistic theocracies resorting to what J.S. Mill and Pareto identify as equating pleasures/sins with grave crimes,[8] as in medieval monasticism and

---

which thus appears as a functional equivalent of Puritanism/Calvinism and evangelicalism in this and related respects like religious revolutions and wars, as Weber observes. In turn, Puritanism/Calvinism and its heir evangelicalism, like Islam, construe Simmel's 'individual's conscience' as religiously predetermined, God's inscribed Christian or Islamic 'conscience,' and thus effectively denies or perverts freedom of conscience, claiming that there is no thing as non-religious, i.e., non-Christian and non-Islamic 'conscience.' Relatedly, they tend to deny or pervert religious liberty into Christian and Islamic 'liberty' essentially understood and practiced as the 'license to kill' or oppress, exclude, and discriminate against non-Christian and non-Islamic 'infidels,' notably liberals, secularists, progressives, and the like, let alone non-believers and agnostics No wonder that Mueller (2009) identifies Puritan-rooted American evangelicalism and Islamic fundamentalism as the twin major mortal enemy and danger to modern liberal democracy and civil society, political freedom as well as individual liberty. Moreover, Mueller (2009) observes that whenever and wherever 'Puritanical' American evangelicalism and Islamic fundamentalism prevail, as in 'evangelical America' and Muslim theocracies since the 1980s, liberal democracy and civil society, i.e., political freedom and individual liberty, are effectively extinguished or perverted.

7 Also, Mueller (2009, p. 392) suggests that 'if religion strengthens moral convictions, it should produce morally superior behavior—a lower proclivity to commit crime, for example. In the US state-level evidence suggests a negative correlation between church attendance and various crime statistics.' Mueller (2009, p. 394) elaborates that the US 'stands out as a dramatic outlier (in) the homicide rate. Attending church regularly and believing that God is very important to their lives does not appear to make Americans less likely to murder one another than people in other rich countries but quite the reverse. One reason for the high homicide rates in the US is, of course, the Constitution Second Amendment, which makes it easier for Americans to acquire guns than in most other developed countries. This does not save the hypothesis that religion makes people behave morally, however, because a religious person who believes that God forbids killing should presumably not use a gun to kill his neighbor just because he owns one.'

8 Referring to the 'fanatical moral intolerance of the Puritans' and their suppression of 'all public, and nearly all private, amusements,' J.S. Mill (1991, p. 77) suggests 'mind their own business is precisely what should be said to every government and every public, who have the

Calvinist Puritanism, and consequently severely punishing them and their enjoyers through the state enforcement of moral conduct, i.e., the government coercion of individuals and thus civil society into morality by legal rules and sanctions.

To that extent, morality, like civil society overall, becomes within modern free society the only or most suitable sphere where the laissez-faire principle of personal liberty and privacy unrestricted by state repression and intrusion and religious coercion and invasion truly holds and is sustained. This is by analogy, but not equation and even in contrast, to the economy/market in view of, by virtue of being a public domain, its external societal consequences (externalities) that are by definition and in reality non-existent or minimal in their physical forms[9] in the private life sphere. That is what the inventor of the phrase and doctrine, a 18th century French Enlightenment philosopher precisely meant when stating that 'laissez-faire should be the principle of all public power since the world has been civilized'[10]—i.e., primarily civil, moral, thus non-economic and secondarily, if at all, market, economic laissez-faire.

---

pretension that no person shall enjoy any pleasure which they think wrong.' Pareto (2000, p. 106) remarks that 'religious and sectarian sentiments can be decried' in various 'follies' and 'certain men experience great delight in tormenting themselves and others.' Pareto (2000, p. 107) as an example cites the Scotch Presbyterian clergy noting that 'according to their code,' 'all the natural affections, all the pleasures of society, all the pastimes, all the gay instincts of the human heart were so many sins.'

9   Mueller (2013, p. 9) remarks that 'harmful actions (cause) negative externalities (i.e.) physical damage. Traditionally, in economics, negative externalities have been thought of as causing physical damage—the smokey factory soils the laundry's wash etc.' In turn, he suggests that 'religious beliefs are a great source of psychological externalities. The religious person sees someone dressed in a "wanton" manner and becomes offended. Even contemplating an action by others, say two homosexuals having a sexual relationship, can distress a person with strong religious convictions. Thus, religious beliefs have led those holding them to demand, and often obtain, legislation restricting the freedom to act of other individuals, even when the prohibited actions cause no physical harm' (Mueller 2013, p. 9).

10   Keynes (1972, p. 278) reports that 'the first writer to use the phrase laissez-faire in clear association with the doctrine was the Marquis d'Argenson about 1751,' an Enlightenment philosopher, citing the French original *Laissez-faire, telle devrait etre la devise de toute puissance publique, depuis que le monde est civilize* (laissez-faire should be the maxim of all public power since the world has been civilized), and not the 'British political economists' like Adam Smith. Similarly, Hicks (1969, pp. 97.-8) comments that the 'liberal or non-interference principles were not economic principles; they were an application to economics of principles that were thought to apply over a much wider field. The contribution that economic freedom made for economic efficiency was no more than a secondary support.'

On account of such near-zero or minimal adverse external consequences of the individual freedom of moral choice between 'sainthood' and 'sins,' 'virtues' versus 'vices,' the argument for laissez-faire in morality[11] seems more compelling than in the economy/market where if the latter is totally unregulated such negative 'externalities' for society tend to be more numerous or severe, including lethal. The case is stronger because morality is intrinsically the most private realm of life, that of what can be called the individual 'soul'[12] with no or minimal 'spillovers' to society or interferences with other individuals' liberties and lives[13] and precisely because of the liberal principle of universal, equal freedom. By contrast, the economy/market represents a public setting (the 'market square') generating often negative external consequences and thus requiring extraneous societal, including state, intervention and regulation.[14] Pragmatically, what Americans and Westerners call 'home sweet home' as the

---

11   According to Popper (1973, p. 109) liberal theory 'has nothing to do with the *policy of strict non-intervention* (often, but not quite correctly, called *"laissez faire"*). Liberalism and state-interference (in economy) are not opposed to each other.' Popper (1973, p. 137) observes that 'laissez-faire capitalism being replaced by interventionism' such that economic policy *'laissez-faire* has disappeared from the face of the earth,' thus unwittingly agreeing with Keynes' (1972) diagnosis even prior (in 1926) to the Great Depression of the 'end of *laissez-faire*' as the ultimate case of this economic catastrophe, just as for that matter, its proxy sequel the Great Recession as suggested by Akerlof and Shiller (2009), De Long (1996), Eggertsson (2008), Stiglitz (2010) and other contemporary economists. Notably, Popper (1973, p. 237) recommends that the moral ('higher') values 'should very large be considered (state) "non-agenda", and should be left to the realm of *laissez-faire*,' thus in apparent contrast to the economy and markets.

12   Simmel (1955, p. 25) proposes that the 'deepest and finest content' of morality or ethic consists in the 'behavior of the individual soul in and to itself, which does not enter into its external relations' both to society, notably the state, and to the divine, thus having nothing to do with politics and religion, (positive) laws and religious dogmas and their sanctions or punishments.

13   Mueller (2009, p. 13) observes that 'in a liberal democracy citizens not only participate in a democratic process but also get great freedoms to think and do as they please' so long as they do not constrain or interfere with such freedom of others, thus having no negative externalities for a free civil society. In this connection, Mueller (2009,17) cites J.S. Mill's statement that 'liberalism (is) the liberty to do, think and say what one wants so long as the exercise of such liberty does not do undue harm to other.'

14   For example, Mankiw (2013, pp. 32–33) admits that the 'role of government arises as the economy departs from this classical benchmark (of competitive equilibrium without any without any externalities or public goods). Pigovian taxes and subsidies are necessary to correct externalities, and progressive income taxes can be justified to finance public goods based on the benefits principle. Transfer payments to the poor have a role as well, because fighting poverty can be viewed as a public good.'

epitome of the private moral sphere of life and the microcosm of civil society is 'sweet' because or insofar as it entails comprehensive, universal, unrestricted, and inviolable personal liberties and choices a la laissez-faire so long as they do not interfere with or restrict those of other individuals in virtue of the principle of equal freedom in contrast to the economy/market and the polity/state as public spheres.[15] In this respect, a condition and indicator of a free civil society is that people's homes form the genuine oasis or island of individual freedom of choice between alternative 'right' and 'wrong' moral actions, including sins- and non-sins, virtues and vices, and in that sense the genuine and sole domain of laissez-faire, thus being the 'non-agenda' of the modern state,[16] just as of a pre-modern theocratic church-state. Negatively stated, therefore a definite condition and indicator of a free civil society is that private homes are not subject to intrusion, invasion, interference, control, or surveillance by state and/or church on any grounds, from 'patriotism' and 'national security' to 'greater than humans and life' moralistic and religious justifications.

Generally, its negative condition and indicator is *no* criminalization and punishment of sins and vices (alcohol, drugs, abortion, pre- and extra-marital sex, homosexuality, prostitution, pornography, etc.) as morally 'wrong' and religiously proscribed 'ungodly' behaviors, because such penal practices deny and suppress the personal freedom of choice between alternative moral actions and privacy defining and constituting a free civil society. A free civil society is precisely typified by that various human sins and vices—what Pareto calls personal sensual and related 'pleasures,' including 'sexual enjoyments'[17]

---

15   This is what essentially Habermas suggests by his consistent, clear, and relative sharp differentiation between the 'life-world' and 'system,' the first primarily referring to the private sphere and the second to economic and political spheres. Specifically, Habermas (2001, p. 152) proposes that the 'rationalization of the life world' is different from 'rationalizing economic or administrative activities or their action systems' in that it 'encompasses the three components of cultural traditions, socialization of individuals and social integration.' In turn, Habermas (2001, p. 53) suggests that economy and politics as 'functionally integrated action systems transformed themselves into self-regulating systems steered by money and administrative power' and notably that the 'balance tips to the negative when (these systems) spill over into the life-world's core areas.'

16   Keynes (1972, p. 288), referring to Bentham, suggests to 'distinguish afresh the Agenda of government from the Non-Agenda, and the task of politics is to devise forms of government within a democracy which shall be capable of accomplishing the Agenda,' and Popper (1973, p. 237) that the moral values 'be considered' 'non-agenda.'

17   An implied rationale why sensual and other pleasures are not criminalized, penalized, and coercively suppressed in a free civil society is that for Pareto (1932, p. 1577) the 'desire for sexual enjoyments (plus material goods) is almost constant.'

(the 'sex residue')—no longer are legally prohibited and severely punished by
state, even if condemned and proscribed by church on the assumption of a
formal or effective differentiation between politics and religion. If they are, in
so doing the moralistic state—typically fused with or controlled by church—
eliminates a free civil society as an independent sphere of individual liberty
and privacy epitomized by private home, notably the freedom of choice between alternative courses of moral action, including pleasures or sins and non-
sins, or perverts it into a proxy all-embracing monastery and a total open (and
true) prison.

Equating pleasures and sins with crimes and punished severely represents
the shared historical Calvinist, particularly Puritan, and Islamic (as Weber[18]
suggests in his comparative sociology of religion), and consequently the common contemporary evangelical and Islamist pattern and syndrome. Such a
puritanical syndrome (in the general sense) acts as the theocratic-moralistic
deadly poison of a free civil society, notably personal freedom of choice and privacy, thus of the autonomy and inviolability of private home, just as of liberal-
secular democracy. On account of such a lethal effect on a free civil society,
historically what were Calvin's Geneva in the 16th century and Puritan-ruled
England and New England (e.g., Salem) in the 17th century and Mohammad's
Medina[19] and medieval Islam overall (as Weber observes) are today Islamic
fundamentalism[20] in various Muslim countries or regions and Puritan-rooted

---

18   This is what Weber (1968, p. 594) suggests by observing that 'inner-worldly asceticism
     reached a similar solution (like Islam) wherever, as in radical Calvinism, it represented
     as God's will the domination over the sinful world by religious virtuosi belonging to the
     "pure" church.'

19   In Weber's (1968, p. 444) view, like Calvinism 'the religion of Muhammad' is 'fundamen-
     tally political in its orientation,' with 'his position in Medina' being almost the same as
     that of 'Calvin at Geneva.' Thus, Weber (1968, p. 574) observes that 'Calvin and Muham-
     mad, each of whom (was) convinced that the certainty of one's own mission in the world
     came not from any personal perfection but from his situation in the world and from god's
     will.'

20   Mansbach (2006, p. 112) considers Calvinism a historical 'precedent' for contemporary
     Islamic radicalism, noting that, for example, in Geneva under Calvin's theocratic rule
     'taverns were banned temporarily, and gambling was forbidden much as Afghanistan's
     Taliban banned all outward shows of luxury and entertainment during their reign. Begin-
     ning in 1545, church officials began visiting private homes to determine citizens' moral
     rectitude, and, like Iran's and Saudi Arabia's religious police, reported any offenses.' Also,
     Mansbach (2006, p. 113) observes that 'Calvinism would then make its way to the New
     World with the Puritans. Its legacy continues to motivate many US evangelicals in their
     efforts to infuse politics and government with religion. Fundamentalism, after all, is not
     unique to Islam and can be seen today in evangelical Christianity (etc.).'

evangelicalism in Western societies, above all 'conservative America' and in part Great Britain.

In relation to a free civil society, comparatively what Islamic fundamentalism is and does in its settings revived evangelicalism is and does in these Western societies (first and foremost, the US South cum the 'Bible Belt'). In this respect, Calvinism, including Puritanism, and Islam constitute the historical (as in Weber's context), and contemporary Islamic fundamentalism and revived evangelicalism comparative, functional equivalents by exerting the identical 'function' (effect) of negating and destroying a free civil society, just as liberal-secular democracy. The shared Puritan-Islamic, Evangelical-Islamist (and any religious) syndrome of equating sensual pleasures and sins, most notably 'sexual enjoyments,' with crimes invariably subject to Draconian punishment to the point of death far from being neutral to or compatible with (as believed in evangelical America) civil society ultimately poisons and destroys it, just as liberal-secular democracy and modern free society. To understand and explain the common Evangelical-Islamist syndrome of criminalizing and severely punishing pleasures or sins (above all 'sexual enjoyments,' plus alcohol, drugs, etc.) and thus suppressing individual liberty and privacy constitutive of a free civil society requires taking account of the shared historical pattern and precedent of Calvinism, including Puritanism, and Islam, such as Calvin's Geneva, Puritan New England, medieval Islamic states, etc.

The preceding suggests that what typifies a free civil society, as well as a genuine democratic state in moral terms, is that the latter as a rule does not criminalize pleasures or sins and severely punish them through the legal-penal system but only does so with respect to anti-social and violent behaviors.[21] Conversely, a free civil society is effectively vanished without trace or dramatically subverted beyond doubt and recognition through what Pareto observes as government coercively enforcing 'morality by law' resulting in 'malignant power' and 'gross abuses of power,' typifying undemocratic and illiberal, especially moralistic and religiously grounded, states.[22]

---

21   Tönnies (2001, p. 255) observes that 'inner morality is hardly a direct concern of the (modern) state. Its task is only to suppress and punish aggressive and anti-social behavior (on the conclusion that) dead morality and religion cannot be revived by coercion or education.'

22   Pareto (1935, p. 1608) predicts that 'uses and abuses of power will be the greater, the more extensive the government's interference in private (life),' particularly observing that in the 'United States where the government tries to enforce morality by law, one notes gross abuses that are not observable in countries where there are no such restrictions.' Moreover, Pareto (1935, p. 1429) observes in the US a 'mass of hypocritical laws for the enforcement of morality that are replicas of laws of the European Middle Ages (sic).' Akin to

This means that the most moralistic ('moral'), ascetic states are actually the least moral in the sense of human or the most immoral-inhuman, simply the 'worst,'[23] in terms of human liberty and dignity and humane life as the essence of morality. This is epitomized by governments under Calvinism (Calvin's Geneva, etc.), including Puritanism (Salem, New England), Islam (Mohammad's Medina and medieval Muslim states), revived evangelicalism and sectarianism (the US 'Bible Belt,' Mormon-ruled Utah), Islamic fundamentalism (Taliban, etc.). No wonder, most proponents and defenders of a free civil society and liberal-secular democracy, notably the Enlightenment figures from Voltaire, Condorcet, and Hume to Jefferson and Madison, repudiate such moralistic and theocratic governments, particularly the Calvinistic-Puritan vision of 'Christian Sparta' (Geneva, New England, and America), as effectively immoral through depreciating and eliminating human liberty, dignity, joy, and life, and Calvinism overall on moral grounds as deeply inhuman, as Franklin[24] does, for example.

Therefore, this condition and indicator of a free civil society involves the effective existence and legal protection of privacy in personal morality and life generally, and in that sense the 'peace of mind' undisturbed, unthreatened, and unconstrained by state surveillance and invasion, religious coercion and intrusion, as well as market-economic compulsion and imperatives. Legally, in a free civil society conjoined with liberal democracy moral and all-encompassing privacy is invariably enshrined in the constitution and other

---

Pareto, Popper (1973, p. 237) argues that 'the use of political (and legal) means for imposing our scale of values upon others is a different matter,' specifically inadmissible in and incompatible with a free open society, notably its civil sphere.

23   This is what US critical journalist Mencken implies in his oft-cited observation that 'the worst government is often the most moral. One composed of cynics is often very tolerant and humane. But when fanatics are on top there is no limit to oppression,' particularly referring to Puritan-evangelical governments. Thus, Mencken (1982, pp. 624–25) describes *Puritanism* as the 'haunting fear that someone, somewhere, may be happy' suggesting 'show me a Puritan and I'll show you a (SOB),' and considers its sequel 'evangelical Christianity' to be 'founded upon hate.' In passing, the 'show me a Puritan and I'll show you a (SOB)' maxim was confirmed by some US Southern Puritanical evangelicals being depicted by some of their colleagues as the 'miserable SOB' (and 'Lucifer in the flesh') during the 2010s.

24   According to Slack (2013, pp. 364–65), Franklin relinquishes Calvinism because in the latter 'God's omnipotence negated the order of nature and the agency of man (i.e.) the capacity of human reason.' Likening Calvinism to idolatry, Franklin opines: 'Surely it is not more difficult to believe the World was made by a God of Wood or Stone, than that the God who made the World should be such a God as this.'

legal documents, and substantively is effectively protected and promoted and its violations prevented or sanctioned.

Minimally, this entails *no* Orwellian totalitarian surveillance, control, constraint, repression, and punishment of individuals' 'immoral' private, especially intimate, lives, enjoyments, and activities through the government enforcing of morality and punishing of immorality by moralistic and religiously based anti-privacy laws and penal systems. For instance, global privacy rankings can be taken to indicate the extent to which Western and related societies, specifically their states, legally recognize and effectively protect individuals' private liberties and choices in moral and other life, as the crucial condition, ingredient, and indicator of a free civil society.

As a corollary and particular application of the first, the second condition, element, and indicator of a free civil society comprises personal bodily liberties, choices, and rights. Generally, this is the freedom of choice with respect to the physical dimension of individuals, specifically the right of free possession, control, and use one's own body according to their needs, preferences, and decisions.[25] In particular, this condition consists of the freedom of choice with respect to human reproduction in the sense of the private liberty and right to procreation and to non-procreation alike. Negatively stated, it means that a free civil society is characterized with that individuals and families are not prohibited and punished by the state and its laws and penal system either in spontaneous and unrestricted procreation or in deliberate and unconstrained non-procreation. More specifically, this condition incorporates the comprehensive freedom and right of birth control and family planning and thus of controlled and planned biological reproduction, simply reproductive liberties and rights. The condition also involves the freedom of choice between procreation and non-procreation as presumably 'right' and 'wrong' alternative types of moral decisions and actions, including the right to the second decision and action. The latter thus signifies in a free civil society individuals are granted legally recognized and effectively protected freedom and right of 'abortion' as the particular form and expression of that of possession, management, and employment of their own bodies as they need, prefer, and decide.

Within a free civil society, the freedom of choice in this and any respects overrides any principles and activities denying and suppressing such and other individual liberties and choices, specifically the religiously construed 'right

---

25 Tönnies (2001, p. 189) defines individual freedom 'either as possession of one's *own* body and its organs or as power over one's own actions,' and Giddens (1984, p. 186) suggests that personal liberty includes free possession and management of the 'physical qualities of the body.'

to life' for the *un*born—yet denying or suppressing such rights for the born like the 'godless,' etc.—while in unfree (so 'uncivil') societies being overridden by this spurious 'right.' At this juncture, a free civil society is diagnosed or expected with a high degree of certainty if the freedom and right of 'abortion' is allowed and protected, for this expresses and realizes the free possession, management, and employment of one's own body, and conversely, its unfree alternatives by the absence or suppression of such and related reproductive liberties and rights (e.g., birth control, family planning, etc.).

Consequently, free Western and related civil societies are observed or predicted to have 'abortion' and related reproductive freedoms and rights, and their unfree alternatives lacking or suppressing them through moralistic and theocratic or religious negation and suppression. On this account, the freedom of choice in relation to 'abortion' appears as perhaps the single most salient and disputed proof, indicator, or test of modern free civil society, as well as liberal-secular democracy. The above far from being either a value-laden defense of or attack on 'abortion' is a factual statement that the freedom of choice and right of it derives from that of possession, management, and employment of one's own body, i.e., personal bodily liberties, choices, and rights as the specific constitutive condition, element, and indicator of a free civil society.

The third condition, element, and indicator of a free civil society represents the corollary and particular application of the first and to some degree of the second—i.e., the personal freedom of choice in the specific domain of alcohol production, distribution, and consumption. This holds true insofar as alcohol production, distribution, and consumption is in virtually all societies and times—with Islamic, Calvinist-Puritan, evangelical, and other ascetic aberrations—not only a basic economic activity and so an elemental aspect of consumer freedom and choice, as it tends to be in a pure market economy/capitalism without anti-alcohol moralistic and religious exhortations and prohibitions or restrictions. Furthermore, especially alcohol consumption becomes a pertinent and often controversial or sensible moral decision and action so long as such an economic activity is also considered an example of the general pattern of freedom of choice between—from the moralistic viewpoint—morally 'right' and 'wrong' or alternative conducts, 'virtue' and 'vice' or 'sin' (simply, drinking and non-drinking respectively).

At first sight, this seems to be a trivial and even redundant and bizarre condition, element, and indicator of a free civil society, as has increasingly become in contemporary Western and related societies. However, this impression is not necessarily correct, as indicated by that at least some of these societies— or certain regions within them—continue to treat alcohol as a non-trivial and even serious and grave matter to be condemned, prohibited or restricted and its production, distribution, and consumption legally punished on various moralistic and religious grounds. This is exemplified by alcohol legal, moreover constitutional, puritanical Prohibition with its harsh penalties for drinking violations (up to life in prison) and its various regional vestiges in the US until the present, especially in the evangelical South, as well as its also total prohibitions and severe punishments in most Islamic countries. This indicates that if puritanical America, notably the evangelical South (and Mormon-ruled Utah, etc.), and Islamic theocracies, thus Puritanism or evangelicalism and Islam, converge and agree on anything in the context of civil society, it is the historical and current prohibition or restriction and Draconian punishment of alcohol, though this is not the only instance of their convergence that extends to prohibiting and punishing virtually all sensual pleasures (especially 'sexual enjoyment' for others, plus drugs, etc.). On this account, the personal freedom, choice, and right of alcohol production, distribution, and consumption as a specific seemingly trivial condition, element, and indicator of a free civil society is not as completely established, protected, and unproblematic yet—at least in Puritan-rooted evangelical and Islamic countries or regions—as it perhaps appears especially in European civil societies.

This condition of a free civil society incorporates free alcohol production, distribution, and consumption in general as a private moral as well as economic freedom, the exercise and domain of privacy in personal morality, just as business entrepreneurship and consumer choice. Negatively, it entails *no* moralistic and religiously driven prohibitions or excessive restrictions and punishment of this activity by government (e.g., banning or restricting alcohol sale and consumption on specific days or times like Sundays driven by puritanical religion) as the instance of the coercive enforcement of 'morality by law' in Pareto's sense, though he derides the 'morality' of drinking non-alcohol and the imputed 'immorality' of drinking alcohol.[26]

---

26   Effectively anticipating Prohibition in America, Pareto (2000, pp. 43–44) remarks that 'anti-alcoholics religious groups (and hygienists) reach religious exaltation. They are (even) ready to kill a person only to keep him healthy. They thus show less sense than the inquisition, which buried men in order to save their souls.' He adds that their 'ideal is a population of ascetics who (e.g.) drink no wine' and asks 'what do you expect from people who (say) drink no wine and modestly lower their eyes when they see a beautiful woman? They may go and become monks (yet) cannot fight and win the battle of life' (Pareto 2000, pp. 46/92). Pareto (2000, p. 106) concludes that that 'it is not only abuse that (anti-alcoholic groups) wish to combat but even the most moderate use, and it is herein that the religious and sectarian sentiments can be decried' and notes that 'very few (of great men) drank only water.'

In addition, the condition involves free private and public alcohol production and consumption after a certain common legal age in modern civil
societies (usually 18 year or slightly earlier). It also includes no legal prohibitions or excessive restrictions and punishments such as coerced non-alcohol
regions and drastically raising the limit for this moral and consumer freedom
to unreasonably or unusually high levels, and harshly punishing violations in
contradiction' to or deviation from the prevalent reasonable pattern. Hence,
the absence of coerced non-alcohol zones and a lower age limit for alcohol
production, distribution, and consumption indicate a more universal and
higher degree of personal freedom of choice in this respect and consequently
a freer civil society on such a dimension of individual liberties and rights, and
conversely.

The fourth condition, element, and indicator of a free civil society, also a
corollary and particular yet controversial application of the first and in part
second conditions, pertains to the freedom of production, distribution, and
consumption of certain chemical substances termed 'drugs,' 'narcotics,' and
the like. Prima facie, this appears, along with abortion and personal freedom in
sexual activities, to be the probably most controversial and disputable condition, element, and indicator of a free civil society in light of the near universal
moralistic-religious condemnation and political-legal prohibition and punishment of non-medical 'drugs' (with some rare exceptions) on various grounds
like morality, religion, health, law and order, etc. Thus understood, it can be
treated as the prerequisite, component, and index of a perfectly, ideally free
civil society, so of a utopia of complete unconstrained individual liberty and
choice, though what are utopias in the present can become realities in the future, as exemplified by Enlightenment utopian liberal-democratic and rationalistic ideals inducing and realized in the French and American Revolutions.
Hence, in actually existing civil societies this dimension of individual freedom
and privacy is practically non-existent and a taboo, despite some recent episodes of partial de-criminalization or relaxation of legal prohibitions of some
'drugs' in Western and other countries, including a few US states.

However, the aforesaid about the production, distribution, and consumption of alcohol likely holds true for these processes applied to 'drugs,' though
with some qualifications about the relative scope and degree of health dangers
of the two. First, economically both represent economic activities in which
the supply of such goods and services respond and adapt to their effective
demand[27] and to that extent to actual or potential elements of consumer

---

27   As an instance of precluding the 'substitution of naive moral judgments for sociological
      analysis' (by the concept of latent functions), Merton (1968, p. 133) remarks that 'it would

freedom and choice, as in a pure, ideal-typical market economy, notably capitalism, minimizing or neglecting moralistic and religious exhortations and prohibitions or restrictions against alcohol and drugs. For example, most economists typically treat the production, distribution, and consumption of alcohol and other chemical and narcotic 'substances' like drugs as identical economic activities, Prohibition as the equivalent of the 'war on drugs,' and consequently the repeal of the first due to its dismal failure as the ground and precedent for presumably ending the second, and so the de-criminalization or regulation of illicit drugs after the model of its application to alcohol.[28]

Second, like that of alcohol, the production, distribution, and consumption of 'drugs' exemplifies the pattern of freedom of choice between, from a moralistic standard, morally 'right' and 'wrong' alternative courses of behavior, 'virtue' and 'vice' or 'sin' (i.e., using and non-using drugs). To that extent, it simply represents a case of individual liberties and personal preferences, choices, and responsibilities. Third, the criminalization of drugs, like alcohol, is the matter and product of social construction, above all political definition and power constellations, being socially contingent, politically determined and historically variable rather than invariant and universal among Western and other societies and within the same country such as the US, etc.

Fourth, the argument and evidence for the higher degree of lethality or health harm of illicit 'drugs' relative to alcohol is well-established and convincing, though recently questioned. Still, it does not provide a compelling ground for their criminalization and severe punishment of their use in a *free* civil

---

be peculiar to argue that prior to 1920 (Prohibition) the provision of liquor constituted an economic good, that from 1920 to 1933 (not) and that from 1934 to the present (does) once again (just as) would be economically (not morally) absurd to suggest that the sale of bootlegged liquor in the dry state of Kansas is less a response to a market demand that the sale of publicly manufactured liquor in the neighboring wet state of Missouri.' Therefore, he implies that the same economic reasoning applies to the provision of 'drugs.'

28 Friedman (1997, p. 194) suggests that the 'most promising candidate for decriminalization (represents) the current prohibition of the consumption, purchase, or sale of a limited number of chemical substances designated as illegal drugs. In 1991, 30% of the new court commitments to state prisons and 42% of those of federal prisons were drug related violators. The enactment and subsequent repeal of alcohol prohibition provide a highly relevant body of data on possible effects (of the decriminalization of drugs).' Simon (1976, p. 3) invokes the Prohibition Amendment to propose that the 'particular means used to attain this particular end had many consequences (on liberty) other than the specific end sought, and these had to be given their proper weight in considering the desirability of the means.' Levitt and Venkatesh (2000, p. 756) analyze the 'distribution of various narcotic substances' by certain groups (street gangs) in the US.

society as well as liberal democracy, in contrast to their un-free moralistic and un-democratic opposites. This is because of denying personal freedom, choice, and responsibility to individuals and thus treating them as near-children or immature, irresponsible, and incapable of making reasonable, notably non-destructive, decisions and choices in their moral, private life. Consequently, the grounds for recognizing some degree of freedom of choice between 'virtues' and 'vices' in the production, distribution, and consumption of 'drugs' are stronger and more compelling from the prism of a free civil society and liberal democracy—let alone a free market economy or pure capitalism—than the moralistic-religious and even health justifications for denying, violating, and dismissing such personal liberties, choices, and decisions as self-destructive and fantasies. For these justifications overlook that these personal liberties were realities in Western and other societies for long, including the US prior to the 1930s or the 1980s.

In particular, this condition of a perfectly free civil society would conceivably contain some degree of freedom of consumption and possession of recreational, especially relatively less harmful, 'drugs,' negatively no all-encompassing criminalization and/or harsh punishment of non-violent drug uses and users as sins-as-crimes, sinners-as-criminals. This is consistent with the pattern or ideal of a free civil society and liberal democracy not criminalizing and harshly punishing sins and sinners based on the conceptual and legal distinction between these and crimes/criminals. In turn, it is in stark contrast to its unfree opposites and moralistic non-democracies, above all theocracies, performing exactly the opposite equation to the point, as Pareto notes, especially Puritanism equating sensual pleasures with crimes in a display of what he calls 'moralistic insanity.'[29]

On this account, the 'war on drugs' in some Western societies, above all conservative America, has the same or comparable degree of legitimacy as well as rationality and efficiency in a free civil society and liberal democracy as Prohibition and in extension witch-trials in New England's Puritan theocracy—approximately zero.[30] In fact, cynics or critics might comment that the 'war

---

29 Pareto (2000, p. 107) notices that 'long before, the monks had carried this kind of (Puritan) insanity to the utmost limit' citing the observation that 'Pleasure and crime were synonyms in the monastic idiom' and inferring that 'they still are to our modern ascetics'.

30 Even some US conservative economists (Becker, Murphy, and Grossman 2006, p. 39) admit that 'every US president since Richard Nixon has fought a "war" on the production of drugs using police, the Federal Bureau of Investigation, the Central Intelligence Agency, the military, a federal agency (the Drug Enforcement Administration), and the military and police forces of other nations (and) Despite the wide scope of these efforts—and

on drugs,' like Prohibition, and generally 'tough on crime' policy operates as a sequel or replica of Puritan witch-trials, with non-violent drug users becoming new 'witches' figuratively understood as the only difference from those literally defined so in Puritanism.

Probably, future sociologists and other social scientists—and perhaps Americans and other Westerners—a century or so from now will regard the puritanical 'war on drugs' the same way these contemporary colleagues regard Puritan witch-trials and puritanical alcohol Prohibition—as a paradigmatic instance of moralistic devaluation, disregard, and suppression of individual liberty, privacy, dignity and life driven and sanctified by religious fanaticism, extremism, and superstition or irrationalism. They will probably be both perplexed and bemused with 'war on drugs' and related culture warriors, just as their counterparts today are with Puritan witch-hunters or prosecutors and anti-alcohol temperance fanatics. In this sense, the 'war on drugs' will likely end in the historical 'hall of infamy,' alongside Puritan witch-trails, puritanical Prohibition, the 'blue laws,' and other instances of what Weber calls the moralistic and theocratic 'tyranny of Puritanism' and its sequel evangelicalism.

Second and seemingly a fantasy given the taboo, this condition of a perfectly free civil society would involve the freedom of choice in the production and distribution of recreational drugs as opposed to the criminalization and punishment of drug trade and traders. While the usual ground for this freedom is primarily economic such as market 'free enterprise,' it also has a basis in a free civil society in the sense of the liberty of preference, choice, and decision-making between morally 'wrong' and 'right' alternative actions, 'sins' and 'virtues' (i.e., producing and marketing drugs or not doing so). By contrast, the rationale for denying and proscribing this freedom through the 'war on drugs' and its Draconian punishment appears to be as unconvincing and the resulting action as self-defeating as prohibiting and defeating alcohol production and distribution during Prohibition and exorcising 'witches' and 'Satan' through Puritan witch-trials.

Lastly and less controversially, this condition of a free civil society includes the individual freedom and right of consumption and possession of legal, medical drugs in the function of health, physical wellbeing, or preferred lifestyle. Negatively stated, this is *no* prohibition or undue restriction of medical drugs and procedures promoting and sustaining human health, physical wellbeing, or preferred lifestyle, thus their benefits being typically greater than their costs of actual or possible misuses and abuses, as proven by their official approval

---

major additional efforts by other nations—no president or drug "czar" has claimed victory, nor is a victory in sight.'

and continued legitimate applications. This hence implies *no* criminalization and excessive punishment of the improper use or overuse of legal drugs like prescription medicines (e.g., pain medications) on non-medical moralistic, religious, political, financial, and other grounds disregarding or overriding personal freedoms and rights, thus spurious justifications in a free civil society.

This holds true because such criminalization—like and even more than that of illicit drugs—denies and suppresses individuals' personal freedom of choice, dignity, and privacy in matters of health, physical wellbeing, and lifestyle. Consequently, it tends to eventually negate and eliminate individuals' preference for and right to good health and health care, physical wellbeing, and thus self-possession, self-control, and self-employment of their bodies, assuming no negative, unhealthy externalities or spillovers to other persons from the use of medical drugs and preferred lifestyles.[31] In sum, in a free civil society the freedom and right of access to and use of medical drugs and procedures is promoted for the reason of human health, health care, and wellbeing, and limited only for the same reasons, but not on moralistic, religious, and related false non-medical grounds (e.g., humans experiencing 'pleasure' or 'feeling high and good' as 'immoral' or 'ungodly' while taking medications).

The fifth condition, element, and indicator of free civil society constitutes the individual liberty, choice, and responsibility in the sphere of sexual, intimate relationships. This represents the corollary and special application of the condition of individual liberty, choice, and privacy in general. In particular, it is the resultant of personal bodily liberties and choices, like the freedom of self-possession, self-control and self-employment of one's own body as biological property in the sense of the 'happiness, life, and property' right according to the preferences and wishes of the 'owner' of such a resource. No doubt, sexual freedom or act exhibits the most manifest dimension of a morally 'wrong' conduct, an ultimate, grave, and even deadly moral 'sin' for moralistic, ascetic, and theocratic religions. These include (as in Weber's sociology of religion) above all Islam and Calvinism, especially its English-American hyper-moralistic sect Puritanism and the latter's sequel evangelicalism, and Christianity as a whole

---

31   Such a negativity represents what Pareto (2000, p. 107) would call the ultimate form of
      Puritan-evangelical 'moralistic insanity' in view of Puritanism's and evangelicalism's mor-
      alistic and theocratic devaluation, suppression, and sacrifice of human health, wellbeing,
      and life, just as personal liberty, privacy and enjoyment, to the 'will' and 'glory' of the
      absolute, omnipotent, and despotic God in Calvinism. At this juncture, such a 'moralistic
      insanity' against human health and wellbeing exhibits a sort of logic or 'method to the
      madness' of Puritan and generally Calvinist characteristic anti-humanism, inhumanity,
      and brutality. Recall that Weber (1930, pp. 104/223) detects Puritan 'hatred' and 'misan-
      thropy' and the 'extreme inhumanity' of Calvinism, including its dogma of predestination.

on account of the apparent obsession with sex cum 'original sin' and the consequent punishment both of the initial sinner, the 'natural man' and by association of subsequent sinners for the same act and so all humans, minus God's puritanical self-proclaimed agents as saints-rulers. Consequently, the freedom or act of sex has been historically subjected to strong condemnation, systematic suppression, and severe punishment by church and state, especially the theocratic and moralistic church-state.

Still, individual sexual freedoms form a necessary condition, integral element, and salient indicator of modern free civil society conjoined with effective, liberal democracy that as a rule does not criminalize or harshly punish such 'immoral' pleasures and 'sins,' including Pareto's 'sexual residues and enjoyments,' in contrast to its opposites, especially moralistic theocracy, above all Puritan-evangelical and Islamic theocracies. Negatively stated, this signifies no criminalization or severe punishment—for example, death, long imprisonment, and the like—of free consensual sexual or intimate relationships between individuals as the particular realm and exercise of individual liberty, choice, and privacy, namely those between consenting, adult, and legally competent actors in their private lives and settings.

Simply, a free civil society is typified by that state as well as church does not invade its private sphere in order to monitor, control, restrict, and punish what individuals and families do in the intimacy and privacy of their homes, actions deeply incompatible with and contradictory and destructive to genuine, liberal democracy and modern free society. Instead, such actions epitomize and enforce a sort of moral proto-fascism through moralistic theocracy such as Islamic fundamentalist and Calvinist, Puritan-evangelical theocracies, as exemplified by medieval Muslim states or cities and Calvin's Geneva as the prototype generating its sequel Puritan-ruled New England—both being 'Christian Sparta'—historically, and by Iran or Taliban and the US 'Bible Belt' contemporaneously.

The individual freedom of sexual relationships encompasses the personal liberty of choice and responsibility in premarital sex between consenting, adult, and legally competent persons, negatively no criminalization or harsh punishment of what Puritan-evangelical and Islamic moralistic theocracies criminalize and punish as 'fornication' or 'copulation.' Also, it comprises the personal freedom of choice and responsibility in extramarital sexual relations between consenting and legally competent persons, and conversely, no criminalization or harsh punishment of this, as in these and other theocracies, condemned, proscribed, and severely punished moral sin termed 'adultery,' usually with cruel death or torture, as in Puritan New England and Islamic states. Prima facie, this appears to be the most controversial, disputable, and disapproved immoral or repugnant personal conduct from a moralistic and religious viewpoint proscribed and punished as a grave sin-crime in all major religions, including Islam and Christianity; after all, even in a perfectly free, completely liberal civil society, not many would openly approve of and defend 'adultery.'

Yet, aside from such moralistic adverse judgments, as a rule a free civil society is typified by such personal liberty and civic non-criminal responsibility as a particular, perhaps ultimate expression of the general freedom of choice between morally right and 'wrong' behavior, 'virtues' and 'sins.' A free civil society, more precisely genuine liberal democracy does not criminalize and harshly punish this moral 'sin,' even if so morally repugnant and disapproved. This is in accordance with the principle that sins, however 'immoral' or religiously prohibited and sanctioned, still are no crimes, sinners not criminals, and individuals have both the liberty and responsibility for their actions in the domain of sexual and all actions and relations.

At this juncture, what distinguishes a free civil society and liberal democracy from unfree moralistic societies and theocracies is that the second, especially their Islamic and Puritan-evangelical[32] forms, condemn, criminalize, and severely punish—typically with brutal death like stoning, burning as 'witches,' etc.—extramarital sex. Yet, the first do not do so and instead threat the latter as a special aspect and exercise of the individual freedom and responsibility of choice between alternative courses of moral actions. In Durkheim's terms, extramarital sex in a free civil society and liberal democracy has become the matter of modern civil law characterized with restitution as non-criminal sanction and responsibility (e.g., a ground for divorce), while in unfree moralistic societies and theocracies being within the scope of primitive penal law and subjected to 'expiation' through death and other severe punishment. Treating 'adultery' as a dimension of the individual freedom of intimate relationships and so an indicator of a free civil society is a statement of fact—i.e., the latter is typified by recognizing this 'sin' as such. Conversely, this is not a value judgment in Weber's sense, being 'beyond good and evil,' neither approval nor disapproval on the ground that mature and legally competent individuals are both free and responsible for their decisions and choices in this and any domain of their private lives.

Ina addition, the present indicator of a free civil society incorporates the personal freedom of choice and responsibility in homosexual relations between

---

32   Adut (2012, p. 253) finds that 'adultery scarcely figured in the English novel,'—by contrast
        to French novels, for example—especially in Victorian England described as a case of
        'puritanical cultures,' even though Puritanism was militarily defeated and politically dis-
        credited during the late 17th century.

consenting and legally competent persons, negatively no state criminalization and/or harsh punishment of 'sodomy,' also a disapproved and 'immoral' conduct from a moralistic standpoint, though decreasingly so during recent years. The aforesaid of pre- and extra-material sexual relations applies, with necessary qualifications, to those of a homosexual nature. The above indicator also comprises the personal freedom and responsibility in adult entertainment by adult and legally competent persons, and conversely no state criminalization and/or harsh punishment of such 'sin' as 'pornography,' 'obscenity,' and the like on moralistic, religious, and other grounds denying the liberty of choice between morally 'right' and 'wrong' actions, 'virtues' and 'vices.' In addition, this indicator entails the personal freedom of providing and using sexual 'goods' and services between consenting and legally competent individuals, negatively no government criminalization or harsh punishment of 'prostitution'[33] on such grounds negating the liberty of choice between alternative moral actions, and also denying the right to practicing the 'oldest profession' as an economic 'free enterprise.'[34]

No doubt, the last two dimensions of sexual freedom are also controversial, disputable, and even disapproved and sanctioned as more or less grave 'sins' and 'vices' from a moralistic and religious viewpoint. Yet, incorporating them into a free civil society is not a value judgment, neither positive nor negative approving or condemning them. In a free civil society individuals have both the freedom and responsibility to decide and choose morally 'right' or 'wrong' actions and thus know what is the best or worst for them in this respect. Instead, it is a statement of fact in the sense that a free civil society, at least as an ideal, pure type in Weber's sense, is defined and typified in its most intimate realm by such and related individual freedoms, choices, and responsibilities, and effective democracy legally permits or does not criminalize and harshly punish them.

This is in stark contrast to unfree societies and non-democracies like theocracies, in which such sins and vices are condemned and punished as grave crimes and often capital offenses. No truly free civil society and effective democracy criminalizes or harshly punishes adult entertainment and generally what people do in the privacy and intimacy of their homes, as well as (with qualifications) whether they supply and consume sexual 'goods' and services as an economic transaction, which is in turn what unfree societies, above all theocracies, precisely do. As before, this is a statement of fact rather than a value judgment. Even those disapproving and punishing such personal sexual

---

33   Benabou and Tirole (2011, p. 811) register 'changing attitudes' toward 'legalized prostitution.'

34   Two female economists, Edlund and Korn (2002, p. 183) outline an economic theory of prostitution considered an 'alternative female (earnings) strategy.'

freedoms and activities can and do make such statement as when condemning the 'decadence' or 'immorality' of modern free civil society and liberal democracy and glorifying the 'purity,' 'morality' of their moralistic, theocratic opposites and antecedents.

In sum, a free civil society in its most private aspect is conditional on and indicated by personal sexual freedoms, choices, and responsibilities as the special dimension and exercise of individual liberty and choice, as well as of the freedom of property and use of one's own body according to individuals' necessities and desires. These freedoms may appear 'immoral,' 'sinful,' 'disgusting' and 'repulsive,' but modern free civil society in its most intimate dimension, as well as liberal democracy, becomes a logical non sequitur and an empirical impossibility when they are denied, suppressed, and harshly punished, as in unfree societies such as moralistic Puritan-evangelical and Islamic theocracies.

The sixth condition, element, and indicator of a free civil society consists of the individual freedom and right to peaceful, joyful, happy existence and to life compatible and non-interfering with such lives of other individuals. Negatively formulated, this entails the personal freedom from violence, suffering, and death committed and inflicted by other individual, groups, as well as states through physical coercion, violent repression, and state terror. Evidently, this condition restates the personal freedom and right to 'life, property (of economic resources and one's body), and happiness' in Jefferson's sense, notably what Weber calls the Enlightenment's 'joy of life'[35] in relation to other persons, groups, and above all coercive and repressive states. Alternatively, it represents the freedom from violent death, coercive or arbitrary seizure of one's material and related property—also discussed in the context of economic freedoms—and control and constraint of one's own body, and being inflicted with violence, pain, and suffering by other individuals, groups, and repressive states.

This condition incorporates the individual freedom from the aggressive use or threat of lethal weapons and other means of personal, group and government violence and aggression. In negative Hobbesian terms, this means *no* universal 'war of everyone against everyone' by lethal weapons, as the primitive pre-social 'state of nature' governed by the 'law of the jungle' as the 'law of the strongest.' In positive terms, it signifies the modern social constellation of civilized society governed by the law of civility, non-violence, safety, and peaceful conflict resolution establishing and sustaining societal peace within society and in relation to other societies denoted pacifism. Consequently, this involves the individual freedom from random and arbitrary death and the right

---

35   Similarly, Phelps (2007, p. 554) comments that joys of life and creativity called *vitalism* 'is reflected to a degree by Thomas Jefferson and Voltaire among other Enlightenment figures.'

to life and existence, negatively *no* anarchy and thus lack of high probability of murders and massacres, destruction, and suffering by lethal weapons, simply the absence of an anarchic weapon and violent culture. Generally, it comprises the individual and group freedom and right to 'live and enjoy life and let others live and enjoy it' in the sense of tolerance of and peaceful coexistence with other individuals and groups within civil society, overcoming the opposite barbarian rule of 'live and let (make others) die and suffer' through the 'license to kill' and the 'law of the strongest' as the 'law of the jungle.'

In general, a free civil society is 'civil' precisely because of being non-violent and in that sense civilized and thus typified by peace, safety, and peaceful conflict resolution. Conversely, a violent, non-peaceful civil society is an inner contradiction and actual perversion of its essence and functioning, a sort of 'uncivil society.'[36] Consequently, its necessary condition and crucial indicator is, to paraphrase Weber, 'peace in civil society,' just as in his words, 'peace in the market' being an imperative for the latter's existence and operation, namely what he calls the process of 'pacification' of social relations and in that sense 'pacifism' within society, as well as in relation to other societies.[37] In sum, for its persistence and effective functioning a free civil society is also conditional on and indicated by the individual freedom and right to non-violent existence, life, material and bodily property, and happiness consistent and non-interference with and respect for the equal freedoms, choices, and rights of other individuals.

Comparative Estimates and Types of Civil Society

At this juncture, the provisional agnostic position on the question of which particular type of civil society most completely and consistently fulfills and exhibits the preceding conditions, elements, and indicators is suspended. This is done by observing and predicting that liberal-secular civil society intrinsically and systematically realizes and manifests them and hence individual liberties, rights, and privacy. On this basis, any liberal-secular civil society intrinsically constitutes or ultimately becomes a free civil society, alternatively the second representing invariably the first.

---

36   McCann (2000, p. 1) uses the term 'uncivil society' in reference to the destruction or prevention of civil society, in particular personal liberty and privacy, by Mormon theocracy pervading and persisting in Utah during its entire history.

37   In fact, in Hegel-Marx-Tönnies' and other original definitions of civil society, the latter encompasses the market, thus commercial activity and private property, as its integral element in counter-distinction from the public sphere of the state.

Conversely, anti-liberal and anti-secular or theocentric civil societies do not meet the above conditions due to involving all-encompassing moralistic and religiously sanctified control, coercion, and repression, as epitomized by fundamentalist theocracy and moral fascism sharing this totalitarian pattern of individual illiberty, indignity, and non-privacy. On account of such a shared pattern, any fundamentalist theocracy, as epitomized by Islamic and Puritan-evangelical theocracies, represents or is equivalent to moral and religious fascism, just as all moralistic fascisms are typically theocentric or religiously grounded, as exemplified by fascism, including Nazism, in interwar Europe, as well as neo-fascism and neo-Nazism in postwar times. In this respect, to paraphrase Michels' 'iron law of oligarchy,' 'who says/imposes theocracy does moral-religious fascism and therefore an unfree, dead civil society, individual un-freedom.' Theocracy/moral fascism acts as the deadly poison of a free civil society and thus of individual liberty, dignity, and privacy, with the only and most effective antidote being a liberal-secular civic sphere as the sole domain of such liberties.

Therefore, like the equivalent type of democracy with respect to the polity, the liberal-secular variant of civil society is observed or expected to truly and solely epitomize a free civil society as the autonomous private-life sphere of personal liberty and choice. By stark contrast and vehement opposition, anti-liberal and anti-secular or theocentric civil societies through their moralistic and religiously driven control and repression epitomize its unfree, eliminated or subverted variant, a kind of 'uncivil society.' Just as this type of democracy is the historically and empirically sole genuine and viable democratic project and system, so is its liberal-secular variant the only truly free civil society, autonomous private-life sphere, in the history and reality of Western and related societies. Conversely, anti-liberal and anti-secular societies through their moralistic-religious control and coercion inherently aim at and eventually result in the negation and destruction or perversion of the domain of individual liberty, choice, rights, and privacy, thus being the ersatz substitutes of a free civil society. In essence, a free civil society only emerges, exists, and persists among liberal-secular societies, and there is no such thing—even civil society itself—in their anti-liberal and anti-secular opposites, particularly theocracies and moral fascisms.

In consequence, liberal-secular civil societies are observed or expected to be invariably and drastically freer—i.e., more 'libertarian' in the true sense of comprehensive liberalism rather than false 'libertarianism' as the overt eulogy of capitalist dictatorship or plutocracy—than those pervaded and eliminated by moralistic-religious control, repression, and severe sanction. More specifically, the preceding raises the question as to whether and to what extent Western and related societies succeed to fulfill and display the conditions, elements, and indicators of a free civil society, how they rank on the dimension of individual liberties, choices, rights, and privacy. As implied, such Western and similar societies as typified with a liberal-secular civic-private life sphere tend to more systematically, fully, and coherently satisfy and evince these conditions and indicators by ranking higher on the dimension of individual liberties, choices, rights, and privacy than those characterized with its opposite, notably moralistic-religious control and repression. These observations and expectations are strongly confirmed, as seen in this and next chapter.

Classification of Modern Civil Societies

As before, a classification of Western and similar societies into particular types of civil society can be made as follows (Table 8.2).

TABLE 8.2   *Classification of Western and related societies in free civil society/individual liberty.*

I Liberal-secular civil societies (15 and ½ cases)
  Australia, Austria, Belgium, Canada, Denmark, Finland, France, Germany, Iceland, Luxembourg, Netherlands, New Zealand, Norway, Sweden, Switzerland, the US in in liberal and secular civic dimensions, weak, transient or exceptional, and regions, minority or decreasing (e.g., the Coast, parts of the North, etc.).

Expected free civil society/individual liberty overall ranking	highest, I—completely or largely free

II Anti- or non-liberal, anti- or non-secular (theocratic, theocentric, religious) civil societies (4 and ½ cases)
  South Korea, Mexico, Poland, Turkey, the US in anti-liberal anti-secular or theocentric prevalent dimensions civic dimensions and majority regions (the conservative, Southern United States)

Expected free civil society/individual liberty overall ranking	lowest, III—unfree or quasi-free

III   Intermediate, eclectic, mixed civil societies (13 cases)
  Chile, Czech Republic, Greece, Hungary, Estonia, Ireland, Italy, Japan, Portugal, Slovakia, Slovenia, Spain, the UK

Expected free civil society/individualliberty overall ranking	intermediate, II—quasi- or largely free

---

First, the following countries are classified in liberal-secular civil society: Australia, Austria, Belgium, Canada, Denmark, France, Germany, Iceland, Luxembourg, the Netherlands, New Zealand, Norway, Sweden, Switzerland, and the US. The US is so classified in its liberal and secular dimensions (weak, transient or exceptional) and regions (minority or decreasing) contrasted to their anti-liberal, anti-secular opposites, as an observation or assumption of the coexistence and contradiction of the 'two Americas' in civic terms. As a whole, these societies are primary exemplars of this type of civil society in the Western and entire world because they are consistently or increasingly liberal and secular in respect of the private sphere of life, notably individual liberty, personal choice and privacy. They are hence experienced and designated as 'liberal-secular civil societies' and commonly witnessed and realistically predicted to exhibit the highest degree of individual liberty, personal choice and privacy and thus superior overall ranking (I) on a free civil society among all countries. Evidently, this classification indicates that liberal-secular civil society is basically intertwined with liberal, secular, and universalistic democracy, by being its equivalent or complement in the private sphere of life, and conversely, as all these societies are classified into this political system as well. It also suggests that liberal-secular civil society is closely linked to rationalistic, liberal, and secular culture, and to some degree to rationally regulated and egalitarian welfare capitalism, in that they are also classified in these two cultural and economic types.

Second, classified into anti-liberal and anti-secular or theocentric civil society are these countries within OECD: Mexico, Poland, South Korea, Turkey, and the US. The US is so classified in its strong and prevalent dimensions and majority regions of anti-liberalism and anti-secularism or moralistic control, such as the conservative, Southern United States, that coexist with but seek to vanquish, by a religiously driven war on sin-as-crime—especially since Reaganism's war on drugs and other moral sins—against, liberal and secular civil society within the 'two Americas' in individual liberty, personal choice and privacy. Overall, these countries or regions (as within the US) exemplify this type of civil (for cynics and critics 'uncivil') society, for they are persistently or growingly anti-liberal and anti-secular or theocentric and eventually theocratic in relation to individual liberty, personal choice and privacy, so the private lifeworld. They are perceived and denoted as 'anti-liberal and anti-secular or theocentric civil societies,' and widely noted and reasonably anticipated to display the lowest degree of individual liberty, personal choice and privacy and thus inferior overall ranking (III) on a free civil society within the Western world and beyond. As the observe of the previous, all these countries are classified into anti-liberal, anti-secular, and anti-universalistic 'democracy,' which is indicative of the fact that anti-liberal and anti-secular or theocentric civil society is entwined with this political regime whose equivalent or complement it is in the private sphere, just as conversely. In addition, they are classified into anti-rationalistic, anti-liberal, and anti-secular culture as well as unregulated and inegalitarian plutocratic or oligarchic capitalism, indicating that this type of civil society is related closely to such cultural and to some degree to economic types.

Third, into intermediate, eclectic or mixed civil society are classified countries such as Chile, Czech Republic, Greece, Hungary, Estonia, Ireland, Italy, Japan, Portugal, Slovakia, Slovenia, Spain, and the UK. They represent or approximate this type of civil society among OECD and other countries by virtue of combining the features of the previous two types, although in varying ways and degrees, with some of them tending to approach more the first and the others the second. Deemed and depicted as simply 'mixed civil societies,' they are found and expected to show the intermediate degree of individual liberty, personal choice and privacy and thus medium overall ranking (II) on a free civil society among these countries. In turn, all these societies are also classified in mixed democracies, as well as cultures and economies, suggesting that this type of civil society relates or coincides with such political, cultural, and in part economic systems.

Comparative Estimates of Free Civil Society for Western and Related Societies

The comparative estimates of a free civil society for Western and related societies such as OECD countries are constructed on the basis of the above conditions and indicators (Table 8.3).

Like in terms of democracy, these societies display significant variations with respect to their estimates on a free civil society, and thus individual liberty, choice, rights, and privacy (on the 0–10 scale). On the basis of these estimates, they are classified in a descending order into, first, 'completely free' (scores 8 and higher), second, 'mostly free' (scores 7–7.99), third, 'pseudo-free' (scores 6–6.99), and fourth, 'unfree' (scores under 6) civil societies (Table 8.4).

The highest category of 'completely free civil societies' encompasses the following eight countries in a descending order: Luxembourg (8.82), Norway (8.62), Canada (8.54), Portugal (8.49), the Netherlands (8.42), Denmark (8.34), and New Zealand (8.08), all having scores 8 or higher (Table 8.5).

In the present classification, with a single exception of Portugal, all of these countries are classified as liberal-secular civil societies, along with several

TABLE 8.3 *Comparative estimates of a free civil society, OECD countries.*

Country	Civil liberties	Individual liberty	Privacy	Worst privacy	Abortion rights	Alcohol freedom	Death pena for drugs
Australia	10	8	5	8	10	7	10
Austria	9.41	5	6	9	10	9	10
Belgium	9.41	5	8	8	10	NA	10
Canada	10	10	9	10	10	3	10
Chile	9.71	4	NA	NA	0	7	10
Czech Republic	9.41	2	7	8	10	7	10
Denmark	9.41	8	4	5	10	10	10
Estonia	8.82	2	8	10	10	7	10
Finland	9.71	5	7	9	2	2	10
France	8.82	4	4	6	10	9	10
Germany	9.12	6	8	10	10	9	10
Greece	9.41	0	10	9	10	8	10
Hungary	7.65	0	9	8	10	7	10
Iceland	9.71	9	8	9	2	2	10
Ireland	10	9	7	9	0	7	10
Italy	8.53	2	8	8	10	9	10
Japan	8.82	3	5	8	2	2	10
Korea, South	8.53	1	NA	NA	1	2	2
Luxembourg	9.71	9	8	10	10	9	10
Mexico	6.76	1	NA	NA	0	7	10
Netherlands	9.41	7	5	6	10	9	10
New Zealand	10	10	6	10	1	7	10
Norway	10	10	5	7	10	7	10
Poland	9.12	3	6	7	1	7	10
Portugal	9.41	6	8	10	10	9	10
Slovakia	8.82	1	5	7	10	7	10
Slovenia	8.82	3	8	10	10	10	10
Spain	9.41	4	6	7	10	9	10
Sweden	9.71	8	5	9	10	2	10
Switzerland	9.41	7	6	8	10	9	10
Turkey	2.94	0	NA	NA	10	7	10
UK	9.41	7	1	2	2	7	10
US	8.24	6	2	2	10	1	2

I Average free civil society scores 8 and higher—Completely free civil societies.
II Average free civil society scores 7–7.99—Mostly free civil societies.

tramarital	Same-sex marriage	Prostitution	Safety	Homicides	Firearm murders	TOTAL	Rankings	Average
0	5	7	8	8	96.00	13	7.38
0	10	6	9	5	98.41	13	7.57
10	10	5	7	3	95.41	12	7.95
10	10	8	7	4	111.00	13	8.54
0	10	1	3	3	57.71	11	5.25
0	10	4	9	8	94.41	13	7.26
10	10	9	9	4	108.41	13	8.34
0	10	1	1	10	87.82	13	6.76
10	10	10	6	7	97.71	13	7.52
10	10	2	8	9	100.82	13	7.76
0	10	5	9	5	101.12	13	7.78
0	10	3	7	4	90.41	13	6.95
0	10	1	8	10	90.65	13	6.97
10	5	10	9	10	103.71	13	7.98
10	10	10	9	2	103.00	13	7.92
0	10	0	9	0	84.53	13	6.50
0	5	4	10	10	77.82	13	5.99
0	0	6	5	10	45.53	11	4.14
10	10	8	9	2	114.71	13	8.82
5	10	0	0	0	49.76	11	4.52
10	10	5	9	9	109.41	13	8.42
10	10	8	9	4	105.00	13	8.08
10	10	9	6	8	112.00	13	8.62
0	10	3	8	9	83.12	13	6.39
10	10	6	8	4	110.41	13	8.49
0	10	2	7	8	85.82	13	6.60
0	0	7	9	8	93.82	13	7.22
10	5	4	9	6	99.41	13	7.65
10	5	9	9	4	100.71	13	7.75
0	10	7	9	0	95.41	13	7.34
0	10	0	4	7	60.94	11	5.54
10	10	3	8	9	88.41	13	6.80
10	1	2	1	0	50.24	13	3.86

III Average free civil society scores 6–6.99—Quasi-free, semi-free civil societies.
IV Average free civil society scores under 6—Unfree civil societies.

TABLE 8.4   *Average free civil society estimates and classification, OECD countries.*

I   Average free civil society scores 8 and higher—Completely free civil
     societies (7 cases)
        Canada, Denmark, Luxembourg, Netherlands, New Zealand, Norway,
        Portugal

II   Average free civil society scores 7–7.998—largely free civil societies
     (13 cases)
        Australia, Austria, Belgium, Czech Republic, Finland, France, Ger-
        many, Iceland, Ireland, Slovenia Spain, Sweden, Switzerland

III Average free civil society scores 6–6.99—Quasi-free civil societies
     (cases 8)
        Estonia, Greece, Hungary, Italy, Japan, Poland, Slovakia, UK

IV   Average free civil society scores under 6—Unfree civil societies (cases 5)
        Chile, South Korea, Mexico, Turkey, the US (conservative America)

TABLE 8.5   *Free civil society ranking, OECD countries.*

Rank	Country	Index (0–10)	Category of civil society	Classification
1	Luxembourg	8.82	Completely Free	Liberal-Secular
2	Norway	8.62	Completely Free	Liberal-Secular
3	Canada	8.54	Completely Free	Liberal-Secular
4	Portugal	8.49	Completely Free	Intermediate
5	Netherlands	8.42	Completely Free	Liberal-Secular
6	Denmark	8.34	Completely Free	Liberal-Secular
7	New Zealand	8.08	Completely Free	Liberal-Secular
8	Iceland	7.98	Mostly Free	Liberal-Secular
9	Belgium	7.95	Mostly Free	Liberal-Secular
10	Ireland	7.92	Mostly Free	Intermediate
11	Germany	7.78	Mostly Free	Liberal-Secular
12	France	7.76	Mostly Free	Liberal-Secular
13	Sweden	7.75	Mostly Free	Liberal-Secular
14	Spain	7.65	Mostly Free	Intermediate
15	Austria	7.57	Mostly Free	Liberal-Secular

Rank	Country	Index (0–10)	Category of civil society	Classification
16	Finland	7.52	Mostly Free	Liberal-Secular
17	Australia	7.38	Mostly Free	Liberal-Secular
18	Switzerland	7.34	Mostly Free	Liberal-Secular
19	Czech Republic	7.26	Mostly Free	Intermediate
20	Slovenia	7.22	Mostly Free	Intermediate
21	Hungary	6.97	Quasi-Free	Intermediate
22	Greece	6.95	Quasi-Free	Intermediate
23	UK	6.80	Quasi-Free	Intermediate
24	Estonia	6.76	Quasi-Free	Intermediate
25	Slovakia	6.60	Quasi-Free	Intermediate
26	Italy	6.50	Quasi-Free	Intermediate
27	Poland	6.39	Quasi-Free	Anti-Liberal
28	Japan	5.99	Unfree	Intermediate
29	Turkey	5.54	Unfree	Anti- Liberal
30	Chile	5.25	Unfree	Intermediate
31	Mexico	4.52	Unfree	Anti-Liberal
32	South Korea	4.14	Unfree	Anti-Liberal
33	US	3.86	Unfree	Anti-Liberal[a]

a Conservative America.

others as mixed cases, which largely confirms the expectations. These are also fulfilled by the fact that none of those countries classified as anti-liberal and anti-secular or theocentric civil societies belong to this top category. In regional terms, this category comprises, first and foremost, Scandinavia epitomized by Norway and Denmark (but minus the missing link of Sweden probably due to the pernicious long-term effect of militant feminism on a free civil society such as individual liberty and privacy), and other parts of Northwestern Europe like Luxembourg and the Netherlands, joined with Portugal whose unique drug liberalization indicates a larger liberating process within civil society, as well as Canada and New Zealand. As known, Scandinavia and Northwestern Europe overall, along with Canada and New Zealand, are exemplary liberal-secular civil societies—with Portugal as the latest candidate for joining this club— with the highest degrees of individual liberty, choice, rights, and privacy in the Western and entire world and probably in social history since classical civilization and its proto-liberalism, for example, the democracy of Athens.

They therefore validate the current expectations and also confirm the prior sociological observations that liberal-secular civil societies represent as a whole the sole true and viable types of a free civil society by having the highest levels of individual liberty, choice, rights, and privacy in both social space and time, comparatively and historically. In this respect, a free civil society since Hegel and Hobbes as the complex of individual liberty, choice, rights, and privacy has been fully established and sustained only or primarily in contemporary liberal-secular civil societies typifying most of Western Europe (recently adding Portugal) and Canada and New Zealand. Notably, it has reached its highest comparative and historical point of development and consolidation in those civil societies characteristic of Scandinavia today, as in Norway and Denmark. Simply, if one does not know what a free civil society really is, one knows it when seeing liberal-secular Scandinavian countries like Norway and Denmark, and other Northwestern Europe societies such as the Netherlands, plus their non-European equivalents, notably Canada, along with the mixed and striking case of Portugal moving in this direction by overcoming the opposite vestiges of cultural traditionalism and religious anti-liberalism.

The second category of 'largely free civil societies' contains these countries in a descending order: Iceland (7.97), Belgium (7.95), Ireland (7.92), Germany (7.78), France (7.76), Sweden (7.75), Spain (7.65), Austria (7.57), Finland (7.52), Australia (7.38), Switzerland (7.34), Czech Republic (7.26), and Slovenia (7.22). These countries are presently classified mostly as liberal-secular (9 out of 13) civil societies, except for a few mixed cases, but no single case of the opposite, which for most part supports the expectations. These are even more completely supported when taking into account both categories. Overall, all liberal-secular civil societies belong to the two highest categories of 'completely' and 'largely' free civil societies, along with several mixed cases, but absolutely no instance of the anti-liberal and anti-secular type.

The category of 'pseudo-free civil societies' incorporates the following countries also in a descending order: Hungary (6.97), Greece (6.95), UK (6.80), Estonia (6.76), Slovakia (6.60), Italy (6.50), and Poland (6.39). Of these, six countries are in the present classification mixed cases, and one is an instance of anti-liberal and anti-secular or theocentric civil society, which generally supports the expectations. These also supported by the fact that no liberal-secular civil societies appear in this second lowest category. The comparatively low ranking on a free civil society of these countries can be probably explained by that they continue to be over-determined or affected by religious anti-liberalism, namely Catholic (Italy and Poland), Orthodox (Greece) and Protestant-Puritan (the UK) anti-liberal influences or legacies, as well as by (post-Communist) culture traditionalism or path-dependence (Estonia, Hungary, and Slovakia), thus consistent with the expectations.

Generally, they represent mostly eclectic, incoherent mixtures of liberal-secular and illiberal, non-secular civil societies with intermediate, medium degrees of individual liberty, choice, rights, and privacy, confirming both the present expectations and previous observations. On the one hand, compared with liberal-secular civil societies such as Scandinavia and Western Europe, they reveal themselves as almost unfree, with the low or minimal level of individual liberty, choice, rights, and privacy. On the other hand, they reappear as nearly 'free' by comparison with strictly anti-liberal and anti-secular 'civil' societies like the remaining OECD countries, including 'conservative America' of the 'two Americas.' Thus, if coming from Western Europe such as Scandinavia to this intermediate class of civil societies, they are likely experienced as 'unfree,' yet as almost 'free' if arriving often literally from 'conservative America' (e.g., from the repressive-moralistic 'Bible Belt' to less coercive, more morally relaxed Estonia, Hungary, Slovakia, and Greece), so these cases of the pseudo-free category are expected and show to be both 'unfree' and 'free' depending on the comparison. On this account, they are generally mixed, semi-free civil societies.

The last category of 'unfree civil societies' comprises a certain number of countries arranged in an ascending order of un-freedom such as Japan (5.99), Turkey (5.54), Chile (5.25), Mexico (4.52), South Korea (4.14), and the US (3.86). Simply, these are the least free/most unfree civil societies in the Western world and beyond within OECD. It is indicative that most of these countries, including America in the conservative-religious, Southern rendition, are classified into anti-liberal and anti-secular or theocentric civil society, while no instances of its liberal-secular opposite and two cases of its mixed counterpart appear in this category, thus generally confirming the expectations. Thus, except for Japan that anyway substantively belongs or comes close to a quasi-free civil society judging by its estimate, most of these countries are non-liberal and religiously determined or path-dependent moralistic civil societies with the lowest or diminishing degrees of individual liberty, choice, rights, and privacy in the Western world and beyond.

They also strongly confirm the present expectations and previous observations that anti-liberal and anti-secular civil societies are exemplars of unfree— or alternatively, spurious ersatz forms of a free civil society—and moreover no 'civil' societies at all. Instead, they present cases of an 'uncivil society' due to their non-existent or minimal level of individual liberty, choice, rights, and privacy as elements precisely defining civil society. At this juncture, civil society has not only failed to realize but vanished almost without trace or degenerated into these illiberal, non-secular bogus 'civil' societies observed in Europe and 'conservative America.' Their defining element and ultimate outcome is denying and suppressing individual liberty, choice, rights, and privacy on moralistic and religious (e.g., Catholic and Biblical, respectively) grounds. So, if one still does not know what an unfree civil society is in reality among Western and related societies, one knows it when seeing Catholic-determined Mexico and to some extent Chile, religious or traditionalist South Korea, and 'evangelical America,' first and foremost the Southern and other 'Bible Belt.' Notably, the three least free/most unfree civil societies are found to be Mexico, South Korea, and 'evangelical America,' with the latter actually being such a single society.

As a particular curiosity, the neighbors, Mexico and 'evangelical America' appear together in the same category and notably rock-bottom-of 'unfree civil societies,' with the second ranked even ranked lower (33) than the first (31). Moreover, when comparing the South to its neighbor Mexico in terms of the freedom of alcohol consumption and related 'sins,'[38] the picture becomes even bleaker for the first. To that extent, this indicates a near-catastrophic failure or elimination of a free civil society in 'evangelical America' so that what it denounces and disdains as 'unfree' and 'backward' Mexico appears and is usually experienced by visiting 'sinful' Americans as relatively freer, in particular with a higher degree of individual freedom of choice between moral 'virtues' and 'vices' like alcohol consumption, etc. Yet, such a dismal failure is predicted by and demonstrates that a Puritan-evangelical, like any religiously overdetermined, civil society since New England never has been—and likely will be in the US South—free, as well as democratic in the form of liberal-secular democracy. In light of such enduring Puritan oppressive ghost perpetuated through evangelicalism, it is no wonder or shock that 'evangelical America' as the exemplar and last vestige of an anti-liberal and anti-secular civil society and 'democracy' within the Western world is ranked on civil and individual liberties below Catholic Mexico, overall the last out of 33 countries within OECD.

---

38   Anecdotal evidence for this is that many Texans and other Southern college and high-school students and others prefer spending their spring breaks and graduation in Mexican resorts like Cancun, etc., because of their perceived higher degree of freedom of alcohol use and related private freedoms and choices, and its outright prohibitions or harsh restrictions in Texas and the 'Bible Belt' overall, especially (but not solely) in its 'dry' counties. At least on this account, they 'vote by their feet'—literally, fleeing Texas, the 'Bible Belt' for these and other occasions—that 'even' Mexico appears as a freer civil society than their anti-liberal theocratic 'godly' states, almost an oasis of personal freedom compared to the repressive moralistic desert, as Baudrillard (1999) depicts Puritan-inspired America, they flee, at least temporarily and many others even permanently.

Sources and Grounds for Free Civil Society Estimates

Civil Liberties in General

The comparative estimates of civil liberties regarded as a defining prerequisite, essential ingredient, and diagnostic criterion of civil society as well as political democracy are derived from their global indexes comprised in the previously noted 'Democracy Index 2015' (Table 3.10). As seen, the following ten countries within OECD—Australia, Canada, Ireland, New Zealand, Norway, Chile, Finland, Iceland, Luxembourg and Sweden—have the highest civil liberty indexes, with the first five reaching the maximum index (10). In the present classification, almost all of them are categorized as liberal-secular civil societies, with only two exceptions, Chile and Ireland, belonging to their mixed counterparts, which, especially the first, can be interpreted as 'outliers.' Notably, this applies to the countries having the maximum indexes of civil liberties, with four of them being classified in the first, none in the second, and only one, Ireland in the third type of civil society. This therefore largely confirms the anticipation that liberal-secular civil societies as a whole tend to exhibit the relatively highest level of civil liberties, with some reaching the absolute maximum and thus 'perfection' in this respect, simply being the freest overall and 'perfect' in part, with some secondary variations.

In regional terms, it is striking that the above top ten countries in civil liberties include almost all of, with Denmark as a single exception, Scandinavia universally deemed an exemplar of liberal-secular civil society, just as of the equivalent type of political democracy. This strongly reaffirms Samuelson's prior observation and clearly confirms the present prediction that Scandinavia overall as a region attains civil liberties, just as economic and political freedoms, 'second to none' comparatively among present Western and all societies and perhaps historically over time since classical Athens democracy and proto-liberal society.

Conversely, as also noted, these ten or so countries—Turkey, Mexico, Hungary, the US, Italy, South Korea, Estonia, France, Japan, Slovakia, and Slovenia—have the lowest civil liberty indexes. Presently, almost all of them are categorized either in anti-liberal and anti-secular civil society, including the conservative,

Southern US, or its mixed version, with only one, France in its opposite. This generally supports the expectations that the anti-liberal/anti-secular and mixed types of civil society tend to have overall the lower level of civil liberties than the liberal-secular type as a whole, again with secondary variations. In particular, the majority of the five countries with the lowest indexes are classified as anti-liberal and anti-secular civil societies—Turkey, Mexico, and the conservative US—which strongly support the expectation that this type has overall the lowest level of or even ultimately no civil liberties and is in that sense truly an 'un-civil' society. In turn, the cases of Hungary and Italy confirm that mixed civil societies overall are less free than their liberal-secular counterparts as a whole.

Their indexes indicate or predict that Turkey under Islamic theocratic rule, Catholic-pervaded Mexico, and the Southern theocentric US belong to the same category of a religiously-overdetermined and hence basically un- or quasi-free civil society invaded and disturbed in its inherent liberty and autonomy from religion and politics (and the economy) by a form or proxy of theocracy cum 'godly democracy' in the political system. Curiously, this reveals that the Southern theocentric US is not only because of its geographic proximity but also on account of its apparently lower level of civil liberties closer to Catholic-pervaded Mexico, just as to Islamic-ruled Turkey, than to its Northern neighbor liberal-secular Canada as well as Western Europe, notably 'post-Christian' Scandinavia. This also reaffirms casual observations, experiences, and perceptions or 'stereotypes' about the illiberality and the consequent illiberty of this part of the 'two Americas.'

Particularly striking is the fact that the 'godly,' mostly (but not only) Southern, US has the lowest index of civil liberties among all Western and related societies, including Australia, Canada, Germany, France, Italy, Japan, Spain, and the UK, as well as Scandinavia. If these is a 'consolation prize,' this might be that the American index is still higher than those of Turkey and Mexico, but one doubts that this is a sufficient compensation for US 'libertarian' economists and ethnocentric 'we are the only free society' politicians. Yet, this fact reaffirms the observations and expectations that anti-liberal and anti-secular or religiously-overdetermined—as by Puritan-rooted evangelicalism and Islam as theocratic equivalents—civil society is what US sociologist Ross connotes (referring to 'Puritan tyranny') the negative 'antidote,' so poison to civil liberties, just as to political freedom and democracy, thus operates as an 'un-civil' society. In addition, qualitative considerations are presented on particular civil liberties with missing or insufficient data, rankings, or reports are missing (Appendix 9.1).

Individual Liberty and Privacy

The comparative estimates of individual liberty are derived from personal freedom rankings by the Legatum Institute (Table 9.1).

As before, ten countries with the highest and with the lowest degrees of individual liberty, i.e., personal freedom are identified and considered. First, among the top ten countries in terms of personal freedom are the following in a descending order: Canada,[1] New Zealand, Norway, Luxembourg, Iceland, Ireland, Sweden, Denmark, Australia and Switzerland. In turn, the two supposed models of personal freedom are missing in this top ranking—the UK ranked 11 out of 33 countries and the US ranked 13. Therefore, virtually all of these most highly ranked countries, with a single exception of Ireland, in the present framework constitute liberal-secular civil societies, which almost completely confirms the expectation that these as a whole enjoy the highest degree of individual liberty. Consequently, the seemingly surprising 'missing links' of the UK and the US in the top ten club of individual liberty is actually unsurprising and predicted by being categorized not in liberal-secular civil society but in its intermediate type (the first) and its opposite ('conservative America'), respectively.

Second, these are ten countries with the lowest degree of personal freedom in an ascending order: Greece, Turkey, Hungary, Mexico, Korea, Slovakia, Estonia, Italy, Czech Republic, and Japan. Hence, nearly all of these lowest ranked countries, again with a single exception of Italy, are either non-liberal and non-secular civil societies such as Mexico, South Korea, and Turkey or intermediate instances like Czech Republic, Estonia, Greece, Hungary, Japan, and Slovakia, thus largely consistent with the expectations that the latter two types as a whole have the lower degrees of individual liberty than the former.

In addition, the comparative estimates of this essential component of civil society take into consideration some global rankings of Western and other countries in terms of privacy[2] and by implication individual liberty and dignity or personal choice, and in that sense 'individualism' (Table 9.2).

---

1 The Legatum Institute discloses in its latest 2015 report that 'Canada is now the freest country in the world, having risen five places to 1st in the Personal Freedom sub-index. The country is the most tolerant of immigrants in the world. 92 of people think the country is a good place for immigrants. It is also the fifth most tolerant of ethnic minorities. 92 of people think that the country is a good place for ethnic minorities. 94 of Canadians believe that they have the freedom to choose the course of their own lives—the fifth highest in the world.'

2 The source is Privacy International.

TABLE 9.1   *Personal freedom ranking, OECD countries, 2015*

Country	Rank	Point[a]
Canada	1	10
New Zealand	2	10
Norway	3	10
Luxembourg	4	9
Iceland	5	9
Ireland	6	9
Sweden	7	8
Denmark	8	8
Australia	9	8
Switzerland	10	7
United Kingdom	11	7
Netherlands	12	7
United States	13	6
Portugal	14	6
Germany	15	6
Finland	16	5
Austria	17	5
Belgium	18	5
France	19	4
Spain	20	4
Chile	21	4
Slovenia	22	3
Poland	23	3
Japan	24	3
Czech Republic	25	2
Italy	26	2
Estonia	27	2
Slovakia	28	1
Korea, South	29	1
Mexico	30	1
Hungary	31	0
Turkey	32	0
Greece	33	0

a Rank 1–3 = 9 points, rank 4–6 = 9 points, rank 7–9 = 8 points, rank 10–12 = 7 points, rank 13–15 = 6 points, rank 16–18 = 5 points, rank 19–21 = 4 points, rank 22–24 = 3 points, rank 25–27 = 2 points, rank 28–30 = 1 point, rank 31–33 = 0 points.
SOURCE: LEGATUM HTTP://WWW.PROSPERITY.COM.

The most striking and seemingly 'shocking' finding is that virtually all Western and other societies, excluding those for which no scores are provided like Chile, South Korea, and Mexico, have significantly and often dramatically higher 'privacy scores' than do the UK and the US. Conversely, the most conspicuous and

TABLE 9.2   *Global privacy rankings, OECD countries, 2007.*

Country	Overall Score	Point[a]
Greece	3.1	10
Canada	2.9	9
Hungary	2.9	9
Slovenia	2.8	8
Portugal	2.8	8
Luxembourg	2.8	8
Germany	2.8	8
Italy	2.8	8
Estonia	2.8	8
Belgium	2.7	8
Iceland	2.7	8
Czech Rep.	2.5	7
Finland	2.5	7
Ireland	2.5	7
Switzerland	2.4	6
New Zealand	2.3	6
Poland	2.3	6
Spain	2.3	6
Austria	2.3	6
Australia	2.2	5
Japan	2.2	5
Netherlands	2.1	5
Slovakia	2.1	5
Sweden	2.1	5
Norway	2.1	5
Denmark	2.0	4
France	1.9	4
US	1.5	2
UK	1.4	1
Chile	NA	NA

TABLE 9.2   *Global privacy rankings, OECD countries, 2007.* (cont.)

Country	Overall Score	Point[a]
Korea, South	NA	NA
Mexico	NA	NA
Turkey	NA	NA

a Score higher than 3 = 10 points; scores 2.9–3.0 = 9 points, scores 2.7–2.8 = 8 points, scores 2.5–2.6 = 7 points, scores 2.3–2.4 = 6 points, scores 2.1–2.2 = 5 points, scores 1.9–2.0 = 4 points, scores 1.7–1.8 = 3 points, scores 1.5–1.6 = 2 points, scores 1.3–1.4 = 1 point, scores under 1.2 = 0 points.

Note: 5 no invasive policy or widespread practice/leading in best practice 4.1–5.0 Consistently upholds human rights standards.

4 comprehensive efforts, protections, and safeguards for privacy 3.6–4.0 Significant protections and safeguards.

3 some safeguards, relatively limited practice of surveillance 3.1–3.5 Adequate safeguards against abuse.

2 few safeguards, widespread practice of surveillance 2.6–3.0 Some safeguards but weakened protections 2.1–2.5 Systemic failure to uphold safeguards. 1.6–2.0 Extensive surveillance societies 1.1–1.5 Endemic surveillance societies.

SOURCE: NATIONAL PRIVACY RANKING 2007.

at first glance 'stunning' are the lowest 'privacy scores' of the UK and the US among these societies. For example, Canada has a privacy score (2.9) twice as high that of its former colonizer the UK (1.4) and also almost double of that of its supposedly 'freer' neighbor the US (1.5), as do Germany (2.8), Italy (2.8), and even Greece (3.1), Hungary (2.9), Slovenia (2.8), Portugal (2.8), Luxembourg (2.8), Estonia (2.8), Slovenia (2.8), Belgium (2.7), and Iceland (2.7). Curiously, countries having higher privacy scores than do the UK and the US include not only Scandinavian and other Western European liberal-secular civil societies, as well as Australia (2.2), Canada, New Zealand (2.3), and Japan (2.2), as fully predicted. They also comprise all continental European countries, including those in Southern and Eastern Europe, for example, Greece and Hungary with the first and the second highest scores, and even Catholic-dominated nations like Ireland (2.5) and Poland (2.3).

Relatedly, the UK and the US are found to be the two 'countries with the worst records in privacy,' specifically in its various dimensions such as constitutional

TABLE 9.3   *Countries with the worst records in privacy, OECD countries, 2007.*

Constitutional protection:	UK, Australia
Statutory protection	Japan, US
Privacy Enforcement:	US
Identity Cards and Biometrics:	Belgium, Poland, Spain, Netherlands, Slovakia, UK, US
Data-sharing:	Belgium, Czech Republic, Finland, Austria, Netherlands, Denmark, France, UK, Norway
Visual surveillance:	Hungary, UK, Switzerland, US
Communication interception:	Greece, Hungary, Italy, Czech Republic, Poland, Spain, Netherlands, UK, New Zealand, US
Communication Data Retention:	Slovenia, Germany, Italy, Ireland, Poland, Netherlands, Slovakia, Sweden, Denmark, France, UK
Government Access to Data:	Slovakia, Sweden, Denmark, France
Workplace monitoring:	Sweden, US
Surveillance of Medical, Financial, and Movement:	Spain, Sweden, Denmark, UK, Australia, Norway, US
Border and trans-border issues	Denmark, France, UK, Iceland, Switzerland, Japan, Australia, Norway, US

SOURCE: NATIONAL PRIVACY RANKING 2007.

and statutory protection, privacy enforcement, surveillance, communication interception and data retention, and the like (Table 9.3).

For illustration, both have the worst records—seemingly incredibly but true—in most dimensions of privacy (8 out of 12), by far the highest figure among OECD countries, for example, twice as many as does France (4) and three or more times than do others (Table 9.4).

Evidently, no other country comes even close to matching the UK and the US supposedly the 'freest' and most 'individualistic' Western societies in such massive violations and disrespect of privacy and thus individual liberty and dignity and 'individualism.' It is particularly indicative and disturbing from the prism of a free civil society that the two putative 'beacons of liberty' and 'individualism' have the worst records, alongside some other countries, in constitutional (the UK) and statutory (the US) protection of privacy, privacy enforcement

TABLE 9.4 *Number of the worst records in privacy, OECD countries, 2007.*

Country	Number worst	Point[a]
Australia	2	8
Austria	1	9
Belgium	2	8
Canada	0	10
Chile	NA	NA
Czech Republic	2	8
Denmark	5	5
Estonia	0	10
Finland	1	9
France	4	6
Germany	0	10
Greece	1	9
Hungary	2	8
Iceland	1	9
Ireland	1	9
Italy	2	8
Japan	2	8
Korea, South	NA	NA
Luxembourg	0	10
Mexico	NA	NA
Netherlands	4	6
New Zealand	0	10
Norway	3	7
Poland	3	7
Portugal	0	10
Slovakia	3	7
Slovenia	0	10
Spain	3	7
Sweden	1	9
Switzerland	2	8
Turkey	NA	NA
UK	8	2
US	8	2

a Number 0 = 10 points, number 1 = 9 points, number 2 = 8 points, number 3 = 7 points, number 4 = 6 points, number 5 = 5 points, number 6 = 4 points, number 7 = 3 points, number 8 = 2 points, number 9 = 1 point, number more than 10 = 0 points.
SOURCE: NATIONAL PRIVACY RANKING 2007.

(the US), data-sharing (the UK), visual surveillance (both), communication interception (both), communication data retention (the UK), workplace monitoring (the US), surveillance of medical, financial, and movement (both), and border and transborder issues (both). Notably, both have the worst record in legal protection of privacy, namely the UK in its constitutional and the US in its statutory protections, as a likely legacy of their shared common law, especially its master-servant dimension treating political subjects and laborers as servants versus masters and thus denied substantial private liberty and individuality, as well as anti-privacy Puritanism as their common religious heritage. As regards the US, especially striking and disturbing is its worst record in statutory protection of privacy, privacy enforcement, and surveillance.

This seems surprising at first glance given the conservative perennial claim to 'American exceptionalism' in superior individual freedom and individualism but less so in light of the revelations of systematic and massive violations of private liberty by a proxy totalitarian police-surveillance state engaged in total and constant high- (and low-) tech spying on its citizens and others.[3] In

---

3 Furthermore, not only that of the US government, but also the conduct of virtually all Western governments in the case of Showden has appeared disgraceful and shameful by refusing to provide protection from apparent persecution in the evidently undignified, unprincipled, and seemingly cowardly attempt not to displease the first, while this person only being protected by a putative undemocratic non-Western state (Russia). Equally, if not more, disturbing was the treatment by especially British and Swedish governments of WikiLeaks founder Assange convicted of an Orwellian crime (sex without protection cum 'rape') in Sweden and detained in Britain for no rational legal reason, other than, as in the previous case, the rationale of 'cooperating' with the persecuting US government likely seeking to execute him for revealing that the 'emperor has no cloths,' and granted refuge only by a Third-World government's embassy. Thus, the United Nations panel, the Working Group on Arbitrary Detention, as reported by the press in February of 2016, found that 'Assange's detention was arbitrary because of "a substantial failure to exercise due diligence" by both governments, in particular Swedish prosecutors; five years after issuing an arrest warrant, Swedish prosecutors still had not pressed charges; prosecutors didn't show Mr Assange the evidence collected against him or give him a chance to respond; and prosecutors should have taken more seriously Mr Assange's fears of possible extradition to the United States.' These cases confirm that, contrary to its freedom claims, anti-liberal, conservative 'American exceptionalism' and 'imperialism' (Steinmetz 2014), joined by most Western countries within NATO, above all the UK, poses the gravest imminent threat to both political and individual liberty, democracy and free civil society on a global scale. (They also show that Western governments are as 'independent' and 'autonomous' of the US government as were the former Eastern communist states in relation to the Soviet Union—i.e., minimally—and in that sense represent no less 'satellites' than these did, often appearing as 'banana republics.') This applies to Western militarism, imperialism, and colonialism as a whole that as an instinct or vestige persists or reinvents

short, the 'state's reach into private lives'[4] in the US in its, anti-liberal, anti-secular pole is reportedly unmatched among major Western societies and only matched by that in the UK.

While admittedly this ranking does not fully corroborate the prediction that all Western European and other liberal-secular civil societies have higher privacy scores than do others, including Southern and Eastern Europe, it does clearly and strongly support the expectation that they do so compared to the UK and especially the US in the second specification classified in their mixed and opposite categories. In particular, if the US, specifically 'evangelical America,' is considered the 'only remaining primitive,' more specifically pre-liberal and pre-secular Puritan-rooted, civil society[5] modern among Western societies, then the ranking is consistent with the expectation that liberal-secular types are invariably freer, more protective of privacy and individual liberty, than their non-liberal, hyper-religious opposites or antecedents.

Thus, the US and the UK have the lowest privacy scores among Western and all other countries probably as the shared legacy of Puritanism's theocratic denial, disrespect, suppression, and violation of individual liberty and dignity, privacy,[6] and personal choice in the name and for the 'glory of God' after Calvin's model and precedent, manifesting path-dependence in this respect. To that extent, these scores indicate that Puritan-rooted societies—with the

---

itself in old and new forms—as manifested in NATO's 1999 unlawful bombing of Yugoslavia as an act of inter-state terror on behalf of an ethnic Islamic terrorist group, the US/UK 2003 illegal invasion and occupation of Iraq based on 'true lies,' etc.—and continues to eliminate or subvert political and civil liberties and rights both at home and abroad. In this respect, persistent American conservative and other Western nationalism, militarism, and imperialism by apparently not forgetting its 'good old ways' acts as the nemesis of modern free civil society and democracy in America and the West itself, let alone the non-Western world still despised as an 'inferior' and 'unfree' proxy colonial or imperial space to be placed under its military and political control or the 'sphere of influence' (e.g., the Balkans, South America, etc.).

4 Baker and Mezzetti (2012, p. 514) state that in the US 'judicial decisions set the ground rules for the political process and define the state's reach into private lives,' but evidently do not significantly reduce such overreach and instead legitimize it, primarily in the anti-liberal, anti-secular conservative section of America.

5 Contemporary conservative America as the 'only remaining primitive' Puritan society is described in Baudrillard (1999, p. 7); similar observations are found in Mueller (2009) and Munch (2001).

6 Walzer (1963, p. 64) observes that Puritan theological individualism 'never led to respect for privacy' in England and by implication New England, such as the 'list of offenses which merited excommunication' included 'for being overtaken in beer,' thus prefiguring US Prohibition in the 1920s, 'for dancing and other vanities,' etc.

evangelical-Southern US reportedly more than the UK[7]—seem still unable or unwilling to overcome such an adverse and destructive pattern to a free civil society due to their path-dependence on or remembrance of anti-privacy, anti-individual moral liberty, and anti-personal choice Puritanism. In this sense, these scores are not random in both comparative and historical terms, but systemic indicators by indicating that these two societies fail to create or sustain a truly liberal-secular society as a configuration of individual liberty and dignity, personal choice, and privacy comparatively and primarily because they remain more or less Puritan path-dependent historically.

The preceding justifies the seemingly dubious US and UK scores on individual liberty and privacy, while contradicting the usual claims to 'exceptional' America and Great Britain having the highest, maximal levels in this respect and generally as the freest and even the only free civil societies in the Western and entire world—and presumably because of their shared Puritan past and heritage and thus path-dependence on Puritanism. Hence, through these estimates and their grounding the above demonstrates the opposite, namely that UK and US strikingly low privacy scores probably are such primarily because of their shared Puritan background, reflections of the anti-privacy pattern and ghost of Puritanism, as Hume, Mill, and Weber, among others, classically show and emphasize (and Presbyterian Adam Smith admits). In their account, Puritanism in England and New England, just as its parent Calvinism in parts of France, Geneva, Holland, etc., never recognized or respected but denied and suppressed the right to privacy, individual liberty and dignity, and personal choice, and evidently historically Puritan societies like the UK and especially 'evangelical America,' with some adaptations, still do not, as indicated by their lowest privacy scores among Western and related countries.

In light of that all Western and related societies have higher and Canada twice as high scores on privacy and to that extent on individual liberty and dignity and personal choice, i.e., 'individualism,' the UK and the US record on this essential condition and dimension of free civil society can only be described as dismal, and the claims to being the most or only privacy-liberty-choice 'protecting' and 'individualist' democracies in the world and history as

---

7 According to Munch (2001, p. 224), 'in no other country did Puritanism attain significance comparable to (that) in the (US) as the carrier of modern normative culture.' Munch (2001, p. 231) elaborates that 'even today, a special characteristic of American society is that the various institutions of society are more thoroughly penetrated by such a generally binding (religious) morality, rooted in Puritanism yet generalized beyond it, than is the case in the societies of Europe.'

baseless.[8] At this juncture, scientific observers and peoples in other countries may be perplexed or wonder if the UK and the US do not promote privacy and thus individual liberty and dignity and personal choice to the same degree as do the above Western and related societies, what kind of 'freedom,' 'choice,' and 'individualism' within free civil society they claim to sustain as the 'freest' and most 'individualist' ever. For the only kind of genuine 'freedom,' 'choice,' and 'individualism' within free civil society as the sphere of free private life is individual liberty and dignity (and happiness) and personal choice as approximated by privacy and its scores as reported above.

Consequently, a society's failure or success in privacy and thus individual liberty and personal choice is also one in 'freedom,' 'choice,' and 'individualism' in a free civil society. There is no such thing as 'freedom,' 'choice,' and 'individualism' in a free civil society as the free private sphere distinct from and outside of privacy, individual liberty and dignity (and happiness) and personal choice. Hence, if among Western and related societies the UK and the US in the second rendition fail most dismally on privacy, individual liberty and dignity and personal choice, they also do so on 'freedom,' 'choice,' and 'individualism' as their alleged comparative and historical superiority within a free civil society. The above is instructive to emphasize because the UK and 'conservative America' are claimed or perceived to establish and promote privacy and thus individual liberty and personal choice, simply 'individualism,' within civil society more than any or even solely among Western and all societies. These findings and many other observations and events, including the recent disclosure of near-totalitarian government surveillance and systematic egregious and unrepentant Puritan-style violations of privacy and individual liberty in the conservative US and in part the UK demonstrate that such claims or perceptions are without merit.

---

8   In sociology this empirically ungrounded non sequitur or wishful thinking of American exceptional individual liberty and individualism overall, as well as individualistic democracy, within 'conservative America' has been especially promoted by Parsons (1951) and his disciples in postwar times, and Lipset (1996; Lipset and Marks 2000) more recently, along with Friedman (1982) and the Chicago School overall in economics. Giddens (1984, pp. 273–74) describes 'Parsons's view that half a million years of human history culminate in the social and political system of the United States' as 'more than faintly ridiculous.' Similarly, Lipset's (1996) self-professed super-patriotism contaminates and distorts sociological analysis and allows to promote the fiction of conservative 'American exceptionalism' in superior individual liberty, privacy, and individualism in civil society, as well as political freedom and individualistic democracy, as the supposed 'model' for Western and all societies.

In sum, the striking—seemingly shocking but actually, in light of the anti-privacy legacy of Puritanism, not surprising—finding that the UK and the US have the lower degrees of privacy and to that extent individual liberty and dignity and personal choice defining 'individualism' in civil society than all Western and related societies cast doubt on the claims that the two are the most or even only 'individualistic' countries in the world. This also applies to the revelations of near-totalitarian government surveillance and violations of privacy and individual liberty and dignity in the US and the UK on 'national security' grounds, actually driven by the compound of aggressive nationalism, militarism, and imperialism or expansionism as another shared legacy of nativist, militarist, and expansionist Puritanism[9] with its proxy genocide of Native Americans as 'heathen' and its parent Calvinism as Weber's 'Church Militant.' In a way, as regards privacy and hence individual liberty and personal choice, what Weber refers to Germans' perception of 'pure hypocrisy' of 'Americanism' perhaps best describes the claims of American and English 'exceptionalism' in superior and even sole 'individualism' in civil society and beyond.

Alternatively, virtually all other Western and related societies, including Canada and Germany (plus even Greece[10]), surpass the UK and the US in

---

9   Tiryakian (2002, p. 1630) remarks that the 'Puritan-based ethic,' by being 'devoid of the norms of *caritas* and *compassion* that are in the lineage of the welfare state,' has a 'very dark side. It has been and can be even today a ubiquitous and insidious codeterminant of American and British bellicose but moralistic foreign policy, including various old and new manifestations of imperialism and aggressive use of "smart" weapons of mass destruction against demonized non-Western settings.' Munch (2001, p. 235) notes the 'expulsion of the (American) Indians from their lands, their oppression, and the destruction of their culture' initiated by Puritanism and continued under the influence of the notion of 'manifest destiny'. Mann (2005) also treats Puritanism's initial (and subsequent) war against the Native Americans as a prototypical case of genocide.

10   Greece's highest privacy score is as puzzling as are (seemingly) the UK and US lowest scores, and contradicts the expectation that non-liberal and non-secular civil societies have lower degrees of privacy and individual liberty than the liberal-secular. A partial explanation maybe that the Christian Orthodox church as Greece's official one is observed to be less coercive and intrusive in private life, as well as less theocratic in politics, than was Puritanism during its rule in England and especially America, and perhaps even Catholicism, as seen in Poland and Ireland. In Weber's terms, the Orthodox church is more characterized with 'other-worldly' asceticism as through monasticism, and generally focused on the 'spiritual Kingdom of God' in the world beyond, and consequently less interested in this life, including less intrusive into privacy and individual liberty, plus less politically ambitious and involved, in stark contrast to Puritanism and Calvinism overall

privacy and in that sense individual liberty and dignity, and personal choice, simply 'individualism' in civil society, and thus appear as models for the last two rather than conversely as in English and American individualistic 'exceptionalism.' In particular, Canada by virtue of having twice as high degree of privacy can serve as a model for both its former colonizer and its 'individualistic' neighbor and consequently in terms of individual liberty and dignity and personal choice, i.e., 'individualism' in the life-world, as the essential dimension of a free civil society. Canada can be such a model because it has probably overcome the partial past and legacy of anti-privacy Puritanism—anyway, a weaker historical factor in this society than in the UK and especially the US—and also evidently does not find it necessary or prudent to deny and violate privacy and individual liberties and rights on 'national security' grounds by contrast to the two. Canada's lesson is that the anti-privacy and anti-individual liberty past and 'ghost' of 'Puritanism is not necessarily a destiny but can be overcome,' and 'national security' such as the 'war of terror,' just as the Cold War, does not represent a necessary cause or valid rationale for privacy and individual freedom suppressions, in contrast to the UK and the US in both respects.

Ultimately, the overarching reason why Canada exhibits twice as high score of privacy and thus individual liberty as the two is that it has become a more liberal-secular civil society than the UK and especially the US in the second rendition, even if sharing (albeit less) with them a Puritan anti-privacy history and heritage, as well as current 'national security' concerns and participation

---

as 'inner-worldly' asceticism seeking to recreate the 'Dominion of God' in this world and hence more 'curious' and intruding in people's private lives and theocratic. Relatedly, in Weber's framework the Orthodox church belongs to religions of 'passive adaptation' and 'accommodation' to the world, including private life, while Calvinism, including Puritanism, represents the (sole) religion of 'mastery of the world,' notably the 'domination of the sinful world,' which evidently explains and rationalizes its denial and suppression of privacy and individual moral liberty as the sphere or potential of sins equated and punished as crimes. Hence, the higher privacy score of Greece than those of the UK and above the US is not as surprising as it seems at first sight to the extent that religion, even if official, mostly adapts to private life or civil society in the first case, and, regardless of not being formally a state one, dominates it in the second cases. In passing, such a stark difference in privacy contradicts the 'rational choice' theory cum economics of religion that countries with state religions such as European ones have no or lower private and political freedoms, while those with no such religion, notably the US, being superior in this respect, overlooking that the first churches may suppress or invade privacy less, as in Greece (plus Italy, etc.) than the second through their effective capture of or strong influence on a formally separate state, as precisely observed in 'conservative America,' above all the neo-Puritan South turned the theocratic 'Bible Belt.'

in the 'war of terror.' To that extent, the dramatic difference between Canada and the UK and the US in privacy scores provides an equivalent of a confirmatory laboratory test or of controlled cross-national experiment that a liberal-secular civil society tends to attain and sustain higher individual liberty and privacy than do its opposites, at least the conservative 'Southern United States' within America, or mixed cases, including Britain.

At this juncture, perhaps nothing among Western and related societies or regions more clearly and strongly demonstrates and illustrates this divergent impact on individual liberty and privacy of liberal-secular civil society and its opposite than the divergence between Canada and 'conservative America' as exemplars of the first and second type. If Canada's privacy score is almost as twice as high as that of the US, it is probably even higher compared to 'conservative America' like the South given that this region is commonly observed to be the most non-liberal and anti-secular or hype-religious form of regional civil society within the country, and thus likely to dramatically depress its overall degree of privacy and individual liberty and personal choice, just as all other, economic, political, and cultural, liberties and rights.

The degrees or scores of privacy and in extension of individual liberty and personal choice deserve more attention and elaboration than seemingly justified because they form the defining, essential prerequisite, component, and dimension of a free civil society. Furthermore, they do so because they are necessary to and constitutive of a free society as a whole in that they give further substance, value, vigor, or meaning to all other, i.e., economic, political, and cultural liberties, choices, and rights. Conversely, without substantial privacy, individual liberty and personal choice virtually all other liberties, choices, and rights, economic, political, and cultural, becomes emptied or reduced in value and meaning. Simply, one wonders if people do not enjoy basic privacy at their home and individual liberty and personal choice in their life, what is the substance, value, point or meaning of their having and realizing economic, political, and cultural liberties, choice, and rights.

At the minimum, their substance, value, or meaning is, even if not reduced to zero, devalued and diminished greatly, when privacy and individual liberty are denied or suppressed. This sheds a new light on those societies actually or potentially denying or suppressing them, even if they are really or hypothetically permitting and promoting all other liberties, choices, and rights. As seen, this problem or dilemma is especially evident in the UK and the UK in the conservative rendition due to having the lowest scores of privacy and thus individual liberty among Western and related societies, notably by comparison to their former colony and closest neighbor Canada, which justifies their lengthy comparative discussion above.

Reproductive Liberties and Rights

The comparative estimates of reproductive liberties and rights such as the freedom and right of abortion among Western and related countries take into consideration some reports on this indicator of a free civil society. Generally, these countries, except for only a few, recognize the freedom and right of abortion, although in different degrees. Notably, Western and related societies that recognize full, unrestricted abortion rights are mostly are classified into liberal-secular civil societies, with certain exceptions, which at least in part confirms the expectations.

Virtually all Western and related countries classified as liberal-secular civil societies establish the right to abortion 'without restriction as to reason' (Table 9.5).

TABLE 9.5   *Abortion rights in OECD countries, 2013.*

I To save woman's life or prohibited	Point[a]
Chile	0
Ireland	0
Mexico	0
II To preserve health or prohibited	
New Zealand	1
Poland	1
Korea, South	1
III Socioeconomic grounds (also to save the woman's life and health)	
Finland	2
Great Britain	2
Iceland	2
Japan	2
IV Without restriction as to reason	
Australia	10
Austria	10
Belgium	10
Canada	10
Czech Rep.	10
Denmark	10
Estonia	10
France	10

Germany	10
Greece	10
Hungary	10
Italy	10
Luxembourg	10
Netherlands	10
Norway	10
Portugal	10
Slovakia	10
Slovenia	10
Spain	10
Sweden	10
Switzerland	10
Turkey	10
United States	10

a Without restriction as to reason = 10 points, socioeconomic grounds = 2 points, to preserve health or prohibited =1, to save woman's life or prohibited = 0 points.
SOURCE: THE CENTER FOR REPRODUCTIVE *RIGHTS* HTTP://REPRODUCTIVERIGHTS.ORG.

Among these societies, New Zealand is the sole exception by allowing it only 'to save woman's life' and 'to preserve health,' and Finland and Iceland partial exceptions permitting it, in addition, on 'socioeconomic grounds,' along with Japan the UK within the mixed category. Concerning, New Zealand's exception, it seems puzzling but perhaps can be explained by the recent rise or import of anti-liberal neo-conservatism from the UK and the conservative US, mixing unrestricted freedom for capital in the economy with repression and restrictions in civil society, particularly associated with a version of American Draconian 'three strikes laws,' the only two countries having such laws among Western societies. Alternatively, among more than twenty societies having abortion rights 'without restriction as to reason' only two are not classified into liberal-secular or eclectic civil societies, but instead in their opposites, namely Greece and Turkey, along with the US in the double liberal-conservative specification. These exceptions perhaps merit more attention.

First, Greece's exception in unrestricted abortion rights, as in high privacy, can probably be explained by what Weber calls the 'other-worldly asceticism,' including monasticism, and passive 'accommodation to the world' of its dominant religion (the Orthodox Church) tending to be non-coercive or non-intrusive and uninterested in personal reproductive and related acts and decisions. In Weber's contact, this is in sharp contrast to 'inner-worldly asceticism' and the 'mastery of the world' attributed to Calvinism, including Puritanism, resorting to intense coercion and totalitarian intrusion in people's moral lives. On this account, the case of Greece actually reaffirms that a secular civil society—i.e., one not coerced or invaded by religion as well as the state—is associated with greater abortion and related personal rights. Second, Turkey's exception in unrestricted abortion rights is evidently the legacy of a historically secular civil society and state since Ataturk through the 2000s, a heritage that the Islamic-rooted government has attempted but not succeeded yet to completely erase or reverse during recent times, and thus cannot be assumed to survive indefinitely under such theocratic attacks. In this regard, Turkey's case represents a confirmation of, rather than being an exception to, the pattern that a secularized civil society promotes abortion and other individual rights, in this case the first as the recent past leaving a strong legacy of such rights that even subsequent theocratic forces have not been able to fully eradicate yet. Third, the US case of abortion rights 'without restriction as to reason' represents the evident legacy of a relatively secularized and liberalized civil society and polity from the 1960s to the 1980s, as reflected in the pertinent Supreme Court decision during that period. As in the case of Turkey under Islamic-rooted government since the 2000s, this is a liberal-secular legacy that revived religious forces, above all 'born again' evangelicals joined with orthodox Catholics within the 'Christian right,' consistently and vehemently attempt to eradicate by federal and state abortion restrictions in 'conservative America' culminating during the 2010s, reaffirming the coexistence and conflict between the 'two Americas' in this respect.

On the other hand, among those Western and related countries either prohibiting or severely restricting abortion rights most are classified into non-liberal and non-secular civil societies, thus at least partly confirming the expectations. Thus, countries that either prohibit or permit abortion only in exceptional situations such as to 'to save woman's life' or 'to preserve health' include Chile, Ireland, Mexico, and Poland,[11] in addition to South Korea and

---

11   Ruling conservatives in Poland banned and criminalized abortion in most cases as one of their first acts once in power almost immediately after the end of communism, during the early 1990s. Moreover, literally immediately upon returning to power in 2015 Polish ruling ever-more extreme conservatives have attempted and are still attempting at the time of writing these lines to prohibit and criminalize abortion in all cases, absolutely, totally and forever, as they and their 'brothers in arms' in the US (as noted by Mueller 2009) love to say or imply. At least on account of abortion rights and thus a free civil society overall, the end of communism in Poland far from bringing liberty and liberation only substituted religious oppression through effective theocracy for communist dictatorship,

New Zealand. Most of these countries, except for two, are classified as non-liberal and non-secular highly religious civil societies, or at least not belonging to a liberal-secular type.

For example, the first four are predominantly Catholic societies and even, especially post-communist Poland, to some extent proxy theocracies or theocentric states, thus forming the polar opposite and negation of liberal-secular civil society and democracy, so their prohibition or severe restriction of abortion rights fully confirms the prediction. In turn, South Korea is seemingly a more ambiguous instance but still seems closer to a non-liberal or non-secular civil society and 'democracy' than to its liberal-secular type by being mostly conservative or religious—including evangelical and other Christian penetration and influence—coupled with a persistently authoritarian state until recently, thus confirming in part the expectation. This leaves New Zealand as the sole exception to the pattern of non-liberal and non-secular civil society and lack of abortion and related moral rights, but turns out to be less so in that its liberal-secular type is perverted into the opposite or distorted by anti-liberal and anti-secular conservatism imported from the UK and the US, including American-style conservative 'three strike laws.'

In sum even if the overall picture is more complex than perhaps expected, with certain unexpected yet mostly seeming rather than actual exceptions as those mentioned, it is evident that liberal-secular civil societies as a whole tend to promote and protect the freedom and right of abortion more than do their opposites or eclectic cases, which is consistent with the predictions.

Freedom of Alcohol Production, Distribution, and Consumption

The comparative estimates of the freedom of alcohol production, distribution, and consumption as both an economic action and a personal liberty in Western and related societies take into account the statistical data on global alcohol prohibitions and restrictions, including age limits.[12] For example, according to

---

thus one form of totalitarianism and terror was just substituted with another equally and perhaps even, because of its ultimate Divine justification (as suggested by Juergensmeyer 2003), more severe and extensive. Generally, Poland's tragedy under both communism and anti-communism shows that substituting one anti-liberal, totalitarian social system with another while a necessary is not a sufficient condition for individual liberty and so a free civil society unless and until this substitute is a liberal and secular type.

12   The source is World Health Organization.

a global report (Table 9.6), the lowest legal age limits for free alcohol purchase and consumption are found in Western and other European countries here classified as liberal-secular societies.

TABLE 9.6   *Age limit for purchasing alcoholic beverages by country, OECD countries, 2004.*

Country	Beer	Wine	Spirits	Point[a] (Lowest limit)
Australia	18	18	18	7
Austria	16	16	18	9
Belgium	NA	NA	NA	NA
Canada	19	19	19	3
Chile	18	18	18	7
Czech Republic	18	18	18	7
Denmark	15	15	15	10
Estonia	18	18	18	7
Finland	18	18	20	2
France	16	16	16	9
Germany	16	16	18	9
Greece[b]	17	17	17	8
Hungary	18	18	18	7
Iceland	20	20	20	2
Ireland	18	18	18	7
Italy	16	16	16	9
Japan	20	20	20	2
Korea, South	19	19	19	3
Luxembourg[b]	16	16	16	9
Mexico	18	18	18	7
Netherlands	16	16	18	9
New Zealand	18	18	18	7
Norway	18	18	20	7
Poland	18	18	18	7
Portugal	16	16	16	9
Slovakia	18	18	18	7
Slovenia	15	15	15	10
Spain	16	16	16	9
Sweden	20	20	20	2
Switzerland	16	16	18	9

Country	Beer	Wine	Spirits	Point[a] (Lowest limit)
Turkey	18	18	18	7
United Kingdom	18	18	18	7
United States	21	21	21	1

a Age limit 15 = 10 points, age limit 16 = 9 points, age limit 17 = 8 points, age limit 18 = 7 points, age limit 19 = 3 points, age limit 20 = 2 points, age limit 21 = 1 points, age limit higher than 21 = 0 points.
b On-premise.
Note: Off-Premise, except.
SOURCE: WORLD HEALTH ORGANIZATION, GLOBAL STATUS REPORT: ALCOHOL POLICY 2004, GENEVA.

For example, France (16), Germany (16), Austria (16), Switzerland (16), the Netherlands (16), Luxembourg (16), Slovenia (15), Spain (16), Italy (16), and Portugal (16), have lower age alcohol limits than other countries (mostly 18 with some variations).

Conversely, certain non-liberal and non-secular or hyper religious societies have the highest legal age limits for free alcohol purchase and consumption. For example, the US classified in this category in its conservative rendition has by far the highest age limit (21) among all Western and even non-Western countries, being dramatically higher than that of Europe overall, for example, no less than 6 years compared to Slovenia, and 5 years by comparison to France, Germany, Austria, Switzerland, the Netherlands, Luxembourg, Spain, and Italy. It therefore represents a 'deviant case' and striking outlier on this dimension, just as in most dimensions, of individual liberty and personal choice. In addition, the US age alcohol limit is 2 and 3 years higher than those of its neighbors Canada (19) and Mexico (18), as well as 3 years higher even than that of its former colonial ruler and also historically Puritan Great Britain (18).

In particular, this significant difference from the latter confirms the observation that Puritanism has eventually been more tempered in its moralistic prohibitions and theocratic coercion, as by Anglicanism as well as liberalism and secularism, in the UK than in the US, namely 'evangelical America,' where, in spite or because of its disestablishment as the official religion in New England, it has been succeeded by neo-Puritan evangelicalism[13] adopting

---

13   Munch (2001, p. 119) finds that 'Puritan radicalism was tempered by the maintenance of the Anglican Church order.' In turn, he observes that 'even today, a special characteristic

'Puritanical beliefs.' As a particular curiosity, even Islamic Turkey has the lower age limit for free alcohol purchase and consumption (18) than the US. However, like unrestricted abortion rights, this is apparently the result and legacy of a previous relatively liberal-secular civil society or state in Turkey—exemplified by its founder's permission of and Islamist-imputed penchant for alcohol—and is under attack by the recent and present moralistic Islamic-based government, which therefore confirms the expected link between the two in this case. In the meanwhile, even Turkey under Islamic moralistic rule, including the most recent anti-alcohol attacks, continues to have a low age limit for alcohol consumption than the US, including less outright prohibitions than the neo-Puritan South.

In general, these data support the observation and expectation that liberal-secular Western European civil societies as a whole tend to have the higher degrees of freedom of legal alcohol consumption than do their illiberal, non-secular opposites like 'evangelical America' a la the 'Bible Belt'[14] where not only age and other restrictions persist and are zealously enforced by special anti-alcohol commissions and police forces, but Prohibition[15] continues ('dry' counties). In particular, the unmatched and unreasonably or contradictory

---

of American society is that the various institutions of society are more thoroughly penetrated by such a generally binding (religious) morality, rooted in Puritanism yet generalized beyond it, than is the case in the societies of Europe' (Munch 2001, p. 231). Munch (2001, p. 270) concludes that contemporary US Puritan-rooted 'fundamentalist Protestant movements' arise and act 'against the reality of a liberal and pluralist society.' Archer (2001, p. 277) remarks that in the America during the 'Great Awakenings,' the 'new (evangelicalism) carried forward the Puritan idea that the Bible revealed the will of God, and that government should act to reorganize society in accordance with that will (which) remained a central element of American culture to this day.' In particular, Archer (2001, pp. 282–83) notes that these US 'neo-Puritan social movements demanded that the government act to end a wide range of sinful practices (i.e.) to draw the state into pietistic moral crusades,' including 'prohibition of alcohol,' as well as 'sexual morality,' etc. Samuelsson (1961, p. 149) refers to the 'Puritan South' as being for long 'much more Puritan than the states of the North' and also economically 'under-developed.' Mueller (2009, p. 392) registers the 'Puritanical beliefs' of today's US evangelical fundamentalists.

14   Bailey and Snedker (2011, p. 845) cite the observation (by theologian Neibhur) that 'if there were a drunken orgy somewhere, I would bet ten to one a (Southern) church member was not in it. But if there were a lynching, I would bet ten to one a church member was in it'—and with some variations, this still applies to today's South, replacing lynching with shooting in accord with the 'God and guns' bumper-sticker.

15   Mueller (2013, p. 8) remarks that Puritan-inspired 'religious fundamentalists were behind the Prohibition movement in the United States at the start of the twentieth century. Not only did Prohibition infringe on the rights of those with less strong religious convictions, it resulted in a great increase in crime in the United States.'

highest legal age limit and a myriad of other post-Prohibition alcohol prohibitions and restrictions perpetuating the ghost and dismal failure of Puritanical Prohibition highlights the US estimate on this seemingly trivial but integral indicator of a free civil society, so a dimension of personal freedom, choice, and privacy.

Freedom of Drug Production, Distribution, and Consumption

The Death Penalty for Drug Offenses

The death penalty for drug offenses can be taken as an indication or proxy of the freedom of production, distribution, possession, and consumption of drugs at the minimum, existential level in the sense that such activities are not punished with government executions, even if they are usually otherwise such as imprisonment and other sanctions. Thus, no death penalty for such offenses indicates that at the minimum drug offenders, including producers and distributors of drugs, have the freedom and right to life, simply are 'free to live' at least, and conversely, its application denies this most basic, existential liberty just because of such moral sins-as-crimes. In short, this is the existential minimum of freedom, a matter of life and death in respect of such activities.

For instance, a global report (Table 9.7) suggests that virtually all Western and related societies, with only a few exceptions, refrain from applying the death penalty for drug offenses.

TABLE 9.7   *The death penalty for drug offences worldwide*

High commitment states	Point[a]
China	
Iran	
Saudi Arabia	
Viet Nam	
Singapore	
Malaysia	
Low Commitment States	
Indonesia	
Kuwait	
Thailand	
Pakistan	
Egypt	

TABLE 9.7   *The death penalty for drug offences worldwide.* (cont.)

High commitment states	Point[a]
Syria	
Yemen	
Bangladesh	
Symbolic Commitment States	
Lao People's Democratic Republic	
Cuba	
Taiwan	
Oman	
United Arab Emirates	
Bahrain	
India	
Qatar	
Gaza (Occupied Palestinian Territories)	
Myanmar	
Korea, South	2
Sri Lanka	
Brunei-Darussalam	
United States of America	2
Insufficient Data	
North Korea, South	
Iraq	
Libya	
No Commitment to the death penalty	
Other OECD countries	10

a High commitment states = 0 points, low commitment states = 1
point, symbolic commitment states = 2 points, no commitment to
the death penalty = 10 points.
SOURCE: THE DEATH PENALTY FOR DRUG OFFENCES:
GLOBAL OVERVIEW 2010, THE INTERNATIONAL HARM
REDUCTION ASSOCIATION (IHRA).

More specifically, it divides countries on this basis into, first, 'High Commitment States,' second, 'Low Commitment States,' third, 'Symbolic Commitment States,' and fourth, likely Commitment States but with 'Insufficient Data.' No Western and related societies such as OECD countries are listed in 'High Commitment' or 'Low Commitment' States comprising mostly Islamic theocracies or nations (Iran, Saudi Arabia, Malaysia, Indonesia, Kuwait, Pakistan, Egypt, Syria, Yemen, Bangladesh) and other non-Western authoritarian governments (China, Vietnam, Singapore).

In turn, the only OECD countries found in 'Symbolic Commitment States' legally or symbolically committed to applying the death penalty for drug offenses are South Korea and the US, together with Islamic theocracies or nations (Oman, United Arab Emirates, Bahrain Qatar, Gaza, Brunei) and other non-Western authoritarian or religious and traditionalist governments (Myanmar, Sri Lanka, Lao, Cuba, Taiwan, India). As known, South Korea and the US in the second rendition are classified in anti-liberal and anti-secular civil societies, which thereby fulfills the expectation that the latter permit lower individual liberty, choice, and privacy than do others, above all their liberal-secular opposites. Thus, none of OECD countries classified as liberal-secular civil societies is found to be legally, symbolically committed to using the death penalty for drug offenses. Evidently, the above two anti-liberal and anti-secular societies deny, at least legally or symbolically, the minimal, existential freedom and right to life in respect of drug offenses, especially production and distribution of drugs—simply, denying that such offenders are 'free to live' because of such actions—while their liberal-secular opposites preserve this basic and related individual freedoms and rights typifying a free civil society. Lastly and predictably, no Western and related societies are listed in likely 'Commitment States' but with 'Insufficient Data,' again represented by Islamic theocracies or nations (Iraq, Libya) and other non-Western authoritarian countries (North Korea).

The above report thus reaffirms the well-known fact that the level of punishment for producing, distributing, possessing, and consuming criminalized drugs is becoming increasingly less severe and thus common or convergent among Western societies, often due to partial or full drug decriminalization, with the sole salient, perpetual exception of the US (minus a few states). Most of these societies punish such activities, especially the possession and consumption of drugs, with growing mildness, not just applying no death penalty, except for the US within the Western world and South Korea beyond, but also no or relatively short imprisonment, compared to violent and other crimes and to their punishments in non-Western countries, especially Islamic theocratic and other authoritarian Third-World states punishing them often with executions. Moreover, some European and other countries (e.g., Australia and Canada) classified as liberal-secular civil societies reportedly open 'drug consumption rooms' permitting individuals 'who use drugs to inject in a safe space and under medical supervision,'[16] but this is evidently a taboo and

---

16   Harm Reduction International's 2014 Global State of Harm Reduction (p. 16) reports the
     following: 'In 2014 there are now 88 drug consumption rooms (DCRs) operating worldwide.'

unheard-of in their non-liberal and non-secular opposites like the US in the second rendition.

Such punitive mildness, notably opening 'drug consumption rooms,' recognizes some degree or proxy of freedom or legitimacy of drugs, especially their possession and consumption, at the minimum, it admits that such activities are no genuine, serious crimes or minor offenses. To that extent, a higher level of punitive mildness indicates or predicts an implicit or eventual recognition of such freedom, as well as an admission of these acts as non- or quasi-crimes, simply moral sins or vices not to be criminalized or harshly punished, just as alcohol, etc. While Western and related countries exhibit a comparatively common or convergent pattern of punitive mildness in this regard, still those presently classified as liberal-secular civil societies tend to the mildest[17] in punishing non-violent drug offenses, often even applying no physical punishment such as imprisonment, as especially and growingly witnessed in Western Europe and Canada (and a few US liberal states), which thus confirms the expectations. Hence, the above report suggesting a shared mild level of punishment in the sense of applying no death penalty for drug offenses and thus an implicit recognition of some modicum of individual freedom with respect to drugs provides grounds for the estimates on this dimension of a free civil society for Western and related countries.

As indicated, the virtually sole exception to the pattern of growingly mild punishment of no death penalty and no long incarceration for drug offenses among Western societies represents 'conservative America' (so minus a few

---

DCRs form a vital part of harm reduction services in some parts of Western Europe, allowing people who use drugs to inject in a safe space and under medical supervision. Outside of Europe two DCRs are in operation, one in Australia and one in Canada. In Western Europe, Denmark saw the implementation of five DCRs, and both Spain and Switzerland, who had previous DCRs in operation increased their site provision by six each. Between 2012–2014 a DCR was also opened in Greece but closed due to political pressures, and a reduction of DCRs has been seen in Germany with a decrease of 3 between 2012 to 2014, and the Netherlands, which saw a decrease of 10 in the same time period.' Generally, the *Economist*'s 2013 report on drugs notes 'the other big policy innovation in Europe has been to drop punitive policies in dealing with heroin and cocaine addiction, in favour of harm reduction' as through drug consumption rooms.

17   The *Economist* (April 25, 2015) comments that 'trading cannabis, which earns beheading in Saudi Arabia, has been legalised for recreational use in four states of America, as well as in Uruguay, and decriminalised in much of Europe and Latin America. Heroin addiction is increasingly treated as an illness rather than a crime: clean needles are available in many rich countries, and a few, including Britain and Switzerland, even prescribe heroin to a small number of addicts. In most areas of social policy, such different regional policies would not matter much.'

liberal states), where such acts are typically punished with observed Draconian severity by comparison to these societies and almost equivalent to Islamic theocracies and other Third-World countries. Thus, the possession and consumption of drugs are usually punished with long and even, if repeated, life imprisonment ('three strikes' laws), and their production and distribution potentially with the death penalty[18] via the 'war on drugs' as (the war on) crimes. One might plausibly expect that Turkey under Islamic governance will be another exception in this respect. Yet, anti-drug wars and punishments in 'conservative America' appear, just as its anti-alcohol prohibitions and the national legal age alcohol limit, more encompassing and Draconian than even their Turkish versions due to a prior legacy of a partly liberal-secular civil society not yet totally erased by the ruling Islamists.

Other possible exceptions could be post-communist Poland, Mexico, Chile, and in part Ireland, all dominated by Catholicism, and Greece influenced by the Orthodox Church. Still, they apparently show less severity than the conservative pole of the US, probably because Catholic as well as Orthodox societies seem less Draconian-punitive and repressive of sins and vices (except for abortion), including drugs and alcohol, than their Puritan-rooted evangelical variant in America (the 'Bible Belt') and their Islamic counterparts, as Weber notes and predicts by citing the 'indulgent to the sinner' moral maxim of Catholicism. In turn, the actual exception of South Korea among OECD countries through its legal, symbolic commitment to the death penalty for drug offenses indicates that its authoritarian, illiberal legacy still persists despite its formal democracy, and justifies its being classified in anti-liberal, anti-secular civil societies.

By contrast to growing punitive mildness characterizing all Western and related societies (excluding South Korea), the exceptional severity of punishment in the conservative half of the US implies categorical, uncompromising denial and total suppression of any degree or proxy of freedom of drug possession and consumption as personal 'irrational' choice, let alone production and distribution as 'free enterprise.' It also results in a redefinition and reclassification of such behaviors as grave crimes deserving severe punishment to the literal no-return point of life-long imprisonment through Draconian 'three strikes laws' and potentially the death penalty. To that degree, such a Draconian level of punitive severity in the conservative 'war on drugs' since Reaganism indicates and predicts no actual existence or realistic prospect of this freedom,

---

18   In the 2016 the US government criticized the executions of drug traders by police forces in the Philippines but did not make any attempts to change the law providing for the use of the death penalty for trade in drugs in America.

and a refusal to admit or resign to these behaviors as non-violent sins-vices, so non- and quasi-crimes hence not to be criminalized or not as severely punished potentially with death as violent crimes.

This reveals striking and persistent conservative 'American exceptionalism' in Draconian severity of punishment and generally all-encompassing criminalization of drugs, like alcohol, not only in relation to Western Europe and Canada as liberal-secular civil societies but even Turkey under Islamic governance classified, like the US in the second rendition, into their opposites, with South Korea as the sole match in this regard.

In turn, this peculiar, seemingly surprising variation within the category of non-liberal and non-secular civil societies is explained and predicted by that their Puritan or evangelical forms in conservative America tend to be more severely punitive and generally moralistic and repressive than their Catholic versions, as in Poland and Mexico, and equally so as their Islamic counterparts, except still in Turkey due to its prior liberal-secular legacy. Apparently, within this category of non-liberal and non-secular civil societies, Mexico, Poland, and Turkey, along with intermediate instances Chile and Greece, contradict the expectations in terms of the severity of punishment for drugs (plus alcohol), but the conservative half of the US does fully confirm them. This suggests that not all such illiberal, hyper-religious civil societies are 'created equal,' equally severe, with their Puritan-evangelical form being 'more equal' in Draconian severity than others within the religious setting. In sum, while even most other non-liberal and non-secular civil societies, including Islamic-ruled Turkey, are not exceptions to the pattern of no death penalty for drug offenses, 'conservative America' is the salient and sole exception among all Western countries, which sheds light on its 'American exceptionalism' in this respect. (Additional qualitative considerations of the freedom of production, distribution, possession, and consumption of drugs are provided in Appendix 9.1.)

Sexual Freedoms and Rights

Legal Status of Extramarital Sex

The legal status of extramarital sex can be taken as an indicator or proxy, among others, of sexual freedoms and rights in the framework of a free civil society. Thus, observations (Table 9.8) show that extramarital sex or adultery is fully 'legal' in virtually all Western and related societies, such as OECD countries.

The only exception where it is illegal or semi-legal is the US, more precisely 'conservative America' such as more than 20 states and parts of the federal government, still criminalizing and occasionally or regularly (as in the military) punishing it, with the punishment potentially reaching life imprisonment.

TABLE 9.8   *Legal status of extramarital sex (Adultery), OECD countries, 2015.*

Legal	Point
Australia	10
Austria	10
Belgium	10
Canada	10
Chile	10
Czech Republic	10
Denmark	10
Estonia	10
Finland	10
France	10
Germany	10
Greece	10
Hungary	10
Iceland	10
Ireland	10
Italy	10
Japan	10
Korea, South	10
Luxembourg	10
Mexico	10
Netherlands	10
New Zealand	10
Poland	10
Portugal	10
Slovakia	10
Slovenia	10
Spain	10
Sweden	10
Switzerland[a]	10
Turkey	10
UK	10
Illegal	
US (21 state, military)	5

a   Adultery not ground for divorce.

SOURCE: WEISBROD (1999), *NEW YORK TIMES* (NOVEMBER 15, 2012)
FOR THE US, VARIOUS PRESS REPORTS FOR OTHER COUNTRIES.

Evidently, with this single exception, all Western and related societies permit the individual freedom and responsibility for extramarital sex, as none of them criminalizes and punishes adultery but treats it, like all forms of sex, as the matter of individual freedom of choice, consent, responsibility, and privacy, not of government enforcement and legal sanction. For example, adultery has a non-criminal legal status in all of the member countries of the European Union which also has prevented Turkey's Islamic government to recriminalize it as a violation of individual rights. In addition, according to the UN,[19] defining and punishing adultery 'as a criminal offence violates women's human rights.'

Conversely, some countries classified as non-liberal and non-secular or hyper-religious civil societies deny or restrict the individual freedom and responsibility for extramarital sex, as shown by its effective prohibition in 'conservative America' and its attempted proscription in Islamic-ruled Turkey. As a persistent exemplar of such societies 'conservative America' is the sole Western society that criminalizes, as in the military segment of the Federal government and various states, extramarital sex by, as typical, the Puritan-era adultery laws seen as unenforced and unenforceable but occasionally enforced on some adulterers to prove that Americans can never underestimate Puritanism or its heir evangelicalism and their obsession with sex with impunity. In turn, Islamic states are the only or main such examples within the non-Western world. Even among non-liberal, non-secular civil societies, the US in the conservative pole is a strikingly exceptional case, as Mexico, Poland, South Korea, and Turkey, as well as Chile and Greece as mixed cases, do not criminalize and so legally punish adultery, though, as noted, the Turkish Islamic government attempted to do so but failed under the external pressure of the European Union so far to reverse yet another legacy of a prior relatively liberal-secular civil society and state.

In sum, extramarital sex is legal in all Western countries but still remains a criminal offense, including a felony punishable with life and other imprisonment, in many (21) of the US states,[20] plus the military[21] branch of the Federal government, just as in most Islamic countries, minus Turkey so far.

---

19   This statement is from the United Nations Working Group on discrimination against women in law and in practice.

20   Weisbrod (1999, p. 143) notes, for example, 'Utah's adultery statute.' Adultery remains a felony crime in Puritan-founded Massachusetts as well as Idaho, Oklahoma, Wisconsin, and Michigan, with rare but still continuing prosecutions and potential punishments from monetary fines to life imprisonment, as in the last state.

21   The Associated Press (January 21, 2013) reports that 'at least 30 percent of military commanders fired over the past eight years lost their jobs because of sexually related offenses, including harassment, adultery, and improper relationships.' *New York Times* (November

Legal Status of Same-sex Marriage

The legal status of same-sex marriage can be taken as another indicator or proxy of sexual freedoms and rights within a free civil society. The information on the legal status of same-sex marriage in Western and related countries (Table 9.9) shows that countries where it is legal (through 2015) include Belgium, Canada, Denmark, France, Iceland, Ireland, Luxembourg, the Netherlands, New Zealand, Norway, Portugal, Spain, Sweden, the UK, and the US.

Since the vast majority of them (10 out of 14), including the US in its liberal pole, are classified as liberal-secular civil societies, except for several mixed instances, this largely confirms the prediction that these societies permit the highest degree of sexual and related individual freedoms and privacy. Conversely, none of countries classified in anti-liberal, anti-secular civil societies, Mexico, Poland, South Korea, Turkey, and the US in its conservative pole (until and unless forced by judicial decisions), as well as their mixed cases Chile and Greece, grant such legal status to same-sex marriage.

Next, countries where same-sex marriage is legal only in some jurisdictions are Mexico and the US until recently. In both, it is (was) legalized in some regions but not in others and even legally prohibited, as in most Southern and related conservative American states[22] until the series of judicial judgments of such prohibitions as unconstitutional, notably the 2015 Supreme Court ruling, including the persistence of sodomy, anti-homosexuality, and related Puritanical laws. Since these two countries, including the US in the second rendition, are classified as anti-liberal, anti-secular civil societies, this contradicts the expectations but only seemingly, as their neighbor Canada, belonging to liberal-secular society, grants a fuller and uncontested legal status to same-sex

---

15, 2012) comments that '(w)hen David H. Petraeus resigned as CIA director because of adultery, he was widely understood to be acknowledging a misdeed but not a crime. Yet in his state of residence, Virginia, as in 22 others including Massachusetts, adultery remains a criminal act, a vestige of the way US law has anchored legitimate sexual activity within marriage.' In addition, it remarks that Petraeus, 'a retired four-star general who gets a military pension (still) remains subject to military codes of conduct that prohibit adultery.' Moreover, *New York Times* suggests that even premarital sex was not legal in the US until the early 2000s observing that 'most states have purged their codes of laws regulating cohabitation, homosexual sodomy and fornication—sex between unmarried adults—especially after a 2003 Supreme Court decision in Lawrence v. Texas, which made sexual activity by consenting adults in private legal across the country.' If so, it took almost four centuries since the coming of the Puritans to the new world and their criminalization of 'fornication' to legalize premarital sex.

22   McVeigh and Diaz (2009, p. 898) remarks that 'all of the southern states have voted to ban same-sex marriage.'

TABLE 9.9   *Legal status of same-sex marriage, OECD countries, September 2016.*

Countries Where Same-Sex Marriage is Legal	Point[a]
Belgium (2003)	10
Canada (2005)	10
Denmark (2012)	10
England/Wales (2013)	10
Finland (2015)	10
France (2013)	10
Iceland (2010)	10
Ireland (2015)	10
Luxembourg (2014)	10
Netherlands (2000)	10
New Zealand (2013)	10
Norway (2009)	10
Portugal (2010)	10
Scotland (2014)	10
Spain (2005)	10
Sweden (2009)	10
United States (2015)	10
Countries Where Same-Sex Marriage is Legal in Some Jurisdictions	
Mexico (2009)	5

a   Legal = 10 points, partially legal = 5 points, illegal = 0 points.
SOURCE: HTTP://WWW.PEWFORUM.ORG.

marriage than Mexico and 'conservative America' where it is still contested in spite or because of the Supreme Court ruling. Overall, confirming the expectations, most liberal-secular civil societies grant full legal status to same-sex marriage, but none of their opposites or mixed counterparts do, such as Catholic-dominated Poland and Chile, Orthodox Greece, and Turkey under Islamic rule.

Legal Status of Prostitution

Yet another indicator or proxy of sexual freedoms and rights within a free civil society can be taken to be the legal status of prostitution. The legal status of prostitution in Western and related countries ranges from completely legal through limited legality and to illegal (Table 9.10).

The group of countries in which prostitution is completely legal includes Austria, Belgium, Canada, Chile, Czech Republic, Denmark, Estonia, Finland, Germany, Greece, Hungary, Ireland, Italy, Luxembourg, Mexico, the Netherlands, New Zealand, Poland, Portugal, Slovakia, Turkey, and the UK. Evidently, this is a mix of countries classified as liberal-secular, eclectic, and opposite civil societies, which evidently does not fully support the expectations. In turn, such

TABLE 9.10   *Legal status of prostitution by country, OECD countries, 2009.*

Legal	Point[a]
Austria	10
Belgium	10
Canada	10
Chile	10
Czech Republic	10
Denmark	10
Estonia	10
Finland	10
Germany	10
Greece	10
Hungary	10
Ireland	10
Italy	10
Luxembourg	10
Mexico	10
Netherlands	10
New Zealand	10
Poland	10
Portugal	10
Slovakia	10
Turkey	10
United Kingdom	10
Limited legality	
Australia	5
France	5
Iceland	5
Japan	5
Norway	5

TABLE 9.10 *Legal status of prostitution by country, OECD countries, 2009.* (cont.)

Legal	Point[a]
Spain	5
Sweden	5
United States	1 (the state of Nevada only)
Illegal	
Korea, South	0
Slovenia	0

a Legal = 10 points, partially legal = 5 points, illegal 0 points.
SOURCE HTTP://PROSTITUTION.PROCON.ORG.

exceptions as Chile, Mexico, and Poland can be probably explained by that Catholic-dominated societies are less fixated on or proscriptive and punishing of sex, including prostitution, than their Puritan and Islamic versions like the US in the conservative rendition and Iran, etc. With regard to Turkey, it is not really an exception since the legality of prostitution and other sexual freedoms is another legacy of a relatively liberal-secular civil society and state that the Islamic government has not yet entirely reversed. To that extent, the preceding in part confirms the prediction that liberal-secular civil societies or stages in the development of the same society (as in Turkey) more allow this form of individual sexual freedom as well as personal economic activity than do others.

Next, the groups of countries with 'limited legality' of prostitution comprises Australia, France, Iceland, Japan, Norway, Spain, Sweden, and the US, thus a mix of those classified as liberal-secular and eclectic civil societies, keeping in mind the double specification of America. Still, the US can be exempted from this group of countries so long as its 'limited legality' of prostitution is so limited, for example to one state (Nevada) or even city (Las Vegas), that ceases to be effective or meaningful legality. This leaves only liberal-secular civil societies, Australia, France, Iceland, Norway, and Sweden, along with their eclectic counterparts, Japan and Spain, and thus partly confirms the expectations that the first at the minimum permit to some degree or do not fully proscribe this sexual and economic freedom.

Alternatively, the explanations why these five liberal-secular civil societies do not grant complete legality to such sexual-economic freedom, as do most of their counterparts, probably include vestiges of traditional religion and morality, as in Australia, and the growing influence of militant feminism in

France, Iceland, Norway, and especially Sweden as the seeming leader[23] (just as California in the US). Lastly, countries in which prostitution is illegal include South Korea and Slovenia, to which the US, especially in its conservative pole, can be added, thus forming a mix of the last two types of civil society and generally supporting the expectations. These expectations are supported so long as such a status in South Korea can be explained as the vestige of a relatively anti-liberal and non-secular civil society and in Slovenia by that of non-liberal communism, while that in the conservative pole of the US fully confirms them.

---

23 Militant feminism has been primarily instrumental in Sweden's backward movement—from the stance of sexual freedom and thus a free civil society—from complete to limited legality of prostitution in recent years. In addition, it attempts and seemingly succeeds to redefine rape as 'unprotected' even if consensual sex (as shown by the rape accusation against the WikiLeaks founder because of such an act), which is an unprecedented and expansive definition seeking to define as 'rapes' virtually all voluntary (let alone non-consensual) sexual acts of which feminists do not approve. This is not an isolated case, however, but a growing trend and pattern of militant feminism. It has engaged in such an anti-liberal, irrational, and often hateful conduct in other liberal and even non-liberal societies, including Canada, the US, the UK, etc., and proposing Orwellian 'rape prevention' laws (e.g., 'yes means yes' starting in 'liberal' California, etc.) seeking to reduce consensual spontaneous sexual and related interaction to a legal-like contract of initially verbal, eventually written consent, thus converging with its assumed adversary Puritanism. In another example, radical feminists and their allies in California succeeded to enact an Orwellian-style law treating any sexual assaults as 'rapes' (which the Governor disapproved but still signed!). This seems an Orwellian law because it effectively treats non-rapes as rapes, and so conceivably sexual non-assaults, i.e., consensual sex acts, will be treated as 'assaults,' an apparent victory for radical feminism but a defeat for a free civil society or criminal justice in California, as many innocent men will be mandatorily and long imprisoned for falsely defined or non-existing crimes and thus their lives ruined because of feminist militancy. In sum, militant feminism is a growing threat to universal sexual and other personal individual freedom and a free civil society as a whole in Sweden and other Scandinavian and Western liberal-secular societies or regions, like California in the US, thus acting as the substitute of its nominal adversary, religious-moral conservatism, including Puritanism, as the original and perpetual enemy of individual liberty. At this point, anti-liberal totalitarian opposites, 'liberal' feminism, actually a negation or perversion of liberalism, and anti-liberal conservatism, converge on suppressing or subverting individual liberty and thus free civil society and in that sense creating or sustaining puritanical 'moral fascism.' The fact that US conservatives brand militant feminists 'femi-Nazis' does not contradict but unwittingly affirms their convergence and often alliance against individual liberty, because conservatism has proven to intrinsically constitute or ultimately evolve into fascism spanning from Nazi Germany to evangelical America, including 'Tea Party' ultra-conservatism as eventually proto-fascism.

Generally, the above confirms that social conservatism remains the implacable perennial enemy of universal sexual and related individual liberty, just as it reveals militant feminism as the emergent adversary. Both generate adverse outcomes for a free civil society, even if being nominal adversaries, alongside Western nationalism, militarism, and imperialism threatening liberal democracy. To that extent, a new threat to modern free civil society emerges in the form of radical feminism formally in opposition to, but actually in alliance with, conservatism against this and related individual liberties. Perverting and compromising liberalism, militant feminism as supposedly 'liberal' actually acts as a functional equivalent of conservatism in these related societies, just as the latter does as one of fascism, and inflicts a free civil society with almost equivalent destructive consequences as these two anti-liberal ideologies and systems.

Peace and Peaceful Conflict Resolution in Civil Society

The comparative estimates of peace and peaceful conflict resolution in civil society among Western and related countries take into account, for example, the 2015 Global Peace Index, previously considered in connection with the degree of peace in the polity and pacifism in relation to other societies as an indicator of democracy. Prima facie, the degree and so index of peace and peaceful conflict resolution in civil society is closely associated with that of peace in the polity and pacifism in relation to other societies. As seen, the highest ranked countries on these indexes are those presently classified as liberal-secular civil societies, Iceland, Norway, Denmark, Austria, New Zealand, Switzerland, Finland, Canada, Australia, along with two mixed cases, Czech Republic and Japan. This hence largely supports the expectation that the first are most peaceful and least violent in civic terms, just as equivalent democracies are so politically and in relation to other societies. For instance, Scandinavian countries like Iceland and Norway rank the first on both peace indexes.

Conversely, the lowest ranked are non-liberal and non-secular civil societies, South Korea, Mexico, Turkey, plus the US in the conservative rendition, joined with some mixed instances like Chile, Estonia, Greece, Italy, and the UK, and only one liberal-secular case, France. This thus at least in part confirms the expectation that the first are less peaceful and more violent in social life, as are their political equivalents in the polity and versus other countries. For example, the US, Mexico, and Turkey rank the last, with the first country featuring the lowest ranking among all Western societies on both peace indexes.

TABLE 9.11   *Safety and security ranking, OECD, 2015.*

Country	Rank	Point[a]
Iceland	1	10
Finland	2	10
Ireland	3	10
Sweden	4	9
Denmark	5	9
Norway	6	9
Luxembourg	7	8
New Zealand	8	8
Canada	9	8
Switzerland	10	7
Slovenia	11	7
Australia	12	7
Austria	13	6
Korea, South	14	6
Portugal	15	6
Netherlands	16	5
Belgium	17	5
Germany	18	5
Japan	19	4
Czech Republic	20	4
Spain	21	4
Poland	22	3
Greece	23	3
United Kingdom	24	3
France	25	2
Slovakia	26	2
United States	27	2
Estonia	28	1
Hungary	29	1
Chile	30	1
Italy	31	0
Mexico	32	0
Turkey	33	0

a Rank 1–3 = 10 points, rank 4–6 = 9 points, rank 7–9 = 8 points, rank
10–12 = 7 points, rank 13–15 = 6 points, rank 16–18 = 5 points, rank 19–21 = 4
points, rank 22–24 = 6 points, rank 25–27 = 6 points, rank 28–30 = 1 point,
31 and more = 0 points.
SOURCE: LEGATUM HTTP://WWW.PROSPERITY.COM.

In addition, in another similar index indicating or approximating peace (Legatum Safety and Security Ranking in Table 9.11), ten or so most highly ranked OECD countries are Iceland, Finland, Ireland, Sweden, Denmark, Norway, Luxembourg, New Zealand, Canada, Switzerland, and Australia.

This high-end ranking hence strongly confirms the expectations with respect to peace and its correlates of safety and security, because most of these countries are classified as liberal, secular, universalistic civil societies and democracies, with only two exceptions such as Ireland and Slovenia. Conversely, ten or so OECD countries ranked the lowest in these terms are Poland, Greece, the UK, France, Slovakia, the US, Estonia, Hungary, Chile, Italy, Mexico, and Turkey. Thus, this low-end ranking is generally consistent with the expectations in this respect, since most of these countries, including 'conservative America'[24] according to the specification of the 'two Americas,' are classified either as anti-liberal, anti-secular, and anti-universalistic or mixed civil societies and political systems, with only a single exception being in the previous category, France.

In particular, the present estimates take account of the data on global homicide rates and the proportion of them committed by guns. Thus, countries with the lowest homicide rates (Table 9.12) typically belong to the category of liberal-secular civil societies, thus confirming the expectation that these are characterized with a higher degree of social peace and safety and a lower extent of violence and physical insecurity than others.

For example, the countries with the lowest homicide rates (per 100,000 population in 2011) are Austria, Czech Republic, Denmark, France, Germany, Iceland, Ireland, Italy, Luxembourg, the Netherlands, Portugal, Slovenia, Spain, Sweden, and Switzerland, alongside the UK, Australia Japan, and New Zealand. This shows that most of them are in Europe and presently classified as liberal-secular or mixed civil societies. Evidently, the inner pacifism or peacefulness and the general atmosphere of openness, civility, and happiness or enjoyment of life—i.e., what Weber calls Enlightenment-style 'joy of life'—of liberal-secular and to some degree eclectic civil societies result in less murders and related violent actions than in their opposites. Negatively, liberal-secular civil societies' lack or lowest level of latent, symbolic violence translates in a lower degree of manifest, physical violence in the form of homicides than in

---

24   The Legatum Institute comments that 'this year (2015) the United States ranks 33rd on
      the Safety & Security sub-index, down from 31st last year. Safety & Security is the only
      sub-index in which the US ranks outside the top 30. It is also the only Western country to
      register high levels of state-sponsored political violence. According to Amnesty International the country has the same level of political violence as Saudi Arabia.'

TABLE 9.12 *Homicide rates (Murders per 100,000 Population),* OECD *countries, 2006–2011.*

Country	2006	2007	2008	2009	2010	2011	Point[a]
Australia	1.4	1.2	1.2	1.2	1.0	1.1	8
Austria	0.7	0.5	0.5	0.5	0.6	0.8	9
Belgium	2.1	2.0	1.9	1.7	1.7	1.8	7
Canada	1.7	1.6	1.7	1.6	1.4	1.5	7
Chile	3.6	3.7	3.5	3.7	3.2	3.7	3
Czech Republic	1.2	1.1	1.0	0.9	1.0	0.8	9
Denmark	0.5	0.7	1.0	0.9	0.8	0.8	9
Estonia	6.8	6.9	6.3	5.2	5.2	4.8	1
Finland	2.3	2.4	2.5	2.3	2.2	2.2	6
France	1.4	1.3	1.4	1.1	1.1	1.2	8
Germany	1.0	0.9	0.9	0.9	0.8	0.8	9
Greece	1.0	1.1	1.2	1.3	1.6	1.6	7
Hungary	1.7	1.5	1.5	1.4	1.3	1.4	8
Iceland	0.0	0.7	0.0	0.3	0.6	0.9	9
Ireland	1.5	1.8	1.1	1.3	1.2	0.9	9
Italy	1.1	1.1	1.0	1.0	0.9	0.9	9
Japan	0.5	0.5	0.5	0.4	0.4	0.3	10
Korea, South	2.3	2.3	2.3	2.3	2.9	2.6	5
Luxembourg	1.9	1.5	1.6	1.0	2.0	0.8	9
Mexico	9.7	8.1	12.7	17.7	22.7	23.7	0
Netherlands	1.1	0.8	0.9	0.9	0.9	0.9	9
New Zealand	1.2	1.1	1.2	1.5	1.1	0.9	9
Norway	0.7	0.6	0.7	0.6	0.6	2.3	6
Poland	1.3	1.4	1.2	1.3	1.1	1.2	8
Portugal	1.5	1.7	1.2	1.2	1.2	1.1	8
Slovakia	1.6	1.6	1.7	1.5	1.6	1.8	7
Slovenia	0.6	1.2	0.5	0.6	0.7	0.8	9
Spain	1.1	1.1	0.9	0.9	0.8	0.8	9
Sweden	1.0	1.2	0.9	1.0	1.0	0.9	9
Switzerland	0.8	0.7	0.7	0.7	0.7	0.6	9
Turkey	4.6	3.6	3.3	NA	NA	NA	4
UK (England)	1.3	1.4	1.2	1.1	1.1	1.0	8
US	5.8	5.7	5.4	5.0	4.7	4.7	1

a 2011 Rate 0–0.4 = 10 points, rate 0.5–0.9 = 9 points, rate 1.0–1.4 = 8 points, rate 1.5–1.9 = 7 points, rate 2.0–2.4 = 6 points, rate 2.5–2.9 = 5 points, rate 3.0–3.4 = 4 points, rate 3.5–3.9 = 3 points, rate 4.0–4.4 = 2 points, rate 4.5–4.9 = 1 point, rate 5 or higher = 0 points.
SOURCE: UNODC HOMICIDE STATISTICS 2013 (HTTPS://WWW.UNODC.ORG/UNODC/EN/DATA-AND-ANALYSIS/HOMICIDE.HTML).

others, simply does not explode or escalate in murders and other violent acts. In this sense, what some sociologists call the 'law of conservation of violence' is reversed or neutralized in liberal-secular and in part mixed civil societies in that their lack of or lower symbolic violence predicts the lowest rate of physical violence like murders.

Conversely, countries with the highest homicide rates are generally those belonging to non-liberal, non-secular hyper-religious civil societies, which confirms the opposite expectation that these are deprived of basic social peace and safety and plagued with chronic and pervasive violence and physical insecurity more than others. For illustration, countries with the highest homicide rates (per 100,000 population in 2011) include Mexico, Estonia, the US, Chile, and South Korea, of which the majority, including America in the conservative pole, are classified into non-liberal or non-secular civil societies. Apparently, the intrinsic non-pacifism or tension and the overarching climate of closure, incivility, and unhappiness of non-liberal and non-secular over-religious civil societies are linked to more murders and other violent act than in their liberal-secular counterparts. In particular, 'conservative America' continues to have by far the highest homicide rate, in spite of decreasing in recent years, among all Western societies (thus not counting Mexico and Estonia), for example, higher than those of the UK, Germany, France, Italy, Spain,

TABLE 9.13   *Percentage of homicides by firearm and homicide by firearm rate, OECD countries, 2005–10.*

Country	2005	2006	2007	2008	2009	2010	Point[a]
Australia		8.9	16.4	13.3	11.8	11.5	8
		0.1	0.2	0.2	0.1	0.1	
Austria	24.1	29.5					5
	0.2	0.2					
Belgium	39.5 (2004)						3
	0.7 (2004)						
Canada	36.2	33.5	34.7	35.3	32.0		4
	0.7	0.6	0.6	0.6	0.5		
Chile	37.3						3
	2.2						
Czech Republic		12.4	14.3	16.3	16.8	11.0	8
	0.2	0.3	0.3	0.3	0.2		
Denmark		20.8	27.6	17.9	11.1	31.9	4
	0.2	0.1	0.1	0.1	0.3		

Country	2005	2006	2007	2008	2009	2010	Point[a]
Estonia	3.9						10
			0.2				
Finland	10.3	15.8	18.8	22.7	19.8		7
	0.2	0.4	0.5	0.6	0.4		
France		9.6					9
		0.1					
Germany		29.4	26.9	26.1	29.9	26.3	5
	0.3	0.3	0.2	0.2	0.2	0.2	
Greece		34.9					4
		0.3					
Hungary	12.8	5.7	7.8	8.2	5.0	10	
	0.2	0.1	0.1	0.1	0.1		
Iceland	0.0	0.0	0.0	0.0	0.0		10
	0.0	0.0	0.0	0.0	0.0		
Ireland	42.3	43.5	23.4	42.0			2
	0.5	0.6	0.4	0.5			
Italy	66.2	66.7					0
	0.7						
Japan				1.8			10
				0.0			
Korea, South			1.7				10
		0.0					
Luxembourg			11.1	28.6	42.9		2
	0.2	0.4	0.6				
Mexico	28.5	30.7	39.4	38.6	54.6	54.9	0
	3.0	3.3	3.7	4.6	7.9	10.0	
Norway		8.1					9
		0.1					
Netherlands		26.9	28.7	29.5	30.7		4
	0.4	0.3	0.3	0.3	0.3		
New Zealand	18.4	10.4	13.5				8
	0.2	0.1	0.2				
Poland	9.7	9.8	10.3	7.0	7.1		9
	0.1	0.1	0.1	0.1	0.1		
Portugal	51.6	28.6	43.5	33.8			4
	0.8	0.5	0.5	0.4			
Slovakia	11.3	11.2					8
	0.2	0.2					

TABLE 9.13 *Percentage of homicides by firearm and homicide by firearm rate, OECD countries, 2005–10.* (cont.)

Country	2005	2006	2007	2008	2009	2010	Point[a]
Slovenia	25.0	36.0	18.2	15.4			8
	0.1	0.4	0.1	0.1			
Spain	17.9	17.4	16.7	21.8			6
	0.1	0.1	0.2	0.2			
Sweden	33.9 (2004)						4
	0.4 (2004)						
Switzerland	72.2 (2004)						0
	0.8 (2003)						
Turkey	14.9	16.9					7
	0.7	0.8					
United Kingdom		7.1	8.3	7.1	5.9	6.6	9
	0.1	0.1	0.1	0.1	0.1		
United States of America	67.9	67.8	67.9	67.0	66.9	67.5	0
	3.8	3.9	3.8	3.6	3.3	3.2	

a 2010 Percentage 0–5 = 10 points, percentage 6–10 = 9 points, percentage 11–15 = 8 points, percentage 16–20 = 7 points, percentage 21–25 = 6 points, percentage 26–30 = 5 points, percentage 31–35 = 4 points, percentage 36–40 = 3 points, percentage 41–45 = 2 points, percentage 46–50 = 1 point, percentage higher than 50 = 0 points.
SOURCE: UNODC HOMICIDE STATISTICS 2013.
HOMICIDE BY FIREARM RATE PER 100,000 POPULATION.

and other European countries, as well as other immigrant nations like Canada, Australia, and New Zealand, plus Japan. Alternatively, only its neighbor Mexico (23.7) has a significantly higher murder rate than the US (4.7), which is in turn more three times higher than that of its other neighbor Canada (1.5).

In addition, the data on homicides committed by guns reveal an almost identical pattern as above and in that sense can be taken to indicate or approximate the degree of a gun-ridden violent civil society or 'gun culture.' They show that the lowest percentages of homicides committed by guns and homicide by gun rates (Table 9.13) and to that extent the weakest 'gun culture' are characteristic for liberal-secular societies such as Western European countries, with some exceptions, consistent with their expected highest level of social peace, non-violence, safety, openness and civility.

For instance, ten countries with the lowest percentage of homicides by guns (based on available data for the last years given) and thus the weakest 'gun culture' include Iceland (0.0), Republic of Korea (1.7), Japan (1.8), Estonia (3.9), Hungary (5.0), the UK (6.6), Poland (7.1), Norway (8.1), France (9.6), Czech Republic (11.0). Admittedly, not of all these are classified as liberal-secular civil societies, but the majority (6 out of 10) still are, which supports in part or at least does not contradict the expectations. Relatedly, ten countries with the lowest homicide by gun rates (per 100,000) and so the weakest 'gun culture' are Iceland (0.0), Japan (0.0), Republic of Korea (0.0), Australia (0.1), France (0.1), Hungary (0.1), Norway (0.1), Poland (0.1), Slovenia (0.1), and the UK (0.1). As before, the majority of these countries (6 out of 10) are classified as liberal-secular societies, thus at least in part supporting the expectations.

Conversely, ten countries with the highest percentage of homicides by guns and thus the strongest 'gun culture' include Switzerland (72.2), the US (67.5), Italy (66.7), Mexico (54.9), Luxembourg (42.9), Ireland (42.0), Belgium (39.5), Chile (37.3), Sweden (33.9), and Portugal (33.8). Apparently, this group contains a mixture of civil societies, and this seemingly does not support the expectations. Some of those countries classified as non-liberal and non-secular civil societies, however, belong to this group—for example, the US in the conservative rendition, Mexico—which in part supports the expectations, along with several mixed cases. Alternatively, only a few of the countries classified as liberal-secular civil societies do so, namely 6 out of 20 or so—Switzerland, Italy, Luxembourg, Belgium, Sweden, and Portugal—thus supporting partly the expectations.

Similarly, ten countries with the highest homicide by gun rates (per 100,000) and so the strongest 'gun culture' are Mexico (10.0), the US (3.2), Chile (2.2), Switzerland (0.8), Turkey (0.8), Belgium (0.7), Italy (0.7), Luxembourg (0.6), Canada (0.5), and Ireland (0.5). As before, this group comprises a mix of civil societies, thus apparently not confirming the expectations. Yet, some of the countries classified as non-liberal, non-secular civil societies are included in this group, with moreover two of them, Mexico and the US in the conservative pole, having (along with Chile) by far the highest homicide by gun rates, drastically higher than those of their liberal-secular counterparts. For example, Mexico's rate is more than 10 times, that of the US 4 times higher than those of Switzerland, Belgium, Italy, Luxembourg, and Canada. In turn, only a few of the countries classified as liberal-secular civil societies are in this group, namely 5 of 20 or so, such as Switzerland, Italy, Luxembourg, Belgium, and Canada, which partly confirms or does not contradict the expectations.

In particular, these data document that the US continues to have the highest homicide by gun rate and on that account the strongest 'gun culture' among all Western societies and even beyond, if not counting Mexico. If counting Mexico, then its higher rate may be either a reason for partial 'could be worse' consolation to gun-control advocates or for strong 'we must be best' dissatisfaction and envy by 'gun rights' groups in the conservative half of the US but in any case both cases strongly confirm the expectations. Like that of Mexico, the US exceptional homicide by gun rate and so 'gun culture' and violence exemplifies and strongly reaffirms the association of non-liberal and non-secular hyper-religious civil societies with violence, notably attacks and murders by guns, and the consequent physical insecurity.

At the minimum, within the US this holds true for the conservative Southern and related illiberal and hyper-religious regions and (per)versions of civil society,[25] just as does for Mexico during its recent drug-related violence and anarchy among other countries. While Mexico only recently, these regions for long resurrect the Hobbesian primitive 'state of nature' ruled by the 'law of the jungle' and of the 'strongest' approximated by the pervasive gun culture and gun-committed violence in this and related regions, as symbolized—not only in movies—by the 'Wild West' of 'open carry' guns, as among favorite children toys, Christmas presents, and adult gadgets, and perpetual and mass murders, including of children in schools. Simply, if one does not know what the 'law of the jungle' is or if it persists among Western and related societies one knows it when seeing drug-related violence and anarchy in Mexico and the gun culture, notably 'open carry' and 'concealed' guns sacrificing the rights to social peace, physical safety, and life within civil society to the 'right to bear arms' in conservative America such as the South.

This region hence appears much closer to its hated or despised—driven by chronic xenophobic paranoia—Southern neighbor in this respect than to Western societies, including Canada and Europe. Thus, the risk of innocent, uninvolved persons, even children, being killed by guns both in homes

---

25   Munch (1994, p. 69) suggests referring to contemporary America that 'a society in which each believes he can police other's actions on his behalf by relying on the firepower on his own weapons is in danger of destroying its liberties, because everybody has to fear everybody else. Such a society is close to Hobbes's state of nature.' Also, Mueller (2009, p. 392) observes that 'in the US state-level evidence suggests a negative correlation between church attendance and various crime statistics.' Mueller (2009, p. 394) adds that the 'US stands out as a dramatic outlier (in) the homicide rate. Attending church regularly and believing that God is very important to their lives does not appear to make Americans less likely to murder one another than people in other rich countries but quite the reverse. One reason for the high homicide rates in the US is the Constitution Second Amendment, which makes it easier for Americans to acquire guns than in most other developed countries.'

and public places, including shopping malls, schools, and universities, in the US South is comparable to or just slightly lower than in Mexico, or anarchic Third-World countries, during its drug-induced violence, moreover being more permanent since the latter is more recent than the perennial Southern gun culture a la primitive 'open carry' and 'concealed' weapons causing the constant hazard of random and mass gun-induced death or harm. Conversely, such a risk is dramatically lower in Canada as well as Europe and the UK after its comprehensive gun control measures than in both Mexico and the US South and 'conservative America' overall.

Appendix 9.1. Qualitative Considerations of Civil Liberties

Freedom of Production, Distribution, Possession, and Consumption of Drugs

The freedom of drug production, distribution, possession, and consumption probably displays the highest degree of convergence of Western and related societies in terms of a free civil society. Unlike in the previous cases, virtually all these restrict this probably most controversial element and indicator of free civil society and a dimension of personal liberty, choice, and privacy. The only but growing[26] exceptions are Holland, Spain, Portugal, and the Czech Republic, plus a few US states, as the only European and Western countries or regions decriminalizing the personal possession and use of certain narcotic drugs. While Holland being an earlier, partial, and famous case in point, Spain, Portugal, and the Czech Republic are newer, more complete, and relatively unknown and surprising instances of decriminalization of certain drugs (alongside Uruguay among non-Western countries). On this account, they represent

---

26   The *Economist*'s 2013 report 'Winding down the war on drugs' suggests that 'Experiments in legalisation are showing what a post-war approach to drug control could look like.' For example, it reports that 'Spain's approach now rivals that of the pioneering liberal Dutch. Though selling is illegal, buying is not. One result is hundreds of cannabis "social clubs," which allow members to pool their purchases. Similar experiments are under way in France, Belgium, Italy and Germany. In much of Britain, especially its big cities, the risk of prosecution for those using small quantities of soft drugs is vanishingly low. But the most comprehensive policy comes from Portugal. In 1997 opinion polls rated drug use the country's biggest social problem. Now, 12 years since the decriminalisation of personal use of small amounts (meaning less than ten days' worth) of all drugs, it ranks 13th. All parties now support the policy of treating drug use as a health issue, not a crime.' The report adds that 'in 2009 the Czech Republic decriminalised possession of most drugs along Portuguese lines. In December it went further, fully legalising medicinal cannabis.'

sole examples of a completely free civil society and protectors of individual liberty, choice, and privacy in terms of freedom of production and distribution, especially possession and consumption of narcotic drugs among Western and related societies.

The major exception is 'conservative America' due to the most encompassing criminalization, minus a few states, and Draconian punishment—as through harsh 'three strikes' laws—of the possession and consumption, not to mention production and distribution, of drugs among Western and related societies, and solely matched or surpassed in Islamic theocracies and other unfree Third-World countries. Moreover, US anti-drug laws and punishments are so total and severe, including the military style Puritanical 'war on drugs' and life in prison for repeated drug use and the death penalty for production and distribution, that appear 'exceptional' compared to even those of Turkey under Islamic government due, like the legal age alcohol limit, to the legacy of a prior relatively liberal-secular Turkish civil society the ruling Islamists have not succeeded to completely erase yet. Notably, the US is the only one among Western societies that legally imposes (even if not practically applies yet) the death penalty for drug production and especially distribution; within OECD even Turkey under Islamic governance does not, and only South Korea does. In extension, on the whole American continent, only the US and Cuba impose the death penalty for drug trade,[27] revealing a surprising commonality in Draconian punishment for drugs, but no real surprise so long as, as often said, authoritarian or repressive, i.e., conservative-religious and communist, opposites 'meet' (i.e., 'Bible Belt' theocracy and Cuban dictatorship) precisely because of their shared anti- or pre-liberalism in civil society, as well as politics.

In turn, the totality and severity of American 'exceptional' anti-drug laws, wars, and punishments are only rivalled or exceeded in most other Islamic theocracies or states such as Iran, Saudi Arabia, Indonesia, Sudan, etc., as well as China, Cuba, North Korea, Singapore, the Philippines, and other unfree, anti-liberal Third-World countries.[28] This confirms the functional equivalence

---

27   The *Economist* (from April 25, 2015) comments that America and Cuba 'have the death penalty on the books for drug traffickers but do not apply it in practice.'

28   According to the International Harm Reduction Association's The Death Penalty for Drug Offences Global Overview 2010 no Western country, except for the US, and only about 30 non-Western Third-World countries provide the death penalty for such offenses. Thus, it 'identifies 32 jurisdictions that currently have legislation prescribing capital punishment in drug cases, including five countries considered abolitionist in practice. These are Bahrain, Bangladesh, Brunei-Darussalam, China, Cuba, Egypt, Gaza (Occupied Palestinian Territories), India, Indonesia, Iran, Iraq, Kuwait, Lao PDR, Libya, Malaysia, Myanmar, North Korea, Oman, Pakistan, Qatar, Saudi Arabia, Singapore, South Korea, Sri

or congruence of what Pareto diagnosed as the American conservative Puritanical government—and its precedent Puritanism—constantly imposing Puritan 'morality by law' and Islamist governments and Islam overall, as well as authoritarian communist states, on total and intense moralistic repression through criminalization and Draconian punishment of sins-as-crimes, in particular criminalizing drugs (plus alcohol, sexuality, etc.) and in that sense moral fascism as the lethal poison of a free civil society, notably individual liberty, choice, and privacy. At this juncture, 'conservative America' manifests itself as the exact inverse of Holland, Spain, Portugal, the Czech Republic, etc.—the sole 'exceptional' example of a completely unfree civil society and the realm of individual un-freedom, non-choice, and non-privacy in respect of freedom of possession and consumption, let alone production and distribution, of narcotic drugs among Western and related societies. This is demonstrated by the striking, unrepentant—despite the evident dismal failure analogous to Prohibition—persistence, totality and Draconian severity of the American conservative government Puritanical 'war on drugs' as a unique anomaly or unparalleled phenomenon on this scale among these societies, and only matched or surpassed in Islamic theocracies and other Third-World dictatorships like Iran and North Korea.

In general, the preceding expresses two common tendencies among Western and related societies, first, the low but growing degree of freedom of drug production, distribution, possession, and consumption, and second, the continuing yet decreasing severity of punishment for these activities, especially possessing, and consuming drugs if criminalized. Thus, the effective freedom of drug production, distribution, possession, and consumption as an indicator of a free civil society, particularly individual liberty and privacy, is minimal—or has been revoked historically—in most Western and related societies, though growing in a few cases like Holland, Spain, Portugal, and the Czech Republic. This indicates that such a freedom overall remains an unrealistic, utopian vision or distant historical memory, not (re)incorporated into individual liberty and privacy, and hence most Western and related countries are not completely

---

Lanka, Sudan, Syria, Taiwan, Thailand, United Arab Emirates, United States of America, Viet Nam and Yemen' (p. 6). The *Economist* (April 25, 2015) comments that 'all but four (America, Cuba, Sudan and South Sudan) are in Asia or the Middle East. But in most of these countries executions are extremely rare. Fourteen, including America and Cuba, have the death penalty on the books for drug traffickers but do not apply it in practice. Only in six countries—China, Iran, Saudi Arabia, Vietnam, Malaysia and Singapore—are drug offenders known to be routinely executed, according to HRI's most recent analysis. (Indonesia will soon join this list, following its recent executions.) In Iraq, Libya, North Korea, Sudan, South Sudan and Syria the data are murky.'

free civil societies in this specific dimension. Even those classified as liberal-secular civil societies fall short in this respect, which apparently contradicts the expectations, though probably in short or medium terms so long as they are plausibly predicted to recognize or restore some modality of this individual freedom in the long run, as exemplified and anticipated by Holland and Portugal (plus some liberal US states), more so than their opposites or eclectic cases. Alternatively, the fact that the only completely free Western and related civil societies (and US regions) in terms of this individual freedom are Holland, Spain, Portugal, and the Czech Republic (and liberal American states) classified into the liberal-secular category in part confirm the expectations.

Sexual Freedoms and Rights

Generally, the comparative estimates of sexual freedoms and rights in Western and related societies take into consideration studies and observations of the freedom of premarital and extramarital sex, the data on adultery, legal status of same-sex marriage, and legal status of prostitution, and the like. In general, Western and most other European countries, plus Canada, Australia, etc., classified as liberal-secular civil societies exhibit the highest degree of sexual freedoms and rights, with secondary variations. To that extent, this confirms the expectations that such civil societies by virtue of their liberalism and secularism in respect of individual liberty and choice inherently establish, promote, and sustain the strongest and most extensive sexual liberties and rights. Conversely, countries, including the US in the second rendition, classified as non-liberal and non-secular civil societies show the lowest degree of sexual freedoms and rights, again with some variations. Hence, this supports the prediction that these civil societies due to their anti- or pre-liberalism and anti- or pre-secularism or hyper-religiosity with regard to individual liberty and choice intrinsically tend to have no or minimal sexual liberties and rights.

First, those Western and related countries classified as liberal-secular civil societies display consistently the greatest degree of freedom of consensual sex outside formal marriage. Thus, none of these societies criminalizes and punishes premarital and extramarital sex, but leaves it individual freedom of choice, consent, and responsibility, and privacy. Conversely, those countries classified as non-liberal and non-secular or hyper-religious civil societies evince consistently the lowest degree of such sexual freedom. Thus, at least some of these societies criminalize and punish consensual premarital and extramarital sex, and hence refuse to leave it to individual freedom of choice, consent, and responsibility, and privacy, but instead treat it as within the scope of government action and the matter of legal definition and sanction, as exemplified by 'conservative America.' Alongside alcohol, this is what Pareto probably meant when diagnosing the US conservative government Puritan-rooted pattern of

enforcing 'morality by law'—coercing Puritanical sexual purity by criminalization of non-marital sex.

For instance, studies show that hyper-religious Christian societies such as
'conservative America' and most Muslim countries continue the strict, respectively Puritan and Islamic, moral-religious proscription, punishment, and condemnation of non-marital sex by proscribing and sanctioning or condemning
extramarital and premarital sex.[29] Comparatively, the conservative half of the
US and Islamic countries are the only ones in the Western and entire world that
criminalize non-marital sex. The first does partly through the Puritan-era laws
criminalizing premarital and extramarital sex ('fornication' and 'adultery')—
which are widely regarded as unenforced and unenforceable but occasionally
still enforced—and the second completely by harsh anti-sex proscriptions
and punishments. At this juncture, an exception both within non-liberal and
non-secular civil societies and among Islamic countries is Turkey where neither premarital nor extramarital sex are proscribed, as another liberal-secular
legacy of the past that its Islamic government has not succeeded to fully erase
yet by attempting but failing to criminalize adultery. By virtue of this enduring,
if threatened, legacy of a liberal-secular civil society/state, Turkey appears to
have a higher level of such sexual freedoms than 'conservative America' due to
its even more durable anti-liberal theocratic heritage of Puritanism and the resurgence of its heir Puritanical evangelicalism. Also, as with respect to alcohol
and drugs, the less harsh proscription and punishment of non- and especially
pre-marital sex in Chile, Mexico, Poland, and Ireland than in the conservative
pole of the US is probably explained by the same factor—the weaker sexual
and other moralistic repression of Catholic as compared to Puritan or evangelical, as well as Islamic, theocracies and societies.

Predictably, Western and other liberal-secular civil societies by allowing
most fully such a stronger, maximal form of sexual freedom as non-marital
sex also allow to the same extent its weaker, minimal forms or proxies such
as that of consensual sexually-connoted social interaction as a minimum and
condition in this respect. None of these societies criminalizes and punishes
consensual social interactions seeking or leading to, but not involving, actual
non-marital sex, such as interacting with actual or potential sexual partners legally defined by age, agency, etc. In turn, some non-liberal and hyper-religious
civil societies not only proscribe non-marital sex as the stronger, maximal form
of sexual freedom but consensual sexually-connoted social interactions as the
minimal weaker forms or proxies, as exemplified by 'conservative America'

---

29   Adamczyk and Hayes (2012, pp. 729–30) observe that 'both Islam and Christianity pro-
       scribe sex outside of marriage, and some conservative Christian groups have been highly
       effective at persuading individuals to delay first sex (sometimes until marriage).'

(plus 'feminist' California) among Western countries and Islamic states within the Third-World.

Thus, these are the only ones within their respective settings that criminalize and punish to some extent even consensual sexual-connoted and related social interactions seeking or leading to but not involving actual sex, including interacting with actual or potential legally defined sexual partners, as proxy Orwellian crimes of thought, intention, solicitation, or attempt. For example, many of convicted or registered sexual offenders in 'conservative America' (plus 'feminist' California) seem punished—and then their normal life ruined or disrupted due to perpetual Puritan-style punishment for their sins—for such Orwellian crimes, viz., 'intention to get sex,' 'solicitation for sex' in person or by phone and digital communication, 'attempt at sex,' and the like without actually engaging in any acts of non-marital sex.[30] As with respect to proscribing non-marital sex, this is a kind of double Puritanical 'American exceptionalism' not only in relation to Western liberal-secular civil societies but also to their opposites, as for example, Islamic Turkey and Catholic Mexico and Poland, do not criminalize and punish sexually-connoted social interaction or communication such as 'solicitation for sex,' etc. This confirms that what Durkheim might call the Puritan 'morbid' obsession with sex and its proscription and punishment persists and expands through Puritanical evangelicalism in 'conservative America' (plus 'feminist' California) more than anywhere else, including Britain, and any other religion like Catholicism and ideology such as liberalism and secularism, as does that of Islam in Islamic states, as in Turkey (though its theocratic government not being able yet to reverse the legacy of a liberal-secular past, including legal non-marital sex and prostitution).

Notes on US Estimates of a Free Civil Society

Individual Liberty and Privacy
A likely expression of the anti-privacy legacy of and path-dependence on Puritanism in 'conservative America' is that its declared heirs, religious

---

30   That is not just an Orwellian dystopia, for some persons in the 'Bible Belt' are actually punished for Orwellian crimes of thought, intention, solicitation, or attempt in respect of sex. For example, one person in Texas was reportedly imprisoned to 90 years—not days—for 'attempting to get sex' (from a police officer). This confirms that in a Puritan-evangelical anti-liberal civil society and theocracy, as in its Islamic equivalent, sex is a graver sin-crime than violent crimes, including sometimes murder. Thus, it is unheard-of even in the 'Bible Belt,' including Texas, that someone was imprisoned to 90 years for 'attempting to kill,' but now heard of this for 'attempting to get sex.'

conservatives typically deny that there is such thing any right to privacy and thus to individual liberty and dignity, and personal choice and to that extent to individualism in the Constitution and the supposedly most 'individualist' society in the world and history. Yet, even if there is such a constitutional right to privacy and thus individual liberty and dignity as the matter of legal interpretation, evidently it is far from being fully promoted or protected and instead systematically denied and violated, above all in the conservative pole of the US, in the reality of civil society, and thus almost becoming not worth the paper on which it is written. The point is that it is difficult to fully understand and explain the comparatively lowest, 'shocking' US (and UK) scores on privacy in the ranking without considering the strong anti-privacy pattern of Puritanism as their shared religious-moral past and legacy and thus path-dependence, though more enduring and intense in 'conservative America' such as the South cum the neo-Puritan 'Bible Belt' through revived evangelicalism and conservatism overall. In general, the US ranking on this crucial dimension of civil society highlights the observations of the persistent and growing problem and violation of individual liberty and dignity, personal choice, and privacy in 'conservative America,' above all the South, the continuing 'obsession with sin and vice' equated with and severely punished as crimes from Puritanism through neo-conservatism, the persisting or reemerging vice-police and security state, and the like.

Conversely, one can speculate that without the 'Southern United States,' the US privacy score would be definitely and substantially higher, although not necessarily identical to that of Canada so long as civil society even in Dixie-less America does not seem yet as liberal-secular and consequently such a realm of high degree of privacy and individual liberty as in the northern neighbor and most other Western societies. If so, this yields the sober non-ethnocentric prediction or expectation that America either with or without the South will reach the degree of privacy and individual liberty of Canada only when and if it as a whole somehow becomes as a truly and fully liberal-secular civil society as the latter. This seems, however, a far more realistic outcome and less protracted process for Dixie-less America, insofar as, in light of its past and present, the South may reach Canada's style of liberal-civil society in a much longer time, say, equal to the period since the end of the Civil War through the present, or from the Puritan Salem witch-trials of the late 17th century to the Jeffersonian Enlightenment and the demise of theocratic Puritanism. Or given the 'Southern pride' in anti- or pre-liberal and anti- or pre-secular hyper-religious civil society, the South perhaps never will reach this stage within the timespan equivalent to that of the Christian Dark Middle Ages, viz., around 15th centuries since their beginning with the establishment of Christianity in the 4th century AD through their demise due to the Enlightenment and the

French Revolution during the 18th century. After this period, the historical though counterfactual logic or reasoning is if even the Christian Dark Middle Ages eventually ended after 15 or so centuries, the prediction is that so will likely the Southern 'Bible Belt' often seen as their sequel or the evangelical New Dark Ages.

Reproductive Liberties and Rights

Like in Islamic-ruled Turkey, this civil and legal legacy of abortion rights in America under evangelical and generally conservative resurgence and domi-nance (as in the 'Bible Belt') cannot be taken as established beyond doubt and contestation, as in most other Western societies, and presumed to endure in-tact indefinitely under such theocratic or theocentric threats and assaults at both national and state levels. In fact, this legacy has been so attacked, com-promised, and distorted by resurgent and growingly prevalent religious and political anti-abortion forces that unrestricted abortion rights are through various federal and especially state laws, plus violent attacks, greatly reduced, if not even effectively eliminated, in a myriad of persistent violations of the Supreme Court decision, as in 'conservative America,' thus approximately half of the 'two Americas.' At the minimum, abortion freedoms and rights 'with-out restriction as to reason' tend to become a threatened and to some extent extinct species of individual liberty and rights in the 'Bible Belt' and related regions due to perennial and even intensifying and expanding anti-abortion wars, including violent attacks on medical facilities and personnel, by conser-vative religious-political forces driven by theocratic and intolerant 'Puritanical beliefs.'[31]

The ground for the US maximal score of reproductive liberties and rights is that at least abortion is still legal and practiced in America in spite of further

31   Bell (2002, pp. 484–85) suggests that in the US 'what is troublesome is the politicization of
       moral and cultural issues (like abortion), for by their very nature they are non-negotiable
       and serve to polarize society. If such moral and cultural questions cannot be privatized,
       then the country may remain in trouble as new wars of religion take hold. That is the pros-
       pect of the continuing involvement of the radical right in politics.' Mueller (2009, p. 392)
       points to those in America 'whose Puritanical beliefs cause hardship, suffering, and often
       death by denying others the possibility of having safe and cheap abortions (plus) means
       of birth control.' Specifically, Mueller (2013, p. 8) notes that the 'religious fundamentalists
       in the US have turned their attention to preventing abortions. Extremists in this move-
       ment have broken US laws by blocking access to public buildings, damaging property,
       harassing young pregnant women, and workers in abortion clinics and, on occasion, mur-
       dering doctors who perform abortions.' In turn, Boyle, Kim, and Longhofer (2015) docu-
       ment the trend to abortion liberalization in the world as a whole during 1960–2009.

escalating anti-abortion laws, hysterias, and violent or culture wars at federal and state levels, especially (though not only) in the 'Bible Belt,' at the time of writing these lines. Hence, like Greece and especially Turkey, upon closer inspection, the US turns out to actually confirm the pattern of liberal-secular civil society more sustaining abortion and other personal freedoms and rights than do its opposites, rather than being an exception to the rule. Specifically, like in the case of Turkey, it does so by its liberal-civil society as a recent past bequeathing a civics lesson or legal legacy of such and related freedoms and rights that is evidently threatened, attacked, and attempted to eradicate or reverse, but not eradicated yet (e.g., the Supreme Court abortion decision prior to the 1980s) by anti-liberal and anti-secular forces, laws, and wars at all levels, above all in the 'Bible Belt' and similar conservative regions.

Freedom of Alcohol Production, Distribution and Consumption

At this juncture, both Americans and non-Americans may be mystified and wonder why such drastic or significant differences in the legal age of alcohol use exist between the US and other Western and even non-Western societies. Hence, it would be informative to know the US federal government's and states' true explanation why Americans must be 5–6 years older than many Europeans and 2–3 years than Canadians and Mexicans, notably 3 years than also the historically Puritan English people, to be able to legally purchase and consume alcohol in the privacy of their homes or in public, including no more than beer and wine, let alone why they should be prohibited from doing so regardless of any age, as in much of the South. One wonders what is the real political reason why Americans are treated as more immature—i.e., from 2 to 6 years—and thus untrustworthy and irresponsible than other Western persons in terms of alcohol purchase and consumption, but more mature, trustworthy, and responsible in many other respects, including purchasing, owning, and carrying guns. Simply, one expects the US conservative government, above all the 'Southern United States,' to explain or justify why Americans must be between 2–6 years older than Europeans, Canadians, Mexicans, and Britons, to purchase and consume beer or vine, while being allowed to buy and carry, including openly and publicly, ever-more deadly guns at the of equal or even younger age than their counterparts.

In expectation of such a genuine (as distinct from false, Prohibition-style) explanation—perhaps futile waiting, since it has not been provided since the increasing legal alcohol age limit in the 1980s—one can only hypothesize what is inside the 'beautiful minds' of US anti-alcohol temperance and other conservative forces cum 'culture warriors' who make Americans the least mature, trustworthy, and responsible persons with respect to alcohol (but the most as regards guns) in the Western world and beyond, including Europe, Canada, Mexico, the UK, and even Islamic Turkey. One hypothesis traced to Pareto is that the true reason for the US highest legal age limit for alcohol is that the conservative government and Southern and other states continue to follow, as he notes, Puritanism's equation (adopted from Calvin) of sensual pleasures, thus including alcohol consumption, just as sex, with sins and these with crimes, as shown by persistent 'Puritanical beliefs' in these and other moral maters such as abortion. Hence, the hypothesized explanation is what Pareto describes as 'religious exaltation,' 'religious and sectarian sentiment' to the no-return point of Hume's classically diagnosed 'madness with religious ecstasies,' specifically 'wretched' and 'wild 'fanaticism' of Puritanism and its legacy evidently still pervasive in the US conservative government and states alike, notably the 'Bible Belt.'

Another hypothesis, also traced to Pareto, is the US highest legal age limit for alcohol maybe be attributed to what he detects as the tendency for ascetics or 'elated moralists,' in this case anti-alcohol groups, to torment and show 'bitter hatred' for 'less ascetic men,' originating, aside from 'religious and sectarian sentiment,' in the 'envy' of non-enjoyers for enjoyers, for example, for young— and in the case of prohibition all—alcohol drinkers. If so, the hypothesized explanation would a kind of sadism involving a ruling group of sadistic personalities whose dream-world or ideal is what Pareto names a 'population of ascetics who (e.g.) drink no wine,' as totally implemented during Prohibition and much of the 'Bible Belt' today, and expressed or approximated in what many Americans perceive as the government Puritan-rooted credo of 'if it feels good (to individuals), ban it and punish it' arguably precisely because they enjoy it. This also applies, since ultra-conservative Reaganism, to the US government criminalization of and Draconian punishment, including potentially execution and actually life-long imprisonment, for drug production, purchase, and consumption (with the partial exception of marihuana in a few states recently).

An opposite hypothesis, implied in Hume and Weber, for the puzzle is that self-declared ascetic saints or moralists such as anti-alcohol temperance persons and groups punish for and deny to others, in this case young and via prohibition all alcohol users, what they actually commit and enjoy themselves, including alcohol and other sins and vices (drugs, sex) they condemn and criminalize if committed and displayed by anyone but themselves. To that extent, the hypothesized explanation would be Puritan-rooted or style duplicity or hypocrisy, as Hume anticipates by classically detecting the 'cant and hypocrisy' of Puritanism, and Weber implies by referring to the 'pure hypocrisy' of 'Americanism,' including by implication the hypocritical prohibition for and punishment of younger and other Americans what the 'all-American' prohibiting groups engage in themselves, such as alcohol consumption and other prohibited activities (sex, drugs, etc.).

Yet another hypothesis concerning the US highest legal age limit for alcohol is what Pareto diagnoses and predicts as the government perennial pattern of enforcing 'morality by law,' including non-alcohol and other temperance by legal sanctions, as epitomized by Prohibition enforced no less than by the Constitution, resulting in 'gross abuses' of power that are not observed in societies with 'no such restrictions,'[32] thus subverting democracy into moralistic tyranny. If so, the hypothesized explanation would be the systemic, systematic, and perpetual imposition of morality by legal mechanisms, and the corresponding criminalization and sanction of its violations, including alcohol purchase and consumption by 'immature' people such as those under 21; and all Americans were made such during Prohibition, and many are still in much of the prohibitive 'Bible Belt' ('dry' counties).

These hypothesized explanations may be useful to help both non-Americans and Americans better understand or make sense of what is seemingly non-understandable or non-sense and atypical in comparative terms, namely the by far highest legal age limit for alcohol, including its dramatic increase, from 18 to 21, by the Puritanical Reagan administration during the 1980s. They are more or less plausible and probable until and unless the US government at both federal and state level fully and clearly explains what is the true reason or rationale that in order to purchase and consume alcohol, simply buy and drink mere beer or wine, Americans must be from 2–6 years older than their Western and even non-Western counterparts, including both continental Europeans and Canadians, Mexicans, Britons, and even Turks. And regardless of the explanation or justification, a higher (lower) legal age limit for alcohol indicates—as does the absence (presence) of prohibitions—a higher (lower) degree of this individual freedom and personal choice, and thus of a free civil society, in conjunction with other such freedoms.

At this juncture, peoples from Western and related countries, including Canada (except for Muslims) are probably both perplexed and bemused at the Orwellian spectacle of police presence in and surveillance of alcohol-serving establishments to enforce the age-limit for alcohol in 'conservative America' such as the South, because they have seen nothing of sorts in their societies but only in Third-World dictatorships like Islamic theocracies. (They may be even

---

32   Pareto (1935, p. 1608) observes states that 'in the United States where the government tries to enforce morality by law, one notes gross abuses that are not observable in countries where there are no such restrictions.'

more puzzled and amused to observe such police presence and monitoring in non-alcohol-serving establishments to enforce outright alcohol prohibitions as in the 'Bible Belt,' Utah, etc.). They may be perplexed that public resources are not employed in more rational or effective crime-control activities— simply if the police had 'nothing better to do' than to prevent people younger than 21 year from drinking alcohol and arresting them if they do—given that the homicide rate and the percentage of murders by guns are the highest in the Western world. Yet, as always in 'conservative America,' there is a 'rationale and method to the anti-liberal, antirational, repressive madness' in civil and all society obliterating or perverting the domain of individual liberty and privacy.

Generally, the bizarre—from the Western viewpoint—example of alcohol-consumption police surveillance in the US South and beyond illustrates that the state in 'conservative America' invariably tends to be the Orwellian police state and to that extent a proxy totalitarian or authoritarian government comparable to those in fascism and communism in the past and Third-World dictatorships today. Particularly, it reaffirms that the police force in 'conservative America' essentially represents Puritanical vice-police historically descending from the Puritan anti-sin archetype and comparatively equivalent or comparable to that in Islamic theocracies. Thus, observations indicate that most of material and personnel police resources are spent on the Puritanical warfare on moral sins and vices, as distinct from crimes, in 'conservative America,' as were in the old Puritan theocracy as its evident model, and are in today's Islamic theocracies. This is indicated by that the vast majority of prisoners in 'conservative America' are sinners like non-violent drug offenders and others rather than ordinary criminals, and most arrests[33] are made for sins and offenses other than violent or property crimes (murder, rape, assault, robbery, etc.). And this Puritanical warfare on sins and generally human weakness and imperfection is couched as 'war on crime' in 'conservative America,' as was in the Puritan theocracy and is in Islamic theocracies. Therefore, this compromises and exposes any 'war of crime' and being 'tough on crime' in 'conservative America'—as did in the Puritan theocracy and does in Islamic theocracies—as a moral-religious warfare ('crusade,' 'jihad') on human sins and vices construed as Orwellian crimes, and thus a moralistic attack on individual liberty and privacy typifying a free civil society.

---

33   Levitt (1997, p.) finds that 'less than one-quarter of all arrests are for crimes' such as 'murder and nonnegligent manslaughter, forcible rape, assault, robbery, burglary, larceny, and motor vehicle theft' (reported in *Uniform Crime Reports* by the Federal Bureau of Investigation).

The above shows that the Puritanical war on sins-as-crimes and vice-police in 'conservative America' is irrational, inhuman, and anachronistic historically in view of the death of the Puritan theocracy and comparatively given that it is unknown in Western societies and only found in Islamic theocracies. So, the Orwellian police surveillance of alcohol-serving and related vice environments is an absurdity and a cause for perplexity for Westerners, while making perfect sense in 'conservative America,' as in the dead Puritan theocracy and present Islamic theocracies.

Freedom of Drug Production, Distribution, and Consumption
In general, studies and observations suggest the military-style expansive, persisting, and expensive war on drugs and severe Draconian[34] punishment for their possession, use, and trade in America as opposed to the reportedly more humane treatment of drug use and users as mostly non-criminal health issues in most other Western societies. The US war on drugs is an instance and continuation of various temperance[35] and culture wars and movements since moralistic and theocratic Puritanism and Prohibition and consequently tends to deny and suppress personal liberty, choice, and privacy, in sharp contrast to alternative, less violent, coercive, and repressive approaches to the problem of drugs typifying most Western European countries. In short, it does by redefining and harshly punishing drug use as a crime rather than a health problem

---

34   Mueller (2013, p. 9) remarks that 'many of those in jail in the US are guilty of drug-related crimes, and so this latter statistic can be attributed to the draconian nature of US policies with respect to drugs in comparison to other rich democracies. But these draconian policies can also be traced to the much stronger religious beliefs in the US. Evangelical Americans, a significant fraction of the population, see the world in terms of good and evil. Evil must be punished. Drugs are evil. Send the users and sellers to jail.' He infers therefore that a 'casual visitor to religious America and secular Europe (will) find it difficult to identify the social benefits that America reaps from its greater religiosity compared with Europe' (Mueller 2013, p. 9).

35   Young (2002, pp. 660–61) observes that 'the movements for temperance were the first national movements in the US, but they emerged in interaction with religious and civil institutions, not the state,' particularly emphasizing the 'centrality of evangelical Protestantism,' but Tilly (2002, p. 690) objects that 'temperance movement leaders called on state and national governments to enact moral policies on behalf of such moral programs,' thus enforcing their 'morality by law' and criminalizing pleasures-sins, as Pareto noted and illustrated by Prohibition. In a way, Young (2002, p. 661) implicitly admits the Puritan-style criminalization of pleasures-sins noting that 'the evangelical schemas of public confession (against sin and of faith) and the special sins of the nation mobilized support for these (temperance) movements within a national infrastructure of Protestant institutions,' as culminated by the Constitutional enactment of alcohol Prohibition.

like addiction, just as all Puritan temperance wars criminalize various human sins and so pleasures[36] and sinners. On account of its destructive impact on personal liberty, choice, privacy, and even life, the 'war of drugs'—no matter how justified politically, morally, religiously, or medically—like all wars or repressions, objectively attacks and ultimately vanquishes or subverts, just as did its model or precedent Prohibition, free civil society in America and beyond, as expanded during recent times.

Sexual Freedoms and Rights

As implied, the continuing and exceptional criminalization of such sexual freedom as adultery, however morally repugnant, in 'conservative America' (i.e., more than 20 states and the military) reflects the legacy of Puritanism—and its functional equivalence to detested Islam—that punished with death such an offense, as Tocqueville[37] classically observes for New England's Puritan theocracy, and generally fixated on condemned and punished sex as a supreme sin-crime and near-taboo.[38] This provides the rationale for the US medium score on this perhaps most controversial, dubious, and 'revulsive' or 'immoral' dimension of sexual freedom and generally individual liberty, choice, responsibility, and privacy.

---

36   Scitovsky (1972, p. 66) notes that 'it seems a strange irony of fate that our Puritan rejection of pleasure as the ultimate aim of life should have led to a preference system in which the making of money is the main challenge and effortless, pleasureless comfort the main reward. We usually trade quality of life to save effort or obtain extra safety; (and) are forced into such trade-offs by restrictions of our authorities impose, supposedly to protect people from their own folly and with never a thought of the pleasure they force people sacrifice for what often are insignificant increments of safety.' For example, Scitovsky (1972, p. 66) observes that in vacations 'when the US is compared to Europe, we rank among the poorest European countries, with Portugal and Italy—as though our high standard of comfort and safety were an irreducible minimum, absorbing so s such of our income that, measured by what's left over for the enjoyment of life, we seem worse off than many others poorer than we are,' inferring that US 'less good vacation amenities (are) partly explained in turn by our authorities' less tolerance for citizens' taking risks for pleasure.'

37   In his *Democracy in America* Tocqueville observes that in Puritan New England adultery, together with blasphemy, sorcery, and rape, was 'punished with death,' and comments that the 'legislation of a rude and half-civilized people was thus applied to an enlightened and moral community.'

38   Swedberg (2005, p. 21), referring to Weber analysis in the *Protestant Ethic*, comments that the Puritans 'were not, however, allowed to indulge their senses—just as they were not allowed to enjoy sex, even if they were allowed to procreate.'

In general, sociological and other observations suggest that ruling political and religious groups in 'conservative America' exploit 'sexual mores' as the 'footholds for intolerance' reaching the point of their 'sadistic intolerance to cultural otherness,' the degree of freedom of adult entertainment cum 'pornography,' etc.[39]

Peace and Peaceful Conflict Resolution in Civil Society

'American exceptionalism' in the highest homicide rate is associated with that in an exemplary non-liberal and non-secular hyper-religious civil society in 'conservative America' like the South, with the first being conditioned and predicted by the second. In this sense, the 'law of conservation of violence'[40] asserts itself with a vengeance in that latent, symbolic violence as well as closure, incivility, and unhappiness in a non-liberal and non-secular ultra-religious conservative society ultimately explode, escalate, or translate in manifest, physical violence through homicides. To paraphrase Clausewitz's definition of war

---

39   Bauman (2000, p. 106) alerts to the 'sadistic intolerance to cultural otherness widespread in American society,' in particular that 'sexual mores were no doubt exploited as one of the more important footholds for intolerance.' Edelman (2009, p. 211) reports that in most US states, 'producers of adult entertainment face possible charges of "pandering" (and so) the production of adult entertainment in (these) states continues to present significant legal risk.' Also, Edelman (2009, p. 211) observes that 'US consumers also receive substantial adult entertainment from firms in Montreal, where zoning and immigration laws tend to facilitate production of adult entertainment. Through 2004, Canada issued visas to would-be adult entertainers.' Edelman (2009, p. 219) finds that adult entertainment subscriptions are 'more prevalent in states where surveys indicate conservative positions on religion, gender roles, and sexuality. In states where more people agree that "Even today miracles are performed by the power of God" and "I never doubt the existence of God," there are more subscriptions to this service. Subscriptions are also more prevalent in states where more people agree that "I have old-fashioned values about family and marriage" and "AIDS might be God's punishment for immoral sexual behavior."' Evidently, these are the same people and states that publicly seek to outlaw adult entertainment and punish its producers and distributors, perpetuating what Weber refers to as Puritan 'pure hypocrisy' (perhaps the only purity in Puritanism as the delusional, pretended 'pure' church and morality). Merton (1968, p. 134) asks the questions: 'Can it be held that in European countries with registered and regulated prostitution the prostitute contributes an economic service, whereas in this country lacking legal sanction the prostitute provides no such service?' and suggests a negative answer.

40   Bourdieu (1998, p. 40) suggests that one 'cannot cheat with the law of the conservation of violence: all violence is paid for (e.g.) the structural violence exerted by the financial markets (layoffs, loss of security) is matched sooner or later in the form of a whole host of minor and major everyday acts of violence (suicide, crime).'

of which it is an equivalent proxy within a society, the exceptional homicide rate in the US is, other things equal, a continuation of the 'politics' of symbolic violence, closure, incivility, and unhappiness of a non-liberal and non-secular 'godly' society by 'other (violent) means' in 'conservative America,' such as the Southern 'Bible Belt.'

In particular, the US exceptional homicide rate, notably the percentage of homicides by guns, supports the expectation of an association between non-liberal and non-secular overly-religious civil societies and a high level of violence expressed in their higher murder rate than others. At the minimum, 'conservative America' does so by being the most intense, pervasive, and persistent exemplar of a pre- and anti-liberal and non-secular, religiously over-determined civil society[41] within the US and among Western societies and also having the highest homicide rate in both contexts. In this regard, the compound of anti-liberalism and anti-secularism or religious over-determinism ('religion and guns') in 'conservative America' appears to cause and predict a higher rates of murders than liberal-secular alternatives, simply 'kill' more than anything else both in the US and among Western societies.

An additional factor explaining the US striking and highest percentage of homicides by guns consists of so-called 'stand your ground' laws enacted in the conservative-religious US states during recent times. These laws effectively give gun-owners, a relatively small subset of the US population in which gun-ownership is extremely concentrated in one or so percent, just like wealth and income, 'license to kill' with legal impunity and generally to terrorize and intimidate non-owners, so most Americans. On this account, in spite or rather because of their professed intentions to defend the Constitutional 'right to bear arms,' these laws legalize and the conservative states sponsor and spread murder, terror, and intimidation in civil society by an armed part of the population over the rest, a comparatively unknown and unheard-of phenomenon

---

41   Bailey and Snedker (2011, pp. 845–50) register the historically decisive 'impact that Chris-
      tian organizations had on Southern social life and local power structures' such that 'in
      the case of the American South, the connection between religion and society was strong
      and not unlike what Durkheim described of earlier historical periods when everything
      social was religious' and, one can add, what Simmel denoted the 'primitive identity' of
      religion and politics. Bailey and Snedker (2011, p. 878) add that 'white Southerners have
      historically used religious expression and structures as barriers against the tides of social
      change, and nonreligious civil society developed more slowly (if at all) in the South than
      in other regions of the United States.' They also note that 'Southern Christianity largely
      rejected the Social Gospel that swept the North, choosing instead to focus on saving indi-
      vidual souls' (Bailey and Snedker 2011, p. 878).

in Western and related societies, including even neighboring Mexico where state-sponsored gun violence is replaced by that between various non-state groups (drug gangs, etc.). Historically, these laws/states aim and apparently succeed to make the US descend into the barbarian Hobbesian state of nature ruled by the 'law of the strongest' and the 'law of the jungle,' simply the 'Wild West' of what Spencer notes as 'unavenged murders, rifle duels, and Lynch law,' as an exemplar of the 'barbarizing of colonists.'

The preceding, above all the perpetual, pervasive, and conservative gun culture and violence, justifies the US estimate of peace, peaceful conflict resolution, security, and the appreciation of human life, as the condition and indicator of free civil society. It is also supported by the observations about various violent and apocalyptic, rapture-expectant sects and cults, as epitomized by the violence and self-destruction of a fundamentalist cult in Texas during the 1990s inspiring the 1995 Oklahoma bombing and many subsequent acts of anti-government religiously induced terrorism.[42] These instances could be taken into account for the US estimate especially so long as the risk of such sect and cult followers being killed, gravely harmed, or dispossessed by their 'holy' leaders in the 'name of God,' 'rapture,' the 'second coming,' 'Biblical law,' and the like is probably higher than that of members of any groups in Western and related societies, except for Mexico. Simply, this applies so long as one is more likely to get murdered, gravely harmed and dispossessed belonging to a fundamentalist sect and cult a la Jones and Koresh in 'conservative America' than being member of other religious and secular group in these countries, minus Mexico. Such examples of sect violence are pertinent if the risk of followers' death in US evangelical sects and cults is comparable to the hazard of members of a drug gang or cartel being killed by their leaders or other such gangs in Mexico.

Both tendencies indicate the negation and breakdown of the above condition of a free civil society by violence, personal unsafety and physical insecurity, and notably the depreciation and elimination or degradation of human life, though for different reasons. These are the 'glory of God' in US evangelical denominations, sects, and cults, and monetary gain in Mexican drug cartels or gangs, albeit 'God and money' can be merged in the first, as exemplified

---

42   Gorski and Türkmen-Dervişoğlu (2013, p. 197) cite 'modern episodes of sacrificial violence, such as the (Puritan) New England witch craze' and the 'violent cults of the 1980s, such as those in Jamestown and Waco.' Juergensmeyer (2003) identifies and analyzes the religious sources and justifications of anti-government terrorism in America and elsewhere (for a review of the sociological literature on the subject see Turk 2004).

'conservative America' by the Koresh Waco cult, the Southern 'Christian coalition,' 'prosperity gospel,' and the like as what Pareto[43] calls the 'method of clip-
ping the sheep' economically and spiritually, taking followers' resources and
soul and mind, body and eventually, as by a self-proclaimed 'Divine leader,'
their life. Pareto might add that this is precisely what Protestant pastors and
their Catholic and other religious equivalents are for—to 'clip the sheep' of its
possessions and ultimately to 'kill (them) in the name of the divine master.'[44]
On this account, both the deadly violence perpetrated by Mexican drug gangs
and the perennial mass death in evangelical sects and cults within 'conservative America' should be considered in respect of a peaceful free civil society.

---

43   Pareto (2000, p. 69) remarks that the sums which the ruling class of bourgeoisie 'appropri-
      ates illicitly are enormous and certainly comparable to the sums which, during other pe-
      riods, were extorted by other ruling classes. The only advantage for the nation is the fact
      that the method of clipping the sheep has been perfected; hence for the same amount of
      extorted wealth the amount squandered is smaller.'

44   Pareto (2000, p. 55) states that following the establishment of Christianity, its 'warlike
      prelates donned armor over their stoles and went out to kill in the name of the divine
      master.'

CHAPTER 10

Summary and Conclusion

Summary of Findings

> Forty years after Friedrich Hayek wrote down his nightmare of the welfare
> state leading remorselessly to the totalitarian murder of freedom, Scandi-
> navians enjoy freedom second to none that the world has ever seen.
>
> SAMUELSON 1983

The comparative estimates of modern free society in its four component
parts—i.e., democracy, free economy, free culture, and free civil society—
are aggregated in a composite estimate for Western and related countries
(Table 10.1). Such composite estimates are calculated from almost 50 rankings,
taken or derived from multiple sources, of these countries on various dimensions of modern free society, which ensures their high degree of representative-
ness and objectivity, and accounts for some seemingly surprising or 'shocking'
results, as shown next.

Based on such aggregate estimates, one can categorize the latter into, first,
'completely free' (aggregate scores 8 or higher on a 0–10 scale), second, 'mostly
free' (scores 7–7.99), third, 'pseudo- or semi-free' (scores 6–6.99), and fourth,
'unfree' societies (scores under 6) (Table 10.2).

First and foremost, 'completely free societies' are demonstrated to be following countries in a descending order: Norway (8.87), Sweden (8.43), Denmark
(8.29), Iceland (8.27), the Netherlands (8.21), and Belgium (8.01) (Table 10.3).

As noted, all of these six totally free countries are considered and classified
as 'liberal societies' in the present classification, which entirely and dramatically fulfills the prediction or expectation that the latter tend as a whole to be
the freest modern societies in the Western and entire world. Notably, the top
five 'completely free societies' are four Scandinavian countries and one similar
country, the Netherlands, which are widely observed or described, both by liberals approvingly and anti-liberals, especially conservatives (as in the US and
Islamic countries), with condemnation, as the most liberal in the Western and
all world. To that extent, this fully and dramatically fulfills the expectation that
the most liberal societies are as a whole also the freest among Western and
related countries, as within OECD. In particular, the single most 'completely
free, freest society out of 33 Western and related countries is shown to be

TABLE 10.1   *Comparative aggregate estimates of a free society, OECD countries.*

	Democracy	Free economy	Free culture	Civil society	TOTAL	Rankings	Average
Australia	131.52	51.29	64.75	96.00	343.56	48	7.16
Austria	141.63	61.24	41.50	98.41	332.78	43	7.74
Belgium	134.29	75.00	63.88	95.41	368.58	46	8.01
Canada	131.78	60.32	67.75	111.00	370.85	47	7.89
Chile	106.96	31.73	23.88	57.71	220.28	42	5.24
Czech Republic	113.34	45.00	46.88	94.41	299.63	44	6.81
Denmark	142.07	75.14	47.38	108.41	373.00	45	8.29
Estonia	102.21	35.00	42.88	87.82	267.91	42	6.38
Finland	135.95	68.55	75.75	97.71	377.96	48	7.87
France	117.76	51.45	79.25	100.82	349.28	49	7.13
Germany	131.89	64.04	78.13	101.12	375.18	49	7.66
Greece	107.42	27.23	29.25	90.41	254.31	43	5.91
Hungary	102.71	48.00	52.88	90.65	294.24	44	6.69
Iceland	132.20	73.12	55.00	103.71	364.03	44	8.27
Ireland	132.91	63.52	58.38	103.00	357.81	48	7.45
Italy	124.85	47.67	47.13	84.53	304.18	46	6.61
Japan	119.66	34.27	69.50	77.82	301.25	46	6.55
Korea South	101.21	29.79	48.50	45.53	225.03	42	5.36
Luxembourg	120.47	53.08	44.75	114.71	333.01	42	7.93
Mexico	94.20	21.25	24.38	49.76	189.59	42	4.51
Netherlands	137.72	67.00	88.13	109.41	402.26	49	8.21
New Zealand	137.71	62.21	61.13	105.00	366.05	46	7.96
Norway	142.51	79.66	74.00	112.00	408.17	46	8.87
Poland	99.06	37.01	36.38	83.12	255.57	46	5.56
Portugal	112.06	39.18	49.88	110.41	311.53	45	6.92
Slovakia	110.97	48.00	26.00	85.82	270.79	43	6.30
Slovenia	113.95	39.00	46.63	93.82	293.40	43	6.82
Spain	113.46	46.95	66.13	99.41	325.95	46	7.09
Sweden	141.42	75.73	95.00	100.71	412.86	49	8.43
Switzerland	132.21	64.37	67.38	95.41	359.37	46	7.81
Turkey	87.20	28.01	20.63	60.94	196.78	44	4.47
UK	116.48	51.98	81.75	88.41	338.62	49	6.91
US	82.35	38.32	32.13	50.24	203.04	49	4.14

I   Average free society scores 8 and higher—Completely free societies
II   Average free society scores 7–7.99—Mostly free societies
III   Average free society scores 6–6.99—Pseudo-, semi-free societies
IV   Average free society scores under 6—Unfree societies

TABLE 10.2 *Average free society estimates and classification, OECD countries.*

I   Average free society scores 8 and higher—Completely free societies
    (6 cases)
    Belgium, Denmark, Iceland, Netherlands, Norway, Sweden

II Average free society scores 7–7.99—mostly free societies (11 cases)
    Australia, Austria, Canada, Finland, France, Germany, Ireland,
    Luxembourg, New Zealand, Spain, Switzerland

III Average free society scores 6–6.99—Pseudo-free societies (9 cases)
    Czech Republic, Estonia, Hungary, Italy, Japan, Portugal, Slovakia,
    Slovenia, the UK

IV Average free society scores under 6—Unfree societies (7 cases)
    Chile, Greece, South Korea, Mexico, Poland, Turkey, the US ('conser-
    vative America')

TABLE 10.3 *Aggregate free society ranking, OECD countries.*

Rank	Country Index (0–10)		Type of society	Classification
1	Norway	8.87	Completely Free	Liberal
2	Sweden	8.43	Completely Free	Liberal
3	Denmark	8.29	Completely Free	Liberal
4	Iceland	8.27	Completely Free	Liberal
5	Netherlands	8.21	Completely Free	Liberal
6	Belgium	8.01	Completely Free	Liberal
7	New Zealand	7.96	Mostly Free	Liberal
8	Canada	7.89	Mostly Free	Liberal
9	Luxembourg	7.93	Mostly Free	Liberal
10	Finland	7.87	Mostly Free	Liberal
11	Switzerland	7.81	Mostly Free	Liberal
12	Austria	7.74	Mostly Free	Liberal
13	Germany	7.66	Mostly Free	Liberal
14	Ireland	7.45	Mostly Free	Intermediate
15	Australia	7.16	Mostly Free	Liberal
16	France	7.13	Mostly Free	Liberal
17	Spain	7.09	Mostly Free	Intermediate
18	Portugal	6.92	Pseudo-Free	Intermediate

TABLE 10.3   *Aggregate free society ranking, OECD countries.* (cont.)

Rank	Country index (0–10)		Type of society	Classification
19	UK	6.91	Pseudo-Free	Intermediate
19	Slovenia	6.82	Pseudo-Free	Intermediate
21	Czech Republic	6.81	Pseudo-Free	Intermediate
22	Hungary	6.69	Pseudo-Free	Intermediate
23	Italy	6.61	Pseudo-Free	Intermediate
24	Japan	6.55	Pseudo-Free	Intermediate
25	Estonia	6.38	Pseudo-Free	Intermediate
26	Slovakia	6.30	Pseudo-Free	Intermediate
27	Greece	5.91	Unfree	Intermediate
28	Poland	5.56	Unfree	Anti-Liberal
29	South Korea	5.36	Unfree	Anti-Liberal
30	Chile	5.24	Unfree	Intermediate
31	Mexico	4.51	Unfree	Anti-Liberal
32	Turkey	4.47	Unfree	Anti-Liberal
33	US	4.14	Unfree	Anti-Liberal[a]

a 'Conservative America'.

Norway that is commonly or frequently regarded as the most liberal country in the West and entire world, alongside Sweden, Denmark, Iceland, or the Netherlands ranked just below it in this ranking, or alongside or above it in some other rankings. Yet again, this entirely and dramatically fulfills the expectation that the most liberal country—Norway, or Sweden or the Netherlands in other observations or perceptions—invariably is/will be the single freest modern society in the Western and entire world. Most importantly, 'liberal society' as a societal type or whole proves to be the most 'completely free,' the freest form of society or group of societies among all Western and related countries.

Conversely, no countries classified as a 'mixed' and 'anti-liberal conservative' society belong to 'completely free societies,' which hence fully and dramatically supports the negative expectation that they are hardly ever such and drastically less free than their liberal alternatives. Notably, not a single 'anti-liberal conservative' society, including the US in the sense of 'conservative America,' particularly Dahrendorf's 'Southern United States,' is ranked among 'completely free societies,' as is neither in those 'mostly free' nor even 'pseudo-free,' but instead invariably in 'unfree' ones identified next, which hence entirely fulfills the expectations.

In general, this aggregate ranking is similar but not identical to some non-academic rankings of 'liberal' societies in the Western world and beyond (Table 10.4).

For example, one of these rankings identifies the Netherlands as the 'most liberal' and consequently the freest country (score 8.57) among Western and other countries in the world, which is in the present ranking among the five freest ones and classified in liberal societies. That ranking includes Sweden (8.01), Belgium (7.31), Norway (7.02), Denmark (6.95), and Iceland (6.93) either in 'very liberal' or 'liberal' and therefore very free or free countries, which are also presently among the six freest OECD countries and classified in liberal societies. As a particular curiosity, the above ranking incorporates the USA in 'non-liberal countries close to liberal' (score 5.39) and thus non-free close to free countries—which intimates the 'two Americas'—and ranked 47 overall below South Korea, Mexico, and Italy, but above Chile and Greece belonging to this group and such 'non-liberal countries close to anti-liberal' and so unfree as Poland and Turkey.

Second, 'mostly free societies' are found to be these countries in a descending order:

New Zealand (7.96), Canada (7.89), Luxembourg (7.87), Finland (7.88), Switzerland (7.81), Austria (7.74), Germany (7.66), Ireland (7.15), Australia (7.16), France (7.13), and Spain (7.08). Recall that in the present classification nine out of these eleven countries are deemed and classified as 'liberal societies,' and only two as the 'intermediate, mixed,' thus none as 'anti- or non-liberal,' specifically conservative, society. Therefore, this result largely fulfills the expectation that 'liberal societies' as a whole tend to be essentially free, either completely or mostly, and relatively freer than others, including both their intermediate counterparts and especially their anti-liberal, conservative opposites as wholes.

Thus, all the 15 countries (except for 'liberal America' as evidently the weaker or transient one of the 'two Americas') considered and classified as 'liberal societies' belong to 'completely' or 'mostly free societies,' proving to be essentially free and comparatively freer than others, while none belonging to pseudo- or un-free societies, which hence almost entirely fulfills the positive expectations in this respect. Conversely, these results fulfill the negative expectations that the other two types of society are overall less free than the liberal, as shown by that only 2 out of 13 mixed and none of anti-or non-liberal, conservative societies belong to 'mostly free societies,' and, as seen, not a single one of either to 'completely free societies.' In sum, these findings show that 'liberal societies'

TABLE 10.4 *Liberal societies, OECD countries, 2014.*

Most liberal country	Score
1. Netherlands	8.57
Very liberal countries	
2. Sweden	8.01
3. New Zealand	7.63
4. Belgium	7.31
5. Canada	7.26
6. Spain	7.26
8. Luxembourg	7.17
9. Switzerland	7.14
10. Finland	7.04
11. Norway	7.02
Liberal countries	
12. Ireland	6.99
13. Denmark	6.95
14. Iceland	6.93
15. Czech Republic	6.9
16. Slovenia	6.84
18. Germany	6.69
19. Japan	6.56
20. UK	6.52
21. Austria	6.51
22. France	6.50
23. Portugal	6.45
25. Hungary	6.41
26. Estonia	6.31
28. Australia	6.15
30. Slovakia	6.12
Non-liberal countries close to liberal	
40. Korea South	5.68
41. Mexico	5.58
45. Italy	5.44
47. US	5.39
58. Chile	5.20
63. Greece	5.04

Most liberal country	Score
Non-liberal countries close to anti-liberal	
68. Poland	4.90
95. Turkey	4.39

SOURCE: HTTP://SAMBAWALKER.COM/LIBERAL/LIBERAL-INDEX.

are 'mostly free' at the minimum—and 'completely free' otherwise—while their mixed counterparts being only at the maximum or in exceptional rare cases, and their conservative opposites not in any respect, thus conclusively confirming the predictions.

Third, 'pseudo-, semi-free societies' involve certain countries in a descending order, for example, Portugal (6.92), the UK (6.91), Slovenia (6.82), Czech Republic (6.81), Hungary (6.69), Italy (6.61), and Japan (6.55), Estonia (6.38), and Slovakia (6.30). As also noticed, the present classification considers and classifies all of these 9 countries as 'intermediate, eclectic, mixed' societies, which means that virtually all of them are pseudo- or semi-free, except for only 2 of them being 'mostly free,' as seen earlier. Therefore, the results entirely support the expectation that these societies as a whole tend to be ranked in respect of freedom between their liberal and anti-liberal versions, simply to be quasi- or half-free overall. Conversely, no countries classified as 'liberal societies' are shown to be 'pseudo-, semi-free,' which strongly reaffirms the prediction that these are instead either 'completely free' or at the minimum 'mostly free.' This also holds for countries classified as 'anti-liberal, conservative societies,' which dramatically confirms the opposite prediction that these as a whole are invariably, drastically, and completely unfree, and not even pseudo-, semi- or minimally free as confirmed by their missing from this group of quasi- or minimal freedom, as from the previous two groups.

Fourth and last, 'unfree societies' are hence identified to be the remaining subset of OECD countries in a descending order of freedom or rather an ascending order of un-freedom, namely, Greece (5.91), Poland (5.56), South Korea (5.36), Chile (5.24), Mexico (4.51), Turkey (4.47) and the US (4.14). To recall, most of these countries,[1] including the US in the sense of 'conservative

---

[1] This bottom ranking indicates that that Chile has not fully emancipated from Catholic dominance and the vestige of, as Pryor (2002, p. 10) notes, an 'authoritarian government' during Pinochet's brutal military dictatorship, as neither has Mexico from such religious influence, as reported in Inglehart (2014). It also reaffirms that Greece is plagued by what Bloemraad et al. (2008, p. 158) identify as 'ethnic nationalism' sustaining a primitive closed mono-ethnic

America,' particularly the 'Southern United States,' out of the 'two Americas,' in the current classification are considered and classified as 'anti-liberal conservative societies,' along with two mixed cases. Alternatively, *all* the 'anti-liberal conservative societies' in this classification, including 'conservative America,' prove to be 'unfree,' only two of their mixed counterparts, namely Chile and Greece, and none of their liberal opposites. Accordingly, the results essentially fulfill the negative expectation that 'anti-liberal conservative societies' as a whole tend to be 'unfree' and comparatively less free than their liberal opposites as well as their mixed counterparts, thus least free of all within the Western and related context of OECD. In other words, they confirm that these societies represent or approach dictatorships, often religiously grounded and sanctified, simply theocracies or theocentric social systems, as shown by many of the above cited countries, in particular Poland, Turkey, and 'conservative America.'

Notably, the two most 'unfree societies' are identified as Turkey and the US, which are exactly and commonly experienced or perceived as the most 'anti- or non-liberal,' the first during theocratic Islamic rule, and the second as 'conservative America' epitomized by the 'Southern United States' as effective theocracy (the 'Bible Belt'), along with Poland under Catholic dominance. This therefore entirely and dramatically supports the expectation that the most 'anti- or non-liberal conservative societies' invariably tend to be as a whole the most unfree or least free among Western and related countries.

---

rather than a modern open multi-ethnic society, that South Korea remains what Habermas (2001, p. 38) denotes 'a developmental dictatorship,' and that in Poland, as Mueller (2009, p. 378) observes, religion persists in exerting a 'strong hold on a large segment of the population' making it a theocratic antithesis of liberal-secular democracy and a free society overall, and a pariah, along with Greece due to its nationalist negation and suppression of ethnic minority existence and rights, within the European Union. In addition, it confirms the fears, as Acemoglu et al. (2012, p. 1464) register, that 'any constitutional guarantees can be changed in the future' in Turkey under Islamic rule, as dramatically proven after the failed military coup attempt in 2016, and Dahrendorf's (1979) depiction of the 'Southern United States' and in extension 'conservative America' as a non-democratic, illegitimate government owing to the violation of 'fundamental human rights,' as again witnessed during the 2010s. Coincidentally or rather not, all these anti-liberal, undemocratic states and unfree societies (except for Mexico) have been military and related allies, with many installed (e.g., Chile under Pinochet's dictatorship) or supported (South Korea, Turkey, etc.) by the US conservative government. This shows that illiberal undemocratic 'misery needs company,' or what Bauman (1997, p. 184) calls 'protototalitarian' theocratic opposites, such as Islamic Turkey and 'evangelical America,' or in his words, the 'Islamic integrisme of ayatollahs' and 'evangelist churches of the Bible Belt,' 'attract each other.'

Their two lowest ranks indicate that Islamic-ruled Turkey and 'conservative America' as a consequence of being profoundly anti-liberal are basically
totalitarian societies. Due to the anti-liberal and anti-secular resurgence and
dominance in the 2000s obliterating a relatively liberal-secular legacy and history, Turkey has become an Islamic theocracy couched as formal 'democracy'
(almost like Iran) but eradicating substantive democracy in the sense of effective political and civil liberties and rights, as well as a free civil society and
culture. In turn, because of its perennial anti-liberalism 'conservative America'
like the 'Southern United States' has always been a proxy totalitarian ('proto-
fascist'[2]) compound of capitalist dictatorship combining anarchy for capitalists and oppression of labor, evangelical theocracy with absolute power of the
'godly' and oppression, exclusion, and discrimination against the 'godless,'
Puritan moral fascism in war on individual liberty and privacy, 'sins and vices'
('war on crime'), and religious superstition, overarching irrationalism, and vehement anti-rationalism against science after the vestige or image of the Dark
Middle Ages. And it has not only perpetuated itself as such but further escalated and intensified, as its last rank on modern free society indicates, since
the 1980s with anti-liberal Reaganism, particularly the 'Southern United States'
during the 2010s with the 'Tea Party' extremist resurgence and seizure of power.

In particular, the single most 'unfree society' is found to be—seemingly surprisingly and even shockingly—the US commonly observed, experienced, or
perceived as the most 'anti- or non-liberal' in the form of 'conservative America' both by liberals with despair or regret and by conservatives with celebration or approval among these countries, at least in the Western world. Thus,
the society that ranks[3] the last out of 33 countries in this respect is, in the prevalent form of 'conservative America' such as the 'Southern United States,' typically ranked by anti-liberals with 'pride and joy' the 'best' ('No 1' a la Reagan)
in 'anti- or non-liberal conservative' dimensions among Western countries and
perhaps beyond. To that extent, this finding entirely and drastically fulfills

---

2 Putnam (2000, p. 350) describes 'conservative America' during the 1950 as 'protofascist.'
3 No doubt, the US ranking is 'shocking' at first glance. Still, it becomes less so if considering,
   for example, Pryor (2002, p. 13) observation that 'in almost all cases' of comparison with OECD
   countries in the various indicators or covariates of modern free society the 'US appears almost alone at one [negative] extreme,' indicating what he calls 'American exceptionalism' in
   an inverse form of that usually supposed and celebrated. In addition, this 'shock' is overcame
   or diminished if one considers the coexistence and opposition between the 'two Americas' of
   which authoritarian and theocratic 'conservative America,' as epitomized by what Dahrendorf (1979) connote the 'Southern States of America,' has prevailed over or at least countered
   its liberal, democratic, and secular opposite since the 1980s, as Mueller (2009) observes.

the negative expectation that the single most 'anti- or non-liberal conserva-tive' society is invariably the most unfree or least free among contemporary Western and related societies. Conversely, no 'liberal society' is found in 'un-free societies,' which clearly fulfills the expectations that this societal type is completely or mostly free, and never unfree, but an antithesis and antidote of these as its lethal poison. Also, no mixed society is listed in 'unfree societies,' which is also consistent with the expectations that this type is comparatively freer than its 'anti- or non-liberal' variant as the invariably most unfree among these comparative societal types.

Conclusions

In theoretical sociological terms, like any other, modern free society consti-tutes a total social system of interconnected and interactive subsystems, and thus an holistic, integral category, as does its defining attribute, societal liberty. Alternatively, it is not simply democracy or capitalism because the first is its in-tegral political and the second its economic subsystem, each being component part of the whole in interconnection and interaction with the others, includ-ing a free culture and civil society. This indicates that a sociological, holistic conception of modern free society regarded as a total social system has com-parative advantages to alternative economics and political-science concep-tions that tend to conceive it in reductive terms as capitalism and democracy, respectively. Evidently, modern free society represents a four-fold complex of, first, liberal, secular, and universalistic democracy, second, rationally regulat-ed and egalitarian welfare capitalism, third, rationalistic-liberal culture, and fourth, liberal-secular civil society. These form its political, economic, cultural and civic conditions, elements, and indicators typically in interconnection and interaction within it as a total social system.

In essence, therefore, modern free society constitutes a liberal social system. It is the practical implementation of liberalism as the principle and system of integral, universal liberty and what Mannheim connotes its complement equality and by implication justice in society. On this account, it provides a strong reaffirmation and reminder that liberalism originally was (classical) and substantially remains (contemporary) such a principle and system, what Smith denotes as the 'liberal plan' of 'liberty, equality, and justice' in society. This holds true in spite or because of anti-liberal, particularly conservative-fascist, enemies, and detractors construing liberalism, by deliberate miscon-structions and deceptions or delusions and fantasies, as the exact opposite ('tyranny,' 'big government'), as in the UK during Thatcherism and especially the US from neo-conservative Reaganism through the 'conservative revolution' of the 1990s to proto-fascist 'Tea Party' extremism in the 2010s.

The above reaffirms and reminds that liberalism by virtue of being a project and system of liberty conjoined with equality and justice constitutes the sole or the strongest and most viable foundation, condition, and predictor of a free society among contemporary Western and related societies, as did in the past and can be predicted to do in the foreseeable future. Conversely, it confirms and reminds that anti-liberalism forms the prevailing and most enduring basis and rationale of an unfree society among these societies, as did in retrospect and can be expected to continue in prospect. This primarily applies to conservatism as the most vehement, lasting, and tenacious kind of anti-liberalism, including its extreme subtypes or outcomes and allies such as theocratic religious fundamentalism and fascism. Conservatism, spanning from paleo-conservatism through fascism to neo-conservatism and revived religious fundamentalism and neo-fascism, invariably is, to paraphrase Smith, a vehemently anti-liberal plan and practice of illiberty, inequality, and injustice, although with what Michels diagnoses and prophetically predicts as a conservative 'mask' and rhetoric of 'freedom,' 'democracy,' 'justice,' 'life,' and the like to actually destroy or pervert freedom, democracy, justice, and life in society.

Modern free society is essentially an integral of liberal political, economic, cultural, and civic fields in conjunction and mutual reinforcement, as has been in the distant and recent past. This period spans from classical liberal-democratic civilization (Athens) through the proto-liberal Renaissance, Enlightenment liberalism, the liberal French and American Revolutions and to the postwar time of accelerating liberalization and democratization after WW II. Notably, all of today's free societies are liberal, liberalized, and liberalizing. They are in the sense of classical and contemporary liberalism as the ideal and system of holistic, universal, and comprehensive liberty and liberalization as the process of liberation, conjoined with equality, justice, inclusion, material and non-material well-being, happiness and joy of life, reason and scientific rationalism, and progress in society. Thus, the freest modern societies are the most liberal, liberalized, and liberalizing such as Western European countries, particularly Scandinavia, along with Canada, etc. This proves that these societies are the freest precisely because of being the most liberal, liberalized, and liberalizing by consistently embracing, implementing, and sustaining the liberty principle and system of liberalism, or the most advanced in the societal process of liberalization as liberation and emancipation.

Notably, the single freest modern society in the Western world and beyond in the present estimation and ranking, as in many others, is also observed to be the most liberal, liberalized, liberalizing—for example, Norway or the

Netherlands occupying the top rank in societal liberty. Hence, if Norway or the Netherlands—or the closest counterparts Belgium, Denmark, Iceland, Sweden, Finland, and Canada—appears to be the freest, most liberated modern Western and any society, it is exactly by virtue of being the most liberal, liberalized, and liberalizing in this societal context and beyond. It is such because of its most fully adopting and most consistently implementing the liberty principle of liberalism or the most advanced in the global and especially Western process of accelerating liberalization as intrinsically liberation and democratization.

Simply, if one does not know what is/are the freest, most liberated modern society/societies, one knows it/them by seeing the most liberal, liberalized, liberalizing one/ones such as Norway or the Netherlands and Western-Northern Europe, particularly Scandinavia. In sociological terms, a liberal, liberalized, liberalizing total social system explains and predicts a free, liberated society, with the extent of liberalism or the pace of liberalization of the first unambiguously explaining and predicting the degree of freedom or liberation of the second. For example, the observed greatest scope of liberalism or the fastest process of liberalization of Norway or the Netherlands today (and before after the demise of theocratic Calvinism) in the West and the world overall explains and predicts its estimated greatest degree of freedom or liberation, thus being the freest, most liberated society, among contemporary Western and all societies.

Evidently, being the most liberal country and region within this comparative setting and beyond represents the 'secret' of why Norway or the Netherlands and Western-Northern Europe, particularly Scandinavia, is estimated to be the freest modern society and a group of societies.[4] On this account, this specific country and region illustrates that the link between a liberal *and* free society is virtually axiomatic, essentially an identity, equation, or equivalence by virtue of liberalism's principle and practice of liberty and its complements equality and justice, as in Smith's classical 'liberal plan' encompassing all the three, just as does its modern version since the development of the welfare state, including Keynesianism and the New Deal in the US. This striking continuity and consistence of liberalism as the holistic trilogy of liberty, equality and justice from Smith to Keynes, Jefferson to Franklin Roosevelt dispels conservative, 'libertarian' detractors' accusations (as by Friedman et al.) that its

---

4   This may be the 'best kept' secret for anti-liberals such as US conservatives denying or overlooking above, so a self-inflicted perpetual mystery, but the 'worst kept secret' to liberals and thus a manifest, self-evident explanation, so an 'indecent proposal for the first and 'preaching to the converted' for the second.

modern, including Keynesian, welfare state, and New Deal, variant violates the classical and that conservatism or 'libertarianism' is the only heir and guardian of classic liberal heritage and so of 'freedom' and 'free society.' In short, it proves that by its trilogy of liberty, equality, and justice liberalism emerges and remains as both liberating (so truly libertarian) and egalitarian-equitable, which defines modern free society.

Consequently, the present estimates and findings clearly and strongly confirm that liberal society is the only truly free or the freest total social system as a complex of political, economic, cultural, and civil systems in historical and comparative terms. First, they confirm that liberal, secular, and universalistic democracy, defined by universal political and civil liberties and rights and structural differentiation between religion and politics, constitutes the solely genuine or the most democratic, freest political system. Thus, the estimated most democratic political systems such as Western-Northern European states, including Scandinavia, Canada, etc., prove to be such precisely because they are the most liberal, secular, and universalistic democracies.

Second, the estimates confirm that rationally regulated and welfare capitalism, defined by symmetrical freedom and agency for capital and labor as the factors of production, emerges as the sole truly free or the freest, the most egalitarian, equitable or fair, efficient, and the least crisis-plagued, self-destructive, and shared-prosperity economic system in the modern economy. The estimated freest economic systems such as those of Western-Northern Europe, particularly Scandinavia, show to be so exactly because of being the most rationally regulated and egalitarian welfare capitalisms. Third, the results confirm that the sole truly free or the freest culture constitutes the rationalistic, liberal, and secular. It is by virtue of representing the most rationalistic, liberal, and secular cultures that Western-Northern European, particularly Scandinavian, countries represent the freest ones. Fourth, the estimates confirm that the solely free or the freest civil society is the liberal-secular. Precisely because of being the most liberal-secular civil societies that Western-Northern European countries, in particular Scandinavia (except in part Sweden and Iceland due to the adverse impact of militant feminism on universal individual liberty), constitutes the freest.

To that extent, the preceding reaffirms that liberalism forms the necessary and sufficient condition, the main explanation and prediction of a present and future free society. As implied, this may sound—which it is—as a self-evident axiom and so redundant inference in light of that liberalism originates, develops, and remains as the project and institution of integral, indivisible, and universal liberty, as well as its complementary values of equality and justice. Yet, what is axiomatic and evidence as the principle of liberty and the prime foundation of a free society for classical and contemporary liberals has become questionable, obscured, and even denied as 'lie' with the resurgence of anti-liberalism, especially in America, redefining 'liberalism' in opposite terms ('anti-freedom,' 'big government'), thus defaming or distorting it. Anti-liberal defamations and detractors are unable to deny or obscure the overwhelming and consistent evidence about or tendency of liberalism.

This is that liberalism continues to be the sole true or foremost ideal and practice of liberty, and solely or primarily explains and predicts modern free society in the present and future, while continuously evolving, for example, relinquishing laissez-faire in the economy, integrating freedom with equality and justice as complements, etc. Notably, these anti-liberal attacks are helpless in denying or useless in accounting for the fact that the freest modern societies/society are/is also the most liberal one(s)—Scandinavian countries and Norway or the Netherlands. In a way, they are analogous to using geocentric the 'sun revolves-around-the earth' theory to explain actual astronomical movements in the opposite direction, 'head-in-sand' approaches living in a fantasy universe and the 'golden past,' and oblivious of reality, the historical and empirical equivalence of a liberal and a free society, liberalism and the idea/state of liberty. In the delusionary world of anti-liberalism, above all conservatism, including religious fundamentalism and fascism, Scandinavia, in particular Norway or the Netherlands, would never be the freest modern societies/society, but the opposite because of being the most liberal one(s). Conversely, in this fictitious universe the most-anti-liberal countries, for example, conservative-evangelical America (the 'Bible Belt,' etc.), Islamic-ruled Turkey, and Catholic-dominated Poland, must be the 'freest' according to such delusions. In short, this is 'true' or possible only in such a fiction of American and other conservative anti-liberalism but evidently not in the reality of modern Western and related societies.

At any rate, the present findings clearly and strongly contradict such anti-liberal claims as delusions and deceptions, and reaffirm that liberalism continues to be the sole or prime basis and predictor of universal liberty, equality, and justice. Consequently, they confirm that the more liberal a society is, the freer it will be, as demonstrated by those and that being the freest of all, Scandinavian countries and Norway or the Netherlands. Needless to say—but needed for anti-liberal objections—this is a statement of fact based on the preceding data and estimates, and not a value judgment expressing 'liberal' bias. It is no promotion and advocacy of liberalism but doing justice to the presented data and observations and derived estimates confirming its strong and invariant association with modern free society; and if conceivably anti-liberalism exhibits such a connection, it will be considered the same way as its opposite through statements of fact.

The fact of the matter seems so overwhelming and strong that it amounts to Michels' like 'iron' sociological law or historical pattern—'who says a (most) liberal society, says a free (freest) society' among modern Western and related societies. On this account, it provides a powerful vindication of liberalism long maligned and defamed in the US and the UK with the rise of anti-liberalism such as neo-conservatism in the form of Reaganism and Thatcherism, including neo-fascism and fundamentalism, and in part perverted or compromised by spurious 'liberal' ideas and practices (especially radical feminism), causing its partial discredit, as witnessed in America. In light of such anti-liberal defamations and 'liberal' distortions, one cannot emphasize and reiterate enough that liberalism reemerges as a sole genuine program and realization of liberty, and a (most) liberal social system as the only truly free (freest) society among contemporary Western and all societies.

Conversely, modern unfree society appears as the four-fold compound of, first, anti-liberal, anti-secular, and exclusionary 'democracies' or 'republics,' second, anarchic and plutocratic capitalism, third, irrational and pre-liberal culture, and fourth, illiberal and non-secular civil society. They form unfree political, economic, cultural, and civic conditions and subsystems interconnected and mutually reinforced within modern un-free society as a total—more precisely, totalitarian—social system. Essentially, the latter represents a pre- and anti-liberal, more specifically conservative, societal system. It is the composite of illiberal, conservative political, economic, cultural, and civic systems, just as has always been since the Christian and Islamic Dark Middle Ages through the post-bellum US 'Bible Belt,' interwar fascist Europe, neo-fascist South America, and evangelical America and Islamic theocracies. Briefly, practically all modern un-free societies are illiberal, conservative societies, creations or expressions of anti-liberalism in the primary and specific form of conservatism. The latter spans from medieval-rooted arch-conservatism through interwar fascism, including Nazism, and to neo-conservatism, in particular neo-fascism and religious fundamentalism embodied by Islamic fundamentalists and 'born again' US evangelicals as putative enemies yet allies in the shared 'holy' war and terror against liberal-secular democracy and civil society and rationalistic culture.

The preceding therefore identifies or predicts the main implacable adversary, the most lethal poison, and the gravest threat to modern free society—contemporary conservatism. The latter is and will certainly continue to be such an adverse and destructive force to this society for two related reasons. First, this is because conservatism's 'parent' or origin is, as Mannheim shows, feudalism and medievalism and in that sense the Dark Middle Ages, including theocracy and aristocracy (as fervently defended by the conservative role model Burke) as its class basis. Second, it is because conservatism's 'child' or destination is fascism, including neo-fascism, and in that sense the New Dark Ages, with the shared fascist ideal being medievalism, as shown by Nazism.

Contemporary conservatism operates as a functional equivalent of feudalism and medievalism, notably aristocracy and theocracy, and/or of fascism and neo-fascism in those societies where it prevails such as evangelical America (above all, the South), the UK during Thatcherism and its sequels, Catholic Poland, Turkey under Islamic governance, etc. As a result, conservatism generates and sustains equivalent adverse and ultimately destructive consequences for modern free society in these settings as did feudalism and medievalism and do fascism and neo-fascism. Alternatively, conservatism represents an equivalent or analogue of feudalism and medievalism and fascism and neo-fascism precisely because it tends to reproduce identical or analogous effects on this society as did and do these pre- and anti-liberal forces. Overall, they are all equivalents in that they express or (in factor-analytic terms) 'load on' the same overarching underlying variable, anti-liberalism as the generic and persistent antithesis of a free society.

As a corollary, liberalism reaffirms itself as both the necessary and sufficient condition, the chief explanatory factor and the strongest predictor of modern free society, including democracy defined by universal political and civil liberties. In turn, secularism and rationalism form the necessary, but not, if not conjoined with liberalism, the sufficient conditions. They are both the necessary and sufficient conditions insofar as they are, as typical, interconnected and mutually reinforced with liberalism within the framework of modernity and modernization. Therefore, a liberal social system intrinsically and universally constitutes, and a secular and rationalistic one tends to ultimately become, as when being liberal, a free society.

Conversely, an anti-liberal society actually never has been and probably will be a truly and lastingly free one, as epitomized by the conservative half of the 'two Americas' (above all, the evangelical South[5]) during most of its history,

---

5   As noted, an exemplar of the logic and pattern of modern unfree society is the US South, i.e., the Southern self-consistent syndrome of economic, political, individual, and cultural illiberty, as well as unreason and irrationality through religious superstition and anti-science. This is the methodical and coherent mix of, first, unfettered pro-capital, anti-labor aristocratic capitalism elevating capitalists into absolute masters as aristocrats of capital and reducing non-capitalists to proxy slaves through coercion and repression like anti-labor 'right to work' laws, low wages and benefits, etc. The second component is theocratic 'godly' oppression, exclusion, and discrimination by God's self-assigned agents against the 'godless.' The third involves severe moralistic religiously driven control and repression, including imprisonment and executions for sins-crimes, simply 'moral fascism.' The forth comprises 'monkey trials' against 'ungodly' physical and social science and scientists driven by religious superstition

Catholic-dominated Poland and also Mexico, and to some extent Chile and Ireland (in civil society), and Turkey under Islamist rule, plus in part Orthodox Greece. Relatedly, a non-secular, ultra-religious, and anti-rationalistic society hardly ever—and even more so when, as typical, being an anti- or pre-liberal one—represents or becomes a free society, as exemplified by these societies.[6]

likely eventuating, as typical in history, in societal extinction or petrification. No modern Western society reveals or even approximates such a syndrome of systematic oppression as does the US South cum the 'Bible Belt' self-situated—and with 'Southern pride and joy'—outside the orbit of Western liberal democracy and civilization, and substantively within that of the conservative non-Western 'Third' world, specifically Islamic theocracies exhibiting a comparable totalitarian pattern. Thus, Bauman (1997), Moulitsas (2010), Phillips (2006), Turner (2002), and other analysts suggest that the 'Bible Belt' and 'evangelical America' as a whole is experienced as a sort of American, Christian substitute for Taliban, Iran, or Saudi Arabia, including 'Christian Sharia law' cum 'Biblical law' as the effective or prospective 'law of the land' and 'jihadic' politics and war through fundamentalist culture wars against 'sins' and 'ungodliness,' and 'crusades' on the 'evil' world. For example, as noted, Dahrendorf (1979, p. 110) places the US South in the company of Nazi Germany as well as Third-World dictatorships on account of its past and legacy of 'Divinely ordained' slavery, segregation, exclusion, and discrimination still glorified as the 'golden past' or not truly recanted and their official demise never mourned enough with monuments and remembrance. Analogously, this region can be placed today alongside in part resurging neo-Nazism in Germany and Europe, and especially Islamic religious dictatorships not so much because of racial exclusion and discrimination officially diminished, but the four-fold syndrome of capitalist dictatorship, fundamentalist theocracy, Puritan moral fascism, and superstitious cultural irrationalism. On account of its syndrome of illiberty, self-perpetuated and self-justified as glorious Southern anti-liberalism, mixed with unreason and religious superstition expressed in anti-science, the South likely will render America a dramatically less free society than otherwise, and drastically so compared to most Western societies. Alternatively, what Lloyd (2012, p. 494) notes as the perceived 'persistently insular and reactionary nature of the American South' likely will remake America as a proxy non-Western Third-World country, at least closer to this than to Western societies, in terms of modern free society as a composite of democracy with a free economy, civil society, and culture, i.e., holistic liberty composed of universal political, economic, individual, and cultural liberties and rights. To avoid misunderstanding, this is a statement of fact or plausible expectation, and not a value judgment, expressing no animus for this region, simply value-free and neutral in Weber's sense. If 'judgment' or 'evaluation' can be used, it is only in the meaning of judging or evaluating this region, just as all America, like any regions and societies, by standards of modern free society defined by universal and holistic social liberty, not in itself and its supposed 'uniqueness.'

6 The conservative half of the US and thus America as a whole may never become a genuinely and consistently free society so long as it remains an anti-liberal ultra-conservative as well as an anti-secular hyper-religious and anti-rationalistic society, as witnessed in the South cum the 'Bible Belt' as instead an exemplar of an unfree, even probably the most unfree, region, among all Western societies from Europe to Canada. Conversely, it can become a free

In short, there is only modern free-as-liberal society, but no such thing as the illiberal-free.

In retrospect, this is 'nothing new under the sun.' Since the Enlightenment and the French and American Revolutions, classical liberals like Condorcet, Montesquieu, Voltaire, Diderot, Hume, Kant, Smith, Jefferson, Saint Simon, Comte, etc. know well and predict accurately that modern free society is and will be only a liberal as well as secular and rationalistic one. And conversely, they know and predict that unfree societies are invariably pre- and anti-liberal, particularly medievalist and conservative, ones contrary to aristocratic proto-conservatives (Burke, de Maistre, in part Tocqueville, etc.). In Smith's words, a free society is and can only be founded and sustained on the basis of the 'liberal plan' and practice of 'liberty, equality, and justice' in conjunction and reciprocal reinforcement rather than mutual exclusion and opposition as in 'libertarian' economic misinterpretations a la Mises, Hayek, Freidman, et al. This is also implied in Jefferson's principle of 'liberty *and* justice (and equality) for all,' and not 'liberty *or* justice' as 'libertarianism' as the pretended and spurious heir of classical liberalism insinuates. Alternatively, these and other classical liberals perfectly know and predict precisely that a liberal as well as secular and rationalistic society is and will be the sole type of a truly free modern social system, in particular liberal-secular democracy as the only form of a genuine democratic political system. To paraphrase Smith, the 'liberal plan' and institution of conjoined 'liberty, equality, and justice' provides the only program, foundation, and preservation of a free society.

Hence, liberal-as-free society has been a theoretical axiom and an historical-empirical law or pattern for classical liberalism and remains so for its contemporary, essentially identical version, except for its modification of economic liberalism in the direction of substituting government rational regulation of the economy for laissez-faire since Keynesianism and the Great Depression, including the New Deal in the US. Conversely, illiberal-as-free society has been a logical non-sequitur and an historical-empirical non-entity or monstrosity for classical liberals, and remains so for their contemporary descendants. Anti-liberalism, above all American and British conservatism since Reaganism

---

society, a 'land of freedom,' only when and if it becomes a liberal non-conservative, secular or non-religious, and rationalistic society—which could be 'never' given American history since pre- and anti-liberal theocratic Puritanism and the resurgence of its heir evangelical fundamentalism and conservatism in general during recent times, including proto-fascism, just as was so reportedly 'postwar America' (Putnam 2000), like 'Tea Party' extremism and totalitarian, theocratic and Hitler-style (as described) Presidential candidates in the 2010s, etc.

and Thatcherism, however, has attempted and to some extent, especially in America, succeeded to reverse or obscure the classical axiom and pattern of a liberal-as-free society, liberalism as the ideal and institution of liberty. Instead, it reasserts the non-sequitur and monstrosity of an illiberal, notably conservative 'free' society, following aristocracy-apologist Burke as the role model, along with more sophisticated apologists like Tocqueville.

While liberalism posits and proves that liberal-secular democracy is the sole genuine type of democracy, conservative anti-liberalism in America defames, attacks, and perverts the latter and the basically minimal non-comprehensive and non-generous US welfare state as 'tyranny' and 'big government,' and alleges that the anti-liberal police-warfare state represents 'freedom,' 'small government,' etc. In light of such anti-liberal conservative defamations and attacks, in the US and in part elsewhere—substantively equivalent to reasserting that the 'sun revolves around the earth'—it is necessary and useful to revisit the classical axiom and historical pattern of liberal-as-free society and liberalism as the principle and system of liberty. Most importantly, the present results fully and unequivocally confirm this classical liberal axiom and historical pattern, while also completely and unambiguously rejecting these anti-liberal conservative claims as delusions and deceptions, namely what US proto-conservative Emerson calls 'universal seeming and treachery' admitted as inherent to conservatism.

In a way, liberal society is the only truly, fully, consistently, and viably modern free society—and liberalism the sole consistent principle of liberty—because it solely 'knows' and appreciates what human liberty or freedom is or must be to be genuine. It is only liberal society and liberalism that 'knows' and appreciates that liberty is or must be holistic and inseparable, integral and indivisible. Specifically, only this social system and principle 'knows' that liberty in society is or must be a composite of entwined and mutually reinforcing political, economic, cultural, and civic liberties and rights, and not just one of these artificially or arbitrarily separated from the whole and emphasized as the 'most important,' for example, freedom in the market and economy according to 'libertarianism' thereby appearing as false, partial liberalism. In short, liberty in society is either integral and inseparable or not real for a liberal social system and liberalism. Consequently, only a liberal social system and liberalism 'knows' and appreciates that a truly and consistently free society constitutes the whole of a free polity, economy, culture, and culture, and not just one of them in separation and isolation like laissez-faire or 'free market' capitalism in 'libertarianism.' This social system solely creates and sustains such a whole in the form of a composite of mutually connected and reinforced liberal-secular democracy, rationally regulated welfare capitalism, rationalistic-liberal culture, and liberal-secular civil society as the fields of realization of political, economic, cultural, and civic liberties and rights, respectively.

It follows that liberal societies are the only free ones—and liberalism the sole ideal of liberty—because they 'know' and value freedom as an integral, indivisible whole of political, economic, cultural, and civic liberties. This is epitomized by Western-Northern Europe, notably Scandinavia and in particular Norway or the Netherlands, as the freest region and society in the world. For instance, they 'know' that liberty involves not only or primarily market-economic freedom—as pretended 'libertarianism' or spurious 'neo-liberalism' alleges—but also non-economic political and civil, individual, and cultural liberties and rights. Moreover, even with respect to economic liberty, they 'know' that the latter contains not just 'free enterprise' for capital, but also symmetrical freedom for labor as another factor of production, in contrast to 'libertarianism' maximizing the first and minimizing the second facet of its 'liberty' thereby misconstrued or divided as anarchy for capitalist plutocracy and Leviathan for non-capitalists. As a consequence, liberal social systems like Scandinavia such as Norway, Sweden, Denmark, and others, the Netherlands, Belgium, and Western-Northern Europe overall, plus Canada, New Zealand, etc., are free societies because they 'knows' that the latter are an integral, inseparable complex of liberal-secular and universalistic democracy, rationally regulated and egalitarian welfare capitalism, rationalistic-liberal culture, and liberal-secular civil society realizing such liberties.

Conversely, anti-liberal, particularly conservative, society is an unfree social system—and anti-liberalism, notably conservatism, the doctrine of illiberty—because it does not (want to) 'know' and appreciate what human liberty is or must be to be genuine. It does not 'know' that liberty is or must be holistic and inseparable, an indivisible integral of interconnected and mutually reinforcing political, economic, cultural, and civic liberties. As a result, an anti-liberal, particularly conservative, social system and doctrine does not 'know' that a truly free society forms the whole of a free polity, economy, culture, and culture altogether rather than only one part, including a 'free market,' unregulated capitalism. This is exemplified by 'conservative America' (the South's 'God and capitalism' credo), Poland and Mexico (and some extent Chile and Ireland) under Catholic dominance, Turkey during Islamic-rule (plus Orthodox Greece), etc. Notably, anti-liberalism refuses to 'know' and to appreciate that modern free society represents the complex of reciprocally related and reinforced realms of liberal-secular democracy, rationally regulated welfare capitalism, rationalistic-liberal culture, and liberal-secular civil society realizing the integral of political, economic, cultural, and civic liberties. An anti-liberal conservative social system, just as false 'libertarianism,' does not (want to) 'know' that modern free society constitutes more than just a 'free enterprise' economy, but also the non-economic, non-capitalist trinity of free political, cultural, and civic systems in the form of liberal-secular democracy, rationalistic-liberal culture, and liberal-secular civil society, alongside regulated, welfare capitalism.

Thus, anti-liberal conservative countries invariably tend to be un- or at best semi-free because they do not (or refuse to) 'know' that liberty is an inseparable whole of political, economic, cultural, and civic liberties, hence modern free society a complex of a free polity, economy, culture, and culture in the form of liberal-secular universalistic democracy, rationally regulated welfare capitalism, rationalistic-liberal culture, and liberal-secular civil society. This lack or refusal of 'knowledge' of the nature of liberty and thus modern free society essentially explains and predicts the ranking of these countries, such as those mentioned above, among the least free contemporary Western and related societies.

First, anti-liberal conservative countries are unfree because they do not seem (or refuse) to 'know' that economic liberty itself is also integral, indivisible, and universal in that it pertains to both capital and labor as the necessary and complementary factors of production. Instead, they permit and maximize economic freedom only for the first production factor, while denying or minimizing it to the second, as observed in the conservative half of the US (above all, the anti-labor/anti-union South), South Korea, Mexico, Poland, Turkey, etc. By doing so, they divide and thereby pervert economic freedom into anarchy as unrestrained 'license to kill'—figuratively and sometimes literally—for capital as the preferred production agent and Leviathan in the form of systematic oppression and depreciation of non-capitalist agents, as exemplified in 'conservative America' (the labor oppressive South, etc.), as well as these non-Western countries. In this sense, these societies show that they do not (want to) 'know' what economic liberty really is or must be in a modern economy to be genuine. In the process, they violate the principle of universal, equal freedom for all economic agents, and consequently reproduce unfree or pseudo-free economies contrary to the opposite claims, especially by pretended 'libertarian' economists a la Friedman et al. about the US economy.

Accordingly, they are un- or pseudo-free economies because they do not (or refuse to) 'know' what a free economy really is in contemporary society. Thus, anti-liberal conservative countries or periods of a country do not (want to) 'know' that economic freedom and thus a 'free market' economy consists not only of capital 'free enterprise' but also of labor liberties and rights, as epitomized in the US since Reaganism (above all, the anti-labor South), the UK during Thatcherism, Chile under Pinochet's military rule, South Korea, Mexico, Turkey, etc. Consequently, they represent un- or quasi–free economies in the form of capitalist dictatorship/absolute power. For example, they do not seem (or want) to 'know' that such freedom comprises not only capital action and association (e.g., trade associations) but also labor agency and organization, including union organizations, collective bargaining, industrial protest and democracy, etc. This is exemplified by the above countries, in particular 'conservative America' pervaded with vehemently anti-union practices and regions (as in the South, etc.) where these and related elements of economic freedom are practically eliminated or systematically violated—outlawed or suppressed unions, no capital-labor wage and other collective negotiations, no worker participation in management, and so on.

Second, anti-liberal conservative countries are unfree because they do not appear (or refuse) to 'know' that political and civil liberty is or must be to be genuine, namely a holistic, inseparable, and universal category in that it equally applies, like justice and equality, to 'all,' as Jefferson states, including both 'godly' and 'godless' subjects. Instead, they exclusively permit and monopolize political and civil liberties for the 'godly' (declared 'Christians' in the US, at least the 'Bible Belt,' Catholics especially in Poland and to some degree Mexico (plus in part Chile and Ireland), Muslims in Turkey during Islamic rule, etc. Conversely, they deny or minimize these liberties to the 'godless,' including non-believers, those with no organized religion ('nones' in America), liberals, secularists, progressives, rationalists, and similar groups, all oppressed, excluded, and discriminated against in the 'name and mind of God' and 'faith-based' government. This especially (though not solely) holds true for the freedom and right to seek and hold state power or public office that the 'godly' monopolize in these societies and the 'godless' effectively 'need not apply' to exercise this component of political liberty.

This is observed in both Christian and Islamic countries, such as persistently in evangelical America (the 'Bible Belt' and similar regions), completely in Catholic-dominated Poland and to a lesser extent Mexico (and Chile and Ireland), growingly in Islamic-ruled Turkey (plus Orthodox Greece), etc. These societies in so doing divide and pervert political freedom into an ersatz Christian and Islamic 'liberty' only for the 'godly' and systematic and unapologetic oppression, exclusion, and discrimination against the 'ungodly.' Apparently, their ruling groups do not (want to) 'know' that the 'ungodly' also may be entitled to such liberties and rights on constitutional and other legal and democratic grounds, as especially observed in evangelical America with its 'Bible Belt' suppression, exclusion, and discrimination against the 'godless,' Catholic-dominated Poland, and Islamic-ruled Turkey.

On this account, these societies do not (or refuse to) 'know' what political liberty really is or must be in a modern inclusive democracy to be genuine by their denials and violation of the principle of universal, equal freedom for all subjects. As a result, they reproduce un- or quasi-free polities contrary to their claims, especially by US conservative politicians, to their 'only and superior' democracies and freedoms. Accordingly, they are un- or quasi-free political systems because they do not (want to) know what genuine democracy really is in contemporary society. Thus, anti-liberal conservative countries do not 'know' that political freedom and thus genuine democracy consists not just of freedoms and rights for the 'godly' and 'us' overall, but also of those for the 'godless' or with no religion and 'them,' as epitomized in evangelical America (the Southern and other 'Bible Belt'), Catholic-dominated Poland, Islamic-ruled Turkey, and other theocratic or theocentric exclusionary ersatz 'democracies.' For example, they do not show to 'know' that this involves not just the freedom and right to pursue and hold political position or public office by 'true believers' and other 'us' but also 'infidels' and 'them' forced or expected to 'need not apply.' This is paradigmatically and persistently and even growingly witnessed in these countries, including the conservative/evangelical half of America spanning from the 'Bible Belt' to the federal government, from state governments to the Presidency and Congress.

Third, anti-liberal conservative countries are unfree because they do not seem (or refuse) to 'know' what cultural freedom is or must be in order to be genuine within culture, namely being integral, indivisible, universal, and comprehensive. Instead, they seek to dissolve, fragment and so disfigure the whole of cultural freedom into some parts, invariably its religious forms, for example, 'Christian' and 'Islamic' liberty, science, and education, with 'freedom of religion' meaning primarily these religions. In turn, they deny, suppress, or restrict most other, notably secular forms of cultural freedom, such as artistic, academic, educational, and ideological freedoms, as well as that from religion as a non-entity and taboo in anti-liberal countries, in particular evangelical America, Catholic-dominated Poland, and Islamic-ruled Turkey.

As typical, in doing so, they divide and thereby pervert integral and indivisible cultural freedom into an ersatz religious liberty or reductive freedom of religion and denied and suppressed non-religious freedoms and that from religion. Thus, they do not (want to) 'know' that cultural freedom involves not only 'Christian' and 'Islamic' liberty, science, education, and art, but also artistic, academic, educational, and ideological freedoms, and religious liberty involving both freedoms of and from religion. For example, it does not occur to them that it comprises not only freedom of holding 'creationism,' 'intelligent design,' 'Satan,' and related 'godly' conceptions, practicing religious home schooling and art, but also that of adopting biological evolution, global warming theory, and other 'godless' scientific theories, and pursuing secular public

education and 'ungodly' arts. In this respect, anti-liberal conservative countries do not (or refuse to) 'know' what cultural freedom really is or must be in
modern culture to be genuine in that they negate or violate its integral, indivisible, universal, and comprehensive character, resulting in the reproduction of
un- or quasi-free cultures contrary to their pretensions to the opposite. In short,
precisely because they do not (want to) know what a free culture is in contemporary society—a liberal-secular one—they are un- or quasi-free cultures.

Fourth, anti-liberal conservative countries are unfree because they do not
(or refuse to) 'know' that individual liberty, including privacy, is, or must be to
be genuine, namely integral, indivisible, and comprehensive. Instead, they tend
to reduce and fragment individual liberty into some of its dimensions, while
denying, suppressing or restricting all the others primarily on 'sacred' religious
grounds. These practices particularly target privacy, reproductive (abortion
and birth control) liberties and rights, freedom of alcohol consumption, sexual
liberties, and generally free personal moral action and responsibility, as especially observed in evangelical America (the 'Bible Belt' and beyond), Catholic
Poland and Mexico (plus Chile and Ireland) and Islamic-ruled Turkey. In so
doing, these anti-liberal countries apparently do not (or refuse to) 'know' that
individual liberty may also include these other dimensions, notably personal
moral freedom and choice, free private agency and responsibility in morality.
Moreover, some of them, such as 'conservative America,' construe individual
liberty and privacy in a form and way (exemplified by the 'right to bear arms')
adverse and ultimately destructive to its exercise and elements, manifestly
to peace, safety, security, and life within civil society, implicitly to all or most
other liberties and rights.[7] By so doing, they divide, fragment, and thus pervert
individual liberty into a partial, destructive, and threatening ersatz freedom
and a pattern of denial and suppression of its other forms, particularly privacy
and personal moral liberties and choices, all for 'higher' religious causes.

In this sense, these anti-liberal conservative countries do not (or refuse to)
'know' what individual liberty really is or must be to be genuine within the
'lifeworld' in that they deny, suppress, or violate its nature as an integral, inseparable, and comprehensive category. Thereby, they create and sustain un- or
quasi-free civil societies contradicting their opposite claims, especially by US
politicians about 'conservative America' as the 'land of freedom' in this and all
respects. In brief, due to not (or refusing to) 'knowing' what a free civil society

---

7   Since none of these countries does so, by virtue of its individual 'right to bear arms,' 'conser-
    vative America' is an exceptional case or outlier even among such anti-liberal conservative,
    let alone other Western and related, societies.

really is, they represent un- or quasi-free and in that sense 'uncivil' societies. They do not 'know' that individual liberty and thus a truly free civil society comprises not only some limited, including ersatz (if ever), forms, but also many others constitutive of it. For example, they do not seem or want to 'know' that this involves not just 'free speech' if they ever recognize or respect it, or the 'right to bear arms'—yet exclusively in 'conservative America'—potentially subverting or threatening all individual freedoms and rights, notably that to peace, safety, and life. They 'forget' or deny that a free civil society also comprises reproductive rights denied or restricted in evangelical America, Catholic Poland and Mexico (plus Chile and Ireland), Islamic Turkey, etc., freedom of alcohol consumption prohibited mostly in the American 'Bible Belt,' personal sexual liberties and choices suppressed in most of them, and generally privacy violated in all of them, and the like.

Simply, these societies do not 'know' what makes individuals free and thus civil society a space of individual freedom, choice, agency, and privacy. In this sense, in particular, 'conservative America,' along with Catholic Poland and Islamic Turkey, does not seem yet to 'know,' realize, and appreciate what, in spite of the rhetoric, a 'land of freedom' 'for all' in Jefferson's sense really is in terms of individual liberty, choice, agency, and privacy and in extension of economic, political, and cultural liberties. For illustration, it does not 'know' or realize that the individual 'right to bear arms,' or even 'free speech' if ever respected, does not only or mostly makes a civil society the 'land of freedom,' but that additional personal liberties, choice, agency, and privacy as those above are also necessary for that purpose. Similarly, it does not 'know' that political freedoms monopolized for the 'godly,' capital's unrestricted 'free enterprise,' and exclusive 'Christian liberty' and partial 'freedom of religion' do not suffice to make America and any society the 'land of freedom' in political, economic, and cultural terms, if they are not complemented by other corresponding liberties and rights as mentioned. While being the most evident for 'conservative America,' this applies, with certain qualifications, to other anti- or non-liberal countries such as Poland, and in part Chile, Mexico (and Ireland) under Catholic dominance, Turkey during Islamic governance, etc.

In sum, contemporary liberal societies such as those in Western Europe, particularly Scandinavia, notably Norway, and the Netherlands, plus Canada, etc., may be free and the freest precisely because they 'know,' realize and appreciate what human social liberty and so modern free society truly and really is. Thus, they 'know' that liberty is a holistic, indivisible category involving intertwined and mutually reinforce political, economic, cultural, and individual liberties, and consequently a free society being a whole of a free polity, economy, culture, and civil society. More precisely, they both 'know' and prove that such liberty is solely or most fully and consistently realized and this society only or best represented in the complex of liberal-secular and universalistic democracy, rationally regulated and egalitarian welfare capitalism, rationalistic-liberal culture, and liberal-secular civil society.

By stark contrast, anti-liberal conservative countries spanning from the conservative proximate half of the US (above all, the South) through Poland to Turkey among others, may well be the least free or the most unfree among Western and related societies exactly because they do not (or refuse to) 'know,' realize and appreciate the preceding about liberty and modern free society and its only genuine form. Simply, the first, in particular Scandinavia, notably Norway or the Netherlands as the freest region and country, are what they are probably because they 'know' genuine liberty and thus a truly free society, and act accordingly. Conversely, the second, including 'conservative America' in the prime form of Dahrendorf's 'Southern United States,' Poland, and Turkey as among the most unfree in the present setting, are also what they are because they do not (want to) 'know' this, and behave in accordance with this self-inflicted ignorance or refused knowledge. In this sense, precisely because they 'know' what the nature and societal space of liberty—i.e., the 'land of freedom' in US terms—actually is, liberal societies become such societal spaces. Conversely, their anti-liberal opposites, including America in its conservative face, Poland under Catholic dominance, and Turkey during Islamic rule, because of not 'knowing' or refusing this knowledge, do not become such lands, in spite of their lofty clams to being the most or even only 'free,' as in 'American exceptionalism' advanced by conservatism and false 'libertarianism.' This appears to be proof of Comte's classic and enduring principle of 'knowledge as (societal) power' in respect of liberty and a free society, and conversely its lack as a corresponding weakness and even fatal defect and curse in this sense, thus a far cry from and disproof of the religious or other 'ignorance-as-bliss' equation.

At the end, perhaps more realistically, both liberal and anti-liberal societies 'know' or realize what liberty and thus modern free society really is, as defined throughout. The difference, however, is that liberal societies take account, appreciate, and implement this knowledge or realization in reality, and hence intrinsically constitute or invariably become truly free social systems, as exemplified by the freest among them, Scandinavia as the region, and Norway or the Netherlands as the single country. By stark and dark contrast, anti-liberal societies do the opposite by discounting, devaluating, and failing or refusing to practically implement that knowledge. Instead, they aim at or succeeded in creating and living in a parallel world of Orwellian fantasies, delusions, and deceptions in the manner of 'oppression is freedom,' 'exclusion and discrimination are justice,' 'war is peace,' etc., compounded with superstitions a la 'Satan' or 'witches' descending from the Dark-Middle Ages, as especially witnessed in theocracies like evangelical America, Catholic-dominated Poland, and Islamic-ruled Turkey. Hence, they also inherently represent or invariably become unfree, authoritarian social systems, as exemplified by Poland, Mexico, South Korea, Turkey, and 'conservative America,' all classified as anti-liberal societies, along with Chile and Greece as the only eclectic cases.

Consequently, liberal and anti-liberal societies are essentially as different, distant, mutually exclusive, and opposite as modern free and unfree society, liberty and illiberty or freedom and un-freedom, including democracy and non-democracy, simply as 'heaven and earth' in this sense. (Theocracies like 'evangelical America' and Islamic Turkey claim to be 'paradise on earth' and condemn liberal democracies like Canada and Scandinavia as 'hell.') Thus, the contradiction, tension or friction, and even open or covert battle between liberal and anti-liberal societies arises and continues as that between a free and an un-free society, liberty and illiberty, including democracy and non-democracy. This expresses the sociological 'law' or historical pattern that liberalism intrinsically generates and nurtures a truly free society and full liberty, including genuine and viable democracy, and anti-liberalism in the prime and the most vehement and tenacious form of conservatism, including fascism and religious fundamentalism, inherently destroys or perverts this. Therefore, this is an objective statement of fact or tendency rather than a 'liberal' and 'anti-conservative' value judgment or evaluation, as it might be perceived both by liberals and especially conservatives.

And so the freest societies/society are/is: the most liberal such as Western-Northern European, in particular Scandinavian, countries as the group or region, and Norway or the Netherlands as the single country. Conversely, the most unfree societies/society are/is (within OECD): the most anti-liberal like 'Christian,' 'Islamic,' and other theocentric countries as a group, and Turkey under Islamic rule or 'conservative America' as the single country or region. The answer to the main question in this book is thus clear and grounded.

References

Abbott, Andrew. 2005. Linked Ecologies: States and Universities as Environments for Professions. Sociological Theory 23, 245–74.

Acemoglu, Daron. 2001. Good Jobs Versus Bad Jobs. Journal of Labor Economics 19, 1–21.

Acemoglu, Daron. 2005. Constitutions, Politics, and Economics: A Review Essay on Persson and Tabellini's the Economic Effects of Constitutions. Journal of Economic Literature 43, 1025–48.

Acemoglu, Daron, and David Autor. 2012. What Does Human Capital Do? A Review of Goldin and Katz's *the Race Between Education and Technology*. Journal of Economic Literature 50, 426–63.

Acemoglu, Daron, Georgy Egorov, and Konstantin Sonin. 2009. Do Juntas Lead to Personal Rule? American Economic Review 99, 298–303.

Acemoglu, Daron, Georgy Egorov, and Konstantin Sonin. 2010. Political Selection and Persistence of Bad Governments. Quarterly Journal of Economics 12, 1511–75.

Acemoglu, Daron, Georgy Egorov, and Konstantin Sonin. 2012. Dynamics and Stability of Constitutions, Coalitions, and Clubs. American Economic Review 102, 1446–76.

Acemoglu, Daron and James Robinson. 2006. De Facto Political Power and Institutional Persistence. American Economic Review 96, 325–30.

Acemoglu, Daron and James Robinson. 2008. Persistence of Power, Elites, and Institutions. American Economic Review 98, 267–93.

Acemoglu, Daron, and Pierre Yared. 2010. Political Limits to Globalization. American Economic Review 100, 83–88.

Acemoglu, Daron, Philippe Aghion, Leonardo Bursztyn, and David Hemous. 2012. the Environment and Directed Technical Change. American Economic Review 102 131–66.

Acemoglu, Daron, and Pischke Jorn-Steffen. 1998. Why Do Firms Train? Theory and Evidence. the Quarterly Journal of Economics 113, 79–119.

Adamczyk, Amy and Brittany Hayes. 2012. Religion and Sexual Behaviors: Understanding the Influence of Islamic Cultures and Religious Affiliation for Explaining Sex Outside of Marriage. American Sociological Review 77, 723–46.

Adorno, Theodor. 1991. the Culture Industry. London: Routledge.

Adut, Ari. 2012. A Theory of the Public Sphere. Sociological Theory 30, 238–62.

Aghion, Philippe, Howitt Peter, and Mayer-Foulkes David. 2005. the Effect of Financial Development on Convergence: Theory and Evidence. the Quarterly Journal of Economics 120, 173–222.

Aizer, Anna and Joseph J. Doyle Jr. 2015. Juvenile Incarceration, Human Capital, and Future Crime: Evidence from Randomly Assigned Judges. the Quarterly Journal of Economics 130, 759–803.

Akerlof, George. 2002. Behavioral Macroeconomics and Macroeconomic Behavior. American Economic Review 92, 411–33.

Akerlof, George. 2007. the Missing Motivation in Macroeconomics. American Economic Review 97, 5–36.

Akerlof, George and Robert Shiller. 2009. Animal Spirits. Princeton, Princeton University Press.

Alesina, Alberto and Roberto Perotti. 1997. the Welfare State and Competitiveness. American Economic Review 87, 921–39.

Alesina, Alberto, Enrico Spolaore and Romain Wacziarg. 2000. Economic Integration and Political Disintegration. American Economic Review 90, 1276–96.

Alesina, Alberto and George-Marios Angeletos. 2005. Fairness and Redistribution. American Economic Review 95, 960–80.

Alesina, Alberto and Eliana La Ferrara. 2014. A Test of Racial Bias in Capital Sentencing. American Economic Review 104, 3397–3433.

Alvaredo, Facundo, Anthony B. Atkinson, Thomas Piketty, and Emmanuel Saez. 2013. the Top 1 Percent in International and Historical Perspective. Journal of Economic Perspectives 27, 3–20.

Amenta, Edwin, Chris Bonastia, and Neal Caren. 2001. US Social Policy in Comparative and Historical Perspective: Concepts, Images, Arguments, and Research Strategies, Annual Review of Sociology 27, 213–34.

Andrews Kenneth T. and Charles Seguin. 2015. Group Threat and Policy Change: The Spatial Dynamics of Prohibition Politics, 1890–1919, American Journal of Sociology 121, 475–510.

Archer, Robin. 2001. Secularism and Sectarianism in India and the West: What Are the Real Lessons of American History? Economy and Society 30, 273–87.

Arrow, Kenneth and Gerard Debreu. 1954. Existence of An Equilibrium for A Competitive Economy. Econometrica 22, 265–90.

Ashenfelter Orley and Kathryn Graddy. 2003, Auctions and the Price of Art. Journal of Economic Literature 41, 763–86.

Bailey, Amy and Karen Snedker. 2011. Practicing What They Preach? Lynching and Religion in the American South, 1890–1929. American Journal of Sociology, 117, 844–87.

Baily, Martin and Robert Solow. 2001. International Productivity Comparisons Built from the Firm Level. Journal of Economic Perspectives 15, 151–172.

Baker, Jonathan. 2003. the Case for Antitrust Enforcement. Journal of Economic Perspectives 17, 27–50.

Baker, Scott and Mezzetti Claudio. 2012. A Theory of Rational Jurisprudence. Journal of Political Economy 120, 513–51.

Baldassarri, Delia and Peter Bearman. 2007. Dynamics of Political Polarization. American Sociological Review 72, 784–811.

Baldassarri, Delia and Peter Bearman. 2008. Partisans Without Constraint: Political Polarization and Trends in American Public Opinion. American Journal of Sociology 114, 408–46.

Banerjee, Abhijit and Somanathan Rohini. 2001. A Simple Model of Voice. the Quarterly Journal of Economics 116, 189–227.

Baudrillard, Jean. 1999. America. London: Verso.

Bauman, Zygmunt. 1997. Postmodernity and Its Discontents. New York: New York University Press.

Bauman, Zygmunt. 2000. Community. Cambridge: Polity Press.

Bauman, Zygmunt. 2001. the Individualized Society. Cambridge: Polity Press.

Baumol, William. 2000. What Marshall Didn't Know: On the Twentieth Century's Contributions to Economics. the Quarterly Journal of Economics 115, 1, 1–44.

Baxter, Vern and A.V. Margavio. 2000. Honor, Status, and Aggression in Economic Exchange. Sociological Theory 18, 399–416.

Bebchuk, Lucian and Jesse Fried. 2003. Executive Compensation as An Agency Problem. Journal of Economic Perspectives 17, 71–92.

Beck, Ulrich. 2000. the Brave New World of Work. Cambridge: Polity Press.

Becker, Gary., Murphy Kevin, and Grossman Michael. 2006. the Market for Illegal Goods: the Case of Drugs. Journal of Political Economy 114, 38–60.

Becker, Howard. 1974. Art as Collective Action. American Sociological Review 39, 767 76.

Becky, Pettit and Bruce Western. 2004. Mass Imprisonment and the Life Course: Race and Class Inequality in U.S. Incarceration. American Sociological Review 69, 151–69.

Bell, Daniel. 2002. Afterword in Daniel Bell (ed.), the Radical Right (pp. 447–503). New Brunswick: Transaction Publishers.

Benabou, Roland. 2003. Human Capital, Technical Change, and the Welfare State. Journal of the European Economic Association 1, 522–32.

Benabou, Roland and Jean Tirole. 2011. Identity, Morals, and Taboos: Beliefs as Assets. the Quarterly Journal of Economics 126, 805–55.

Bendix, Reinhard. 1974. Inequality and Social Structure: A Comparison of Marx and Weber. American Sociological Review 39, 149–61.

Benjamin, Daniel, Ori Heffetz, Miles Kimball, and Alex Rees-Jones. 2012. What Do You Think Would Make You Happier? What Do You Think You Would Choose? American Economic Review 102, 2083–2110.

Berezin Mabel. 1997. Politics and Culture: A Less Fissured Terrain. Annual Review of Sociology 23, 361–83.

Berger, Daniel, William Easterly, Nathan Nunn, and Shanker Satyanath. 2013. Commercial Imperialism? Political Influence and Trade During the Cold War. American Economic Review 103, 863–96.

Bertrand, Marianne, Matilde Bombardini, and Francesco Trebbi. 2014. Is It Whom You Know or What You Know? An Empirical Assessment of the Lobbying Process. American Economic Review 104, 3885–3920.

Besley, Timothy, and Preston Ian. 2007. Electoral Bias and Policy Choice: Theory and Evidence. the Quarterly Journal of Economics 122, 1473–510.

Besley, Timothy and Torsten Persson. 2009. Repression or Civil War? American Economic Review 99, 292–97.

Besley, Timothy, Ethan Ilzetzki and Torsten Persson. 2013. Weak States and Steady States: The Dynamics of Fiscal Capacity. American Economic Journal: Macroeconomics 5, 205–35.

Bhagwati, Jagdish 2011. Markets and Morality. American Economic Review 101, 162–65.

Bivens, Josh and Lawrence Mishel. 2013. the Pay of Corporate Executives and Financial Professionals as Evidence of Rents in Top 1 Percent Incomes. Journal of Economic Perspectives 27, 57–78.

Blau, Francine and Lawrence Kahn. 2000. Gender Differences in Pay. the Journal of Economic Perspectives 14, 75–99.

Blau, Judith, Peter Blau and Reid Golden. 1985. Social Inequality and the Arts. American Journal of Sociology 91, 309–31.

Blaug, Mark. 2001. No History of Ideas, Please, We're Economists. Journal of Economic Perspectives 15, 145–64.

Blee, Kathleen and Kimberly Creasap. 2010. Conservative and Right-Wing Movements. Annual Review of Sociology 36, 269–86.

Bloemraad, Irene, Anna Korteweg, and Gokce Yurdakul. 2008. Citizenship and Immigration: Multiculturalism, Assimilation, and Challenges to the Nation-State. Annual Review of Sociology 34, 153–79.

Bollen, Kenneth. 1980. Issues in the Comparative Measurement of Political Democracy. American Sociological Review 45, 370–90.

Bollen, Kenneth. 1990. Political Democracy: Conceptual and Measurement Traps. Studies in Comparative International Development, 25, 7–25.

Bollen, Kenneth. 1998. Liberal Democracy Indicators 1950–1990. Ann Arbor, MI: Inter-University Consortium for Political and Social Research. Http://Webapp.Icpsr .Umich.Edu/Cocoon.

Bollen, Kenneth and Pamela Paxton. 1998. Detection and Determination of Bias in Subjective Measures, American Sociological Review 63, 465–78.

Bollen, Kenneth and Robert Jackman. 1985. Political Democracy and the Size Distribution of Income. American Sociological Review 50, 438–57.

Bollen, Kenneth and Robert Jackman. 1989. Democracy, Stability, and Dichotomies. American Sociological Review 54, 612–21.

Boudon, Raymond. 2011. Ordinary Rationality: The Core of Analytical Sociology. in Pierre Demeulenaere (ed.), Analytical Sociology and Social Mechanisms (pp. 33–49). New York: Cambridge University Press.

Bourdieu, Pierre. 1998. Acts of Resistance. New York: Free Press.

Bourdieu, Pierre and Hans Haacke. 1995. Free Exchange. Stanford: Stanford University Press.

Boyle, Elizabeth, Minzee Kim, and Wesley Longhofer. 2015. Abortion Liberalization in World Society, 1960–2009. American Journal of Sociology 121, 882–913.

Brady, David, Jason Beckfield, and Martin Seeleib-Kaiser. 2005. Economic Globalization and the Welfare State in Affluent Democracies, 1975–2001. American Sociological Review 70, 921–48.

Brady David, Jason Beckfield, and Wei Zhao. 2007. the Consequences of Economic Globalization for Affluent Democracies. Annual Review of Sociology 33, 313–34.

Brady, David, Regina S. Baker, and Ryan Finnigan. 2013. When Unionization Disappears: State-Level Unionization and Working Poverty in the United States. American Sociological Review 78, 872–96.

Brooks, Clem. 2000. Civil Rights Liberalism and the Suppression of a Republican Political Realignment in the US, 1972 To 1996. American Sociological Review 65, 483–505.

Brooks, Clem. 2006. Voters, Satisficing, and Policymaking: Recent Directions in the Study of Electoral Politics. Annual Review of Sociology 32, 191–211.

Brooks, Clem and Jeff Manza. 1997. the Social and Ideological Bases of Middle-Class Political Realignment in the U.S., 1972–1992. American Sociological Review 62, 191–208.

Brooks, Clem and Jeff Manza. 2006. Social Policy Responsiveness in Developed Democracies. American Sociological Review 71, 474–94.

Brooks, Clem and Jeff Manza. 2013. A Broken Public? Americans' Responses to the Great Recession. American Sociological Review 78, 727–48.

Bruce, Steve. 2002. God Is Dead. London: Blackwell.

Bruch Sarah, Myra Marx Ferree, and Joe Soss. 2010. From Policy to Polity: Democracy, Paternalism, and the Incorporation of Disadvantaged Citizens. American Sociological Review 75, 205–26.

Bruni, Luigino and Robert Sugden. 2013. Reclaiming Virtue Ethics for Economics. Journal of Economic Perspectives 27, 141–64.

Buchanan, James and Gordon Tullock. 1962. the Calculus of Consent. Ann Arbor: University of Michigan Press.

Carlton, Dennis. 2007. Does Antitrust Need to Be Modernized? Journal of Economic Perspectives 21, 155–76.

Cassel, Gustav. 1927–8. the Rate of Interest, the Bank Rate, and the Stabilization of Prices. Quarterly Journal of Economics 42, 511–29.

Caves, Richard. 2003. Contracts Between Art and Commerce. Journal of Economic Perspectives 17, 73–83.

Centeno, Miguel. 1994. Between Rocky Democracies and Hard Markets: Dilemmas of the Double Transition. Annual Review of Sociology 20, 125–47.

Ceobanu Alin and Xavier Escandell. 2010. Comparative Analyses of Public Attitudes Toward Immigrants and Immigration Using Multinational Survey Data: A Review of Theories and Research. Annual Review of Sociology 36, 309–28.

Chamberlin, Edward. 1948 (1933). the Theory of Monopolistic Competition. Cambridge: Harvard University Press.

Chaves, Mark. 1999. Religious Congregations and Welfare Reform: Who Will Take Advantage of 'Charitable Choice'? American Sociological Review 64, 836–47.

Coate, Stephen, and Knight Brian. 2007. Socially Optimal Districting: A Theoretical and Empirical Exploration. the Quarterly Journal of Economics 122, 1409–471.

Coats, A.W. 1967. Sociological Aspects of British Economic Thought (Ca. 1880–1930). Journal of Political Economy 75, 706–29.

Cochran, Augustus. 2001. Democracy Heading South. Lawrence: University Press of Kansas.

Cohen, Daniel. 2003. Our Modern Times. Cambridge: MIT Press.

Cole, Wade. 2005. Sovereignty Relinquished? Explaining Commitment to the International Human Rights Covenants, 1966–1999. American Sociological Review, 70, 472–95.

Cole, Wade and Francisco O. Ramirez. 2013. Conditional Decoupling: Assessing the Impact of National Human Rights Institutions, 1981 to 2004. American Sociological Review 78, 702–25.

Collins, Patricia. 2010. the New Politics of Community. American Sociological Review 75, 7–30.

Cooney, Mark and Callie Harbin Burt. 2008. Less Crime, More Punishment. American Journal of Sociology 114, 491–527.

Corak, Miles. 2013. Income Inequality, Equality of Opportunity, and Intergenerational Mobility. Journal of Economic Perspectives 27, 79–102.

Dahrendorf, Ralph. 1959. Class and Class Conflict in Industrial Society. Stanford: Stanford University Press.

Dahrendorf, Ralph. 1979. Life Chances. Chicago: Chicago University Press.

Darnell, Alfred and Darren Sherkat. 1997. the Impact of Protestant Fundamentalism on Educational Attainment. American Sociological Review 62, 306–15.

Davis, Arthur. 1945. Sociological Elements in Veblen's Economic Theory. Journal of Political Economy 53, 132–49.

Dayton, Cornelia. 1999. Excommunicating the Governor's Wife: Religious Dissent in the Puritan Colonies Before the Era of Rights Consciousness, in McLaren John and Coward, Harold (eds.), Religious Conscience, the State, and the Law (pp. 29–45). Albany: State University of New York.

De Long, Bradford. 1996. Keynesianism, Pennsylvania Avenue Style: Some Economic Consequences of the Employment Act of 1946. Journal of Economic Perspectives 10, 41–53.

Desai, Mihir. 2005. the Degradation of Reported Corporate Profits. Journal of Economic Perspectives 19, 171–92.

DiMaggio, Paul. 1987. Classification in Art. American Sociological Review 52, 440–55.

DiPrete, Thomas, Andrew Gelman, Tyler Mccormick, Julien Teitler, Tian Zheng. 2011. Segregation in Social Networks Based on Acquaintanceship and Trust. American Journal of Sociology 116, 1234–83.

Dixit, Avinash and Joseph Stiglitz. 1977. Monopolistic Competition and Optimum Product Diversity. American Economic Review 67, 297–308.

Dobbin, Frank and Dowd, Timothy. 2000. the Market That Antitrust Built: Public Policy, Private Coercion, and Railroad Acquisitions, 1825 To 1922. American Sociological Review 65, 631–57.

Dombrowski Daniel. 2001. Rawls and Religion. New York: State University of New York Press.

Dreiling, Michael and Derek Darves 2011. Corporate Unity in American Trade Policy: A Network Analysis of Corporate-Dyad Political Action. American Journal of Sociology 116, 1514–63.

Dube, Arindrajit, Ethan Kaplan, and Suresh Naidu. 2011. Coups, Corporations, and Classified Information. the Quarterly Journal of Economics 126, 1375–1409.

Dustmann, Christian, Bernd Fitzenberger, Uta Schönberg, and Alexandra Spitz-Oener. 2014. From Sick Man of Europe To Economic Superstar: Germany's Resurgent Economy. Journal of Economic Perspectives, 28, 167–88.

Duverger, Maurice. 1972. De Janus. Paris: P.U.F.

Edelman, Benjamin 2009. Markets: Red Light States: Who Buys Online Adult Entertainment? Journal of Economic Perspectives 23, 209–20.

Edgell, Penny. 2012. A Cultural Sociology of Religion: New Directions. Annual Review of Sociology 38, 247–65.

Edgell, Penny, Joseph Gerteis and Douglas Hartmann 2006. Atheists as Other: Moral Boundaries and Cultural Membership in American Society. American Sociological Review 71, 211–34.

Edlund, Lena, and Korn Evelyn. 2002. A Theory of Prostitution. Journal of Political Economy 110, 181–214.

Eggertsson, Gauti. 2008. Great Expectations and the End of the Depression. American Economic Review 98, 1476–1516.

Eggertsson, Gauti. 2012. Was the New Deal Contractionary? American Economic Review 102, 524–55.

Einolf, Christopher. 2007. the Fall and Rise of Torture: A Comparative and Historical Analysis. Sociological Theory 25, 101–121.

Eisenstadt, Shmuel. 1998. the Paradox of Democratic Regimes: Fragility and Transformability. Sociological Theory 16, 211–38.

Ellman, Matthew and Leonard Wantchekon. 2000. Electoral Competition Under the Threat of Political Unrest. the Quarterly Journal of Economics 115, 499–531.

Eriksson, Stefan, and Dan-Olof Rooth. 2014. Do Employers Use Unemployment as a Sorting Criterion When Hiring? Evidence from a Field Experiment. American Economic Review 104, 1014–39.

Esteban, Joan and Debraj Ray. 2008. On the Salience of Ethnic Conflict. American Economic Review 98, 2185–2202.

Etzioni, Amitai. 1999. Essays in Socio-Economics. New York: Springer.

Evans John and Michael Evans. 2008. Religion and Science: Beyond the Epistemological Conflict Narrative. Annual Review of Sociology 34, 87–105.

Fearon, James. 2011. Self-Enforcing Democracy. the Quarterly Journal of Economics 126, 1661–1708.

Fischer, Claude and Greggor Mattson. 2009. Is America Fragmenting? Annual Review of Sociology 35, 435–55.

Fishman, Robert and Omar Lizardo. 2013. How Macro-Historical Change Shapes Cultural Taste: Legacies of Democratization in Spain and Portugal. American Sociological Review 78, 213–39.

Fitzpatrick Martin. 1999. Enlightenment and Conscience. in McLaren, John and Coward, Harold (eds.), Religious Conscience, the State, and the Law (pp. 46–61). Albany: State University of New York Press.

Flanagan, Robert. 1999. Macroeconomic Performance and Collective Bargaining: An International Perspective. Journal of Economic Literature 37, 1150–1175.

Fligstein, Neil. 2001. the Architecture of Markets. Princeton: Princeton University Press.

Frank Reanne, Ilana Redstone Akresh, and Bo Lu. 2010. Latino Immigrants and the U.S. Racial Order: How and Where Do They Fit In? American Sociological Review 75, 378–401.

Friedland, Roger. 2001. Religious Nationalism and the Problem of Collective Representation, Annual Review of Sociology 27, 125–52.

Friedman, John and Richard Holden. 2008. Optimal Gerrymandering: Sometimes Pack, But Never Crack. American Economic Review 98, 113–144.

Friedman, Milton. 1982. Capitalism and Freedom. Chicago: University of Chicago Press.

Friedman, Milton. 1997. Economics of Crime. Journal of Economic Perspectives 11, 194.

Garcelon Marc. 2010. the Missing Key: Institutions, Networks, and the Project of Neoclassical Sociology. Sociological Theory 28, 326–53.

Garrard, Graeme. 2003. Rousseau's Counter-Enlightenment. Albany: State University of New York Press.

Gauchat, Gordon. 2012. Politicization of Science in the Public Sphere: A Study of Public Trust in the United States, 1974 To 2010. American Sociological Review 77, 167–87.

Giddens, Anthony. 1984. the Constitution of Society. Berkeley: University of California Press.

Giddens, Anthony. 2000a. the Third Way. Malden. Blackwell Publishers.

Giddens, Anthony. 2000b. the Third Way and Its Critics. London: Polity Press.

Glaeser, Edward., Giacomo Ponzetto, JesseShapiro. 2005. Strategic Extremism: Why Republicans and Democrats Divide on Religious Values. the Quarterly Journal of Economics 120, 1283–1330.

Glenn, Evelyn. 2011. Constructing Citizenship: Exclusion, Subordination, and Resistance. American Sociological Review 76, 1–24.

Goldberg, Chad Alan. 2001. Social Citizenship and A Reconstructed Tocqueville. American Sociological Review 66, 289–315.

Goldstein, Adam. 2012. Revenge of the Managers: Labor Cost-Cutting and the Paradoxical Resurgence of Managerialism in the Shareholder Value Era, 1984 To 2001. American Sociological Review 77, 268–94.

Goolsbee, Austan D. and Alan B. Krueger. 2015. A Retrospective Look at Rescuing and Restructuring General Motors and Chrysler. Journal of Economic Perspectives 29, 3–24.

Gorski, Philip and Gülay Türkmen-Dervişoğlu. 2013. Religion, Nationalism, and Violence: An Integrated Approach. Annual Review of Sociology 39, 193–210.

Gottdiener, Mark. 1985. Hegemony and Mass Culture: A Semiotic Approach. American Journal of Sociology 90, 979–1001.

Gowrisankaran, Gautam, Aviv Nevo, and Robert Town. 2015. Mergers When Prices Are Negotiated: Evidence from the Hospital Industry. American Economic Review 105, 172–203.

Grossman, Gene and Giovanni Maggi. 2000. Diversity and Trade. American Economic Review 90, 1255–75.

Habermas, Jurgen. 2001a. the Postnational Constellation: Political Essays. Cambridge: MIT Press.

Hart, Oliver. 1985. Monopolistic Competition in the Spirit of Chamberlin: A General Model Review of Economic Studies 52, 529–46.

Hayek, Friedrich. 1960. the Constitution of Liberty. South Bend: Gateway Editions.

Hedges, Chris. 2006. American Fascists. New York, Free Press.

Hendel, Igal and Lizzeri, Alessandro. 1999. Adverse Selection in Durable Goods Markets. American Economic Review 89, 1097–1115.

Hess, Gregory D., and Orphanides Athanasios. 2001. War and Democracy. Journal of Political Economy 109, 776–810.

Hicks, Alexander. 2006. Free-Market and Religious Fundamentalists Versus Poor Relief. American Sociological Review 71, 503–10.

Hicks, John. 1961. Value and Capital. Oxford: Oxford University Press.

Hill, Steven. 2002. Fixing Elections. New York: Routledge.

Hodgson, Geoffrey. 1999. Economics and Utopia. New York: Routledge.

Hoff, Karla and Joseph Stiglitz. 2010. Equilibrium Fictions: A Cognitive Approach to Societal Rigidity. American Economic Review 100, 141–46.

Hout Michael and Claude Fischer. 2002. Why More Americans Have No Religious Preference: Politics and Generations. American Sociological Review 67 165–90.

Hull, Mary. 1999. Censorship in America. Boulder: NetLibrary.

Inglehart, Ronald (ed.). 2004. Human Beliefs and Values. México: Siglo XXI.

Inglehart, Ronald and Wayne Baker. 2000. Modernization, Cultural Change and the Persistence of Traditional Values. *American Sociological Review* 65, 19–51.

Jacobs, David and Daniel Tope. 2007. the Politics of Resentment in the Post–Civil Rights Era: Minority Threat, Homicide, and Ideological Voting in Congress. American Journal of Sociology 112, 1458–94.

Jacobs, David, Jason Carmichael, and Stephanie Kent. 2005. Vigilantism, Current Racial Threat, and Death Sentences. American Sociological Review 70, 656–77.

Janssen, Susanne, Giselinde Kuipers, Marc Verboord. 2008. Cultural Globalization and Arts Journalism: The International Orientation of Arts and Culture Coverage in Dutch, French, German, and U.S. Newspapers, 1955 To 2005. American Sociological Review 73, 719–40.

Johnson, Victoria. 2007. What Is Organizational Imprinting? Cultural Entrepreneurship in the Founding of the Paris Opera. American Journal of Sociology 113, 97–127.

Juergensmeyer, Mark. 1994. the New Cold War? Berkeley: University of California Press.

Juergensmeyer, Mark. 2003. Terror in the Mind of God. Berkeley: University of California Press.

Kaplan, Benjamin. 2002. 'Dutch' Religious Tolerance: Celebration and Revision. in Hsia Po-Chia and Henk Van Nierop (eds.), Calvinism and Religious Toleration in the Dutch Golden Age (pp. 8–27). New York: Cambridge University Press.

Kaufman, Jason. 2008. Corporate Law and the Sovereignty of States. American Sociological Review 73, 402–25.

Kenworthy, Lane. 2002. Corporatism and Unemployment in the 1980s and 1990s. American Sociological Review 67, 367–88.

Kerrissey Jasmine. 2015. Collective Labor Rights and Income Inequality. American Sociological Review 80, 626–53.

Keynes, John M. 1960 (1936). the General Theory of Employment, Interest and Money. London: Macmillan.

Keynes, John M. 1972 (1931). Essays in Persuasion. London: Macmillan St.Martin's Press.

Kim, Hyojoung and Steven Pfaff. 2012. Structure and Dynamics of Religious Insurgency: Students and the Spread of the Reformation. American Sociological Review 77, 188–215.

Kimeldorf Howard. 2013. Worker Replacement Costs and Unionization: Origins of the U.S. Labor Movement. American Sociological Review 78, 1033–62.

King, Mervyn. 2004. the Institutions of Monetary Policy. American Economic Review 94, 1–13.

King, Ryan, Michael Massoglia, and Christopher Uggen. 2012. Employment and Exile: U.S. Criminal Deportations, 1908–2005. American Journal of Sociology 117, 1786–1825.

Klandermans, Bert, Jojanneke Van Der Toorn, Jacquelien Van Stekelenburg. 2008. Embeddedness and Identity: How Immigrants Turn Grievances into Action. American Sociological Review 73, 992–1012.

Kleven, Henrik. 2014. How Can Scandinavians Tax So Much? Journal of Economic Perspectives 28, 77–98.

Kloppenberg, James. 1998. the Virtues of Liberalism. New York: Oxford University Press.

Knight, Frank. 1967. Laissez Faire: Pro and Con. Journal of Political Economy 75, 782–95.

Kohler-Hausmann, Issa. 2013. Misdemeanor Justice: Control Without Conviction. American Journal of Sociology 119, 351–93.

Koopmans, Ruud 2013. Multiculturalism and Immigration: A Contested Field in Cross-National Comparison. Annual Review of Sociology 39, 147–69.

Korpi, Walter. 1989. Power, Politics, and State Autonomy in the Development of Social Citizenship: Social Rights During Sickness in 18 OECD Countries Since 1930. American Sociological Review 54, 309–28.

Krasa, Stefan, and Mattias Polborn. 2014. Social Ideology and Taxes in A Differentiated Candidates Framework. American Economic Review, 104, 308–22.

Kurzman, Charles and Erin Leahey. 2004. Intellectuals and Democratization, 1905–1912 and 1989–1996. American Journal of Sociology 109, 937–86.

La Porta, Rafael, Florencio Lopez-De-Silanes, and Andrei Shleifer. 2008. the Economic Consequences of Legal Origins. Journal of Economic Literature 46, 285–332.

Lane, Robert. 2000. the Loss of Happiness in Market Democracies. New Haven: Yale University Press.

Leijonhufvud, Axel. 2004. Celebrating Ned. Journal of Economic Literature 42, 811–21.

Lenski, Gerhard. 1966. Power and Privilege. New York: McGraw Hill.

Levitt, Steven. 1997. Using Electoral Cycles in Police Hiring to Estimate the Effect of Police on Crime. American Economic Review 87, 270–90.

Levitt, Steven and Sudhir Alladi Venkatesh. 2000. An Economic Analysis of a Drug-Selling Gang's Finances. the Quarterly Journal of Economics 115, 755–89.

Llavador, Humberto, and Oxoby Robert. 2005. Partisan Competition, Growth, and the Franchise. the Quarterly Journal of Economics 120, 1155–89.

Lichterman, Paul. 2008. Religion and the Construction of Civic Identity. American Sociological Review 73, 83–104.

Lim, Claire. 2013. Preferences and Incentives of Appointed and Elected Public officials: Evidence from State Trial Court Judges. American Economic Review 103, 1360–97.

Lindsay, Michael. 2008. Evangelicals in the Power Elite: Elite Cohesion Advancing a Movement. American Sociological Review 73, 60–82.

Lipset, Seymour. 1955. the Radical Right: A Problem for American Democracy. the British Journal of Sociology 6, 176–209.

Lipset, Seymour. 1996. American Exceptionalism. New York: Norton.

Lipset, Seymour and Gary Marks. 2000. It Didn't Happen Here. Norton.

Lizzeri, Alessandro, and Persico Nicola. 2001. the Provision of Public Goods Under Alternative Electoral Incentives. American Economic Review 91, 225–39.

Lizzeri, Alessandro, and Persico Nicola. 2004. Why Did the Elites Extend the Suffrage? Democracy and the Scope of Government, with an Application to Britain's Age of Reform. the Quarterly Journal of Economics 119, 707–65.

Lloyd, Richard. 2012. Urbanization and the Southern United States. Annual Review of Sociology 38, 483–506.

Lyness, Karen., Janet Gornick, Pamela Stone, and Angela Grotto. 2012. It's All About Control: Worker Control Over Schedule and Hours in Cross-National Context. American Sociological Review 77, 1023–49.

McDaniel, Cara. 2011. Forces Shaping Hours Worked in the OECD, 1960–2004. American Economic Journal: Macroeconomics 3, 27–52.

Madestam, Andreas, Daniel Shoag, Stan Veuger, and David Yanagizawa-Drott. 2013. Do Political Protests Matter? Evidence from the Tea Party Movement. Quarterly Journal of Economics 128, 1633–85.

Mailath, George, Larry Samuelson, and Avner Shaked. 2000. Endogenous Inequality in Integrated Labor Markets with Two-Sided Search. American Economic Review 90, 46–72.

Makowski, Louis and Joseph Ostroy. 2001. Perfect Competition and the Creativity of the Market. Journal of Economic Literature 39, 479–535.

Mandel, Benjamin R. 2009. Art as An Investment and Conspicuous Consumption Good. American Economic Review 99, 1653–63.

Manent, Pierre. 1998. Modern Liberty and Its Discontents. Lanham, MD: Rowman & Littlefield.

Mankiw, Gregory. 2013. Defending the One Percent. Journal of Economic Perspectives 27, 21–34.

Mann, Michael. 2005. the Dark Side of Democracy. New York: Cambridge University Press.

Mannheim, Karl. 1986. Conservatism. London: Routledge and Kegan Paul.

Mansbach, Richard. 2006. Calvinism as A Precedent for Islamic Radicalism. Brown Journal of World Affairs 12, 103–15.

Marshall, Alfred. 1961 (1891). Principles of Economics. London: Macmillan.

Martin, John. 2002. Power, Authority, and the Constraint of Belief Systems. American Journal of Sociology 107, 861–904.

McCann, Sean. 2000. Gumshoe America. Durham: Duke University Press.

McLaughlin, Neil. 1996. Nazism, Nationalism, and the Sociology of Emotions: Escape from Freedom Revisited. Sociological Theory 14, 241–61.

McMurtry, John. 1999. the Cancer Stage of Capitalism. London: Pluto Press.

McVeigh, Rory and Diaz Maria-Elena. 2009. Voting To Ban Same-Sex Marriage: Interests, Values, and Communities. American Sociological Review 74, 891–915.

Melitz, Marc and Stephen Redding. 2014. Missing Gains from Trade? American Economic Review 104, 317–21.

Menjívar, Cecilia and Leisy J. Abrego. 2012. Legal Violence: Immigration Law and the Lives of Central American Immigrants. American Journal of Sociology 117, 1380–1421.

Merton, Robert. 1939. Review of *the Protestant Crusade, 1800–1860*. By Ray Allen Billington. *American Sociological Review* 4, 436–38.

Merton, Robert. 1968. Social Theory and Social Structure. New York: The Free Press.

Merton, Robert. 1976. Sociological Ambivalence. New York: The Free Press.

Milanovic, Branko. 2014. the Return of Patrimonial Capitalism: A Review of Thomas Piketty's Capital in the Twenty-First Century. Journal of Economic Literature 52, 519–34.

Mill, John Stuart. 1991 (1859). On Liberty. Oxford: Oxford University Press.

Miller, Jon. Eugenie Scott, and Shinji Okamoto. 2006: Public Acceptance of Evolution. Science 313, 765–66.

Mises, Ludwig. 1962. the Ultimate Foundation of Economic Science. Princeton: Van Nostrand Co.

Mokyr, Joel. 2009. Intellectual Property Rights, the Industrial Revolution, and the Beginnings of Modern Economic Growth. American Economic Review 99, 349–55.

Mokyr, Joel. 2014. A Flourishing Economist: A Review Essay on Edmund Phelps's Mass Flourishing: How Grassroots Innovation Created Jobs, Challenge, and Change. Journal of Economic Literature 52, 189–96.

Mooney, Chris. 2005. the Republican War on Science. New York: Basic Books.

Moulitsas, Markos. 2010. American Taliban. New York. Polipoint Press.

Mueller, Dennis. 2007. Democracy, Rationality and Morality. Max Planck Institute of Economics. MPI Jena.

Mueller, Dennis. 2009. Reason, Religion, and Democracy. Cambridge: Cambridge University Press.

Mueller, Dennis. 2013. the State and Religion. Review of Social Economy 71, 1–19.

Mulligan, Casey, Ricard Gil and Xavier Sala-I-Martin. 2004. Do Democracies Have Different Public Policies Than Nondemocracies? Journal of Economic Perspectives 18, 51–74.

Munch, Richard. 1994. Sociological Theory. Chicago: Nelson-Hall Publishers.

Munch, Richard. 2001. the Ethics of Modernity. Lanham: Rowman & Littlefield.

Myles, John and Adnan Turegun. 1994. Comparative Studies in Class Structure. Annual Review of Sociology 20, 103–24.

Naidu, Suresh, and Noam Yuchtman. 2013. Coercive Contract Enforcement: Law and the Labor Market in Nineteenth Century Industrial Britain. American Economic Review 103, 107–44.

Nicholas, Tom 2008. Does Innovation Cause Stock Market Runups? Evidence from the Great Crash. American Economic Review 98, 1370–96.

Obstfeld, Maurice. 2012. Does the Current Account Still Matter? American Economic Review 102, 1–23.

Orren, Karen. 1994. Institutions, Antinomies, and Influences in Labor Governance. Law and Social Inquiry 19, 187–93.

Osborne, William. 2002. Marketplace of Ideas: But First, the Bill, A Personal Commentary on American and European Cultural Funding. ArtsJournal http://www.artsjournal .com/artswatch/20040311-11320.shtml

Owens, Timothy, Dawn Robinson, and Lynn Smith-Lovin. 2010. Three Faces of Identity. Annual Review of Sociology 36, 477–99.

Pak, Michael. 2007. Academic Freedom and the Liberation of the Nation's Faculty. the NEA Higher Education Journal 83–93.

Pareto, Vilfredo. 1932 (1916). Traité De Sociologie Generale. Paris: Payot.

Pareto, Vilfredo. 1935. the Mind and Society. New York: Dover Publications.

Pareto, Vilfredo. 2000 (1901). the Rise and Fall of Elites. New Brunswick: Transaction Publishers.

Parkera, John and Edward Hackettb. 2012. Hot Spots and Hot Moments in Scientific Collaborations and Social Movements. American Sociological Review 77, 21–44.

Parsons, Talcott. 1951. the Social System. New York: The Free Press.

Paxton, Pamela. 2002. Social Capital and Democracy: An Interdependent Relationship. American Sociological Review 67, 254–77.

Pegram, Thomas. 1998. Battling Demon Rum. Chicago: Dee.

Pencavel, John 2011. Real Wage Index Numbers. American Economic Review 101, 565–70.

Perrucci, Robert and Earl Wysong. 2008. The New Class Society. Lanham: Rowman & Littlefield.

Persson, Torsten and Guido Tabellini. 2006. Democracy and Development: The Devil in the Details. American Economic Review 96, 319–24.

Phillips, Kevin. 2006. American Theocracy. New York: Viking.

Pichardo, Nelson. 1997. New Social Movements: A Critical Review. Annual Review of Sociology 23, 411–30.

Phelps, Edmund. 2007. Macroeconomics for A Modern Economy. American Economic Review 97, 543–61.

Pigou, Alfred. 1960. Economics of Welfare. London: Macmillan.

Piketty, Thomas. 2014. Capital in the Twenty-First Century. Cambridge, MA: Harvard University Press.

Plotke, David. 2002. Introduction, in Daniel Bell (ed.), the Radical Right (pp. Vi–Lxxvi). New Brunswick: Transaction Publishers.

Pontikes, Elizabeth, Giacomo Negro, and Hayagreeva Rao. 2010. Stained Red: A Study of Stigma By Association To Blacklisted Artists During the Red Scare in Hollywood, 1945 To 1960. American Sociological Review 75, 456–78.

Popper, Karl. 1973. the Open Society and Its Enemies. London: Routledge and Kegan Paul.

Prasad, Monica. 2005. Why Is France So French? Culture, Institutions, and Neoliberalism, 1974–1981. American Journal of Sociology 111, 357–407.

Pryor, Frederic. 2002. the Future of U.S. Capitalism. New York: Cambridge University Press.

Putnam, Robert. 2000. Bowling Alone. New York: Simon & Schuster.

Putterman, Louis, John E. Roemer, and Joaquim Silvestre. 1998. Does Egalitarianism Have a Future? Journal of Economic Literature 36, 861–902.

Ragan, Kelly. 2013. Taxes and Time Use: Fiscal Policy in a Household Production Model. American Economic Journal: Macroeconomics 5, 168–92.

Reskin, Barbara. 2003. Including Mechanisms in Our Models of Ascriptive Inequality. American Sociological Review 68, 1–21.

Robinson, Joan. 1933. the Economics of Imperfect Competition. London: Macmillan.

Rogers Joel and Wolfgang Streeck. 1995. Works Councils. Chicago: University of Chicago Press.

Rudel, Thomas, Timmons Roberts, and Joann Carmin. 2011. Political Economy of the Environment. Annual Review of Sociology 37, 221–38.

Rydgren, Jens. 2007. the Sociology of the Radical Right. Annual Review of Sociology 33, 241–62.

Samuelson, Paul. 1964. Personal Freedoms and Economic Freedoms in the Mixed Economy in Cheit, E.F. (ed.), the Business Establishment (pp. 193–227). New York: Wiley.

Samuelson, Paul. 1983a. Foundations of Economic Analysis. Cambridge: Harvard University Press.

Samuelson, Paul. 1983b. the World Economy at Century's End. in S. Tsuru (ed.), Human Resources, Employment and Development (pp. 58–77). Macmillan, London.

Samuelson, Paul. 1994. the Classical Classical Fallacy, Journal of Economic Literature 32, 620–39.

Samuelson, Paul. 2004. Where Ricardo and Mill Rebut and Confirm Arguments of Mainstream Economists Supporting Globalization. Journal of Economic Perspectives 18, 135–46.

Samuelsson, Kurt. 1961. Religion and Economic Action. New York, Basic Books.

Sandel, Michael. 2013. Market Reasoning as Moral Reasoning: Why Economists Should Re-engage with Political Philosophy. Journal of Economic Perspectives, 27, 121–40.

Schelling, Thomas. 2006. An Astonishing Sixty Years: The Legacy of Hiroshima. American Economic Review 96, 929–37.

Schumpeter, Joseph. 1949(1911). the Theory of Economic Development. Cambridge: Harvard University Press.

Schumpeter, Joseph. 1950. Capitalism, Socialism and Democracy. New York: Harper and Brothers.

Schumpeter, Joseph. 1954. History of Economic Analysis. New York: Oxford University Press.

Schutz, Eric. 2001. Markets and Power. Armonk: M.E. Sharpe.

Scitovsky, Tibor. 1972. What's Wrong with the Arts Is What's Wrong with Society. American Economic Review 62, 62–69.

Sen, Amartya. 1994. the Formulation of Rational Choice. American Economic Review 84, 385–90.

Senior, William. 1951 (1836). An Outline of the Science of Political Economy. New York: A.M. Kelley.

Simmel, Georg. 1955 (1923). Conflict. the Web of Group Affiliations. New York: The Free Press.

Simon, Herbert. 1976. Administrative Behavior. New York: The Free Press.

Skrentny, John. 2006. Law and the American State. Annual Review of Sociology 32, 213–44.

Slack, Kevin. 2013. On the Origins and Intention of Benjamin Franklin's on the Providence of God in the Government of the World. the Pennsylvania Magazine of History and Biography 137, 345–79.

Smeeding, Timothy. 2006. Poor People in Rich Nations: The United States in Comparative Perspective. Journal of Economic Perspectives 20, 69–90.

Smelser, Neil and Mitchell, Faith. 2002. Terrorism. Washington, D.C. National Academies Press.

Smits, Heroen, Wqout Ultee and Jan Lammers. 1998. Educational Homogamy in 65 Countries: An Explanation of Differences in Openness Using Country-Level Explanatory Variables, American Sociological Review 63, 264–85.

Solow, Robert, Alan Budd, and Christian von Weizsacker. 1987. the Conservative Revolution: a Roundtable Discussion. Economic Policy 2, 181–200.

Somerville, Peter. 2000. Social Relations and Social Exclusion. New York: Routledge.

Spence, Michael. 2002. Signaling in Retrospect and the Informational Structure of Markets. American Economic Review 92, 434–59.

Spiegler, Ran. 2013. Placebo Reforms. American Economic Review 103, 1490–1506.

Steckel Richard. 2008. Biological Measures of the Standard of Living. Journal of Economic Perspectives 22, 129–52.

Steinberg Marc. 2003. Capitalist Development, the Labor Process, and the Law. American Journal of Sociology 109, 445–95.

Steinfeld, Robert. 2001. Coercion, Contract, and Free Labor in the Nineteenth Century. Cambridge: Cambridge University Press.

Steinmetz, George. 2005. Return to Empire: The New US Imperialism in Comparative Historical Perspective. Sociological Theory 23, 339–67.

Stepan-Norris, Judith and Caleb Southworth. 2010. Rival Unionism and Membership Growth in the United States, 1900 To 2005: A Special Case of Inter-Organizational Competition. American Sociological Review 75, 227–51.

Stern, Nicholas. 2008. the Economics of Climate Change. American Economic Review 98, 1–37.

Stiglitz, Joseph. 1979. Equilibrium in Product Markets with Imperfect Information. American Economic Review 69, 339–45.

Stiglitz, Joseph. 2002. Information and the Change in the Paradigm in Economics. American Economic Review 92, 460–501.

Stiglitz, Joseph. 2010. Freefall. New York: Norton.

Sutton, John. 2004. 2013. the Transformation of Prison Regimes in Late Capitalist Societies. American Journal of Sociology 119, 715–46.

Swedberg, Richard. 2005. Markets as Social Structures. in Neil Smelser and Richard Swedberg (eds.), the Handbook of Economic Sociology (pp. 233–53). Princeton: Princeton University Press.

Throsby, David. 1994. the Production and Consumption of the Arts: A View of Cultural Economics. Journal of Economic Literature 32, 1–29.

Tilly, Charles. 2002. Buried Gold: Comment on Young. American Sociological Review 67, 689–92.

Tilman, Rick. 2001. Ideology and Utopia in the Social Philosophy of the Libertarian Economists. Westport: Greenwood Press.

Tiryakian, Edward. 2002. Review of the Ethics of Modernity: Formation and Transformation in Britain, France, Germany and the United States. By Richard Munch. American Journal of Sociology 107, 1629–31.

Tönnies, Ferdinand. 2001 (1887). Community and Civil Society. Cambridge: Cambridge University Press.

Trebbi, Francesco, Aghion Philippe, and Alesina Alberto. 2008. Electoral Rules and Minority Representation in U.S. Cities. the Quarterly Journal of Economics 123, 325–57.

Trigilia Carlo. 2002. Economic Sociology. Malden: Blackwell Publishers.

Turk, Austin. 2004. Sociology of Terrorism. Annual Review of Sociology 29, 271–86.

Turner, Bryan. 2002. Sovereignty and Emergency: Political Theology, Islam And American Conservatism. Theory, Culture & Society 19, 103–19.

Uggen, Christopher And Jeff Manza. 2002. Democratic Contraction? Political Consequences of Felon Disenfranchisement in The United States. American Sociological Review 67, 777–803.

Van Dyke, Vernon. 1995. Ideology and Political Choice. Chatham: Chatham House.

Wacquant, Loýc. 2002. Scrutinizing the Street: Poverty, Morality, And the Pitfalls Of Urban Ethnography. American Journal of Sociology 107, 1468–1532.

Wakefield, Sara And Christopher Uggen. 2010. Incarceration and Stratification. Annual Review of Sociology 36, 387–406.

Waldman, Michael. 2003, Durable Goods Theory for Real World Markets. Journal of Economic Perspectives 17, 131–54.

Wall, Steven. 1998. Liberalism, Perfectionism and Restraint. New York: Cambridge University Press.

Walras, Leon. 1926 (1874). Elements D'économie Politique Pure. Paris: R. Pichon Et R. Durand-Auzias.

Walzer, Michael. 1963. Puritanism as A Revolutionary Ideology. History and Theory 3, 59–90.

Weber, Max. 1930 (1905). The Protestant Ethic and The Spirit of Capitalism. New York: Charles Scribner's Sons.

Weber, Max. 1946. From Max Weber. New York: Oxford University Press.

Weber, Max. 1968. (1921–2) Economy and Society. New York: Bedminster Press.

Weisbrod, Carol. The Law and Reconstituted Christianity: The Case of the Mormons, in McLaren, John, Coward, Harold (eds.), 1999. Religious Conscience, The State, and the Law (pp. 136–53). Albany: State University of New York Press.

Welch, Finis. 1999. In Defense of Inequality. American Economic Review 89, 1–17.

Wolff, Edward. 1998. Recent Trends in The Size Distribution of Household Wealth, Journal of Economic Perspectives 12, 131–50.

Wolff, Edward. 2002. Top Heavy. New York: New Press.

Wright, Erik. 2000. Working-Class Power, Capitalist-Class Interests, And Class Compromise. *American Journal of Sociology* 105, 957–1002.

Wright, Erik. 2013. Transforming Capitalism Through Real Utopias. American Sociological Review 78, 1–25.

Young, Michael. 2002. Confessional Protest: The Religious Birth of US National Social Movements. American Sociological Review 67, 660–88.

Zaret, David. 1989. Religion and The Rise of Liberal-Democratic Ideology In 17th Century England. American Sociological Review 54, 163–79.

Index

www.ingramcontent.com/pod-product-compliance
Lightning Source LLC
Chambersburg PA
CBHW070857030426
42336CB00014BA/2244